Deep Learning for Targeted Treatments

Scrivener Publishing
100 Cummings Center, Suite 541J
Beverly, MA 01915-6106

Publishers at Scrivener
Martin Scrivener (martin@scrivenerpublishing.com)
Phillip Carmical (pcarmical@scrivenerpublishing.com)

Deep Learning
for Targeted Treatments

Transformation in Healthcare

Edited by
Rishabha Malviya
Gheorghita Ghinea
Rajesh Kumar Dhanaraj
Balamurugan Balusamy
and
Sonali Sundram

Scrivener
Publishing

WILEY

This edition first published 2022 by John Wiley & Sons, Inc., 111 River Street, Hoboken, NJ 07030, USA and Scrivener Publishing LLC, 100 Cummings Center, Suite 541J, Beverly, MA 01915, USA
© 2022 Scrivener Publishing LLC
For more information about Scrivener publications please visit www.scrivenerpublishing.com.

Wiley Global Headquarters
111 River Street, Hoboken, NJ 07030, USA

For details of our global editorial offices, customer services, and more information about Wiley products visit us at www.wiley.com.

Limit of Liability/Disclaimer of Warranty
While the publisher and authors have used their best efforts in preparing this work, they make no representations or warranties with respect to the accuracy or completeness of the contents of this work and specifically disclaim all warranties, including without limitation any implied warranties of merchantability or fitness for a particular purpose. No warranty may be created or extended by sales representatives, written sales materials, or promotional statements for this work. The fact that an organization, website, or product is referred to in this work as a citation and/or potential source of further information does not mean that the publisher and authors endorse the information or services the organization, website, or product may provide or recommendations it may make. This work is sold with the understanding that the publisher is not engaged in rendering professional services. The advice and strategies contained herein may not be suitable for your situation. You should consult with a specialist where appropriate. Neither the publisher nor authors shall be liable for any loss of profit or any other commercial damages, including but not limited to special, incidental, consequential, or other damages. Further, readers should be aware that websites listed in this work may have changed or disappeared between when this work was written and when it is read.

Library of Congress Cataloging-in-Publication Data

ISBN 9781119857327

Cover image: Pixabay.Com
Cover design by Russell Richardson

Set in size of 11pt and Minion Pro by Manila Typesetting Company, Makati, Philippines

Printed in the USA

10 9 8 7 6 5 4 3 2 1

Contents

Preface

Given the digital availability of knowledge today, deep learning (DL) has become a hot topic in the field of medicine in recent years. Deep learning is the general-purpose automatic learning procedure that is currently being widely implemented in a number of fields, including science, industry, and government. Since pharmaceutical formulation data consists of formulation combinations and methodological approaches that are neither image nor sequential data, this fully connected broad feed-forward network is a good option to predict pharmaceutical formulations. Moreover, targeted delivery of drugs to diseased tissues is another major challenge that can be solved by utilizing the deep learning framework. This book describes the importance of this framework for patient care, disease imaging/detection and health management. Since deep learning can play a major role in a patient's healthcare management by controlling drug delivery to targeted tissues or organs, the main focus of the book is to leverage the various prospects of the DL framework for targeted therapy of various diseases. In terms of its industrial significance, this general-purpose automatic learning procedure is being widely implemented in pharmaceutical healthcare.

This book provides the direction for future research in deep learning in terms of its role in targeted treatment, biological systems, site-specific drug delivery, risk assessment in therapy, etc. The profusely referenced and copiously illustrated 13 chapters are subdivided into various sections that were written by renown researchers from many parts of the world. It should be noted that since all chapters were deliberately reviewed and suitably revised once or twice, the information presented in this book is of the highest quality and meets the highest publication standards. Therefore, this book should be both immensely interesting and useful to researchers and those in industry working in the areas of clinical research, disease management, pharmaceuticals, R&D formulation, deep learning analytics, remote healthcare management, healthcare analytics, and deep learning in the healthcare industry.

Finally comes the best part, which is to thank everyone who helped to make this book possible. First and foremost, we express our heartfelt gratitude to the authors for their contributions, dedication, participation, and willingness to share their significant research experience in the form of written testimonials, without which this book would not have been possible. Lastly, we want to express our gratitude to Martin Scrivener of Scrivener Publishing for his unwavering support.

The Editors
July 2022

Acknowledgement

Our sincere thanks to

Prof. P. K. Sharma
Pro-VC
Galgotias University
Without his encouragement and support
This task wouldn't have been possible

Having an idea and turning it into a book is as hard as it sounds. The experience is both internally challenging and rewarding. At the very outset, we fail to find adequate words, with limited vocabulary to our command, to express our emotion to almighty, whose eternal blessing, divine presence, and masterly guidelines helps us to fulfill all our goals.

When emotions are profound, words sometimes are not sufficient to express our thanks and gratitude. We especially want to thank the individuals that helped make this happen. Without the experiences and support from my peers and team, this book would not exist.

No words can describe the immense contribution of our parents, friends, without whose support this work would have not been possible.

Last but not least, we would like to thank, our publisher for their support, innovative suggestions and guidance in bringing out this edition.

Deep Learning and Site-Specific Drug Delivery: The Future and Intelligent Decision Support for Pharmaceutical Manufacturing Science

**Dhanalekshmi Unnikrishnan Meenakshi[1]*, Selvasudha Nandakumar[2],
Arul Prakash Francis[3], Pushpa Sweety[4], Shivkanya Fuloria[5],
Neeraj Kumar Fuloria[5], Vetriselvan Subramaniyan[6] and Shah Alam Khan[1†]**

*[1]College of Pharmacy, National University of Science and Technology,
Muscat, Oman
[2]Department of Biotechnology, Pondicherry University, Puducherry, India
[3]Department of Biochemistry and Molecular Biology, Pondicherry University,
Puducherry, India
[4]Anna University, BIT Campus, Tiruchirappalli, India
[5]Faculty of Pharmacy, AIMST University, Bedong, Malaysia
[6]Faculty of Medicine, Bioscience and Nursing, MAHSA University, Selangor,
Malaysia*

Abstract

Site-specific drug delivery [SSDD] is a smart localized and targeted delivery system that is used to improve drug efficiency, decrease drug-related toxicity, and prolong the duration of action by having protected interaction between a drug and the diseased tissue. SSDD system in association with the computational approaches is employed in discovery, design, and development of drugs to improve treatment outcomes. Artificial intelligence [AI] networks and tools are playing a prominent role in developing pharmaceutical products by employing fundamental paradigms. Among many computational techniques, deep learning [DL] technology utilizes artificial neural networks [ANN], belongs to machine learning [ML] approach that holds the key to measuring and forecasting a drug's

*Corresponding author: dhanalekshmi@nu.edu.om; ORCID: 0000-0002-2689-4079
†Corresponding author: shahalam@nu.edu.om; ORCID: 0000-0002-0729-3403

Rishabha Malviya, Gheorghita Ghinea, Rajesh Kumar Dhanaraj, Balamurugan Balusamy
and Sonali Sundram (eds.) *Deep Learning for Targeted Treatments: Transformation in Healthcare,*
(1–38) © 2022 Scrivener Publishing LLC

affinity for specific targets. It can reduce both cost and time by speeding up the drug development process rationally with careful decisions. DL is considered as the primary strategy to predict bioactivity as it shows improved performance compared with other technologies in the field. DL can assist in evaluating the success of a target-based drug design and development before the actual laboratory synthesis or production of the drug molecule. This chapter highlights the potential applications of DL in assigning a specific drug target site by predicting the structure of the target protein and drug affinity for a successful treatment. It also spotlights the impactful applications of many types of DL in SSDD and its advantages over conventional SSDD systems. Furthermore, some formulations that are intended to lead to the target or site-specific delivery and DL role in docking and pharmacokinetics profiling are also addressed. Ongoing challenges, skepticism about the likelihood of success, and the paths to overcome by future technological advancements are also dealt with briefly. Due emphasis is given to the use of DL in reducing the economic burden of pharmaceutical industries to overcome costly failures and in developing target specific new drug candidate[s] for a successful therapeutic regimen beneficial to human life.

Keywords: Site-specific, target, drug delivery, deep learning, machine learning, artificial intelligence, computational approach, precision medicine

1.1   Introduction

Site-specific drug delivery (SSDD) is an almost a century-old strategy but successful delivery of drugs to the target site without producing off-site unwanted adverse effects has not been realized yet. Random testing assays in the traditional development of SSDD identify only 3% of compounds that warrant further laboratory tests, and hence, it is vital to explore the drug-target interactions for every single pharmaceutical molecule. Modern drug discovery, which includes identifying and preparing drug-molecular targets with precision, is emerging to fill traditional SSDD gaps. Target-specific drug delivery promotes the delivery of medications to target sites without creating unwanted side effects elsewhere. Despite numerous publications and attention paid to the site-specific delivery that promises to "deliver" the medicine at the diseased site, the generation of target-specific therapeutic products has still been a challenge for researchers [1]. The obstructions met during the drug formulation process are mainly associated with the inability to foresee the impact of the combination of active pharmaceutical ingredients [APIs] and materials on the formulation parameters. A new drug formulation development process and the associated procedures need to satisfy the site-specific delivery and release profile. Moreover, it is a laborious task and the protocols to perform *in vitro* characterizations or modifications to obtain the desired profile are difficult for the formulators [2]. To bridge the knowledge gap and reduce the time required for selecting the best molecule for drug development, researchers have devised computational modeling approaches like molecular dynamics simulations, docking studies [3], and cheminformatics [4]. These helps in the evaluation of novel insights about the complex drug delivery systems, especially in atomic/cellular scale which experimental techniques cannot provide [5–7]. A revolution in data science has been observed in the last decades due to the usage of the graphics processing unit [GPU]. A large volume of drug-related data and techniques were generated and analyzed using artificial intelligence [AI] to predict drug interaction with the diseased targets in drug discovery. AI networks and tools are playing a prominent role in the development of pharmaceutical products by employing fundamental paradigms. In medicinal chemistry, several computational methods contributed to designing new drug candidates by relating the drug candidate's physicochemical properties, biological activity, and binding affinity [8]. Machine learning [ML], the branch of AI, has gained importance in drug discovery protocols and has become the most attractive and prominent research areas. ML supports the advancement of effective formulation through data-driven predictions using experimental data. A well-designed ML technique can significantly speed up the optimization of formulations with reduced cost [9]. Knowledge acquisition about the molecular characteristics of lead molecules has been made with the help of ML techniques like partial least squares [PLS], k-nearest neighbors [kNN], and artificial neural networks [ANN] [10]. ANN is the most prevalent ML technique in formulation prediction [9, 10].

Among the various methodologies of AI, deep learning [DL] had gained significant attention in several areas because of its ability to extract features from data [11]. Leading pharmaceutical industries in collaboration with different AI organizations are trying to develop effective and ideal drug candidates in the field of oncology and CNS complications. In recent years, several trials involving the combination of nanotechnology and DL are underway to study their potential role in drug formulation with SSDD. The role of DL in drug development and manufacturing is depicted in Figure 1.1. DL methods are representation-learning techniques that can discover multiple-level representations of increasing complexity from the raw data using nonlinear models [12]. Several recent trials have connected nanotechnology and DL to study their potential role in drug formulation with site-specific drug delivery [SSDD]. DL can predict the probable drug carrier candidate through target-based drug designing and development.

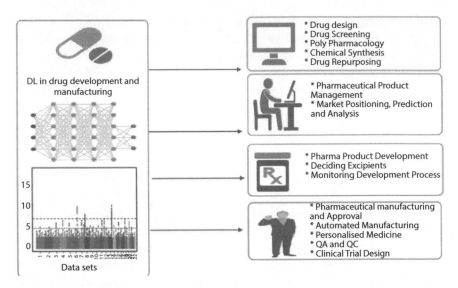

Figure 1.1 Role of DL in drug development and manufacturing.

DL methods play a significant role in drug delivery by predicting (i) drug loading in the carrier, (ii) the enhancement in permeability through the body barriers, and choosing the stable drug delivery systems from different carriers and matrices [13].

DL has proved to be an effective tool for virtual screening and predicting quantitative structure-activity relationships from large chemical libraries [14]. Golkov *et al.* reported that the DL is very useful in predicting the biological functions of several chemical compounds from the raw data based on their electronic arrangements [15]. A previous study on DL revealed that it has collected evidence from the vast amount of data sets related to the genome and utilized for drug repurposing and precise treatments [16]. Various DL models have been used to forecast interactions between protein-ligand, scoring docking poses, and virtual screenings. Thus, DL has been utilized to discover several endpoints in medicinal chemistry [17].

A study on predicting protein-ligand interactions using molecular fingerprints and protein sequences as vector input showed that the essential amino acid residues responsible for drug-target interactions were predicted using vectors obtained from the model [18]. A previous study by Lee *et al.* detailed a predictive model to represent the DeepConv-drug-target interactions [DTIs] in ligand-target complex. The predictive models were built using over 32,000 drug-target structures from the DrugBank, IUPHAR, and KEGG data sets. DNN outperforms similarity-based models and traditional protein representations, according to the findings [19]. For the prediction of novel DTIs between marketed medications and targets, Wen *et al.* used a successful DL method called deep belief network [DBN] and developed a methodology called DeepDTIs. This method was tested using an appropriate method and associated to suitable algorithms, such as random forest [RF], Bernoulli Naive Bayesian [BNB], and decision tree [DT]. Results showed that the algorithm used in this method achieves comparatively high prediction performance and could be used for drug repositioning in the future [20]. Another study proved that DNN surpasses support vector machines [SVM] used internal testing to predict the drugs and therapeutic categories after ten-fold cross-validation using gene expression data [16]. Recently, the combination of DL-based predictors with the conformal prediction framework to create highly extrapolative models and further evaluated their performance on toxicology in the 21st century [Tox21] data [21]. The results suggested that the utility of conformal predictors is an appropriate way to provide toxicity predictions with assurance. Another study introduced QuantitativeTox (a DL-based framework) to predict toxicity endpoints like LD_{50}, IGC_{50}, LC_{50}, and LC_{50}-DM [22].

Many researchers reported the applications of DL in drug design using different models. The development of new applications and methodologies makes this system a reliable tool in the collections available to discover new drug candidates. In terms of drug discovery and development, DL techniques still have a long way to go and the applications of DL methods in target-specific drug delivery are focused on in this chapter. It also discusses how DL can be used to assign a specific drug target site by estimating the target protein's structure and drug affinity for successful therapy. It also highlights the important applications of DL in SSDD, as well as the benefits of DL over traditional SSDD systems. Furthermore, some formulations intended to lead to the target or site-specific delivery and DL role in docking and pharmacokinetic profiling are also addressed. Ongoing challenges, skepticism about the likelihood of success, and the paths to overcome by future technological advancements are also dealt with. The application of DL in minimizing the economic burden of pharmaceutical enterprises to overcome costly failures and produce target-specific new drug candidate[s] for a successful therapeutic regimen beneficial to human life is discussed briefly in this chapter.

1.2   Drug Discovery, Screening and Repurposing

Drug discovery is a complex, tedious, lengthy, costly, and challenging multistep process with a very high failure rate. That is why a new drug approximately requires 10 to 15 years to enter from the bench to the bedside. Despite rapid development in the field of chemical and biological sciences, only an average of 25 new molecular entities [NME] per year were approved over the last two decades, indicating obvious challenges and obstacles associated with the currently used methods for the discovery of drugs [23]. In the late 20th century, target-based drug discovery programs [TBDD] focused on the identification of promising target proteins trailed by high-throughput screening [HTS] to recognize potential drug candidates based on their interaction with the target protein. However, HTS screening program is a costly, time-consuming process with low success rates. Therefore, pharmaceutical industries during 2001 to 2020 mainly relied on virtual screening [VS], i.e., *in silico* computational methods to design and discover new drugs that resulted in the approval of 498 NME by the US-FDA. VS predicts drug-target interaction and is carried out just before the HTS to increase success rate with less cost. One study reported that the hit rate to identify a suitable protein tyrosine phosphatase-1B enzyme inhibitor by VS approach was much higher [34.8%] than the HTS method [0.021%] [24]. The chemical [small bioactive molecules] and biological [protein target structures] databases are expanding at a rapid pace [high volume, velocity, and variety] due to advancements in technology. To speed up drug discovery, DL seems to be a popular approach for mining suitable drug targets from big data. DL is helpful in drug discovery process, prediction of physicochemical characteristics, quantitative structure-activity relationship [QSAR] studies, bioactivities, ligand-based and structure-based virtual screening, toxicity, mechanism of action, drug-target interaction, protein-protein interactions, design of dosage form, etc. Zhavoronkov and co-workers in 2019 used DL method namely generative tensorial reinforcement learning [GENTRL] and discovered potent inhibitors of discoidin domain receptor 1 [DDR1] merely in 3 weeks. One of the inhibitors showed promising activity against fibrosis and a favorable pharmacokinetic profile in experimental animals [25]. Stokes *et al.* in 2020 discovered a broad-spectrum antibiotic halicin employing a DNN model of DL. The chemical structure of bactericidal halicin is very different from the core of existing antibiotic molecules and was identified from the drug-repurposing hub through the prediction of antibacterial activities [26].

DL uses chemical and protein data to accelerate the drug design and development protocols. The big data in chemical space are stored in databases, such as ChemSpider, ChEMBL, ChemMine, ChemBank, DrugCentral, GDB-17, ZINC, and PubChem, while 3D images of proteins are available in protein data bank PDB, BindingDB, and KEGG ligand. DisGeNET database provides useful information on the relationship between human disease-associated genes and variants [27]. Another important database for drug discovery is STITCH, which provides information on interactions between small chemical molecules and target proteins along with binding affinity [28]. For drug discovery, DL employs several subsets of ANNs, including deep neural networks [DNNs], recurrent neural networks [RNNs], and convolutional neural networks [CNNs]. DNN can be used either to generate the structure of bioactive compounds from the pool of chemical libraries and training sets [generative DNN] or to predict physicochemical properties of novel bioactive chemicals [predictive DNN] [29, 30]. RNNs are primarily used to process sequential data. It works on a self-learning method and helps to create a descriptive simplified molecular-input line-entry system [SMILES] for characterization and synthesis of molecules [4, 31]. CNNs are the most effective tool of DL that can convert 2D to 3D data. CNN is used to differentiate data for the identification of gene mutations, disease target, lead candidate, and their interaction based on microscopy images and fingerprints. It is a very good DL algorithm for handling 2D data but requires a long training time [32–34]. In the recent past, graph neural networks [GNNs] are preferred over RNNs and CNNs that present model data in a graph instead of representation in Euclidean space [35]. GNN molecular graphs for small bioactive molecules are a useful drug development process to predict molecular attributes and generate molecular tasks [36].

QSAR modeling is a computational technique used in drug discovery. It develops a quantitative relationship between the physiochemical features of tiny chemical compounds and their biological activities using mathematical models. Some of the web-based models developed for QSAR studies include; Cloud 3D-QSAR, FL-QSAR, QSAR-Co-X, Meta-QSAR, and Vega platform, etc., [37]. AlphaFold is an AI-based tool developed by Google's DeepMind to identify protein interaction [38]. This CNN-based tool can help in structure-based VS for drug discovery. Al Quraishi in 2019 also developed a similar DL-based tool, known as Recurrent Geometric Network, for the prediction of 3D structures of proteins [39].

The Monte Carlo tree search (MCTS) technique is a computational-based NN system and is very effective in generating various chemical synthetic pathways and in providing a solution to the total synthesis problems [40]. AiZynthFinder is recently developed by Genheden *et al.*, using MCTS approach for retrosynthesis planning [41]. DeepScreening is a DL algorithm-based, user-friendly online server developed by Liu *et al.*, in 2019 for drug discovery. It assists in VS of chemical compounds either from the public database or as defined by the user for a particular target protein [42]. The deep Reinforcement Learning for Structural Evolution

[ReLeaSE] program, which is based on the stack-augmented RNN, could be used to develop chemical libraries. ReLeaSE performs the *de novo* drug design through generative and predictive DNNs [43, 44]. Bai *et al.* in 2020 designed a soft tool called MolAIcal to design 3D drugs in 3D protein pockets. It utilizes DL and genetic algorithms for *de novo* drug design using US- FDA-approved drugs followed by DL-based molecular docking [45]. Drug discovery applications of DL are briefly presented in Table 1.1.

As discussed, conventional drug design and development might take a long period, expensive, off-target delivery, and high risk, with enormous difficulties and challenges; as a result, efforts are made to repurpose existing medications [60, 61]. Drug repurposing [or drug repositioning] is an approach that helps to speed up the applications of an already approved existing drug for a new indication, thus reducing the difficulties of discovering new drug molecules [62]. The advancement in the large-scale, heterogeneous biological networks provided unique opportunities in *in silico* drug repurposing methods as discussed elsewhere in this chapter [60]. These appealing properties have piqued biopharmaceutical companies' interest in scanning existing medications for potential repurposing applications. According to an estimate, approximately 30% of FDA-approved new drug products were made available through medication repurposing [63]. Using various biological networks, significant data collection from molecular, genomic, and phenotypic data facilitates the advanced development in drug repurposing [62]. Mechanism-based repurposing approaches are likely to find new indications for individual patients, given the current demand for PM and personalized therapy. These approaches consider the patient's complexity and heterogeneity, lowering the risk of drug toxicity and interpatient variability therapeutic efficacy [62].

Computer-assisted drug repositioning plays a leading role to improve the safety and efficacy of repurposing approaches utilizing the advantage of computational modeling through the data obtained from preclinical and clinical studies. With the advancement of computational drug design, various anticancer drugs, like Gefitinib, Erlotinib, Sorafenib, Crizotinib, and so on, were profitably discovered, which has been considered a milestone in this area. Collaboration of computational and AI methods are creating new promising outcomes in drug development research, and the role of DL is valued by pharma industries [37, 64]. DL creates a unique perspective on how drug molecules bind to target molecules, the changes in their physicochemical characteristics that result, and how these changes impact phenotypic alterations. Furthermore, this technique aids in the identification of novel therapeutic targets from large-scale data sets gathered by numerous programs [65].

Table 1.1 Applications of DL in drug discovery.

Method	Application	Purpose	Ref
Undirected graph recursive neural networks [UGRNNs]	Ligand-based approach	Prediction of solubility (aqueous) of organic compounds	[46]
DNNs	Ligand-based approach	Prediction of binary toxic effects using Tox21 Data Challenge	[47]
UGRNNs	Ligand-based approach	Prediction of drug induced liver injury	[48]
Molecular graph convolution DNNs	Ligand-based approach	Prediction of binary toxic effects using Tox21 Data Challenge	[49]
CNNs and Random forest [RF]	Ligand-based approach	Prediction of Tox21, SIDER, and MUV data sets	[50]
Graph convolutional DNNs	Ligand-based approach	Prediction of bioactivity and toxicity using Tox21, MUV, and PubChem BioAssay data sets	[51]
Convolutional 3D layer DL method	Structure-based approach	Prediction of structural features of a pharmacophore evaluated by AutoDock Vina score	[52]
DeepVS- DNNs	Structure-based approach	To identify active compounds from inactive using molecular descriptors.	[14]

(*Continued*)

Table 1.1 Applications of DL in drug discovery. (*Continued*)

Method	Application	Purpose	Ref
DL architecture with four hidden layers	Ligand-target interaction prediction	Prediction of binding affinity of ligand-protein target interactions	[53]
DBN models	Ligand-target interaction prediction	Prediction of drug target interactions were better than RF and BNB.	[20]
CNN and GNN	Ligand-target interaction prediction	Prediction of protein residues at the binding site	[18]
DeepConv-DTI	Ligand-target interaction prediction	Prediction of binding affinity	[19]
RNNs combined with reinforced learning	Chemical synthesis	*De Novo* drug design of bioactive compounds	[54, 55]
Transformer-CNN	QSAR modeling	QSAR modeling	[56]
A dual CNN	Drug repurposing	Disease-drug association via Chou's five-step rule	[57]
Graph NN based DeepCE	Drug repurposing	Prediction of the differential gene expression profile and to identify novel lead compounds through drug repurposing	[58]
Rotation Forest and DNNs	Ligand-based approach	Prediction of QSAR models to identify dipeptidyl peptidase-4 [DPP-40 inhibitors	[59]

Drug candidates for medical repurpose could be ordered using information from the biological literature and databases. The information was then transferred to several sources, allowing it to be incorporated into a knowledge graph [KG]. As a result, it covers all known links between biomedical concepts including medications, diseases, genes, and so on [66]. Constructing drug KG is a key pace to utilize existing and discrete drug information [67]. These graphs, which are made up of nodes and edges, represent biomedical concepts and relationships and can aid researchers in solving a variety of issues, assisting in patient diagnosis, and establishing links between diseases and drugs [68]. Moridi *et al.* reported the advantages of the DL technique to extract the drug and disease features and explore their logical relationship in drug repurposing [69]. Such techniques are used to a wide range of data, including genomics, phenotypic statistics, and chemical statistics [67]. By using good drug data representation techniques, KG aids in converting knowledge into useful inputs for ML algorithms that may accurately forecast drug repurposing possibilities.

1.3   DL and Pharmaceutical Formulation Strategy

1.3.1   DL in Dose and Formulation Prediction

Even though there is a variety of successful pharmaceutical formulations with efficient delivery, inappropriate dose recommendation to a patient is the key reason for most adverse reactions and toxicity. Therefore, it is essential to regulate the administration of right dose for treating specific diseases. For more than a few decades, the determination of the optimum dose of a drug to accomplish the preferred and successful pharmacological action with the least toxicity is a challenging task [70]. The most widely used ML technology in pharmaceutical formulation prediction is ANN. DL algorithms could be applied to determine proper drug doses with minimal toxicity. Telemetry observation of the antiarrhythmic medication dofetilide has been done for 3 days because of its intensified toxicity risk. Levy *et al.* studied the ML algorithms role and dofetilide dose adjustment patterns for successful commencement of the medication and its dose prediction [71]. A reinforcement learning algorithm that is familiar with unsupervised learning can predict dosing decisions with an accuracy of 96.1%. A data-driven prediction system using an ML technique proficient of modeling pathogen-drug dynamics and projecting efficiency of dosage fixing and medication administration systems were developed. Using metronidazole and Giardia lamblia, the approach was confirmed for cell-drug interaction, with an accuracy of 85% [72].

Ter-Levonian and Koshechkin analyzed articles on ML and DL and reported that DL has the competence to select the required dosage regimen and can decide the proper combinations for any treatment strategies [73]. Drug Synergy Combinations strongly prove that DL approach is the best for dose prediction and therapeutic action. CoSynE and INferring Drug Interactions using chemoGenomics and Orthology (INDIGO) algorithms are employed for the synergistic combination selection of antibacterial agents. INDIGO identified that the combination of antagonistic antibiotics moxifloxacin and spectinomycin could turn into extremely synergistic by adding Clofazimine as a third drug. Comparison between DeepSynergy approaches and a few other ML approaches like elastic nets, gradient boosting machines, RF, and SVM evidenced the implication of deep synergy over other methods for envisaging novel therapeutic interactions of drugs and cell lines that have been studied. In the NCi ALMANAC database, 2620 medication combinations were evaluated in 60 cancer cell lines, yielding 3.04 million data points. *In vitro*, synergistic drug interaction between Navelbine and Iressa in the SK-MEL-5 melanoma cell line was also confirmed by Ter-Levonian and Koshechkin [73].

Treatments for many life-threatening diseases are done by prescribing/dispensing multiple drugs and it has become a routine practice especially in cancer treatment. In contrast to single-agent trials, finding a dose for combinatorial drugs poses various encounters. Lin and Yin proposed a novel Bayesian adaptive drug-combination trial design based on a resilient dimension-reduction algorithm [74]. Weight, height, and age are the key factors for precise calculation of dose to avoid toxicity primarily in children. Pediatricians have piloted endless wide-ranging medical literature reviews and data to gather proof-based drug dosage data and to deliver a platform that recommends drug dosing. Rodle *et al.* defined the design of a model for the recommendation of pediatric drug selection and dosing based on clinical medication data. They launched an Extract-Transform-Load (ETL) process to offer data for ANNs, which includes patients' age, weight, and full medication characteristics (e.g., dosage and route of application) and emphasis on three active substances, namely paracetamol, ibuprofen, and cefotaxim. The genetic algorithm with backpropagation has reached the maximum accuracy among other learning algorithms [75]. The transplantation of organs is a major source of apprehension in the medical industry, especially liver and kidney transplantation as it is very vital for their survival. For transplantation protocol, tacrolimus (an immunosuppressant drug) is generally prescribed for suppressing immunity. DNN enables the optimization of these kinds of drugs concerning the characteristics of patients. This strategy improves the ability to overcome numerous risk factors by properly predicting the formulation requirements of tacrolimus for organ transplants in a tailored manner. This prediction technique will take into account minute details that influence tacrolimus dosage variance [76]. Boosted regression trees, Bayesian additive regression trees, multivariate adaptive regression splines are other ANN approaches to decide the optimal dose of tacrolimus [77].

Antibiotics are essential in the cure of various ailments, but clinicians observed failures of antibiotics secondary to bacterial resistance. The advanced tools of DL are reported to address these issues. At Hokkaido University Hospital, a study was conducted by enrolling 654 patients with the rationale to develop an algorithm for primary dose sets of vancomycin [VCM] and was called VCM decision tree [DT] analysis. VCM daily doses calculated by DT algorithm ranged from 20.0 to 58.1 mg/kg while with nomogram range of 15 to 40 mg/kg with eGFR ≥50.13. As a result, the amounts suggested by the DT are higher than nomogram, which tend to be underdosing. Therefore, it was concluded that ML is beneficial for dose fixation and DT algorithm attained the maximum therapeutic range for vancomycin in comparison to conventional methods of dose setting [78]. Prediction of the dose was performed using 40 patients with the Bayesian network [BN] and compared with body weight-adjusted doses calculation. The BN seems to be an optimal approach to estimate the first dose of amikacin and proves its probable utilization for other antibiotics doses calculation, which was not involved in clinical practice blood parameter detection [79].

AI-PRS, an AI-based platform, was introduced by Shen *et al.* for selecting optimal doses and combinations of drugs for antiretroviral therapy [HIV] [80]. It is an NN-driven method, which links efficacy to drug dosage and its combinations by employing a parabolic response curve [PRS]. Using the PRS method, a combination of antiviral drugs, including efavirenz, lamivudine, and tenofovir, was administered to 10 HIV patients. The starting dose of tenofovir decreased by 33% without causing virus relapse, and it was concluded that AI-PRS optimal drug dosage platform can also be conveniently applied to other ailments. DL has extensive application in screening the dose of cancer drugs and radiation therapy. Pantuck *et al.* established CURATE. AI to guide the selection of optimum drug dose from the patient's data records. A combination of ZEN-3694, an investigational drug and chemotherapeutic drug enzalutamide, was administered to a patient with prostate cancer [81]. Applying CURATE. In AI, it was discovered that a 50% lower dose of ZEN-3694 than the beginning dose is adequate to stop cancer development. Lu *et al.* suggested a DL method created using neural ordinary differential equations [neural-ODE] and concluded that neural-ODE is the perfect pharmacokinetic tool for the prediction of untested treatment regimens prediction [82]. Timing and dosing data are incorporated directly at the decoder stage to enable the adoption of this method to a different treatment regimen. This model will have future scope in *in vitro/in vivo* extrapolation and pharmacokinetic profiling. DeepDose is a DL-based approach for rapid dose calculations in radiation therapy [83]. An ML approach based on dose demands was used to detect the ideal starting dose of the anticoagulant warfarin [84]. Similarly, a perfect dose of heparin is obtained with the help of a deep reinforcement learning approach [85]. ML approaches, like multilayer perceptron network, classification, regression trees, and k-nearest neighbor, were used by Hu *et al.* to establish a safe beginning dose of the cardiac medication digoxin [86]. Zhu *et al.* used noninvasive quantifiable features to validate the amount [C/D ratio] of lamotrigine by employing a dose-adjusted ML approach. For drug monitoring, 15 ML models were optimized using an extra tree regression algorithm, and the results of these studies can direct the clinicians for suitable dose adjustment in patients to minimize adverse reactions and can be conveniently used for other drugs in the future [87].

Using AttPharm, drug formulation data sets among eight groups of cyclodextrins [CD] and 1320 different ranges of distinct molecules were retrieved through academic literature published between 1990 and 2018. AttPharm used representation learning to manage the feature values and physical meaning separately. AttPharm came in three different flavors: AttPharm, AttPharm-formula, and AttPharm-formula-ResNet. The AttPharm-formula-ResNet was used to estimate the CD binding-free energy, which also took into account weight distributions that may be characterized as feature level, as well as sample level interpretability. Preparation into CD inclusion complexes can increase insoluble drug solubility and bioavailability, improve drug stability, mask undesirable odors, and lessen medication irritation and side effects. The findings revealed that in the pharmaceutical data set, lipophilic contact among sender and the receiver compounds, steric hindrance, testing temperature, and hydrogen bonds all have a substantial influence on the development of CD complexation [88]. This is the starting point toward developing pharmaceutical formulations utilizing attention-based DNNs. Several pharmaceutical and nutrition operations can potentially benefit from the proposed strategy.

Because of inadequate experimental data, ANNs' formulation prediction accuracy is low. Pharmaceutical data in formulation consists of various compositions and production procedures, which are neither visual nor sequence data. As a result, the fully-connected deep feed-forward network is a nice option regarding pharmaceutical formulation prediction. DNNs beat ANNs with one hidden layer in the prediction of orally disintegrating tablet, according to a recent study [89]. Further comparisons of DL with other ML approaches are required to predict good formulations. The small data set with imbalanced input space is one of the most difficult formulation prediction elements. The data splitting algorithm and assessment parameters appropriate for pharmaceutical formulation data sets should be examined for improved performance. DNNs [SRMT] were trained using the data. Compared with other ML methods, DL can uncover the complex relationship among formulations and their *in-vitro* characteristics, indicating that DL has a bright future in pharmaceutical formulation prediction [78, 89].

1.3.2 DL in Dissolution and Release Studies

The poor solubility of APIs poses a significant barrier in dosage form development. Model formulation technology development using DL, especially investigational and predictive tools, is advantageous to solve several difficulties that pharmaceutical manufacturers face. Computational approaches performed by Mendyk *et al.* (2019) to predict bicalutamide dissolution from solid dispersion formulated using different carriers [90]. AI techniques like decision trees, ANN, DNN, evolutionary computations, and rule-based systems were utilized for dissolution and release studies, which select all fundamental variables by default for successful pharmaceutical formulation. *In silico* simulations based on ab initio modeling were piloted to expose excipients and drug interactions. Three ML methods, including ensemble of regression trees [ERT], ANN, SVM, were applied to forecast the *in vitro* dissolution data of sustained-release formulations, among which ANN produced the exact results. In addition, the release rate of the drug from the formulation is influenced by the nature of API, matrix polymer content, polymer particle size distribution in a matrix [PSD], and compression force and all these parameters can be easily evaluated by ML-based techniques [91].

ANN is used as a suitable predicting model for the design of solid dosage formulation and also for evaluating the impact of numerous features such as compression parameters, physicochemical properties, etc. With the application of Chem software, the ANN model gets upgraded based on the input [hardness, particle size, and moisture] and output [percentage of drug release, mechanism of release pattern] data units. Based on optimal *in-vitro* disintegration time, as well as *in vivo* release profiles, trained ANN model is utilized to predict the most effective tablet compositions for effective pharmacokinetic action. Combination of fuzzy logic with neural networks provides an effective tool, which offers powerful and flexible results. Model drugs *viz.* naproxen, carbamazepine, chlorpropamide, ketoprofen, diazepam, and ibuprofen were formulated and subjected to their dissolution performance using Expert Network and the results suggested poor prediction with error. This led to the development of new data with an intelligent hybrid, which was found to be appropriate for the investigation of multiple BCS class II drugs [92] OXPIRT was used to produce an immediate-release generic tablet in pilot-scale production [93]. Commercially available software used a four-layered artificial neural network [4LNN] to forecast the disintegration data from physicochemical characteristics of drugs. The outcomes demonstrated that the 4LNN approach is a superior model for predicting dissolution data when compared to traditional three-layered models [94].

1.3.3   DL in the Manufacturing Process

Following the discovery of a novel therapeutic molecule, the inclusion of these drug molecules into a suitable dosage form with desirable delivery characteristics is a technological art. In this case, AI can take the role of the classic trial-and-error method. Stability, dissolution, porosity, and other formulation design apprehensions can be solved using a variety of computational techniques for the successful production of various pharmaceutical formulations.

As manufacturing processes become more complex and there is a greater desire for effectiveness and superior product quality, advanced manufacturing techniques attempt to deliver human expertise to machineries, which is continually changing industrial practice. AI integration in industrial processes, especially product production, could benefit the pharmaceutical business. Reynolds-Averaged Navier-Stokes solvers expertise has been used to investigate the effect of agitation and stress levels in various machinery, allowing many pharmaceutical activities to be automated. Advanced ways to resolve problems in the pharmaceutical manufacturing process are used in related systems, like large eddy and direct numerical simulations [95].

Discrete element modeling has been widely used in the pharmaceutical manufacturing process, particularly for isolation of powders in a binary mixture, predicting tablets coating techniques, the effects of varying blade speed and shape, and analyzing time consumed by tablets in the spray region. To reduce tablet capping, ANNs and fuzzy tools are being used to investigate the association between machine characteristics with capping concerns on the manufacturing line. Meta classifiers and tablet classifiers are AI technologies that contribute to regulating the final product's quality standard. AI can also be used to regulate in-line manufacturing processes to attain anticipated product quality. In the total quality management (TQM) skilled method, deep data mining and diverse knowledge discovery protocols can be employed to formulate complicated judgments, including developing new methods for pharmaceutical quality control [88, 95].

DL-based decision-support techniques utilize rule-based systems to choose the type, nature, and quantity of excipients for manufacturing process depending on the drugs' physical and chemical characteristics. They use a response tool to continuously observe and change the procedure [57, 95]. Guo *et al.* combined Expert Systems [ES] and ANN to establish a hybrid system to advance direct-filling hard gelatin capsules containing piroxicam that successfully meet dissolving profile parameters. Based on the input parameters, MODEL EXPERT SYSTEM [MES] prepares formulation development recommendations, as well as judgments [95, 96].

Continuous Manufacturing [CM] of pharmaceutical formulation is a novel method in the pharma sector. To examine the process and characterize the impact on quality characteristics, DL techniques are utilized to forecast the quality [output] with numerous critical process parameters [input]. DL reduces noise and simplifies data interpretation for proper understanding of the process. With 2500 epochs, the Rectified Linear Unit [ReLU] activation function and ADAM optimizer have been utilized [number of learning cycles]. With less calibration error [10%], API concentrations, polydispersity index values, and loss on drying values were estimated. The amount of inaccuracy allows DNN to monitor the process effectively, and the most important process parameters may be determined at a complex level of process comprehension [97]. The synergy between process analytical technology and data science creates a superior monitoring framework of the continuous manufacturing line. This raises awareness of this cutting-edge production process, as well as the advancement of AI/ML/DL in pharmaceutical formulation design and is depicted in Figure 1.2.

A hot-melt extrusion [HME], an ML model created by the utilization of ANN, and decision trees can successfully manufacture the drug products. The role of ANNs in preformulation studies helps to identify

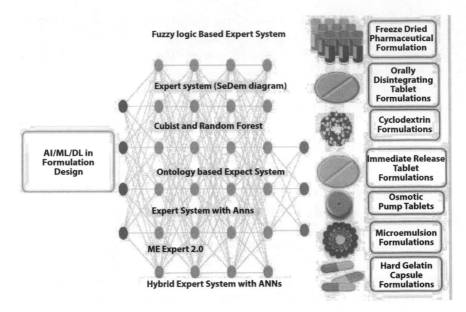

Figure 1.2   Applications of AI/ML/DL in the design of pharmaceutical formulations.

physicochemical characteristics of polymers of amorphous nature, glass transition temperature, and flow characteristics [98]. It is also utilized to see how excipient amount, as well as process restrictions, affects medication [prednisolone] release from pellets. ANNs are also applied to evaluate the process parameters of HME for a vaginal film [99]. In all these cases, it has a 1% error for the predicted values compared to experimental data. The application of ANNs for the improvement of [BCS] class IV drugs properties is another breakthrough. ANNs have meritorious applications for ranitidine hydrochloride polymorphic form quantification in multicomponent tablets [100].

3D printing [3DP] is a new production method for accurate personalized drug-loaded formulation production. The application of DL in 3D technology has the advantage to reduce costs and rationalize the formulation parameters of drug-loaded products. In an ML model, generative adversarial networks [GANs] can generate novel chemical structures similar to a drug. It is utilized to enhance film-forming formulations and the DNNs could accomplish prognostic precision, with f2 score of 99.99 [101]. A software, namely M3DISEEN based on ML technique, was applied on a data set containing 145 exclusive excipients with 614 drug-loaded formulations. Supervised ML techniques, like DL, k-nearest neighbors, multivariate linear regression, SVM, traditional neural networks, and random forest, were utilized in rationalizing the pharmaceutical 3DP procedure [102]. Even though the biopharmaceutical industry is hesitant to adopt ML as a standard tool for bioprocess development due to the potentially catastrophic consequences of faulty products, biopharmaceutical manufacturing continues to surprise us with new applications and case studies every year. Technological advancements in DL and computing will inevitably lead to greater use of these techniques, and case studies like this are critical in giving meaningful benchmarking material to the community. In terms of quality control, root cause analysis, predictive maintenance, and waste reduction, as well as optimizing the automation process, DL can provide a greater variety of benefits. This technology appears to work best when combined with standard algorithms to improve process performance and reduce waste and expenses of the pharmaceutical industry.

1.4   Deep Learning Models for Nanoparticle-Based Drug Delivery

Prediction of biological processes including drug delivery and toxic off-target effects are possible nowadays through intelligent data management systems using automated microscopy imaging. Researchers widely utilize these modern DL-based models for nanoparticle and SSDD applications. This is because they highly suggest the probability to monitor the cell's response or the expression of some desired protein is potentially high when each cell is followed over time. In this regard, time-lapse microscopy has been recently utilized in identifying the cellular expression based on the time-lapse data of the liver cell lines treated with mRNA-loaded lipid nanoparticles. This advanced research phenomenon using data sets and corresponding experimental data prediction always leads to a newer perspective of biological insights. Jones *et al.*, illustrates the potential and efficiency of data extraction and ML methods in predicting nanoparticle morphological and anatomical feature [109].

Moreover, optimization of DL to a relatively smaller data set will play a dramatic role with the list of important advantages. It includes reduced processing time and storage requirement that ultimately leads to a faster acquisition time. However, the application of DL methodologies to the images of cells and tissue is having its limitations due to the unavailability of annotated data. This could be addressed through the usage of larger annotated data sets, for example, ImageNet [103].

CNNs and RNNs are highly applied in the area of biomedical image analysis. More importantly, RNN is used for functional DNA sequence quantification, owing to its ability to analyze sequential data followed by its ubiquitous usage in machine translation and speech recognition. The time series-based sequential data prediction has revolutionized the modern era, providing the exploration of the hidden biological mechanisms involved in the specific processes. Therefore, modeling of the cell dynamics through the cell imaging process at the time-lapse scale would provide a suitable evaluation of the nanoparticle function for appropriate formulation and model development initiation.

1.4.1   Nanoparticles With High Drug Delivery Capacities Using Perturbation Theory

DL is an automated learning procedure that could alter the low-level representation to a more abstract level. However, in the case of nanoparticle formulation prediction, the fully connected deep feed-forward network is preferred as these data are neither image nor sequential data. The nanoparticle formulation data, which often deal with the formulation composition and manufacturing process, are found to be better analyzed through DNNs as compared to ANN. In the case of the developing stage of the nanoparticle-based formulation, a deep convolutional network was established for predicting the epoxidation reactivity of molecules to subsequently decrease the toxicity of the drug. Recently, DL has also been used in the prediction of pharmaceutical formulation through the construction of regression models [89].

Santana *et al.* identified a nanoparticle drug release system using perturbation theory machine learning [PTML] models [104]. Here, the researchers made a detailed analysis using more than 30,000 preclinical from ChEMBL. For comparative purposes, linear and nonlinear PTML representations were trained using R studio scripts. This study based on the multilabel PTML model was found novel, and it is the first study to make a suitable choice of drug, their coating agent, metal and metal-oxide nanoparticles [MONP] for the designing of a proper SSDD system. The methodology involves drug data preprocessing, MONP data preprocessing, the fusion of MONP-drug information, and eventually the creation of the PTML linear model. This model additionally stands out from other previously built models as it provides optimal activity/toxicity profiles [104]. Apart from getting SSDD, nanoformulation might be observed for its limitations because of its enormous adverse/side effects related data.

With human intelligence, it is not that effective in managing the positive results data along with their side effects in the later stages. AI drives and supports clinicians in operating huge data sets. Thus, an integrated approach with AI could help in making the right decision for the rapid treatment and also help to identify and reduce the long-term side effects [1].

1.4.2 Artificial Intelligence and Drug Delivery Algorithms

The success of the nanoparticle-based drug delivery system critically depends on the initial stages of formulation development. Here, the expert systems [ESs] and ANN are the two major tools for the process of formulation development. Integration of AI and nanotechnology would probably aid in the advancement of nanosystems through smarter technological ideas [2]. Moreover, ANN is also being considered as an important and popular ML tool in formulation prediction as it could stimulate the structure/function of biological neural networks. In nanomedicine, ANN is playing a crucial role in overcoming the physical limitations of nanotechnology. ANN is particularly used in the creation of a mathematical model, which could foresee the particle size along with the polydispersity index [PDI]. These two are the critical parameters in deciding the suitability of drug release from the prepared nanoformulation. Also, it is understood that the polymer drug ratio and the molecular weight of polymers will be determining the above said critical parameters in attaining efficient nanoparticle formation.

In the visualization aspect, scanning probe microscopy has been considered a powerful tool in imaging sample-probe interactions. However, the application of AI with this microscopy would provide a deeper knowledge through estimation of not only the image data but also the dielectric constants and sample–tip distance [105]. It is noteworthy to mention that the interaction of AI with nanotechnology is a bidirectional approach. It is also possible with the trained ANN to predict the entrapment efficiency, which would greatly aid in the development of efficient therapeutics [101]. AI-based techniques and their paradigms were also found useful at nanoscale level simulations for sensory information processing. ML algorithms deal with the diverse data types to successfully predict disease risk, diagnosis, and appropriate management. This also provides data processing, model training, and system management. It makes it possible in pooling the patients' phenotypic and genotypic data for a better understanding of the disease condition by proper maintenance of the integrated data sets. These algorithms of AI along with the DL infrastructure confer flexibility and scalability in dealing with complex data sets for solving diverse clinical

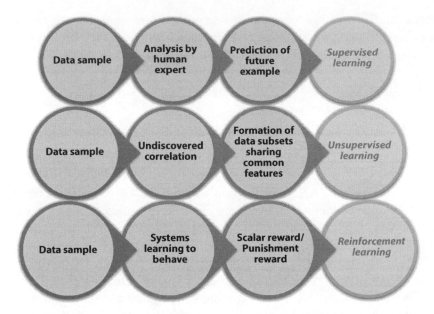

Figure 1.3 Categories of ML algorithms in learning relationship of input and output data.

problems. AI-based algorithms when coupled with modular ML tools will derive some of the unique ML features [106]. ML algorithms have been categorized based on how it learns the association or relationship between the input and output data [Figure 1.3].

Although these modern techniques have shown many benefits in maintaining healthcare data, ethical-based considerations also need to be taken into account. It includes the data privacy and management system, medicolegal complications, doctors' interests, and knowledge in the practical application of these ML tools [107].

1.4.3   Nanoinformatics

Drug delivery and yield optimization are aided by nanoinformatics, which makes decision making easier in several areas of research. Nanomedicine has benefited from information and data science in several aspects especially formulation, encapsulation, characterization, and biological outcomes. These efforts aid academic and pharmaceutical industry researchers in determining which medications to encapsulate, what carrier to use, and what conditions to proceed for a successful manufacturing process [108].

More than genomic, phenotypic, and disease-based data processing, the ML approach helps in the estimation of *in-vitro* and *in-vivo* data through IVIVC. The integrated IVIVC and ANN would provide the researcher with the pharmacokinetic parameters in deriving complex relationships of the patients' data with the nanoparticle drug formulation. This helps in the understanding of the release kinetics of the drug from the nanoformulation and its probability in site-specific delivery at the targeted site. In this regard, generalized regression neural network [GRNN] is a tool employed in analyzing *in vivo* data. This is a multiunit particle system in optimizing formulation parameters for getting the suitable drug release profile at the targeted site of delivery [72]. When it comes to the future of nanoinformatics, data mining will play a considerably larger role and it holds immense promise for further breakthroughs and discovery. PM and innovative treatments with molecular precision could also have substantial consequences for nanomedicine and SSDD. It appears likely that nanomedicine and medication delivery will change from a trial-and-error method to a digital, tailored, and automated approach using AI/ML/DL in the coming decade. It will change how we select pharmaceuticals, match carriers to diseases, and fine-tune variables in the preparation process [108]. Several review publications have focused on the difficulties in developing nano-QSARs, such as a deficiency of quality experimental information, a nonexistence of information about nanoparticle interactions, such as aggregation, polydispersity index, and so on [72, 109]. These are unquestionably substantial challenges in the field of nanoinformatics.

1.5   Model Prediction for Site-Specific Drug Delivery

1.5.1   Prediction of Mode and a Site-Specific Action

The process of designing a drug delivery system is fraught with difficulties, including forecasting the connection among formulation constraints and treatment consequences, as well as unforeseen events [72]. It has also been documented that microchips are useful to monitor the precise distribution of medications related to blood thinning category and thereby helps in reducing the danger of life-threatening illnesses or complications [110]. For automated regulation of the venous and arterial circulation, a fuzzy logic-based automated medication administration system was developed and tested [72]. The ability of trained ANN to anticipate the particle size of nanoparticles and entrapment efficiency could be crucial in the creation of more effective nanotherapeutics. Determining appropriate physicochemical characteristics of nanoparticles and ensuring maximum accumulation at the target region is crucial for theranostic applications. ANNs were used to detect appropriate particle size and to target the sick microvasculature [72, 110]. The impact of process parameters on papain loaded alginate beads was assessed using an ANN model, resulting in increased stability and site-specific delivery. Alginate beads can be used to deliver papain to the small intestine, according to dissolution tests using the ANN model. The shelf life of entrapped papain was significantly improved after accelerated and long-term stability tests, confirming the method's utility in the manufacture of beads capable of SSDD. For monitoring the persistent release of chemotherapeutic drugs, an ANN-based predictive controller was described. The development of DNN models allows for the prediction of drug pharmacological characteristics, including modes of action and indications. The undirected graph recursive neural networks approach can foresee drug-induced liver damage in addition to offering predictive solubility models [72, 87, 108, 110]. On small data, DL models have been effectively created to forecast pharmaceutical formulations. The external data sets demonstrated the models' high generalization performance. Because DL can discover the complicated association in the data, the created models were more effective in predicting essential characteristics in regression situations than models trained using conventional ML methods. Quality by design [QbD] elements must be incorporated throughout the drug development process for modern pharmaceutical development to be successful. Not only may ML technologies aid in the prediction of *in vivo* and *in vitro* features created on process and formulation data, but they could also aid in pharmaceutical experimental strategy and product quality control. In the implementation of QbD, DL has a lot of promise. The time takes to generate a therapeutic product, as well as the amount of material used, can be drastically reduced using DL. Furthermore, the integration of pharmaceutics and AI across disciplines may transform the paradigm of pharmaceutical research away from experience-based studies and toward data-driven techniques [89].

Primary research among healthcare professionals and persons working with AI is the identification of personalized treatment along with the SSDD method. However, the computer-based prediction of drug response in the patient become challenging due to the unavailability of clinical data and algorithm. Later on, the advancement of DL approaches helps in the accurate prediction of the computational drug response. Improvement of these kinds of ML techniques has been made through its comparison for its practical application for clinicians. Here, the incorporation of modalities like single-cell profiling could rapidly find some effective drug combinations in cancer care improvement. The basic workflow of building a DL model in cancer prognosis prediction involves the preliminary step in the collection of input data. This comprises clinical data, image data, and multi-omics data. It is followed by the feature examination through the handling of missing data and the building of the DL model. Finally, the built model will be subjected to model validation for its suitable and significant application [111].

Xu *et al.* have recently explained the application and significance of the ML approach in predicting the drug-target interaction [112]. The larger amount of data incorporated accompanied with the modern computer-based techniques is playing a vigorous role in the latest biological and medical research. Utilization of existing data background has been immensely identified as a significant feature in the successful prediction of drug-target interaction, i.e., databases like UniProt, PubChem, DrugBank, KEGG, etc. These databases would give comprising information about the metabolism and action potential of the chosen drug when subjected to a particular disease or information. Based on the available literature and experimental data, understanding the appropriate mechanism of action, dosage requirement followed by the finding that any other drug toxic effects to the patient could become possible [110–112]. A web server like ADMETsar, which explains the fate of any drug along with its toxic effect is also much useful in estimating the severity of the drug before the usage with the patient. This computer-based prediction significantly helps the researchers and clinical experts by minimization of the preliminary laboratory diagnostics for every patient. If proper healthcare electronic data are maintained for every individual across the country, whenever a person gets a disease or accident, immediate analysis through ML followed by appropriate treatment becomes a greater success in the field of medicine and healthcare. Some governing toolkits, like SwissTargetPrediction, RDkit, OpenChem, iFuture, etc., are contributing much to the progress of the interdisciplinary field of bioinformatics or cheminformatics. Most of these toolkits that are working based on python aim in providing a comprehensive history and action potential of the biologically active molecules when entering the human system. The complete metabolic profile, its site-of-action, followed by the disease controlling mechanism. helps the researchers to classify and use the drug based on the varied requirement of patients and their disease severity rate [4, 113]. The role of ANN nowadays is widely being applied in controlled drug delivery systems. *In vitro* estimation of drug release profiles is a time-consuming and tedious process. However, ANN a combination of fully interconnected artificial neurons could provide its function in analyzing the pharmaceutical as well as pharmacokinetic areas. Accordingly, Rafienia *et al.* (2010) have studied the application of ANN called feed-forward neural networks, which comprises multilayer perceptron, radial basis function network, and generalized regression neural network. In this particular study, the release of drugs, like betamethasone and betamethasone acetate, have been studied which are present in the *in situ* forming systems [2]. More importantly, input vectors of the ANNs of this study include drug concentration, gamma irradiation, additive uses, and drug type.

ML is a widely used big data analysis tool that may be used to analyze huge quantities of complicated healthcare data. Conversely, to utilize it effectively in patient care, some of the critical key issues and several kinds of limitations need to be considered while its implementation. The data-driven prediction system could help in determining the drug dosing effectiveness based on the computational and ML approach. This suitably aids in reducing the experimental time taken to study every dosing scenario of the drug selected for the study. This method is scalable and robust in understanding the drug-pathogen dynamics along with the effectiveness of drug treatment. A data-driven system has been developed with two distinct states lime drug concentration and pathogen population. These states would be accordingly analyzed for the understanding of drug-cell interaction over time using a temporal model [36, 113]. Additionally, this data-driven Variable Length Markov Model [VLMM] has been observed for increased flexibility which is opposite to the Hidden Markov Models. It is developed to interpret dynamic-based drug-pathogen samples rather than dealing with the static data sets. This technique adopts Fuzzy-C-Mean [FCM] clustering protocol to develop the online learning algorithms. Here, online learning algorithms were found suitable compared to offline-based algorithms like Bayesian.

1.5.2 Precision Medicine

Precision medicine deals with treatments appreciably designed for diagnosis and treatment of small groups, rather than larger populations. In this regard, proper maintenance of an individual's clinical data is mandatory for diagnosis, treatment, and intermittent check-ups for complete monitoring of the patient. This becomes possible nowadays through the maintenance of electronic health records [EHRs], which could help in sharpening the doctor's picture over the individual patient. It is achieved through ML encompassing algorithmic methods without the requirement of computer programming [114, 115]. However, AI-based PM is now in its primary phase of development, especially AI-based treatments. Although AI-based diagnostic tools and methods are introduced in hospitals, complete utilization and getting promising clinical data are still not much attained.

For example, deep genomics, a startup company is using AI in drug discovery through analyzing large genomic databases. But, it is still working on its implementation to develop a complete precision-based treatment strategy. Researchers have discovered the potential of the DL model in cancer precision medicine. It helps in accurate analysis of tumor data followed by recommending the suitable and best possible treatment aiding in the accelerated cancer precision medicine. Due to the varied responses of cancer therapeutic drugs with different patients, approval by FDA is a time-consuming process. This is successfully overcome based on the development of the DL model with a variety of drug combinations to various patients' metabolism for the drug response. A clear understanding of drug choice for each patient is available through the proper DL model, as it recommends the suitable drug target for the particular cancer type and its rate of severity which depends on each patient. The specific model developed by researchers is the DrugCell, where the team trained it with over 1,200 tumor cell lines and their significant response to FDA-approved drug moieties. This could provide the best-possible drug when the researcher input the particular tumor data. It helps in attaining SSDD followed by a minimal rate of drug toxicity at healthier sites. In addition, this DrugCell model could show the biological pathways involved in the drug metabolism, which is much helpful in the identification of other possible pathways to block further cancer progression.

1.6 Future Scope and Challenges

Many pharmaceutical companies are concentrating on artificial intelligence [AI] and related technologies to cut costs and reduce the risk of failure in pharmaceutical formulation, SSDD, and development. The need for AI and related technologies has increased, and its expected development since 2017 shows that these technologies undoubtedly transform the pharmaceutical industries [95]. Numerous pharmaceutical companies make significant investments in computation-based technologies to reduce the obstacles they confront in the pharmaceutical research, drug development, and manufacturing process [40]. In recent years, DL has become more widely used in pharmaceutical formulation research. When compared to other methodologies, DL methodology correctly predicts physiochemical properties, pharmacokinetic and pharmacodynamics functionalities of the drug molecule and has been considered as an important aspect in the pharmaceutical manufacturing process. DL has outdone different computational methods like BN, SVM, and RF in predicting toxicity in the 2016

Tox21 Data Challenge. Furthermore, researchers can use DL to explore the expanding data sets in drug discovery and development, allowing them to not only learn from previous experience but also forecast drug repurposing. Almost all recent researches suggested that DL outperformed other ML approaches in terms of prediction performance [108, 116].

AI/ML/DL technologies involved in the drug discovery, development, and it is possible to picture the process of developing a therapeutic product from the lab to the patient's bedside. These technologies help to assist in decision-making, support rational drug design, precise treatment, including PM, and accomplish the application of data created for future drug development. E-VAI is decision making and systematic AI approach that employs ML algorithms and a simple user interface to construct analytical roadmaps based on related stakeholders and current market share to forecast significant drivers in pharmaceutical trades. This aids marketing executives in allocating resources for improving sales, increasing market share, and projecting where to invest [95, 117].

Personalized drugs and their necessary dose, release characteristics, and additional features can be completed with the integration of DL in pharmaceutical product manufacturing. Using the most up-to-date tools will reduce the period it takes for pharmaceutical products to reach the market and improve product quality and safety of the formulation process. It also maximizes available resources while being cost-effective, highlighting the need for automation [95, 117–120]. By processing massive volumes of data from scientific journals and tests, DL is used to uncover potential medications and narrow down the design of new drugs. People must determine the direction research and development should go.

Alternative ML approaches like interpretable and explainable ML, are more prominent, hence formulation improvement efforts concentrated solely on prediction accuracy. Several research reports are expected to emphasize on the analysis of ML models to gain scientific comprehension, as well as precise predictions. These experiment-planning algorithms will almost certainly be employed in the production of drug formulations to advise researchers on which trials to conduct to achieve desired formulation attributes with the least amount of effort [119, 120].

DL can also help with the subsequent inclusion of the medicine in its right dose form, as well as its optimization and swift decision making, resulting in speedier production of higher-quality items with consistent batch-to-batch consistency [119–122]. It can also help establish the product's safety and efficacy in clinical studies, as well as ensure correct market positioning and costs through detailed market analysis and forecasting. DL is predicted to become a vital tool in the pharmaceutical industry shortly, even though no drugs have been launched based on these approaches so far, and specific issues in the implementation of this technology persist.

1.7   Conclusion

In recent decades, DL technologies have unquestionably changed pharmaceutical drug discovery platforms, and they are now increasingly being integrated into drug delivery systems. More inventive techniques and strategies are required due to the vast amounts of time and money spent on drug research and development. Modern computational methods are used for drug toxicity screening, categorization, and prediction in addition to virtual screening methods. In drug discovery and delivery, DL models are rapidly gaining prominence. DL could be used to assess the success of a target-based drug design, forecast the dynamics of the drug-pathogen/target cells, and estimate the efficacy of various drug delivery strategies. An ideal dosing strategy could be developed using DNN algorithms, balancing the trade-off between side effects and dosage. The development of DNN models allows predicting drug pharmacological characteristics, including modes of action and indications. In the future, DL will be a critical part of drug discovery, development, and PM and will be a critical component of drug formulation and personalized therapy. Furthermore, pharmaceutical experts have yet to fully use several recent developments in AI/ML/DL in the development of medication formulations and SSDD. In the fields of oncology, cardiovascular illnesses, and CNS disorders, leading pharmaceutical companies are collaborating with various AI organizations to discover effective and optimum medication candidates. Pharmaceutical experts may be able to use ML/DL algorithms to focus the impact of API-material amalgamations on formulation constraints, thus speeding up the drug formulation/manufacturing process. We believe that introducing more DL models into the pharmaceutical sciences will provide us with the tools we need to produce successful medications, as well as accelerate the pace of data-driven formulations. Strong multidisciplinary association between pharmaceutical, data, and computer scientists will be required for the success and increasing usage of DL as smart and intelligent decision support for pharmaceutical manufacturing science in the future.

References

1. Petrak, K., Artificial intelligence and disease-site specific targeting of drugs. *ASCB.*, 3, 12–14, 2019.
2. Rafienia, M., Amiri, M., Janmaleki, M., Sadeghian, A., Application of artificial neural networks in controlled drug delivery systems. *Appl. Artif. Intell.*, 24, 807, 2010.
3. Kitchen, D.B., Decornez, H., Furr, J.R., Bajorath, J., Docking and scoring in virtual screening for drug discovery: Methods and applications. *Nat. Rev. Drug Discovery*, 3, 935, 2004.
4. Chen, H., Engkvist, O., Wang, Y., Olivecrona, M., Blaschke, T., The rise of deep learning in drug discovery. *Drug Discovery Today*, 23, 1241, 2018.
5. Casalini, T., Not only *in silico* drug discovery: Molecular modeling towards *in-silico* drug delivery formulations. *J. Control Release.*, 332, 390, 2021.
6. Gapsys, V., Pérez-Benito, L., Aldeghi, M., Seeliger, D., van Vlijmen, H., Tresadern, G., de Groot, B.L., Large scale relative protein ligand binding affinities using non-equilibrium alchemy. *Chem. Sci.*, 11, 1140, 2020.
7. Hossain, S., Kabedev, A., Parrow, A., Bergström, C.A.S., Larsson, P., Molecular simulation as a computational pharmaceutics tool to predict drug solubility, solubilization processes and partitioning. *Eur. J. Pharm. Biopharm.*, 137, 46, 2019.
8. Maltarollo, V.G., Kronenberger, T., Wrenger, C., Honorio, K.M., Current trends in quantitative structure–activity relationship validation and applications on drug discovery. *Future Sci. OA.*, 3, FSO214, 2017.
9. Han, X., Jiang, H., Han, L., Xiong, X., He, Y., Fu, C., Xu, R., Zhang, D., Lin, J., Yang, M., A novel quantified bitterness evaluation model for traditional Chinese herbs based on an animal ethology principle. *Acta Pharm. Sin. B.*, 8, 209, 2018.
10. Lima, A.N., Philot, E.A., Trossini, G.H.G., Scott, L.P.B., Maltarollo, V.G., Honorio, K.M., Use of machine learning approaches for novel drug discovery. *Expert Opin. Drug Discovery*, 11, 225, 2016.
11. Sharma, S. and Sharma, D., Intelligently applying artificial intelligence in chemoinformatics. *Curr. Top. Med. Chem.*, 18, 1804, 2018.
12. Goodfellow, I., Bengio, Y., Courville, A., *Deep Learning*, pp. 201–208, Cambridge, MA, USA: MIT Press, 2016.
13. Hathout, R.M., Machine learning methods in drug delivery, in: *Applications of Artificial Intelligence in Process Systems Engineering*, pp. 361–380, Netherlands, Elsevier, 2021.
14. Pereira, J.C., Caffarena, E.R., dos Santos, C.N., Boosting docking-based virtual screening with deep learning. *J. Chem. Inf. Model.*, 56, 2495, 2016.
15. Golkov, V., Skwark, M.J., Mirchev, A., Dikov, G., Geanes, A.R., Mendenhall, J., Meiler, J., Cremers, D., 3D deep learning for biological function prediction from physical fields. *arXiv.*, 1704.04039, 2017.

16. Aliper, A., Plis, S., Artemov, A., Ulloa, A., Mamoshina, P., Zhavoronkov, A., Deep learning applications for predicting pharmacological properties of drugs and drug repurposing using transcriptomic data. *Mol. Pharm.*, 13, 7, 2524, 2016.

17. Lipinski, C.F., Maltarollo, V.G., Oliveira, P.R., da Silva, A.B.F., Honorio, K.M., Advances and perspectives in applying deep learning for drug design and discovery. *Front. Robot. AI.*, 6, 108, 2019.

18. Tsubaki, M., Tomii, K., Sese, J., Compound–protein interaction prediction with end-to-end learning of neural networks for graphs and sequences. *BION.*, 35, 309, 2018.

19. Lee, I., Keum, J., Nam, H., DeepConv-DTI: Prediction of drug-target interactions via deep learning with convolution on protein sequences. *PloS Comput. Biol.*, 15, e1007129, 2019.

20. Wen, M., Zhang, Z., Niu, S., Sha, H., Yang, R., Yun, Y., Lu, H., Deep-learning-based drug–target interaction prediction. *J. Proteome Res.*, 16, 1401, 2017.

21. Zhang, R., Li, J., Lu, J., Hu, R., Yuan, Y., Zhao, Z., Using deep learning for compound selectivity prediction. *Curr. Comput. Aided Drug Des.*, 12, 5, 2016.

22. Karim, A., Riahi, V., Newton, M.A.H., Dehzangi, A., Balle, T., Sattar, A., Quantitative toxicity prediction via meta ensembling of multitask deep learning models. *ACS Omega.*, 6, 12306, 2021.

23. Mullard, A., FDA drug approvals. *Nat. Rev. Drug Discov.*, 20, 85, 2021, 2020.

24. Doman, T.N., McGovern, S.L., Witherbee, B.J., Kasten, T.P., Kurumbail, R., Stallings, W.C., Connolly, D.T., Shoichet, B.K., Molecular docking and high-throughput screening for novel inhibitors of protein tyrosine phosphatase-1B. *J. Med. Chem.*, 45, 2213, 2002.

25. Zhavoronkov, A., Ivanenkov, Y.A., Aliper, A., Veselov, M.S., Aladinskiy, V.A., Aladinskaya, A.V., Terentiev, V.A., Polykovskiy, D.A., Kuznetsov, M.D., Asadulaev, A., Volkov, Y., Zholus, A., Shayakhmetov, R.R., Zhebrak, A., Minaeva, L.I., Zagribelnyy, B.A., Lee, L.H., Soll, R., Madge, D., Xing, L., Guo, T., Aspuru, Deep learning enables rapid identification of potent DDR1 kinase inhibitors. *Nat. Biotechnol.*, 37, 1038, 2019.

26. Stokes, J.M., Yang, K., Swanson, K., Jin, W., Cubillos-Ruiz, A., Donghia, N.M., MacNair, C.R., French, S., Carfrae, L.A., Bloom-Ackermann, Z., Tran, V.M., Chiappino-Pepe, A., Badran, A.H., Andrews, I.W., Chory, E.J., Church, G.M., Brown, E.D., Jaakkola, T.S., Barzilay, R., Collins, J.J., A deep learning approach to antibiotic discovery. *Cell.*, 180, 688, 2020.

27. Piñero, J., Bravo, Á., Queralt-Rosinach, N., Gutiérrez-Sacristán, A., Deu-Pons, J., Centeno, E., García-García, J., Sanz, F., Furlong, L.I., DisGeNET: A comprehensive platform integrating information on human disease-associated genes and variants. *Nucleic Acids Res.*, 45, D833, 2017.

28. Szklarczyk, D., Santos, A., Von Mering, C., Jensen, L.J., Bork, P., Kuhn, M., STITCH 5: Augmenting protein-chemical interaction networks with tissue and affinity data. *Nucleic Acids Res.*, 44, D380, 2016.

29. D'Souza, S., Prema, K.V., Balaji, S., Machine learning models for drug-target interactions: Current knowledge and future directions. *Drug Discovery Today*, 25, 748, 2020.

30. Baskin, I.I., Winkler, D., Tetko, I.V., A renaissance of neural networks in drug discovery. *Expert Opin. Drug Deliv.*, 11, 785, 2016.

31. Yuan, W., Jiang, D., Nambiar, D.K., Liew, L.P., Hay, M.P., Bloomstein, J., Lu, P., Turner, B., Le, Q.-T., Tibshirani, R., Khatri, P., Moloney, M.G., Koong, A.C., Chemical space mimicry for drug discovery. *J. Chem. Inform. Model.*, 57, 875, 2017.

32. Dana, D., Gadhiya, S.V., St Surin, L.G., Li, D., Naaz, F., Ali, Q., Paka, L., Yamin, M.A., Narayan, M., Goldberg, I.D., Narayan, P., Deep learning in drug discovery and medicine; scratching the surface. *Mol.*, 23, 2384, 2018.

33. Reher, R., Kim, H.W., Zhang, C., Mao, H.H., Wang, M., Nothias, L.F., Caraballo-Rodriguez, A.M., Glukhov, E., Teke, B., Leao, T., Alexander, K.L., Duggan, B.M., Van Everbroeck, E.L., Dorrestein, P.C., Cottrell, G.W., Gerwick, W.H., A convolutional neural network-based approach for the rapid annotation of molecularly diverse natural products. *J. Am. Chem. Soc*, 142, 4114, 2020.

34. Rathi, P.C., Ludlow, R.F., Verdonk, M.L., Practical high-quality electrostatic potential surfaces for drug discovery using a graph-convolutional deep neural network. *J. Med. Chem.*, 63, 8778, 2020.

35. Wu, Z., Pan, S., Chen, F., Long, G., Zhang, C., Yu, P.S., A comprehensive survey on graph neural networks. *arXiv.*, 00596.37, 2021, 1901.

36. Li, Y., Zhang, L., Liu, Z., Multi-objective *de novo* drug design with conditional graph generative model. *J. Cheminformatics.*, 10, 33, 2019.

37. Gupta, R., Srivastava, D., Sahu, M., Tiwari, S., Ambasta, R.K., Kumar, P., Artificial intelligence to deep learning: Machine intelligence approach for drug discovery. *Mol. Divers.*, 25, 1315, 2021.

38. Powles, J. and Hodson, H., Google deepmind and healthcare in an age of algorithms. *Health Technol. (Berl).*, 7, 4, 351, 2017.

39. AlQuraishi, M., End-to-End differentiable learning of protein structure. *Cell Syst.*, 8, 292, e3, 2019.

40. Chan, H.C.S., Shan, H., Dahoun, T., Vogel, H., Yuan, S., Advancing drug discovery via artificial intelligence. *Trends Pharmacol. Sci.*, 40, 592, 2019.

41. Genheden, S., Thakkar, A., Chadimová, V., Reymond, J.-L., Engkvist, O., Bjerrum, E., AiZynth-Finder: A fast, robust and fexible open-source software for retrosynthetic planning. *J. Cheminformatics.*, 12, 70, 2020.

42. Liu, Z., Du, J., Fang, J., Yin, Y., Xu, G., Xie, L., Deep screening: A deep learning-based screening web server for accelerating drug discovery. *Database (Oxford)*, baz104, 2019, 1, 2019.

43. Popova, M., Isayev, O., Tropsha, A., Deep reinforcement learning for *de novo* drug design. *Sci. Adv.*, 4, eaap7885, 2018.

44. Sarmadi, M., Behrens, A.M., McHugh, K.J., Contreras, H., Tochka, Z.L., Lu, X., Langer, R., Jaklenec, A., Modeling, design, and machine learning-based

framework for optimal injectability of microparticle-based drug formulations. *Sci. Adv.*, 6, eabb6594, 2020.

45. Bai, Q., Tan, S., Xu, T., Liu, H., Huang, J., Yao, X., MolAICal: A soft tool for 3D drug design of protein targets by artificial intelligence and classical algorithm. *Brief. Bioinf.*, 22, 1, 2021.

46. Lusci, A., Pollastri, G., Baldi, P., Deep architectures and deep learning in chemoinformatics: The prediction of aqueous solubility for drug-like molecules. *J. Chem. Inf. Model.*, 53, 1563, 2013.

47. Unterthiner, T., Mayr, A., Klambauer, G., Hochreiter, S., Toxicity prediction using deep learning. *arXiv*, 1503.01445, 2015.

48. Xu, Y., Dai, Z., Chen, F., Gao, S., Pei, J., Lai, L., Deep learning for drug-induced liver injury. *J. Chem. Inf. Model.*, 55, 2085, 2015.

49. Kearnes, S., McCloskey, K., Berndl, M., Pande, V., Riley, P., Molecular graph convolutions: Moving beyond fingerprints. *J. Comput. Aided Mol.*, 30, 595–608, 2016.

50. Altae-Tran, H., Ramsundar, B., Pappu, A.S., Pande, V., Low data drug discovery with one-shot learning. *ACS Cent. Sci.*, 3, 283, 2017.

51. Ohue, M., Ii, R., Yanagisawa, K., Akiyama, Y., Molecular activity prediction using graph convolutional deep neural network considering distance on a molecular graph. *arXiv*, 1907, 01103, 2019.

52. Wallach, I., Dzamba, M., Heifets, A., AtomNet: A deep convolutional neural network for bioactivity prediction in structure-based drug discovery. *arXiv*, 1510.02855, 2015.

53. Tian, K., Shao, M., Wang, Y., Guan, J., Zhou, S., Boosting compound-protein interaction prediction by deep learning. *Methods.*, 110, 64, 2016.

54. Merk, D., Friedrich, L., Grisoni, F., Schneider, G., *De Novo* design of bioactive small molecules by artificial intelligence. *Mol. Inform.*, 37, 1700153, 2018.

55. Maragakis, P., Nisonoff, H., Cole, B., Shaw, D.E., A deep-learning view of chemical space designed to facilitate drug discovery. *J. Chem. Inf. Model.*, 60, 4487, 2020.

56. Karpov, P., Godin, G., Tetko, I.V., Transformer-CNN: Swiss knife for QSAR modeling and interpretation. *J. Cheminformatics.*, 12, 17, 2020.

57. Xuan, P., Cui, H., Shen, T., Sheng, N., Zhang, T., HeteroDualNet: A dual convolutional neural network with heterogeneous layers for drug-disease association prediction via chou's five-step rule. *Front. Pharmacol.*, 10, 1301, 2019.

58. Pham, T.H., Qiu, Y., Zeng, J., Xie, L., Zhang, P., A deep learning framework for high-throughput mechanism-driven phenotype compound screening and its application to COVID-19 drug repurposing. *Nat. Mach. Intell.*, 3, 247, 2021.

59. Bustamam, A., Hamzah, H., Husna, N.A., Syarofina, S., Dwimantara, N., Yanuar, A., Sarwinda, D., Artificial intelligence paradigm for ligand-based virtual screening on the drug discovery of type 2 diabetes mellitus. *J. Big Data.*, 8, 74, 2021.

60. Zeng, X., Zhu, S., Liu, X., Zhou, Y., Nussinov, R., Cheng, F., deepDR: A network-based deep learning approach to *in silico* drug repositioning. *Bioinformatics.*, 35, 24, 5191, 2019.
61. Lavecchia, A., Deep learning in drug discovery: Opportunities, challenges and future prospects. *Drug Discovery Today*, 24, 10, 2017, 2019.
62. Park, K., A review of computational drug repurposing. *Transl. Clin. Pharmacol.*, 27, 2, 59–63, 2019.
63. You, J., McLeod, R.D., Hu, P., Predicting drug-target interaction network using deep learning model. *Comput. Biol. Chem.*, 80, 90, 2019.
64. Cui, W., Aouidate, A., Wang, S., Yu, Q., Li, Y., Yuan, S., Discovering anti-cancer drugs via computational methods. *Front. Pharmacol.*, 11, 733, 2020.
65. Issa, N.T., Stathias, V., Schürer, S., Dakshanamurthy, S., Machine and deep learning approaches for cancer drug repurposing, in: *Paper presented at the Seminars in cancer biology*, 2021.
66. Malas, T.B., Vlietstra, W.J., Kudrin, R., Starikov, S., Charrout, M., Roos, M., AC't Hoen, P., Drug prioritization using the semantic properties of a knowledge graph. *Sci. Rep.*, 9, 1, 2019.
67. Zhu, W., Xie, L., Han, J., Guo, X., The application of deep learning in cancer prognosis prediction. *Cancers*, 12, 603, 2020.
68. Shen, Y., Liu, T., Chen, J., Li, X., Liu, L., Shen, J., Wang, J., Zhang, R., Sun, M., Wang, Z., Song, W., Qi, T., Tang, Y., Meng, X., Zhang, L., Ho, D., Ho, C.-M., Ding, X., Lu, H.-Z., Harnessing artificial intelligence to optimize long-term maintenance dosing for antiretroviral-naive adults with HIV-1 infection. *Adv. Ther.*, 3, 1900114, 2020.
69. Moridi, M., Ghadirinia, M., Sharifi-Zarchi, A., Zare-Mirakabad, F., The assessment of efficient representation of drug features using deep learning for drug repositioning. *BMC Bioinform.*, 20, 577, 2019.
70. Dimmitt, S., Stampfer, H., Martin, J.H., When less is more– efficacy with less toxicity at the ED50. *Br. J. Clin. Pharmacol.*, 83, 1365, 2017.
71. Levy, A.E., Biswas, M., Weber, R., Tarakji, K., Chung, M., Noseworthy, P.A., Newton-Cheh, C., Rosenberg, M.A., Applications of machine learning in decision analysis for dose management for dofetilide. *PloS One*, 14, e0227324, 2019.
72. Hassanzadeh, P., Atyabi, F., Dinarvand, R., The significance of artificial intelligence in drug delivery system design. *Adv. Drug Deliv. Rev.*, 151, 169, 2019.
73. Ter-Levonian, A.S. and Koshechkin, K.A., Review of machine learning technologies and neural networks in drug synergy combination pharmacological research. *Res. Result Pharmacol.*, 6, 27, 2020.
74. Lin, R. and Yin, G., Bootstrap aggregating continual reassessment method for dose finding in drug-combination trials. *Ann. Appl. Stat.*, 10, 2349, 2016.
75. Rodlea, W., Caliskan, D., Prokosch, H.U., Kraus, S., Evaluation of different learning algorithms of neural networks for drug dosing recommendations in paediatrics. *Stud. Health Technol. Inform.*, 271, 271, 2020.

76. Nijitha Thomas, K. and Aswathy, W., Automating the drug dosage of tacrolimus for liver, renal transplant patients using neural network. *IJITEE.*, 9, 1115, 2019.

77. Tang, J., Liu, R., Zhang, Y.L., Liu, M.Z., Hu, Y.F., Shao, M.J., Zhu, L.J., Xin, H.W., Feng, G.W., Shang, W.J., Meng, X.G., Zhang, L.R., Ming, Y.Z., Zhang, W., Application of machine learning models to predict tacrolimus stable dose in renal transplant recipients. *Sci. Rep.*, 7, 42192, 2017.

78. Imai, S., Takekuma, Y., Miyai, T., Sugawaraa, M., A new algorithm optimized for initial dose settings of vancomycin using machine learning. *Biol. Pharm. Bull.*, 43, 188, 2020.

79. Debeurme, G., Ducher, M., Jean-bart, E., Goutelle, S., Bourguignon, L., Bayesian network to optimize the first dose of antibiotics: Application to amikacin. *Int. J. Pharmacokinet.*, 1, 35, 2016.

80. Shen, Z., Zhang, Y.H., Han, K., Nandi, A.K., Honig, B., Huang, D.S., miRNA-disease association prediction with collaborative matrix factorization. *Complexity.*, Article ID 2498957, 2017.

81. Pantuck, A.J., Lee, D.-K., Kee, T., Wang, P., Lakhotia, S., Silverman, M.H., Mathis, C., Drakaki, A., Belldegrun, A.S., Ho, C.-M., Ho, D., Modulating BET bromodomain inhibitor ZEN-3694 and enzalutamide combination dosing in a metastatic prostate cancer patient using CURATE. AI an artificial intelligence platform. *Adv. Ther.*, 1, 180 0104, 2018.

82. Lu, J., Deng, K., Zhang, X., Liu, G., Guan, Y., Neural-ODE for pharmacokinetics modeling and its advantage to alternative machine learning models in predicting new dosing regimens. *iScience*, 24, 102804, 2021.

83. Kontaxis, C., Bol, G.H., Lagendijk, J.J.W., Raaymakers, B.W., DeepDose: Towards a fast dose calculation engine for radiation therapy using deep learning. *Phys. Med. Biol.*, 65, 075013, 91, 2021.

84. Sharabiani, A., Bress, A., Douzali, E., Darabi, H., Revisiting warfarin dosing using machine learning techniques. *Comput. Math. Methods Med.*, 560108, 2015.

85. Nemati, S., Ghassemi, M.M., Clifford, G.D., Optimal medication dosing from suboptimal clinical examples: A deep reinforcement learning approach. *Proc Annu Int Conf IEEE Eng Med Biol Soc EMBS*, pp. 2978–2981, 2016.

86. Hu, Y.H., Tai, C.T., Tsai, C.F., Huang, M.W., Improvement of adequate digoxin dosage: An application of machine learning approach. *J. Healthc. Eng.*, 3948245, 2018.

87. Zhu, X., Huang, W., Lu, H., Wang., Z., Ni, X., Hu, J., Deng, S., Tan, Y., Li, L., Zhang, M., Qiu, C., Luo, Y., Chen, H., Huang, S., Xiao, T., Shang, D., Wen, Y., A machine learning approach to personalized dose adjustment of lamotrigine using noninvasive clinical parameters. *Sci. Rep.*, 11, 5568, 2021.

88. Ye, Z., Yang, W., Yang, Y., Ouyang, D., Interpretable machine learning methods for *in vitro* pharmaceutical formulation development. *Food Frontiers.*, 2, 195, 2021.

89. Yang, Y., Ye, Z., Su, Y., Zhao, Q., Li, X., Ouyang, D., Deep learning for *in vitro* prediction of pharmaceutical formulations. *Acta Pharm. Sin. B.*, 9, 177, 2019.

90. Mendyk, A., Pacławski, A., Szafraniec-Szczęsny, J., Antosik, A., Jamróz, W., Paluch, M., Jachowicz, R., Data-driven modeling of the bicalutamide dissolution from powder systems. *AAPS Pharm. Sci. Tech.*, 21, 111, 2020.

91. Elbadawi, M., McCoubrey, L.E., Gavins, F.K.H., Ong, J.J., Goyanes, A., Gaisford, S., Basit, A.W., Disrupting 3D printing of medicines with machine learning. *Trends Pharmacol. Sci.*, 42, 745, 2021.

92. Nagalakshmi, S., Artificial intelligence: A new paradigm for pharmaceutical applications in formulations development. *Indian J. Pharm. Educ. Res.*, 54, 843, 2020.

93. Napphadol Chalortham, N., Ruangrajitpakorn, T., Supnithi, T., Leesawat, P., Aguilar, J.E., Oxpirt: Ontology based expert system for production of a generic immediate release tablet, in: *Formulation Tools for Pharmaceutical Development*, pp. 203–228, Netherlands, Elsevier, 2013.

94. Takayama, K., Kawai, S., Obata, Y., Todo, H., Sugibayashi, K., Prediction of dissolution data integrated in tablet database using four layered artificial neural networks. *Chem. Pharm. Bull.*, 65, 967, 2017.

95. Paul, D., Sanap, G., Shenoy, S., Kalyane, D., Kalia, K., Tekade, R.K., Artificial intelligence in drug discovery and development. *Drug Discovery Today*, 26, 80, 2021.

96. Guo, M., A prototype intelligent hybrid system for hard gelatin capsule formulation development. *Pharm. Technol. Int.*, 6, 44, 2002.

97. Roggo, Y., Jelsch, M., Heger, P., Ensslin, S., Krumme, M., Deep learning for continuous manufacturing of pharmaceutical solid dosage form. *Eur. J. Pharm. Biopharm.*, 153, 95, 2020.

98. Ebube, N.K., Owusu-Ababio, G., Adeyeye, C.M., Preformulation studies and characterization of the physicochemical properties of amorphous polymers using artificial neural networks. *Int. J. Pharm.*, 196, 27, 2000.

99. McKinley, D., Patel, S.K., Regev, G., Rohan, L.C., Akil, A., Delineating the effects of hot-melt extrusion on the performance of a polymeric film using artificial neural networks and an evolutionary algorithm. *Int. J. Pharm.*, 571, 118715, 2019.

100. Akbari Hasanjani, H.R. and Sohrabi, M.R., Artificial neural networks (ANN) for the simultaneous spectrophotometric determination of fluoxetine and sertraline in pharmaceutical formulations and biological fluid. *IJPR.*, 16, 478, 2017.

101. Elbadawi, M., Gaisford, S., Basit, A.W., Advanced machine-learning techniques in drug discovery. *Drug Discovery Today*, 26, 769, 2021.

102. Elbadawi, M., Castro, B.M., Gavins, F.K.H., Ong, J.J., Gaisford, S., Pérez, G., Basit, A.W., Cabalar, P., Goyanes, A., M3DISEEN: A novel machine learning approach for predicting the 3D printability of medicines. *Int. J. Pharm.*, 590, 119837, 2020.

103. Harrison, P.J., Wieslander, H., Sabirsh, A., Karlsson, J., Malmsjö, V., Hellander, A., Wåhlby, C., Spjuth, O., Deep-learning models for lipid nanoparticle-based drug delivery. *Nanomed.*, *16*, 1097, 2021.

104. Santana, R., Zuluaga, R., Gañán, P., Arrasate, S., Onieva, E., González-Díaz, H., Predicting coated-nanoparticle drug release systems with perturbation-theory machine learning (PTML) models. *Nanoscale*, 12, 13471, 2020.

105. Sacha, G.M. and Varona, P., Artificial intelligence in nanotechnology. *Nanotechnology*, 24, 452002, 2013.

106. Alsuliman, T., Humaidan, D., Sliman, L., Machine learning and artificial intelligence in the service of medicine: Necessity or potentiality? *Curr. Res. Transl. Med.*, *68*, 245, 2020.

107. Ngiam, K.Y. and Khor, W., Big data and machine learning algorithms for healthcare delivery. *Lancet Oncol.*, 20, e262, 2019.

108. Sason, H. and Shamay, Y., Nanoinformatics in Drug Delivery. *Isr. J. Chem.*, 6, 1, 2020.

109. Jones, D.E., Ghandehari, H., Facelli, J.C., A review of the applications of data mining and machine learning for the prediction of biomedical properties of nanoparticles. *Comput. Methods Programs Biomed.*, 132, 93, 2016.

110. Rode, A. and Sharma Shatware, K., Artificial intelligence: Microchip based drug delivery through resealed erythrocytes. *Biochem.*, 11, 1, 2017.

111. Zhu, Y., Che, C., Jin, B., Zhang, N., Su, C., Wang, F., Knowledge-driven drug repurposing using a comprehensive drug knowledge graph. *J. Health Inform.*, 26, 2737, 2020.

112. Xu, L., Ru, X., Song, R., Application of Machine Learning for Drug-Target Interaction Prediction. *Front. Genet.*, 12, 680117, 2021.

113. Lin, X., Quan, Z., Wang, Z.J., Huang, H., Zeng, X., A novel molecular representation with BiGRU neural networks for learning atom. *Brief. Bioinf.*, *21*, 2099, 2020.

114. MacEachern, S.J. and Forkert, N.D., Machine learning for precision medicine. *Genome*, 6, 416, 2021.

115. Khosla, M., Jamison, K., Ngo, G.H., Kuceyeski, A, Sabuncu, M.R., Machine learning in resting-state fMRI analysis. *Magn. Reson. Imaging*, 64, 101, 2019.

116. Davenport, T.H. and Ronanki, R., Artificial intelligence for the real world, in: *Harvard Business Review*, vol. 96, p. 108, 2018.

117. Blasiak, A., Khong, J., Kee, T., CURATE., A.I., optimizing personalized medicine with artificial intelligence. *SLAS Technol.*, 25, 95, 2020.

118. Sun, D., Wang, M., Li, A., A multimodal deep neural network for human breast cancer prognosis prediction by integrating multi-dimensional data. *TCBB*, 16, 841, 2018.

119. Mehta, C.H., Narayan, R., Nayak, U.Y., Computational modeling for formulation design. *Drug Discovery Today*, 24, 781, 2019.

120. Guzik, A., Deep learning enables rapid identification of potent DDR1 kinase inhibitors. *Nat. Biotechnol.*, 37, 1038, 2019.

121. Bannigan, P., Aldeghi, M., Bao, Z., Häse, F., Aspuru-Guzik, A., Allen, C., Machine learning directed drug formulation development. *Adv. Drug Deliv. Rev.*, 175, 113806, 2021.
122. Katzman, J.L., Shaham, U., Cloninger, A., Bates, J., Jiang, T., Kluger, Y., DeepSurv: Personalized treatment recommender system using a Cox proportional hazards deep neural network. *BMC Med. Res. Methodol.*, 18, 1, 2018.

2

Role of Deep Learning, Blockchain and Internet of Things in Patient Care

Akanksha Sharma[1]*, Rishabha Malviya[2] and Sonali Sundram[2]

[1]Monad College of Pharmacy, Monad University, Hapur, Uttar Pradesh, India
[2]Department of Pharmacy, School of Medical and Allied Sciences, Galgotias University, Greater Noida, Gautam Buddha Nagar, Uttar Pradesh, India

Abstract

Deep learning is a subfield of machine learning that deals with artificial neural networks, which are algorithms encouraged by the structure and operation of the brain. Health practitioners and analysts are using deep learning to discover the latent opportunities in data and to support the healthcare industry in better way. Deep learning in healthcare enables physicians to correctly analyze any illness to properly manage it which results in better treatment decisions. Blockchain and Internet of things are also used as deep learning models in the healthcare system to manage the large healthcare data, such as electronic medical records. Mobile healthcare system is also a part of deep learning, which is used nowadays by health practitioners to manage the healthcare system by online mode. Therefore, there is a need to concentrate on the knowledge and use of certain methods in order to address the shortcomings of current mainstream approaches to human health monitoring. This chapter describes the role of deep learning in the patient care by using different models and managing the healthcare system effectively.

Keywords: Deep learning, blockchain, Internet of Things, artificial intelligence, neural network, healthcare, diseases

Corresponding author: akankshasona012@gmail.com; ORCID: 0000-0002-5325-427X
Rishabha Malviya: ORCID: 0000-0003-2874-6149

Rishabha Malviya, Gheorghita Ghinea, Rajesh Kumar Dhanaraj, Balamurugan Balusamy
and Sonali Sundram (eds.) Deep Learning for Targeted Treatments: Transformation in Healthcare,
(39–76) © 2022 Scrivener Publishing LLC

2.1   Introduction

Studies have shown that in the coming years, patients with normal illnesses will increase but traditional care of health and recognition cannot efficiently meet each cases. This provides strong understanding that existing patients and prospective patients must be more aware of their healthcare. Because of new healthcare system technology, it is getting easier to cope with each drawbacks and effectively meet all requirements. The idea appears that bio-medical sensors, cloud computing, and Internet of Things (IoT) are needed for storage of data related to healthcare systems. The healthcare system has essentially two kinds of communication protocols, one with the use of biomedical sensors and the other a core device with cloud-based compo-nents of the e-health system. In 2012, IEEE 802.15.6 basic contact proto-col [1] released Wireless Body Area Networks (WBAN). WBAN absorbs less power than Bluetooth and Zigbee [2] WBAN uses 0.1 mW to 10 mW power usage, due to the data and bandwidth, is relatively good [3] WBAN uses 0.1 mW to 10 mW power usage, due to the data and bandwidth, is relatively good [4] and even in big applications a decentralized distributed system. There are still many security problems affecting medical data pro-vided by E-Health. Blockchain technology can be useful in providing a safe and usable medical data application to address this global difficulty. Via confident data exchange between sensors, blockchain-based medical health data can face all challenges, while at the same time providing a dis-tributed database that tracks and records all changes. Privacy also meets the same access control criteria such that only an approved person can display and adjust all privileges. This article suggests a blockchain based e-health framework that works with IoT and WBAN. The same is designed so that WBAN can be used as a front-end sensor device that interacts in the back-end with blockchain. To provide a safe storage, WBAN inter is used with sensors and Blockchain. Although WBAN and Blockchain are orthogonal, they do not deal with each other and eventually face the chal-lenges in e-health systems. The merger between WBAN and Blockchain provides benefits, such as energy efficiency, security, and decentralized data storage. On the contrary, complexity of the algorithm is one of the key problems facing this fusion [5, 6].

Deep learning employs mathematical models that are designed to operate the work like a human brain. The various layers of network and technology enable extraordinary computational power and the ability to sift through massive amounts of data that might have been lost, missed or forgotten. Deep learning networks can tackle complicated problems and extract out the strands of insight from massive amounts of data in the healthcare industry. It is a collection of skills that has not gone ignored by the medical community. Deep learning in healthcare, on the other hand, remains a field brimming with potential and extraordinary innovation. Organizations have harnessed into the strength of algorithms and the capabilities of artificial intelligence (AI) and machine learning (ML) to produce solutions that are well suited to the healthcare industries' stringent requirements.

Deep learning algorithms are already shown in medical imaging solutions, chatbots, which can determine the patterns of symptoms in patient. Deep learning can also identify cancers with specific types, rare diseases or certain types of pathology. Deep learning has proven to have a crucial role in providing medical personnels with insights that enable them to detect problems early on, thereby providing a more tailored and relevant patient care [7].

Along with ensuring the security, privacy, and transmission in data, the main focus in the study is on Blockchain, the Wireless Body Area Network, and IOT. Evolution of Blockchain is 2008, without relying on trusted authorities, which acts as a transaction book for Bitcoin. Later the technology Blockchain focuses on finance emerging areas [8]. And obviously, health systems have also developed countless solutions in Blockchain technology with many research activities. It is also known as Ledger technology distributed [9]. Therefore, such a disruptive technology can also be brought about by risk mitigation, transparency, and also fraud. The chain consists of blocks, which are composed of Data, Nunce, and Hash elements. The details are the information present in the block, the Nuncy number is 32-bit and the Hash number is 256-bit.

Amount of Nonce married. There is a unique Nuncia and Hash for every block in a Blockchain [10] Relation of the preceding blocks chain as long as it was not just easy to mining blocks. Manipulation is also difficult as a shift in a block earlier in the chain involves the remaining of all subsequent blocks, by ensuring the secure handling of health data by means of Blockchain technology.

The data transferred by the patient called medical healing data obtained from the sensors are usually sent to a centralized system for a certain period of time "t" by the medical healthcare monitoring. The centralized device ultimately produces a medical document containing the name of the patient, Id, time, and place. To safely archive this information blockchain is passed this medical record. The medical record can be accessed and updated from this network only by a medical doctor of the patient.

IEEE 802.15.6 standard for wireless body area network (WBAN) defining parameters [11] such as data rate, frequency etc., WBAN is made up of number of sensors in various body parts, which can be used and inserted into different parts of the body [12]. 1 Mb/s and 0.1 mW, respectively are data and power usage up to 0.8 mW; the traditional protocol has a very high energy consumption in relation to that. Validation is required for elliptic curve cryptography (ECC) and advance encryption standard [AES], the most common encoding that is used in the current application. IEEE802.15.6, to be exact, also provides peripheral security for the implementation [13].

The machine users are physicians, patients, pharmacists and emergency services. In Blockchain technology, WBAN supports the data transfer between sensors and the central computer. Sensor-to-central system data are collected in a framework that contains the name and ID of the patient, name of the medical officer, place and time submitted to the network of Blockchain. Health practitioners have access to their records and can provide the corresponding patients with medical instruction.

WBAN is widely used to communicate health data between sensors and a central computer in the proposed work on health monitoring. Another approach is to use a WBAN composed of devices in which people can carry in a number of ways, such as clothes bags, by hand or bags wireless body area networks consisting of a single body central unit and of countable mini-sensor bodies. The doctor can access and track medical information in real time.

As Internet with interconnected entities, the nature of IoT can be conveyed [14]. These organizations have limited resources, power, bandwidth, and protection sources, which simultaneously produce large quantities of data. A centralized data center like a cloud application is typically used to handle these data. The big benefits of IoT are the use of RFI Similarly [15] and sensors can be connected to the network to a wide variety of devices. This can be stored in smart storage systems, such as cloud technologies after data collection, and as IoT technology's potential is sufficiently high, it can be widely used across most ecosystems, such as healthcare, security, etc [16].

2.2   IoT and WBAN in Healthcare Systems

2.2.1   IoT in Healthcare

The concepts of IoT allow every object to be addressed through an Internet Protocol (IP) and to act in a smart space, like an environment for healthcare.

IoT is also characterized as a "self-configured, dynamic global communication system with interoperable standards and communication protocols where physical and virtual "things" have identities, physical attributes and virtual personalities and are integrated with information infrastructure in a seamless way [17].

Fundamental features of the IoT technology

1. In a global framework a real-time solution
2. Wireless solutions in particular: ambient indoors and outdoors
3. Environmental and object monitoring capability remotely.

Various characteristics of IoT are summarized in Figure 2.1.

Because of population growth, urban development, decreasing birth rates, population ageing, economic growth and the use of social capital unbalanced, healthcare is one of the primary concerns for all governments. IoT help in healthcare in many effective ways, which is summarized in Figure 2.2.

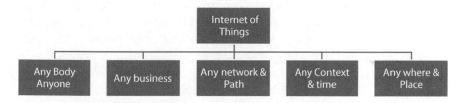

Figure 2.1 Various characteristics of IoT.

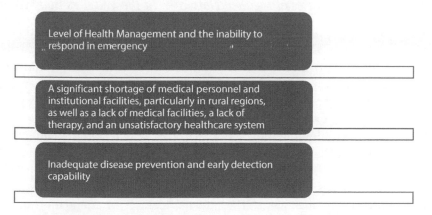

Figure 2.2 Use of IoT in healthcare system.

Figure 2.3 Some innovations used in IoT healthcare systems.

In terms of healthcare, the various applications of technologies and goods related to the Internet of Things (IoT). The IoT presence in the area of healthcare is beneficial to both patients and providers. Some applications of IoT health services include mobile medical applications or wearable devices to allow patients to collect their health information. Hospitals use IoT to tap where medical equipment, staff and patients are located. Some innovations that can be used in IoT healthcare systems are described below in Figure 2.3 [18].

2.2.2   WBAN

WBAN may make important contributions to improving healthcare for patients, including diagnostics and/or therapy supervision. WBAN technology has made its initial steps in medical rehabilitation and patient monitoring in a short period of time. The underlying technology, on the other hand, is still in its early stages of development and is usually dependent on very specific wireless communications technologies. Patients can be comfortably observed at home while going about their regular activities, and medical personnel must monitor a large number of patients at the same time [19].

2.2.2.1   Key Features of Medical Networks in the Wireless Body Area

WBANs are primarily used in patient surveillance activities for healthcare applications. Sensors of the different physiological parameters are distributed in this network on the human body, representing the most commonly used solution within this field [20]. Wireless capabilities with sensors all over the body are of particular interest to the WBAN, as they offer a comfortable and user-friendly way of tracking the health of a patient over long periods, eliminating the use of cables that wire round the patient. In general, there are various concentrations of water in the composition of the human body tissue. For a wireless connection, the transmitting power for body transmission depends on the physical distance of the link and its instantaneous channel status. The internal features of attenuation of RF may directly affect channel conditions in and around the human body.

Patient mobility and posture may also have a major influence on the successful delivery of packages. WBAN radio transmission properties are complex because of the human body movements. Regular activities like running and walking and physiological activities like heartburn and respiration significantly affect wireless spread [21].

2.2.2.2   Data Transmission & Storage Health

Data analysis has several benefits, pledges and potential for healthcare transformations, but it faces multiple obstacles and challenges. In fact, concerns about safety and privacy of large-scale healthcare data are increased annually. Furthermore, health organizations found that the organization and its patients are not covered by a reactive, bottom-up technology approach to the determination of protection and privacy requirements [22].

New information and techniques are therefore required to avoid infringements of confidential information and other kinds of security incidents so that the data on big healthcare are used effectively.

2.2.2.3   Privacy and Security Concerns in Big Data

Big data protection and privacy are main concerns. Privacy is also described as the right to protect information that is subject to personal health information. It focuses on the usage and governance of personal data, such as legislation and authorizations to ensure that the personal information of patients is appropriately recorded, exchanged and used. While security is generally characterized as protection from unauthorized access, with some express reference to integrity and availability. It concentrates on data security from pernicious attacks and benefit robbing. Although healthcare organizations store, manage and distribute enormous quantities of data to support effective and appropriate treatment, technological assistance and safety are insufficient. The health sector continues to be one of the most exposed infringements of publicly revealed data in complicating matters. In reality, attackers may use data mining procedures to detect and reveal confidential data to the public, and thus a violation of the data occurs. Although enforcing security measures is a complex procedure, stakes are constantly increased by the more sophisticated ways of defeating sequence controls. It is also vital that organizations put in place protection solutions for healthcare data that secure valuable properties while meeting mandates for healthcare fulfilment [23].

2.3   Blockchain Technology in Healthcare

Blockchain is one of the most promising and appealing innovations in many research and business studies. The definition was first proposed by Satoshi Nakamoto in a white paper in 2008 [24]. Blockchain is a decentralized, unchangeable booklet that makes transfers and asset monitoring in the company network simpler. A good (a home, a vehicle, currency, land) or intangible may be tangible (intellectual property, patents, copyrights, branding). Almost all of the value of a blockchain network can be tracked and exchanged to reduce the risks and expense for those concerned [25].

As open-source software did a quarter of a century ago, blockchain, which started to exist as a real-world technology alternative in 2016 and 2017, is about to change IT so soon. In addition, it will take blockchain years to be a lower-cost, more effective way to exchange information and data between open and private sector networks, and more than a decade to be one of the cornerstones of digital application growth. Based on the topology of peer-to-peer (P2P), blockchain is a distributed ledger (DLT) technology that allows the worldwide stocking of data on thousands of servers—letting anyone in the network view the entries of all others in almost real time. This makes it hard for one person to monitor the network or game. However, blockchain is committed to transparency in transactions, namely to creating secure, real-time networks with partners across the globe to support all aspects from supply chains through payment networks through to the sharing of property deals and health data [26].

2.3.1   Importance of Blockchain

Corporate intelligence runs. The more easily and accurately it is obtained, the better. It offers instant, shared and fully open information stored on an immutable leader which can only be accessed by approved nets. Blockchain is suitable to provide this information. A network blockchain will trace orders, transfers, accounts and many more. And since Participants have a shared sense of the facts, you can see all the precise descriptions of the transaction end-to-end [27].

Furthermore, blockchain has the following characteristics:

Decentralization: Contrast conventional data stores, which hold information on a central database, blockchain addresses the problem of a centralized point of failure. Without a central point of influence, data is hosted and Sensors 2020, 20, 6538 5 of 24 controlled by consensus among all parties participating in the market flow.

Distributed and scalable: The backend of a distributed ledger system is a collection of servers, each of which stores applications and records. This delivery means that the device is still accessible and that it can be reached easily.

Security and transparency: the blockchain project were born out of the necessity of a safe and stable system, so data privacy, cryptography, and protection are the main aspects of this techniques.

Data immutability and integrity: Since data cannot be modified until all stakeholders in the blockchain achieve consensus, the decentralized and distributed framework guarantees data immutability and authenticity, increasing customer loyalty. While the platform is still in its early stages of growth and validation, it can change market structures and move them away from a centralized to a decentralized method. The banking, logistics/supply chain, healthcare, legal, regulatory, gas and oil industries are the top 5 industries that are currently implementing blockchain service [28, 29].

2.3.2   Role of Blockchain in Healthcare

The use of blockchain in healthcare has tremendous potential to solve a range of existing healthcare problems, such as the immutable preservation and dissemination of patients' medical information, enabling more people to engage in the medical process while simultaneously maintaining data safety and protection [30, 31]. It can get a unique solution to data owners and authorization access across the value chain of health stakeholders dependent Sensors 2020. Blockchain technologies in healthcare can help patients transition from conventional connectivity to patient-centered connectivity by giving them the power of their medical health records and allowing them to determine they have access to the information [32].

Examples of blockchain systems in healthcare-

- MedBlocks—medical records are stored on a sequential file system that has been rendered immutable using distributed ledger technology. To ensure that the network is not overloaded, the consensus process has been improved [33].
- Secure Health Chain—it stores electronic personal health records on a blockchain and guarantees that data may be accessed by authorized individuals only who have been given permission [34].
- Medical Chain—medical data may be stored, exchanged, and used on a decentralized network. It allows the user to

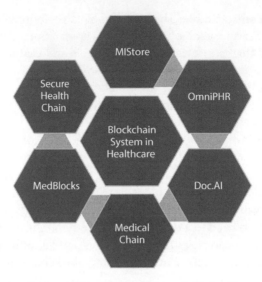

Figure 2.4 Schematic diagram of blockchain systems used in healthcare.

grant access to their health information to healthcare professionals [35].

- Doc.AI—It is an artificial intelligence platform that mines medical data using natural language processing, computer vision, and blockchain technology [36].
- OmniPHR—type of distributed system to store data of patient health. It uses different blocks to store different patient datasets [37].
- MIStore—it is storage system for medical insurance that is based on blockchain [38].

Blockchain system in healthcare are summarized in Figure 2.4.

2.3.3   Benefits of Blockchain in Healthcare Applications

Decentralization is a term used to describe the mechanism of the essence of healthcare, with its multiple stakeholders, necessitating the use of a decentralized control system. Blockchain can become the open medical data storage system, giving all parties managed access to the same health information without the need for a central body to monitor global health information. Data access and privacy have been strengthened [29].

Since the data saved on the blockchain cannot be manipulated, changed, or recovered, the immutability property of blockchain significantly increases the reliability of the health data held on it. On the blockchain, all health information is secure, time-stamped, and appended in sequential order. Furthermore, health data are stored on a blockchain utilizing cryptographic keys, which help to secure patients' identities and privacy. For ownership in clinical records, patients must be the stewards of their data and have the power over how it is used. Patients need confidence that their health records will not be misused by third parties, as well as the ability to detect any abuse. Solid cryptographic protocols and well-defined smart contracts help blockchain satisfy these criteria [39].

Robustness/Availability—The availability of health data stored on the blockchain is assured since the records on the blockchain are mirrored in several nodes, and the machine is stable and resilient to data losses, data manipulation, and any protection attacks on data availability. Transparency and trustworthiness Blockchain fosters faith in collaborative healthcare applications by way of its free and accessible nature, which makes it possible for healthcare stakeholders to consider those applications. The validity of results, the credibility and authenticity of data stored on the blockchain can be checked without even reaching the plaintext of that information [39].

2.3.4   Elements of Blockchain

- **Distributed ledger technology**
  The distributed leader and its permanent database of transactions is open to all network members. This mutual directory tracks transactions only once, which prevents the repetition of effort characteristic of standard business networks.
- **Records are immutable**
  After documenting it in the public ledger, no member can alter or tamper with a transaction. When a transaction record contains a mistake, a new transaction must be inserted in order to reverse the error.
- **Smart contracts**—a variety of rules, referred to as a clever contract, are saved and executed on the blockchain to speed transactions. A smart contract will set conditions for the transfer of corporate bonds, including the terms for payment of travel insurance and many more.

One of the sectors in which blockchain has a wide opportunity is healthcare. The Office of the National Coordinator for Health Information Technology (ONC), which recognized the significance and value of blockchain in health facilities in 2016, composed an ideation task for demanding white papers on the future use of blockchain in healthcare. This challenge culminated in several proposed blockchain medical applications.

- **Electronic Medical Records**—the focus should be given to the management of the health data to transform the health-care system and increase the accuracy of the electronic health records (EHRs). There is a difference between the two terms while EMRs and EHRs are used on an interchangeable basis. First came the EMRs word, which is a graphical representation of the clinic's paper diagrams. An EMR involves patients with one specialty medical and care records. However, the EHRs focus on overall patient wellbeing, which goes beyond traditional clinical statistics gathered in the office of the provider which provides an analysis of patient health.
- **Remote Patient Monitoring**—remote patient tracking may include medical data collection from mobile devices, sensors for the body area and Internet of Things (IoT) items to remotely monitor the status of a patient. Blockchain plays a crucial role in the collection, exchange, and retrieval of biomedical data that are obtained remotely.

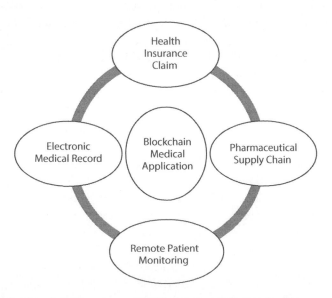

Figure 2.5 Schematic diagram represents blockchain medical applications.

- **Pharmaceutical Supply Chain**—in the pharmaceutical industry, another reported case of blockchain use is. Patients will suffer critical effects if counterfeit or ineffective medicines are administered. The technology from blockchain was found to solve this problem.
- **Health Insurance Claims**—health insurance claims are one of the ways in which health services will benefit, immutability of the blockchain, accountability and auditing of the reported results.

Blockchain medical application are summarized in Figure 2.5.

The information innovation and the rise of the mobile wireless infrastructure have made a major contribution to e-health coverage extension and empowerment. The truth is, the health and social services productivity of the workforce and customers are making a massive shift with insightful remote and mobile healthcare apps. The key goal of such applications is to use IoT, ML, and semantic Web technology to ensure that people can and do what they value in their lives through disease.

2.3.5   Situation Awareness and Healthcare Decision Support with Combined Machine Learning and Semantic Modeling

The academic group focused on the analysis and growth of M-Health programmes and applications. Various scientific subjects pertaining to health, including cardiology, diabetes, obesity, smoking abstinence and elderly treatment and chronic diseases, have garnered substantial findings and contributions from health. These multiple medical specialties use m-Health Essentially for outbreak control, prevention and diagnosis, Basic diagnosis is required in more specialized facilities. In developed countries where healthcare facilities are often distant and unavailable even become popular with m-Health services, apart from all medical applications. Mobile healthcare apps are increasing rapidly. Between 2002 and 2012, the writers carried out a literature analysis of 117 publications in 77 newspapers. The findings revealed that the number of research papers almost doubled between 2007 and 2008 and increased exponentially per year.

This curiosity and momentum has now expanded to information technology in healthcare. In 2016, the Office of the National Health Information Technology Coordinator, acknowledging the potential value and significance of the blockchain in healthcare, held an ideation competition to call for white papers on possible use of the blockchain in healthcare. This challenge led to a range of proposed blockchain medical applications. Although the whole health record may be used as a use case for healthcare inside the blockchain, several possible impediments were found to its adoption, such as privacy issues, compliance with regulatory requirements and data collection and delivery technological hurdles. This has contributed to much of the short-term initiatives focusing on authentication, auditing, and authorization of records. Guardtime, a Netherlands-based data protection organization, has collaborated with Estonia to build a blockchain basis for validating patient identities. One example is applying this method.

A smart card has been provided to all people that connects your EHR data with their blockchain identity. Any update in the EHR will be allocated a hash of a blockchain and registered. This means the information inside the EHR provides an immutable history of auditing and does not alter data maliciously. The immutable, time-stamped data logs often allow the data state from current medical databases to be archived. Thanks to its concern for planning abuse in the management of the veterans and the possibility of data processing of implantable medical devices, such as marrow-creators, the recent exposure to data security has a number of possible advantages to ensure safe and auditable changes to the health records. MedRec, a collaboration launched between the MIT Media Lab and the Beth Israel Deaconess Medical Center, is a second EHR-related implementation. The network incorporates a decentralized approach for the administration, consent, and data sharing of healthcare systems.

The technology uses blockchain to encourage patients to have an entity and to know who will access their healthcare records. These allowances will be shared in a blockchain to establish a more automated solution to clinical and testing data exchange; however, the real patient data are not stored on the blockchain. During blockchain approvals, data storage location and audit records, all patient information is left to EHR systems and requires external technical components in order to allow for effective interoperability.

As a proof of concept for medicine data, the MedRec project has been tested and developers plan to improve the reach of the project by introducing additional data forms, data contributors and users. The use of blockchain to ensure fast and secure access to longitudinal research data may benefit substantially from this proof of conception. Similar to the processing of trade settlements, blockchain is capable of using statements for automatic authentication that can improve transaction reliability and process protection.

In a blockchain used by payers and insurers, the app can store encrypted paten identifiers and health plan details. This configuration could allow automated processing of claims, eligibility tests, and preauthorization almost in real time to be enforced. Researchers may also use subsets of these knowledge for use in biomedical research with sufficient permits [40].

2.3.6   Mobile Health and Remote Monitoring

In the modern technology era, smartphone devices and remote monitoring machines are important for medical care. Blockchain can be used to enhance the reliability and quality of these technologies. For instance, a team of researchers developed and tested a mHealth (mobile health) smartphone program for insomnia cognitive behavioral therapy [41].

The software transfers patient health information to a stable blockchain network. Due to the obvious characteristics of the blockchain, the EMRs in the chain are stable and immune to modification after testing, and the data were open to and monitored by the patient. A patient can store information and transfer it to healthcare professionals in minutes with an app like this one, regardless of the distance between the provider and the patient. Patients will be more responsive to their safety and well-being because they can track their treatment using this system. Also, a smartphone framework called Healthcare Data Gateway (HGD) has been provided for patient data organization [42].

This program includes three layers of data: the database layer, the data processing layer, and the data utilization layer, all of which operate together to ensure the data is safe and usable. Furthermore, enhancing blockchain-based smart contracts could assist in the safe operation of tracking devices. The blockchain operation is checked and tracked by smart contracts. To enhance remote surveillance, a private blockchain based on the ethereum model has been established; in this blockchain, sensors communicate with smart devices that use smart contracts to manage the database in the blockchain [43].

Smart contracts provide for real-time patient tracking by safely submitting critical updates to patients and healthcare professionals. Patients should take control of their health while a medical professional is still available for real-time alerts, which is important for healthcare at home. Since patient health data is processed on mobile devices, security issues are raised. Blockchain has been disrupted in the past by smartphone ransomware, and the blockchain that governs mobile apps must be fully safe until it can be used to maintain health data. The root exploits, the most dangerous form of malicious software, and its associations with blockchain were explored in one study [44].

Because it may get a patient's PKI private key, which the patient needs to access their private, protected data on the blockchain, the root issue is risky to blockchain applications. The biological technique of realistic swarm optimization (PSO) was utilized in this study to find root flaws, as well as enhancers that can increase machine learning activity and discover malware information. Logitboost, a form of boost used in the analysis was observed to have a 93% accuracy rate in detecting root exploits.

2.3.7   Different Mobile Health Application with Description of Usage in Area of Application

1. **Calorie counter and diet tracker:** Used in the area of prevention/healthy lifestyle with the calorie counting diet program, calorie monitoring, exercises and weight targets. It investigates social dimensions as an opportunity, including ties to friends.
2. **Calorie Counter PRO:** Apply for the prevention/healthy lifestyle by means of Diät for calories, diet monitoring and exercise with weight targets as a motivational aspect.

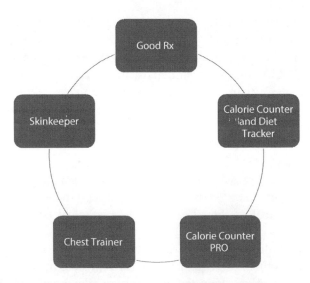

Figure 2.6 Schematic diagram to represent different mobile application in healthcare system.

3. **Chest trainer:** Used for prevention/healthy lifestyle weight and fitness training that aims to replace an individual trainer.
4. **Good Rx:** Used for filling of prescriptions by this app compares and offers prescription drug costs. It also offers discounts and discount tips in many US pharmacies for over 6,000 drugs.
5. **Skinkeeper:** Deal with the oncology sector providing the enables people to track, capture and manage major risk factors of personal and family skin cancer. It also helps a patient with the practitioner to share this knowledge.

Figure 2.6 represents the different mobile application used in healthcare system.

2.3.8 Patient-Centered Blockchain Mode

An efficient medical information management system was designed based on blockchain technology that enables people to keep control of their documents while enabling hospitals quick access. Our framework is based on the Ethereum network, a decentralized platform that makes it possible to create custom blockchains and run applications on them. They hold the original medical records on a decentralized cloud storage network like Ethereum Swarm, a local base layer component of the Ethereum web3 layer that acts as a pooled storage platform since blockchains do not always have adequate storage. The root chunk is created by combining the swarm hash of each health record with the decryption key.

As a result, the root pieces are safely stored in smart contracts on the blockchain and activated only when those requirements are reached. We use multisignature (multisig) contracts to address the issue of data ownership and power. Multisig allows two people, in this situation the patient and the clinic, to sign a document for authentication using their private keys. The patient cannot change the record without the hospital's approval, but he has the power of who has exposure to it. Since the old swarm hash is now identified, a new swarm hash must be created each moment the data are accessed, so they attach a "last accessed" timestamp. The swarm hash should be automatically changed as the data changes, and it could then be protected before it requires the necessary permissions for entry. This paradigm provides a multisig approach to data control and usability, in addition to the protection and immutability offered by blockchain [45].

One of the possible examples connected with Healthcare Data Gateway (HDG) process, proposed by Yue *et al.*, is using a private blockchain to track and archive private clinical information. Patients have the right to view, track, and maintain their defined medical records and healthcare overview, which is held on a private blockchain, through this customized healthcare process (a centralized database system with guided access only entitled to authorized or particular users) [46]. Griggs *et al.* used a private blockchain built on the ethereum protocol to allow for not just the safe and stable use of sensor nodes, but also to remove the security risks involved with a remote patient management scheme. The blockchain-based strategy proposed by them can enable secure real-time monitoring systems, allow practitioners to monitor their patients' health status from afar while also keeping a safe, reliable, and advance patient history [47].

Ivan developed a method for storing protected health data by encrypting it using a public blockchain (a decentralized database system with freely accessible reach to others connected to the network). The encrypted healthcare information is recorded openly in this technique, resulting in a blockchain-based personal health record (PHR). Their proposed solution encouraged patients to have greater autonomy of their health files, allowing them to easily view, track, and add to their records, as well as share them with every related caregiving entity [48].

Chen *et al.* suggested an automated blockchain and cloud connectivity system for storing and exchanging patient medical information in another report. The suggested scheme will be used to store and share confidential patient medical details conveniently and reliably. The proposed solution is innovative in that it offers patients with full access and control of their confidential medical records, obviating the need for any additional third-party intervention [49]. Wang *et al.* recently suggested a blockchain platform for assessing the healthcare condition of patient disorders, which is focused on simultaneous implementation and artificial healthcare networks. The suggested approach measures the patient's overall illness, diagnosis, and recovery process, as well as the rehabilitation interventions associated with them, using simultaneous executions and computational experiments for clinical decision making. To determine the accuracy of care and management efficacy, the proposed method was tested on both actual and artificial health services [50].

BloCHIE, a blockchain-based application for healthcare data sharing, was founded by Jiang *et al.*. The proposed portal assesses healthcare data exchange criteria, specifically for personal healthcare information & electronic medical records, & works with several other information categories by integrating blockchains within different outlets. They merged the framework with on-chain and off-chain authentication mechanisms to ensure that both authenticity and privacy are met. They merged the framework with on-chain and off-chain authentication mechanisms to ensure that both authenticity and privacy are met. Sharing of medical data, protection, and security can be significantly enhanced between clinical experts and healthcare organizations by using blockchain technology as a tool [51].

Cryan, M.A. suggested a systematic and creative architecture leveraging blockchain technologies that are capable of securing confidential medical data, solving essential data protection problems, and integrating a blockchain software framework in a healthcare system, using a similar mechanism. In biomedical science and therapeutic area, blockchain technology has demonstrated exceptional promise. Even before the start of clinical trial or review, it could be possible to store all clinical consents, protocols, and schedules on a blockchain, due to the realistic implementation of blockchain technology. Clinical trial critical data will be more up-to-date, stable, time-stamped, and publicly accessible in this way. Smart contracts, on the other hand, maybe deployed, repeated, and then executed during different stages of a clinical trial to ensure accountability (if followed and validated correctly) [52].

Shubbar proposed a blockchain-based telemonitoring healthcare system for remote patients' cancer tumor detection and treatment in proactive aging, on the other hand, is a blockchain-based network that assists in the active life of the elderly. It should be remembered that blockchain technology can be an ideal and well-suited option in comprehensive medical care procedures, such as chronic disorders (e.g., cancer), surgical procedures, and aging. Furthermore, pharmaceutical firms, drug suppliers, and biomedical researchers will be able to use DNA data stored on blockchains to perform advanced transnational genomic analysis [53, 54].

2.3.9   Electronic Medical Record

The electronic medical record (EMRs) method has been showing an increase in physician-centered growth in recent years with the development and implementation of cloud computing technologies. One of the most divisive problems in this case is how anonymity, protection, and sharability of EMRs can be ensured while finely regulated access is achieved. A powerful approach is to merge cloud computing, ABE and searchable encryption technology. However, in terms of anonymity, protection, and interoperability, this strategy does face some difficulties [55].

In 2008, the Satoshi Nakamoto idea of a blockchain was first proposed, which is known as "Bitcoin" as a crypto-currency technology, which allows transactions amongst peers without centralized third parties. In order to create a trusted distributed system, the mechanism for storage, accounting, maintenances, authentication and delivery of blockchain data relies on the distributed system framework using pure mathematical approaches rather than central institutions. A blockchain, as the title indicates, is made up of numerous blocks, each of which refers to a collection of all communication and information data in the system over a period of time. A block is the fundamental building element of a blockchain, and each block contains a timestamp as its unique mark to ensure the blockchain's traceability [56].

Participants of the network use unlike permissionless blockchain, permissioned blockchain acts as close ecosystem where one cannot join the network if not authorized. New user requires prior permission to join the network. The nodes who participate in the consensus management are also predefined. In permissioned blockchain the nodes that maintain the blockchain are employed and operated by blockchain owner or an ensemble of known entities such as members of a consortium who jointly own the blockchain but these members do not necessarily trust each other.

Hyperledger by Linux Foundation an open source blockchain project is a well-known implementation of permissioned blockchain. Hyperledger with a modular architecture allows consensus and membership services to be pluggable. It leverages container technology to host smart contracts (chaincode) which contains the application logic of the system. Hyperledger modular architecture allows different consensus algorithms to be pluggable, such as practical byzantine tolerance algorithm (PBFT) [12], which is computationally much lighter than proof of work (PoW).

In hyperledger blockchain, all the nodes in the network have an identity. All participating nodes are issued a certificate by the member service provider (MSP), which use a public key infrastructure to issue cryptographic certificates. A username and password pair is issued to every network user. This username/password pair is used to issue enrollment certificate (Ecert). Transaction Certificate Authority issues transaction certificates (TCert) to Ecert owners. Multiple TCerts can be derived from one Ecert.

Electronic medical records (EMRs) are files that include extremely sensitive and confidential information about a patient's diagnosis and treatment that must be exchanged well across colleagues. Because the data might be leaked or modified during operating process, sharing medical records between participants is extremely difficult. The best answer to these problems is a blockchain-based electronic medical records system. In this study, we looked at how blockchain technology may aid in improved data management in the healthcare industry. For effective management and exchange of electronic medical information (EMRs), we proposed a blockchain-based records management system. Using the permissioned blockchain technology "Hyperledger," we developed a prototype of an electronic medical records management system [57].

Blockchain, the fundamental technology of Satoshi Nakamoto's virtual digital currency "Bitcoin," is a peer-to-peer distributed ledger system. Blockchain is a new technology trend that is having an impact on business and society. Financial services, government administration, supply chain management, healthcare, and many more industries have effectively implemented blockchain technology [58].

A blockchain is a distributed database in which cryptographic primitives protect a linear collection of data pieces known as blocks that are linked together to form a chain. As the number of transactions increases, blockchain rises in size. Blocks keep track of the order in which transactions were recorded in the blockchain, as well as when they were recorded. The cryptographic hash that points to the preceding block, as well as the date and transaction data, are all contained in each block. This preceding block's hash pointer connects the blocks, making them tamper-resistant and giving blockchain its immutability property. Only if the majority of the nodes specified for the consensus mechanism (depending on which blockchain platform is used) agree on a transaction by validating the authenticity of transaction data can a new block be added to the blockchain [59].

A single universal blockchain network cannot be utilized for all industries since various firms and consumers have distinct demands. This has resulted in the development of many blockchain systems, each with its own set of protocols, but the underlying principles remain the same. Despite the large number of blockchain platforms now accessible, there are two types of blockchains on the market: permissionless (public) and permissioned (private) blockchains [60].

Electronically defined health record (EMR) systems are likely to bring significant benefits to doctors, cline practices and healthcare organizations, defined as an electronic recording of information relating to the person that can be produced, processed, handled, and consulted by licensed medical practitioners and personnel within a specific healthcare organization. This technologies can enhance patient care and safety and promote workflow. Despite these advantages, the total usage of EMRs in the U.S. is weak. Only 4% of outpatient doctors reported having a broad and completely functioning electronic records and 13% reported having a basic system [61].

The pressure on doctors and hospital personnel has increased significantly as the population and number of patients has expanded. Earlier, when a patient visited a hospital, his information was recorded on paper. The use of IT in health services has contributed to a revolution in the processing of patient data. Patient data are processed online in medical care. It allows physicians and hospital employees provide patients better treatment and support as it provides all the knowledge about patients' previous appointments, prescriptions, and laboratory reports [62].

2.3.9.1   The Most Significant Barriers to Adoption Are:

> ➤ small practices and safety net providers experience high capital costs and low returns on investment,
> ➤ underestimation of organizational skills and the need for change management,
> ➤ failure to incorporate technological systems into clinical processes and workflows,
> ➤ concerns about systems becoming outdated.
> ➤ a scarcity of experienced implementation and support resources
> ➤ concerns that present market mechanisms may not be enough to fulfill the demands of rural health centers or federally qualified health centers (FQHC).

2.3.9.2   Concern Regarding Negative Unintended Consequences of Technology

Integrated clinical workstations are being developed by several healthcare organizations. These are single points of entry into a medical world in which computational tools aid not only clinical issues (reporting of result, order entry, telemedicine applications, access to transcribed reports, and decision support), but also financial and administrative issues (Admission-Discharge-Transfer, personnel, materials management, and payroll), as well as research (result analysis, QA). The medical record in its new incarnation is at the core of the developing clinical workstation: digital, accessible, confidential, secure, acceptable to doctors and patients, and integrated with nonpatient-specific information [63].

As per the human factors paradigm, healthcare work systems and advancements, such as electronic health records, have no significant impact on patient safety. Instead, their impacts are determined by how the clinical work system, whether computerized or not, influencing the execution of cognitive work processes by healthcare professionals. The human factors paradigm was applied to interview data from two hospitals in the

Midwest United States, yielding several examples of how electronic clinical documentation, electronic medical records, and automated provider order input affect performance. The findings show both increases and decreases in the ease and quality of cognitive functioning among the doctors interviewed, as well as their colleagues and patients. Alteration in cognitive function appears to have both positive and negative consequences for patient safety, as well as healthcare quality and other important results. Interactions between work system elements, including new technology, may also be traced to cognitive performance, allowing for the detection of problems with "fit" that can be addressed by design interventions [64].

First, symmetric searchable encryption (SSE) based on stream cypher was introduced to allow accurate recovery of encrypted data. SSE, on the other hand, has a complex key distribution, which means they can't be used in a lot of practical situations. To solve this problem, researchers presented the PEKS (public key encryption with keyword search method) and demonstrated its security using the random oracle model. In this case, although a secure route is required to transfer the key, SCF-PEKS (secure channel free proxy re-encryption with keyword search) was the first model suggested based on fuzzy keyword search, introducing the notion of public key encryption The results of the server's fuzzy keyword search on all ciphertexts are returned to the receiver, who then runs a more accurate keyword search on the results.

As searchable encryption allows users to query encrypted data using a keyword, it may be used in the EMR to secure the patient's personal details, such as identification, conversation, and health records. As certificateless public key cryptography reduces the need for certificates and tackles the key escrow problem, a certificateless searchable public key encryption method for mobile healthcare systems was proposed. The electronic medical record, ciphertext is encrypted by the patient's public key in most EMR data-sharing methods based on searchable encryption, thus only the patient's private key is used to decode. If a patient's condition is critical, more hospitals are required for online consultation, then EMR sharing will become an issue [65].

The application of information processing including both computer hardware and software that deals with the storing, retrieval, exchange, and use of healthcare information, data, and knowledge for communication and decision making has been characterized as healthcare information technology (HIT). From simple charting to more complex decision assistance and interaction with medical equipment, health information technology encompasses a wide range of technologies. Reducing human mistakes, enhancing clinical outcomes, increasing care coordination, enhancing practice efficiency, and collecting data over time are just some of the ways that health information technology may help improve and revolutionize healthcare. There has been a rapid growth and acceptance of health information technology since the initial IOM study, with varied degrees of evidence concerning the influence of health information technology on patient safety [66].

The studies were conducted in both inpatient and outpatient settings, with any of the following interventions:), clinical decision support (CDS), electronic physician orders (CPOE), E-prescribing, electronic sign-out and hand-off tools, smart pumps, automated medication dispensing cabinets (ADC), bar code medication administration (BCMA), electronic medication record (EMR). Safety of patient, medical errors, adverse event, medication errors, ADE, and fatality were the primary outcomes of interest. Systematic reviews, meta-analyses, and randomized clinical trials were given top attention. If no such studies could be found, other types of epidemiological or experimental research method, such as quasi-experimental, nonrandomized controlled trials, before and after studies, case control studies, prospective, and retrospective cohort studies might be used instead [67].

Studies that meet any of the following criteria will be excluded: high risk of bias, nonclinical studies, cointerventions with non-health information technology interventions, research that do not evaluate patient safety outcomes, qualitative or narrative studies. To find both published and unpublished studies, the search strategy was conducted Embase, Medline, and the Cochrane Database were all used in the search. Until studies have been published electronic physician order entry (CPOE), electronic medical records (EMR), clinical decision support (CDS), electronic sign-out and hand-off, e-prescribing, bar code medication administration (BCMA), patient data management systems (PDMS), closed loop medication administration, patient electronic portals, retained surgical items detectors, telemedicine, and electronic incident reporting were among the first keywords used [68].

2.4 Deep Learning in Healthcare

Deep learning is a commonly used artificial intelligence technology, which can discover the associations from data without requiring them to be defined beforehand. The capacity to create predictive models without making strong assumptions about the underlying mechanisms, which are often unknown or inadequately characterized, is the main attraction.

Data harmonization, model fitting, representation learning, and evaluation are the four processes of a typical machine learning workflow [69].

Deep learning varies from traditional machine learning in terms of the representational patterns that are learnt from raw data. Deep learning allows computational models based on neural networks to learn multiple levels of abstraction for data representations by combining many processing layers. The primary distinctions between deep learning and traditional artificial neural networks are the number of hidden layers, their connections, and the capacity to gain meaningful abstractions of the inputs (ANNs). Typical artificial neural networks (ANNs) include three layers and are trained to provide supervised representations that are especially optimized for the work at hand [70, 71].

Because information sources are handled in a forward direction, ANN is also known as a "feed-forward neural system." The ANN is composed of three layers input, hidden and output layer. The information layer receives the information sources, the concealed layer handles the information sources and the yield layer delivers the results. Deep learning and neural networks today provide the finest answers to a wide range of problems in preparing of normal language, picture acknowledgement, discourse acknowledgement. Achievements in important clinical availability have been made in human services also presenting the approach to a potential wise device's new generation–based deep learning for genuine life Medicare [72, 73].

2.4.1   Deep Learning Models

Different types of neural systems in profound learning, such as CNN (convolution neural systems), RNN (intermittent neural systems), and ANN, are altering how we interact with the world. These various types of neural systems are on the verge of a breakthrough, powering applications, such as self-driving vehicles, automated ethereal vehicles, and discourse recognition.

2.4.1.1   *Recurrent Neural Networks (RNN)*

RNNs are useful in data stream processing. They are made up of a single network that does the same thing for each element of a sequence, with each output value determined by prior calculations. RNNs could only look back a few steps in the original formulation due to disappearing and expanding gradient issues. The problem was handled using gated recurrent unit (GRU) and long short-term memory (LSTM) networks, which simulate the hidden state with cells that choose what to maintain in (and what to remove from) memory given the previous state, current memory, and input value. These variations are good at capturing long-term dependencies and have done well in natural language [74].

Furthermore, medicinal interventions were included in the model to dynamically shape the forecasts. Deep care was tested for disease progression modelling, intervention recommendation, and future risk prediction on diabetes and mental health patient cohorts. Choi *et al.* build the Doctor AI, an end-to-end RNN with GRU model that utilises a patient's prior information to forecast, diagnose, and prescribe medications for sickness. By transferring the resultant model from one institution to another without compromising considerable accuracy, the evaluation demonstrated considerably greater recall than shallow baselines, as well as high generalizability [75].

Razavian *et al.* demonstrated that convolutional neural networks and recurrent neural networks with LSTM units performed better than logistic regression with clinically relevant properties that were hand-engineered in predicting sickness onset from laboratory test measurements alone [76, 77].

2.4.1.2   Convolutional Neural Networks (CNN)

The "CNN" or "ConvNet" class in profound learning is a deep neural systems class that is frequently used to deconstruct visual symbols. CNN is a type of neural systems that is widely used in the field of computer vision. It starts the name from the various levels of deception it entails. Convolution layers, totally associated layers, pooling layers, and standardization layers are CNN shrouded layers. Application of CNN are generally in image information, classification of forecast issues and regression expectation issues.

In contrast to a feed-forward neural network (NN), which is only employed in totally connected layers, CNN design has three layers: the pooling layer, the convolutionary layer, and the completely connected layer. The convolutional layers utilized for extracting features from input neurons in CNN have K filters (or kernels) that are smaller in size than the image dimension. The pooling and convolutional layers study extraction features, while the third is a fully connected layer that extracts map attributes and is displayed in the final output. Pixel values are stored in a 2D matrix in the form of digital images, such as a numbers array and a small parameter matrix known as the kernel, and at each image position, an optimizable extractor is utilized.

For example, in a picture, the first layer may be used to recognize corners and lines, the second layer may combine these features into various forms, and the last layer may recognise something like to a high-level complex, such as a dog breed. CNN is the best-performing image recognition algorithm, as demonstrated by GoogLeNetwinning entry into the ImageNet Large Scale Visual Recognition Challenge and Microsoft ResNet's entry. The various chemicals are identified using CNN's protein ligand scoring model. The 3D grid is used to illustrate protein-binding ligand structures that are created via docking with the help of binders or nonbinders. It demonstrates that the AutoDockVina scoring method is utilized to make a prediction, which is then carried out by the CNN scoring algorithm [78].

2.4.1.3   Deep Belief Network (DBN)

Deep belief network (DBN) is one of the most used deep learning techniques. It is based on the restricted Boltzmann machine (RBM), which has only two layers: visible and hidden. The neurons between the two levels are completely connected, whereas neurons in the same layer are not connected. The following properties of determining the neuron state are due to the disconnection between neurons at the same level: when the visible cell state is determined, the hidden unit condition is activated independently; otherwise, when the hidden cell state is determined, the conditions of the visible units are activated independently.

RBMs and profound conviction models can be used for dimensionality reduction and information inspection, among other things. DBNs, for example, have been utilized to extract appropriate depictions from microarray data in order to predict bosom malignancy development [79].

2.4.1.3.1   Auto Encoder

Because it does not use names, auto encoder is an unaided learning model. The model has been successfully employed in applications to reduce dimensionality. When an adequate measure of information is available, auto encoders can achieve a considerably better two-dimensional depiction of cluster data. An example of case for auto encoders used in human services is estimating the likelihood of patients based on reasonable portrayals from electronic social insurance records [80].

2.4.1.4   Contrasts Between Models

They are sufficient when the data include clusters of qualities in an exhibit that are related to one another. for the recording, picture, and sound information situation Using close availability and shared loads, a convolution layer can readily process high-dimensional contributions, while a pooling layer can down-example the contribution without losing critical information.

By stacking many convolution layers, the system may modify the information of image into a representation that preserves essential input designs, resulting in exact forecasts [81].

RNNs are used to solve problems involving consecutive data, such as language and discourse preparation or modelling. RNN associations can frame cycles despite the fact that CNNs and DBNs are feed forward systems. This makes it possible to demonstrate dynamical changes over time.

2.4.1.5   Use of Deep Learning in Healthcare

Deep learning is a strong technology that augments traditional machine learning by allowing computers to learn from data in order to create better applications. These methods have already been used to a variety of applications, including computer vision and natural language processing. According to all of the findings in the literature, deep learning can be utilized to analyze healthcare data. In fact, adopting multilayer neural networks to analyze medical data increased the prediction ability of a number of specialized applications in a variety of clinical sectors. Owing to its hierarchical learning structure, deep architectures also have the capacity to integrate multiple data sets across dissimilar data types and enable higher generalization due to its concentration on representation learning rather than classification accuracy. In an ideal scenario, this depiction would bring together all of the many data sources, like as EHRs, the environment, genetics, wearables, social activities, and so on, to create a holistic and comprehensive picture of a person's health. The deep learning framework would be integrated into a healthcare platform (such as a hospital EHR system), and the models would be updated on a regular basis to account for changes in the patient population.

Disease risk prediction, personalized prescriptions, therapeutic recommendations, clinical trial enrolment, and research and data analysis are just a few domains and applications that might benefit from deep representations. The typical vector or matrix-based strategy may not be the best option since the entries in those vectors/matrices are frequently aggregated over time, making it difficult to capture illness progression trends. In clinical contexts, deep learning may be used as a guiding principle to organise both hypothesis-driven research and exploratory studies (e.g., visualization of patient cohorts, grouping, disease group stratification) [80, 82].

Machine learning models with their advantages and disadvantages are summarized in Table 2.1.

Table 2.1 Machine learning models with their advantages and disadvantages [83, 84].

Machine learning network	Architecture	Advantage	Disadvantage
Recurrent Neural Networks	It has the capability of sequence learning. The weights are sharing across all steps and neurons.	Time dependency may be modeled and sequential occurrences can be understood quickly. RNNs such as LSTM, BLSTM, HLSTM, and MDL-STM are used. They have produce state of art accuracies in speech recognition, character recognition, and a variety of other natural language processing applications.	It requires big databases and falls into the problems because of gradient vanishing.
Convolutional Neural Networks	For 2-D data, they function admirably. Convolution filters are used to convert 2-D data into 3-D data.	Produce great efficiency and more quick learning.	It is a requirement of the classification that all data be labeled.

(Continued)

Table 2.1 Machine learning models with their advantages and disadvantages [83, 84]. (*Continued*)

Machine learning network	Architecture	Advantage	Disadvantage
Deep Belief Network	The top two levels of this model have unidirectional connections. In machine learning, it is utilized in both supervised and unsupervised learning. Each sub-hidden network's layers serve as the visible layer for the next layer.	In each layer greedy strategy are used. The interference tractable maximize the likelihood directly.	It is an expensive method.
Deep Neural Network	Its architecture comprises more than two levels, allowing it to deal with non-linear relationships that are complex. It is widely utilized in both classification and regression analysis.	It offers a wide range of applications and produces great precision.	Because there are more hidden layers in the training process, the error is propagated back to the previous layer and becomes very small. The learning process is also quite long.

(*Continued*)

Table 2.1 Machine learning models with their advantages and disadvantages [83, 84]. (*Continued*)

Machine learning network	Architecture	Advantage	Disadvantage
Deep Boltzmann Machine	This model is based on the Boltzmann family and consists of one-way connections between all hidden layers.	The top-down feedback incorporates with ambiguous data for more robust inference.	Big data sets optimization are not possible.

Table 2.2 Type of deep learning and algorithm with their application [85, 86].

Type of deep learning and algorithm	Applications
Supervised learning	Personalized treatment, in treatment of population health
Convolutional Neural Networks	Radiology-Image Classification, Organ Segmentation, Iris sensor model identification
Recurrent Networks	In precision medicine and medical translation
Unsupervised Learning	Drug discovery
Generative Adversarial Networks	Data augmentation
Reinforcement Learning	Identification of right treatment
Complementary Priors on Belief Networks	Digital classification
Particle filtering and Bayesian-belief propagation	Hierarchical Bayesian inference in the visual cortex
Back propagation and associative memory architecture	Deep belief network for phone recognition
Local filtering and max-pooling infrequency domain	Multi-speaker speech recognition

Type of deep learning and neural network with their application are summarized in Table 2.2.

2.5 Conclusion

Artificial neural networks, which are algorithms inspired by the structure and operation of the brain, are the focus of deep learning, a subset of machine learning. Deep learning in healthcare enables physicians to correctly analyze any disease to properly manage it which results in better treatment decisions. In the healthcare sector, deep learning models, such as blockchain and the Internet of Things are utilized to manage vast amounts of healthcare data, such as electronic medical records. Deep learning is now being utilized by health practitioners to administer the healthcare system in an online way, and mobile healthcare is a part of it. This chapter describes the role of deep learning in healthcare by using different models and managing the healthcare system effectively. It also summarizes the role of blockchain and IoT in health management.

2.6 Acknowledgments

The authors of this chapter are thankful to their respective Departments/ Universities for successful completion of this study.

References

1. Wang, J., Han, K., Alexandridis, A., Zilic, Z., Lin, J., Pang, Y., Yang, X., A baseband processing ASIC for body area networks. *J. Ambient Intell. Humaniz. Comput.*, 10, 10, 3975–3982, 2018.
2. Negra, R., Jemili, I., Abdelfettah, B., Wireless Body Area Network: application and technologies. *Proc. Comput. Sci.*, 83, 1274–1281, 2016.
3. Hasan, K., Biswas, K., Ahmed, K., Nafi, N.S., Islam, M.S., A comprehensive review of wireless body area network. *J. Netw. Comput. Appl.*, 143, 178–198, 2019.
4. Conti, M., Dehghantanha, A., Franke, K., Watson, S., Internet of Things security and forensics: challenges and opportunities. *Future Gener. Comput. Syst.*, 78, 544–546, 2018.
5. Shen, J., Chang, S., Shen, J., Liu, Q., Sun, X., A lightweight multi-layer authentication protocol for wireless body area networks. *Future Gener. Comput. Syst.*, 78, 956–963, 2018.

6. Wang, J., Han, K., Alexandridis, A., Zilic, Z., Pang, Y., Lin, J., An ASIC implementation of security scheme for body area networks, in: *2018 IEEE international symposium on circuits and systems (ISCAS)*, pp. 1–5, 2018, May2018.
7. https://www.aidoc.com/blog/deep-learning-in-healthcare/
8. Ambigavathi, M. and Sridharan, D., Energy efficient and load balanced priority queue algorithm for Wireless Body Area Network. *Future Gener. Comput. Syst.*, 88, 586–593, 2018.
9. Adarsh, T.K. and Vijayakumar, K.P., A classical method for health monitoring on IoT: from architecture, security and application. *Int. J. Innov. Technol. Explor. Eng.*, 8, 11, 2278–3075, 2019.
10. Sicilia, M.A. and Visvizi, A., Blockchain and OECD data repositories: opportunities and policymaking implications. *Libr. Hi Tech.*, 37, 1, 30–42, 2019.
11. Reyna, A., Martín, C., Chen, J., Soler, E., Diaz, M., On blockchain and its integration with IoT. Challenges and opportunities. *Future Gener. Comput. Syst.*, 88, 173–190, 2018.
12. Xie, Z., Dai, S., Chen, H.N., Wang, X., Blockchain challenges and opportunities a survey. *Int. J. Web Grid Serv.*, 14, 4, 352–375, 2018.
13. Wang, J., Han, K., Alexandridis, A., Zilic, Z., Wu, W., Jeon, G., A novel security scheme for Body Area Networks compatible with smart vehicles. *Comput. Netw.*, 143, 74–81, 2018.
14. https://info1.exlservice.com/blockchain-the-concept-for-health-plan-cmos-2017-thank-you?submissionGuid=e5a4fca9-1b87-4a20-aef1-c6de03d0ed23
15. Laplante, P.A. and Laplante, N.L., A Structured approach for describing healthcare applications for the Internet of Things, in: *Internet of Things, WF-IoT, 2015 IEEE 2nd World Forum on*, Milan, pp. 621–625, 2015, http://dx.doi.org/10.1109/WF-IoT.2015.7389125.
16. Barchetti, U., Bucciero, A., De Blasi, M., Mainetti, L., Patrono, L., RFID, EPC and B2B convergence towards an item-level traceability in the pharmaceutical supply chain, in: *2010 IEEE International Conference on RFID-Technology and Applications, Guangzhou*, China, pp. 194–199, 2010.
17. Commission, E., Internet of things strategic research roadmap, *Internet of things-global technological and societal trends*, 1, 9–52, 2009. http://www.internet-ofthingsresearch.eu/pdf/IoT_Cluster_Strategic_Research_Agenda_2009.pdf.
18. Nogueira, V.B. and Carnaz, G., An overview of IoT and Healthcare. 1–12, 2016.
19. Filipe, L., Fdez-Riverola, F., Costa, N., Pereira, A., Wireless body area networks for healthcare applications: Protocol stack review. *Int. J. Distrib. Sens. Netw.*, 11, 10, 1–23, 2015.
20. Custodio, V., Herrera, F.J., López, G., Moreno, J.I., A review on architectures and communications technologies for wearable health-monitoring systems. *Sensors*, 12, 10, 13907–13946, 2012.

21. Nie, Z., Ma, J., Li, Z., Chen, H., Wang, L., Dynamic propagation channel characterization and modeling for human body communication. *Sensors*, 12, 12, 17569–17587, 2012.

22. Houlding, D., *Health information at risk: successful strategies for healthcare security and privacy*, pp. 1–8, Healthcare IT Program Office Intel Corporation, white paper, 2011.

23. Abouelmehdi, K., Beni-Hessane, A., Khaloufi, H., Big healthcare data: preserving security and privacy. *J. Big Data*, 5, 1, 1–18, 2018.

24. Mazlan, A.A., Daud, S.M., Sam, S.M., Abas, H., Rasid, S.Z.A., Yusof, M.F., Scalability challenges in healthcare blockchain system-a systematic review. *IEEE Access*, 8, 23663–23673, 2020.

25. https://www.ibm.com/in-en/blockchain/what-is-blockchain

26. https://www.computerworld.com/article/3191077/what-is-blockchain-the-complete-guide.html

27. https://www.ibm.com/in-en/blockchain/what-is-blockchain

28. Gupta, M., Blockchain for Dummies. *Jpn. J. Nurs. Sci.*, 14, 257–266, 2017.

29. Cernian, A., Tiganoaia, B., Sacala, I.S., Adrian, P., Iftemi, A., Patient data chain: A blockchain-based approach to integrate personal health records. *Sensors*, 20, 1–24, 2020.

30. Yoon, H.J., Blockchain technology and healthcare. *Healthc. Inform. Res.*, 25, 59–60, 2019.

31. Stan, O. and Miclea, L., New era for technology in healthcare powered by GDPR and blockchain, in: *Proceedings of the 6th International Conference on Advancements of Medicine and Healthcare through Technology*, Cluj-Napoca, Romania, pp. 311–317, 17–20 October2018.

32. Tiganoaia, B. and Cernian, A., Computer systems for business and data management, in: *Transaction and Security*, vol. 170, University Publishing House, Bucharest, Romania, 2019.

33. MedBlocks. https://medblocks.org/ (accessed on 10 FEB 2021).

34. Secure Health Chain. https://secure.health/ (accessed on 10 FEB 2021).

35. MedicalChain. https://medicalchain.com/en/ (accessed on 10FEB 2021).

36. Doc.AI. https://doc.ai/ (accessed on 10 FEB 2021).

37. OmniPHR. https://www.sciencedirect.com/science/article/pii/S1532046417301089 (accessed on 10 FEB 2021).

38. MIStore. https://www.ncbi.nlm.nih.gov/pmc/articles/PMC6028902/ (accessed on 10 FEB 2021).

39. Leeming, G., Cunningham, J., Ainsworth, J., A ledger of me: Personalizing healthcare using blockchain technology. *Front. Med.*, 6, 1–10, 2019.

40. https://www.ahajournals.org/doi/full/10.1161/circoutcomes.117.003800

41. Stan, O. and Miclea, L., New era for technology in healthcare powered by GDPR and blockchain, in: *Proceedings of the 6th International Conference on Advancements of Medicine and Healthcare through Technology*, Cluj-Napoca, Romania, pp. 311–317, 2018.

42. Abadi, D.J., Data management in the cloud: Limitations and opportunities. *IEEE Data Eng. Bull.*, 32, 1, 3–12, 2009.
43. Fan, K., Wang, S., Ren, Y., Li, H., Yang, Y., Medblock: Efficient and secure medical data sharing via blockchain. *J. Med. Syst.*, 42, 8, 1–11, 2018.
44. Blobel, B. and Roger-France, F., A systematic approach for analysis and design of secure health information systems. *Int. J. Med. Inform.*, 62, 1, 51–78, 2001.
45. Chen, H.S., Jarrell, J.T., Carpenter, K.A., Cohen, D.S., Huang, X., Blockchain in healthcare: A patient-centered model. *Biomed. J. Sci. Tech. Res.*, 20, 3, 15017–15022, 2019.
46. Yue, X., Wang, H., Jin, D., Li, M., Jiang, W., Healthcare data gateways: Found healthcare intelligence on Blockchain with novel privacy risk control. *J. Med. Syst.*, 40, 10, 1–8, 2016.
47. Griggs, K.N., Ossipova, O., Kohlios, C.P., Baccarini, A.N., Howson, E.A., Hayajneh, T., Healthcare blockchain system using smart contracts for secure automated remote patient monitoring. *J. Med. Syst.*, 42, 7, 1–7, 2018.
48. Ivan, D., Moving toward a blockchain-based method for the secure storage of patient records, in: *ONC/NIST use of blockchain for healthcare and research workshop; ONC/NIST: Gaithersburg*, MD, USA, pp. 1–11, 2016.
49. Chen, Y., Ding, S., Xu, Z., Zheng, H., Yang, S., Blockchain-based medical records secure storage and medical service framework. *J. Med. Syst.*, 43, 1, 1–9, 2018.
50. Wang, S., Wang, J., Wang, X., Qiu, T., Yuan, Y., Ouyang, L., Guo, Y., Wang, F.Y., Blockchain-powered parallel healthcare systems based on the ACP approach. *IEEE Trans. Comput. Soc Syst.*, 99, 1–9, 2018.
51. Jiang, S., Cao, J., Wu, H., Yang, Y., Ma, M., He, J., Blochie: A blockchain-based platform for healthcare information exchange, in: *Proceedings of the 2018 IEEE International Conference on Smart Computing (SMARTCOMP)*, Taormina, Italy, pp. 49–56, 2018.
52. Cyran, M.A., Blockchain as a foundation for sharing healthcare data. *Blockchain Healthc. Today*, 1, 1–6, 2018.
53. Shubbar, S., *Ultrasound medical imaging systems using telemedicine and blockchain for remote monitoring of responses to neoadjuvant chemotherapy in women's breast cancer: Concept and implementation*, Master's thesis, Kent State University, Kent, OH, USA, 2017.
54. Ianculescu, M., Stanciu, A., Bica, O., Neagu, G., Innovative, adapted online services that can support the active, healthy and independent living of ageing people. A case study. *Int. J. Econ. Manage. Syst.*, 2, 321–329, 2017.
55. Mark, A.E., Hitching healthcare to the chain: an introduction to blockchain technology in the healthcare sector. *Technol. Innov. Manage. Rev.*, 7, 10, 22–34, 2017.
56. Lefeuvre, D., Pavillon, G., Aouba, A., Lamarche-Vadel, A., Fouillet, A., Jougla, E., Rey, G., Quality comparison of electronic versus paper death certificates in France, 2010. *Popul. Health Metr.*, 12, 1, 1–8, 2014.

57. Vukoli, M., Rethinking permissioned blockchains, in: Proceedings of the ACM workshop on blockchain, in: *Cryptocurrencies and Contracts*, New York, NY, United States, pp. 3–7, 2017.

58. Wong, J.Q., Uy, J., Haw, N.J.L., Valdes, J.X., Bayani, D.B.S., Bautista, C.A.P., Haasis, M.A., Bermejo III, R.A., Zeck, W., Priority setting for health service coverage decisions supported by public spending: experience from the Philippines. *Health Syst. Reform*, 4, 1, 19–29, 2018.

59. Nakamoto, S., Bitcoin: A peer-to-peer electronic cash system, in: *Decentralized Business Review*, DEBR, 398, Seocho-daero Seocho-gu, Seoul, KR pp. 1–9, 2008.

60. Buterin, V., *A next-generation smart contract and decentralized application platform*, vol. 3, pp. 1–36, White Paper, 2014, https://github.com/ethereum/wiki/wiki/White-Paper.

61. Mane, R.R. and Kulkarni, R.V., A review: electronic medical records (emr) system for clinical data storage at health centers. *Int. J. Comput. Technol. Appl.*, 3, 5, 1837–1842, 2012.

62. Kaushal, R., Kern, L.M., Barron, Y., Quaresimo, J., Abramson, E.L., Electronic prescribing improves medication safety in community-based office practices. *J. Gen. Intern. Med. United States*, 25, 530–536, 2010.

63. Strom, B.L., Schinnar, R., Aberra, F., Bilker, W., Hennessy, S., Leonard, C.E., Pifer, E., Unintended effects of a computerized physician order entry nearly hard-stop alert to prevent a drug interaction: a randomized controlled trial. *Arch. Intern. Med.*, 170, 1578–1583, 2010.

64. Dainty, K.N., Adhikari, N.K.J., Kiss, A., Quan, S., Zwarenstein, M., Electronic prescribing in an ambulatory care setting: a cluster randomized trial. *J. Eval. Clin. Pract.*, 18, 761–767, 2012.

65. Clinical Decision Support (CDS) Office of the National Coordinator for Health Information Technology. https://www.healthit.gov/policy-researchers-implementers/clinical-decision-support-cds.

66. Shojania, K.G., Jennings, A., Mayhew, A., Ramsay, C.R., Eccles, M.P., Grimshaw, J., The effects of on-screen, point of care computer reminders on processes and outcomes of care. *Cochrane Database Syst. Rev.*, 3, 1–68, 2009.

67. Shah, N.R., Seger, A.C., Seger, D.L., Fiskio, J.M., Kuperman, G.J., Blumenfeld, B., Recklet, E.G., Bates, D.W., Gandhi, T.K., Improving acceptance of computerized prescribing alerts in ambulatory care. *J. Am. Med. Inform. Assoc.*, 13, 5–11, 2006.

68. Paterno, M.D., Maviglia, S.M., Gorman, P.N., Seger, D.L., Yoshida, E., Seger, A.C., Bates, D.W., Gandhi, T.K., Tiering drug-drug interaction alerts by severity increases compliance rates. *J. Am. Med. Inform. Assoc.*, 16, 40–46, 2009.

69. Jordan, M.I. and Mitchell, T.M., Machine learning: Trends, perspectives, and prospects. *Science*, 349, 6245, 255–260, 2015.

70. Rumelhart, D.E., Hinton, G.E., Williams, R.J., Learning representations by back-propagating errors. *Nature*, 323, 6088, 533–536, 1986.

71. Miotto, R., Wang, F., Wang, S., Jiang, X., Dudley, J.T., Deep learning for healthcare: review, opportunities and challenges. *Brief. Bioinform.*, 19, 6, 1236–1246, 2018.

72. Bengio, Y., *Learning deep architectures for AI*, vol. 2, pp. 1–127, Now Publishers Inc., Hanover, MA, United States, 2009.

73. Malik, M., Singh, Y., Garg, P., Gupta, S., Deep learning in healthcare system. *Int. J. Grid Distrib. Comput.*, 13, 2, 469–468, 2020.

74. Collobert, R., Weston, J., Bottou, L., Karlen, M., Kavukcuoglu, K., Kuksa, P., Natural language processing (almost) from scratch. *J. Mach. Learn. Res.*, 12, 2493–2537, 2011.

75. Choi, E., Bahadori, M.T., Schuetz, A., Stewart, W.F., Sun, J., Doctor ai: Predicting clinical events via recurrent neural networks, in: *Machine Learning for Healthcare Conference*, 56, pp. 301–318, 2016.

76. Razavian, N., Marcus, J., Sontag, D., Multi-task prediction of disease onsets from longitudinal laboratory tests, in: *Machine learning for healthcare conference*, Presented at 2016 Machine Learning and Healthcare Conference (MLHC 2016), Los Angeles, CA. pp. 73–100, 2016.

77. Dernoncourt, F., Lee, J.Y., Uzuner, O., Szolovits, P., De-identification of patient notes with recurrent neural networks. *J. Am. Med. Inform. Assoc.*, 24, 3, 596–606, 2017.

78. Ragoza, M., Hochuli, J., Idrobo, E., Sunseri, J., Koes, D.R., Protein–ligand scoring with convolutional neural networks. *J. Chem. Inf. Model.*, 57, 4, 942–957, 2017.

79. Lu, P., Guo, S., Zhang, H., Li, Q., Wang, Y., Wang, Y., Qi, L., Research on improved depth belief network-based prediction of cardiovascular diseases. *J. Healthc. Eng.*, 2018, 1–9, 2018.

80. Miotto, R., Li, L., Kidd, B.A., Dudley, J.T., Deep patient: an unsupervised representation to predict the future of patients from the electronic health records. *Sci. Rep.*, 6, 1, 1–10, 2016.

81. Rakhlin, A., *Convolutional neural networks for sentence classification, Mater's thesis*, University of Waterloo, Ontario, Canada, 2016.

82. https://www.michaeljfox.org/grant/subtyping-parkinsons-disease-deep-learning-models-2016-ppmi-data-challenge-winner?grant_id=1518

83. Razzak, M.I., Naz, S., Zaib, A., Deep learning for medical image processing: Overview, challenges and the future, in: *Classification in BioApps*, Computer Vision and Pattern Recognition, pp. 323–350, 2018.

84. Kumar, U., Applications of machine learning in disease pre-screening, in: *Research Anthology on Artificial Intelligence Applications in Security*, IGI Global, USA, pp. 1052–1084, 2021.

85. Vargas, R. and Lourdes, R.U.I.Z., Deep learning: previous and present applications. *J. Aware.*, 2, 3, 11–20, 2017.

86. https://morioh.com/p/dfb35fa50823

3

Deep Learning on Site-Specific Drug Delivery System

Prem Shankar Mishra[1], Rakhi Mishra[2*] and Rupa Mazumder[2]

[1]Department of Pharmacy, Galgotias University, Greater Noida, Uttar Pradesh, India
[2]Noida Institute of Engineering and Technology (Pharmacy Institute),
Greater Noida, Uttar Pradesh, India

Abstract

Nowadays, modern technology with a focus on drug discovery development in novel site-specific drug delivery systems has developed in pharmaceutical research. **Aim:** Nowadays, deep learning technology is accepted worldwide in many exigent branches as it have the specific competency of automatic data extraction. The usual dosage form, such as tablets and capsules, possesses disadvantages of bioavailability, frequent application need, and various side effects that ultimately cause inconvenience to the patient. **Discussion:** Numerous publications continue to appear, which assure to "carry" but have limitation, to facilitate the generation of therapeutic products through developing a new strategy for site-specific drug delivery systems. A deep learning algorithm system enhances the effectiveness of conventional methods of drug discovery, yielding a substitute to the traditional drug delivery systems. The deep learning method can predict the drug stability, shelf lives of drugs, and the stability of whole drug delivery systems. Thus, it becomes a need for the current era to consider the use of deep learning as a necessary instrument to practice facts assets and move ahead in an knowledgeable and balanced manner. **Conclusion:** This paper aims to provide a summarized theory on deep learning, which finds its wide application in discovering and developing site-specific drug delivery systems.

Keywords: Deep learning, site-specific, algorithm, dosage forms, drug delivery system, artificial intelligence, machine learning

*Corresponding author: rakhi.misra84@rediffmail.com

Rishabha Malviya, Gheorghita Ghinea, Rajesh Kumar Dhanaraj, Balamurugan Balusamy and Sonali Sundram (eds.) *Deep Learning for Targeted Treatments: Transformation in Healthcare*, (77–100) © 2022 Scrivener Publishing LLC

3.1 Introduction

At current time, pharmaceutical industries are facing several challenges in developing a more superior and optimized system to embattled drug release with minimum risk and hazards [1]. High cost and more time requirements are other common obstacles faced by the R& D sectors in the drug discovery and development phase [2].

Various methods remain used to design the targeted drug delivery system like sonography, micropump mechanism, and focused drug delivery through microrobot [3, 4]. Targeted drug delivery in the form of nanoparticles, a microfluidic platform, is a promising approach [5, 6]. Microfluidic technology can develop an advanced drug delivery system; for example, a nanoparticle formulation can deliver multiple drugs to a specific target [7–9]. First, an osteoporotic patient used an implantable specific drug delivery system [10].

Nowadays, worldwide several computational approaches are undertaken by researchers to minimalize the price and period in the development of drugs [11]. In traditional computational methods like simulated and *in silico* studies, the rationale of the study is to confirm the binding affinity of targeted protein with drugs. These studies are mostly ignored, while other targeted proteins of selected compounds will be unidentified [12]. Thus, the use of novel- and site-specific delivery of the therapeutic agents with the help of machine learning or AI technique widely encounters all challenges mentioned above.

Information technology and artificial neural network (ANN) play a vital role in producing site-specific drug delivery systems that benefit different conventional treatment strategies. These studies also indicate more options for site-specific drug delivery systems [13, 14].

The technique of artificial intelligence includes using a deep and machine learning algorithm that provides several advantages over the previously used approaches for the site-specific design of the therapeutics, which is one of the surges of the current market of pharmaceuticals [15]. Despite traditional objects for specific site delivery of the drug with minimum side effects, the AI approach has a thing for expanding effective site-specific drug delivery systems [16].

Design and advancement of site-specific drug delivery approaches have attracted the interest of researchers to overcome several hindrances associated with the traditional drug delivery systems [17, 18]. This drug delivery system is advantageous in different kinds of severe ailments requiring monitoring and consistent treatments [19]. This is capable of enhancing pharmaceuticals' effectiveness and protection with more effect on patient's compliance [20].

Researchers suggested that machine learning is a prominent part of AI, while some literature described it as a subdivision of artificial intelligence [21, 22]. Artificial intelligence (AI) is a type of canopy where all the computational program can work and behaves like humans do, while in machine learning (ML), all the data along with algorithm command are set into a machine, such as decision tree, Naïve Bayes, Markov model, etc. and support the devices to acquire deprived programmed [23]. For along with the advancement of neural networks, machines can be categorized and establish data, which imitate like humans' memory and show the development in AI. Around the 20th century, Aizenberg *et al.* introduced, for the first time, artificial neural networks in deep learnings [24–29]. Deep learning is a subdivision of machine learning, and ML itself is a subdivision of artificial intelligence. The ability of AI, ML, and DL is as follows: artificial intelligence (AI) > machine learning (ML) > deep learning (DL) [30, 31].

Sometimes, automatic adjustment of the concentration of open program, site-specific drugs, and automatic control of drug proclamation prove to be an effective method for enhancing the efficacy and safety of drug profiles [32].

For all these controls, there is a need for an intelligent control scheme based on the deep learning method, including the use of the technique of artificial intelligence [33]. The design of competent drug delivery and control system based on the modification of dose or rate of site-specific drug release and steadiness of medications could be considered [34]. A suitable algorithm can be applied to control the drug release through self-control drug delivery systems [35].

Under the deep learning technique, neural network, logic integrator, and differentiator have been used to develop a new site-specific delivery system of different therapeutics [36–38].

Artificial Neural Networks (ANNs) containing the interrelated dispensation essentials, which are formed through pretending the computational system of designed nerve cells [39–43], are pragmatic to create software program, representing the pharmacological progressions, producing the regulated algorithm, pharmacological model, measured site-specific drug delivery, which assess the efficacy of diagnostic and treatment approaches [44, 45].

ML strategies are used to predict target-based ligands focused on target fishing; the dataset of ligands, receptor protein, and describes the ligand-target relationship, which envisages various pharmacological activity of newly designed compound to find out receptor proteins [46, 47].

Certainly, advanced methodologies are important for generating novel drugs and modern site-specific drug delivery systems [48, 49].

Deep learning is generally computer learning, which thinks similar to structures modeled on the human brain. DL is a part of artificial intelligence that imitates the behavior of the human brain in data algorithms to diagnose and detect things, sound recognition, language molding, taking decisions [50, 51]. DL can memorize itself and design the data algorithm, which is deep learning AI can learn without human supervision, illustration from data that is both amorphous or shapeless and unlabeled [52, 53].

DL is a programmed software for the general purpose, extensively accepted in other drug discovery development and government areas. Distinctly, ML is an approach needing other places to get the output of the study in a more acceptable high-level representation [54]. Compared to ML methods, deep learning possesses more sensitivity to either unacceptable or variable data [55].

In 2013, the first comparison of conventional ML methods and deep learning was carried out by doing a solubility study of drugs [56]. The result showed that comparatively, deep learning methods are far superior to other approaches, which leads to the expansion of pharmaceutical studies using the concept of deep learning [57]. In some investigation, it was reported that toxicity of the drugs could be reduced by the forecasting of the ability of drug molecule to undergo epoxidation reaction for which deep convolution network (DCN) method of deep learning was used [58, 59].

In 2016, it was also concluded that deep learning techniques can be used to envisage the toxicity of the molecule more accurately when compared to other computational methods [60]. The deep learning method enormously helps produce results of many patient insights, which further supports the researchers and healthcare system analyze and improve the different patient care areas. Collectively, this method data insights of the increased number of patients can be explored [61]. Other wearable pharmaceutical companies also use this technology to ultimately serve the need of patients [62, 63].

In the domain of cancer or chemo preventive technologies, deep learning technology paved a path by which any type of cancer be diagnosed specifically and for identifying any rare or specific kind of health issue [64–66]. To fulfill the emerging need for deep learning technology, different study programs are finding a place in the country with varying courses on deep learning, data engineering, and artificial intelligence [67]. In India, Maharashtra alone is where deep learning and data science are the most prominent courses undertaken by individuals [68, 69].

3.2   Deep Learning

DL alone can easily copy the working of the human brain and is regarded as a type of Artificial Intelligence. It is also known as a deep neural network or deep neural learning. Like a human brain, it works and helps the scientist process the data and create some pattern that allows a person for any decision [70]. Deep learning always works with the help of neural networks of different types. The artificial neural network in its structure resembles the human brain's anatomical structure, having millions of its units as neuron connected in a web [71]. Compared to conventional machine learning methods, which carry their data analysis linearly, the deep learning systems allow the machines to process data advantageously in a nonlinear way [72]. Because of its ability to assess data in a nonlinear way, it proved to be very useful for a researcher who needs to collect, analyze, and interpret any massive data and needs a lot of time when read and studied by any other classical methods [73, 74].

Deep learning is preferably used in instances of collection and analysis of a large amount of data, sometimes also in situations where there is a loss of data introspection knowledge and in some composite harms of speech recognition and NLP [75, 76].

With the deep learning process, a data scientist or analyst can:

1) identify the problem,
2) collect the relevant and necessary data set and organize the collected data for investigation,
3) select the type of deep learning algorithm suitable to carry the task,
4) correlate and set the chosen algorithm for the labeled data,
5) analyze and compare the results of labeled data against the unlabeled data by repeating the above procedure [77, 78].

Deep learning technology uses many algorithms and models according to the task and type of data chosen and collected [79]. Every model of deep learning technique is suitable for different applications, like drawing, speech recognition, language modeling, drug activity, toxicity prediction, etc. [80]. Other types of algorithms used are discussed below [81, 82]:

3.2.1   Types of Algorithms Used in Deep Learning

Different types of deep learning models/algorithm are shown in Figure 3.1 and these are as follows:

1) Convolutional neural networks (CNNs),
2) Long short-term memory networks (LSTMs),

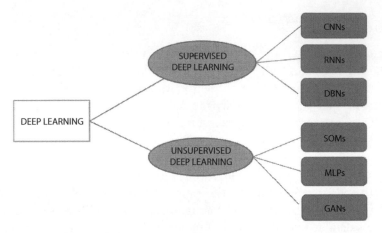

Figure 3.1 Shows different deep learning models.

3) Recurrent neural networks (RNNs),
4) Generative adversarial networks (GANs),
5) Radial basis function networks (RBFNs),
6) Multilayer perceptron (MLPs),
7) Self-organizing maps (SOMs),
8) Deep belief networks (DBNs).

3.2.1.1   Convolutional Neural Networks (CNNs)

The year 1959 proved to be a turning point for AI when two neurophysiologists, D. Hubel and T. Wiesel, concluded in their study in the form of a research paper that the building block of the brain, i.e., the neurons are present and organized in the form of layers inside the brain [83]. Neurons present in the form of layers are first used to extract the confined data and then combine all the small extracted features to visualize a specific pattern.

Later on, this concept becomes the fundamental of the program of DL [84].

The deep learning model works on the principle of multilayer neural network, the same as the working of the human ophthalmic system. In the CNN model, artificial neurons are designed in the form of multiple neurons layers. The multilayer of artificial neurons at the last part of the study gives a calculated value, an added value of multiple input and outputs [85].

In this deep learning method, the images are represented as tensors, which make an essential part of CNNs. In this, all the data, either input, output, or any other parameters, are all tensor. In this model, normally, tensors having a value of 3 or more than 3 are commonly used. One processing step of CNNs is regarded as a layer, which may be of the following types:

- a convolution layer,
- a pooling layer,
- a normalization layer,
- a fully connected layer,
- a loss layer, etc.

The methods end when the processing of the layers in the CNN has been finished. For backward error propagation, one additional layer is also added in this method of deep learning.

In present studies, this proved to be a tool of getting very fruitful and hopeful results in different kinds of optical applications using a computer and also is very useful in specific image-related tasks, like image classification, semantic image segmentation, two object detection in images [86]. The importance of these applications lies in the fact that they can be used to design a model or a system that can further predict the disease and its severity and differentiate the progression of the same condition in different subjects.

In the technique of CNN, the processing of both the layer of classification and feature extraction occurs together, making the result of the model dependant on the features of the extracted layer; thus, the results are obtained in a very organized form. The organized type of result data gives an advantage to this method for its use to an extensive network of unorganized data [87].

3.2.1.2   Long Short-Term Memory Networks (LSTMs)

This is another class and more advanced version of recurrent neural networks as in RNNs, back signal either got vanished so RNNs can only look back in time for approximately 10 timesteps [88, 89]. To overcome this problem of RNNs, long short-term memory recurrent neural network (LSTM-RNN) is one of the most potent dynamic classifiers publicly known [90]. Recently risen to prominence with state-of-the-art performance in early learning tasks, cognitive learning tasks, speech recognition, handwriting recognition, machine translation, language modeling, translation, image captioning [91].

3.2.1.3   Recurrent Neural Networks

Recurrent neural networks (RNNs) is a model which provides a very fruitful advantage over plain CNNs as the concurrent neural networks are not suitable for a very lengthy input and output, both of which are strongly correlated in the sequence [92]. The RNN model in this situation is compelling because it can assemble more information of unorganized data successfully in their hidden state for dynamics of the complicated and nonlinear pattern [93]. Thus, this model helps gather and fix all past inputs that were not resolved earlier. The architecture of a recurrent neural network (RNN) has one feedback connection in the network for the forward and backward loop movement of information. This type of network system exists in many forms, out of them standard multilayer perceptron (MLP) method is universal type having supplementary loops benefit [94]. This class's other kind of network system possesses more systemic structures, having a well-organized system of neurons with all necessary stochastic activation functions [95].

3.2.1.4   Generative Adversarial Networks (GANs)

The generative model is a network that can detect and find the clustered and hidden forms of data. This model is used for unorganized data processed by the GANs, just like the production and use of fake currency [96].

In its earlier use, this model uses two probable latent variables, z, and x, noisy with one real variable as x. All three variables are identified and differentiated based on their inputs [97].

With the advancement in the features of this method, many new techniques are developed, among which, Pix-to-Pix is a model developed based on GANs deep learning method. This advanced Pix-to-Pix model can be used to generate deep high contrast images with the pairing of two shots in a single. The technique is widely used to produce various medical images that need deep neural network fitting [98]. The hidden layer of the functions of the same use that have the basis of the radial function of Gaussian type [99].

3.2.1.5   Radial Basis Function Networks

Radial basis function network (RBFN) is a type of deep neural network, the idea of which is taken from function approximation theory. This network consists of two layers that can work in the forward direction. The performance of RBFNs is high-speed and divided into two stages [100]. The first involves the transfer of data from the input layer to the hidden layer, and the second stage causes the transfer of data from the hidden to the output layer. This model is outstanding at interpolation [101].

For the processing of an RBFN, the operator needs to enter the hidden unit activation function, the number of the processing units, the modeling algorithm for specific work, and an algorithm for training that collectively will produce the required parameters of the network. This whole process of obtaining different parameters value is known as network training.

Network training process is used for completion of the given task and also for collection of the different criteria parameters. In the above training process, the radial basis function network system can be used with identification of the hidden unit and the total number of processing units [102].

3.2.1.6 Multilayer Perceptron

Multilayer perceptrons (MLPs) is a multilayer model based on feedforward learning. In this model, multiple layers of unorganized data are present with some identical units in each layer. All the units are connected in a whole network. The first and last layers are the input and output layers, respectively. Hidden layers are present in between input and output layers [103]. This network model works on the backpropagation method for deep learning of nonlinear activation. This model works on the principle of adaptive learning [104]. It can fastly differentiate between linear and nonlinear data [105].

3.2.1.7 Self-Organizing Maps

Self-organizing maps (SOMs) are used for deep learning of unorganized data based on competitive learning, which involves the activation of single neurons among all output neurons at a single time [106, 107]. The activated neuron is known as the winner or winning neuron. Activation of neurons is induced by the adverse feedback pathway, which is present among the multiple neurons. After their activation, neurons start to organize themselves, because of which, this network system is known as a self-organizing map (SOM) [108]. SOMs usually work for the organization and visualization of unorganized data [109]. The data containing neurons are well connected because a minute change in the weight of one neuron affects all other neurons present in its vicinity with the most negligible effect on far neurons [110]. This characteristic feature of the neurons presents in SOMs model causes reduction of the problem of overfitting among the data sets [111, 112].

3.2.1.8 Deep Belief Networks

Deep belief networks (DBNs) model of deep learning involves the use of several latent variables. The used latent variables in this model can be binary. The variables used invisible layers of this model can be binary or accurate in the heart [113]. Latent and visible layers of this model are not interconnected, but the top 2 layers have a unidirectional connection in the direction toward the data [114]. This model system is not having its layers interconnection. The deep belief network system can be used for deep learning various objects, documents, etc. [115]. DBNs are a generative model that, in combination with some other algorithms like unsupervised greedy learning algorithm CD-k, can attain deep learning of objects [116].

3.3   Machine Learning and Deep Learning Comparison

Machine learning and deep learning differs from each other as shown in Figure 3.2 and the basic difference between the two are as follows:

S. no.	Deep learning	Machine learning
1.	Denoted by DL	Denoted by ML.
2.	It is a subset of ML	It belongs to superset of DL
3.	This learning works on the principle of "artificial neural network"	Machine learning uses different algorithms to work on the basis of data.
4.	It on the basis of neural neuron network can take its own decision	This method cannot take its own decision. It gives decisions on the basis of its learning
5.	This learning has a human brain like structure with the presence of artificial neurons	This has a simple algorithm based linear tree like structure.
6.	There is a need of more input data for obtaining good results	It works with less input data
7.	Requires more time	Need less time
8.	Trains on GPU for proper training	Trains on CPU
9.	The output is obtained in the form of any free form elements such as free text and sound.	The output is in numerical form for classification and scoring applications.
10.	Can be tuned in various ways	Limited tuning capability for hyperparameter tuning

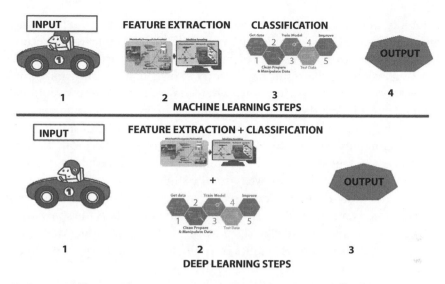

Figure 3.2 Difference in machine learning and deep learning methods [117, 118].

3.4 Applications of Deep Learning in Drug Delivery System

In the current practice of the development of pharmaceuticals, the scope of deep learning is increasing as the traditional approach for pharmaceutical development is very costly with the requirement of more human resources and time also [119]. The deep learning method possesses advantages over the limitations of the traditional way as it has automatization features [120].

Artificial neural network models are finding their role in the area of pharmaceutical and pharmacokinetic studies. ANNs can predict the relationship dependence and nondependence of the model under the study areas to sculpt multifaceted affairs and specify the nonlinear relationship between underlying factors and reaction variables.

For 5 years, the first beckon of deep learning uses in pharmaceuticals and related research has occurred, and its applications have gone ahead of bioactivity predictions. They have also shown they swear in addressing varied troubles in drug discovery [121, 122]. This method provides more accuracy when compared to machine learning as this method possess the ability to detect any variation in each second of its processing [123].

Since the last few years, many wide applications of deep learning in the advancement of pharmaceutical formulation preparations have been reported [124]. In 2013, this method was used to predict the drugs' water solubility and predicted values compared with other machine learning approaches [125]. Some studies also concluded that deep learning performance is superior when compared to other machine learning models. All the conclusions of the result have clearly shown that deep learning possesses more and better performance when compared to other conventional methods [126]. The deep learning technique nowadays finds its application in drug discovery also as it can predict better results of quantitative structure-activity relationship (QSAR) study, which is a critical study in the process of drug discovery [127, 128]. It can use multitask learning with insufficient data for drug discovery despite single-task knowledge [129]. It can also do future drug repurposing by enabling the scientist to learn from the past study data of the drug [130]. All obtained results of the study done in the last 5 years showed that deep learning had more advantages over other machine learning techniques in predicting different types of effects of the drugs [131, 132] as shown in Figure 3.3.

Deep learning finds its application in predicting the chemical process of epoxidation of molecules, which causes drug toxicity [133]. The prediction of drug toxicity can be made by using a deep convolution network [134]. This model can also be applied to predict any damage in liver tissues caused by drugs [135].

Various DL methods are recently used and reported for their wide application in reaction prediction. The results obtained in multiple studies

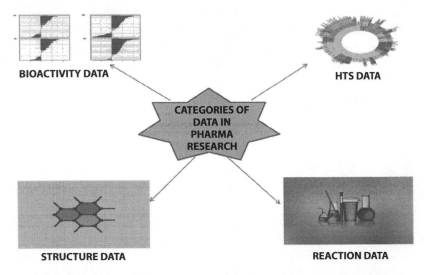

Figure 3.3 Different types of research data in pharmacy, which can be managed by the deep learning algorithms [136].

showed that DL, compared to other machine learning methods, can predict and give superior results in the prediction of reactions [137].

Deep learning finds its wide application in the field of cheminformatics also [138] with the help of different neural networks in the deep learning generation of new structures that can have more promising biological properties [139]. Among the type of deep learning, generative adversarial networks (GANs) are used in many studies to produce novel chemical entities with their anticancer action [140].

Encouraging results are obtained by applying deep learning neural networks in detecting the protein-ligand interactions [141]. With the inspiration from molecular docking programs, which are widely used for the interaction prediction between ligand and target protein among deep learning methods, complex neural networks are also gaining popularity for doing the same with more efficiency [142, 143].

From Research & Development to clinical trials, images with high pixels, contrast, and analysis of those images are crucial for drug discovery [144]. With the help of biological photos, a scientist can judge the type of phenotype and learn the features of organs, tissues, cells, and other cellular components [145]. The technique of deep learning has made all these processes easy, efficient, and satisfactory. With the help of deep learning, the hidden pathology responsible for the occurrence of any disease can be studied with superior performance when compared to old classical image reading and analyzing techniques [146, 147].

In the whole drug discovery process, the application of deep learning can be utilized for the following studies [148]:

1. study of drug properties,
2. design of novel drugs,
3. defining drug-target interaction.

The properties of drugs can be studied by deep learning in the form of supervised problems. In the method of deep understanding, when one wants to inspect the property of medicine, then the "input" is done in the form of a drug, and by using the algorithm used in this study, "output" can be obtained in the form of "Drug Properties." The output gives an idea of various properties of a drug like its solubility, toxicity, etc. [149, 150].

Drug target interaction can also be obtained with this DL method. In the process, both "drug" and "target" are used as input, and then the output can be obtained in the form of their interaction, but the difference is observed when different types of neural networks are used [151]. *In silico* drug-target interactions information can also be obtained impressively with the help of this deep learning method.

3.5   Conclusion

In summary, deep learning covers many algorithms with their extensive and comprehensive applications in drug design and delivery system domains, which forecast the need and use of this technology in future drug discovery and development.

This chapter has discussed different deep learning algorithms that provide many innovative techniques and strategies for reducing the excess time and cost in the research and drug discovery process. These models are an efficient tool to analyze a large amount of data to reduce the complexity and various problems related to developing a drug delivery system [152]. Deep learning methods manage to rapidly decide more accurate biomarkers, drug targets, and significant drug moieties. It also indicates the correlation between drug therapeutics and different formulations types with identification of optimized dose, other process variables with a comprehensive study of various diseases, cellular responses, and their outcomes.

References

1. Li, Y., Lenaghan, S.C., Zhang, M., A data-driven predictive approach for drug delivery using machine learning techniques. *PloS One*, 7, 2, e31724, 2012.
2. Ratsch, G., *A Brief Introduction into Machine Learning*, Friedrich Miescher Laboratory of the Max Planck Society, Germany, 2005.
3. Dearden, J.C. and Rowe, P.H., Use of artificial neural networks in the QSAR prediction of physicochemical properties and toxicities for REACH legislation. *Methods Mol. Biol.*, 1260, 65–88, 2015.
4. Yang, Y., Ye, Z., Su, Y., Zhao, Q., Li, X., Ouyang, D., Deep learning for *in vitro* prediction of pharmaceutical formulations. *Acta Pharm. Sin. B*, 9, 1, 177–185, 2019.
5. Zhang, W., Zhao, Q., Deng, J., Hu, Y., Wang, Y., Ouyang, D., Big data analysis of global advances in pharmaceutics and drug delivery 1980–2014. *Drug Discov. Today*, 22, 1201–1208, 2017.
6. Rowe, R.C. and Roberts, R.J., Artificial intelligence in pharmaceutical product formulation: Knowledge-based and expert systems. *Pharm. Sci. Technol. Today*, 1, 153–159, 1998.

7. Bengio, Y., Courville, A., Vincent, P., Representation learning: A review and new perspectives. *IEEE Trans. Pattern Anal. Mach. Intell.*, 35, 1798–1828, 2013.

8. Lecun, Y., Bengio, Y., Hinton, G., Deep learning. *Nature*, 521, 436–444, 2015.

9. Schmidhuber, J., Deep learning in neural networks: An overview. *Neural Netw.*, 61, 85–117, 2015.

10. Ekins, S., The next era: Deep learning in pharmaceutical research. *Pharm. Res.*, 33, 2594–2603, 2016.

11. Mamoshina, P., Vieira, A., Putin, E., Zhavoronkov, A., Applications of deep learning in biomedicine. *Mol. Pharm.*, 13, 1445–1454, 2016.

12. Gawehn, E., Hiss, J.A., Schneider, G., Deep learning in drug discovery. *Mol. Inform.*, 35, 3–14, 2016.

13. Ma, J., Sheridan, R.P., Liaw, A., Dahl, G.E., Svetnik, V., Deep neural nets as a method for quantitative structure–activity relationships. *J. Chem. Inf. Model*, 55, 263–274, 2015.

14. Zhu, K.Y., Zheng, H., Zhan, D.G., A computerized drug delivery control system for regulation of blood pressure. *Int. J. Intel. Comput. Med. Sci. Image Process.*, 2, 1–13, 2007.

15. Nihar, S., Nishith, P., Patel, K.R., A sequential review on intelligent drug delivery system. *J. Pharm. Sci. Biosci. Res.*, 3, 158–162, 2013.

16. Ibric, S., Jovanovic, M., Djuric, Z., Parojcic, J., Solomun, L., Lucic, B., Generalized regression neural networks in prediction of drug stability. *J. Pharm. Pharmacol.*, 59, 745–750, 2007.

17. Mendyk, A., Jachowicz, R., Dorozyński, P., Artificial neural networks in the modeling of drugs release profiles from hydrodynamically balanced systems. *Acta Pol. Pharm.*, 63, 1, 75–80, 2006.

18. Ibric, S., Djuris, J., Parojcic, J., Djuric, Z., Artificial neural networks in evaluation and optimization of modified release solid dosage forms. *Pharmaceutics*, 4, 531–550, 2012.

19. Ekins, S., The next era: Deep learning in pharmaceutical research. *Pharm. Res.*, 33, 11, 2594–603, Nov 2016.

20. Chen, H., Engkvist, O., Wang, Y., Olivecrona, M., Blaschke, T., The rise of deep learning in drug discovery. *Drug Discov. Today*, 23, 6, 1241–1250, Jun 2018.

21. Chen, H., Engkvist, O., Wang, Y., Olivecrona, M., Blaschke, T., The rise of deep learning in drug discovery. *Drug Discov. Today*, 23, 6, 1241–1250, 2018.

22. Fernández, S. *et al.*, An application of recurrent neural networks to discriminative keyword spotting. *Proceedings of the 17th International Conference on Artificial Neural Networks*, Springer-Verlag, pp. 220–229, 2007.

23. Ma, J. *et al.*, Deep neural nets as a method for quantitative structure–activity relationships. *J. Chem. Inf. Model.*, 55, 263–274, 2015.

24. Ramsundar, B., Is multitask deep learning practical for pharma? *J. Chem. Inf. Model.*, 57, 2068–2076, 2017.

25. Koutsoukas, A., Deep-learning: Investigating deep neural networks hyper-parameters and comparison of performance to shallow methods for modeling bioactivity data. *J. Cheminformatics*, 9, 42, 2017.
26. Aliper, A., Deep learning applications for predicting pharmacological properties of drugs and drug repurposing using transcriptomic data. *Mol. Pharm.*, 13, 2524–2530, 2016.
27. Lusci, A., Deep architectures and deep learning in chemoinformatics: The prediction of aqueous solubility for drug-like molecules. *J. Chem. Inf. Model.*, 53, 1563–1575, 2013.
28. Xu, Y., Deep learning-based regression and multiclass models for acute oral toxicity prediction with automatic chemical feature extraction. *J. Chem. Inf. Model.*, 57, 2672–2685, 2017.
29. Kadurin, A., druGAN: An advanced generative adversarial autoencoder model for de novo generation of new molecules with desired molecular properties *in silico*. *Mol. Pharm.*, 14, 3098–3104, 2017.
30. Jiang, F., Jiang, Y., Zhi, H., Dong, Y., Li, H., Ma, S. *et al.*, Artificial intelligence in healthcare: Past, present and future. *Stroke Vasc. Neurol.*, 2, 4, 230–43, 2017.
31. Lo, Y.-C., Rensi, S.E., Torng, W., Altman, R.B., Machine learning in chemoinformatics and drug discovery. *Drug Discov. Today*, 23, 8, 1538–46, 2018.
32. Ye, Z., Yang, Y., Li, X., Cao, D., Ouyang, D., An integrated transfer learning and multitask learning approach for pharmacokinetic parameter prediction. *Mol. Pharm.*, 16, 2, 533–41, 2018.
33. Ekins, S., The next era: Deep learning in pharmaceutical research. *Pharm. Res.*, 33, 11, 2594–2603, 2016.
34. Jing, Y., Bian, Y., Hu, Z., Wang, L., Xie, X.Q., Deep learning for drug design: An artificial intelligence paradigm for drug discovery in the big data era. *AAPS J.*, 33, 9, 20–58, 2018.
35. Li, Y., Lenaghan, S.C., Zhang, M., A data-driven predictive approach for drug delivery using machine learning techniques. *PloS One*, 7, 2, e31724, 20122012.
36. Ron, D., Singer, Y., Tishby, N., The power of amnesia: Learning probabilistic automata with variable ꞌemory length. *Mach. Learn.*, 25, 117–149, 1996.
37. Chen, H., Engkvist, O., Wang, Y., Olivecrona, M., Blaschke, T., The rise of deep learning in drug discovery. *Drug Discov. Today*, 23, 1241–1250, 2018.
38. Machine learning poised to accelerate drug discovery. *Novartis*, May 7, 2018.
39. Pennachin, C. and Goertzel, B., Contemporary approaches to artificial general intelligence. *Cogn. Technol.*, 8, 1–30, 2007.
40. Pham, D. and Afify, A., Machine-learning techniques and their applications in manufacturing. *Proc. Inst. Mech. Eng. B J. Eng. Manuf.*, 219, 5, 395–412, 2005.
41. Khurana, U., Samulowitz, H., Turaga, D., Feature engineering for predictive modeling using reinforcement learning. *32nd AAAI Conference on Artificial Intelligence*, 2017.

42. Aliper, A., Plis, S., Artemov, A., Ulloa, A., Mamoshina, P., Zhavoronkov, A., Deep learning applications for predicting pharmacological properties of drugs and drug repurposing using transcriptomic data. *Mol. Pharm.*, 13, 2524–2530, 2016.

43. Altae-Tran, H., Ramsundar, B., Pappu, A.S., Pande, V., Low data drug discovery with one-shot learning. *ACS Cent. Sci.*, 3, 283–293, 2017.

44. Caruana, R., Multitask learning. *Mach. Learn.*, 28, 41–75, 1997.

45. Collobert, R. and Weston, J., A unified architecture for natural language processing: Deep neural networks with multitask learning, in: *Proceedings of the 25th International Conference on Machine Learning*, Helsinki, pp. 160–167, 2008.

46. Duch, W., Swaminathan, K., Meller, J., Artificial intelligence approaches for rational drug design and discovery. *Curr. Pharm. Des.*, 13, 1497–1508, 2007.

47. Gertrudes, J.C., Maltarollo, V.G., Silva, R.A., Oliveira, P.R., Honorio, K.M., Da Silva, A.B.F., Machine learning techniques and drug design. *Curr. Med. Chem.*, 19, 4289–4297, 2012.

48. Golkov, V., Skwark, M.J., Mirchev, A., Dikov, G., Geanes, A.R., Mendenhall, J. *et al.*, 3D deep learning for biological function prediction from physical fields, in: *International Conference on 3D vision (3DV)*. IEEE, Fukuoka, Japan on 25-12 Nov 2020, 2017. arXiv: 1704.04039.

49. Hinton, G.E., Osindero, S., Teh, Y.-W., A fast learning algorithm for deep belief nets. *Neural Comput.*, 18, 1527–1554, 2006.

50. Kearnes, S., McCloskey, K., Berndl, M., Pande, V., Riley, P., Molecular graph convolutions: Moving beyond fingerprints. *J. Comput. Aided Mol. Des.*, 30, 595–608, 2016.

51. Lavecchia, A., Machine-learning approaches in drug discovery: Methods and applications. *Drug Discov. Today*, 20, 318–331, 2015.

52. LeCun, Y., Bengio, Y., Hinton, G., Deep learning. *Nature*, 521, 436–444, 2015.

53. Lee, I., Keum, J., Nam, H., Deep Conv-DTI: Prediction of drug-target interactions via deep learning with convolution on protein sequences. *PloS Comput. Biol.*, 15, e1007129, 2019.

54. Lima, A.N., Philot, E.A., Trossini, G.H.G., Scott, L.P.B., Maltarollo, V.G., Honorio, K.M., Use of machine learning approaches for novel drug discovery. *Expert Opin. Drug Discov.*, 11, 225–239, 2016.

55. Lusci, A., Pollastri, G., Baldi, P., Deep architectures and deep learning in chemoinformatics: The prediction of aqueous solubility for drug-like molecules. *J. Chem. Inf. Model.*, 53, 1563–1575, 2013.

56. Maltarollo, V.G., Gertrudes, J.C., Oliveira, P.R., Honorio, K.M., Applying machine learning techniques for ADME-Tox prediction: A review. *Expert Opin. Drug Metab. Toxicol.*, 11, 259–271, 2015.

57. Maltarollo, V.G., Kronenberger, T., Wrenger, C., Honorio, K.M., Current trends in quantitative structure–activity relationship validation and applications on drug discovery. *Future Sci. OA*, 2017.

58. Mayr, A., Klambauer, G., Unterthiner, T., Hochreiter, S., DeepTox: Toxicity prediction using deep learning. *Front. Environ. Sci.*, 2016, 3, 80.

59. Ohue, M., Ii, R., Yanagisawa, K., Akiyama, Y., Molecular activity prediction using graph convolutional deep neural network considering distance on a molecular graph, *Int' Conf. Par. and Dist. Proc. Tech. and Appl.(PDPTA'19)*, 122-128 vol. 1907, p. 01103, 2019, arXiv preprint arXiv.

60. Pereira, J.C., Caffarena, E.R., dos Santos, C.N., Boosting docking-based virtual screening with deep learning. *J. Chem. Inf. Model.*, 56, 2495–2506, 2016.

61. Rawat, W. and Wang, Z., Deep convolutional neural networks for image classification: A comprehensive review. *Neural Comput.*, 29, 2352–2449, 2017.

62. Sharma, S. and Sharma, D., Intelligently applying artificial intelligence in chemo informatics. *Curr. Top. Med. Chem.*, 18, 1804–1826, 2018. Tsubaki, M., Tomii, K., Sese, J., Compound–protein interaction prediction with end-to-end learning of neural networks for graphs and sequences. *Bioinformatics*, 35, 309–318, 2018.

63. Kirchmair, J., Göller, A.H., Lang, D., Kunze, J., Testa, B., Wilson, I.D., Glen, R.C., Schneider, G., Predicting drug metabolism: Experiment and/or computation? *Nat. Rev. Drug Discov.*, 14, 387, 2015.

64. Loging, W., Harland, L., Williams-Jones, B., High-throughput electronic biology: Mining information for drug discovery. *Nat. Rev. Drug Discov.*, 6, 220–230, 2007.

65. Schmidhuber, J., Deep learning in neural networks: An overview neural networks. *Neural Netw.*, 61, 85– 117, 2015.

66. Mamoshina, P., Vieira, A., Putin, E., Zhavoronkov, A., Applications of deep learning in biomedicine. *Mol. Pharm.*, 13, 5, 1445– 1454, 2016.

67. Leung, M.K.K., Xiong, H.Y., Lee, L.J., Frey, B.J., Deep learning of the tissue-regulated splicing code. *Bioinformatics*, 30, i121– i129, 2014.

68. Wang, S., Weng, S., Ma, J., Tang, Q., Deep CNF-D: Predicting protein order/disorder regions by weighted deep convolutional neural fields. *Int. J. Mol. Sci.*, 16, 8, 17315–17330, 2015.

69. Hughes, T.B., Miller, G.P., Swamidass, S.J., Modeling epoxidation of drug-like molecules with a deep machine learning network. *ACS Cent. Sci.*, 1, 4, 168–180, 2015.

70. Solovyeva, K.P., Karandashev, I.M., Zhavoronkov, A., Dunin-Barkowski, W.L., Models of innate neural attractors and their applications for neural information processing. *Front. Syst. Neurosci.*, 215–25, 2015.

71. Newby, D., Freitas, A.A., Ghafourian, T., Comparing multilabel classification methods for provisional biopharmaceutics class prediction. *Mol. Pharm.*, 12, 187 – 102, 2015.

72. Broccatelli, F., Cruciani, G., Benet, L.Z., Oprea, T., II, BDDCS class prediction for new molecular entities. *Mol. Pharm.*, 9, 3, 570– 580, 2012.

73. Glorot, X. and Bengio, Y., Understanding the difficulty of training deep feedforward neural networks. *Int. Conf. Artif. Intell. Stat*, pp. 249– 256, 2010.

74. Hinton, G.E. and Salakhutdinov, R.R., Reducing the dimensionality of data with neural networks. *Science*, 313, 5786, 504– 507, 2006.

75. Cortes, C. and Vapnik, V., Support-vector networks. *Mach. Learn.*, 20, 3, 273– 297, 1995.

76. Wang, F., Diao, X.M., Chang, S., Xu, L., Recent progress of deep learning in drug discovery. *Curr. Pharm. Des.*, 27, 17, 2021.

77. Ching, T., *et al.*, *Opportunities and obstacles for deep learning in biology and medicine*, bioRxiv, J R Soc Interface. 2018;15(141):20170387. 2017.

78. Goh, G.B. *et al.*, Deep learning for computational chemistry. *J. Comput. Chem.*, 38, 1291–1307, 2017.

79. Wan, L., Regularization of neural networks using drop connect, in: *Proceedings of the 30th International Conference on Machine Learning*, vol. 28 PMLR, pp. 1058–1066, 2013.

80. Ekins, S., The Next Era: Deep learning in pharmaceutical research. *Pharm. Res.*, 33, 11, 2594–603, 2016.

81. Kamerzell, T.J. and Middaugh, C.R., Prediction machines: Applied machine learning for therapeutic protein design and development. *J. Pharm. Sci.*, 110, 2, 665–681, 2021.

82. Jiang, D., Wu, Z., Hsieh, C.-Y., Chen, G., Liao, B., Wang, Z., Shen, C., Cao, D., Wu, J., Hou, T., Could graph neural networks learn better molecular representation for drug discovery? A comparison study of descriptor-based and graph-based models. *J. Cheminformatics*, 13(1), 2021.

83. Deng, H. and To, A.C., A parametric level set method for topology optimization based on deep neural network. *J. Mech. Des.*, 143, 9, 2021.

84. Wen, M., Zhang, Z., Niu, S., Sha, H., Yang, R., Yun, Y., Lu, H., Deep-learning-based drug–target interaction prediction. *J. Proteome Res.*, 16, 4, 1401–1409, 2017.

85. Zheng, L., Fan, J., Mu, Y., OnionNet: A multiple-layer intermolecular-contact-based convolutional neural network for protein–ligand binding affinity prediction. *ACS Omega*, 4, 14, 15956–15965, 2019.

86. Ciallella, H.L. and Zhu, H., Advancing computational toxicology in the big data era by artificial intelligence: Data-driven and mechanism-driven modeling for chemical toxicity. *Chem. Res. Toxicol.*, 32, 4, 536–547, 2019.

87. Donner, Y., Kazmierczak, S., Fortney, K., Drug repurposing using deep embeddings of gene expression profiles. *Mol. Pharm.*, 15, 10, 4314–4325, 2018.

88. Alberga, D., Trisciuzzi, D., Montaruli, M., Leonetti, F., Mangiatordi, G.F., Nicolotti, O., A new approach for drug target and bioactivity prediction: The multifingerprint similarity search algorithm (MuSSeL). *J. Chem. Inf. Model.*, 59, 1, 586–596, 2019.

89. Wang, S., Jiang, M., Zhang, S., Wang, X., Yuan, Q., Wei, Z., Li, Z., MCN-CPI: Multiscale convolutional network for compound–protein interaction prediction. *Biomolecules*, 11, 8, 1119, 2021.

90. Tripathi, N., Goshisht, M.K., Sahu, S.K., Arora, C., Applications of artificial intelligence to drug design and discovery in the big data era: A comprehensive review. *Mol. Divers.*, 25, 3, 1643–1664, 2021.

91. Hooshmand, S.A., Ghobadi, M.Z., Hooshmand, S.E., Jamalkandi, S.A., Alavi, S.M., Masoudi-Nejad, A., A multimodal deep learning-based drug repurposing approach for treatment of COVID-19. *Mol. Divers.*, 25, 3, 1717–1730, 2021.

92. Li, P., Li, Y., Hsieh, C.-Y., Zhang, S., Liu, X., Liu, H., Song, S., Yao, X., TrimNet: Learning molecular representation from triplet messages for biomedicine. *Brief. Bioinformatics*, 22, 4, 225, 2021.

93. Yu, Z., Lu, J., Jin, Y., Yang, Y., KenDTI: An ensemble model for predicting drug-target interaction by integrating multi-source information. *IEEE/ACM Trans. Comput. Biol. Bioinform.*, 18, 4, 1305–1314, 2021.

94. Pliakos, K., Vens, C., Tsoumakas, G., Predicting drug-target interactions with multi-label classification and label partitioning. *IEEE/ACM Trans. Comput. Biol. Bioinform.*, 18, 4, 1596–1607, 2021.

95. Li, P., Wang, J., Qiao, Y., Chen, H., Yu, Y., Yao, X., Gao, P., Xie, G., Song, S., An effective self-supervised framework for learning expressive molecular global representations to drug discovery. *Brief. Bioinformatics*, 39, 109, 2021.

96. Zeng, Y., Chen, X., Luo, Y., Li, X., Peng, D., Deep drug-target binding affinity prediction with multiple attention blocks. *Brief. Bioinformatics*, 8, 202–215, 2021.

97. Yang, S., Zhu, F., Ling, X., Liu, Q., Zhao, P., Intelligent healthcare: Applications of deep learning in computational medicine. *Front. Genet.*, 12, 2021.

98. Liu, Z., Chen, Q., Lan, W., Pan, H., Hao, X., Pan, S., GADTI: Graph auto-encoder approach for DTI prediction from heterogeneous network. *Front. Genet.*, 12, 2021.

99. Luo, H., Li, M., Yang, M., Wu, F.-X., Li, Y., Wang, J., Biomedical data and computational models for drug repositioning: A comprehensive review. *Brief. Bioinformatics*, 22, 2, 1604–1619, 2021.

100. Junejo, A.R., Li, X., Madiha, H., Mohamed, S., Molecular communication networks: Drug target scalability based on artificial intelligence prediction techniques. *J. Nanopart. Res.*, 23, 3, 2021.

101. Chu, Y., Kaushik, A.C., Wang, X., Wang, W., Zhang, Y., Shan, X., Salahub, D.R., Xiong, Y., Wei, D.-Q., DTI-CDF: A cascade deep forest model towards the prediction of drug-target interactions based on hybrid features. *Brief. Bioinformatics*, 22, 1, 451–462, 2021.

102. Hudson, I.L., *Data Integration Using Advances in Machine Learning in Drug Discovery and Molecular Biology. Methods Mol. Biol.*, 2020, 21(90), 167-184 pp. 167–184, 2021.

103. Cheng, K., Wang, N., Li, M., *Interpretability of Deep Learning: A Survey*, pp. 475–486, 2021.

104. Parisapogu, S.A.B., Annavarapu, C.S.R., Elloumi, M., *1-Dimensional Convolution Neural Network Classification Technique for Gene Expression Data*, pp. 3–26, 2021.

105. Li, A., Lin, X., Xu, M., Yu, H., Drug-Target Interactions Prediction with Feature Extraction Strategy Based on Graph Neural Network, in: *Intelligent Computing Theories and Application. ICIC 2021*, pp. 561–569, 2021. Lecture Notes in Computer Science, 12838. Springer, Cham. https://doi.org/10.1007/978-3-030-84532-2_50

106. Cong, H., Liu, H., Chen, Y., Cao, Y., Self-evoluting framework of deep convolutional neural network for multilocus protein subcellular localization. *Med. Biol. Eng. Comput.*, 58, 12, 3017–3038, 2020.

107. Kim, H., Kim, E., Lee, I., Bae, B., Park, M., Nam, H., Artificial intelligence in drug discovery: A comprehensive review of data-driven and machine learning approaches. *Biotechnol. Bioprocess Eng.*, 25, 6, 895–930, 2020.

108. Pliakos, K. and Vens, C., Drug-target interaction prediction with tree-ensemble learning and output space reconstruction. *BMC Bioinform.*, 21, 1, 2020.

109. Ji, B.-Y., You, Z.-H., Jiang, H.-J., Guo, Z.-H., Zheng, K., Prediction of drug-target interactions from multi-molecular network based on LINE network representation method. *J. Transl. Med.*, 18, 1, 2020.

110. Abbasi, K., Razzaghi, P., Poso, A., Amanlou, M., Ghasemi, J.B., Masoudi-Nejad, A., Deep, C.D.A., deep cross-domain compound–protein affinity prediction through LSTM and convolutional neural networks. *Bioinformatics*, 36, 17, 4633–4642, 2020.

111. Wang, C. and Kurgan, L., Survey of similarity-based prediction of drug-protein interactions. *Curr. Med. Chem.*, 27, 35, 5856–5886, 2020.

112. Huang, W., Power system Frequency prediction after disturbance based on Deep Learning. *Int. J. Circuits Syst. Signal Process.*, 14, 716–725, 2020.

113. He, S., Wen, Y., Yang, X., Liu, Z., Song, X., Huang, X., Bo, X., PIMD: An Integrative approach for drug repositioning using multiple characterization fusion. *Genomics Proteomics Bioinformatics*, 18, 5, 565–581, 2020.

114. Zhao, L., Ciallella, H.L., Aleksunes, L.M., Zhu, H., Advancing computer-aided drug discovery (CADD) by big data and data-driven machine learning modeling. *Drug Discov. Today*, 25, 9, 1624–1638, 2020.

115. Piroozmand, F., Mohammadipanah, F., Sajedi, H., Spectrum of deep learning algorithms in drug discovery. *Chem. Biol. Drug Des.*, 96, 3, 886–901, 2020.

116. Low, Z.Y., Farouk, I.A., Lal, S.K., Drug repositioning: New approaches and future prospects for life-debilitating diseases and the COVID-19 pandemic outbreak. *Viruses*, 12, 9, 1058, 2020.

117. Liang, S. and Yu, H., Revealing new therapeutic opportunities through drug target prediction: a class imbalance-tolerant machine learning approach. *Bioinformatics*, 36, 16, 4490–4497, 2020.

118. Shi, C., Chen, J., Kang, X., Zhao, G., Lao, X., Zheng, H., Deep learning in the study of protein-related interactions. *Protein Pept. Lett.*, 27, 5, 359–369, 2020.

119. Wang, J., Wang, H., Wang, X., Chang, H., Predicting drug-target interactions via FM-DNN learning. *Curr. Bioinform.*, 15, 1, 68–76, 2020.
120. Pichler, M., Boreux, V., Klein, A.-M., Schleuning, M., Hartig, F., Machine learning algorithms to infer trait-matching and predict species interactions in ecological networks. *Methods Ecol. Evol.*, 11, 2, 281–293, 2020.
121. Zhu, H., Big data and artificial intelligence modeling for drug discovery. *Annu. Rev. Pharmacol. Toxicol.*, 60, 1, 573–589, 2020.
122. Lin, X., Xu, M., Yu, H., Prediction of Drug-Target Interactions with CNNs and Random Forest, in: *Intelligent computingTheories and Application- 16th International Conference, ICIC 2020, Bari, Italy, 2-5, 2020, Proceedings, Part-II*. vol. 12464 pp. 361–370, Lecture Notes in Computer Science, 2020.
123. Hu, S., Zhang, C., Chen, P., Gu, P., Zhang, J., Wang, B., Predicting drug-target interactions from drug structure and protein sequence using novel convolutional neural networks. *BMC Bioinform.*, 20, S25, 2019.
124. Chaoming, L., Prediction and analysis of sphere motion trajectory based on deep learning algorithm optimization. *J. Intell. Fuzzy Syst.*, 37, 5, 6275–6285, 2019.
125. Lipinski, C.F., Maltarollo, V.G., Oliveira, P.R., da Silva, A.B.F., Honorio, K.M., Advances and perspectives in applying deep learning for drug design and discovery. *Front. Robot. AI*, 6, 2019.
126. Wang, L., Ding, J., Pan, L., Cao, D., Jiang, H., Ding, X., Artificial intelligence facilitates drug design in the big data era. *Chemometr. Intell. Lab. Syst.*, 194, 103850, 2019.
127. Wan, F., Zhu, Y., Hu, H., Dai, A., Cai, X., Chen, L., Gong, H., Xia, T., Yang, D., Wang, M.-W., Zeng, J., DeepCPI: A Deep Learning-based framework for large-scale *in silico* drug screening. *Genomics Proteomics Bioinformatics*, 17, 5, 478–495, 2019.
128. Luo, P., Li, Y., Tian, L.-P., Wu, F.-X., Enhancing the prediction of disease–gene associations with multimodal deep learning. *Bioinformatics*, 35, 19, 3735–3742, 2019.
129. Rifaioglu, A.S., Atas, H., Martin, M.J., Cetin-Atalay, R., Atalay, V., Doğan, T., Recent applications of deep learning and machine intelligence on *in silico* drug discovery: Methods, tools and databases. *Brief. Bioinformatics*, 20, 5, 1878–1912, 2019.
130. Mei, S. and Zhang, K., A multi-label learning framework for drug repurposing. *Pharmaceutics*, 11, 9, 466, 2019.
131. Lee, H. and Kim, W., Comparison of target features for predicting drug-target interactions by deep neural network based on large-scale drug-induced transcriptome data. *Pharmaceutics*, 11, 8, 377, 2019.
132. Ezzat, A., Wu, M., Li, X.-L., Kwoh, C.-K., Computational prediction of drug–target interactions using chemogenomic approaches: an empirical survey. *Brief. Bioinformatics*, 20, 4, 1337–1357, 2019.

133. Lee, I., Keum, J., Nam, H., Deep Conv-DTI: Prediction of drug-target interactions via deep learning with convolution on protein sequences. *PloS Comput. Biol.*, 15, 6, e1007129, 2019.

134. Jang, H.-J. and Cho, K.-O., Applications of deep learning for the analysis of medical data. *Arch. Pharm. Res.*, 42, 6, 492–504, 2019.

135. You, J., McLeod, R.D., Hu, P., Predicting drug-target interaction network using deep learning model. *Comput. Biol. Chem.*, 80, 90–101, 2019.

136. Zhang, W., Lin, W., Zhang, D., Wang, S., Shi, J., Niu, Y., Recent advances in the machine learning-based drug-target interaction prediction. *Curr. Drug Metab.*, 20, 3, 194–202, 2019.

137. Zhao, Q., Yu, H., Ji, M., Zhao, Y., Chen, X., Computational model development of drug-target interaction prediction: A review. *Curr. Protein Pept. Sci.*, 20, 6, 492–494, 2019.

138. Ekins, S., Puhl, A.C., Zorn, K.M., Lane, T.R., Russo, D.P., Klein, J.J., Hickey, A.J., Clark, A.M., Exploiting machine learning for end-to-end drug discovery and development. *Nat. Mater.*, 18, 5, 435–441, 2019.

139. Nelson, W., Zitnik, M., Wang, B., Leskovec, J., Goldenberg, A., Sharan, R., To embed or not: Network embedding as a paradigm in computational biology. *Front. Genet.*, 10, 2019.

140. Zhou, L., Li, Z., Yang, J., Tian, G., Liu, F., Wen, H., Peng, L., Chen, M., Xiang, J., Peng, L., Revealing Drug-target interactions with computational models and algorithms. *Molecules*, 24, 9, 1714, 2019.

141. Wu, Q., Ke, H., Li, D., Wang, Q., Fang, J., Zhou, J., Recent progress in machine learning-based prediction of peptide activity for drug discovery. *Curr. Top. Med. Chem.*, 19, 1, 4–16, 2019.

142. Saikin, S.K., Kreisbeck, C., Sheberla, D., Becker, J.S., Aspuru-Guzik, A., Closed-loop discovery platform integration is needed for artificial intelligence to make an impact in drug discovery. *Expert Opin. Drug Discov.*, 14, 1, 1–4, 2019.

143. Ezzat, A., Wu, M., Li, X., Kwoh, C.-K., *Computational prediction of drug-target interactions using chemogenomic approaches: an empirical survey. Brief Bioinformatics,* 20, 4, 1337–1357, 239–254, 2019.

144. Savva, K., Zachariou, M., Oulas, A., Minadakis, G., Sokratous, K., Dietis, N., Spyrou, G.M., *Computational Drug Repurposing for Neurodegenerative Diseases, In Silico* Drug Design, Academic Press, pp. 85–118, 2019.

145. Wang, N., Li, P., Hu, X., Yang, K., Peng, Y., Zhu, Q., Zhang, R., Gao, Z., Xu, H., Liu, B., Chen, J., Zhou, X., Herb target prediction based on representation learning of symptom related heterogeneous network. *Comput. Struct. Biotechnol. J.*, 17, 282–290, 2019.

146. Chiu, Y.-C., Chen, H.-I.H., Zhang, T., Zhang, S., Gorthi, A., Wang, L.-J., Huang, Y., Chen, Y., Predicting drug response of tumors from integrated genomic profiles by deep neural networks. *BMC Med. Genomics*, 12, S1, 2019.

147. Chang, Y., Park, H., Yang, H.-J., Lee, S., Lee, K.-Y., Kim, T.S., Jung, J., Shin, J.-M., Cancer drug response profile scan (CDRscan): A deep learning model that predicts drug effectiveness from cancer genomic signature. *Sci. Rep.*, 8, 1, 2018.
148. Yasuo, N., Nakashima, Y., Sekijima, M., *CoDe-DTI: Collaborative Deep Learning-Based Drug-Target Interaction Prediction*, 2018 IEEE International Conference On Bioinformatics And Biomedicine, 2018, 792-797 pp. 792–797, 2018.
149. Wu, Z., Li, W., Liu, G., Tang, Y., Network-based methods for prediction of drug-target interactions. *Front. Pharmacol.*, 9, 2018.
150. Ghasemi, F., Mehridehnavi, A., Pérez-Garrido, A., Pérez-Sánchez, H., Neural network and deep-learning algorithms used in QSAR studies: Merits and drawbacks. *Drug Discov. Today*, 23, 10, 1784–1790, 2018.
151. Öztürk, H., Özgür, A., Ozkirimli, E., DeepDTA: Deep drug–target binding affinity prediction. *Bioinformatics*, 34, 17, i821–i829, 2018.
152. Kalinin, A.A., Higgins, G.A., Reamaroon, N., Soroushmehr, S., Allyn-Feuer, A., Dinov, I.D., Najarian, K., Athey, B.D., Deep learning in pharmacogenomics: From gene regulation to patient stratification. *Pharmacogenomics*, 19, 7, 629–650, 2018.

4

Deep Learning Advancements in Target Delivery

Sudhanshu Mishra[1], Palak Gupta[2], Smriti Ojha[1], Vijay Sharma[3], Vicky Anthony[4] and Disha Sharma[5*]

[1]Department of Pharmaceutical Science & Technology, Madan Mohan Malviya University of Technology, Gorakhpur, Uttar Pradesh, India
[2]National Institute of Pharmaceutical Science and Research, Mohali, Punjab, India
[3]Hygia Institute of Pharmaceutical Education and Research, Lucknow, Uttar Pradesh, India
[4]School of Pharmaceutical Science, Rajiv Gandhi Technical University Bhopal, Madhya Pradesh, India
[5]Gahlot Institute of Pharmacy, Navi Mumbai, Maharashtra, India

Abstract

Artificial intelligence (AI) could also aid in the subsequent assimilation of the produced medicine in its proper pharmaceutical formulations, as well as its optimization, as well as quick decision making, leading to speedier manufacture of relatively high goods with consistent batch-to-batch stability and consistency. AI may also assist in establishing the product's efficacy and safety in clinical trials, and also some maintain proper placement and pricing in the market, through detailed market analysis and forecast. Despite of the fact that not much advancement has been discovered using AI-based methodologies, and particular issues exist in the technology's application, artificial intelligence (AI) is expected to become a formidable tool in the pharmaceutical business in the future. In the fields of drug discovery and production, machine learning technologies have been used to produce novel therapeutic candidates. Machine learning and deep learning algorithms are

Corresponding author: dishasharma.3003@gmail.com
Sudhanshu Mishra: ORCID: (0000-0001-5009-4736)
Palak Gupta: ORCID: (0000-0002-4551-2072)
Smriti Ojha: ORCID: (0000-0002-8125-7822)
Vijay Sharma: ORCID: (0000-0002-1689-6716)
Vicky Anthony: ORCID: (0000-0002-3828-7743)
Disha Sharma: ORCID: (0000-0001-9874-1875)

Rishabha Malviya, Gheorghita Ghinea, Rajesh Kumar Dhanaraj, Balamurugan Balusamy and Sonali Sundram (eds.) Deep Learning for Targeted Treatments: Transformation in Healthcare, (101–126) © 2022 Scrivener Publishing LLC

increasingly extensively used in approaches for generating therapeutic targets and new drug development to improve the efficiency, efficacy, and quality of developed outputs. Machine understanding and deep learning approaches have become more reliable as a result of the use of slightly elevated screening and high-throughput computational analysis of databases for lead and target identification.

Keywords: Artificial intelligence, deep learning, machine learning, pharmaceutical formulations

4.1   Introduction: Deep Learning and Targeted Drug Delivery

Deep learning is a prominent strategy for handling machine learning and artificial understanding challenges that makes optimal use of neural network models in today's world.

Deep learning is an emerging new methodology that has gained popularity in predictive modeling. Predictions made through the complex and sophisticated artificial neural networks are being considered as a precise tool to hit the desired complication and procure the number of possibilities for meticulously achieving the same.

A variety of neural network types is being developed and exploited to their full potential to be applied and utilized for improving the existing treatment strategies, such as to enhance the recovery rate, multiplying the effectiveness subsiding the existing anomalies and resultant side effects when drug therapy comes into play.

Deep learning through the artificial neural networks apart from enhancing competencies and slashing down drawbacks, has focused on drug discovery by the use of deep learning, which, unlike conventional methods, has foreshortened the efforts and the duration to reach a competent molecule of interest. Due to the differences in obtained results from various types of neural networks, and their application to drug discovery, it requires expert knowledge and carefully examined opinion to be able to choose the most appropriate approach [1].

The automatic extraction of the desired unvarying properties from the pool of available and constantly augmenting data, by intelligent use of representation learning methodology is considered as the greatest assurance of the use of machine learning. Deep-learning artificial neural networks work in the form of multiple levels of representation existing into hidden layers. Each subsequent layer forms a representation of a higher, more complex and abstract, level than the previous one, such neural networks are capable of learning extremely complex functions of their inputs with all necessary invariance properties, which are due to the presence of multiple (up to several dozen or more) hidden layers of nonlinear units. So, deep learning can be considered an important step toward artificial intelligence. However, on the contrary, the selection of sparse features is something that cannot be easily performed but is considered important for optimization of new data prediction and simple interpretation of models.

Creating effective, reliable, safe, and promising targeted drug delivery strategies becomes an integral component of the overall process of using machine learning for drug development. There are certain key requirements of an efficient and effective drug delivery system, which can be broadly grouped under the four pillars of retention, evasiveness, target, and release.

The goal, which has always been a concern to the researchers, is increasing the therapeutic index (TI) of a delivered compound. It can be achieved by selectively delivering the molecule of interest to the target areas, without letting the molecule concern unintended areas of the body. But the goal itself is a challenge, which has many obstacles throughout its way [2].

In recent developments, some of the abovementioned concerns hindering the goal of targeted drug delivery have been addressed in various areas, including but not limited to liposomes, nanosomes, prodrugs, external drug targeting, controlled gene expression, and antibodies.

Some of the relevant inventions and researches are being analyzed to understand and represent these innovations in a new light,various domains comprising of materials science, pharmaceutical and medical intervention, and engineering approaches have been combined and used to analyzed the patents and help discuss their advantages and disadvantages concerning further possibilities of improvement. There are certain patents concerning the manipulation, alteration, and engineering of genes and proteins, some patents concerning the targeted drug delivery by the machine learning approaches, which involves understanding of the human body and the action of medicinal moieties by the combined use of artificial intelligence and neural networks are at the core of this research and are an integral part of the upcoming possibilities and treatment strategies soon [3].

Specific targeting of therapeutic molecules is possible when working through this level of approach to reach our goal. This forms the most interesting and exciting strategy since it combines all the aspects of seeking a problem and solving it at all levels of medicinal, engineering, artificial intelligence, and computer science. The developments through these help in combining targeting strategies for delivery systems, which will be enriched with many layers of specificity, thereby increasing their targeting potential.

It is indeed crucial to investigate and comprehend (and maybe exploit) the prospective regions where distinct delivery systems are now being targeted various techniques, as well as to understand from nature's natural delivery methods within the body.

Following the aspects of all these targeted delivery within the human body include, but are not confined to, transport through red blood cells, neutrophils, and secretion granules, as well as many others that have been researched and debated utilizing a materials science approach. This in-depth examination illustrates how crucial it is to comprehend and interpret a variety of traits that nature has built into its targeted delivery, which manifest together within species, and whether these are essential to remember and comprehend when constructing man-made commodities.

When compiling the understanding about all these natural delivery mechanisms within the body at a deeper level, along with the mechanisms of deep learning neural networks exposing the same towards natural mechanisms such that it could learn and expand its neural network to analyzed and create a more specific path to deliver the intended molecule at a concise target. This could also be achieved if machine learning could gradually be made to learn how to use and exploit to its full potential body's delivery mechanism for targeted delivery approaches, rather than designing new routes and methods. The more layers of machine learning algorithms increase with learning body mechanisms, the more reliable, safe, and efficient drug-targeted approaches will come into existence.

Drug discovery and development based on the targeted delivery system will overall result in enhanced therapeutic action with minimized or ultimately zero unwanted and unintended effects for major ailments, including various types of cancer, genetic disorders, autoimmune disorders, diabetes, various neuronal and cardiovascular ailments, and many more, may be cured efficiently with the full potential of therapeutic agent being utilized [4].

4.2   Different Models/Approaches of Deep Learning and Targeting Drug

Deep learning (DL) is one of the most reducing areas of research and development in practically every scientific and technical discipline. The artificial neural network (NN) is a critical pillar of DL, and AI-based integration of common methodologies is key to the company's continued development. Deep neural networks (DNNs), recurrent neural networks (RNNs), and convolutional neural networks are the three main types of artificial neural networks employed in drug design today (CNNs) [5].

4.3   QSAR Model

DNNs are a sort of feed forwarding neural network that uses a solitary path data flow from the input layer to the hidden layer(s) and finally to the output units.

The outputs generated are typically identified using trained supervised learning algorithms. DL algorithms function through neural networks, which can incorporate other ML techniques for training. Through supervised and reinforcement learning guided methods, a DNN can be trained to complete complex tasks. QSAR models are presently being employed to search out the correlation between the compounds' chemical structure and activity. QSAR analysis is one of the foremost advanced kinds of DL-based AI in current drug discovery and development. It has allowed researchers to acquire 2D chemical structures and find out the physicochemical descriptors associated with the molecule's activity.

Typically, established supervised classification technologies are used to identify the outputs generated. For retraining, DL algorithms use neural networks, which would combine other ML approaches. A DNN can be programmed to execute complex operations using guided and encouragement feedback-guided approaches [6]. QSAR models are currently being used to look for a link between a compound's molecular structure and its activity. In today's drug discovery and development, QSAR assessment is amongst the most developed types of DL-based AI. Researchers have attempted to obtain 2D chemical characteristics and determine the physicochemical characteristics linked only with the molecule's action.

The first is the availability of surplus descriptors, which causes NN redundancy and, as a result, prevents outputs. This redundancy will significantly reduce the NN's efficiency while also producing non-ideal outcomes. These issues have been attempted to be overcome by employing a more precise technique to get a smaller number of higher quality descriptors; however, NN-based QSAR will continue to confront this challenge. The second challenge is to establish optimum model parameters without overfitting [7].

4.3.1   Model of Deep Long-Term Short-Term Memory

Drug targeting is the foundation for drug discovery and development, and people have depended on a variety of drug candidates that are recognized to recognize medications over the years.

One machine learning method for novel drug interactions is the deep learning methodology (DTIs). Drug target relationships are divided into two categories: interactions and noninteractions. Using machine learning algorithms, such tactics learn the probable patterns of known compound-target combinations, develop prediction models through iterative optimization, and infer potential DTIs.

Wang *et al.* proposed a deep learning-based mechanism for identifying unknown DTIs. The suggested technique is as follows:

(i)   Presentation of drug-target couples whereby the drug particles are represented as biometric features and the proteins sequences alternatives are derived by applying legendre moments (LMs) to the position-specific marking

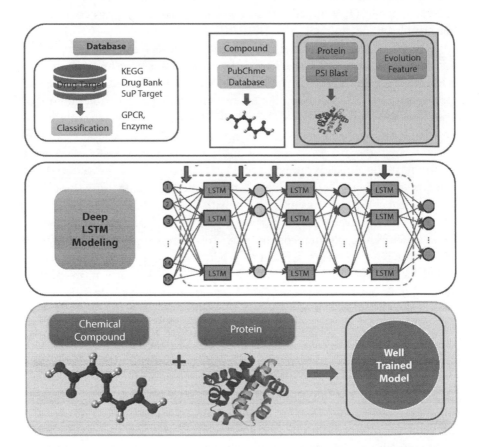

Figure 4.1 Schematic diagram of drug targets predicted by the proposed method.

matrix (PSSM), which includes biological details about just the proteins.

(ii) Compression and lamination are included. To reduce the computational complexity of the attributes and the informational redundancy, the sparse principal component analysis (SPCA) is being used [8].

(iii) Prediction. Predictions tasks are to be carried out using the deep long short-term memory (deep LSTM) paradigm. Figure 4.1 depicts the flow of the predicted model. Enzymes, ion channels, GPCRs, and nuclear receptors are among the four DTI datasets that are being used to test this approach. The findings demonstrate that the proposed approach outperforms current framework DTI forecasting techniques.

(iv) On the DTI problem, deep LSTM outperformed older machine learning techniques due to its superiority in feature representation and interpretation. It will also operate effectively with a condensed sample, and forecasting quality improves as the dataset size grows. The proposed approach and, as a consequence, the results of the experiment provide sufficient empirical and conceptual information on the effectiveness of utilizing this practice to foresee DTIs [9].

4.3.2 RNN Model

Recurrent neural networks (RNNs) are a type of NN that employs a self-learning system based on successive processing of inputs and the development of hidden nodes. For the production of unique chemical structures, RNN-type long immediate memory has become a dependable, standardized process. In contrast to DNNs and feedback control machine learning, which have no connections between identical layers and just push outputs, RNNs have the potential to use neurons connected in the very same hidden state to generate a continuous loop of processing endpoints. These synthetic RNNs have demonstrated encouraging results in the development of novel smile structures that were not included in the previous SMILE training sets. Segler *et al.* developed possible molecular structures that potentially show activity against *Staphylococcus aureus* (*S. aureus*) and *Plasmodium falciparum* using generative RNN models (*P. falciparum*). Their models were given condensed collections of chemical structures with known activity against all of these target species, and they created 14% of the 6051 possible molecule possibilities for *S. aureus* developed by medicinal chemists using these sources. The model, moreover, generates 28% of the known compoundsdeveloped for *P. falciparum*.

4.3.3   CNN Model

Convolutional neural networks (CNNs) is a type of deep neural network (DNN) that takes inputs, assigns weights to different components of the input, and then builds the power to differentiate the data. While classical DNNs are limited in their ability to perform appropriately on higher-dimensional data sources, CNN's offer a brilliant solution to this problem by preserving input complexity. A CNN model requires less retraining than DNNs and RNNs and is allowed to implement with accuracy and effectiveness. Because of these advantages, it has emerged as a standout learning optimization technique for picture identification, outperforming a variety of computer vision tasks. CNNs are becoming cost-effective methods for target finding, lead characterization, in silico performance in defined assessment, and protein-ligand assessment in the drug discovery process.

The use of a mixture of multiple techniques, such as CNNs, has been very useful in identifying gene alterations and disease targets. CNNs have been frequently used in later stage drug development, not simply for discovery. CNNs have been used to assist in the creation of cancer cell motility models that respond to treatment.

A recent study demonstrated the use of deep learning-based drug interface (DDI) predictors to address a wet research laboratory challenge that is often costly and time-consuming throughout the drug development process. Graph convolutional networks and DNN models were used to produce a new method. The graphene convolutional network was designed to extract structure features from medications found in DDI networking, learning low-dimensional approximations of the alternatives. The data are then sent into the DDN model, which functioned as the actual predictor; the program's ability to demand feature vectors and link them to matching feature vectors of prospective medication combinations allowed it to anticipate interactions. And, what is more encouraging, their technique's forecasts outperformed the most widely used state-of-the-art methodologies [10].

4.4   Deep Learning Process Applications in Pharmaceutical

Medication targets are the basis of drug research and development, and humans have depended significantly on scores of drug objectives known to detect medicines throughout the drug goals for the last few centuries. While the number of possible medicines that interact with target proteins keeps going up, only a portion of the human proteome remains in a number of authorized therapeutic targets. The initial stage in developing novel medication and one of the essential components in drug screening and drug-oriented synthesis is the identification of interactions between medicines and targets. Benefits from increased tests, a growing insight into the pharmaceutical compound's structural area, and genomic area of target proteins have been completed. Several free datasets, such the ChEMBL, Drug Bank, Super Target, focus on the connection between medicines and targets. The contents of these databases are the golden datasets necessary for developing computational techniques for predicting DTIs [11]. Biological pathways are a complex source of information during adaptation and sickness. These data are now being systemically monitored and retrieved at unprecedented levels, thanks to a wide range of "omics" and sophisticated technology. The application of these high technologies to biology and illness presents both challenges and opportunities for the pharmaceutical industry to uncover feasible therapeutic assumptions that lead to the development of drugs. Recent advancements in a variety of areas have sparked increased interest in the use of machine learning approaches in the healthcare business.

4.5   Techniques for Predicting Pharmacotherapy

There are only a few commercially accessible methods for predicting pharmaceutical responsiveness. Biomarker assays, which analyze quantities, such as gene expression and suggest whether or not a specific medicine connected with the biomarker essay will be beneficial for a given patient, are the most widely available procedures. Only a few multivariate assays rely on simple statistical and machine learning methods, while the majority of these tests and prediction models are univariate (the OncotypeDx21 and MAMMAPRINT22 models for breast cancer are based on a linear regression model and the nearest centroid model, respectively).

Given the higher measurement to sample ratio (N > D) and architectures that mimic the human brain and restrict overfitting, such as convolutional neural networks, deep learning has proved successful in sectors like image classification and translation software [12]. The complicated fundamental cancer pathophysiology would just be especially marked by neural network models with an appropriate inductive bias for genomics than linear regression, which limits the risk of overloading but odd significant modeling biases. Using feature pick is another way to deal with the limited number of tests available in drug response forecasting trials. Feature extraction excludes factors like gene genetic expression that are thought to be inaccurate for the phenotype being studied. This improves the functionality ratio, and univariate image segmentation is a common attribute selection strategy that maintains those properties that are strongly adjusted by the phenotype. Multivariate component methodological approaches exist as well, and they examine different types of features at the same time because a single feature may not be predictive of an event on its own; however, this does not rule out a combination of attributes [13].

4.6   Approach to Diagnosis

The last centuries or so have seen the huge success of conventional treatments, an approach that has surpassed previous remedies like medical purgatory and homeopathy in order of popularity. Nonetheless, this method's flaws, combined with the omics and bioinformatics explosion, spurred precision medicine, a framework whereby each patient's genetic background controls pharmaceutical choice. Indeed, precision medicine-based medicines, which were first used to treat cancer, are now being utilized to treat autoimmune, renal, and other disorders. A new reformation is transforming daily life, and it has now worked its way into healthcare. The last centuries or so have seen the huge success of conventional treatments, an approach that has surpassed previous remedies like medical purgatory and homeopathy in order of popularity. Nonetheless, this method's flaws, combined with the omics and bioinformatics explosion, spurred precision medicine, a framework whereby each patient's genetic background controls pharmaceutical choice. Indeed, precision medicine-based medicines, which were first used to treat cancer, are now being utilized to treat autoimmune, renal, and other disorders. A new reformation is transforming daily life, and it has now worked its way into healthcare.

Artificial intelligence (AI) has evolved from primarily scientific frameworks to practical applications in recent years. The widespread availability of new computer technologies, including such graphics processing units (GPUs), which accelerate parallel processing, particularly in numerically complex computations, can be credited for most of the exponential increase. Advances in new machine learning algorithms, including deep neural networks (DL), that build powerful predictive models, as well as the demonstrated success of these research methods in numerous public contests, have contributed to a significant increase in the use of ML in the pharmaceutical sector in the last few years [14].

Currently, the three primary groups of computational techniques for predicting DTIs are ligand-based, docking simulation, and chemogenomic approach. Ligand-based techniques, such as Quantitative Structure-Activity Relationship (QSAR), are based on the notion that comparable compounds bind to similar proteins. These techniques, in particular, anticipate interactions by comparing a novel ligand to existing protein ligands. However, when the number of known ligands is inadequate, ligand-based approaches perform poorly. In the case of docking simulation techniques, the three-dimensional (3D) structures of proteins are necessary for simulation, making them inapplicable when there are many proteins with inaccessible 3D structures. Furthermore, they are inapplicable to membrane structures such as ion channels and G-Protein Coupled Receptors (GPCRs), the architectures of which are too complicated to acquire. Docking simulators often take a long time, making them particularly wasteful.

Many public databases have been published, and the majority of them provide instructions for researchers to utilize in analysis and testing. The databases for retinal disorders include fundamental pathological characteristics that typically give information about the seven retinal pigment epithelium, as well as the choroid and sclera. This sort of data is gathered by a process known as "segmentation," which was formerly accomplished through manual image processing but is increasingly being accomplished through computer algorithms. In the 1980s, the early foundation for deep learning was developed on artificial neural networks (ANNs), and the true effect of deep learning became obvious in 2006. Deep learning has been used in a variety of disciplines since then, including automatic speech recognition, picture identification, natural language processing, drug discovery, and bioinformatics. Table 4.1 enlists different applications, methodologies and its benefits.

Table 4.1 Different applications, methodologies and its benefits.

Application	Method/techniques	Benefits
Disease Detection System (DDS)	Specialists or health professionals utilize DDS's Graphical User Interface (GUI) to detect illnesses in patients.	For treatment of Liver disorder, Hepatitis, Diabetes, Cardiac disease, Chronic renal disease.
Magnetic Resonance Spectroscopy Imaging (MRSI)	Enables the noninvasive characterization and measurement of molecular markers with potentially significant clinical value for improved illness identification, diagnosis, and therapy.	For treatment of Brain Cancer
cNMTF (corrected nonnegative matrix tri-factorization)	To find loci-trait correlations, this technique analyzes the interrelatedness of genotypes, phenotypes, the negative effect of variations, and gene networks.	Utilized in two demographic cohorts to select genes related to lipid characteristics by accounting for the individuals' lineage, the algorithm worked efficiently against significant population structures
Neurological and Neuromuscular Diseases (NND)/Juvenile Idiopathic Arthritis (JIA)	Multilayer Perceptron (MLP), boosting, Random Forest (RF), and Support Vector Machine (SVM) classifiers	Detection of definite illnesses and gait analysis
Optic nerve head identification/ segmentation	DRIONS-DB	Supplies the characteristics that define the papilla's form
Fundus image database through precise gold standards of optic nerve head	Provide precise ONH segmentations and its estimation method	Glaucoma detection

4.7   Application

Drug research and development pipelines are long, intricate, and dependent on several factors. Machine learning (ML) technologies provide a set of tools for improving exploration and decision-making for situations with well-defined parameters and lots of high-quality data. ML has the potential to be used at numerous stages of drug development. Target validation, the development of prognostic biomarkers, and the interpretation of digital imaging data are all instances of developing drugs. The context and manner of applications have varied, with certain techniques producing accurate forecasts and observations. Figure 4.2 illustrates a variety of deep learning applications. A conventional approach to pharmaceutical research has been used, with a focus on holistic therapy. The world's healthcare organizations began to utilize an allopathic technique in treatment and therapy in the previous century. This shift resulted in the successful treatment of illnesses, but it also resulted in high medication expenditures, which became a healthcare burden. Despite being highly variable and candidate-specific, the expense of drug development has regularly and substantially grown. Target recognition and categorization, lead

Figure 4.2 Illustrates a variety of deep learning applications.

detection, and lead enhancement are fundamental components of early drug discovery [15].

Biomedical data became an interesting candidate for deep learning applications early because deep learning requires large datasets. However, because different types of medical datasets necessitate different types of data analysis and implementation of existing machine learning algorithms, it is critical that deep learning and pharmaceutics specialists share relevant insights around each ground for deep learning should be used satisfactorily manner in pain medications.

The research of molecular structure and core physiological functions, interpretation, signaling, metabolic processes, and so on—in individuals and molecular techniques will have a long-term influence on the development of various diseases. Anticipating how cellular networks respond to environmental disturbance and how genetic differences affect them remains a difficult task. Deep learning provides innovative techniques for modeling biochemical reactions and assimilating multiple types of omic data, which might eventually aid in predicting that these processes are hindered in disease. Recent research has since improved our potential to recognize and perceive genetic changes, investigate bacterial species, and forecast protein structure. Furthermore, unattended deep learning has immense potential for identifying novel cellular states from gene regulation, fluorescence microscopy, and some other types of information, which may eventually prove clinically applicable. In genomics and imaging, where required elements are readily adaptable to some well deep learning paradigms, development has been rapid [16, 17].

4.7.1   Deep Learning in Drug Discovery

Machine technology is used to find and prioritise bioactive components with the best pharmacological effects, as well as to improve their performance as drug-like leads. Two emerging techniques are biological target categorization and protein configuration. Chemocentric strategies give a broad array of applications in molecular informatics, including various machine-learning algorithms. In order to construct descriptions descriptors or quantitative structure-activity association (QSAR) models, a comprehensive sense machine-learning aim is to determine the connection between the molecular descriptors utilized and the measured operation of the compounds. In truth, neural networks have a long and illustrious history in drug discovery and development. Other approaches, like as SVM models, have frequently been utilized in their stead because they run the risk of being easily overtrained and viewed as a "black box." Deep learning approaches will almost certainly be completely grasped if the user comprehends the underlying molecular properties that enable pattern correlation and categorization. The development of revolutionary deep learning theories, such as RBMs and CNNs, has brought game winning tactics to the molecular modeler's arsenal [18].

4.7.2   Medical Imaging and Deep Learning Process

Deep learning technique can be implemented to evaluate medical images in a range of sectors in recent years, and it excels in tasks like segmentation and registration. Edge identification filters and a number of mathematical methods are used in the standard image segmentation method. In some visual and aural classification methods, AI has the ability to surpass humans, that would lead to implications in medicine and healthcare, notably in diagnostic imaging. Deep learning technology could be used in a variety of ways in medical imaging to reduce the burden on doctors, improve the quality of the healthcare system, and improve patient outcomes. Furthermore, this type of intelligent technology could be used in precision medicine, which involves prevention and treatment strategies that take individual variability into account. Despite many promising results from previous studies, the following issues must be addressed before deep learning can be used in medical imaging: To begin, the high reliance on the quality and quantity of training datasets, as well as the proclivity for outliers and bias, should be taken into consideration.

Furthermore, also because integrity of the information will be so important to efficiency, there could be moral and constitutional questions about using clinical imaging data for marketing purposes viability. Third, the black-box character of the current deep learning approach should really be acknowledged.

Even while deep learning-based decisions have produced remarkable results, expressing the logical foundation for the conclusion is difficult or even impossible in many circumstances. Finally, products liability problems might arise if we deployed a deep learning technology in a certain clinical practice method even without direction of a medical.

At the moment, the physician is dealing with an increasing number of complex observations. This makes it very hard to complete reading and to provide acceptable reports on time. Deep learning, on the other hand, is intended to help radiologists have a much more precise diagnosis by providing a quantitative analysis of suspicious lesions, and it may also allow for a shorter time in the operating room [19].

4.7.3   Deep Learning in Diagnostic and Screening

Computational pathology and the use of AI for tissue analytics are rapidly expanding and have the potential to transform pathology with applications that speed up workflow, improve Provisional diagnostics, and improve patient clinical outcomes. There is a significant gap between research studies and those required to provide safe and dependable AI to the pathology community. This gap will close as the demands of clinical AI become better understood. Pathology AI is still very much in early stages and will keep going to grow up as investigators, physicians, industry, regulatory agencies, and patient advocacy groups cooperate to innovate and deliver emerging innovations to healthcare providers.

As per the research results, deep learning-based models have had a helpful content to provide an efficient and accurate method for the detection and diagnostic test of COVID-19, which might result in a significant increment in accuracy and sensitivity values if used in the processing of modalities. Early diagnosis and treatment of COVID-19 using DL techniques at the lowest feasible cost and consequences are the basic stages in preventing the disease and the spread of the pandemic, as previously indicated. With the rapid implementation of DL algorithms in radiology centre machinery, a faster, more cost-effective, and secure diagnosis of this disease will be achievable. The application of such technologies in quick COVID-19 diagnostic decision could be a useful tool for radiologists to reduce human participation and assist us in making choices in crucial situations and at the peak of illness. Machine learning algorithms are a viable technique to optimise healthcare and improve clinical procedure outcomes, according to this study. Although DL, notably COVID-19, are among the most advanced computer tools for diagnosing pneumonia, developers must be cautious to avoid overfitting and to improve the generalization and usefulness of COVID-19 DL diagnostic approaches. To cover all efficient communication space, these characteristics must be informed on huge, diverse datasets [20].

4.7.4   Clinical Trials Using Deep Learning Models

The excellence of epidemiological studies and clinical proceedings is dependent on selecting the appropriate patients. Medical researchers must undertake this variety thoroughly by critically examining a large quantity of information from various sources. This is an affordable and time process. To lighten the stress on academic professionals in cohort availability, rules-based procedures or machine teaching classifiers related to the selection criteria can also be used. There are few prospective deep learning studies and randomized trials in medical imaging. The bulks of nonrandomized trials are not prospective, are biased, and do not follow established reporting guidelines. The majority of research lack data and code, and human comparator groups are typically in short supply. Use of cases and the assurance of screening and delivering speedy remedies to service users through the use of enhanced AI and ML approaches are provided by the latest findings at the intersection of computer science and medicine, an assertive regulatory backdrop, and the provision of big databases. This point of view aims to educate and involve researchers from several domains, including business research, biology, treatment, engineering, biostatistics, and policymakers, about the importance of evolving AI and machine learning approaches in tackling critical challenges in the clinical development cycle. The FDA's strategic marketing policy focuses on consolidating innovation, advancing health technology technologies, and developing next-generation analytical methods in order to improve healthcare, expand funding, and promote public health goals. For regulatory needs of AI, ML, and computer vision algorithms, the FDA has established SaMD and digital health mechanisms. To date, the FDA in the United States has cleared or approved a number of AI/ML-based SaMD. Only algorithms that are trapped prior to sales advertising have traditionally been included in these. The FDA, for example, has certified IDx's machine learning-based software application for entirely independent diabetic retinopathy identification.

4.7.5   Learning for Personalized Medicine

The recent digitalization of medical information, on the other hand, has offered a great platform for evaluating the application of such strategies in healthcare. As a result, the large number of studies using deep learning on electronic records to benefit in the form of health accelerations is increasing. While this is a positive trend, enormous paper-to-paper variation has impeded the field's capacity to assess and contrast such predictions for a specific design of interest (from data sets and models used to clinical questions they attempt to answer). The availability of additional data (EHR and beyond), developments in DL (particularly, models for pattern classification), and new ways of combining the two trends have all benefited any use of DL to analyse EHR data in recent years. In this study, we applied important machine learning algorithms to learn a good patient representation for predicting emergency admission and heart failure. Our goal was to provide a comparison of these approaches to the sector, and to also analyse their benefits and drawbacks in regards of EHR [21]. The Health

Information Technology for Economic and Clinical Health (HITECH) Act of 2009, which provided $30 billion in subsidies for health facilities and physician practices to implement EHR systems, has boosted hospital acceptance of electronic health record (EHR) technologies over the last decade. Furthermore, workplace physician adoption of basic and authorized EHRs will have more than doubled, from 42% to 87%. EHR systems store activities collected during each patient's care, as well as demographic information, diagnoses, diagnostic procedures and results, medication, radiological images, medication lists, and more. Though many studies have suggested secondary uses for healthcare information applications, they were originally developed to maximize healthcare efficiency from an operational standpoint. Patient data contained in EHR systems, in distinctive, has been used tasks such as medical concept extraction. Until recently, the majority of techniques used to analyse large amounts of EHR data depend on traditional machine learning and data mining techniques, such as logistic regression, support vector machines (SVM), and regression trees [22]. Deep learning techniques have recently achieved great success in many domains by constructing deep hierarchical features and retrieving lengthy interconnections in data in an impact.

The invention of efficient and innovative systems for the targeted administration of therapeutic drugs with maximum effectiveness, and little danger has been a big challenge for biological and chemical scientists around the world in latest generations.

When considering the process of drug design and drug development, the major drawbacks in the development of novel therapeutic agent was identified as the cost required for development and the time consumed for the improvement method.

To overcome these obstacles, researchers all over the world have turned to computational methods, such as virtual screening (VS) and molecular docking, which are commonly referred to as traditional methods because they have been used for centuries but are the most common types of computational analysis [23]. Apart from being the most used techniques around the globe, they also possess various challenges for the computational analysis, most common of which includes the inefficiency and inaccuracy.

Thus, there is a need for the implementation of advanced and more developed novel techniques, which unlike the traditional techniques, are autonomous and works unaided, thereby eliminating the challenges and hurdles put up by the conventional models.

Artificial intelligence (AI), which includes deep learning (DL) and machine learning (ML) algorithms, is the most trustworthy solution that has evolved in our period to overcome this barrier. These potential solutions can effectively manage the problems and vaults that arise during the drug design and development phase.

It also consists of long and complex steps in drug discovery and design, including selection and validation of targets, therapeutic testing and optimization of lead compounds, preclinical and clinical trials, and manufacturing practices. Figure 4.3 illustrates the applications of AI in pharmaceuticals.

Another considerable challenge imposed by all these steps in identifying effective drugs for the disease. Therefore, the biggest problem, which arises for the pharmaceutical companies, is the question of controlling the price and speediness of the procedure.

Artificial intelligence has efficiently addressed all of these issues in a straightforward and systematic fashion, by delivering practical solutions that have decreased the process's complexity and expenses.

Digitization is gradually increasing its hold among all the sectors of pharmaceutical companies and healthcare sector in all over the world which has encouraged the implementation of Artificial Intelligence to overcome the problems of scrutinizing the complex data [24].

Computational modeling techniques, which are based on the incorporation of AI and ML principles, provide a great avenue for some of the below mentioned [25, 26]:

- identifying, evaluating, and validating the target chemical compounds of interest;
- accurate and precise identification of target;

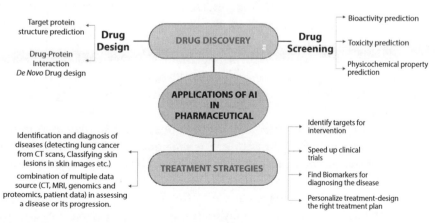

Figure 4.3 Applications of AI in Pharmaceuticals.

- drug monitoring based on pharmacological and toxicological profile;
- peptide synthesis;
- assessment of drug toxicity and physiochemical properties;
- drug efficacy and effectiveness;
- drug repositioning.

Screening of target chemical compounds from the chemical libraries comprising of more than 106 million compounds using conventional methods has always been a tedious task. With the development of AI values additionally along with the machine learning and DL algorithms, the tedious process of virtual screening of compounds has become effortless and time efficient. AI can detect hit and lead compounds, allowing for faster therapeutic target validation and structural design optimization. In addition, the off-target interactions, resulting into toxicity issues, were also tackled and eliminated with the use of AI models [27].

Despite its benefits, AI confronts major data problems, including the data's volume, growth, variety, and unpredictability. Pharmaceutical firms' drug research data sets can contain millions of chemicals, and standard machine learning methods may not be able to handle them.

A mathematical model based on the quantitative structure-activity relationship (QSAR) can predict a large number of therapeutic chemical entities or basic physicochemical features like log P or log D in a short amount of time. However, these models are developed in part from complex biological properties such as chemical efficacy (compound performance) and adverse effects [28].

Several in silico approach for virtual screening of substances from virtual chemical spaces, as well as architecture and ligand-based procedures, improve profile analysis, speed up the removal of non-lead compounds, and reduce costs while selecting therapeutic molecules. Nearest-neighbor classifications, RF, supervised learning models, SVMs, and deep neural networks (DNNs) are some examples of AI-based techniques, which are used to predict in vivo application and toxicity depending on synthesis possibility.

The creation of computer functions imbued with human reasoning, learning, and problem-solving abilities is a major contribution of AI, which has demonstrated its supremacy in a variety of fields, including gaming, sociology, and neurological research [29].

It has had a tremendous influence in the medical field in recent years. Different illnesses can be accurately identified, and the proper therapy can then be provided for the same. There is little question that the use of AI in the treatment of illnesses will become more generally accepted and will be widely recognized in the future years.

The use of various AI approaches on various forms of data, both structured and unstructured, is one of the main reasons for its broad flexibility. This feature expands the scope of the disease's diagnosis. AI has the capability of learning rapidly using ML hence adding new data and connections to its database for a quick diagnosis and treatment strategy. A rapid diagnosis of disease allows for speedier and less expensive therapy.

The amount of healthcare data being collected is continuously increasing. The AI-based method aids in the learning of characteristics from a vast volume of medical data necessary for clinical practice assistance. Furthermore, these algorithms include self-correction capabilities, which increases their accuracy and efficiency based on feedback obtained for the given amount of data [30].

The AI-based system may also aid clinicians by collecting, organizing, analyzing, and generating the most up-to-date medical knowledge from sources such as journals, textbooks, clinical practices, and other sources, resulting in optimal patient care. AI methods can forecast a person's DNA and propose appropriate therapy, allowing for completely customized care.

Various functions are associated with human intelligence while they are being developed in AI, such as problem-solving ability, learning, and reasoning, and therefore, they aid in enhancing the efficiency and capacities of medical personnel.

Rule-based systems, case-based reasoning, fuzzy models, artificial neural networks, multiagent systems, cellular automata, swarm intelligence, genetic algorithms, hybrid systems, reinforcement learning, and other approaches are examples of diverse methodologies [31, 32].

4.8   Conclusion

The subsequent inclusion of a novel drug molecule into a suitable dosage form with desirable delivery characteristics follows the discovery of a novel therapeutic molecule. In this case, AI can take the role of the classic trial-and-error method. With the use of QSPR, various computational techniques may handle challenges encounter in the formulation intend field, likeconstancy concerns,porosity, dissolution, and likewise. Decision-sustain equipment employs rule-supporting systems to pick the kind, environment, and measure of excipients based on the drug's physicochemical properties, and they use a reaction method to continuously monitor and change the process. Current manufacturing systems are attempting to impart human knowledge to machines, which is constantly changing the manufacturing practice, as manufacturing processes get more complex, and there is a greater desire for competence and higher product value. AI integration in developed could be beneficial to the pharmaceutical business.

Clinical trials, which take 6 to 7 years and a significant economic speculation, are designed to determine the security and efficiency of a therapeutic invention in humans for a specific illness circumstance. However, just one out of every ten molecules that enter these trials gets cleared, resulting in a substantial loss for the industry. Inappropriate patient selection, a lack of technological needs, and bad infrastructure can all contribute to these failures. However, given the large amount of digital therapeutic data accessible, AI can be used to lessen these failures.

The corporation chooses the ultimate price of the product depending on market assessment and costs involved in the creation of the pharmaceutical merchandise. The key to using AI to estimate this price is to use it to examine the aspects that govern the pricing of a product after it is manufactured by using its capacity to replicate the reasoning of a human expert.

Acknowledgment

The authors are highly thankful to all the contributors School of Pharmaceutical Sciences, Rajeev Gandhi Prodygiki Viswavidlaya, Bhopal, Dr. M.C. Saxena College of Pharmacy, Lucknow and Madan Mohan Malviya University of Technology Gorakhpur for providing library facility for literature survey.

References

1. Knowles, J. and Gromo, G., A guide to drug discovery: Target selection in drug discovery. *Nat. Rev. Drug Discov.*, 2, 1, 63–9, 2003.
2. Dana, D., Gadhiya, S.V., St. Surin, L.G., Li, D., Naaz, F., Ali., Q., Paka, L., Yamin, M.A., Narayan, M., Goldberg, I.D., Narayan, P., Deep learning in drug discovery and medicine: Scratching the surface. *Molecules*, 23, 9, 2384, Sep 2018.
3. LeCun, Y., Bengio, Y., Hinton, G., Deep learning. *Nature*, 521, 436, 2015.

4. Chen, R., Liu, X., Jin, S., Lin, J., Liu, J., Machine learning for drug-target interaction prediction. *Molecules*, 23, 9, 2208, 2018.

5. Ekins, S., The next era: Deep learning in pharmaceutical research. *Pharm. Res.*, 33, 11, 2594–2603, Nov 2016.

6. Tsou, L.K., Yeh, S.-H., Ueng, S.-H., Chang, C.-P., Song, J.-S., Wu, M.-H., Chang, H.-F., Chen, S.-R., Shih, C., Chen, C.-T., Ke, Y.-Y., Comparative study between deep learning and QSAR classifications for TNBC inhibitors and novel GPCR agonist discovery. *Sci. Rep.*, 10, 16771, 2020.

7. Lipinski, C.F., Maltarollo, V.G., Oliveira, P.R., da Silva, A.B.F., Honorio, K.M., Advances and perspectives in applying deep learning for drug design and discovery. *Front. Robot. AI*, 6, 108, 2019.

8. Wang, Y.B., You, Z.H., Yang, S., Yi, H.C., Chen, Z.H., Zheng, K., A deep learning-based method for drug-target interaction prediction based on long short-term memory neural network. *BMC Med. Inform. Decis. Mak.*, 20, Suppl2, 49, Mar 2020.

9. Abbasi, K., Razzaghi, P., Poso, A., Ghanbari-Ara, S., Masoudi-Nejad, A., Deep learning in drug target interaction prediction: Current and future perspectives. *Curr. Med. Chem.*, 28, 11, 2100–2113, 2021.

10. An, J.Y., Meng, F.R., Yan, Z.J., An efficient computational method for predicting drug-target interactions using weighted extreme learning machine and speed up robot features. *BioData Min.*, 14, 1, 1–17, 2021.

11. Vamathevan, J., Clark, D., Czodrowski, P., Dunham, I., Ferran, E., Lee, G., Li, B., Madabhushi, A., Shah, P., Spitzer, M., Zhao, S., Applications of machine learning in drug discovery and development. *Nat. Rev. Drug Discov.*, 18, 6, 463–477, Jun 2019.

12. Mamoshina, P., Volosnikova, M., Ozerov, I.V., Putin, E., Skibina, E., Cortese, F., Zhavoronkov, A., Machine learning on human muscle transcriptomic data for biomarker discovery and tissue-specific drug target identification. *Front. Genet.*, 9, 242, 2018.

13. Jeon, J., Nim, S., Teyra, J., Datti, A., Wrana, J.L., Sidhu, S.S., Kim, P.M., A systematic approach to identify novel cancer drug targets using machine learning, inhibitor design and high-throughput screening. *Genome Med.*, 6, 7, 1–18, 2014.

14. Ferrero, E., Dunham, I., Sanseau, P., In silico prediction of novel therapeutic targets using gene–disease association data. *J. Transl. Med.*, 15, 1, 1–16, 2017.

15. Morgan, S., Grootendorst, P., Lexchin, J., Cunningham, C., Greyson, D., The cost of drug development: A systematic review. *Health Policy*, 100, 1, 4–17, 2011.

16. Gawehn, E., Hiss, J.A., Schneider, G., Deep learning in drug discovery. *Mol. Inform.*, 35, 1, 3–14, 2015.

17. Hudson, I.L., Data integration using advances in machine learning in drug discovery and molecular biology. Artificial neural networks. *Methods Mol. Biol.*, 2190, 167–184, 2021.
18. Baskin, I., II, The power of deep learning to ligand-based novel drug discovery. *Expert Opin. Drug Discov.*, 15, 7, 755–764, 2020.
19. Kim, M., Yun, J., Cho, Y., Shin, K., Jang, R., Bae, H.J., Kim, N., Deep learning in medical imaging. *Neurospine*, 16, 4, 657–668, 2019.
20. Ghaderzadeh, M. and Asadi, F., Deep learning in the detection and diagnosis of COVID-19 using radiology modalities: A systematic review. *J. Healthc. Eng.*, 116, 2021.
21. Ayala Solares, J.R., Diletta Raimondi, F.E., Zhu, Y., Rahimian, F., Canoy, D., Tran, J., Salimi-Khorshidi, G., Deep learning for electronic health records: A comparative review of multiple deep neural architectures. *J. Biomed. Inform.*, 101, 103337, 2020.
22. Eraslan, G., Avsec, Z., Gagneur, J., Theis, F.J., Deep learning: New computational modelling techniques for genomics. *Nat. Rev. Genet.*, 20, 7, 389–403, 2019.
23. Li, Y., Shi, W., Wasserman, W.W., Genome-wide prediction of cis-regulatory regions using supervised deep learning methods. *BMC Bioinform.*, 31, 19(1), 202, 2018.
24. Sadeghi, Z. and Testolin, A., Learning representation hierarchies by sharing visual features: A computational investigation of Persian character recognition with unsupervised deep learning. *Cogn. Process.*, 18, 3, 273–284, 2017.
25. Miotto, R., Wang, F., Wang, S., Jiang, X., Dudley, J.T., Deep learning for healthcare: Review, opportunities and challenges. *Brief. Bioinformatics*, 19, 6, 1236–1246, 2018.
26. Gawehn, E., Hiss, J.A., Schneider, G., Deep learning in drug discovery. *Mol. Inform.*, 35, 1, 3–14, 2016.
27. Kim, M., Yun, J., Cho, Y., Shin, K., Jang, R., Bae, H.J., Kim, N., Deep learning in medical imaging. *Neurospine*, 16, 4, 657–668, 2019.
28. Ghaderzadeh, M. and Asadi, F., Deep learning in the detection and diagnosis of COVID-19 using radiology modalities: A systematic review. *J. Healthc. Eng.*, 120, 2021.
29. Shah, P., Kendall, F., Khozin, S., Goosen, R., Hu, J., Laramie, J., Ringel, M., Schork, N., Artificial intelligence and machine learning in clinical development: A translational perspective. *NPJ Digit. Med.*, 2, 1, 1–5, 2019.
30. Fumero, F., Alayón, S., Sanchez, J.L., Sigut, J., Gonzalez-Hernandez, M., RIM-ONE: An open retinal image database for optic nerve evaluation, in: *2011 24th international symposium on computer-based medical systems (CBMS)*. *IEEE*, pp. 1–6, 2011.

31. Wen, M., Zhang, Z., Niu, S., Sha, H., Yang, R., Yun, Y., Lu, H., Deep-learning-based drug–target interaction prediction. *J. Proteome Res.*, 16, 4, 1401–1409, 2017.

32. Morgan, S., Grootendorst, P., Lexchin, J., Cunningham, C., Greyson, D., The cost of drug development: A systematic review. *Health Policy*, 100, 1, 4–17, 2011.

5

Deep Learning and Precision Medicine: Lessons to Learn for the Preeminent Treatment for Malignant Tumors

Selvasudha Nandakumar[1], Shah Alam Khan[2], Poovi Ganesan[3], Pushpa Sweety[4], Arul Prakash Francis[5], Mahendran Sekar[6], Rukkumani Rajagopalan[5] and Dhanalekshmi Unnikrishnan Meenakshi[2*]

[1]Department of Biotechnology, Pondicherry University, Puducherry, India
[2]College of Pharmacy, National University of Science and Technology, Muscat, Oman
[3]Mother Theresa Postgraduate and Research Institute of Health Sciences, Puducherry, India
[4]Anna University, BIT Campus, Tiruchirappalli, India
[5]Department of Biochemistry and Molecular Biology, Pondicherry University, Puducherry, India
[6]Department of Pharmaceutical Chemistry, Faculty of Pharmacy and Health Sciences, Royal College of Medicine Perak, Universiti Kuala Lumpur, Ipoh, Malaysia

Abstract

The healthcare system is transforming as a result of new technology invention and implementation, which promotes therapeutic interventions and treatment outcomes for improved patient care. Numerous diverse parameters like gene variation, sociodemographics, lifestyle/environmental elements, should be measured to expedite precision/personalized medicine (PM). As a result, one of the most important difficulties in PM is bridging the translational gap in the clinical context by transforming big, multimodal data into decision support tools. Deep learning (DL) offers a novel technique to overcome these challenges, enabling the building or acquisition of accuracy, multimodal predictive models that could help the PM vision become a reality shortly. DL along with modern artificial intelligence (AI), in particular, provides tools in the form of algorithms that could pave the way for an individualized malignancy treatment in a more

Corresponding author: dhanalekshmi@nu.edu.om; ORCID ID: 0000-0002-2689-4079

Rishabha Malviya, Gheorghita Ghinea, Rajesh Kumar Dhanaraj, Balamurugan Balusamy and Sonali Sundram (eds.) Deep Learning for Targeted Treatments: Transformation in Healthcare, (127–170) © 2022 Scrivener Publishing LLC

precise and customized manner by allowing early diagnosis and precise treatment options. Machine learning (ML) techniques applied to genomic datasets have a lot of potentials to deliver PM. DL has the power to accurately analyze tumor data and recommend the best possible treatment for cancer patients with a personalized approach.

The capacity to anticipate how a patient will respond to a medication using DL techniques will aid in the reevaluation of treatment decisions, as well as the reduction of errors and disease-related financial burden. This chapter discusses the overall characteristics of DL and PM, as well as the importance of DL in precision oncology drug discovery and development, genomics, and biomarker datasets. It also outlines the potential of different technologies of DL in cancer diagnosis, detection, and prediction. It also highlights the applications of DL in translational oncology and its clinical benefits. Various challenges and limitations associated with DL techniques, such as like unique genomic patterns, small sample size, multidisciplinary expertise, and clinical trials, are also addressed.

Keywords: Deep learning, precision medicine, artificial intelligence, biomarkers, oncology, cancer, personalized treatment, clinical trials

5.1   Introduction

Cancer is a multifaceted ailment characterized by massive genome aberrations. A recent study estimated that cancer-related deaths in 2020 were nearly 10 million [1]. Molecular mechanisms governing the normal physiological processes are transformed in cancer pathology due to mutation of the DNA, as well as changes in the expression of genes such as proto-oncogenes and tumor suppressor genes. Despite the cancer type, different molecular and genetic patterns among the patient population are hurdles in the treatment of cancer [2]. In cancer cells, genetic variations, such as amplification, gene rearrangement, and point mutation with subsequent alteration in the cellular processes, i.e., cell division and proliferation, manifest the biomarkers released in a major group of patients [3]. Most of the newly discovered cancer drugs that underwent different phases of clinical trials are not qualified for market approval due to incomplete understanding and reporting of the signaling mechanisms governing the drug response. However, the drug's compatibility and requirements differ between individuals, making sensible approaches impossible to match. It occurs mostly due to the intricate nature of the human biosystem, the complexity of cancer cells, and individual variance, making it even more difficult to forecast [2]. In recent times, the personalized medicine approach is used in cancer research to address the aforementioned issues by considering the genetic composition with preferences, knowledge, social context, whereas precision medicine (PM) relies on a model considering the analytics, diagnostics, data, and information contributing to healthcare delivery in a smarter way.

PM is defined as adapting therapeutics to each patient's unique traits. It is based on vulnerability to disease and/or reaction to the particular treatment among the patients in groups. Hence the variation in the treatment among the groups is observed. The approach of PM is highly dependent on the sorting of disease into its subclass, and the process is influenced by clinical, genotypic, and phenotypic data [4]. Preventative or therapeutic measures can then be focused on individuals who will benefit, while those who will not be spared the expenditure and adverse effects. PM comprises the use of genomic, immunological, and proteomic profiling in the treatment of cancer to provide therapeutic options as well as prognostic information for each patient and their tumor's gene mutations by combining data from multiple patients [5]. The ability to forecast how a patient will react to medicine would lessen disease-related health and cost burdens by moving treatment decisions away from trial and error. Machine learning (ML) techniques applied to genetic information have a lot of potential for personalized treatment [6]. ML methods are designed and used to detect specific genetic changes and predict the probability of developing cancer. The researchers use ML to look at the framework of cancer diagnosis and treatment because of its ability to accurately predict the treatment outcomes. ML is a relatively modern approach to assessing centuries-old issues [7]. The prompt emergence of ML technologies like Tensorflow, H2O, as well as high-end hardware like NIVIDIA GPU Cards (using CUDA) running on Amazon Web Services Cloud (AWS) is highly supportive to manage the previously unknown findings. High-quality tailored anticancer treatments, such as radiotherapy and chemotherapies, have been planned using ML approaches [8, 9]. It is believed that a deep learning (DL) algorithm combined with modern ML technologies will result in accurate and exact tumor data analysis. Pharmaceutical drug discovery and development centres have not been successful to date in matching the right combinations of drugs to the right patients in a smart way. Scientists are oblivious in predicting which drug will work uniquely against cancer cells in an individual patient to produce the best therapeutic response.

DL is a specialized ML method that customs numerous layers (algorithms) of artificial neurons to practice data and learn by improving the precision of an intelligent process and adjusting each synapse [9]. In addition, it helps to learn and process big data, similar to the human brain such as conceptualization and application of the concepts to new data with high precision. By using current DL systems, the heterogeneous data obtained from the individual patients can be integrated across modalities and different times manifesting better predictions and therapies that can be customized based on the individual patients' needs and characteristics. Clinical workflow in oncology relies on predictive and prognostic biomarkers, which are costly. Modest and cutting-edge analysis of images for cancer histology investigations is achieved by extracting biomarkers directly from conventional histology images and summarizing using DL. Furthermore, an integrated layer is added to the DL structure to allow active genetic data processing and biomarker development. It can match different tumors to the best drug combinations and enable targeted therapy. An AI tool DrugCell model is planned to meet the possible requirements of the healthcare system in recent years. It is also used to predict the data about the tumor and the biological pathways that control the effect of the drug and the combination of drug effects on the malignant cells. This demonstrates DL's potential to transform enormous amounts of healthcare data into helpful tools for enhancing PM and personalized therapy [9, 10]. A model known as Drug Cell was specifically designed to provide the best possible treatments for patients, potentially accelerating cancer precision medicine using AI systems [10]. Drug Cell model is used to input data on a specific tumor, and the system provides the best and effective drug, the molecular pathways that influence response to that drug, and drug combinations that will be effective to treat cancer. Computer-extracted features are used as a response in algorithms of ML, which uses advanced statistical methodologies to facilitate computers to excel at certain jobs by learning data patterns [11]. Deep convolutional neural networks (dCNNs) turned into the option for computer visualizations since the launch of the 2012 ImageNet Large Scale Visual Recognition Challenge [11]. Automated analysis tools based on DL diminish the substantial work in the cancer early diagnosis for healthcare workers [12]. When given raw data, dCNNs employ representation learning to characterize or predict a specific outcome to complete the task if a sufficient amount and quality of data are supplied [13]. Figure 5.1 depicts an overview of the uses and interrelationships of AI, ML, and DL in precision oncology.

PM therapies have been shown to enhance cancer patient outcomes better than traditional medicines. However, designing medication based on a patient's unique genetic pattern is difficult, and the technique necessitates interdisciplinary competence, as well as access to pharmaceuticals or clinical trials that are not usually available in smaller practices [10, 14]. Biomarkers are also needed for cancer diagnosis and response prediction

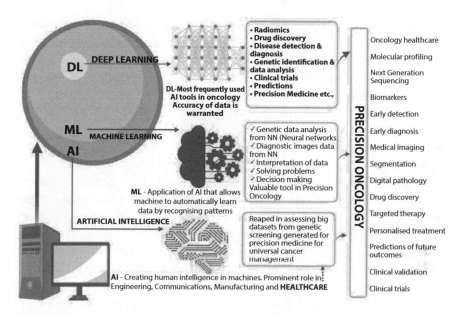

Figure 5.1 Applications for an effective clinical decision making in a humane like manner using data sets.

to various therapies as it relates to specific cancer. DL is helpful to overcome the above difficulties, as it can retrieve hidden data directly using commonly available data in molecular biology assays using biomarkers. DL biomarkers are utilized in the genetic investigation to pre-screen individuals and would necessitate significantly better test performance than the conventional test that has been achieved so far. To detect mutations directly from histology slides, DL principles are utilized as conclusive testing procedures [3].

Drug development and multidrug resistance challenges in cancer therapy are the domains that are suitable for ML algorithms implementation. Developing anticancer drugs and conducting clinical trials involve a significant amount of time and resources. To create an acceptable test scenario, AI-based DL may synthesis patient data and clinical trial data. Most significantly, AI can assess the efficacy of medication before clinical trials. To predict cancer cell susceptibility to treatments, NNs can be trained on genomic and chemical characteristics. As a result, it may be used to locate suitable experimental drugs for a specific patient's cancer treatment. Using DNA blueprint or RNA response profiles, these algorithms can propose a tailored treatment that is more likely to result in favorable outcomes. NNs may be used to decipher biological activities by interpreting genetic variations and trends. CRISPR is a technique that is now being evaluated to determine if gene mutations may be reversed. AI is not just considerably faster than humans in reading and analyzing massive amounts of medical data. It can also more correctly predict the results of a patient's medical interventions and the therapy's potential consequences [15]. With Watson for Drug Discovery, IBM and Pfizer have teamed up to boost immuno-oncology research using a DL methodology. Scientists are employing DL approach in predicting which drug will work uniquely against cancer cells in an individual patient to produce the best therapeutic response. It has been documented that AI and DL systems could assist the medical team to quickly arrive at an accurate and effective treatment decision [9]. This chapter focuses on the overall aspects of DL and PM, the role of DL in genomics, biomarker as well as diagnosis datasets related to the field of oncology. It also outlines the potential of DL and PM for better understanding and cohesiveness of different technologies. It also deals with future research to use DL as a pharmaceutical and diagnostic tool in the real world. Various challenges associated with DL techniques, such as like unique genomic pattern, sample size, multidisciplinary expertise, and clinical trials are also addressed.

5.2   Role of DL in Gene Identification, Unique Genomic Analysis, and Precise Cancer Diagnosis

DL-based techniques in cancer diagnosis include convolutional neural networks (CNNs), autoencoders, restricted Boltzmann machines (RBMs), and sparse coding. CNN and autoencoders are frequently used in oncology for molecular imaging. CNN models are the most widely used techniques owing to their more sophisticated architecture and supple setup enabling them to study more discriminative characteristics for more precise identification [16]. Molecular imaging and tumor segmentation using DL is very useful as it inevitably and appropriately outlines lesions for better analysis and therapy. MRI data of multimodality, comprising contrast-enhanced T1W, has been used to train DL models for superior brain tumor segmentation. In breast and lung cancer, DL approaches have been successfully utilized for image analysis in the treatment of difficult areas in tumors, tubules mitotic activity lymphocytes [17, 18]. Deep neural networks (DNN) were considered to be competent to provide high-level task-specific feature learning, utilizing data from multimodal MRI to recognize brain-pathology aspects of MRI. To forecast the development of brain tumors, multiple incremental learning models and DNN models have been employed in patients [19]. Three phases are involved in extracting a multiform learning system feature: statistical sampling techniques are used to choose the benchmarks, multiple skeletons are identified from the points of view, and the LLE algorithm is used to inject out-of-bag data into the skeleton [15, 17]. The Fisher Score and the Gaussian Mixing Model (GMM) were used to select and classify features, respectively. In PM approach analysis, genomic fingerprints of patients are progressively being used for risk prediction, diagnostics, and the creation of targeted medicines, due to better advancements in DL [19].

5.2.1   Gene Identification and Genome Data

Gene expression is an imperative component of a patient's genetic profile; therefore, ML classification techniques for gene expression profiles are not novel. The use of AI and natural language processing (NLP) in the field of genomics is escalating, and they are considered as the foundation of PM because of their ability to transmute a variety of clinical datasets [20]. Data scientists compete to detect diverse genetic variations using machine learning algorithms trained on real-world evidence (RWE) clinical data [21]. Next-generation sequencing (NGS) is increasingly used as a way to learn more about a tumor's genetic composition. Some NGS-based panels associated with oncology like Praxis Extended RAS Panel, Oncomine Dx Target Test, MSK-IMPACT are widely used. FDA approval for tumor agnostic evidence for NTRK gene fusions also widens the use of NGS, and these data were used to clarify oncogenic pathways of functional relevance across several cancer types [22, 23].

NLP methods in cancer genomics automate entities such as genes, genetic variations, therapies, and diseases for PM. Determining genetic variations is critical for tumor molecular profiling and analyzing subsequent gene–protein or disease relationships. The basis of evidence extraction for PM is biomedical named entity recognition (Bio-NER). Integration of unsupervised and supervised features is done using DL through the application of nonlinear functions (multilayered) for classification and analysis. Promising results have been observed while applying DL methods like recurrent neural networks (RNNs) and CNNs in the relation extraction field [20, 24, 25]. According to Lee *et al.* [2018], for sentence-level correlations, CNN is the best option [25]. Peng *et al.* [2017] used graph LSTM for drug-gene-mutation ternary connection extraction and achieved an accuracy of 0.75 in a cross-sentence context [24].

ML techniques have recently been used to investigate the functions of F-box/WD repeat-containing protein 7 (Fbw7) in oxidative cancer cell metabolism [26]. The patient's survival outcome and personalization of the therapy can be assisted by the various data reports obtained from molecular profiling. Novel biomarkers' discovery, including tumor mutational burden (TMB) and mutation signatures, is supported by NGS. The process of detecting variations in NGS data is known as variant calling. To prepare for variant calling, the reads from raw sequences were initially brought into line with the reference genome and run via a series of quality enhancement procedures. Several ML methods have been trained on features that encode secondary structures, DNA binding, intrinsic disorders, conservation, phosphorylation, predicted structure, and homolog counts by various research groups for improving variant classification, incorporating great-dimensional data sets, and unifying diverse elucidation across test centre. In lung cancers, DL framework may be used to assess the gene mutation [27]. DNNs are well known for their use in logistic regression, random forests, and aid vector machines. The MERGE machine learning algorithm was created to find effective cancer medications by detecting genetic variants that are important for a patient's response to treatment for acute myeloid leukaemia (AML) [28].

AI approaches have shown to be beneficial in terms of accurate and scalable genomic analysis and hence important in PM. As recently noted by Zou and colleagues [2019], DL has been used to suggest 3D protein topologies, determine transcription start sites, predict gene expression and model regulatory elements, and form genomic data by incorporating data from the research literature with insights from sequencing [29]. These interpretations play a crucial role in identifying the links between variation in genes, the success of therapy, presentation of the disease and prediction. Radiogenomics has indeed greatly contributed to the first successful AI model in imagery recognition. In the topic of accuracy research, radiogenomics emphasizes the connection of cancer imaging characteristics with an expression of genes to forecast the potential for an individual to acquire toxicity following radiation therapy. A study suggested using MRI (multimode) datasets to foresee isocitrate dehydrogenase genotype in non-invasive degrees glioma (II-IV.) Furthermore, AI has been utilized to identify radiogenomic correlations in tumors, such as liver, breast, and colorectal cancer [30]. Data availability is now the most challenging barrier for AI radiogenomics, and DL is playing a significant role in data acquisition and analysis [31–33].

5.2.2   Image Diagnosis

In addition to cancer detection, computers are effective in cancer diagnosis. Computer-assisted diagnosis (CADx) aids clinicians in accurately detecting cancer by analysing comprehensive picture information and predicting the likelihood that certain features correspond to a given disease state, such as whether a tumor is cancerous or not. Developments in modern computer technology, as well as image collecting and analysis tools, have made it feasible to learn more from medical images than ever [34]. The data from the image is important for diverse applications in cancer such as diagnosis, detection, therapy, prognosis, risk assessment and scientific research. In computer-aided detection (CADe), quantitative image analysis techniques are employed to spot patterns in mammograms of breast cancer that radiologists might miss. CADe is an AI-based cancer detection technology that was first created in 1980 for lungs and breast pictures. More than 80% of mammography screenings today are read by a "second reader." Multiple strategies for the diagnosis and follow-up of lung nodules on thoracic radiography and computed tomography (CT) scans are also being translated [35]. According to the healthcare data repository [31], digital imagery is used in the majority of diagnosis. Convolutional neural network (CNN) is a type of ML design to interpret images by analysing pixels, accounting for them, and accurately recognizing dots, curves, and lines. Moreover, further training of CNN mechanisms can be applied to the accurate prediction of outcomes for various malignancy treatments and immunotherapy methods. Companies are developing a low-invasive cancer screening device that uses ML to evaluate blood samples. DL methods applied in medical images processing and investigation over the years because they overcome the limitations of traditional ML methods by extracting hierarchical characteristics with powerful representational capabilities [36–38]. Because the target to background ratio in the images is not achievable, subtle changes in molecular imaging techniques may be difficult to detect in clinical practice through visual inspection. The emergence of intelligent methods is showing promising potential to overcome the problems through automation of image interpretation (Figure 5.2). DL is an advanced ML method to resolve the aforementioned challenges through improving and abstracting high-end features on data with a profound complex neural network [9]. In comparison to past systems based on manually built features, the key advantage of the DL-based method is the automated learning of prognostic characteristics [39].

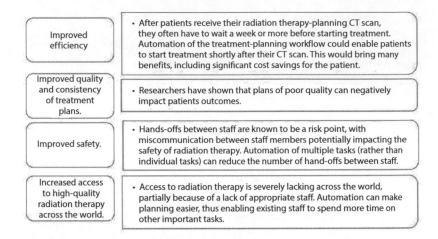

Improved efficiency	• After patients receive their radiation therapy-planning CT scan, they often have to wait a week or more before starting treatment. Automation of the treatment-planning workflow could enable patients to start treatment shortly after their CT scan. This would bring many benefits, including significant cost savings for the patient.
Improved quality and consistency of treatment plans.	• Researchers have shown that plans of poor quality can negatively impact patients outcomes.
Improved safety.	• Hands-offs between staff are known to be a risk point, with miscommunication between staff members potentially impacting the safety of radiation therapy. Automation of multiple tasks (rather than individual tasks) can reduce the number of hand-offs between staff.
Increased access to high-quality radiation therapy across the world.	• Access to radiation therapy is severely lacking across the world, partially because of a lack of appropriate staff. Automation can make planning easier, thus enabling existing staff to spend more time on other important tasks.

Figure 5.2 Applications of DL in radiation oncology.

Even though AI-based tools and PM have been already in the clinical sector but to date, they are found to be foundational, in which PM based upon AI encompasses medicine, statistics, biology, and computing. Numerous organizations have started to explore approaches based on AI to PM. Through the analysis of massive genomic databases and clinical trials, deep genomics leverages AI to lower the cost and errors associated with drug discovery. The National Institutes of Health (NIH) research effort intends to collect data from one million patients in order to further research in the field of PM. From May 2018, it started the enrolment of patients to construct a massive database with patient data which can be utilized by the researchers through various approaches, such as AI and DL, to develop treatment methods for PM. DNA sequence data collected from an individual through mining is used to generate a gene-based diagnosis of disease [40]. Furthermore, AI-based blood analysis could help in cancer diagnosis and has been demonstrated to have a lot of promise [41]. There are still several obstacles to AI in PM, one of which is that the technology is not sophisticated enough. AI can grasp organized games like chess and go by observing moves on a board; however, it cannot easily observe physician moves. If it could, it could reproduce that research and recommend better for more tailored treatment based on patient data [42]. Another barrier is electronic health records (EHRs) platforms used by different hospitals. An additional issue is about data compilation in which one platform for specific data sets, such as patient information and another platform for cancer patients, is not easily accessible by AI regarding the data, which is needed for suggesting a personalized treatment.

Artificial Neural Network (ANN), Convolutional Neural Network (CNN); Deep Q-Network (DQN), Fully Convolutional Neural Network (FCN); Generative Adversarial Network (GAN); IIFDL, Intra- and Inter-fraction Fuzzy Deep Learning (IIFDL); Radiotherapy Artificial Environment (RAE) and Support Vector Machine (SVM) DL applications and their clinical outcomes are related to toxicity, response, and planning in patients with prostate, lung and pelvis cancer [43].

5.2.3   Radiomics, Radiogenomics, and Digital Biopsy

Despite the advances in technology, there is still potential to use the medical image information for making clinical decisions in malignant tumors, and it can be used along with DL to mine patient data spaces. CAD has also expanded its application to the area of radiomics which involves the production of minable data from converted images for a more complete diagnosis. To generate radiomic data, computer segmentation of a tumor from its backdrop, followed by computer extraction of multiple tumor features, such as size, form, texture, and margins (morphology), as well as other aspects related to physiological activities, can be used. A fundamental goal of radiomics is to identify image-based properties that are characteristic to cancer. Furthermore, these image-based elements are combined using ML techniques to produce tumor signatures [44, 45]. Employing ML approaches in analyzing medical images are significantly useful for physicians for opting for better diagnosis or treatment strategies. Integrated DL and radiomics along with radiological parameters are helpful for personalized diagnosis of a patient. DL and radiomics are fast-evolving technologies that are transforming medical imaging and its applications, with the potential to revolutionize PM [46].

Datasets in the Cancer Imaging Archive (CIA) are collections of data that often reflect groups of patients with a common condition. It is a significant resource for radiomics researchers. This project compiles deidentified cancer clinical photos, as well as crucial data, such as patient outcomes, treatment information, genetics, pathophysiology, and expert opinions. Researchers are employing this resource, like The Cancer Genome Atlas (TCGA), to make breakthroughs that lead to image-based clinical indicators [47]. Another important goal of radiomics and machine learning is to develop diagnostic or prognostic tools by combining image data with clinical, pathologic, and genomic data. This is known as radiogenomics. The first step is to compare radiomic features to those from a biopsy and other tests to see which ones correspond and complement one another. Radiogenomics includes DL tools to learn the most useful quantitative representation and utilizing that data to create prediction models [48]. A characteristic feature shared by an established genetic marker corresponds to the tumor image that could be used in devising treatment options. It is also known as "virtual digital biopsy" because it is utilized to track responses and forecast future recurrence risk. It is a non-invasive, reproducible procedure that covers the entire tumor and may add value to the information gained from various tests and biopsies. It will not be able to substitute an actual biopsy, but it will be valuable when an actual biopsy is not possible during repeated therapeutic assessments to determine the response. More tailored targeted therapy will be aided by comprehensive data sets of molecular tumor profiles. Various studies contribute to the idea of PM to personalize the early detection of disease to provide effective treatment and clinical decisions at the right time [41, 48].

5.2.4   Medical Image Analysis in Mammography

Ada Boost, Decision Tree (DT), Fuzzy Method, K-Nearest Neighbor (KNN), Linear Discriminant Analysis (LDA), Logistic Regression (LR), Naive Bayes (NB), Support Vector Machine (SVM), and Random Forest (RF) are the most often utilized ML techniques in mammography. Existing ML algorithms are unreliable for accurately detecting breast densities; nevertheless, DL methods offer a promising advancement in bulk segmentation, reducing the false-positive ratio (FPR). Shen *et al.* [2019] used an "end-to-end" training strategy that takes training data from either an extensive clinical recording or the cancer status label of the entire picture to create a DL algorithm that can reliably identify breast cancer [49]. The single model provided an image AUC of 0.88 in an autonomous testing set of digital mammograms from the Mammography Screening Digital Database (CBIS-DDSSM), while the average four-model AUC was improved to 0.91. AUC of 0.95 was reached on the best single model in an independent testing set using full-field DIMM (FFDM) pictures from the INbreast database, and the average four-model AUC was increased to 0.98. A whole image classifier trained on CBIS-DDSM digitized film mammograms uses an end-to-end method and is translated to INbreast FFDM images. Several mammographic algorithms based on AI convincingly indicated a decrease in human breakdown and computer diagnostic performance. Studies have revealed that the interpretation of CAD based on AI has increased the diagnostic performance of radiologists by commercially available DL CAD algorithms for mammography analysis in comparison with studies without AI-CAD [34]. In the DM dialogue on reverse assessment and methodologies (DM-DREAM), the current investigation of AI algorithms, AI-CAD performance in screening contexts, was explained. Comparison research was conducted using top-performing AI algorithms and radiologists' memory assessments. It was discovered that AI did not outperform radiologists and did not improve mammography identity accuracy. The potential of applying machine learning technologies to improve mammography screening interpretation is highlighted in this work [50]. The use of CNN in medical imaging has grown highly promising. InceptionV3 outperforms the other two widely used CNNs (VGG16 and ResNet50) in categorizing the mass and non-mass breast regions for CBIS-DDSM (digital mammography) [51].

DL models were introduced in mammographic breast density analysis to allow for a more objective and quantitative density evaluation. With a total accuracy of 72% [52], DL CNN with mammography outperformed a radiologist (odds ratio, 4.42 vs. 1, 67). Hybrid DL models integrating traditional risk factors and mammograms [53] have displayed higher diagnostic efficiency (AUC, 0.70) than a clinical risk factor model (AUC, 0.62–0.67) and the image-only DL (AUC, 0.68). DL algorithm with a larger number of inputs from health records data is adopted to link the mammographic data (AUC, 0.09) and hence the researchers were able to estimate breast cancer at levels equivalent to radiologists [54]. Recently, cancer patients are provided treatment using customized radiation therapy (Figure 5.2). DL algorithms are precise and able to pair to patient clinical risk variables to access and analyze digital images. A separate radiation dose for each patient is produced by the algorithm. This strategy has demonstrated a reduction in the negative effects and failure rates of cancer treatment are reduced [54].

5.2.5   Magnetic Resonance Imaging

Based on image characteristics, ML algorithms are applied to categorize magnetic resonance imaging (MRI) images as malignant or benign. The ML model generated is based on a mathematical approach that can predict the outcome through generalizing the experience gained in a data set and delivering an optimal prediction from new MRI images unnoticed by the models established. Among ML models, DL can perform both tasks, such as analysis of image and use a prediction algorithm to eliminate additional steps for the extraction of radiomic characteristics, which can deliver high performance without any preceding future extraction. The size of the filters and involved parameters in the pooling needs massive pooling data sets, which is nonoptimal for pilot studies with small datasets and in addition, it is computationally expensive [30]. DL is used to lower the radiation dose necessary for computed tomography (CT) imaging or to speed up MRI data acquisition [41].

5.2.6   CT Imaging

Ding *et al.* implicated pathological classification of micropapillary carcinoma has been predicted using CT imaging characteristics, and their identification through AI has not been included [55]. Luo *et al.* and Yu *et al.* implicated that AI can be used for the prognosis prediction of lung cancer patients from pathological image analysis which showcases that CT and pathological diagnosis are crucial for lung cancer treatment. It is much predictable that AI can offer additional functionalities in the future for accurate diagnosis. In 2019, Chen *et al.* reported the effectiveness of biological samples examination through AI integrated microscopy and can be used to diagnose cancer [56]. Cancers would be diagnosed with this technology. The deployment of AI in the diagnosis of cancer pathology was sooner and much more sophisticated in breast cancer and AI diagnostic approach had great application in the breast cancer diagnosis [57].

DNN, which is based on AI, has established a more efficient way for constructing classification models from data matrices. Surprisingly, these models are better at detecting, monitoring, and forecasting the progression of cancer. As a result, DL gives the best and most timely treatment to cancer patients [58]. By utilizing these models' abilities to analyze massive quantities of data, solve complicated issues, and predict with high accuracy, doctors can minimize misdiagnoses. The use of a DNN, today's most advanced AI approach, to extract data from images is extremely advantageous. Many medical professions, such as radiology and pathology, often use DL algorithms for screening. Furthermore, high performance in executing DL systems for clinical imaging in cancer biology has been achieved [59, 60]. DL can perform cancer diagnosis in three steps viz. (i) Pre-process step, which involves the improvisation of quality of the image by removing the unwanted information commonly called image sounds [61]. (ii) Image segmentation: This is taking part in the partition of a zone. The threshold, pixel, region, and image model decide the partition. Some of the additional approaches like Histogram threshold, adaptive threshold, gradient flow vector, and edge detection utilized in image segmentation [61–63]. (ii) Step of postprocessing: island removal, area merging, border enlargement, and smoothing are all part of this procedure. In addition, the ABCD rule, the 7-point checklist approach, the Menzies method [64], and pattern analysis [61] are all used to diagnose cancer.

CNN algorithms have been widely utilized to segment, categorize, denoise, and find anomalies and diseases from medical images derived from MRI, CT scan, PET, mammography, ultrasound, radiographic imaging, mass-spectrometry imaging (MSI), and X-ray [65].

5.3   DL in Next-Generation Sequencing, Biomarkers, and Clinical Validation

5.3.1   Next-Generation Sequencing

Next-generation sequencing (NGS) is the ideal platform for predicting cancer early by identifying novel biomarkers and target sites that require oncology experts' assistance with ML background to design algorithms. NGS data considering the patients' genetic variability helps develop a specific drug to target specific cancer cells. Hence AI is the most cutting-edge method for predicting and pinpointing cancer diagnosis, prognosis, and treatment. The future of digital healthcare and clinical practices is being updated to include algorithm-based AI help for various medical activities to provide a more specific cancer treatment option [66]. The use of NGS in genome sequencing is quickly rising in the clinical field, allowing for gene profiling and showing promise for precision oncology in the future. It offers a plethora of advantages by revealing prognostic and predictive biomarkers. Short and long readings are supported by NGS. Short readings are quite useful in the PM for detecting changes in population screening and clinical benefits. The Sanger sequencing method (first generation) is very time-consuming as it uses fragment cloning. NGS (second generation) is capable of sequencing large DNA and RNA sequences and high throughput screening (HTS) of the data at affordable costs [67]. Clinical trials following precision oncology protocols sequencing RNA facilitates better clinical prediction shows the beneficial effects of RNA profiling in oncologic samples. Vaske *et al.* [2019] link precision oncology to RNA profiling and show that it can help treat cancer in young people and children [68]. In addition, it also displayed that 70% (approx.) of gene expression data have potential implications in the clinical area. A predominant drawback of the second-generation sequencing method is the requirement of library preparation from either DNA or RNA samples. Third-generation sequencing methods were introduced to alleviate the shortcomings by providing a cost-effective and streamlined sequencing technology. Oxford nanopore technology is the only one of its kind capable of doing sequencing in a portable device. Because NGS creates vast amounts of complicated genomic data, AI can be used to identify and correlate data. For big data sets, file formats like BAM (the binary version of sequence alignment/map), FASTQ (to align reference sequences), and variant call format (VCF) is utilized [69]. In addition, bioinformatics tools enhanced with ML approaches are capable of correlating the severity of gene variations and assigning clinical relevance, which utilizes supervised and unsupervised method approaches for the classification of data [70]. To predict the missense variants computational algorithms, such as AlignGVGD, SIFT, and Polyphen 2, are commonly employed [71]. Compared to deep sequencing, nowadays, shallow RNA sequencing is used for the prediction of disease outcomes as it generates sufficient data for disease prediction and personalized medicine. In addition, computational tools, such as NNSPLICE, MaxEntScan, are used to predict intrinsic and silent variants [72]. A study using the NGS platform revealed the need to adjust cancer therapy for 46% of patients, emphasizing the need for precision oncology in cancer treatment. Patients with reverted and recalcitrant haematological tumors (leukemia, lymphoma) as well as solid tumor patients (sarcoma, ovarian, brain, renal, neuroblastoma, and liver cancer) were studied. In many tumors, NGS was utilized to find critical gene fusions, germline mutations, and harmonizing RNA transcriptional marks of vital molecular pathways. According to the study, 15% of the cancer patients needs adjustments in their treatment regimen, and 10% needs genetic counselling to assess upcoming risk indicating the significance of PM in decision making for better treatment outcomes in cancer patients [9].

5.3.2   Biomarkers and Clinical Validation

Screening is needed to address the essential biomarker candidates and to know more about cancer drug resistance and enhance therapeutic regimens. The main objectives of PM are to predict the response from cancer patients to diverse therapy and biomarker identification to drug sensitivity. In addition, diagnostic biomarkers play a crucial role in clinical practice, as no biomarkers meet the requirements criteria such as high clinical sensitivity and specificity, short half-life, organ or tissue-specific, discriminate metastasis, etc. All these parameters should be carefully evaluated for diagnostic biomarker selection.

Poor reproducibility is caused by physical examination and elucidation of disease classification and related tissue biomarkers [73]. On the other hand, computational pathology, with the help of complex image analysis algorithms, describes the morphological and biomarker interpretation of the digital histopathological images. Pixels are classified and segmented into nuclei, cells, and tissue using algorithms. As a result, a set of measures defining tissues, tissue components, morphological patterns, and cancer variations is generated [8, 73]. Numerical data obtained using computational image analytics are more reproducible, consistent, and dependable than data obtained through visual interpretation. Image analytics was employed to objectively quantify tissue marker expression. Analytical algorithms could be applied in both fluorescence and chromogenic images to detect ISH labeling of nucleic acid sequences.

Numerous studies proved that quantitative interpretation of tissue biomarkers should be improved using digital image analysis [74, 75]. Similar studies found improved uniformity in the evaluation of HER2, Ki6, ER, and PR, in breast cancer. Following deep learning, membrane boundary modeling based new segmentation methods is developed to assess cell membrane borders [76, 77]. Image analytics has been used to detect a variety of biomarkers in different tissue types PD-L1, p53, MED1, BCL2, and CD39 [78, 79].

Image analytics has been developed as the gold standard for tissue biomarker investigations to assure uniformity, reproducibility, and dependability. AI-based computational image analysis, based on DNN, has changed the field. CNN architectures segment pictures using numerous layers of processes (convolutional kernels, nonlinear activation functions, and subsampling). The network strength between these layers is modified to improve the network's segmentation or classification accuracy [80]. In the field of computational pathology, the DL technique has proven to be useful [81]. DL techniques, in essence, employ data to train the image characteristics that will be used for classification as well as the classifier itself. However, for training and validation, DL requires a huge amount of annotations. Many early image analysis examples used extremely large-scale image sets like ImageNet, which cannot be duplicated in the pathology domain [82]. FDA-sanctioned biomarkers for immune-checkpoint inhibitor therapy, such as micro satellite instability (MSI) and mismatch-repair deficiency (dMMR), can be utilized to identify any cancer. It also accounts for the morphological change inside the cancer microenvironment which can be easily detected from the histology reports in various cancers [83]. Various studies have validated these findings and extended DL-based genotyping across different tumors [84, 85].

The most difficult component of the development process for DL systems is clinical validation in the digital pathology of cancer. Three separate studies have shown that DL systems can be used to detect and grade prostate cancer in large patient cohorts, including pathologists and outside validation. The efficiency of DL systems grows with the number of patients in the training package and hits a performance plateau after training on over 10,000 histological images, which is a significant aspect for this work [86, 87], indicating the prerequisite for huge quantities of images and data to be produced to achieve adequate performance.

5.4   DL and Translational Oncology

Unsurpassed explosion in cancer biology supported in the development of PM, which favors accurate detection techniques in the diagnosis as well treatment of cancer individually [88–90]. PM relies on a thorough understanding of tumor biology and the detection techniques promote the close monitoring of the development of disease and its significant scientific changes in the therapeutic effect followed by development in either new drugs or new targets [90]. Also, Precision oncology knowledge provides a systematic platform for both oncologists and patients, to understand the clinically relevant genetic information for genetic-based clinical decision making [89]. The data obtained from the genomics, proteomics, microarray information, and clinical trials showed its complexity and challenging prospect for the maintenance of big data [91]. In this situation, a new method is needed to increase the availability of novel and effective anticancer treatments in a cost-efficient manner [92].

5.4.1   Prediction

DL techniques are useful for predicting gene diversity, drug design, protein-DNA and RNA interactions, and cancer progression [93]. Different DL designs in systems in bioinformatics are utilized depending on the forms of cancer. For the early identification and prediction of brain malignancies (glioma type), researchers suggest a three-dimensional evolving NNs architecture that uses consulting learning and huge datasets. The study also had an 89.9% accuracy rate in predicting the patient's survival time [94]. There has been documented a novel multilevel featured selection strategy based on DL for selecting genes/miRNAs based on expression patterns [95]. In comparison to traditional methods, the findings demonstrated a 9% (liver cancer), a 6% (lung cancer), and a 10% (breast cancer) improvement in cancer diagnosis. Deep faith networks provided more promising findings in the genetic diagnosis of breast cancer. Yildiz presented the C4Net model, a DNN-based approach that has a 96.94% success rate in detecting skin cancer (kind of melanoma) [96]. Recent research focuses on clinical cancer to determine the prognosis or predict the precise outcome concerning the treatment. Prediction of accurate prognoses of different patients may lead to a customized treatment for the patient. AI can assess a variety of characteristics from many patient examination data and assist in more precisely predicting cancer prognosis, survival duration, and disease progression in patients. When researchers evaluated a range of algorithms to traditional techniques for ovarian cancer prediction, they discovered that AI gives better accurate results [97]. Many decision tree rules, fuzzy membership functions, and inference approaches were used in the analysis of breast cancer survival. The study results revealed that predictions of weighted fuzzy decision trees (wFDT) are more accurate and showed a significant prediction towards cancer prognosis [98]. Comparison of artificial neural network results of breast cancer datasets with nuclear morphometric features of two different patients successfully predicted recurrence probabilities between patients with good and bad prognoses [99]. Hostallero et al. constructed and trained TINDL a DL structure over preclinical cell cancer cell lines to predict the effect on patients for various therapies [100]. SiRNA knockdown experiment showed that 10 genes influenced the drug (tamoxifen) sensitivity of the MCF7 cell line identified by the model and confirmed the prediction of aforementioned attributes in cancer through the DL framework. Recurrent neural networks (RNN) are built for sequential analysis, and they train the hidden state to make predictions by updating it frequently. Durr et al. used CNNs [101] to investigate the phenotypic classification of cells treated with various biological substances. Godinez et al. developed CNN's methodologies to study the accurate prediction of the small-molecule mechanism of action [102].

The role of DL in the determination of toxicity plays a major role to finalize valuable clinical decisions [103]. Pella and colleagues used neural networks and SVM-based algorithms to investigate gastrointestinal and genitourinary acute toxicities in prostate cancer patients [104]. Zhen and colleagues predicted rectal toxicity in cervical cancer radiation by transfer learning using a CNN model and calculated dose distribution in 42 patients' rectum with predictive relative > G2 rectal toxicity with an AUC of 0.7 [105].

Prediction models have been updated from 2D to 3D models due to modernization. Automated treatment planning (ATP) approaches based on DL helps to overcome the challenges of manual treatment in cancer and can develop a treatment plan in an efficient and precise manner with high consistency. It has been documented and proved that the 3D CNN model combined with Rapid Plan™ used for the prediction of intensity-modulated radiotherapy (IMRT) in prostate cancer based on the specific patients using only contours in planning CT was superior [106]. It has also been supported that the deep CNN-based dose prediction model produced a significant result compared to the contour-based method [107]. Also, for 3D dose distribution predictions, the most frequently used technique reported was CNN technique. Furthermore, the designs belonging to the category of CNN such as Alex-Net, VGG-Net, U-Net, V-Net, and Res-Net are studied well in all categories [72].

For omics prediction analysis a huge number of samples is required and omics datasets are luxurious to generate. But this is challenging to obtain in the real world [6]. Using regression-based methodologies, the major features utilized to develop the prediction model were pre-selected from the entire data set. However, this strategy runs the danger of overestimating how effectively the algorithm will predict the answer (overfitting), a methodological problem known as double-dipping. Focusing on significant features of the patient and excluding those that are not necessary for the prediction analysis might relieve the difficulty of a small sample size.

5.4.2   Segmentation

Medical imaging acquired using various modalities is segmented using DL approaches, ensuring quality, reducing inherent inter-observer variability and controlling treatment planning time. Auto segmentation is the most common application of DL techniques [28, 108]. It also helps with the segmentation of brain tumors and subsequent lesions in diagnostic neuroradiology. The identification and segmentation of brain metastases were greatly aided by multimodal MR imaging [109]. DL techniques and prior knowledge in the image segmentation of head and neck malignancies help to overcome the difficulties in radiotherapy such as modification of normal anatomy of the site during the surgical procedures associated with large primary or nodal lesions [110]. Men *et al.* employed the deep deconvolutional neural network (DDNN) technique to analyze the gross tumor volume of nasopharyngeal and metastatic lymph nodes in nasopharyngeal carcinoma patients [230 numbers] and found significant consistent results than other methods of segmentation [111]. Similarly, DL techniques are used in the segmentation of lungs, abdomen, pelvic and rectal region and they used deep dilated convolutional neural network planning CTs with very high segmentation speed [45s].

The Deep Neural Networks (DNN) method performed well in the lung cancer finding in the context of computed tomography data. This technology's advancement could help to boost lung cancer screening efforts [112]. A model for segmenting basal cell carcinoma in histopathology images was introduced using a DNN. They were able to segment with excellent accuracy using this model. As a result, they were able to use the DL technique to diagnose the pathology of basal cell carcinoma with a high precision rate [113]. Ghoneim *et al.* designed an approach using CNN and extreme learning machines and achieved high accuracy in detecting and classifying cervical cancer. In this system, images were sent to CNN, and input images were categorized using extreme learning machines [114]. A new image processing model based on CNN has been designed for the early detection of skin cancer. To examine the proposed method, the whale optimization algorithm was used to optimize the CNN and compare it to various ways in different data clusters [115]. The performance over the conventional models was discovered with deep models which provide insides over biological data with increased interpretation capability. Huang *et al.* projected an algorithm (SALMON [Survival Analysis Learning with Multi-Omics Network]), to predict breast cancer survival in which this algorithm predicted better cancer survival with prognosis accuracy and good concordance index compared to the other models [116]. Lee *et al.* used the DeepHit approach using DNN for the survival analysis which showed better performance when applied on METABRIC, UNOS, SYNTHETIC compared to other survival models [28]. Yousefi *et al.* used a risk propagation technique, for the interpretation of the deep survival model through the SurvivalNet framework and also compared this Bayesian optimized model with ML. It was concluded that a more precise prediction of cancer outcomes can be achieved from deep survival models [117]. Through methylation data, miRNA, and RNA sequencing from the TCA dataset [118], Chaudhary *et al.* developed a DL tool to predict the survival of liver cancer patients. The survival class labels were acquired from the TCGA dataset in the first step, and the SVM model was used in the second step. The suggested model's accuracy was tested on five distinct datasets, and it revealed variables that were associated with lung cancer patient survival. Drug Ranking Using Machine Learning (DRUML) can rank cancer medicines by efficacy across a variety of cancer types accurately. It's feasible to forecast which medicine will be most effective at slowing cancer cell growth using DRUML.

5.4.3   Knowledge Graphs and Cancer Drug Repurposing

To date, Computational and AI methods are creating new promising outcomes in anticancer drug development research [119]. Apart from various applications in technology development, DL is also focused and implemented in drug discovery effectively [65]. Significant data collection of the pharmacological compounds from the molecular, genomic and phenotypic data supports the cancer drug repurposing and facilitates advanced development. This process is referred to as computational drug repurposing [120]. At present, with the need for PM and personalized drugs, mechanism-based repurposing approaches are anticipated to find the new indication for the individual patients because these repurposing approaches consider the patient's heterogeneity and complexity, reduce the drug toxicity risk and inter-patient variability along with better efficacy [120, 121]. Computational approaches aid in the interpretation of the biology of existing and new cancer targets, as well as their mechanisms of action, for in-silico prediction of repurposing medicinal molecules into their next sophisticated use. Various computational tools are available to design cancer-related drug repurposing based on diverse data kinds and approaches. The data can be of two forms: traditional data like drug chemical structures, physical qualities, and molecular targets, and new data like omics data types (for computational analysis] like drug-induced transcriptional responses or metabolic simulations). Moreover, in the past few years, the research on drug repurposing gained more benefit by adopting computational strategies such as ML and DL technique to analyze the vast amount of available complex data for drug repurposing [88, 120, 121].

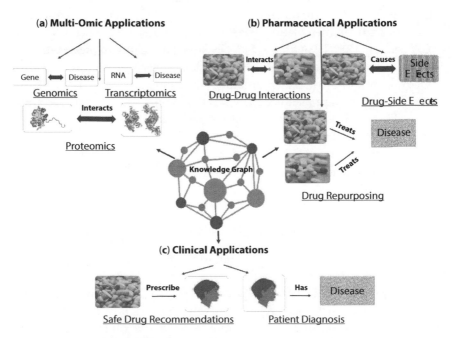

Figure 5.3 KG and its applications.

Computational techniques have the potential to find new drug-target interactions and speed up the process of drug repurposing and DTIs [122]. The accumulation of a significant quantity of biological experimental data and accompanying literature enriches the biological database, allowing computational methods to be used more effectively [123]. Also available are the ChEMBL, DrugBank, and SuperTarget databases, which aid in the correlation of medicines and targets [72]. To predict DTIs, several DL methods are established, including CNN to investigate the characteristics of individual drug-protein pairs [124].

Knowledge graphs (KGs) are a key step in weaving the constantly rising, fragmented, and dispersed drug-related data to make the best use of existing knowledge. By using good data representation techniques to drug KGs, it is possible to convert information into informative inputs for machine learning algorithms that may accurately forecast medication repurposing candidates [32]. Field experts create KGs from preexisting databases, utilizing manual curation or automated processes [125]. Figure 5.3 shows how the use of DL techniques for graph data has risen dramatically in recent years [126].

5.4.4   Automated Treatment Planning

The process of radiotherapy highly depends on treatment planning (RT) [67]. RT treatment plan is the result of a complex design process that involves multiple medical professionals and several software systems. This includes specialized optimization software to deliver the final dose distribution. The model outputs a treatment plan that is subsequently evaluated by an oncologist. The oncologist usually proposes modifications to the plan, which then requires the treatment planner to resolve the optimization model using updated parameters [127]. The quality of the treatment plan, on the other hand, has a direct and significant impact on patient treatment outcomes [67]. Contouring, planning, and assessing the final plan are all parts of the radiation therapy planning process, and each one takes a lot of time and work from a lot of people [128]. The existing planning paradigm's time and manpower demands can expose patients to delays and potentially poor treatments, all while appearing to be insurmountable hurdles to adaptive RT [129]. It is also unrealistic to construct all conceivable treatment regimens using available RT techniques and then pick the best one for a given patient [130]. However, automation of treatment planning (ATP) can save time and money while also potentially providing more consistent and higher-quality plans, as shown in Figure 5.4 [128]. AI, which includes ML and DL, has recently been utilized to automate RT planning

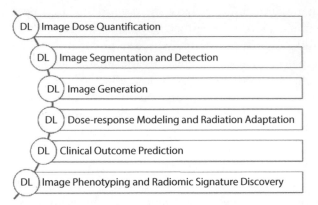

Figure 5.4 Significant advantages of ATP in radiation therapy.

and has sparked a lot of interest in the RT community due to its considerable potential for enhancing treatment planning quality and efficiency [67]. Various types of ATP techniques have been investigated during the previous few years [67, 124].

5.4.5   Clinical Benefits

Clinical trials are efficient methods to assess the therapeutic and diagnostic strategies and in-depth mining of data that enable the implementation of AI for diagnosis and treatment of cancer. Emerging data suggests the identification of features via DL models from CT scan images to support accurate outcome predictions. DL may be taught to predict therapy response from histopathologic images, resulting in the formation of a new class of companion diagnostics. However, as a precaution, legal and ethical considerations should be explored in depth before applying any new form of a biomarker to regular clinical practice or clinical studies. Additional investigations are necessary to solve these challenges in particular about the use of DL systems for clinical practice oncology.

The evaluation of patients with advanced NSCLC treated with ICI was done using a DL-radiomic model based on deep radiomics (DR) based on evolutionary AI neural networks. To predict the overall response rate (ORR), progression-free survival (PFS), and overall survival (OS), algorithms were created by including baseline clinical characteristics and DL into several models. The AUC for DR and its clinical manifestations was 0.78 [95% CI 0.70–0.85%], suggesting that DR might be employed as a new clinical approach in immuno-oncology to assess clinical outputs [131].

Table 5.1 Public accessible large-scale cancer databases.

Database	Specification	Application
The cancer genome atlas (TCGA)	Contains clinical data related to 11,000 tumor patients of 33 tumor types	To study genomic, transcriptomic, epigenomic and proteomic profiling.
Gene expression omnibus	Microarray and next generation sequencing (NGS) data	Understanding the process of genome methylation, chromatin structure, genomic mutation, protein profiling and genome-protein interactions.
Genotype-tissue expression	Whole genome sequencing (WGS) as well as RNA sequencing profiles.	Used for the analysis of tissue images from the tissue samples of postmortem adult donors.

General and well-known public accessible large-scale cancer databases comprising patients' multi-omics data are available and are represented in Table 5.1.

A total of 97 registered trials for registered AI tests for cancer diagnostics were included in a study [132]. Of those studies, only 27 [27.8%] were intervention studies and 70 [72.1%] were observer studies. Of the 97 studies, 37 (38.1%) dealt with colorectal cancer, 11 (11.3%) with breast cancer, 43 (44.3%) with imaging diagnoses, 33 (34.0%) with endoscopic diagnoses, and 11 (11.3%) with pathologic diagnoses. Most AI cancer detection trials have discovered that observational designs are required, and further research is needed in this area. The efficiency of an automatic quality control system (AQCS) with colonoscopy was investigated in an interventional trial (NCT03622281). The AQCS group showed a higher rate of adenoma detection, indicating that AQCS might improve the colonoscopy precision realistically [133]. In another trial (NCT03556813), the efficacy of the chatbot was tested on physicians regarding the information provided on the breast cancer patients, which revealed that the chatbot group has a higher success rate than the physicians implicating noninferiority (P < 0.001) [33]. Nagendran *et al.* assessed the performance and its adherence to the reporting standards, design, and claims for medical images with that of clinicians. For randomized and non-randomized studies, the risk of bias has been evaluated using the CONSORT (consolidated standards of reporting trials) and TRIPOD (transparent reporting of a multivariable prediction model for individual prognosis or diagnosis) tools, as well as the Cochrane risk of bias tool and PROBAST (prediction model risk of bias assessment tool) [70]. For 58 of 81 studies, the overall risk of prejudice was considerable, with suboptimal compliance (<50% compliance for 12 out of 29 TRIPOD items). In summary, 61 of 81 research indicated that AI performance was at least comparable to (or better than) that of physicians.

5.5   DL in Clinical Trials—A Necessary Paradigm Shift

Success rates of clinical trials are highly dependent on disease type. Between 2000 and 2015, an exhaustive study looked at 186,000 distinct trials and showed that the overall probability of success (POS) was 13.8%. Oncology studies, on the other hand, had a substantially lower POS of 3.4% [99]. Academic institutions, biopharma corporations, CROs, and smaller biotech firms are increasingly realizing the potential of AI, ML, and DL to transform oncology-based clinical trials. These intelligent techniques have the potential to improve trial success rates and reduce biopharma R&D costs by transforming numerous important phases in clinical trials, from protocol design to study execution. Particular individuals are commonly precluded from interventional cancer clinical trials due to comorbidities, prior or concurrent treatments [33, 134]. AI and other sophisticated analytics tools have previously been shown to help automate clinical trial processes, resulting in more cost-effective cancer research.

DL models have shown promise in learning critical traits for clinical trial cohort selection, potentially saving time and money. A group of researchers decided to put a variety of DL models to test the task of cohort selection, including a simple CNN, a deep CNN, a recurrent neural network (RNN), and a hybrid model that combined CNN and RNN [135]. The study discovered that the RNN and hybrid algorithms produced the best overall outcomes of all the models, while the standard CNN and deep CNN algorithms produced somewhat lower overall results. Moreover, the study revealed that extraction of medical data from human study protocols is also possible with DNN, which may aid practitioners in prescribing cancer medicines [136]. Deep Lens start-up is the AI clinic trial platform that was founded by Dave Billiter, TJ Bowen, and Simon Arkell in 2017.

It enables qualified patients to be autonomously identified for clinical tests and offers Deep Lens's free toolset—Virtual Imaging for Pathology Education and Research (VIPER). In a data-driven investigation, ML was used to foretell results of 2-year treatment from three similar phase III studies on bicalutamide for prostate cancer [137]. This study is an important step toward proving the efficacy of ML and its application in PM but it has several flaws.

Choosing the correct patients is critical to the outcome of epidemiological investigations and clinical trials. Medical researchers must make this decision cautiously after carefully analyzing multiple sets of data from many sources. To address the lack of a sufficient number of training instances, researchers investigated semisupervised DL techniques in the clinical trial process. The tiny amount of the dataset, according to the researchers, was a major weakness of the study [138]. In a publication, it was described how an attentional convolutional network can predict medical codes from clinical literature using possible codes of CNN [127]. Another work [136] shows how DL approaches can be used to do a semantic evaluation of clinical trial eligibility conditions directly. In contrast to traditional methods, they neglected curbs of previous processes including "tokenization, stemming, and syntactic analysis, named entity recognition (NER), concept tagging to ontologies, rule definition, and human feature selection". This CNN model was also tested on an independent clinical data source, paving the way for its eventual inclusion in oncologists' clinical notes, pending clinical support system advances. A new model might be built based on the efficacy data of previous clinical research to create prospective cancer treatments for a given patient condition.

DL notably CNNs and RNNs may foresee survival and clinical outcomes in patients with NSCLC by merging pre-treatment and follow-up CT scans. Individuals with stage III lung cancer with different therapeutic regimens were evaluated in two distinct databases. In the first dataset, they constructed and evaluated DL models in patients receiving final chemoradiation therapy. The network's generalizability and pathologic validation were tested using a second dataset of patients who had chemoradiation followed by surgery [139]. Furthermore, prognostic predictions may aid in the evaluation of patient outcomes in clinical trials, allowing for the assessment of response and, eventually, dynamically changing therapy [139]. They showed how DL can combine imaging data from various time points to improve clinical outcome forecasts. AI-based noninvasive radiomics biomarkers can have a significant influence in the clinic due to their low cost and lack of human input [132, 139]. This sheds more light on applications such as the diagnosis of gross residual disease without the need for surgery, as well as other PM approaches based on DL techniques.

Travel restrictions, social isolation, and even incarceration have all been part of the global response to the COVID-19 pandemic. All of these factors may greatly restrict trial subjects' and staff's ability and willingness to visit clinical sites, affecting data collection: some data will be lost, and some data may be collected in a different method (e.g., remotely vs. on-site). Because of these issues, the US Food and Drug Administration [140] has issued special recommendations for conducting clinical trials during the pandemic. All of these concerns will almost certainly lead to consequences, such as tainted trial data and difficulties interpreting clinical trial outcomes [141, 142]. When a clinical study is interrupted and data are lost, it might be problematic to collect and document predicted data of trial design when the experiment was dropped out. On-site patient assessments may be less frequent during the pandemic, resulting in missing data. Furthermore, because of possible variations in visit frequency before, during, and after the pandemic, patient data may not be captured at the typical intervals. Both of these problems might be solved with existing ML techniques. Missing data in temporal data streams can be imputed using ML approaches. ML approaches using multidimensional recurrent neural networks and generative adversarial imputation nets outperform earlier methods. For extracting insight from data from suspended trials, machine learning algorithms for estimating diverse treatment responses could be effective [143]. The current tendency is for clinical study datasets to be made publicly available. As a result, data from phase III clinical trials may be beneficial in the development of practical ML-based PM systems [137].

The clinical trial enrichment method is also adopted in DL. Although there have not been any FDA approvals of pharmaceuticals that use ML-based clinical trial enrichment, the FDA has praised its applicability. To more clearly address the subject and compare past computational approaches to DL [144], a bigger patient dataset with both gene expression and treatment response data was presented. The Cancer Genome Atlas (TCGA) has datasets for two drugs: cisplatin and paclitaxel. In addition, the Esophageal Cancer Clinical and Molecular Stratification (OCCAMS) consortium have unpublished gene expression and patient response data from [1] a PARP inhibitor clinical study conducted at MD Anderson Cancer Center, and [2] a cohort of oesophageal adenocarcinomas treated with neoadjuvant chemotherapy as a clinical model for cisplatin-based therapy [145, 146]. These datasets could be useful for clinical trials based on DL.

A registry-based approach that enables the group and identifies topics with growing research and investment that could have therapeutic significance in the coming decade has been explored. In light of legislative delays, the study findings may be useful to health decisions and policymakers grappling with ML application regulation and governance issues [147]. The clinical translation of ML-related software and apps has recently made tremendous progress. The translation and market acceptability of ML-based algorithms pose a substantial obstacle in terms of legislation and regulation. Based on statistics from the registry site ClinicalTrials.gov, the number of registered clinical trials in the field of ML and DL has gradually climbed from year to year since 2015, with a particularly substantial increase in the previous 2 years [138, 147].

The critical requirement of hospitalization is well-known to everyone during the present global threat of COVID-19 pandemic. DL-based precision medicine could reduce this need through proper channelling using deep learning-based precision medicine. Hereby, it is possible through identification and usage of appropriate drugs among the clinically approved drugs corticosteroids and remdesivir. Proper maintenance of clinical data as electronic health records could only aid in the success of this kind of deep learning-based PM approach. Otherwise, clinical complications will happen during the treatment at severe conditions. Lam *et al.* [2021] conducted a study on the use of machine learning as a precision medicine strategy in the prescription of COVID-19 medicines such as Remdesivir or corticosteroids. The utility of machine learning algorithms in optimal drug selection for various individuals based on survival time and disease stage was investigated in this study [148].

5.6   Challenges and Limitations

An emerging approach of PM is primarily focused on better understanding and treatment of a disease through multi-modal or multiomics data. Computer-based analysis coupled with the PM could provide big data in the area of genetics, genomics, etc. This technique does not require extensive data processing which critically combines binary, categorical, discrete, and continuous parameters or variables. The property of model adaptability comprises multifaceted, nonlinear patterns in training data. However, this complex model containing non-linear patterns has been observed for lower interpretation capacity compared with the simpler linear models. In the case of genomics, DL-based models are extensively being applied to analyze a wide range of genomic data. The most important example is the application of ML in genome-wide association studies (GWAS). In that case, complex genomic information could be effectively processed or evaluated in identifying the trait or phenotype. Several researchers also have made a study in understanding this GWAS-based machine model, where it has been trained and evaluated in predicting a particular disease type. This is possible through the results of genotype-based disease risk assessment. Recently, due to the increased advancement in this field, random forest models are popularly known as powerful in analyzing datasets with large numbers of variables with fewer observations. Moreover, the developing fields like epigenetics and epigenomics generally comprise the study of mechanisms that aids in the modification of gene expression without modifying the corresponding gene sequence. In this regard, some significant DL-based models have been developed which includes Deep Bind. It is a neural network, designed for identifying the gene sequences recognized by DNA and RNA binding proteins which subsequently helps in predicting any possibility of human disease through genetic variation. Other models like DeepChrome and DeepHistone, are also designed in such a way to find any occurrence of histone protein modification which possibly would develop some kind of health modification and disease condition [149]. When compared to radiology, DL in the field of histology has shown less improvement, but the research area is rapidly improving clinical studies with the addition of technology that is focused on challenges and activities that are relevant for patient care and decision making. Regulatory bodies are approving more DL concepts, clearing the road for clinical implementation [150]. In reality, DL approaches have limitations: To begin with, DL approaches in histology necessitate slide scanners and file format uniformity, which is not currently the case in diagnostic pathology. In addition, DL systems need performance improvements to become usable clinical tools; False-positive forecasts, however, could not be tolerated in a clinical environment by adopting DL systems for pre-screening by subsequent molecular testing. Due to its integrated analysis of complex and larger databases, DL will play a vital role in the future of medicine and healthcare in the coming decade. As there is increasing complexity in understanding the disease condition at the level of genetics, metabolomics, and immunology, precision medicine combined with these ML approaches is highly useful for clinicians. Though these advanced techniques are powerful in managing a wide variety of patients' data, without manpower, knowledge, and critical thinking nothing becomes useful in real-time application in treatment. Advancement of every technique should promise ethical, legal, and moral consideration in clinical application among the patient healthcare. This computer-based learning is not feasible for every clinician in understanding its usage due to its advanced algorithms and complex protocol. So, errors may occur in handling patients' data followed by inappropriate strategies. This leads to the rise of legal and clinical concerns. Also, it is due to its increased advancement, the technique is becoming a costlier business among healthcare professionals, which is limiting its application among economically poor people. Suitable steps should be taken in providing this modern facility to every human without comparing their economic status.

5.7   Conclusion

AI, ML and DL offer great promise in the identification of datasets related to malignant tumors/cancers that might not be possible using traditional statistical techniques. Several techniques in the oncology field as described in this chapter have applied DL and encouraging results have been obtained. Advances in computational processing and programming have made state-of-the-art DL more accessible and popular in precision oncology. However, the use of DL in the field of PM is still in its early stages, and researchers are continually discovering the advantages and disadvantages of various computational model approaches. In the future years, it will be critical to integrate the data collected utilizing the various approaches and platforms mentioned in this chapter to create an integrated data model, particularly for PM. Methodology to integrate the data is very important to confirm that these integrations result in an improved ability for PM and to classify the respondents and non-respondents in the treatment protocol. Lessons learned from the various approaches, application or utilization of standardized techniques, reporting, AUC, accuracy, methodological advantages and disadvantages, sample size, etc., should be optimized to perform a standardized and successful treatment approach in the field of PM. However, these fields must adopt ethical methodology in the future to revolutionize healthcare and precision oncology.

References

1. Sung, H., Ferlay, J., Siegel, R.L., Laversanne, M., Soerjomataram, I., Jemal, A., Bray, F., Global cancer statistics 2020: GLOBOCAN estimates of incidence and mortality worldwide for 36 cancers in 185 countries. *CA Cancer J. Clin.*, 71, 209, 2021.

2. Fassler, D.J., Abousamra, S., Gupta, R., Chen, C., Zhao, M., Paredes, D., Batool, S.A., Knudsen, B.S., Escobar-Hoyos, L., Shroyer, K.R., Samaras, D., Kurc, T., Saltz, J., Deep learning-based image analysis methods for bright-field-acquired multiplex immunohistochemistry images. *Diagn. Pathol.*, 15, 100, 2020.

3. Echle, A., Rindtorff, N.T., Brinker, T.J., Luedde, T., Pearson, A.T., Kather, J.N., Deep learning in cancer pathology: A new generation of clinical biomarkers. *Br. J. Cancer*, 124, 686, 2021.

4. Paracha, R.Z., Obaid, A., Ali., A., Phenotyping in precision medicine, in: *Progress and Challenges in Precision Medicine*, M. Verma and D. Barh (Eds.), pp. 55–77, Academic Press, Elsevier Publications, Netherlands, 2017.

5. Yehia, L. and Eng, C., Largescale population genomics versus deep phenotyping: Brute force or elegant pragmatism towards precision medicine. *NPJ Genom. Med.*, 4, 6, 2019.

6. Plant, D. and Barton, A., Machine learning in precision medicine: Lessons to learn. *Nat. Rev. Rheumatol.*, 17, 5, 2021.

7. Chen, H., Zhang, Y., Kalra, M.K., Lin, F., Chen, Y., Liao, P., Zhou, J., Wang, G., Low-dose CT with a residual encoder-decoder convolutional neural network. *IEEE Trans. Med. Imaging*, 36, 2524, 2017.

8. Fan, J., Wang, J., Chen, Z., Hu, C., Zhang, Z., Hu, W., Automatic treatment planning based on three-dimensional dose distribution predicted from deep learning technique. *Med. Phys.*, 46, 370, 2019.

9. Dlamini, Z., Francies, F.Z., Hull, R., Marima, R., Artificial intelligence (AI) and big data in cancer and precision oncology. *Comput. Struct. Biotechnol. J.*, 18, 2300, 2020.

10. Ballester, P.J. and Carmona, J., Artificial intelligence for the next generation of precision oncology. *NPJ Precis. Oncol.*, 5, 79, 2021.

11. Giger, M.L., Machine learning in medical imaging. *J. Am. Coll. Radiol.*, 15, 512, 2018.

12. Xue, Y., Chen, S., Qin, J., Liu, Y., Huang, B., Chen, H., Application of deep learning in automated analysis of molecular images in cancer: A survey. *Contrast Media Mol. Imaging*, 2017, 9512370, 2017.

13. Mendelson, E.B., Artificial intelligence in breast imaging: Potentials and limitations. *AJR Am. J. Roentgenol.*, 212, 293, 2019.

14. Krzyszczyk, P., Acevedo, A., Davidoff, E.J., Timmins, L.M., Marrero-Berrios, I., Patel, M., White, C., Lowe, C., Sherba, J.J., Hartmanshenn, C., O'Neill, K.M., Balter, M.L., Fritz, Z.R., Androulakis, I.P., Schloss, R.S., Yarmush, M.L., The growing role of precision and personalized medicine for cancer treatment. *Technology*, 6, 79, 2018.

15. Chen, H., Engkvist, O., Wang, Y., Olivecrona, M., Blaschke, T., The rise of deep learning in drug discovery. *Drug Discov. Today*, 23, 1241, 2018.

16. Li, Y., Kang, K., Krahn, J.M., Croutwater, N., Lee, K., Umbach, D.M., Li, L., A comprehensive genomic pan-cancer classification using the cancer genome atlas gene expression data. *BMC Genom.*, 18, 508, 2017.

17. Romo-Bucheli, D., Janowczyk, A., Gilmore, H., Romero, E., Madabhushi, A., A DL based strategy for identifying and associating mitotic activity with gene expression derived risk categories in estrogen receptor positive breast cancers. *Cytometry A*, 91, 566, 2017.

18. Saltz, J., Gupta, R., Hou, L., Kurc, T., Singh, P., Nguyen, V., Samaras, D., Shroyer, K.R., Zhao, T., Batiste, R., Van Arnam, J., Cancer Genome Atlas Research Network, Shmulevich, I., Rao, A., Lazar, A.J., Sharma, A., Thorsson, V., Spatial organization and molecular correlation of tumor-infiltrating lymphocytes using deep learning on pathology images. *Cell Rep.*, 23, 181, 2018.

19. Zhou, H., Lang, C., Liu, Z., Knowledge-guided convolutional networks for chemical-disease relation extraction. *BMC Bioinform.*, 20, 260, 2019.

20. Libbrecht, M. and Noble, W., ML applications in genetics and genomics. *Nat. Rev. Genet.*, 16, 321, 2015.

21. Hough, S.H., Ajetunmobi, A., Brody, L., Humphryes-Kirilov, N., Perello, E., Desktop genetics. *Per. Med.*, 13, 517, 2016.

22. Sanchez-Vega, F., Mina, M., Armenia, J., Chatila, W.K., Luna, A., La, K.C., Dimitriadoy, S., Liu, D.L., Kantheti, H.S., Saghafinia, S., Chakravarty, D., Daian, F., Gao, Q., Bailey, M.H., Liang, W.W., Foltz, S.M., Shmulevich, I., Ding, L., Heins, Z., Ochoa, A., Gross, B., Gao, J., Zhang, H., Kundra, R., Kandoth, C., Bahceci, I., Dervishi, L., Dogrusoz, U., Zhou, W., Shen, H., Laird, P.W., Way, G.P., Greene, C.S., Liang, H., Xiao, Y., Wang, C., Iavarone, A., Berger, A.H., Bivona, T.G., Lazar, A.J., Hammer, G.D., Giordano, T., Kwong, L.N., McArthur, G., Huang, C., Tward, A.D., Frederick, M.J., McCormick, F., Meyerson, M., Van Allen, E.M., Cherniack, A.D., Ciriello, G., Sande, R.C., Schultz, N., Cancer genome atlas research network, oncogenic signaling pathways in the cancer genome atlas. *Cell*, 173, 321, 2018.

23. Cava, C., Bertoli, G., Colaprico, A., Olsen, C., Bontempi, G., Castiglioni, I., Integration of multiple networks and pathways identifies cancer driver genes in pan-cancer analysis. *BMC Genom.*, 19, 25, 2018.

24. Peng, N., Poon, H., Quirk, C., Cross-sentence N-ary relation extraction with graph LSTMs, TACL, 5, arXiv:1708.03743. 2017.

25. Lee, K., Kim, B., Choi, Y., Kim, S., Shin, W., Lee, S., Park, S., Kim, S., Tan, A.C., Kang, J., Deep learning of mutation-gene-drug relations from the literature. *BMC Bioinform.*, 19, 21, 2018.

26. Davis, R.J., Gönen, M., Margineantu, D.H., Handeli, S., Swanger, J., Hoellerbauer, P., Paddison, P.J., Gu, H., Raftery, D., Grim, J.E., Hockenbery, D.M., Margolin, A.A., Clurman, B.E., Pan-cancer transcriptional signatures predictive of oncogenic mutations reveal that Fbw7 regulates cancer cell oxidative metabolism. *Proc. Natl. Acad. Sci. U.S.A.*, 115, 5462, 2018.

27. Coudray, N., Ocampo, P.S., Sakellaropoulos, T., Narula, N., Snuderl, M., Fenyö, D., Moreira, A.L., Razavian, N., Tsirigos, A., Classification and mutation prediction from non–small cell lung cancer histopathology images using deep learning. *Nat. Med.*, 24, 1559, 2018.

28. Lee, S.I., Celik, S., Logsdon, B.A., Lundberg, S.M., Martins, T.J., Oehler, V.G., Estey, E.H., Miller, C.P., Chien, S., Dai, J., Saxena, A., Blau, C.A., Becker, P.S., A machine learning approach to integrate big data for precision medicine in acute myeloid leukemia. *Nat. Commun.*, 9, 42, 2018b.

29. Zou, J., Huss, M., Abid, A., Mohammadi, P., Torkamani, A., Telenti, A., A primer on DL in genomics. *Nat. Genet.*, 51, 12, 2019.

30. Zhang, Y., Oikonomou, A., Wong, A., Haider, M.A., Khalvati, F., Radiomics-based prognosis analysis for non-small cell lung cancer. *Sci. Rep.*, 7, 46349, 2017.

31. Trivizakis, E., Manikis, G.C., Nikiforaki, K., Drevelegas, K., Constantinides, M., Drevelegas, A., Marias, K., Extending 2-D convolutional neural networks to 3-D for advancing DL cancer classification with application to MRI liver tumor differentiation. *IEEE J. Biomed. Health Inform.*, 23, 923, 2019.

32. Zhu, Y., Che, C., Jin, B., Zhang, N., Su, C., Wang, F., Knowledge-driven drug repurposing using a comprehensive drug knowledge graph. *Health Inf. J.*, 26, 2737–2750, 2020.

33. Bibault, J.E., Chaix, B., Guillemassé, A., Cousin, S., Escande, A., Perrin, M., Pienkowski, A., Delamon, G., Nectoux, P., Brouard, B., A chatbot versus physicians to provide information for patients with breast cancer: Blind, randomized controlled noninferiority trial. *J. Med. Internet Res.*, 21, e15787, 2019.

34. Kim, H.E., Kim, H.H., Han, B.K., Kim, K.H., Han, K., Nam, H., Lee, E.H., Kim, E.K., Changes in cancer detection and false-positive recall in mammography using artificial intelligence: A retrospective, multireader study. *Lancet Digit. Health*, 2, 138, 2020.

35. Pacilè, S., Lopez, J., Chone, P., Bertinotti, T., Grouin, J.M., Fillard, P., Improving breast cancer detection accuracy of mammography with the concurrent use of an artificial intelligence tool radiology. *Artif. Intell.*, 2, e190208, 2020.

36. Allahyar, A., Ubels, J., De Ridder, J., A data-driven interactome of synergistic genes improves network-based cancer outcome prediction. *PloS Comput. Biol.*, 15, e1006657, 2019.

37. Hosny, A., Parmar, C., Quackenbush, J., Schwartz, L.H., Aerts, H., Artificial intelligence in radiology. *Nat. Rev. Cancer*, 18, 500, 2018.

38. Mitchell, M.J., Jain, R.K., Langer, R., Engineering and physical sciences in oncology: Challenges and opportunities. *Nat. Rev. Cancer*, 17, 659, 2017.

39. Wulczyn, E., Steiner, D.F., Xu, Z., Sadhwani, A., Wang, H., Flament-Auvigne, I., Mermel, C.H., Chen, P.C., Liu, Y., Stumpe, M.C., Deep learning-based survival prediction for multiple cancer types using histopathology images. *PloS One*, 15, e0233678, 2020.

40. Telenti, A., Lippert, C., Chang, P.-C., Mark, D., DL of genomic variation and regulatory network data. *Hum. Mol. Genet.*, 27, R63, 2018.

41. Cohen, O., Zhu, B., Rosen, M.S., MR fingerprinting deep reconstruction network (DRONE). *Magn. Reson. Med.*, 80, 885, 2018.

42. Robinson, P.N., Piro, R.M., Jager, M., Post processing the alignment, in: *Computational Exome and Genome Analysis*, 1st ed, Chapman and Hall/ CRC, New York, NY, USA, 2017.

43. Boldrini, L., Bibault, J.E., Masciocchi, C., Shen, Y., Bittner, M.I., Deep learning: A review for the radiation oncologist. *Front. Oncol.*, 9, 977, 2019.

44. Gillies, R.J., Kinahan, P.E., Hricak, H., Radiomics: Images are more than pictures, they are data. *Radiology*, 278, 563, 2016.

45. Luo, X., Zang, X., Yang, L., Huang, J., Liang, F., Rodriguez-Canales, J., Wistuba, I.I., Gazdar, A., Xie, Y., Xiao, G., Comprehensive computational pathological image analysis predicts lung cancer prognosis. *J. Thorac. Oncol.*, 12, 501, 2017.

46. Parekh, V.S. and Jacobs, M.A., Deep learning and radiomics in precision medicine. *Expert Rev. Precis. Med. Drug Dev.*, 4, 59, 2019.

47. Russell, P., Fountain, K., Wolverton, D., Ghosh, D., TCIA pathfinder: An R client for the cancer imaging archive REST API. *Cancer Res.*, 78, 4424, 2018.

48. Martin-Gonzalez, P., Crispin-Ortuzar, M., Rundo, L., Delgado-Ortet, M., Reinius, M., Beer, L., Woitek, R., Ursprung, S., Addley, H., Brenton, J.D., Markowetz, F., Sala, E., Integrative radiogenomics for virtual biopsy and treatment monitoring in ovarian cancer. *Insights Imaging*, 11, 94, 2020.

49. Shen, L., Margolies, L.R., Rothstein, J.H., Eugene, F., Russell., M.C.B., Weiva, S., DL to improve breast cancer detection on screening mammography. *Sci. Rep.*, 9, 12495, 2019.

50. Schaffter, T., Buist, D., Lee, C.I., Nikulin, Y., Ribli, D., Guan, Y., Lotter, W., Jie, Z., Du, H., Wang, S., Feng, J., Feng, M., Kim, H.E., Albiol, F., Albiol, A., Morrell, S., Wojna, Z., Ahsen, M.E., Asif, U., Jimeno Yepes, A., Yohanandan, S., Rabinovici-Cohen, S., Yi, D., Hoff, B., Yu, T., Chaibub Neto, E., Rubin, D.L., Lindholm, P., Margolies, L.R., McBride, R.B., Rothstein, J.H., Sieh, W., Ben-Ari, R., Harrer, S., Trister, A., Friend, S., Norman, T., Sahiner, B., Strand, F., Guinney, J., Stolovitzky, G., Mackey, L., Cahoon, J., Shen, L., Sohn, J.H., Trivedi, H., Shen, Y., Buturovic, L., Pereira, J.C., Cardoso, J.S., Castro, E., Kalleberg, K.T., Pelka, O., Nedjar, I., Geras, K.J., Nensa, F., Goan, E., Koitka, S., Caballero, L., Cox, D.D., Krishnaswamy, P., Pandey, G., Friedrich, C.M., Perrin, D., Fookes, C., Shi, B., Cardoso Negrie, G., Kawczynski, M., Cho, K., Khoo, C.S., Lo, J.Y., Sorensen, A.G., Jung, H., Evaluation of combined artificial intelligence and radiologist assessment to interpret screening mammograms. *JAMA Netw. Open*, 3, e200265, 2020.

51. Agarwal, R., Diaz, O., Lladó, X., Yap, M.H., Martí, R., Automatic mass detection in mammograms using deep convolutional neural networks. *J. Med. Imaging*, 6, 031409, 2019.

52. Ha, R., Chang, P., Karcich, J., Mutasa, S., Pascual Van Sant, E., Liu, M.Z., Jambawalikar, S., Convolutional neural network-based breast cancer risk stratification using a mammographic dataset. *Acad. Radiol.*, 26, 544, 2019.

53. Yala, A., Lehman, C., Schuster, T., Portnoi, T., Barzilay, R., A DL mammography-based model for improved breast cancer risk prediction. *Radiology*, 292, 60, 2019.
54. Akselrod-Ballin, A., Chorev, M., Shoshan, Y., Spiro, A., Hazan, A., Melamed, R., Barkan, E., Herzel, E., Naor, S., Karavani, E., Koren, G., Goldschmidt, Y., Shalev, V., Rosen-Zvi, M., Guindy, M., Predicting breast cancer by applying DL to linked health records and mammograms. *Radiology*, 292, 331, 2019.
55. Ding, H., Xia, W., Zhang, L., Mao, Q., Cao, B., Zhao, Y., Xu, L., Jiang, F., Dong, G., CT-Based deep learning model for invasiveness classification and micropapillary pattern prediction within lung adenocarcinoma. *Front. Oncol.*, 10, 1186, 2020.
56. Chen, P.C., Gadepalli, K., MacDonald, R., Liu, Y., Kadowaki, S., Nagpal, K., Kohlberger, T., Dean, J., Corrado, G.S., Hipp, J.D., Mermel, C.H., Stumpe, M.C., An augmented reality microscope with real-time artificial intelligence integration for cancer diagnosis. *Nat. Med.*, 25, 1453, 2019.
57. Liu, Z., Fan, J., Li, M., Yan, H., Hu, Z., Huang, P., Tian, Y., Miao, J., Dai, J., A deep learning method for prediction of three-dimensional dose distribution of helical tomotherapy. *Med. Phys.*, 46, 1972, 2019.
58. Park, A. and Nam, S., Deep learning for stage prediction in neuroblastoma using gene expression data. *Genomics Inform.*, 17, e30, 2019.
59. Huang, S., Yang, J., Fong, S., Zhao, Q., Artificial intelligence in cancer diagnosis and prognosis: Opportunities and challenges. *Cancer Lett.*, 28, 61, 2020.
60. Sompairac, N., Nazarov, P.V., Czerwinska, U., Cantini, L., Biton, A., Molkenov, A., Zhumadilov, Z., Barillot, E., Radvanyi, F., Gorban, A., Kairov, U., Zinovyev, A., Independent component analysis for unraveling the complexity of cancer omics datasets. *Int. J. Mol. Sci.*, 20, 4414, 2019.
61. Munir, K., Elahi, H., Ayub, A., Frezza, F., Rizzi, A., Cancer diagnosis using deep learning: A bibliographic review. *Cancers*, 11, 1235, 2019.
62. Celebi, M.E., Kingravi, H.A., Iyatomi, H., Aslandogan, Y.A., Stoecker, W.V., Moss, R.H., Malters, J.M., Grichnik, J.M., Marghoob, A.A., Rabinovitz, H.S., Menzies, S.W., Border detection in dermoscopy images using statistical region merging. *Skin Res. Technol.*, 14, 347, 2008.
63. Tong, N., Lu, H., Ruan, X., Yang, M., Salient object detection via bootstrap learning. *Proc. IEEE Comput. Soc. Conf. Comput. Vis. Pattern Recognit*, Boston, MA, USA, vol. 1884, 2015.
64. Johr, R.H., Dermoscopy: Alternative melanocytic algorithms—the ABCD rule of dermatoscopy, menzies scoring method, and 7-point checklist. *Clin. Dermatol.*, 20, 240, 2002.
65. Lavecchia, A., Deep learning in drug discovery: Opportunities, challenges and future prospects. *Drug Discov. Today*, 24, 2017, 2019.
66. Iqbal, M.J., Javed, Z., Sadia, H., Qureshi, I.A., Irshad, A., Ahmed, R., Malik, K., Raza, S., Abbas, A., Pezzani, R., Sharifi-Rad, J., Clinical applications of artificial intelligence and machine learning in cancer diagnosis: Looking into the future. *Cancer Cell Int.*, 21, 270, 2021.

67. Wang, Y., Mashock, M., Tong, Z., Mu, X., Chen, H., Zhou, X., Zhang, H., Zhao, G., Liu, B., Li, X., Changing technologies of RNA sequencing and their applications in clinical oncology. *Front. Oncol.*, 10, 447, 2020.

68. Vaske, O.M., Bjork, I., Salama, S.R., Beale, H., Tayi Shah, A., Sanders, L., Pfeil, J., Lam, D.L., Learned, K., Durbin, A., Kephart, E.T., Currie, R., Newton, Y., Swatloski, T., McColl, D., Vivian, J., Zhu, J., Lee, A.G., Leung, S.G., Spillinger, A., Liu, H.Y., Liang, W.S., Byron, S.A., Berens, M.E., Resnick, A.C., Lacayo, N., Spunt, S.L., Rangaswami, A., Huynh, V., Torno, L., Plant, A., Kirov, I., Zabokrtsky, K.B., Rassekh, S.R., Deyell, R.J., Laskin, J., Marra, M.A., Sender, L.S., Mueller, S., Sweet-Cordero, E.A., Goldstein, T.C., Haussler, D., Comparative tumor RNA sequencing analysis for difficult-to-treat pediatric and young adult patients with cancer. *JAMA Netw. Open*, 2, e1913968, 2019.

69. He, K.Y., Ge, G., He, M.M., Big data analytics for genomic medicine. *Int. J. Mol. Sci.*, 18, 412, 2017.

70. Nagendran, M., Chen, Y., Lovejoy, C.A., Gordon, A.C., Komorowski, M., Harvey, H., Topol, E.J., Ioannidis, J., Collins, G.S., Maruthappu, M., Artificial intelligence versus clinicians: Systematic review of design, reporting standards, and claims of deep learning studies. *Br. Med. J. (Clin. Res. Ed.)*, 368, m689, 2020.

71. Xu, J., Yang, P., Xue, S., Sharma, B., Sanchez-Martin, M., Wang, F., Beaty, K.A., Dehan, E., Parikh, B., Translating cancer genomics into precision medicine with artificial intelligence: Applications, challenges and future perspectives. *Hum. Genet.*, 138, 109–124, 2019.

72. Wang, Y.B., You, Z.H., Yang, S., Yi, H.C., Chen, Z.H., Zheng, K., A deep learning-based method for drug-target interaction prediction based on long short-term memory neural network. *BMC Med. Inform. Decis. Mak.*, 20, 49, 2020.

73. Hamilton, P.W., van Diest, P.J., Williams, R., Do we see what we think we see? The complexities of morphological assessment. *J. Pathol.*, 218, 285, 2009.

74. Hamilton, P.W., Bankhead, P., Wang, Y., Hutchinson, R., Kieran, D., McArt, D.G., James, J., Salto-Tellez, M., Digital pathology and image analysis in tissue biomarker research. *Methods*, 70, 59, 2014.

75. Prescott, J.W., Quantitative imaging biomarkers: The application of advanced image processing and analysis to clinical and preclinical decision making. *J. Digit. Imaging*, 26, 97, 2013.

76. Masmoudi, H., Hewitt, S.M., Petrick, N., Myers, K.J., Gavrielides, M.A., Automated quantitative assessment of HER-2/neu immunohistochemical expression in breast cancer. *IEEE Trans. Med. Imaging*, 28, 916, 2009.

77. Vandenberghe, M.E., Scott, M.L.J., Scorer, P.W., Soderberg, M., Balcerzak, D., Barker, C., Relevance of deep learning to facilitate the diagnosis of HER2 status in breast cancer. *Sci. Rep.*, 7, 45938, 2017.

78. Klümper, N., Syring, I., Vogel, W., Schmidt, D., Müller, S.C., Ellinger, J., Shaikhibrahim, Z., Brägelmann, J., Perner, S., Mediator complex subunit

MED1 protein expression is decreased during bladder cancer progression. *Front. Med.*, 4, 30, 2017.

79. Parra, E.R., Behrens, C., Rodriguez-Canales, J., Lin, H., Mino, B., Blando, J., Zhang, J., Gibbons, D.L., Heymach, J.V., Sepesi, B., Swisher, S.G., Weissferdt, A., Kalhor, N., Izzo, J., Kadara, H., Moran, C., Lee, J.J., Wistuba, I.I., Image analysis–based assessment of PD-L1 and tumor-associated immune cells density supports distinct intratumoral microenvironment groups in non–small cell lung carcinoma patients. *Clin. Cancer Res.*, 22, 6278, 2016.

80. LeCun, Y., Bengio, Y., Hinton, G., Deep learning. *Nature*, 521, 436, 2015.

81. Wang, D., Khosla, A., Gargeya, R., Irshad, H., Beck, A.H., Deep learning for identifying metastatic breast cancer, q-bio.QM. arXiv, 1606.05718, 2016.

82. Deng, J., Dong, W., Socher, R., Li, L.-J., Li, K., Fei-Fei, L., ImageNet: A large-scale hierarchical image database. *IEEE Comput. Soc. Conf. Comput. Vis. Pattern Recognit*, Miami, FL, USA, p. 248, 2009.

83. Ström, P., Kartasalo, K., Olsson, H., Solorzano, L., Delahunt, B., Berney, D.M., Bostwick, D.G., Evans, A.J., Grignon, D.J., Humphrey, P.A., Iczkowski, K.A., Kench, J.G., Kristiansen, G., van der Kwast, T.H., Leite, K., McKenney, J.K., Oxley, J., Pan, C.C., Samaratunga, H., Srigley, J.R., Takahashi, H., Tsuzuki, T., Varma, M., Zhou, M., Lindberg, J., Lindskog, C., Ruusuvuori, P., Wählby, C., Grönberg, H., Rantalainen, M., Egevad, L., Eklund, M., Artificial intelligence for diagnosis and grading of prostate cancer in biopsies: A population-based, diagnostic study. *Lancet Oncol.*, 21, 222, 2020.

84. Kather, J.N., Pearson, A.T., Halama, N., Jäger, D., Krause, J., Loosen, S.H., Marx, A., Boor, P., Tacke, F., Neumann, U.P., Grabsch, H.I., Yoshikawa, T., Brenner, H., Chang-Claude, J., Hoffmeister, M., Trautwein, C., Luedde, T., Deep learning can predict microsatellite instability directly from histology in gastrointestinal cancer. *Nat. Med.*, 25, 1054, 2019.

85. Sparano, J.A., Gray, R.J., Makower, D.F., Pritchard, K.I., Albain, K.S., Hayes, D.F., Geyer, C.E., Dees, E.C., Goetz, M.P., Olson, J.A., Lively, T., Badve, S.S., Saphner, T.J., Wagner, L.I., Whelan, T.J., Ellis, M.J., Paik, S., Wood, W.C., Ravdin, P.M., Keane, M.M., Gomez Moreno, H.L., Reddy, P.S., Goggins, T.F., Mayer, I.A., Brufsky, A.M., Toppmeyer, D.L., Kaklamani, V.G., Berenberg, J.L., Abrams, J., Sledge, G.W., Adjuvant chemotherapy guided by a 21-gene expression assay in breast cancer. *N. Engl. J. Med.*, 379, 111, 2018.

86. Campanella, G., Hanna, M.G., Geneslaw, L., Miraflor, A., Werneck Krauss Silva, V., Busam, K.J., Brogi, E., Reuter, V.E., Klimstra, D.S., Fuchs, T.J., Clinical-grade computational pathology using weakly supervised deep learning on whole slide images. *Nat. Med.*, 25, 1301, 2019.

87. Bulten, W., Pinckaers, H., van Boven, H., Vink, R., de Bel, T., van Ginneken, B., van der Laak, J., Hulsbergen-van de Kaa, C., Litjens, G., Automated deep-learning system for Gleason grading of prostate cancer using biopsies: A diagnostic study. *Lancet Oncol.*, 21, 233, 2020.

88. Issa, N.T., Stathias, V., Schürer, S., Dakshanamurthy, S., Machine and deep learning approaches for cancer drug repurposing. *Semin. Cancer Biol.*, 68, 132, 2021.

89. Li, X. and Warner, J.L., A review of precision oncology knowledge bases for determining the clinical actionability of genetic variants. *Front. Cell Dev. Biol.*, 8, 48, 2020.

90. Bai, R., Zheng, L., Xiao, C., Hanfei, G., Ling, B., Huimin, T., Wei, L., Jiuwei, C., Precision detection technology: Equipping precision oncology with wings. *J. Oncol.*, 2020, 9068121, 2020.

91. Gupta, R., Srivastava, D., Sahu, M., Tiwari, S., Ambasta, R.K., Kumar, P., Artificial intelligence to deep learning: Machine intelligence approach for drug discovery. *Mol. Divers.*, 25, 1315, 2021.

92. Mottini, C., Napolitano, F., Li, Z., Gao, X., Cardone, L., Computer-aided drug repurposing for cancer therapy: Approaches and opportunities to challenge anticancer targets. *Semin. Cancer Biol.*, 68, 59, 2021.

93. Kaya, U., Yılmaz, A., ve Dikmen, Y., Deep learning methods used in health. *Eur. J. Sci. Tech.*, 16, 792, 2019.

94. Nie, D., Zhang, H., Adeli, E., 3D deep learning for multi-modal imaging-guided survival time prediction of brain tumor patients. *International Conference on Medical Image Computing and Computer-Assisted Intervention*, 2016, Springer, Cham, pp. 212–220, 2016.

95. Ibrahim, R., Yousri, N.A., Ismail, M.A., Multi-level gene/mirna feature selection using deep belief nets and active learning. *Conf. Proc. IEEE Eng. Med. Biol. Soc*, vol. 2014, p. 3957, 2014.

96. Yildiz, O., Detection of melanoma from dermoscopy images with deep learning methods: Comprehensive study. *J. Fac. Eng. Archit. Gaz.*, 34, 2241, 2019.

97. Enshaei, A., Robson, C.N., Edmondson, R.J., Artificial intelligence systems as prognostic and predictive tools in ovarian cancer. *Ann. Surg. Oncol.*, 22, 3970, 2015.

98. Khan, U., Shin, H., Choi, J.P., Kim, M., wFDT weighted fuzzy decision trees for prognosis of breast cancer survivability. *Proceedings of the 7th Australasian Data Mining Conference*, Australian Computer Society, Glenelg, South Australia, pp. 141–152, 2008.

99. Wong, C.H., Siah, K.W., Lo, A.W., Estimation of clinical trial success rates and related parameters. *Biostatistics*, 20, 273, 2019.

100. Hostallero, D.E., Wei, L., Wang, L., Junmei, C., Amin, E., A deep learning framework for prediction of clinical drug response of cancer patients and identification of drug sensitivity biomarkers using preclinical samples. *bioRxiv*, 2021. https://doi.org/10.1101/2021.07.06.451273.

101. Dürr, O. and Sick, B., Single-cell phenotype classification using deep convolutional neural networks. *J. Biomol. Screen.*, 21, 998, 2016.

102. Godinez, W.J., Hossain, I., Lazic, S.E., Davies, J.W., Zhang, X., A multi-scale convolutional neural network for phenotyping high-content cellular images. *Bioinformatics*, 33, 2010, 2017.

103. Kang, J., Schwartz, R., Flickinger, J., Beriwal, S., Machine learning approaches for predicting radiation therapy outcomes: A clinician's perspective. *Int. J. Radiat. Oncol. Biol. Phys.*, 93, 1127, 2015.

104. Pella, A., Cambria, R., Riboldi, M., Jereczek-Fossa, B.A., Fodor, C., Zerini, D., Torshabi, A.E., Cattani, F., Garibaldi, C., Pedroli, G., Baroni, G., Orecchia, R., Use of machine learning methods for prediction of acute toxicity in organs at risk following prostate radiotherapy. *Med. Phys.*, 38, 2859, 2011.

105. Zhen, X., Chen, J., Zhong, Z., Hrycushko, B., Zhou, L., Jiang, S., Albuquerque, K., Gu, X., Deep convolutional neural network with transfer learning for rectum toxicity prediction in cervical cancer radiotherapy: A feasibility study. *Phys. Med. Biol.*, 62, 8246, 2017.

106. Kajikawa, T., Kadoya, N., Ito, K., Takayama, Y., Chiba, T., Tomori, S., Nemoto, H., Dobashi, S., Takeda, K., Jingu, K., A convolutional neural network approach for IMRT dose distribution prediction in prostate cancer patients. *J. Radiat. Res.*, 60, 685, 2019.

107. Ma, M., Kovalchuk, N., Buyyounouski, M.K., Xing, L., Yang, Y., Incorporating dosimetric features into the prediction of 3D VMAT dose distributions using deep convolutional neural network. *Phys. Med. Biol.*, 64, 125017, 2019.

108. Boldrini, L., Cusumano, D., Cellini, F., Azario, L., Mattiucci, G.C., Valentini, V., Online adaptive magnetic resonance guided radiotherapy for pancreatic cancer: State of the art, pearls and pitfalls. *Radiat. Oncol.*, 14, 71, 2019.

109. Charron, O., Lallement, A., Jarnet, D., Noblet, V., Clavier, J.B., Meyer, P., Automatic detection and segmentation of brain metastases on multimodal MR images with a deep convolutional neural network. *Comput. Biol. Med.*, 95, 43, 2018.

110. Lim, J.Y. and Leech, M., Use of auto-segmentation in the delineation of target volumes and organs at risk in head and neck. *Acta Oncol.*, 55, 799, 2016.

111. Men, K., Dai, J., Li, Y., Automatic segmentation of the clinical target volume and organs at risk in the planning CT for rectal cancer using deep dilated convolutional neural networks. *Med. Phys.*, 44, 6377, 2017.

112. Schwyzer, M., Ferraro, D.A., Muehlematter, U.J., Automated detection of lung cancer at ultralowdose PET/CT by deep neural networks–initial results. *Lung Cancer*, 1, 170, 2018.

113. Jiang, Y.Q., Xiong, J.H., Li, H.Y., Yang, X.H., Yu, W.T., Gao, M., Zhao, X., Ma, Y.P., Zhang, W., Guan, Y.F., Gu, H., Sun, J.F., Recognizing basal cell carcinoma on smartphone-captured digital histopathology images with a deep neural network. *Br. J. Dermatol.*, 182, 754, 2020.

114. Ghoneim, A., Muhammad, G., Hossain, M.S., Cervical cancer classification using convolutional neural networks and extreme learning machines. *Future Gener. Comput. Syst.*, 102, 643, 2020.

115. Zhang, N., Cai, Y.X., Wang, Y.Y., Tian, Y.T., Wang, X.L., Badami, B., Skin cancer diagnosis based on optimized convolutional neural network. *Artif. Intell. Med.*, 102, 101756, 2020.

116. Huang, Z., Zhan, X., Xiang, S., Johnson, T.S., Helm, B., Yu, C.Y., Zhang, J., Salama, P., Rizkalla, M., Han, Z., Huang, K., Salmon: Survival analysis learning with multi-omics neural networks on breast cancer. *Front. Genet.*, 10, 166, 2019.

117. Yousefi, S., Amrollahi, F., Amgad, M., Dong, C., Lewis, J.E., Song, C., Gutman, D.A., Halani, S.H., Velazquez Vega, J.E., Brat, D.J., Cooper, L., Predicting clinical outcomes from large scale cancer genomic profiles with deep survival models. *Sci. Rep.*, 7, 11707, 2017.

118. Chaudhary, K., Poirion, O.B., Lu, L., Garmire, L.X., Deep learning–based multi-omics integration robustly predicts survival in liver cancer. *Clin. Cancer Res.*, 24, 1248, 2018.

119. Cui, W., Aouidate, A., Wang, S., Yu, Q., Li, Y., Yuan, S., Discovering anti-cancer drugs via computational methods. *Front. Pharmacol.*, 11, 733, 2020.

120. Park, K., A review of computational drug repurposing. *Transl. Clin. Pharmacol.*, 27, 59, 2019.

121. Li, Y.Y. and Jones, S.J., Drug repositioning for personalized medicine. *Genome Med.*, 4, 27, 2012.

122. Mahmud Hasan, S.M., Chen, W., Jahan, H., Dai, B., Din, S.U., Dzisoo, A.M., Deep action: A deep learning-based method for predicting novel drug-target interactions. *Anal. Biochem.*, 610, 113978, 2020.

123. Zhao, B.W., You, Z.H., Hu, L., Guo, Z.H., Wang, L., Chen, Z.H., Wong, L., A novel method to predict drug-target interactions based on large-scale graph representation learning. *Cancers*, 13, 2111, 2021.

124. Tanoli, Z., Vähä-Koskela, M., Aittokallio, T., Artificial intelligence, machine learning, and drug repurposing in cancer. *Expert Opin. Drug Discov.*, 16, 977, 2021.

125. Nicholson, D.N. and Greene, C.S., Constructing knowledge graphs and their biomedical applications. *Comput. Struct. Biotechnol. J.*, 18, 1414, 2020.

126. Gao, Y., Li, Y.F., Lin, Y., Hang, G., Latifur, K., Deep learning on knowledge graph for recommender system: A survey, ACM, arXiv, 2004.00387, 2020.

127. Mullenbach, J., Wiegree, S., Duke, J., Jimeng, S., Jacob, E., Explainable prediction of medical codes from clinical text, CSCL, arXiv,1802.05695, 2018.

128. Rhee, D.J., Jhingran, A., Kisling, K., Cardenas, C., Simonds, H., Court, L., Automated radiation treatment planning for cervical cancer. *Semin. Radiat. Oncol.*, 30, 340, 2020.

129. Moore, K.L., Automated radiotherapy treatment planning. *Semin. Radiat. Oncol.*, 29, 209, 2019.

130. Yoganathan, S.A. and Zhang, R., An atlas-based method to predict three-dimensional dose distributions for cancer patients who receive radiotherapy. *Phys. Med. Biol.*, 64, 085016, 2019.

131. Elkrief, A., Phan, K., Di Iorio, L., Simpson, R., Chassé, M., Malo, J., Richard, C., Kosyakov, M., Chandelier, F., Kafi, K., Routy, B., Deep learning model to predict clinical outcomes in patients with advanced non-small cell lung

cancer treated with immune checkpoint inhibitors. *Ann. Oncol.*, 31, suppl_4, S754, 2020.

132. Dong, J., Geng, Y., Lu, D., Li, B., Tian, L., Lin, D., Zhang, Y., Clinical trials for artificial intelligence in cancer diagnosis: A cross-sectional Study of Registered Trials in ClinicalTrials.gov. *Front. Oncol.*, 10, 1629, 2020.

133. Su, J.R., Li, Z., Shao, X.J., Ji, C.R., Ji, R., Zhou, R.C., Li, G.C., Liu, G.Q., He, Y.S., Zuo, X.L., Li, Y.Q., Impact of a real-time automatic quality control system on colorectal polyp and adenoma detection: A prospective randomized controlled study (with videos). *Gastrointest. Endosc.*, 91, 415, 2020.

134. Harrer, S., Shah, P., Antony, B., Hu, J., Artificial intelligence for clinical trial design. *Trends Pharmacol. Sci.*, 40, 577, 2019.

135. Segura-Bedmar, I. and Raez, P., Cohort selection for clinical trials using deep learning models. *J. Am. Med. Inform. Assoc.*, 26, 1181, 2019.

136. Bustos, A. and Pertusa, A., Learning eligibility in cancer clinical trials using deep neural networks. *Appl. Sci.*, 8, 1206, 2018.

137. Beacher, F.D., Mujica-Parodi, L.R., Gupta, S., Ancora, L.A., Machine learning predicts outcomes of phase III clinical trials for prostate cancer. *Algorithms*, 14, 147, 2021.

138. Akacha, M., Branson, J., Bretz, F., Dharan, B., Gallo, P., Gathmann, I., Hemmings, R., Jones, J., Xi, D., Zuber, E., Challenges in assessing the impact of the COVID-19 pandemic on the integrity and interpretability of clinical trials. *J. Biopharm. Stat.*, 12, 419, 2020.

139. Xu, Y., Hosny, A., Zeleznik, R., Parmar, C., Coroller, T., Franco, I., Mak, R.H., Aerts, H., Deep learning predicts lung cancer treatment response from serial medical imaging. *Clin. Cancer Res.*, 25, 3266, 2019.

140. US Food and Drug Administration (FDA), *FDA guidance on conduct of clinical trials of medical products during COVID-19 pandemic guidance for industry, investigators, and institutional review boards*, FDA, US, 2020.

141. Akacha, M., Branson, J., Bretz, F., Dharan, B., Gallo, P., Gathmann, I., Hemmings, R., Jones, J., Xi, D., Zuber, E., Challenges in assessing the impact of the COVID-19 pandemic on the integrity and interpretability of clinical trials. *Stat. Biopharm. Res.*, 12, 419, 2020.

142. Meyer, R.D., Ratitch, B., Wolbers, M., Marchenko, O., Quan, H., Li, D., Fletcher, C., Li, X., Wright, D., Shentu, Y., Englert, S., Shen, W., Dey, J., Liu, T., Zhou, M., Bohidar, N., Zhao, P.L., Hale, M., Statistical issues and recommendations for clinical trials conducted during the COVID-19 pandemic. *Stat. Biopharm. Res.*, 12, 399, 2020.

143. Zame, W.R., Bica, I., Shen, C., Curth, A., Lee, H.S., Bailey, S., Weatherall, J., Wright, D., Bretz, F., van der Schaar, M., Machine learning for clinical trials in the era of COVID-19. *Stat. Biopharm. Res.*, 12, 506, 2020.

144. Theodore, S., Vougas, K., Narang, S., A deep learning framework for predicting response to therapy in cancer. *Cell Rep.*, 29, 3367, 2019.

145. Lagergren, J., Smyth, E., Cunningham, D., Lagergren, P., Oesophageal cancer. *Lancet*, 390, 2383, 2017.

146. Frankell, A.M., Jammula, S., Li, X., Contino, G., Killcoyne, S., Abbas, S., Perner, J., Bower, L., Devonshire, G., Ococks, E., Grehan, N., Mok, J., O'Donovan, M., MacRae, S., Eldridge, M.D., Tavaré, S., Oesophageal Cancer Clinical and Molecular Stratification (OCCAMS) Consortium, Fitzgerald, R.C., The landscape of selection in 551 esophageal adenocarcinomas defines genomic biomarkers for the clinic. *Nat. Genet.*, 51, 506, 2019.

147. Zippel, C. and Bohnet-Joschko, S., Rise of clinical studies in the field of machine learning: A review of data registered in clinicaltrials.gov. *Int. J. Environ. Res. Public Health*, 18, 5072, 2021.

148. Lam, C., Siefkas, A., Zelin, N.S., Barnes, G., Dellinger, R.P., Vincent, J.L., Braden, G., Burdick, H., Hoffman, J., Calvert, J., Mao, Q., Das, R., Machine learning as a precision-medicine approach to prescribing COVID-19 pharmacotherapy with remdesivir or corticosteroids. *Clin. Ther.*, 43, 871, 2021.

149. MacEachern, S.J. and Forkert, N.D., Machine learning for precision medicine. *Genome*, 64, 416, 2021.

150. Couture, H.D., Williams, L.A., Geradts, J., Nyante, S.J., Butler, E.N., Marron, J.S., Perou, C.M., Troester, M.A., Niethammer, M., Image analysis with deep learning to predict breast cancer grade, ER status, histologic subtype, and intrinsic subtype. *NPJ Breast Cancer*, 4, 30, 2018.

6

Personalized Therapy Using Deep Learning Advances

Nishant Gaur*, Rashmi Dharwadkar and Jinsu Thomas

Dy Patil International University, Pune, Maharshtra, India

Abstract

Personalized therapy is the process of providing personalizing medical care to particular patients based on various features including genetics, inheritance, and lifestyle. The core principle of personalized therapy is to provide the right treatment to the right patient at the right time. The concept of personalized therapy dates back to Hippocrates' period. Recent developments in diagnostic medical imaging and molecular medicine are gradually improving healthcare systems by providing knowledge and diagnostic data that allow for individualized patient management. Identifying the best approach to personalize and population medicine requires the ability to interpret detailed patient data together with broader aspects in order to track and differentiate between sick and relatively healthy individuals, leading to a greater understanding of biological markers that can signify health changes. Artificial intelligence (AI) developments in the form of new and emerging technology appear poised to help bring objectivity and precision to various traditionally qualitative analytical techniques. One form of AI in particular, known as deep learning, is achieving expert-level disease classifications in many areas of personalized medicine, relying on algorithms. These algorithms use raw data from an enormous, annotated data set, such as a collection of images or genomes, and then accurately analyze the data and recommend the best possible treatments for patients. Convolutional Neural Network (CNN), Recurrent Neural Network (RNN), Restricted Boltzmann Machine (RBM), and autoencoders are deep learning algorithms. Personalized therapy has a promising future in terms of improving treatment, which is based on patients' specific diagnostic data. This chapter will give an overview of the most common uses of deep learning approaches in personalized therapy, with a focus on data analysis and precision medicine.

---

*Corresponding author: nkgaur29@gmail.com

Rishabha Malviya, Gheorghita Ghinea, Rajesh Kumar Dhanaraj, Balamurugan Balusamy and Sonali Sundram (eds.) *Deep Learning for Targeted Treatments: Transformation in Healthcare*, (171–198) © 2022 Scrivener Publishing LLC

Keywords: DNN, CNN, deep learning, personalized therapy, targeted treatment, machine learning, artificial intelligence

6.1 Introduction

Health intelligence is an essential aspect and significant factor in personalized therapeutic programs. Personalized therapy is prevention and treatment approach that takes into account a person's lifestyle, environment, and genetics [1]. Doctors know it for decades that some medicines work well in certain patients, but they have not worked out why or been able to anticipate which medication would be safe and beneficial for any specific treatment. For example, ten people taking the same medicine for heart disease, epilepsy, cancer and may have different responses. A person may have severe, sometimes dangerous adverse effects while another does not; or a person's tumor may be reduced by an anticancer drug, but it may not be reduced by another [5]. Personalizing a treatment or tailoring treatment to a patient generally requires a comprehensive understanding of that patient's conditions and circumstances, which necessarily involves the use of sophisticated assays that produce huge amounts of data. Essentially, the data generated by these assays must be arranged for studies to be conducted to understand attributes that the patient possesses which can demonstrate the right plan of action [2]. In the twenty-first century, personalized therapy aims to provide "the appropriate kind the right drug, only at right dose, at the right time, and to the right patient." Adopting personalized therapy would change the way physicians diagnose and treat patients, as well as improve the patient's participation during and after treatment. Personalized therapy is a new yet rapidly growing area of medicine in which a physician may choose a genetic profile-based treatment for patients that can not only reduce adverse effects and achieve a better diagnosis but also be less expensive than a "random" tactic to treatment of disease. The ineffective non-PM (error-trail) strategy, result in severe side effects, misdiagnosis, drug toxicity, and reactive treatment is expected to push higher healthcare costs [6].

Humans are in the midst of a significant technology revolution driven by advances in artificial intelligence (AI). As part of the cultural change referred to as digital health, emerging technologies have begun to make different technologies available not just to healthcare professionals but also to their patients. Technologies like wearable sensors, artificial intelligence (AI), biotechnology, and genomics are progressively shifting in three directions [7].

1. Point-of-Care (POC) diagnostics
2. A large amount of data was generated, which necessitated the use of advanced analytics.
3. Precision medicine is built on this framework.

AI is a set of methodologies and computational tools for creating intelligent systems that can grasp, act, think, and analyze problems in a range of fields, including education, training, and, increasingly, healthcare [3].

Doctors and researchers can better predict which treatment and preventive strategies for disease using personalized therapy. It necessarily requires (supercomputers) tremendous computing power; (deep learning) algorithms that can develop at an enormous rate; and, more broadly, an approach that allows the use of physicians' cognitive abilities on a new scale (AI) [7]. AI plays a crucial role in scanning technologies including computed tomography, X-rays, 3D scanners, and magnetic resonance imaging (MRI). These are helpful in determining a more precise diagnosis for a specific patient [4].

The three general methods to artificial intelligence [9]:

1. Symbolism approach (approach based on rules)
2. Connectionism approach (network and connection-based)
3. Bayesian approach (Bayesian theorem based)

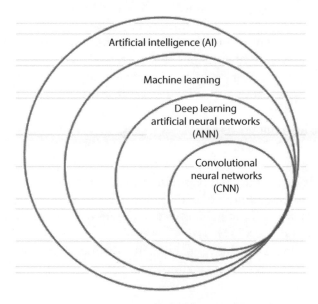

Figure 6.1 The hierarchy of terminology for AI, ML, and DL is depicted in Venn diagram.

AI is a wider term that refers to the area of computer science that focuses on developing algorithms to solve problems that typically need human intelligence. Machine learning is a branch of AI that enable computers toward comprehending information without becoming openly programmed. DL is a subclass of machine learning and technique of training that does not require feature selection [8]. This hierarchy of terminology is shown schematically in Figure 6.1 by a Venn diagram.

6.2   Deep Learning

DL is ideally useful for medical huge datasets, and it has been utilized to extract useful information. The new AI tool can detect abnormalities, perform a differential diagnosis, and provide preliminary radiological reports automatically [9]. DL is a form of ML that processes and learns data using a layered structure (algorithms) of artificial neurons, which were created by merging basic yet nonlinear modules that gradually transfer a presentation from one level to a higher, gain new abstract representation (beginning with the raw input). Very complex concepts can be built by stacking a large number of transformations [10, 11].

An image, for example, is made up of an array of pixels, and the very first level of presentation's learnt properties correctly identify the occurrence of edges at specific positions and places in the image. The second layer spots specific edge arrangements, regardless of tiny changes in edge placements, to identify motifs. After that, the third layer could merge motifs into greater configurations that correlate to components of recognized things, and further stages can detect items as a mix of these elements. Deep learning is distinguished by the fact that these layers of features are learned from data rather than built by human engineers using a general-purpose learning process [10].

This "superintelligence" parameter has been increased to multimodal DL by merging several forms of evidence to promote high-level multimodal decision support and reasoning (images, text, voice, etc.). DL algorithms can now combine and model heterogeneous services from a specific single patient throughout modalities and duration, enabling for more exact diagnoses and therapy [11].

Deep learning is currently separated into distinct approaches in medical data study and analysis [12] (Figure 6.2):

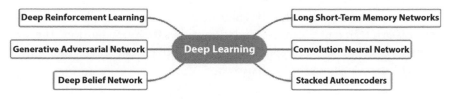

Figure 6.2 Approaches in DL.

6.2.1 Convolutional Neural Networks

CNN is an efficacious example of employing ANN, which represents mammalian visual brain. For many years, artificial neural networks (ANN) have been studied to handle high-level classification issues, such as picture classification. Early research on the visual cortex of cats by Hubel and Wiesel provides substantial physiologically plausible evidence for CNN's design [13, 14]. It has proven to be superior at addressing a variety of difficult image classification issues. In benchmarking studies, CNN-based systems have even outperformed humans in several applications, such as traffic sign identification [15]. CNN's excel at exploiting spatially local correlations in input data for precision medicine, and they have potential futures based on image diagnosis including radiology, dermatology, and pathology [16].

Convolutional neural networks (CNNs) are made up of three layers (or component parts): Pooling, convolution and fully connected. The very first multiple layers, pooling and convolution, extract features, whereas the third, a fully linked layer, converts those characteristics into final outputs such as classification (Figure 6.3).

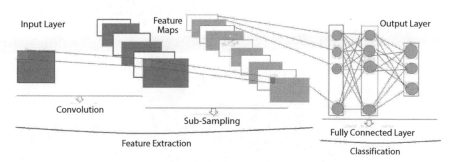

Figure 6.3 Convolutional neural networks structure.

Convention describes the convolution process in CNNs. In mathematics, this is referred to as cross-correlation rather than convolution. The sections go over the various types of layers, how they collaborate, along with some of the principles that CNN uses.

Convolutional Layer

The convolution layer is the initial layer geared to feature extraction via an input image. By understanding the properties of the image based on small squares of a data being entered, convolution preserves the relationships between pixels. Convolution is a mathematical procedure that requires two inputs: a kernel or filter and an image matrix.

We have a dimensioned picture matrix in Figure 6.4 below; width (w), height (h), filter height (fh), filter width (fw) and depth (d) are the dimensions of a filter. We've arrived at a result that includes volume dimensions as $(h - fh + 1) * (w - fw + 1) * 1$.

A set of learnable neurons is used to obfuscate the input image. This provides an output image, which either contains an activation map or feature map that is subsequently supplied as input data to the subsequent convolutional layer.

Subsequent element of the input tensor and kernel is evaluated and added at respective position of tensor to generate output number at the specified location of the output tensor, which is referred to as a feature map [17–19].

Stride-related studies

A stride in CNN denotes the number of pixel changes in the input matrix, as well as the convolution operation. If the stride value is one, the filters are moved one pixel at a time. If the stride value is two, the filters are moved two pixels at a time. Similarly, various stride values are taken into account. Figure 6.5 states the way convolution works when the stride value is two [18].

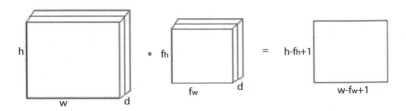

Figure 6.4 Multiplication of image matrix involving filter matrix and kernel.

1	2	3	4	5	6	7
11	12	13	14	15	16	17
21	22	23	24	25	26	27
31	32	33	34	35	36	37
41	42	43	44	45	46	47
51	52	53	54	55	56	57
61	62	63	64	65	66	67
71	72	73	74	75	76	77

Convolve with 3*3 filters filled with ones

108	126
288	306

Figure 6.5 A stride with a value of two pixels as an example.

A. Padding-related studies

In a few cases, the filters do not exactly match the input image. There are two alternatives in this situation:

- Zero padding: To acquire a fit, simply pad the zeros in the image.
- Remove the sections of the image where the filter is not applicable. Valid padding is a technique for reserving only the image's valid portion.

Without changing the architecture structure or fine-tuning the new picture domain, classification performance on low-quality images can be enhanced by using correct padding strategies [20].

B. (Relu) Nonlinearity-related studies

The term "Rectified Linear Unit" comes under the category of nonlinear operation. The goal of ReLU is to improve CNN's nonlinearity. Because the semantic analysis of image is a wildly nonlinear mapping of pixel values in the input, the mapping between CNN inputs and outputs must be nonlinear. By mapping negative values to zero and preserving positive values, ReLU allows for fast and accurate training. Because only the active traits are conveyed to the next layer, this is generally stated to as activation. Figure 6.6 depicts how the ReLU works (6). In place of the ReLU, other

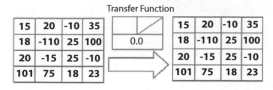

Figure 6.6 ReLU operation.

nonlinearities, such as the (tanh) or (sigmoid) might be utilized. ReLU is used by most researchers and designers because of the better performance it provides [21].

C. Pooling Layer

The pooling procedure has also played an important role, contributing to data invariance and perturbation invariance. Pooling techniques are used in current visual recognition systems to create "downstream" representations that are more resistant to the impacts of data variations while still keeping essential motifs [22]. This section assists in reducing the number of parameters if the photographs are large. Subsampling or downsampling, also known as spatial type pooling, decreases the dimensionality of each map while keeping critical information. Sum pooling, maximum pooling, and average pooling are indeed the three categories of pooling. In featured map, the largest component is considered as max pooling. The average pooling could be assumed if the largest element is assumed. The sum pooling is obtained by adding all feature map elements together [17, 18]. Figure 6.7 illustrates the Max-type pooling.

D. Fully Connected Type Layer (FC)

The output of first phase (which includes repeated convolution and pooling) is passed toward the fully connected layer, which sums the dot product of weight vector and the input vector to get the final output [23]. This is seen in Figure 6.8. Following the pooling layer is the FC layer.

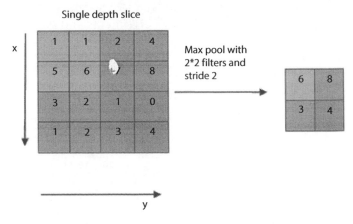

Figure 6.7 Max type pooling.

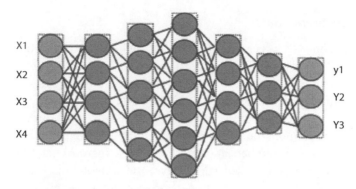

Figure 6.8 The step of flatting the matrix as FC layer.

The fully connected layer's main disadvantage is that it has a huge number of constraints that require extensive calculation in training instances. Accordingly, we strive to decrease the number of nodes and connections. The dropout technique can be used to satisfy the connection after deleting nodes. LeNet and AlexNet, for example, developed a deep and wide network while maintaining a constant computational complexity [24, 26].

Figure 6.9 depicts a comprehensive CNN architecture (9). The feature map's matrix will be converted to vectors in this design (x1, x2, x3). The FC layers are used to create a model out of a mixture of features. As a result, one form of the activation functions, such as "softmax" or "sigmoid," is used to categorize the results, which may be a boat, a home, a cat, a tree, or something else entirely.

CNNs excel at exploiting local correlations in input data [27], and they have promising applications in image-based diagnosis in the fields, like radiology, pathology, dermatology, and Alzheimer's disease [28–31].

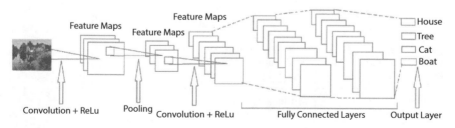

Figure 6.9 Architecture of convolutional neural networks.

6.2.2   Autoencoders

An autoencoder (AE) is a DL methodology, which is comparable to artificial neural network (ANN) and based on unsupervised learning. It's being used to decode and encode input data [32]. Figure 6.10 represents an AE network with layers such as input, hidden and output layers similar to ANN [33] (Table 6.1). Each layer in an AE has a set number of neurons. Because the input and output strands have similar number of neurons, but the hidden layer has lower numbers, it outperforms feed-forward neural networks. Sparse, denoising, zero-biased, contractive, and convolutional autoencoders are all examples of AE [34]. The autoencoder's primary goal is to extract significant features while lowering data size and obtaining noise-free data [35].

The radiologist, in particular, must spend quality time evaluating each image to verify that nodule is properly indicated, which would be essential for diagnostics and a center for research in intelligent healthcare. Autoencoders are advertised as a technique to learn features from massive amounts of data without risking hand-crafted features. Autoencoders successfully address the issue of insufficient dataset created by the difficulties of acquiring labeled medical pictures by combining the benefits of unverified and unlabeled data learning [36]. Kumar *et al.* present AE technique for lung nodule identification and unstructured feature learning [37]. To assess breast pictures, Kalleberg *et al.* suggest a convolutional AE technique [38].

Figure 6.10 shows how AE works in general.

The input is first given to the autoencoder. Assume the value is x.

Table 6.1 A list of CNN parameters and hyperparameters.

	Hyperparameters	Parameters
Convolution layer	Number of kernels, Kernel size, activation function, padding, stride	Kernels
Pooling layer	Filter length, stride, pooling method, padding	None
Fully connected layer	Activation Function, Number of weights	Weights
Others	Model architecture, optimizer, learning rate, loss function, mini-batch size, epochs, regularization, weight initialization, dataset splitting	

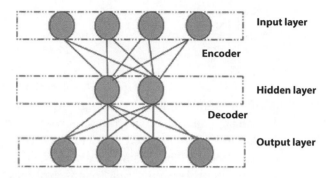

Figure 6.10 Input, hidden, and output layer of autoencoder network.

1. Using the encoder component, this is being sent as an input toward the decoder component to encode the input vector, which is used to attain the hidden code.
2. From the code, the decoder tries to reproduce the actual input, x'.

The autoencoder's primary goal is to extract key features while reducing data size and achieving data free from noise [39].

Equation (6.1) is used to obtain code c during the encoding stage, but equation (6.2) is utilized to recreate the input data, i.e., x', during the decoding phase.

The error are then determined via the back-propagation method, as indicated in eq. (6.3), allowing the network to be fine-tuned and the reconstructed output to be closer toward the input data. The following procedure's primary idea is to extract similar factors from the provided data [40].

$$c = F(wt_x + b) \tag{6.1}$$

$$x' = F(w_c + b') \tag{6.2}$$

$$e = min \sum_{i=1}^{n} (x' - x)2 \tag{6.3}$$

Activation function denoted by F, which specified in [41], b, bias amount; and w, weights between the input and hidden layer in Eqn. (6.1) and (6.2). Using c [42], the x' value involves creating a new form of the input x. The model can be utilized to minimize fitting that is also available in ANN as defined by eq (6.4).

$$min\left[\left\{\sum_{i=1}^{n}(x'-x)2\right\}+\gamma L(w)\right]$$
(6.4)

Autoencoders and their types look promising in a variety of medical applications, including monitoring acute lymphoblastic leukemia treatment with stacked denoising autoencoders. Several researches in the area of cancer data assimilation has emphasized their effectiveness in merging data from many scales to find predictive cancer features, such as liver cancer [43], breast [44], and neuroblastoma cancer [45] subtypes. The goal of these projects is to use AE to solve specific cancer-data integration challenges.

6.2.3   Deep Belief Network (DBN)

This is a specialized system based on artificial neural networks that are both technologically advanced and effective [46]. It uses supervised learning via back propagation after pretraining with unorganized strategies of learning [47]. It is composed of different layers of regulating Restricted Boltzmann machines (RBMs). It sits at the crossroads of supervised and unsupervised learning (whereby the input and label [output] statistics are available, which acquires only by input data). Semisupervised learning [48, 49] is a technique that can be used with both labeled and unlabeled training samples. Because of its exceptional performance, the DBN is employed in a variety of medical sectors, including medical research.

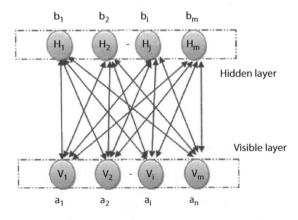

Figure 6.11 Restricted Boltzmann machine.

The energy is used by the RBM that is dependent on the Hopfield network to obtain probabilistic values (using a Boltzmann distribution). Two unit layers make up the RBM, one visible and one concealed, each with a connection intensity of 0 [50]. Figure 6.11 depicts the RBM.

Through the use of an energy function, RBM attempts to learn probability distributions. V H Given the visible unit, hidden unit, and the connection weight between $H(h1,...hn V(v1,...vm)$ each layer, W the function of energy introduced as [51]:

$$E(v,h) = -\sum_{i=1}^{n} a_i v_i - \sum_{j=1}^{m} b_j h_j - \sum_{i=1}^{n}\sum_{j=1}^{m} h_j w_{if} v_i \quad (6.1)$$

where a_i and b_i are terms for the corresponding nodes.

As a result, using the partition function Z, which defines the probability of distribution P (v,h) across visible unit H ($h_1,...h_n$), hidden unit V(v_1...v_m) in terms of the energy function:

$$P(v, h) = e^{-E(v, h)}/z \quad (6.2)$$

$$Z = \sum_{v}\sum_{h} e^{-E(v,h)} \quad (6.3)$$

Therefore, the single probability of activation P ($v_i = 1$|h) and P ($h_j = 1$|v) can be deduced as follows

$$P(v_i = 1|h) = sigm\left(a_i + \sum_{j=1}^{n} w_{ij} h_j\right) \quad (6.4)$$

$$P(h_j = 1|v) = sigm\left(b_j + \sum_{i=1}^{m} w_{ij} v_i\right) \quad (6.5)$$

where sigm denotes the logistic sigmoid function.

DBN approaches can be used to analyze noisy radiography images in real-world circumstances for a variety of medical applications, including disease diagnosis in the lungs, breasts, musculoskeletal system, and pediatric research [52]. Using DBN clinical data and multigenomic platform are the methodologies that may be used to collect both cross-modality and intramodality linkages in order to determine cancer subtypes [53].

By evaluating the ECG predictions findings in depth using the DBN model, we can quantify the relevance of each to the likelihood of CVD, as well as provide personalized treatment to decrease the risk of heart disease.

6.2.4   Deep Reinforcement Learning

A target learning tool in which a computer agent acts as a decision maker is known as RL, evaluating existing knowledge in its defined environment, formulating an action rule, and optimizing long-term rewards [62]. RL is a type of acquisition that straddles the supervised and unsupervised learning spectrum. Learning with a specific aim in mind is the basis for training. Interactions with the environment and observation of status changes result in learning. RL 25 has been used successfully in personalized medicine for the past 10 years. It was initially limited to the dynamic treatment regimes (DTRs), which are multistep clinical decision processes [55–57]. It is now commonly used to refer to a person. In recent years, it has been utilized to modify drug dosage or chemo/radiotherapy for a variety of cancer treatments [58, 59]. Doctors use a succession of medications to treat patients with severe illnesses like hypertension, HIV, anemia, and cancer to achieve the best potential result. Changes in drug dosage, treatment, also other factors may be involved in this process. Because of the variability of patient 35 responses to treatment and the possibility of side effects, determining the appropriate series of medications for a patient is difficult [60]. As a result, physicians should not rely solely on their clinical judgment [61].

The Markov decision process is the mathematical name for this sequential decision-making process (MDP). An MDP is a term used to describe a group of people that work together to achieve

(1) A state that depicts the current situation of the environment;
(2) At any given period, the agent took action that influenced the next phase;
(3) A transition probability that represents the environment where an agent interacts and gives an indication for reaching distinct following stages;
(4) In the case of a state-action pair, a reward function is observed feedback. The MDP's solution is an optimized set of rules.

The generic reinforcement problem is defined as a stochastic control process in discrete time in which agent connects with surrounding in the ways described below:

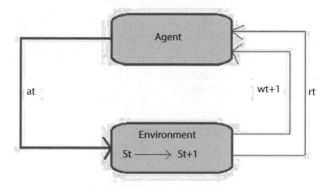

Figure 6.12 In reinforcement learning agent-environment interaction.

The agent starts by collecting early observations $0 \in S$, by collecting early observations $\omega 0 \in \Omega$. The agent must conduct any action $at \in A$ for each time point t [64].

There are three implications, as shown in Figure 6.12:

a. A reward is obtained by the agent $rt \in R$,
b. Transitions between states to $st+1 \in S$, and
c. An observation is obtained by the agent $\omega t+1 \in \Omega$.

Given the vast volume and granularity of recorded data in critical care, for new ICU patients, RL is well adapted to recommending progressive treatment, optimizing therapies, and enhancing outcomes. By automatically evaluating alternative therapeutic choices, RL can increase our understanding of existing clinical protocols. The RL agent analyses patient histories and generates a strategy, or tailored treatment approach, based on trial-and-error that maximizes the possibility of positive clinical outcomes (eg, survival). RL has been dubbed the AI clinician [65] since this computerized method attempts to emulate the cognitive process of a human therapist.

We can think of the state as a patient's well-being or condition. Patients' health may be affected by both static characteristics (eg, patient demographics such as age, ethnicity, gender, and comorbidity that existed previously) and longitudinal assessments (eg, the results of the laboratory tests, vital signs).

Treatment or intervention performed by physicians for patients is referred to as an action (eg, medication prescriptions and laboratory test requests). The transition probability is a forecast that measures the

Figure 6.13 Physician approach and intervention on patient.

likelihood of state transitions. We reward the RL agent if the patient's well-being improves in the new state; however, if the patient's condition worsens or remains steady, we penalize the agent.

Figure 6.13 shows how a physician would treat or intervene (act) on a patient based on his or her current status. Depending on the patient's present state and the activity performed on him, this action would transport him to the next state. While the physician is aware of the patient's next state, he or she must take action following that state. These state-action combinations will be applied throughout time, and the resulting history of state-action pairs might various universities in the patients' health and subsequent treatment decisions made by the clinicians.

The RL algorithm's main goal is to create an operator, which can increase the cumulative future payout from state-action pairings based on the patients' state-action histories. The agent can take immediate action whenever a new state is identified and can choose the operation with the best long-term outcome (eg, survival). It is conceivable for a well-trained RL agent to choose the best action given a patient's state, and we refer to this as a process that follows an optimal policy [66].

6.2.5   Generative Adversarial Network

Generative adversarial networks (GANs) are a recently discovered unsupervised and semisupervised learning technique. They achieve it by implicitly modeling high-dimensional data distributions. The authors of the study [67] recommended that learning be defined by training a pair of competing for neural networks.

GANs provide several advantages over previous techniques, such as the Boltzmann machine and autoencoders. GANs are gaining a lot of traction, and the demand to employ them in a variety of sectors is expanding. Image generation from data, high-resolution photos from low-resolution

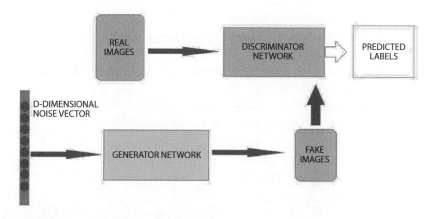

Figure 6.14 The general architecture of GAN.

photographs, medication prediction for a specific disease, detecting objects, and extracting photos with a specific pattern, facial attribute manipulation, anime character generation, image to image translation, and many other tasks have all been successfully implemented using GANs. In the actual world, GANs offer a widespread range of practical applications [68]. The architectural design of GAN is shown in Figure 6.14.

The GAN works on three principles: first, it learns the generative model, and then it generates data using some probabilistic representation. Second, model training can be carried out in any contentious situation. Finally, DL neural networks and AI algorithms were used to train the entire system [69].

GAN behaves similarly to neural networks in that it takes a training dataset as input and learns how to generate new data that is similar to the training set. GAN's picture data training, in particular, they produce different images with features that are akin to human behavior.

The following is a step-by-step explanation of GAN's functioning.

- The users created a generator using the genuine data distribution using a discriminative network generator.
- The system has been taught to enhance the network's liability rate and to deceive the discriminator network by creating candidates that have not been synthesized and are part of data circulation.
- A dataset serves as the discriminator's first training data.
- Datasets are supplied for training samples until accuracy is obtained.

- When the discriminator is deceived and fed random input, the generator is instructed to generate candidates.
- Finally, backpropagation has been used on both generators and discriminators, with the former producing superior images and the latter fading false ones.
- A deconvolutional neural network, which would be a generating channel, uses CNN as a discriminator.
- Mode collapse can occur when a GAN fails to generalize owing to missing entire modes in the input data.
- The researchers provide numerous remedies to a single problem.

Brain tumor images demonstrating that Vox2Vox, a 3D volume segmentation method based on GAN, works with multi-channel 3D MR pictures and finds that if the generator loss is weighed five times the discriminator loss, the best results are produced [71]. GAN is used in a biomedical practice to aid with unconstrained image-to-image information exchange and medical image identification [72]. It has also been proved how these systems helping in Alzheimer's disease (AD) diagnosis by recognizing brain PET images in three phases using artificial medical metaphors (normal, mild, and severe) [73]. Any system that uses a normalizing of spectrum stabilizes feature matching criterion for convergence optimization is considered to be designed on a 3D conditional GAN. Existing 2D conditional GANs and 3D functionality are outperformed by an autonomous conditional GAN, enabling for dynamic 3D deep learning-based neuroimaging synthesis [74].

6.2.6   Long Short-Term Memory Networks

In 1997, The first neural networks with long short-term memory networks (LSTMs) were introduced [75]. LSTM is a kind of RNN designed to address the problem of exploding gradients and vanishing [76, 77]. When the gradients are propagated over time during RNN training employing backpropagation through time (BPTT) [78], they tend to or become unstable and vanish. RNNs have a hard time learning long time dependencies because of this issue. The LSTM, which can react to both long- and short-term dependencies, address this issue (Figure 6.15).

Four layers make up an LSTM cell, commonly known as gates. The gates are described as

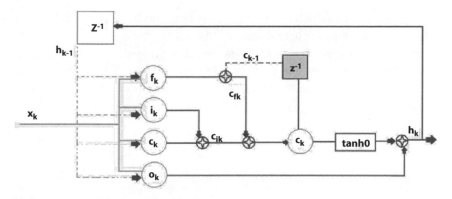

Figure 6.15 Long short-term memory networks (LSTMs).

1. The forget (f_k) gate
2. The input (i_k) gate
3. New cell state candidate gate (c_k)
4. The output gate (o_k)

input value weights (W), biases (b), and weights for the hidden state value (U) are all distinct to each gate.

The cell state acts as the cell's memory, maintaining information throughout time. The x_k vectors are used as inputs to the four gates.

where k is k= {1... τ}

An LSTM cell has the following criteria as me mentioned [79] below:

1. The forget layer decides how much evidence from the cell state should be kept and how much should be left behind. This gate has a sigmoid (σ) activation function.

$$f_k= \sigma(w_f x_k + u_f h_{k-1} + b_f) \tag{6.1}$$

w_f = Weight matrix input,
x_k = Vector input,
u_f = Previous weight matrix output,
h_{k-1} = Previous output,
b_f = Bias

The cell state (c_k) is multiplied element by element by the result of the forget layer (f_k).

$$c_{fk}=f_k{}^o c_{k-1} \tag{6.2}$$

This procedure, which occurs for the output and input gates, deletes the information about the current state of the cell.

The second process is to update the cell state (c_{ik}) with the new information. The new cell state (c_k) candidate gate suggests new information that could be placed in the cell's memory, using a activation function as (tanh) hyperbolic tangent.

$$c_k = \tanh(w_i x_k + u_i h_{k-1} + b_i) \qquad (6.3)$$

The input gate uses a sigmoid (σ) function.

$$I_k = \sigma(w_i x_k + u_i h_{k-1} + b_i) \qquad (6.4)$$

Following that, the state of the cell is determined:

$$c_{ik} = i_k \circ c_k \qquad (6.5)$$

2. The information from the two preceding steps is used to update the new cell state.

$$c_k = c_{fk} + c_{ik} \qquad (6.6)$$

3. The output of the output gate is then calculated using a sigmoid (σ) activation function.:

$$o_k = \sigma(w_o x_k + u_o h_{k-1} + b_o) \qquad (6.7)$$

Activation function is used to change the state of cell represented by ck and hyperbolic agent represented by tanh.

The activation function of hyperbolic tangent (tanh) modifies the cell state (ck). The output (hk) is then computed as follows:

$$h_k = o_k \circ \tanh(c_k) \qquad (6.8)$$

Medical plans with risk-adapted, personalized strategies might benefit from LSTM networks. LSTM networks were applied in personalized therapy to predict various disease states, including results from prostate cancer survival [80] and clinical diagnostic patterns with multivariate time series [81]. LSTM are an effective model for achieving the blood pressure management objectives associated with various blood pressure therapy regimens. Model performances have also been discovered to interact with well-known medical terminologies and ontologies [82].

The development of clinical decision support (CDS) and hypertension management in medical domain is possible with the use of LSTM, because it can remember information from the past over long periods and modulate the amount of information stored in the network overall.

LSTM models can help clinicians make better clinical decisions, reduce significant adverse outcomes, improve early detection and prevention of hypertension-related risks, boost patient awareness, and support lifestyle changes. LSTM models can help physicians make better clinical decisions, detection of hypertension-related risks, reduce significant adverse events and improve early prevention, support lifestyle changes and raise patient awareness [83].

Automated methods can be used in management of rapidly growing wide variety of biological texts in drug-drug interactions (DDI). In recent years, dependency-based deep neural network model have been suggested for extraction of DDI. These models involve three channels, named as, Depth (DFS) and breadth first search (BFS) channel and linear channel. Using this model, they introduced a remarkable state art productivity by an F-score; 72.0% on the 2013 corpus DDI Extraction [84].

Deep learning algorithms can also be applied on electronic healthcare records (EHRs) for prediction of stroke. Overall, there are two primary processes for predicting a stroke, i.e., EHRs are chosen based on risk indicators and the prediction procedure. In medical domain, algorithms with high performances are preferred and Long Short-Term Memory-Recurrent Neural Network (LSTM-RNN) is deemed confident to use with large datasets [85]. In order to learn temporal processing of data for stroke and glioma diagnosis in MRI, an LSTM-based learning model delivers better outcomes. MRI images are collected in a specific order, and LSTM is more effective at learning these patterns. As a result, the proposed method beat the LSTM network in terms of tumor detection [86]. The LSTM method will quickly map the sequence of sounds collected by the device, enabling normal and pathologic cardiac signals to be separated. Memory and gate circuits are the important parts of the deep learning process, enabling LSTM to comprehend the pattern from the sound data [87].

References

1. Shaban-Nejad, A., Michalowski, M., Buckeridge, D.L., Health intelligence: How artificial intelligence transforms population and personalized health. *npj Digital Med.*, 1, 53, 2018.

2. Schork, N.J., Artificial intelligence and personalized medicine, in: *Precision Medicine in Cancer Therapy*, pp. 265–283, Springer, Cham, 2019.

3. Rowe, J.P. and Lester, J.C., Artificial intelligence for personalized preventive adolescent healthcare. *J. Adolesc. Health*, 67, 2, S52–8, Aug 1, 2020.

4. Haleem, A., Javaid, M., Khan, I.H., Current status and applications of artificial intelligence (AI) in medical field: An overview. *Curr. Med. Res. Pract.*, 9, 6, 231–7, Nov 1, 2019.

5. Vogenberg, F.R., Barash, C.I., Pursel, M., Personalized medicine: Part 1: Evolution and development into theranostics. *Pharm. Ther.*, 35, 10, 560, Oct 2010.

6. Mathur, S. and Sutton, J., Personalized medicine could transform healthcare. *Biomed. Rep.*, 7, 1, 3–5, Jul 1 2017.

7. Mesko, B., Expert review of precision medicine and drug development, 2, 5, 2017.

8. Klang, E., Deep learning and medical imaging. *J. Thorac. Dis.*, 10, 3, 1325, Mar 2018.

9. Lee, J.G., Jun, S., Cho, Y.W., Lee, H., Kim, G.B., Seo, J.B., Kim, N., Deep learning in medical imaging: General overview. *Korean J. Radiol.*, 18, 4, 570, Jul 2017.

10. Bengio, Y. and LeCun, Y., Scaling learning algorithms towards AI, in: *Large-Scale Kernel Machines*, vol. 34, pp. 1–41, Aug 2007.

11. Papadakis, G.Z., Karantanas, A.H., Tsiknakis, M., Tsatsakis, A., Spandidos, D.A., Marias, K., Deep learning opens new horizons in personalized medicine. *Biomed. Rep.*, 10, 4, 215–7, Apr 1, 2019.

12. Parekh, V.S. and Jacobs, M.A., Deep learning and radiomics in precision medicine. *Expert Rev. Precis. Med. Drug Dev.*, 4, 2, 59–72, Mar 4 2019.

13. Hubel, D.H. and Wiesel, T.N., Receptive fields of single neurones in the cat's striate cortex. *J. Physiol.*, 148, 3, 574–591, 1959.

14. LeCun, Y. and Bengio, Y., Convolutional networks for images, speech, and time series, in: *The Handbook of Brain Theory and Neural Networks*, vol. 3361, 1995.

15. Li, Q., Cai, W., Wang, X., Zhou, Y., Feng, D.D., Chen, M., Medical image classification with convolutional neural network, in: *2014 13th International Conference on Control Automation Robotics & Vision (ICARCV)*, IEEE, pp. 844–848, Dec 10 2014.

16. Zhang, S., Bamakan, S.M., Qu, Q., Li, S., Learning for personalized medicine: A comprehensive review from a deep learning perspective. *IEEE Rev. Biomed. Eng.*, 12, 194–208, Aug 7 2018.

17. Lin, M., Chen, Q., Yan, S., Network in network, Dec 16 2013, arXiv preprint arXiv:1312.4400. 176, 178, 4 Mar 2014.

18. Yaseen, A.F. and Saud, L.J., A survey on the layers of convolutional neural networks. *Int. J. Comput. Sci. Mob. Computing*, 191–196, Dec 7 2018.

19. Yamashita, R., Nishio, M., Do, R.K., Togashi, K., Convolutional neural networks: An overview and application in radiology. *Insights Imaging*, 9, 4, 611–29, Aug 2018.

20. Tang, H., Ortis, A., Battiato, S., The impact of padding on image classification by using pre-trained convolutional neural networks, in: *International Conference on Image Analysis and Processing*, Springer, Cham, pp. 337–344, Sep 9 2019.

21. Wu, J., *Introduction to convolutional neural networks*, vol. 5, p. 23, National Key Lab for Novel Software Technology, Nanjing University, China, May 1 2017.

22. Lee, C.Y., Gallagher, P.W., Tu, Z., Generalizing pooling functions in convolutional neural networks: Mixed, gated, and tree. *Inartificial Intelligence and Statistics*, PMLR, pp. 464–472, May 2 2016.

23. Zhou, Y., Wang, H., Xu, F., Jin, Y.Q., Polarimetric SAR image classification using deep convolutional neural networks. *IEEE Geosci. Remote Sens. Lett.*, 13, 12, 1935–19, 2016.

24. Guo, Y., Liu, Y., Oerlemans, A., Wu, S., Lew, M.S., Author's accepted manuscript deep learning for visual understanding: A review to appear in. *Neurocomputing*, 2015.

25. Kokkinos, I., Paris, E.C., Group, G., Introduction to deep learning convolutional networks, Dropout, Maxout, vol. 1, pp. 1–70.

26. Russakovsky, O., Deng, J., Su, H., Krause, J., Satheesh, S., Ma, S., Huang, Z., Karpathy, A., Jan, C.V., Krause, J., Ma, S., in ImageNet large scale visual recognition challenge.

27. LeCun, Y., Bengio, Y., Hinton, G., Deep learning. *Nature*, 521, 7553, 436, 2015.

28. Madani, A., Arnaout, R., Mofrad, M., Arnaout, R., Fast and accurate classification of echocardiograms using deep learning, arXiv preprint arXiv:1706.08658. 27 Jun 2017.

29. Prasoon, A., Petersen, K., Igel, C., Lauze, F., Dam, E., Nielsen, M., Deep feature learning for knee cartilage segmentation using a triplanar convolutional neural network, in: *International Conference on Medical Image Computing and Computer-Assisted Intervention*, Springer, Berlin, Heidelberg, pp. 246–253, September 2013.

30. Gulshan, V., Peng, L., Coram, M., Stumpe, M.C., Wu, D., Narayanaswamy, A., Venugopalan, S., Widner, K., Madams, T., Cuadros, J., Kim, R., Development and validation of a deep learning algorithm for detection of diabetic retinopathy in retinal fundus photographs. *JAMA*, 316, 22, 2402–10, Dec 13 2016.

31. Spasov, S.E., Passamonti, L., Duggento, A., Liò, P., Toschi, N., A multi-modal convolutional neural network framework for the prediction of Alzheimer's disease, in: *2018 40th Annual International Conference of the IEEE Engineering in Medicine and Biology Society (EMBC)*, IEEE, pp. 1271–1274, Jul 18 2018.

32. Khamparia, A., Saini, G., Gupta, D., Khanna, A., Tiwari, S., de Albuquerque, V.H.C., Seasonal crops disease prediction and classification using deep convolutional encoder network. *Circuits Syst. Signal Process.*, 32, 1–19, 2019.

33. Liou, C.Y., Cheng, W.C., Liou, J.W., Liou, D.R., Autoencoder for words. *Neurocomputing*, 139, 84–96, 2014.

34. Guo, Y., Liu, Y., Oerlemans, A., Lao, S., Wu, S., Lew, M.S., Deep learning for visual understanding: A review. *Neurocomputing*, 187, 27–48, 2016.

35. Khamparia, A., Saini, G., Pandey, B., Tiwari, S., Gupta, D., Khanna, A., KDSAE: Chronic kidney disease classification with multimedia data learning using deep stacked autoencoder network. *Multimed. Tools Appl.*, 4, 1–6, Jun 2019.

36. Chen, M., Shi, X., Zhang, Y., Wu, D., Guizani, M., Deep features learning for medical image analysis with convolutional autoencoder neural network. *IEEE Trans. Big Data*, Jun 20 2017.

37. Kumar, D., Wong, A., Clausi, D.A., Lung nodule classification using deep features in ct images, in: *12th . IEEE Conference on Computer and Robot Vision (CRV)*, pp. 133– 138, 2015.

38. Kallenberg, M., Petersen, K., Nielsen, M., Ng, A.Y., Diao, P., Igel, C., Vachon, C.M., Holland, K., Winkel, R.R., Karssemeijer, N. *et al.*, Unsupervised deep learning applied to breast density segmentation and mammographic risk scoring. *IEEE Trans. Med. Imaging*, 35, 5, 1322–1331, 2016.

39. Park, C., Lee, S.B., An, K.H., Why organizations should develop its creative ability? Validation of creative thinking process for trading firms. *Information*, 20, 2, 789–818, 2017.

40. Liu, W., Wang, Z., Liu, X., Zeng, N., Liu, Y., Alsaadi, F.E., A survey of deep neural network architectures and their applications. *Neurocomputing*, 234, 11–26, 2017.

41. Bengio, Y., Learning deep architectures for AI. *Found. Trends Mach. Learn.*, 2, 1, 1–127, 2009.

42. Chen, W., Gou, S., Wang, X., Li, X., Jiao, L., Classification of PolSAR images using multilayer autoencoders and a self-paced learning approach. *Remote Sens.*, 10, 1, 2018.

43. Chaudhary, K., Poirion, O.B., Lu, L., Garmire, L.X., Deep learning–based multi-omics integration robustly predicts survival in liver cancer. *Clin. Cancer Res.*, 24, 6, 1248–59, Mar 15 2018.

44. Tan, J., Ung, M., Cheng, C., Greene, C.S., Unsupervised feature construction and knowledge extraction from genome-wide assays of breast cancer with denoising autoencoders, in: *Pacific Symposium on Biocomputing Co-Chairs*, pp. 132–143, 2014.

45. Zhang, L., Lv, C., Jin, Y., Cheng, G., Fu, Y., Yuan, D., Tao, Y., Guo, Y., Ni, X., Shi, T., Deep learning-based multi-omics data integration reveals two prognostic subtypes in high-risk neuroblastoma. *Front. Genet.*, 9, 477, Oct 18 2018.

46. Hinton, G.E., Osindero, S., The, Y.W., A fast learning algorithm for deep belief nets. *Neural Comput.*, 18, 7, 1527–54, Jul 2006.

47. Dahl, G.E., Yu, D., Deng, L., Acero, A., Context-dependent pre-trained deep neural networks for large-vocabulary speech recognition. *IEEE Trans. Audio Speech Lang. Process.*, 20, 1, 30–42, Apr 5 2011.

48. Mishra, C. and Gupta, D.L., Deep machine learning and neural networks: An overview. *Int. J. Hybrid Inf. Technol.*, 9, 11, 401–14, 2016.

49. Song, S.H. and Kim, D.K., Development of a stress classification model using deep belief networks for stress monitoring. *Healthc. Inform. Res.*, 23, 4, 285, Oct 2017.

50. Hinton, G.E., *A practical guide to training restricted Boltzmann machines*, University of Toronto, Toronto, 2010.

51. Nilashi, M., Ahmadi, H., Sheikhtaheri, A., Naemi, R., Alotaibi, R., Alarood, A.A., Munshi, A., Rashid, T.A., Zhao, J., Remote Tracking of Parkinson's Disease Progression Using Ensembles of Deep Belief Network and Self-Organizing Map. *Expert Syst. Appl.*, 159, 113562, Nov 30 2020.

52. Liang, M., Li, Z., Chen, T., Zeng, J., Integrative data analysis of multi-platform cancer data with a multimodal deep learning approach. *IEEE/ACM Trans. Computat. Biol. Bioinform.*, 12, 4, 928–37, Dec 5 2014.

53. Lu, P., Guo, S., Zhang, H., Li, Q., Wang, Y., Wang, Y., Qi, L., Research on improved depth belief network-based prediction of cardiovascular diseases. *J. Healthc. Eng.*, 2018, May 9 2018.

54. Dawson, R. and Lavori, P.W., Dynamic treatment regimes: Practical design considerations. *Clin. Trials*, 1, 1.

55. Chakraborty, B. and Moodie, E.E., *Statistical Methods for Dynamic Treatment Regimes*, Springer, New York, 2013, http://dx.doi.org/10.1007/978-1-4614-7428-9 1450.

56. Saarela, O. and Arjas, E., Optimal dynamic regimes: Presenting a case for predictive inference. 6, 2.

57. Jones, H., O'Grady, K., Tuten, M., Reinforcement-based treatment improves the maternal treatment and neonatal outcomes of pregnant patients en1465 rolled in comprehensive care treatment. *Am. J. Addict./American Acad. Psychiatrists Alcoholism Addict.*, 20, 196–204, 2011.

58. van der Laan, M.J. and Luedtke, A.R., in Super-learning of an optimal dynamic treatment rule, *Int J Biostat.* 2016 May 1; 12(1): 305–332.

59. Qian, M. and Murphy, S.A., Performance guarantees for individualized treatment rules. 39, 2.

60. Laber, E., Davidian, M., Zhang, B., Tsiatis, A.A., The National Center for Biotechnology Information advances science and health, Robust estimation of optimal dynamic treatment regimes for sequential treatment decisions. 100, 3.

61. Montague, P.R., Reinforcement learning: An introduction, by Sutton, R.S. and Barto, A.G, in: *Trends in Cognitive Sciences*, vol. 3, p. 360, Sep 1 1999.

62. Mnih, V., Kavukcuoglu, K., Silver, D., Graves, A., Antonoglou, I., Wierstra, D. *et al.*, Playing Atari with deep reinforcement learning, arXiv preprint 2013:-epub ahead of print, 1312.5602, 19 Dec 2013.

63. Barto, A.G. and R. S. Sutton Neuronlike adaptive elements that can solve difficult learning control problems. *IEEE Trans. Syst. Man Cybern.*, SMC-13, 5, 834–846, Sept.-Oct. 1983.

64. Bellman, R., *Dynamic Programming*, Information and Control, 1, 3, 228-239, September 1958, 1957b.

65. Komorowski, M., Celi, L.A., Badawi, O., Gordon, A.C., Faisal, A.A., The artificial intelligence clinician learns optimal treatment strategies for sepsis in intensive care. *Nat. Med.*, 24, 11, 1716–20, Nov 2018.

66. Liu, S., See, K.C., Ngiam, K.Y., Celi, L.A., Sun, X., Feng, M., Reinforcement learning for clinical decision support in critical care: Comprehensive review. *J. Med. Internet. Res.*, vol. 22, p. e18477, 10 Jun 2014, 2020.

67. Goodfellow, I.J., Pouget-Abadie, J., Mirza, M., Xu, B., Warde-Farley, D., Ozair, S., Courville, A., Bengio, Y., Generative adversarial networks, Jun 10 2014, arXiv preprint arXiv:1406.2661.

68. Alqahtani, H., Kavakli-Thorne, M., Kumar, G., Applications of generative adversarial networks (gans): An updated review. *Arch. Comput. Method. E.*, 19, 1–28, Dec 2019.

69. Liu, M.Y. and Tuzel, O., Coupled generative adversarial networks, Jun 24 2016, arXiv preprint arXiv:1606.07536.

70. Aggarwal, A., Mittal, M., Battineni, G., Generative adversarial network: An overview of theory and applications. *IJIM Data Insights*, 28, 100004, Jan 2021.

71. Cirillo, M.D., Abramian, D., Eklund, A., Vox2Vox: 3D-GAN for brain tumour segmentation, Mar 19 2020, arXiv preprint arXiv:2003.13653.

72. Shin, H.C., Tenenholtz, N.A., Rogers, J.K., Schwarz, C.G., Senjem, M.L., Gunter, J.L., Andriole, K.P., Michalski, M., Medical image synthesis for data augmentation and anonymization using generative adversarial networks, in: *International Workshop on Simulation and Synthesis in Medical Imaging*, Springer, Cham, pp. 1–11, Sep 16 2018.

73. Islam, J. and Zhang, Y., GAN-based synthetic brain PET image generation. *Brain Inform.*, 7, 1–2, Dec 2020.

74. Lan, H., Toga, A.W., Sepehrband, F., Alzheimer Disease Neuroimaging Initiative, *SC-GAN: 3D self-attention conditional GAN with spectral normalization for multi-modal neuroimaging synthesis*, bioRxiv, USC Stevens Neuroimaging and Informatics Institute, USC Keck School of Medicine, University of Southern California, Jan 1 2020.

75. Hochreiter, S. and Schmidhuber, J., Long short-term memory. *Neural Comput.*, 9, 8, 1735–80, Nov 15 1997.

76. Hochreiter, S., The vanishing gradient problem during learning recurrent neural nets and problem solutions. *Int. J. Uncertain. Fuzz.*, 6, 02, 107–16, Apr 1998.

77. Bengio, Y., Simard, P., Frasconi, P., Learning long-term dependencies with gradient descent is difficult. *IEEE Trans. Neural Netw.*, 5, 2, 1, 1994.

78. Werbos, P.J., Backpropagation through time: What it does and how to do it. *Proc. IEEE*, 78, 10, 1550–60, Oct 1990.

79. Carrillo-Moreno, J., Pérez-Gandía, C., Sendra-Arranz, R., García-Sáez, G., Hernando, M.E., Gutiérrez, Á., Long short-term memory neural network for glucose prediction. *Neural Comput. Appl.*, 33, 9, 4191–203, May 2021.

80. Nigam, M., Aschebrook-Kilfoy, B., Shikanov, S., Eggener, S., Increasing incidence of testicular cancer in the United States and Europe between 1992 and 2009. *World J. Urol.*, 33, 5, 623–31, May 2015.

81. Lipton, Z.C., Kale, D.C., Elkan, C., Wetzel, R., Learning to diagnose with LSTM recurrent neural networks, Nov 11 2015, arXiv preprint arXiv:1511.03677.

82. Choi, E., Schuetz, A., Stewart, W.F., Sun, J., Using recurrent neural network models for early detection of heart failure onset. *J. Am. Med. Inform. Assoc.*, 24, 2, 361–70, Mar 1 2017.

83. Ye, X., Zeng, Q.T., Facelli, J.C., Brixner, D.I., Conway, M., Bray, B.E., Predicting optimal hypertension treatment pathways using recurrent neural networks. *Int. J. Med. Inform.*, 139, 104122, Jul 1 2020.

84. Wang, W., Yang, X., Yang, C., Guo, X., Zhang, X., Wu, C., Dependency-based long short term memory network for drug-drug interaction extraction. *BMC Bioinform.*, 18, 16, 99–109, Dec 2017.

85. Goyal, M., Long short-term memory recurrent neural network for stroke prediction, in: *International Conference on Machine Learning and Data Mining in Pattern Recognition*, pp. 312–323, Springer, Cham, Jul 15 2018.

86. Amin, J., Sharif, M., Raza, M., Saba, T., Sial, R., Shad, S.A., Brain tumor detection: A long short-term memory (LSTM)-based learning model. *Neural Comput. Appl.*, 32, 20, 15965–73, Oct 2020.

87. Tobore, I., Li, J., Yuhang, L., Al-Handarish, Y., Kandwal, A., Nie, Z., Wang, L., Deep learning intervention for healthcare challenges: Some biomedical domain considerations. *JMIR mHealth uHealth*, 7, 8, e11966, 2019.

7

Tele-Health Monitoring Using Artificial Intelligence Deep Learning Framework

Swati Verma[1]*, Rishabha Malviya[1], Md Aftab Alam[1] and Bhuneshwar Dutta Tripathi[2]

[1]Department of Pharmacy, School of Medical and Allied Sciences, Galgotias University, Greater Noida, India
[2]Narayan Institute of Pharmacy, Sasaram, Bihar, India

Abstract

Telemedicine is a revolutionary method for optimizing long-distance healthcare access using telecommunications and modern information technology. This method facilitates the contact between patients and healthcare providers while ensuring convenience and dedication. It ensures that the classified information and protection is transmitted from one location to another. Patients in our country's remote regions seek care at public health centers (PHCs). PHCs are permitted in India with just one doctor. A single person cannot handle many people. Hence, it is suggested that an automatic T-health monitoring framework is needed to create. Actual treatment delivery invariably necessitates face-to-face professional contact, the frequency of which varies with conditions. In telehealth, information and communication technologies (ICTs) may be utilized to solve problems of necessity versus availability of healthcare resources. Artificial intelligence could help with this problem by designing algorithms that adapt the supply of care professionals with relevant clinical expertise to the demand for those skill sets in the direct vicinity. AI can mitigate those scenarios by providing mechanisms for human or simulated connections to arise, addressing issues, such as clinician availability and scheduling. AI will aid in the advancement of clinical process awareness. Deep learning has been suggested for the use of automated feature depiction to reduce the difficulty and improve output accuracy. The new period of healthcare is highly dependent on the use of artificial intelligence (AI), such as deep learning and computer science, which are beneficial in the area based on the available data,

Corresponding author: verma22swati@gmail.com

Rishabha Malviya, Gheorghita Ghinea, Rajesh Kumar Dhanaraj, Balamurugan Balusamy and Sonali Sundram (eds.) *Deep Learning for Targeted Treatments: Transformation in Healthcare*, (199–228) © 2022 Scrivener Publishing LLC

this chapter would assist researchers in developing innovative ideas for promoting healthcare in the deep learning framework.

Keywords: Tele-health monitoring, AI, deep learning, data mining, statistical data analysis

7.1   Introduction

Telehealth, often to known as telemedicine and is the use of therapeutic data to enhance a patient's health [1]. Funding and advancements in electronic medical records, restructuring of healthcare delivery, and evidence-based medicine may all help to expedite the integration of telehealth into healthcare [2]. Artificial intelligence and robotic systems may play a significant role in the use and delivery of telemedicine in this scenario.

The name "tele" is derived from the Greek word meaning "distance." Telemedicine then provides different online Medicare services, which often include a variety of telecommunication tools such as laptops, cellular computers, and remote video connections [3]. The traditional method of healthcare delivery was a physician's visit to the client's home, which has been replaced by outpatient physician health clinics. Increased interest and smartphone use have altered a broad variety of sectors, including transit and accounting. Bank employees, for instance, were substituted by the increasing use of automated teller machines in bank lobbies, which have now been completely supplanted using smartphone check deposits and online banking [4]. Similarly, advancements in telemedicine are poised to shift healthcare services away from the physician's office and directly to the patient's bedside.

Multiple tests, such as neurological, imaging, and specific targeting, may be used to diagnose in a systematic approach. In telemedicine, some of these investigations may be too expensive, while others may be unavailable, and to address this multidimensional issue, AI algorithms may serve as an ideal diagnostic tool for future endeavors [5].

7.2   Artificial Intelligence

To better monitor patients, the future of telemedicine, which is a division of computer science that facilitates smart systems (computers) to operate intelligently and deliberately in the same way that people do [6]. As telemedicine has become more common, medical studies have begun to enforce their capacity to manage and disrupt telemedicine data through the use of artificial intelligence in many fields and industries. To address

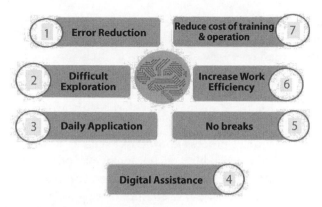

Figure 7.1 Advantages of artificial intelligence.

specific challenges, it has become critical to increase their expertise and develop processes to incorporate telemedicine. In this article, the adaptability of the two technologies is discussed to offer many development opportunities for example artificial intelligence, and telemedicine [7].

According to research, the application of AI in healthcare may result in cost savings of $150 billion [8] conducted by Collier *et al.* In analytical thinking and problem solving, AI outperforms humans and the various advantages of AI are indicated in Figure 7.1 [9]. During the epidemic, telemedicine offered important patient continuity routes in healthcare [10–12]. It also provides aids in the protection of healthcare facilities and the reduction of hazards to healthcare workers [13]. It also helps to reduce the cost burden on the community and healthcare services [14]. Teleconsultations enable physicians to assess patients, identify signs and symptoms of infection, and quickly record individuals who may be at a greater risk of disease [15]. Telemedicine solutions operate quickly, filling out insurance paperwork, allowing physicians to spend more time treating patients. A unique way of medical and healthcare is being provided by it as it also offers interaction with the patient [16].

7.2.1 Types of Artificial Intelligence

7.2.1.1 Machine Intelligence

Machine intelligence (MI), in which a computer performs tasks that are usually believed to require human intelligence, is a hot topic in all fields of science and engineering. Major scientific competitions [17] have shown that computers can achieve human-like picture recognition abilities. MI may help with speech recognition and language processing [18]. All of this evidence suggests that it should be used in healthcare.

We looked at current and future implementations of MI, but we have focused on future ways to address such issues in system deployment. It begins with a broad overview of MI in telehealth before moving on to particular scenarios in which MI may enhance health outcomes while also improving stakeholder experience and adoption. Finally, consider certain social and moral issues. More than any other healthcare service, increased innovation and discovery may complicate treatment [19]. MI will aid in the evolution of clinical process knowledge, such as how to capitalize on new therapeutic and procedural technologies via personalization based on patient associates or user outlines. Increased survival and serious disease treatment in different disease conditions require a multidisciplinary group-based approach to long-term care, ideally at home [20]. Due to a lack of integrated treatment and service development, healthcare equity and consistency are jeopardized. In many sectors of healthcare, seamless communication and connection are required: not all staff members can be present at all times, necessitating the use of teleassistance or remote therapy. Again, MI may assist in meeting demand through facilitating smart data information and collaborating it with an atmosphere in which physicians may link and save virtualized information about patients [21]. As a result, healthcare team members and health system institutions must make use of the increased capacity for health services offered by patient monitoring in the context of intelligence assessment and collaboration. In information and communication technology (ICT), television medical techniques for delivering orders for healthcare services have also been utilized [22].

In this case, MI may help develop algorithms that match healthcare professionals' existing professional competence to the need for such skills in the surrounding region. Similarly, telehealth faces a slew of organizational challenges, such as the loss of a telecommunication link or the scarcity of distant clinics [23]. It has the potential to minimize such problems by providing routes for human or virtual conversations, as well as resolving schedule and availability concerns for doctors (such as the time necessary to comprehend the patient's condition or history) (like the time needed to learn the issue or history of the patient) [24]. Artificial intelligence will aid in the development of clinical process awareness: To begin, consider if patient clusters or consumer profiles correlate with a new therapy and process advancements. To enhance the durability and treatment of chronic illnesses in situations involving several disorders, a multidisciplinary team approach to ongoing social care, particularly at home, is required [25]. Clinical decision making, electronic assistance, and smart support and diagnosis all improve as a consequence of this increasingly complicated, data-rich environment. Telemedicine has the potential to significantly increase the use of information and communication technology (ICT) for online patient diagnosis, control, and treatment [26]. Several framework constraints, however, have hindered the unique telehealth model, which has been extended to fully capitalize on the promise of providing a healthcare system over time at the national and regional levels. According to recent research on TV welfare programs, incorporating new technologies, such as remote healthcare requires organic development, adaptability, and collaboration from community service workers and management [27].

7.2.1.2   Types of Machine Intelligence

According to a survey conducted in around 63% of companies in various sectors, it was noted that the most widely used type of AI is widely used in ML. Deloitte, 2018 conducted a poll of 1,100 US managers whose companies had employed AI in 2018 [28]. Traditional machine learning is often used in healthcare to forecast precision medicine, which is the prediction of therapy procedures based upon treatment environment and patient attributes that are proven to be successful for a patient [29]. Neural network models (NNM) and intensive research are two of the most sophisticated kinds of machine learning with many layers of elements or components predicting conclusions. By increasing the development of cloud infrastructures and today's graphics processing units, tens of thousands of hidden characteristics in such models may be discovered. In medicine, deep learning is often used to detect potentially hazardous tumors in radiological scans [30].

7.2.1.2.1   Natural Language Processing
Since the 1950s, AI researchers have been trying to comprehend human language. Natural language processing (NLP) is divided into two categories: statistical NLP and semantic NLP. Statistical NLP is based on machine learning (particularly deep learning neural networks) and has recently improved recognition accuracy. It seeks a large "dataset" or language from which to learn. The creation, interpretation, and categorization of medical information and published literature are the most common uses of NLP in healthcare [31].

7.2.1.2.2   Rule-Based Expert Systems
In healthcare, for clinical decision support, rule-based expert systems have been widely employed. As a result, their expert programs need individual professionals and expert engineers to provide a broad variety of rules in

a specific field of expertise. They function well and are simple to comprehend, making them very useful today. Many electronic health record EHR firms have also developed a set of system standards [32].

7.2.2 Applications of Artificial Intelligence

Although the bulk of these technologies are directly relevant to the health sector, their specific processes and activities vary significantly [33]. The following list discusses several basic artificial intelligence discoveries with major health consequences as represented in Figure 7.2. Recently, artificial intelligence has been widely utilized in a variety of sectors. Technological advancement can be utilized in a variety of areas of healthcare, such as providing a way to assess patient evidence and identify the source of errors, as well as creating solutions by applying computerized information to medical equipment and resources based on existing results and procedures modifications [30]. The ability to identify patterns with ease and accuracy is a valuable tool in the pursuit of best practice and medical decision-making. Finding patterns in healthcare outputs may help with optimization and forecasting of impending issues. "Hospitals are now utilizing this kind of technology to help experts become even better and more effective," says Dr. Yulun Wang, CEO of in Touch Health in Santa Barbara [34]. Neural networks, deep learning, fluid logic, and others were being employed in tests conducted in references by implementing artificial intelligence.

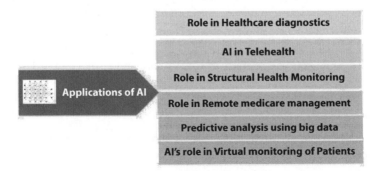

Figure 7.2 Applications of AI in various domains.

7.2.2.1   Role in Healthcare Diagnostics

There have been substantial examples of the potential usefulness of deep learning-based artificial intelligence methods [35] for application in medical diagnostics [36]. While ongoing fundamental research on these techniques is likely to lead to future improvements, we suggest a concurrent, concentrated effort on developing rigorous testing and validation methodologies for AI algorithms in clinical usage. This is required to detect and address any implementation issues as soon as possible [37] to build trust within the medical community and to give input to the basic research community on areas where further development is most needed [38].

7.2.2.2   AI in Telehealth

The new AI concept arose as a result of technical and data processing advances. More areas were used, including voice personal assistants (Alexa, Siri), navigation, photography, internet access, and free driving [39]. While it is now a cliché, Al can make telemedicine completely self-sufficient [40]. Historically, software algorithms were employed to create rules or patterns that experts and specialists might utilize in different circumstances. AI can analyze source data without the need for human intervention using techniques such as deep learning. Based on the circumstances, informing healthcare providers is acceptable [41].

7.2.2.3   Role in Structural Health Monitoring

Structural health monitoring (SHM) is a fast-expanding and creative academic area that is benefiting from advancements in artificial intelligence (AI). The primary aim of SHM is to correctly identify a structure's state and real behavior. It is also aimed at providing suitable tools to help and support the engaged human specialists in performing and monitoring their continuing duties. In terms of computational intelligence-related methods, the identification and quantification of structural defects is a major study area nowadays. A plethora of attempts have been made to enhance damage detection via the use of biologically inspired approaches: For a long time, neural networks have been employed to identify structural deterioration in different engineering constructions, such as bridges [42]. Another approach attempts to use evolutionary computing to provide an accurate estimate of structural damage using evolutionary biology based on mutation, inheritance, and natural selection processes [43].

An SHM system based on AI for monitoring safety-relevant engineering structures has been created. Several suitable AI techniques have been encapsulated and wrapped within the SHM system, utilizing so-called software agents for dependable and efficient monitoring [44]. In general, software agents are proactive software entities that communicate with other agents and, if required, people to get a perspective on their surroundings. The entire collection of interacting software agents is thus referred to as an agent system (the SHM system). A hybrid intelligence method may aid in the implementation of distributed agent-based structural health monitoring for particular job monitoring and automated data interrogation. The application of sophisticated artificial intelligence ideas and techniques to monitoring issues offers novel tools and methods for increasing the efficiency and accuracy of structural health monitoring [45].

7.2.2.4   Role in Remote Medicare Management

Remote health monitoring has been made feasible by the application of recent advances in the field of wireless and sensor technologies. Current medical sensors are being utilized to sense (heart rate, breathing rate, glucose, etc.) the major physiological parameters. Now the collected sensor data can then be transmitted to the central healthcare monitoring systems [46]. Data transmission over a network of central healthcare monitoring not only supports the continuous monitoring of patients but also enables, at the current cost, quick immediate response to the patient's conditions. For remote healthcare monitoring of patients, the reliability of data entered is of utmost importance. Accurate input data can only be produced by using accurate healthcare decisions. Noise and outliers can be present in sensor data, leading to false monitoring [47].

For healthcare monitoring, a preprocessing module has been developed by Nor Faizah *et al.* This preprocessing module is a central gateway that collects all the data provided by medical sensors and is a software-based application [48]. This application resides on the (Patient data application) PDA carried out by each patient. The data collected by monitoring patients based on the monitoring parameters is validated to ensure that the data comes from the right sensor source and is without noise [49]. Deep cleaning of sensor data is suggested as due to poor quality of the sensor and its surroundings, the data are more prone to errors, as well as through deep cleaning, the reliability of sensor data can be increased [50].

To monitor a range of applications, a flexible, robust healthcare monitoring framework has been designed. This monitoring framework is strong enough to support the implementation of monitoring applications. The characteristics of the model are:

1. The model is quite reliable as it minimizes false alerts and guarantees the correctness of the data.
2. The model provides interoperability, i.e., the user can operate it with different sensors.
3. It had an interface where different system settings could be configured to suit different monitoring applications.
4. The model framework has the property of scalability, i.e., it can be able to handle large numbers of users with broad data and mobility over large geographical distances.
5. It ensures that only authorized users have access to the system at appropriate levels.

Other Modules

1. The user interaction module enables caregivers to have access to the system. It not only ensures reliable and dynamic communication among users of the system but is also responsible for delivering alerts and notifications messages by using different communication channels like mail, cell phones, etc., to the patient [51].
2. The active engine module is used to monitor the input data from the preprocessing healthcare module. This healthcare module includes a dataset to store various active rules related to health data. Processing mechanisms are activated as soon as the active rule is triggered to evaluate the trigger and to determine whether an alert should be raised or not [52].
3. To further analyze the active engine algorithms, a preprocessing module is used. This module takes into account the data from various health parameters, including present and historical data, to identify the most appropriate response to the alert [53].

7.2.2.5   Predictive Analysis Using Big Data

Data sets are getting increasingly complicated and harder to evaluate using conventional statistical techniques in the face of greater quantities of diverse and useful data, like for data sequencing, cardiology imaging, and social media. AI techniques based on BIG Data methodologies for automated hypothesis creation have shown encouraging results in terms of analytic and diagnostic capacities [54]. Deep neural networks, for example, can analyze extremely complicated datasets of certain cardiovascular illnesses, extract important risk variables, and give an accurate prediction analysis. ML-based methods for patient monitoring may be utilized to forecast stroke risk and death risk linked to certain cardiac procedures.

7.2.2.6   AI's Role in Virtual Monitoring of Patients

Research carried out at the Pew research center in 2018 indicates the use of smartphones by 81% of US individuals. According to 2015 research, more than 62% of US individuals are using their smartphones for medical and health-related searches [55]. Furthermore, 2018 research on smartphone possession and the usage of health apps among US disadvantaged groups found the involvement of 39% of participants in mobile apps to monitor their health status [56]. Significant advances in the fields of AI, big data, and ML are occurring in this environment to meet the needs of consumers. At the community level, consumers' demands for healthcare technology are influenced by several variables, including demographics and population aging, rising healthcare expenditures, healthcare inequalities, and the growing prevalence of numerous chronic illnesses [57]. Management entails regular monitoring of diet and physical exercise, as well as drug management. Also, there is growing concern regarding labor shortages, such as those witnessed in the healthcare system of the United States [58]. As a result, advanced health monitoring systems can be grown using AI that will assist people in coping with increasing healthcare expenses.

The technologies of interest are primarily concerned with assisting in the stabilization of patients, reducing the duration and cost of hospitalization, conducting therapy and diagnostics under the supervision of a physician, and monitoring the healing process when patients are not in the hospital. Furthermore, there seems to be evidence that poor individuals have worse health, less access to healthcare, and are more likely to be careless about their health, as well as living in hazardous environments [57].

7.2.2.7   Functions of Devices

The utilization and incorporation of artificial intelligence and the IoT for location tracking, social media, mobile applications, and sensors may be utilized for the treatment, early diagnosis, and improved self-management of chronic illness patients [59]. Sensing (i.e., both active and passive) and evaluation based on functions are the two major types of remote healthcare sensing technologies.

Active sensing includes the process of patient monitoring, whereas passive sensing simply gathers the observable data received. Thus, active sensing enables a subjective evaluation of the patient's health status by utilizing questionnaires to characterize their experience at specified time intervals. The patient's reported data are just as essential as the measured data, and it must be included in the models developed for AI so that the appropriate evaluation of the findings can be performed. Passive and active sensing are both included in the functional evaluation. It involves the subjective reporting of the patient with objective data collection using the device's sensor [60].

Smartphones are the most often used passive sensing devices, in which the built-in sensor allows quantum mechanics-based capabilities, for instance. To take a count of the number of steps, a person takes every day as well as geographic localization. An accelerometer, gyroscope, and magnetometer are examples of such smart devices [61]. These devices may also give data about the partial pressure of air, ambient lighting, and speech. The transformation of the smartphone into a fall detector, a sensor based on heart rate, and a spirometer are the innovative applications of these sensors, enabled by the built-in camera [62].

Wrist sensors are examples of wearable sensors that are becoming more popular and include many of the same sensors as those used in smartphones. These sensors can detect motion, such as that caused by smoking or in the case of seizures [63]. According to a US survey in 2017, 17% of US people are using wearable gadgets, such as smart fitness bands or smartwatches [64]. This offers cardiac rhythm parameter measurements [65]. Clinicians also employ wearable sensors. Muscular activity and posture [66] can be detected by wearable patches. To evaluate pulmonary function [67], radiofrequency sensors can be used. Apart from all this, these can be utilized to evaluate the healing phase of various neurological diseases [68]. There is an emerging technique for medication adherence that comprises a tiny sensor implanted on a tablet that sends signals to a wearable patch as it reaches the stomach [69]. To evaluate functional performance, patients must complete standard activities utilizing mobile healthcare technologies. The majority of smartphone applications include assessing the cognitive function of brain training apps that rely on intellectual stimulation. Mental health can be improved via various mental health solutions available, which are proven to have a substantial neurological effect. The mental health of users can be improved by increasing cognitive skills, such as memory and response speed through mobile apps [70]. The use of AI in applications may offer consumers a user-friendly monitoring interface for evaluating their cognitive processes over time.

7.2.2.8   Clinical Outcomes Through Remote Patient Monitoring

Based on clinical research and pilot projects, remote patient monitoring has a wide range of uses and has been shown to enhance clinical results. Simultaneously, many studies show minimal improvements in clinical outcomes, even for the same kind of monitoring instrument or illness. The effectiveness of PMS is difficult to generalize due to the broad variety of applications and disease indications. The bulk of remote patient monitoring systems are focused on a specific technology and a specific illness, showing the market's segmentation [71]. Adherence refers to the monitoring of a patient's dosage regime, i.e., monitoring closely how a patient adheres to medical instructions and medications. It involves medication adherence, as well as the use of other suggested treatment techniques by the patient. Until recently, the discussions about clinical outcomes were based on a reduction in the rate of mortality, morbidity, and biomarkers. The proper implementation of adherence can be ensured via adherence through proper treatment to improve health outcomes [72]. Managing adherence using telemetry systems, such as those used by healthcare providers, has developed in recent years and is now the most prominent application for new web services. Hamie *et al.* discovered that 56% of the trials had a meaningful impact on clinical outcomes after gathering adherence and patient outcome data. Adherence can be increased using different methods that may vary, from text messaging reminders to sensor-based surveillance systems with integrated medical support [73].

Active patient participation is important for enhancing relationships with clients, which results in improving treatment results, as well as adherence with the patients. Many monitoring systems face connection issues due to latency, data loss, and network interactions, resulting in a poor user experience. Accurate data can be provided via body monitoring systems [74]. Clinicians who use the monitoring system developed and tested solely under controlled conditions may be worried about the precision and trustworthiness of clinical decision support as it is based on simulations. Users are often misled into believing that they are metadata catchers, having extremely restricted exposure to the data gathered, which limits their desirability and adoption [75] and, as a result, the inputs from the users and engagement are often lacking. These assessment tools can be upgraded to acquire traction by aiming at the resulting solution and guaranteeing that the product delivers value to the consumer. Inside the healthcare industry, the acceptability and adoption of any product are highly reliant on consumer knowledge and also on approval both from the client and the therapist.

7.2.2.9   Clinical Decision Support

Patients suffering from chronic illnesses, such as chronic obstructive pulmonary disease (COPD), can be monitored via clinical decision support system telemonitoring (CDSS). This CDSS system has been created and built-in in recent years for home telemonitoring of patients [76]. The primary goal of the CDSS is to manage the health of patients via daily monitoring, so that any recurrence or worsening of the illness may be detected and avoided at the earliest [77]. It is based on patient-specific data, computational biological knowledge, and AI models that utilize this knowledge and data to produce relevant information for doctors and provide aid in decision making [78]. The use of AI to analyze huge amounts of data enables clinical decision support systems to function on many levels. ML techniques and neural networks are intended to handle large data sets by using established evaluation metrics [79]. For instance, the neural networks built into a CDSS may utilize the hospital's electrical data to forecast backup admissions on several levels. This would enable the hospital to implement improved decision-making methods for emergency room administration, enhance emergency treatment for patients, and reduce associated costs. Furthermore, these technologies may enhance the patient's quality of life by enabling the app or device to monitor their health status and predict future exacerbations [77].

7.2.3   Utilization of Artificial Intelligence in Telemedicine

The various techniques involved in the utilization of telemedicine's are represented in Figure 7.3.

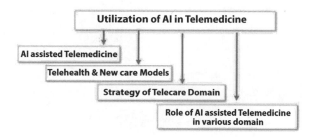

Figure 7.3 Utilization of AI in telemedicine.

7.2.3.1   Artificial Intelligence–Assisted Telemedicine

Any of these studies may be inaccessible in a telemedicine environment, while others may be cheap. Advanced artificial intelligence (AI) data-based algorithms may provide a solution to this challenging multivariate issue by utilizing deep learning on massive data sources in populations with impairments [80, 81]. This approach, which focuses on generalizing prediction for various medical test populations, may acquire information from data without previous statistical modeling, yielding more objective results [82]. Analytical statistical methods, as opposed to traditional statistical hypotheses under single telemedicine constraints, may investigate synergistic variable correlations and needless feature substitution for even more effective diagnosis [83]. Electronic devices are constantly developing, and recent digital developments seem to be essential for achieving information sharing between healthcare professionals and patients [84].

In human subconscious thinking processes such as intuition, experience, contextual judgment, and analysis of ambiguous or qualitative data, the fact that certain problems and therapeutical advice, particularly in new contexts or times, are thought to pose significant challenges for AI in the healthcare system, is thought to pose significant challenges for AI. Telemedicine will reduce the financial burden associated with social and healthcare [85]. Quarantined physicians may provide such services directly to patients at medical facilities through telecommunications, enabling other doctors to provide emergency care to vulnerable patients. Doctors can evaluate patients swiftly, categorize disease signs, and follow patients who are at high risk of illness [86]. The various benefits of using telemedicines are represented in Figure 7.4.

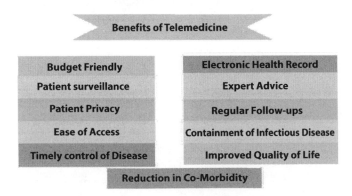

Figure 7.4 Benefits of using telemedicine.

7.2.3.2 Telehealth and New Care Models

In general, the incidence of chronic diseases has increased significantly. This, coupled with an aging population suffering from a variety of morbidities, renders existing healthcare systems inequitable and unsustainable. Telemedicine offers great possibilities to utilize information and communication technology (ICT) effectively for online patient diagnosis, monitoring, and treatment delivery [87]. Nonetheless, numerous framework obstacles have prevented transformative TV models established at the national or regional level from fully realizing the potential of long-distance healthcare. According to recent telehealth method evaluations, the adoption of a complex innovation such as virtual services requires the creation of an organic infrastructure that is adaptive to local health and social care systems [88]. Patient surveillance capabilities that have been enhanced in healthcare must therefore be utilized by representatives of healthcare teams and health service organizations in an intelligence processing and cooperation environment [89].

7.2.3.2.1 Healthcare Services Consequences

Such studies show that, although such work automation is possible, several other external factors, such as automation costs, labor market growth, cost and inflation, and regulatory and social acceptance, are minor [90]. These factors may decrease potential job losses to 5% or less. To the best of our knowledge, no medical personnel has been lost due to AI. So far, the market for AI adoption has been limited, and the obstacles faced in integrating electronic health record (EHR) systems and AI into healthcare processes have had a little positive effect on employment. Controlling positions with direct patient contact, such as multimedia information, radiography, and pathology, is almost ideal [91].

Radiologists are the next in line to read and decode videos. AI radiology systems, like other AI systems, perform individual tasks. Computed tomography for detection of nodules in the chest or through MRI, imaging of hemorrhage in the brain is some of the picture classification tasks for particular laboratories that have been developed through deep education packages. As a consequence, hundreds of these limited-sensing activities must be carried out to recognize all future patient discoveries in their entirety [92].

Second, AI-based imaging and clinical processes are not yet widely available. Many imaging and deep learning algorithm suppliers are interested in the risk of harm, the potential for cancer, or the presence of a nutrient.

Third, advanced picture processing algorithms need "labeled evidence," or millions of photos of individuals with cancer, broken bones, or other illnesses. As a consequence, there is no catalog of radiological photographs that are either titled or nameless. To finish digital image research, significant changes in medical policy and health insurance are needed [91].

7.2.3.3   Strategy of Telecare Domain

7.2.3.3.1   E-health, Intelligence, and New Care Models

The global burden of chronic diseases has increased significantly, which puts an extra burden on healthcare models, especially when combined with an aging population, making them unsustainable and overstressed. Telehealth provides potential options for maximizing the use of ICT in the monitoring, diagnosis, and delivery of healthcare, to reduce the burden on healthcare models. Nonetheless, several system-level constraints have stymied innovative telehealth approaches which have been upgraded at various levels, i.e., regional or national, in a way that increases the promise of delivering care at a distance [93]. A logical step from human-to-human engagement in telehealth is the introduction of computer-based production and comprehension to allow contact between computers and humans. Many additional possibilities exist throughout the care spectrum for automated conversational interactions to enhance and, in some instances, replace human care duties [94]. Patient monitoring's enhanced healthcare skills must thus be used in an information analysis atmosphere and should get cooperation from the team members and the health-related agencies.

These may include

1. responding to health-related questions and providing targeted health information and education;
2. medication, diet, and exercise reminders and encouraging messages;
3. serving as a go-between for several care providers or telecommunications companies;
4. based on personal monitoring data, do routine condition inspections and health maintenance;
5. offering a customized approach for addressing both public engagement and communal quarantine.

Visual or auditory communication is frequently sufficient for basic activities that need nothing but a message or sentence and may be used to communicate a minimum of sophisticated reaction. Some of these technologies include speech-to-text conversion tools and chatbots that can accept audio or written inputs and outputs [95].

Multimodal techniques offering circumstantial consciousness can be utilized to integrate some of the emotional behavioral elements, to allow genuine conversational interaction. While interacting with intellectually disabled people [96], boosting access to online medical health records [97], and offering avatar-based client operatives for senior citizens are some of the examples of Medicare applications where computer systems could provide long-term supplementation or alternatives to traditional clinical care modeling techniques. Such instances depend on a much more sophisticated conversational aim and knowledge base, and the degree of AI complexity grows as the AI agent learns more via data gathering. A customized model based on the patient's past health records can be used while dealing with problems related to patients' previous interactions. A model based on a patient's history could prove beneficial. AI systems for telemonitoring rely on and can extend the capabilities of existing healthcare ICT components. Telemonitoring entrails acquisition of data by using an appropriate sensor, the transmission of data from the patient to the clinician, integration of data, as well as description of the patient's data describing the patient's state. An escalation in the patient's care can be done employing an appropriate action or response taken with associated decision support, either the storage of data [98]. They consistently carry out their orders in a logical manner, being dependent on internal logic tempered by some evidence-based statistics collected from large-scale datasets by machine learning techniques [99]. Tele-health monitoring is now being used to study the remote monitoring of patients suffering from severe diseases like Congestive Heart Failure, Chronic obstructive Pulmonary disorder [100], and Diabetes Mellitus [101]. AI techniques can be used in the case of COPD to manage and monitor the disease state.

7.2.3.3.2   Near-Field Communication in Telehealth

NFCs are also used in contemporary social media applications and medical devices to help with patient self-monitoring processes. NFC is a high-speed networking technology that allows data to be transferred in millimeters between two NFC devices (touching) [102]. Appropriate software, as well as, in the case of NFC, a smartphone, are necessary components of a smart TV device to monitor the patient's detailed treatment data and medication adherence [103]. Passive NFC tags collect and categorize data for objects, such as pharmaceutical packaging [104]. NFC is a critical Internet of Things technology that enables many contacts [105].

7.2.3.4   Role of AI-Assisted Telemedicine in Various Domains

Various roles of AI-assisted telemedicines in healthcare can be presented as Figure 7.5.

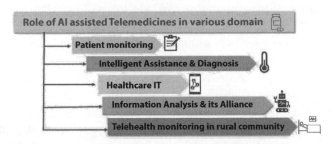

Figure 7.5 Role of AI-assisted telemedicine in various domain.

7.2.3.4.1   Patient Monitoring

One of the earliest and widely used applications of telemedicine is inpatient monitoring. Patient monitoring allows for the most efficient and pocket-friendly regular doctor-to-patient visits [106]. Through this, the patient's health information can be obtained regularly, which may be recorded through face-to-face video conferencing and integrated medical equipment. This design is meant to make patient monitoring accessible, easy, and cost-effective [107]. The most recent prototypes of telecommunication robots have been developed to move around halls and rooms autonomously, utilizing a remote control and a web interface that connects the user to the robot through broadband [108]. Artificial intelligence and visual technologies to detect and navigate barriers have been combined to develop the new design.

7.2.3.4.2   Intelligent Assistance and Diagnosis

The incorporation of assistance mechanic modules, as well as the utilization of medical information and results for smart diagnosis, is another significant advancement in robotic technology. Both characteristics are designed to assist patients physically or in the assessment of early diagnostic examinations by contemporary health infrastructure [109]. These tools may function via the pre-programmed use of neural networks and machine learning. The method's knowledge and the proof will then be used to continuously enhance the technology. Intelligent diagnosis apps for telehealth self-diagnostic technology are now being introduced in many types of gadgets and smartphones [110].

7.2.3.4.3   Healthcare IT

Self-diagnosis technology and human registration have made the process of collection, preservation, and screening of massive amounts of healthcare data quite tedious. Furthermore, the goal of tele sheet connection is to create a centralized record system for all collaborating institutions. Medical practitioners and patients from all around the globe must be connected [111]. The Trend technique for preserving and correctly recovering electronic health information is based on big data analytics (BDA) and the principles of neural networks. The trend toward the application of artificial intelligence (AI) in systemic-based data recovery and its interpretation addresses problems encountered in medical processes as well.

7.2.3.4.4   Information Analysis and its Alliance

The application of telemedicine is in medical research, as well as informal training or consultation. Technology can be used to link medical professionals from different nations, promoting cooperation not only on views and diagnostic information but also on medical data. This will change pharmaceutical research in terms of using data analytics based on big data to consolidate the findings of clinical tests, as well as using hereditary neural networks for analyzing data and recognizing data patterns [112]. This section of the study discusses developments in the application of artificial intelligence to analyze clinical data to evaluate the value of pharmaceutical goods and treatment results. As healthcare information is not only saved and readily accessed but also analyzed, this trend will heavily rely on the pattern recognition feature of artificial intelligence. Because the method is based only on the findings, the use of computer analysis can eliminate prejudice and views about the results.

7.2.3.4.5   Telehealth Monitoring in Rural Community

Telehealth is redefining how medical services and therapeutic training are delivered. Reliable human service is unavailable in many provincial groupings, isolated locations, or postcatastrophe situations. In such locations or situations, telemedicine may be linked to providing crisis social insurance. Patients may get clinical social insurance without having to go to a treatment center [113]. Telemedicine has promoted patient monitoring through PC, tablet, or phone innovation, resulting in fewer outpatient visits. Specialists may now monitor treatment or supervise medication supervision. Furthermore, patients who are confined to their homes may seek medical attention without having to go to a facility in an emergency vehicle. This framework also promotes health education since, at the fundamental level, medical service experts may see the working methodology of social insurance specialists in their specific areas and the professionals can administer it. Telemedicine eliminates the possibility of patients and social insurance specialists contracting contagious diseases [114].

In India, the country still houses 68% of the population. The rustic social insurance framework is afflicted by a few problems. For example, a severe shortage of medical professionals, a scarcity of critical therapeutic supplies, and a lack of nonrestorative foundations. For example, electricity, clean water, a lack of planning, and money. The rural/urban social insurance disparity is mirrored in medical care outcomes, with IMR in urban populations at 27 and 44 in provincial populations [115]. Similarly, the urban populace has a TFR of 1.8, whereas the national population has a TFR of 2.6. The Internet of Things (IoT) is a system of physical goods or "things" outfitted with electronic gadgets, programming innovations, sensors, and system availability that encourages these objects to collect and exchange data for the benefit of various administrators [116, 117].

7.3   AI-Enabled Telehealth: Social and Ethical Considerations

1. Individuals should come forward-AI technology will modify the perspective about how they interact with different healthcare agents. After all, healthcare is all about individuals. We must guarantee that the drive of these tools is on objectives like therapeutic communication and a reduction in provider fatigue. Healthcare is, after all, about people [118].
2. Ensure equity: Although AI and automation might increase the availability and accessibility of goods, they may also expand the gulf between the rich and powerful and the poor and weak [119]. It must be ensured that individuals living in remote and rural areas will benefit from technology-enabled healthcare delivery services, as they are the ones who require them the most, as well as those in underdeveloped countries.
3. Artificial Intelligence is just a weapon: HIT adoption in medical science has been characterized as a voyage instead of an endpoint [120], and so as medical digitalization accelerates, it becomes clearer than before. To be a member of a learning healthcare system [121], we must embrace the idea

of AI while being flexible in the design and implementation of Artificial Intelligence-enabled solutions.

Keeping an eye on technology: A few people are adept at using technology, while others are not, as the world's population is varied. People who are anticipated to gain the most from improvements in telehealth, such as the elderly and the terminally sick, may be restricted by the application of AI technology. There must be a guarantee that the application of AI will not widen the arithmetical gap, but rather improve our capacity to offer high-quality patient-centered care to people.

7.4   Conclusion

AI-enabled telehealth contributes to quality management and the enhancement of the usual approach, as well as the exploration of novel care models. The use of telemedicine is one example of AI's involvement in distant healthcare delivery. More development of integrated science and mathematical modeling will be required for wider use. Most AI methods require a significant learning phase that can only be attained over a lengthy period and therefore needs to be exposed to ongoing testing and adjustment to enhance the human-AI interface. As AI-enabled telemedicine becomes more prevalent, some important social and ethical concerns must also be addressed. AI systems, unlike humans, rarely feel unmotivated. Nevertheless, the lack of emotion leads to an incapability to assess moral virtue or evil, with not enough awareness of the consequences. More and more individuals are being affected by serious illnesses that need lifestyle and pharmacological control, resulting in a greater interest in telemetry systems both for patients and healthcare professionals that may aid in the management of the disease. These screening platforms enable consumers to access medical information at their leisure or the store, or they can communicate it to medical practitioners for therapeutic help. In this chapter, we have discussed a few notable applications of remote patient monitoring, including Glucose Monitoring (for diabetes), ECG monitoring (for heart failure), and movement tracking for Parkinson's disease, but there are plenty more applications that are already in use. Despite its enormous potential, there is a paucity of data demonstrating improved health outcomes and cost savings from remote patient monitoring therapies. As a consequence of the social movement toward web-based services, the widespread demand for automated telemedicine may be seen in the usage rates for online self-diagnosis.

This chapter presents applications of AI techniques derived from traditional AI and also from cyber intelligence to technical challenges in structural health monitoring. It has been shown that a hybrid intelligence method may aid in the implementation of a distributed advisor systemic health monitoring for a particular job monitoring. The application of sophisticated artificial intelligence ideas and techniques to monitoring issues offers novel tools and methods for increasing the efficiency and accuracy of structural health monitoring. Recent interest in telemedicine programs has also been fueled by the possibility of expanding access to underserved areas while simultaneously lowering risk and delivering continuous auditing options for chronic health conditions, thus complementing traditional FTF diagnosis by broadening the purview of medical institutions.

References

1. *Transforming and scaling up health professionals' education and training*, World Health Organization, Geneva, 2013, Available at: https://www.who. int/hrh/resources/transf_scaling_hpet/en/ (accessed September 14, 2020).
2. Tuckson, R.V., Edmunds, M., Hodgkins, M.L., Telehealth. *N. Engl. J. Med.*, 377, 1585–92, 2017. http://dx.doi.org/10.1056/NEJMsr1503323.
3. Kuziemsky, C., Maeder, A.J., John, O., *et al.*, *Role of artificial intelligence within the telehealth domain official 2019 yearbook contribution by the members of IMIA telehealth working group*, Yearbook of Medical Informatics, 28(1), 35–40, 2019. http://dx.doi.org/10.1055/s-0039-1677897.
4. Fogel, A.L. and Kvedar, J.C., Artificial intelligence powers digital medicine. *NPJ Digit. Med.*, 1, 1, 5, 2018.
5. Huys, Q.J.M., Maia, T.V., Frank, M.J., Computational psychiatry as a bridge from neuroscience to clinical applications. *Nat. Neurosci.*, 19, 404–13, 2016.
6. Katharaki, M., A data envelopment analysis model for measuring the efficiency impact of telemedicine on greek obstetric and gynaecology services: Effects on individual. *J. Inf. Technol. Healthcare*, 4, 6, 353–401, 2006. https://www.academia.edu/432787/A_Data_Envelopment_Analysis_Model_for_Measuring_the_Efficiency_Impact_of_Telemedicine_on_Greek_Obstetric_and_Gynaecology_Services_Effects_on_Individual_.
7. Fragella, D., Artificial intelligence in telemedicine and telehealth-4 current applications – 4 current applications, in: *Business Intelligence and Analytics*, Emerj, Boston, 2019.
8. Accenture, Why artificial intelligence is the future of growth, 2020. Available online at: https://www.accenture.com/us-en/insight-artificial-intelligence-future-growth (accessed September 19, 2020).

9. Huang, M.H. and Rust, R.T., Artificial intelligence in service. *J. Serv. Res.*, 21, 155–72, 2018. https://doi.org/10.1177/1094670517752459.

10. Hollander, J.E. and Carr, B.G., Virtually perfect? Telemedicine for Covid-19. *N. Engl. J. Med.*, 382, 1679–81, 2020. https://doi.org/10.1056/NEJMp2003539.

11. Bhaskar, S., Bradley, S., Chattu, B.K. *et al.*, Telemedicine as the new outpa-tient clinic gone digital:position paper from the pandemic health system Resilience PROGRAM (REPROGRAM) international consortium (Part 2). *Front. Public Health*, 8, 410, 2020. https://doi.org/10.3389/fpubh.2020.00410.

12. Bhaskar, S., Bradley, S., Chattu, V.K. *et al.*, Telemedicine across the globe-position paper from the COVID-19 pandemic health system resilience PROGRAM (REPROGRAM) international consortium (Part 1). *Front. Public Health*, 8, 556720, 2020. https://doi.org/10.3389/fpubh.2020.556720.

13. Bhaskar, S., Rastogi, A., Chattu, V.K. *et al.*, Chronic neurology in COVID-19 era: Clinical considerations and recommendations from the REPROGRAM consortium. *Front. Neurosci.*, 11, 664, 2020. https://doi.org/10.3389/fneur.2020.00664.

14. Bhaskar, S., Rastogi, A., Chattu, V.K. *et al.*, Key strategies for clinical man-agement and improvement of healthcare services for cardiovascular disease and diabetes patients in the coronavirus (COVID-19) settings: Recommen-dations from the REPROGRAM consortium. *Front. Cardiovasc. Med.*, 7, 112, 2020. https://doi.org/10.3389/fcvm.2020.00112.

15. Bhaskar, S., Sharma, D., Walker, A.H. *et al.*, Acute neurological care in the COVID-19 era: The pandemic health system Resilience PROGRAM (REPROGRAM) consortium pathway. *Front. Neurosci.*, 11, 579, 2020. https://doi.org/10.3389/fneur.2020.00579.

16. Sinha, S., Kern, L.M., Gingras, L.F. *et al.*, Implementation of video vis-its during COVID-19: Lessons learned from a primary care practice in New York City. *Front. Public Health*, 8, 514, 2020. https://doi.org/10.3389/fpubh.2020.00514

17. Shailaja, K., Seetharamulu, B., Jabbar, M.A. Machine learning in Healthcare: A Review, Proceedings of the Second Intern. Conf. on Elect., Commu. and Aerospace Tech (ICECA 2018).; Coimbatore, India, IEEE Xplore ISBN: 978-1-5386-0965-1910-914, 2018. https://ieeexplore.ieee.org/abstract/document/8474918?casa_token=l5VgUYJeMB8AAAAA:HoLrw4bFm-BLzMMgLKVwb0hxvNPd5ieZu5HRi9qQNPkXGgCiVmvMgbvhStZ4m-BigoJef5UI4I

18. The Great A.I. Awakening - The New York Times, nytimes.com.

19. The Impact of Social and Cultural Environment on Health, in: *Genes, Behavior, and the Social Environment*, NCBI Bookshelf, nih.gov. National Academics Press (US), Washington (DC), 2, 2006.

20. Dwivedi, Y.K., Hughes, L., Ismagilova, E. *et al.*, Artificial Intelligence (AI): Multidisciplinary perspectives on emerging challenges, opportunities, and agenda for research, practice and policy. *Int. J. Inf. Manage.*, 1–47, 2019.

21. Posts - Page 3 of 59 - AI Global Media Ltd.

22. Adly, A.S., Approaches based on artificial intelligence and the internet of intelligent things to prevent the spread of COVID-19: Scoping Review. *J. Med. Internet Res.*, 22, 8, 1–15, 2020. https://doi.org/10.2196/19104.

23. Long, E., Lin, H., Liu, Z. *et al.*, An artificial intelligence platform for the multihospital collaborative management of congenital cataracts. *Nat. Biomed. Eng.*, 1, 2, 0024, 2017. https://doi.org/10.1038/s41551-016-0024].

24. Yu, K., Beam, A.L., Kohane, I.S., Artificial intelligence in healthcare. *Nat. Biomed. Eng.*, 2, 10, 719–731, Oct 2018. https://doi.org/10.1038/s41551-018-0305-z.

25. Wilson, L.S. and Maeder, A.J., Recent directions in telemedicine: Review of trends in research and practice. *Helthc. Infrom. Res.*, 21, 4, 213–22, 2015.

26. goe_telemedicine_2010.pdf (who.int)

27. Hendy, J., Chrysanthaki, T., Barlow, J. *et al.*, An organisational analysis of the implementation of telecare and telehealth: The whole systems demonstrator. *BMC Health Sev. Res.*, 12, 1, 403, 2012.

28. Lee, S., II, Celik, S., Logsdon, B.A. *et al.*, A machine learning approach to integrate big data for precision medicine in acute myeloid leukemia. *Nat. Commun.*, 9, 1–42, 2018.

29. Fakoor, R., Ladhak, F., Nazi, A. *et al.*, Using deep learning to enhance cancer diagnosis and classification. *A conference presentation . The 30th International Conference on Machine Learning*, pp. 1–5, 2013.

30. Davenport, T. and Kalakota, R., The potential for artificial intelligence in healthcare. *Future Healthc. J.*, 6, 2, 94–8, 2019.

31. Almathami, H.K.Y., Win, K.T., Vlahu-Gjorgievska, E., Barriers and Facilitators That Influence Telemedicine-Based, Real-Time, Online Consultation at Patients' Homes: Systematic Literature Review. *J. Med. Internet Res.*, 22, 2, e16407, 2020. https://doi.org/10.2196/16407.

32. Choi, H. and Kim, J., Effectiveness of telemedicine: Videoconferencing for low-income elderly with hypertension. *Telemed. J. E Health*, 20, 12, 1156–1164, Dec 2014.

33. *Artificial Intelligence in Healthcare: Benefits and Challenges of Machine Learning in Drug Development*, Reissued with revisions on Jan. 31, 2020, gao.gov.

34. Jahromi, M.E., Ahmadian, L. Determining the effect of tele-rehabilitation on patients with stutter using the goal attaintment scaling (GAS), BMC Med. Infor. and Decision Making 21 (280), 1–8, 2021. https://doi.org/10.1186/s12911-021-01642-3

35. Jahromi, M.E. and Ahmadian, L., Evaluating satisfaction of patients with stutter regarding the tele-speech therapy method and infrastructure. *Int. J. Med. Inform.*, 115, 128–133, 2018.

36. Kastner, P., Morak, J., Modre, R. *et al.*, Innovative telemonitoring system for cardiology: From science to routine operation. *Appl. Clin. Inform.*, 1, 2, 165–176, 2010.

37. Morak, J., Schwarz, M., Hayn, D. *et al.*, Feasibility of mHealth and near field communication technology based medication adherence monitoring, *Conference Proceedings IEEE Engineering in Medicine and Biology Society*, 272–275, 2012.
38. Stegemann, S., *Developing Drug Products in an Aging Society: From Concept to Prescribing*, Springer, Cham, 2016.
39. Ajami, S. and Lamoochi, P., Use of telemedicine in disaster and remote places. *J. Educ. Health Promot.*, 3, 1–26, 2014.
40. McLean, S., Protti, D., Sheikh, A., Telehealthcare for long term conditions. *BMJ*, 342, d120, 2011.
41. World health organization, *Telemedicine: Opportunities and developments in member states. Report on the second global survey on eHealth*, World Health Organization, Geneva, 2010.
42. Garrett, J.H., Use of neural networks in the detection of structural changes. *Comput. Struct.*, 42, 4, 1–10, 1992.
43. Xia, Y. and Hao, H., *A genetic algorithm for structural damage detection based on vibration data*, Society of Photo Optical Instr. Engineers (SPIE, Bellingham, WA, USA, 2001.
44. Smarsly, K. and Hartmann, D., Artificial intelligence in structural health monitoring. *Computing in civil Engineering*, pp. 1–6, 2007.
45. ChessBase, *Deep Fritz*, ChessBase GmbH, Hamburg, Germany, 2006, online source (http://www.chessbase.de).
46. Australian Institute of Health and Welfare, *Australia's health services expenditure to 1997-98*, 1999. Australian Government, Australia. https://www.aihw.gov.au/
47. Davis, L.J. and Offord, K.P., Logistic regression. *J. Pers. Assess.*, 68, 3, 497–507, 1997. https://doi.org/10.1207/s15327752jpa6803_3.
48. Yongzhen, Z., Chen, L., Wang, X.S. *et al.*, A weighted moving average-based approach for cleaning sensor data. *27th International Conference*, pp. 38–38, 2007, https://doi.org/ 10.1109/ICDCS.2007.83.
49. Tan, Y.L., *SensoClean: Handling noisy and incomplete data in sensor networks using modeling*, University of Maryland, College Park, USA, 2005.
50. Petrosino, A. and Staiano, A., A neuro-fuzzy approach for sensor network data cleaning, In: Apolloni, B., Howlett, R.J., Jain, L. (eds) Knowledge-Based Intelligent Information and Engineering Systems, KES 2007. Lecture notes in Computer Science, Springer, Berlin, Heidelberg, 4694. pp. 140–147, Epdf, 2007.
51. Jeffrey, S.R., Declarative support for sensor data cleaning. *PERVASIVE*, pp. 83–100, 2006.
52. Elnahrawy, E. and Nath, B., Cleaning and querying noisy sensors. *Proceedings in Wireless Sensor Networks and Applications Workshop (WSNA)*, 2003.
53. Zhuang, Y. and Chen, L., In-network outlier cleaning for data collection in sensor networks. *CleanDB*, pp. 1–8, 2006.

54. Jiang, F., Jiang, Y., Zhi, H. *et al.*, Artificial intelligence in healthcare: Past, present and future. *Stroke Vasc. Neurol.*, 2, 230–43, 2017. https://doi.org/10.1136/svn-2017-000101.

55. Research topics. Pew Research centre, 2021. Available from: https://www.pewresearch.org/internet/fact-sheet/mobile/.

56. Vangeepuram, N., Mayer, V., Fei, K. *et al.*, Smartphone ownership and perspectives on Health apps among a vulnerable population in East Harlem, New York. *mHealth*, 4, 31, 2018. https://mhealth.amegroups.com/article/view/20697/20323.

57. Gibbons, M.C. and Shaikh, Y., Introduction to consumer health informatics and digital inclusion, in: *Consumer Informatics and Digital Health*, pp. 25–41, Springer, Cham, 2019.

58. Dall, T., West, T., Chakrabarti, R. *et al.*, *The complexities of physician supply and demand: Projections from 2013 to 2025*, Association of American Meddiacl Colleges, Washington, DC, 2015.

59. Block, V.A., Pitsch, E., Tahir, P. *et al.*, Remote physical activity monitoring in neurological disease: A systematic review. *PloS One*, 11, 4, e0154335, 2016. https://doi.org/10.1371/journal.pone.0154335.

60. Char, D.S., Shah, N.H., Magnus, D. Implementing Machine Learning in Healthcare- Addressing Ethical Challenges, *N. Engl. J. Med.*, 378(11), 981-983, 2018. https://10.1056/NEJMp1714229.

61. Goel, M., Saba, E., Stiber, M. *et al.*, *Spiro-Call: Measuring lung function over a phone call*, pp. 1–11, https://jwfromm.com/documents/spirocall.pdf.

62. Saleheen, N., Ali, A.A., Hossain, S.M. *et al.*, PuffMarker: A multi-sensor approach for pinpointing the timing of first lapse in smoking cessation. *Proceedings of the 13th ACM International Conference on Ubiquitous Computing*, vol. 2015, pp. 999–1010, 2015, https://dl.acm.org/doi/proceedings/10.1145/2030112.

63. mpatica, Embrace2 seizure detection. https://www.empatica.com/.

64. Statista, Wearable user penetration rate in the united states, in 2017, by age. https://www.statista.com/statistics/739398/us-wearable-penetration-by-age/.

65. Alive, C., Detect more arrhythmias than any other EKG. https://www.alivecor.com/.

66. MC10, BioStamp nPoint: Wearable healthcare technology & devices. https://www.mc10inc.com.

67. Gao, J., Ertin, E., Kumar, S. *et al.*, Contactless sensing of physiological signals using wideband RF probes, in: *Forty-Seventh Asilomar Conference on Signals, Systems & Computers*, Pacific Grove, CA, Institute of Electrical and Electronics Engineers, Piscataway, NJ, pp. 86–90, November 3-6, 2013.

68. McLaren, R., Joseph, F., Baguley, C. *et al.*, A review of e-textiles in neurological rehabilitation: How close are we? *J. Neuroeng. Rehabil.*, 13, 59–65, 2016. https://doi.org/10.1186/s12984-016-0167-0.

69. Hafezi, H., Robertson, T.L., Moon, G.D. *et al.*, An ingestible sensor for measuring medication adherence. *IEEE Trans. Biomed. Eng.*, 62, 99109, 2015. https://doi.org/TBME.2014.2341272.

70. Sim, I., Mobile devices and health. *N. Engl. J. Med.*, 381, 10, 956–68, 2019. https://doi.org/10.1056/NEJMra1806949.

71. DiMatteo, M.R., Variations in patients' adherence to medical recommendations: A quantitative review of 50 years of research. *Med. Care*, 42, 3, 200–9, 2004.

72. Baig, M.M., GholamHosseinin, H., Moqeem, A.A. *et al.*, A systematic review of wearable patient monitoring systems-current challenges and opportunities for clinical adoption. *J. Med. Syst.*, 41, 7, 115, 2017. https://doi.org/10.1007/s10916-017-0760-1 10.1007/s10916-017-0760-1.

73. Hamine, S., Gerth-Guyette, E., Faulx, D. *et al.*, Impact of mHealth chronic disease management on treatment adherence and patient outcomes: A systematic review. *J. Med. Internet Res.*, 17, 2, e52, 2015. https://doi.org/10.2196/jmir.3951.

74. Milenkoviac, A., Otto, C., Jovanov, E., Wireless sensor networks of personal health monitoring: Issues and an implementation. *Comput. Commun.*, 29, 13, 2521–33, 2006.

75. Deshmukh, S.D. and Shilaskar, S.N., Wearable sensors and patient monitoring system: A review, in: *International Conference on Pervasive Computing (ICPC)*, IEEE, 2015, https://dl.acm.org/doi/10.1007/s10916-017-0760-1.

76. Sanchez-Morillo, D., Fernandez-Granero, M.A., Leon-Jimenez, A., Use of predictive algorithms in- home monitoring of chronic obstructive pulmonary disease and asthma: A systematic review. *Chron. Respir. Dis.*, 13, 3, 264–83, 2016. https://doi.org/10.1177/1479972316642365.

77. Iadanza, E., Mudura, V., Melillo, P. *et al.*, An automatic system supporting clinical decision for chronic obstructive pulmonary disease. *Health Technol.*, 10, 487–498, 2019. https://doi.org/10.1007/s12553-019-00312-9.

78. Mills, S., Electronic health records and use of clinical decision support. Critical care nursing. *Clinics*, 35, 3, 483–95, 2019.

79. Kindle, R.D., Badawi, O., Celi, L.A. *et al.*, Intensive care unit telemedicine in the era of big data, artificial intelligence, and computer clinical decision support systems. *Crit. Care Clin.*, 35, 3, 48395, 2019. https://doi.org/10.1016/j.ccc.2019.02.005.

80. Lurie, N. and Carr, B.G., The role of telehealth in the medical response to disasters. *JAMA Intern. Med.*, 178, 745–6, 2018. https://doi.org/10.3389/fpubh.2020.00410.

81. Mishra, S., Singh, I., Chand, R. (Eds.), Current Status of Telemedicine Network in India and Future Perspective, *Proceedings of the Asia-Pacific Advanced Network*, 32, 151–163, 2012.

82. Goldberg, L.R., Piette, J.D. *et al.*, Randomized trial of a daily electronic home monitoring system in patients with advanced heart failure: The Weight

Monitoring in Heart Failure (WHARF) trial. *Am. Heart J.*, 146, 705–712, 2003.

83. Lisetti, C., Amini, R., Yasavur, U., Now all together: Overview of virtual health assistants emulating face-to-face health interview experience. *KI-Künstliche Intelligenz*, 29, 2, 161–72, Jun 1 2015.

84. Aractingi, S. and Pellacani, G., Computational neural network in melanocytic lesions diagnosis: Artificial intelligence to improve diagnosis in dermatology? *Eur. J. Dermatol.*, 29, 4–7, 2019. https://doi.org/10.1684/ejd.2019.3538.

85. Luo, E.M., Newman, S., Amat, M. *et al.*, MIT COVID-19 datathon:data without boundaries. *BMJ Innov.*, 0, 1–4, 2020. https//doi.org/10.1136/bmjinnov-2020-000492.

86. Goldstein, B.A., Navar, A.M., Pencina, M.J. *et al.*, Opportunities and challenges in developing risk prediction models with electronic health records data: A systematic review. *J. Am. Med. Inform. Assoc.*, 24, 1, 198–208, 2017.

87. Bensink, M., Hailey, D., Wootton, R., A systemic review of successes and faliures in home telehealth: Preliminary results. *J. Telemed. Telecare*, 12, 3, 8–16, 2006.

88. Bara, A., Klein, B., Proudfoot, J.G., Defining internet-supported therapeutic interventions. *Ann. Behav. Med.*, 38, 1, 4–17, 2009.

89. Ahmad, N.F. and Hoang, D.B., Assistive Healthcare Monitoring Framework Using Active Database Approach. *Proceedings of the IADIS International Conference e-Health*, pp. 19–26, 2009.

90. Deloitte, *State of AI in the enterprise*, Early adopters combine bullish enthusiasm with strategic investments, 2nd Edition, Mumbai, India, 1–28, 2018, www2.deloitte.com/content/dam/insights/us/articles/4780_Stateof-AI-in-theenterprise/AICognitiveSurvey2018_Infographic.pdf.

91. Hosny, A., Parmar, C., Quackenbush, J. *et al.*, Artificial intelligence in radiology. *Perspectives*, 18, 1–11, 2018.

92. Yaghoubzadeh, R., Kramer, M., Pitsch, K. *et al.*, Virtual agents as daily assistants for elderly or cognitively impaired people, in: *International Workshop on Intelligent Virtual Agents*, pp. 79–91, 2013, https//doi.org/10.1007/978-3-642-40415-3_7.

93. Fiscella, K. and Epstein, R.M., So much to do, so litile time: Care for the socially disadvantaged and the 15 minute visit. *Arch. Intern. Med.*, 168, 17, 1843–52, 2008. https//doi.org/10.1001/archinte.168.17.1843.

94. Ricchardi, G., *Towards healthcare personal agents In: Proceedings of the 2014 Workshop on Road mapping the Future of Multimodal Interaction Research including Business Opportunities and challenges*, ACM, pp. 53–6, 2014, https://doi.org/10.1145/2666253.2666266.

95. Bickmore, T.W., Utami, D., Matsuyama, R. *et al.*, Improving access to online health information with conversational agents: A randomized controlled experiment. *J. Med. Internet Res.*, 18, 1, 1–12, 2016. https://doi.org/10.2196/jmir.5239.

96. Shaked, N.A., Avatars and virtual agents-relationship interfaces for the elderly. *Healthc. Technol. Lett.*, 4, 3, 83–87, 2017. https://doi.org/10.1049/htl.2017.0009.

97. Nangalia, V., Prytherch, D.R., Smith, G.B., Health technology assessment review: Remote monitoring of vital signs-current status and future challenges. *Crit. Care*, 14, 5, 233, 2010.

98. Inglis, S.C., Clark, R.A., McAlister, F.A. *et al.*, Which components of heart failure programmes are effective? A systematic review and meta-analysis of the outcomes of structured telephone support or telemonitoring as the primary component of chronic heart failure management in 8323 patients: Abridged Cochrane Review. *Eur. J. Heart Fail.*, 13, 9, 1028–40, 2011.

99. Bolton, C.E., Waters, C.S., Peirce, S. *et al.*, Insufficient evidence of benefit: A systematic review of home telemonitoring for COPD. *J. Eval. Clin. Pract.*, 17, 6, 1216–22, 2011. https://doi.org/10.1111/j.1365-2753.2010.01536.x.

100. Polisena, J., Tran, K., Cimon, K. *et al.*, Home telehealth for diabetes management: A systematic review and meta-analysis. *Diabetes Obes. Metab.*, 11, 10, 913–30, 2009. https://doi.org/10.1111/j.1463-1326.2009.01057.x.

101. van der Wal, M.H., Jaarsma, T. *et al.*, Non-compliance in patients with heart failure; how can we manage it? *Eur. J. Heart Fail.*, 7, 1, 5–17, 2005.

102. Peterson, A.M., Takiya, L., Finley, R., Meta-analysis of trails of interventions to improve medication adherence. *Am. J. Health Syst. Pharm.*, 60, 657–665, 2003.

103. Wilson, L.S. and Maeder, A.J., Recent directions in telemedicine: Review of trends in research and practice. *Healthc. Inform. Res.*, 21(4), 213–22, 2015.

104. Finch, T., May, C., Mair, F., Mort, M., Gask, L., Integrating service development with evaluation in telehealthcare: An ethnographic study. *BMJ*, 327, 7425, 1205–1209, 2003.

105. iRobot Corp. and Business Wire, FDA Clears First Autonomous Telemedicine Robot for Hospitals. [Online]. http://www.businesswire.com/news/home/20130124005134/en/FDA-Clears-Autonomous-TelemedicineRobot-Hospitals. [Accessed: 24-Jun-2017].

106. Labiris, G., Panagiotopoulou, E.K., Kozobolis, V.P., A systematic review of teleophthalmological studies in Europe. *Int. J. Ophthalmol. Clin. Res.*, 11, 2, 314–325, 2018. https://doi.org/10.18240/ijo.2018.02.22.

107. Armstrong, G.W. and Lorch, A.C., A (eye): A review of current applications of artificial intelligence and machine learning in ophthalmology. *Int. J. Ophthalmol. Clin. Res.*, 60, 1, 57–71, 2020. https://doi.org/10.1097/IIO.0000000000000298.

108. Dorsey, E.R. and Topol, E.J., State of Telehealth. *N. Engl. J. Med.*, 375, 2, 154–161, 2016. https://doi.org/10.1056/NEJMra1601705.

109. Pacis, D.M., Subido, E.D., Bugtai, N.T., Trends in telemedicine utilizing artificial intelligence. *AIP Conference Proceedings*, vol. 1993, p. 040009, 2018.

110. Hensel, B.K., Demiris, G., Courtney, K.L., Defining obtrusiveness in home telehealth technologies: A conceptual framework. *J. Am. Med. Inform. Assoc.*, 10, 4, 310–4, 2003. https://doi.org/10.1197/jamia.M2026.

111. Zhang, S., McClean, S.I., Nugent, C.D., Donnelly, M.P. *et al.*, Modelling mobile-based technology adoption among people with dementia. *IEEE J. Biomed. Health Inform.*, 18, 1, 375–383, 2014.

112. Suganthi, M.V., Elavarasi, M.K., Jayachitra, M.J., Tele-Health Monitoring System in a rural community through primary health centre using Internet of Medical Things. *Int. J. Pure Appl. Math.*, 119, 15, 3049–3059, 2018.

113. Jacey-Lynn, M. and Alvin, W.Y., Remote Health monitoring system in a rural population: Challenges and opportunities. *IEEE Conference on Biomedical Engineering and Science*, 2014.

114. Gomez, J., Oviedo, B., Zhuma, E., Patient Monitoring System Based on Internet of Things. *International Conference on Ambient Systems (ANT 2016), Procedia Comput. Sci.*, 83, 90–97, 2016. https://doi.org/10.1016/j. procs.2016.04.103.

115. Muni, K.N. and Manjula, R., Role of Big Data Analytics in Rural Healthcare - A Step Towards Svasth Bharath. *Int. J. Comput. Sci. Inf. Technol., IJCSIT*, 5, 6, 7172–, 20147178.

116. Ranjith, K.M. and Prabu, S., Smart Healthcare Monitoring System for rural area using IoT. *Int. J. Pharm. Technol.* 8(4): 21821–21826, 2017.

117. Epstein, R.M., Fiscella, K., Lesser, C.S. *et al.*, Why the nation needs a policy push on patient-centered healthcare. *Health Aff.*, 29, 8, 1489–95, 2010. https://doi.org/10.1377/hlthaff.2009.0888.

118. Veinot, T.C., Mitchell, H., Ancker, J.S., Good intentions are not enough: How informatics interventions can worsen inequality. *J. Am. Med. Inform. Assoc.*, 25, 1080–8, 2018. https://doi.org/10.1093/jamia/ocy052.

119. McDonald, C.J., Overhage, J.M., Mamlin, B.W. *et al.*, Physicians, information technology, and healthcare systems: A journey, not a destination. *J. Am. Med. Inform. Assoc.*, 11, 121–4, 2004. https://doi.org/10.1197/jamia.M1488.

120. Friedman, C., Rubin, J., Brown, J. *et al.*, Toward a science of learning systems: A research agenda for the high-functioning Learning Health system. *J. Am. Med. Inform. Assoc.*, 22, 43–50, 2015. https://doi.org/ 10.1136/ amiajnl-2014-002977.

121. Epstein, R.M. and Peters, E., Beyond in-formation: Exploring patients' preferences. *JAMA*, 302, 2, 195–7, 2009. https://doi.org/10.1001/jama.2009.984.

8

Deep Learning Framework for Cancer Diagnosis and Treatment

Shiv Bahadur[1]* and Prashant Kumar[2]

[1]Institute of Pharmaceutical Research, GLA University, Mathura,
Uttar Pradesh, India
[2]College of Pharmacy, Teerthanker Mahaveer University, Moradabad,
Uttar Pradesh, India

Abstract

Background: The awareness on deep learning is rapidly increasing day by day and various researchers have explored its application in cancer diagnostics. However, there is a need of exhaustive study in this aspect for real-world medical utility. The cancer is fatal disease and a major cause of bereavement affecting millions of survives every year. Although its early diagnosis may be useful to save the lives of population. This can be facilitated by the application of deep learning (DL) through artificial intelligence (AI) and machine learning (ML) for efficient drug discovery and disease diagnosis.

Aim: The present chapter focuses on the various aspects of deep learning and artificial intelligence in the diagnosis and treatment of cancer.

Discussion: The key challenges in cancer management are foretelling clinical response in case of anticancer drugs in human population. Machine learning refers to complex computer algorithms, which learn from data by learning the way to map input data to generate the desired output predictions. The majority of recent significant deep learning experiments in cancer diagnosis is engaged through input of pictures in the system for the analysis.

Conclusion: Several models of deep learning may be used to track cancer development for the patients undergoing treatment. In comparison to manual segmentation, various investigators found that the DL has significantly enhanced the analysis with recused chances of mistakes. Several studies showed that deep learning can be

*Corresponding author: shiv.pharma17@gmail.com; 0000-0001-9429-2857
Prashant Kumar: ORCID: 0000-0001-9183-0875

Rishabha Malviya, Gheorghita Ghinea, Rajesh Kumar Dhanaraj, Balamurugan Balusamy and Sonali Sundram (eds.) Deep Learning for Targeted Treatments: Transformation in Healthcare, (229–246) © 2022 Scrivener Publishing LLC

used as a potential approach for the improvement of cancer detection accuracy for a variety of cancers, including breast, colon, cervical, and lung cancers.

Keywords: Cancer treatment, cancer diagnosis, machine learning, deep learning, artificial intelligence

8.1 Deep Learning: An Emerging Field for Cancer Management

Deep learning allows systems to leverage complicated patterns in which data input through different dimension to precisely model, allowing for the usage of massive data sets by direct learning of correlations between target output raw and input data. Numerous research data have been published on use of deep learning in cancer management. These claim that such technologies can perform better than physicians but lack to demonstrate real-world medical value [1, 2].

As a result, there is lack of a well-defined review process for transforming promising prototypes into thoroughly evaluated medical systems, which hinders the use of deep learning systems in medicine. There are various new deep learning methods that can be used for the linking of the data input and data output in form of response [3]. Furthermore, deep learning processes are frequently constructed iteratively, with repeated testing and multiple selection methods that may skew outcomes. For many years, similar selection concerns in the medical literature have been recognized as a general concern. Hence, during the selection of design and validation techniques for diagnostic deep learning systems, one must consider both generalization issues and the avoidance of "traditional" data analysis mistakes. However, we shall argue that both sets of problems can be mitigated by following a few easy guidelines. Deep learning was used to successfully identify cancer cell types based on morphological aspects of cells. However, preventing morbidity and mortality requires early detection and treatment of precancerous lesions or early-stage cancer [4, 5].

Physicians frequently use pictorial outline gratitude to recognize problematic scuffs clinically, diagnostically, or radiologically or while diagnosing cancer. Through clinical checkup, dermatologist could notice an uneven border and unusual hues on a lesion that could be melanoma. A radiologist evaluating a mammography notices atypia, which is a significant sign of breast cancer. Biopsies are eventually taken in both cases, as they are in most cancer diagnoses [6]. Further, pathologist examines the tissues in microscope for the analysis. Then results will be predicted based on the pathological and clinical obtained data.

The aforesaid workflows depends on the doctor who have several years of training on enormous amounts of data analysis in order to determine characteristics, which indicate the several symptoms of malignancy [7]. There are huge amount of data used in detection of cancer, which open a scope to machine learning algorithms and increase their predicting concert as data accumulate. Unsupervised and supervised machine learning algorithms are both available. To create predictions, supervised algorithms employ mammograms labeled data (labeled pictures of abnormal and normal) [8]. During application of machine learning cancer diagnosis, to understand the pattern of classification for input data (clinical and pathological report) into prearranged groups is a common goal. The methods of classifications may be based on a precise finding (for example, melanoma). These methods use exercise of labeled data to study the demonstrative structures from groups in a supervised learning framework [9].

Deep learning have a lot of success with image categorization problems. Deep learning is based on multi-layer neural systems having multiple unseen covers, which are connected with simulated neurons and conduct precise actions through input data. Convolutional neural networks (CNNs), a type of neural network that has the ability for the identification of images, are frequently used in image tasks. The CNNs replicate natural graphic dispensation in brain, can understand rich info like relationship between objects and nearby pixels, image classification has performed exceptionally well [10]. Deep learning procedure can be applicable for selecting image of skin lesion. The image is fed into the neural network, which then goes through filtering (convolutions) and subsampling (pooling) phases to study the image attributes. These neuronal network systems correct bulks to other layers of the neural network to maximize link between imaging structures and categorization of the input images, just as it learns the simple image features. The model learns the salient features and how to accurately identify the input images by minimizing that distance or loss [11]. Training a separate validation set is utilized to appreciate the model's presentation and verify the network. After a model has been trained, it is tested on a separate test set to determine its ultimate performance. For example, the independent test set data for a clinical deep learning algorithm may originate from a separate hospital system to ensure that it is generalizable. The abovementioned study models may check through clinical data setting in the future for the establishment of clinical value in a real-world setting [1, 12].

8.2 Deep Learning Framework in Diagnosis and Treatment of Cancer

Cancer is the biggest cause of death, claiming lives of millions of people each year. Its early detection could help many people live longer. Envisaging clinical data in medications of cancer have been considered as major challenging issues nowadays. In cancer treatment, the diagnosis of clinical data has an important role [8, 13]. Deep learning (DL) has a broader applicability in drug discovery and disease diagnosis due to the application of larger artificial intelligence (AI) and machine learning (ML). Computer algorithms that learn from data by learning how to map input data to an output prediction are referred to as machine learning (ML) [1, 7, 14]. Deep learning has the ability to diagnose malignancies like breast, colon, cervical, and lung cancer with high accuracy.

Machine Learning

Machine learning has been considered as one of the most popular type of artificial intelligence in healthcare. Traditional ML has been commonly used in the diagnosis and treatment of several diseases in healthcare, while precision medicine is the most widely used application of artificial intelligence. For many healthcare organizations, being able to forecast which treatment techniques would be successful with patients based on their makeup and treatment framework is a big step forward [15, 16]. The great

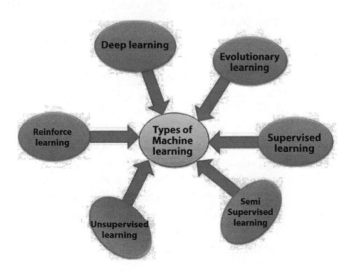

Figure 8.1 Types of machine learning.

majority of AI in healthcare applications that use machine learning and precision medicine require data for training that has a known outcome. This is known as supervised learning. The different types of machine learning have been showed in the Figure 8.1. Natural language processing is another application of artificial intelligence in healthcare that uses deep learning for speech recognition (NLP). Since many features in deep learning models have little value to human observers, hence, interpreting the model's results without adequate interpretation can be difficult [17].

The use of multiparametric magnetic resonance imaging (mpMRI) has been considered to increase ability of persons working in diagnosis of breast cancer clinically. This machine learning work uses mpMRI to paradigm shift to computer-aided diagnosis (CADx) for diagnosis [18]. Precancerous lesions or early-stage cancer should be detected and treated as soon as possible, to reduce morbidity and mortality [19].

8.3 Applications of Deep Learning in Cancer Diagnosis

In the hands of a physician, an AI tool that has been thoroughly assessed to enhance processes, increase precision with reduce charges. Several elements to consider while evaluating AI algorithms for cancer diagnostic jobs. Despite the fact that AI processes discussed have no precise replicate clinical work, the quiet chances for applications of algorithms for the collaboration with healthcare professionals [20]. For example, skin lesions are frequently assessed through doctors before being referred to dermatologists, who are skin specialists. The algorithms may differentiate between the different types of cancer along with various stages of cancer. These algorithms can be prescribed by the doctor the diagnosis and treatment of cancers, which may be preferred [21, 22].

AI offers the potential systems, which will not only advance medical process but also complete jobs, which were very challenging. Artificial intelligence systems can detect patterns that people cannot see, opening up the door to a plethora of creative possibilities. A human pathologist, for example, cannot determine the presence of genetic mutations only by histopathological study. The accurate analysis required specific testing procedures. These AIs may be used for the analysis of different types of mutations at clinical levels. This type of work might be reproduced in various cancer types to give pathologists input on what more testing would be required for a particular tissue [1, 23].

8.3.1   Medical Imaging Through Artificial Intelligence

Presently, AI has attracted a lot of attention in the scientific community. Alan Turing initially proposed artificial intelligence his publication "Computing Machinery and Intelligence" in the 19th century. So many researchers are focusing on the deep learning–based approaches for the management of cancer, hence several publications are coming. In the years 2016 to 2017, this number reached 800, and it is likely to skyrocket in the next years [24]. Medical imaging technology (MIT) benefits greatly from AI, and there are several computer-based models that have been developed, which has the ability to identify biological changes in normal and abnormal cells. Image interpretation and categorization, following data layout, information storage, information mining, and a variety of other applications are all examples of AI's dynamic applications. AI is projected to greatly assist radiologists in boosting diagnosis specificity having its wide opportunity in biomedical technologies. Without radiography, medical organization cannot be completed, particularly the case of tumor [25].

Presently, radiologist must have a wide knowledge about computer-based technology. They are continually on cutting edge of adopting digital medical imaging information. In comparison to other traditional technologies, AI could detect anomalous data at a glance, demonstrating a high sensitivity rate. Naturally, radiologists have important functions for the communication. Presently, AI will not ever completely substitute radiology, diminishing as AI's image interpretation efficiency improves [26]. Experienced technology-oriented radiologists are in high demand to create customized algorithms for high-throughput data processing that are both precise and accurate. Deep learning–based system may discover precise designs to offer information's regarding anomalous discoveries after executing a wide variety of experimental investigation. Traditional computer-assisted detection (CAD) methods may be detected images [27].

8.3.2   Biomarkers Identification in the Diagnosis of Cancer Through Deep Learning

The genome of human being has a complicated nucleotide arrangement. They have 23 chromosomes and encodes as DNA. It is well recognized that gene expression varies depending on the context, and these variations regulate a variety of biological processes. Surprisingly, certain genes only change in response to some specific disease situations (such as tumor). Those specific genes are most commonly known as biomarker. These biomarkers have a different nature, depending on the various types of cancer.

Table 8.1 Machine learning application in diagnosis of various cancers.

S. no.	Technique used	Type of cancer	Reference
1.	Semisupervised learning algorithm	Breast cancer	[33]
2.	Artificial neural networks	Breast cancer	[34]
3.	Bayesian networks	Colon carcinoma	[18]
4.	Support vector machines	Multiple myeloma	[35]
5.	Support vector machines	Breast cancer	[36]
6.	Support vector machines	Oral cancer	[37]
7.	Decision trees	Breast cancer	[38]
8.	Support vector machines	Oral cancer	[39]

The different techniques used in the detection of cancer has been enlisted in Table 8.1. Some researchers from USA have reported that the deep learning approach can be used for the diagnosis of different kinds of breast cancer at genetic level [28].

8.3.3   Digital Pathology Through Deep Learning

Presently, these deep learning and AI-based approaches has been gaining attention in the digital pathology laboratories for the detection of various kinds of diseases. These deep learning systems have various strong neuronal networking, which may generate good quality pictures and could be useful in the characterization of different types of tumors. We can get some novel biomarkers for the diagnosis of different types of cancers [29]. Several pathologies have been digitalized with addition of new modern equipment, which have the ability to produce high-quality images. We can get direct images from the slides of histopathology and further analyzing instruments can be attached to get analytical data at the same time. Hence, the deep learning and artificial intelligence can be integrated for diagnosis and treatment of cancer [30]. Biomarkers are biological indicators that may be used to identify and classify human body tissues and cells. Besides extensive clinical and preclinical studies, drug development today faces a slew of issues, including significant failure rates. To increase the success rate, a new generation of biomarkers must be identified using

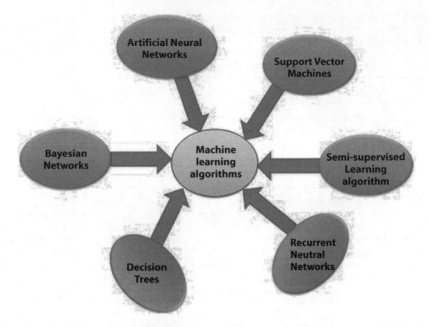

Figure 8.2 Detection of cancer by deep learning.

computational methods for meaningful clinical practice and drug discovery [31]. The AI and deep learning processes function in different steps. Every step is ampule for neurons, and data processing necessitates alliance among altered neuronal layers.

These AI systems have different kinds of layers, such as pooling layer, dense layer, normalizing layer, convolutional layer, recurrent layers, and many other layers. These particular layers have specific functions in the digital pathology for the integration and prediction of data. These layers are all dedicated for the conduction of specific tasks, exactly like human differentiated cells. Imaging data, such as digital pathology images, are processed by convolutional layers. Figure 8.2 illustrates a digital pathology workflow using AI [27, 32].

8.3.4   Application of Artificial Intelligence in Surgery

An exciting area of research is novel AI-based applications and recent advancements in surgery. For decades, oncologists have relied on clinical machine interaction. AI has been shown to reduce the incidence of breast conserving surgery (mastectomy) by 30.6% [40, 41]. Image-based machine learning models can reliably detect and identify different types of cancers, which have a high risk. Presently, there is utmost requirement of updated biopsies needle and updated digital pathology for the efficient clinical practice for cancer management. They can help in the reducing number of unnecessary surgical excisions. Different research groups have constructed random forest ML models for the prediction of survival duration of cancer patients with long-term intellectual outcomes. A random forest ML model was used to examine 335 high-risk cancer patients in a clinical investigation, and it was found that it might avert approximately one-third of unnecessary procedures [42]. Breast cancer has been considered as most commonly happening in women throughout the world. In these investigations, neural networks, extreme boost, decision trees, and support model were employed for the prediction of different types of cancers in order to define new predictive criteria for reliable existence study [43–45].

8.3.5   Histopathological Images Using Deep Learning

The computational technique has been employed in a few clinical contexts, whereas ANN was applied to construct preoperational complete risk assessment based on digital image analysis. ML aid is also possible during surgery; indeed, using investigational camera. Further, this ANN may provide supporting therapeutic results and estimates centered on the entire population. Furthermore, AI and ML can help oncologists assess and forecast morbidity and mortality after surgery [46]. To count immune cells in breast cancer slides, researchers used CNNs, which backs vector analysis technique. They were able to reach up to 90% agreement, which is similar to what pathologists achieve [47]. Deep learning can also be used in the prediction of different types and different stages of cancer [48].

8.3.6   MRI and Ultrasound Images Through Deep Learning

The imaging techniques in the healthcare area, like ultrasound, computed tomography, and magnetic resonance imaging, have been most commonly used for capturing pictures of tumor without invasiveness. Machine learning and artificial intelligence–based approaches may be applied for the detecting tumor progression in cancer patients who are taking therapy. In comparison to manual segmentation, several scientists discovered that deep learning may compact gesture and visual mistake, resulting in extra consistent findings [36, 49]. A study conducted in the chin for the prediction of tumor with elastography on 200 patients with the deep learning approaches, and the result was found to be a precision of 93% [20]. Some significant machine learning algorithms have been shown in Figure 8.3.

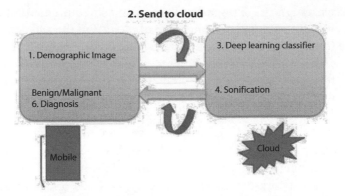

Figure 8.3 Types of algorithms in diagnosis of various cancers.

Several Kaggle competitors were successful in applied in DNN for the set of databases of breast cancer received by University of Wisconsin [50]. The DNN classifier was shaped for the prediction of different types of breast cancer [51].

8.4　Clinical Applications of Deep Learning in the Management of Cancer

Presently, deep learning approaches have been progressively gaining traction in everyday life and are expected to have a significant impact on disease detection and management of cancer in the coming days. Machine learning developments have opened the way for autonomous illness analysis method through exploiting large data sets for upcoming problems and detection of several diseases of human being in initial phase, particularly in tumor [52]. These machine learning methods have been assembled in such algorithms, which will work like a human brain [53]. Clinical oncology research is now more focused on considerate complicated organic building propagation of tumor cell in order to decode molecular beginning of cancer. There are enormously increasing cases of cancer, so these approaches will be very helpful in the identification and treatment of different types of cancer. Further, mortality rate can be reduced with the implementation of these methods in the healthcare sectors [27].

Furthermore, it is thought that incorporating AI into clinical decision-making may improve the odds of early illness detection through different imaging methods. By creating significant data sets and employing specialized bioinformatics tools, can play leading role in introduction of new biomarkers in tumor detection, the invention of novel tailored medications, and the delivery of prospective treatment strategies [54]. Several machines have been developed with the help of improvement of AI systems, which can work same as biological system of human being. We can get real time clinical data and comparison may be done for the large scale data of huge population [55, 56].

In November 2020, renowned international technology firm based in the United States, recently revealed its ambition to create AI-based supercomputer, known as Nvidia, which can be useful in drug delivery.

For DL-based algorithms to identify cancer at an early stage, effective conversion of AI-based applications needs field definite expertise in academics, such as "cancer cell biology." Furthermore, physicians working in cancer management must know AI machinery for minimizing common mistakes and to confirm that it is used safely and ethically [27, 57].

8.5 Ethical Considerations in Deep Learning–Based Robotic Therapy

The impact of machine learning on healthcare procedures is significant. It has the potential to influence treatment and diagnosis, raising severe ethical concerns. The applications of machine learning in healthcare for the management of cancer can be very useful [58, 59]. Clinical applications of several devises have been developed and ethical concerns are mostly focused on long-term, complete patient reliance. Furthermore, because there is a significant difference between human and machine communication, the integration of machine learning device in daily life with medical treatment is shifting public expectations and moral judgment [60, 61].

Transparency in the deep learning has become more difficult and challenging. Several deep learning techniques especially images for the diagnosis can be challenging. Still, the persons working in this area, such as researchers or physicians, cannot understand clear procedure. Several studies demonstrate that these modern methods with machine learning can be harmful in the diagnosis and treatment of cancer [62].

Another area where AI can be used is in mental health clinics, where it can help patients maintain their sovereignty. Hence, these technologies necessitate patient education for the confirmation of the intelligent system. Moreover, harmony for solicitations received external of a therapeutic setting raises a number of issues. AI is vulnerable to erroneous risk assessments [30].

8.6   Conclusion

As we know, there is no substitution for some most commonly used techniques, such as surgery, radiotherapy, and chemotherapy, for the cancer management, while the scientific community is increasingly interested in improving current cancer therapeutic techniques. Deep learning input and support will become a reality in the upcoming new technologies, resulting in substantial new technology insurrection in the prediction and diagnosis of human health-related concerns. There are several issues that can be avoided through deep learning, such as moral, cultural, and emotional issues, exhaustion are all avoided via deep learning. Deep learning may be a modern method in healthcare professionals for the identification and exploration of carcinogenesis with timely manner [48]. The power of the natural human mind to process a large amount of data and available knowledge is restricted. There is a huge interest from the scientific community that are interested in technology. Deep learning–based techniques in the healthcare field have numerous constraints at the microscales and nanoscales [63]. The data obtained from cancer patient confidential are still some of the obstacles that necessitate close attention to the human-computer interaction [64]. Clinically, experiments and their reproducibility are also the most significant roadblocks for drug development, with viable formulations taking many years to reach the market after clinical trials. Calculation that can be repeated with increasing specificity and cheap cost, drug designing has proven to be a viable approach for future drug development. To minimize limitations and false-positive data, big data and deep learning methods can be used to evaluate a vast range of complicated and diverse healthcare data. Deep learning is not fully autonomous, and artificial intelligence cannot completely replace human involvement. Deep learning is a fresh and promising technology in the medical field for achieving a specific cancer diagnosis and treatment with more resized methods [27, 65].

Acknowledgments

The authors would like to thank the Institute of Pharmaceutical Research, GLA University, Mathura for the support and for providing the necessary facilities.

References

1. Daneshjou, R., He, B., Ouyang, D., Zou, J.Y., How to evaluate deep learning for cancer diagnostics - factors and recommendations. *Biochim. Biophys. Acta Rev. Cancer*, 1875, 2, 188515, 2021.

2. Tolios, A., De Las Rivas, J., Hovig, E., Trouillas, P., Scorilas, A., Mohr, T., Computational approaches in cancer multidrug resistance research: Identification of potential biomarkers, drug targets and drug-target interactions. *Drug Resist. Updat.*, 48, 100662, 2020 Jan.

3. Levine, A.B., Schlosser, C., Grewal, J., Coope, R., Jones, S.J.M., Yip, S., Rise of the machines: Advances in deep learning for cancer diagnosis. *Trends Cancer*, 5, 3, 157–169, 2019.

4. Currie, G., Hawk, K.E., Rohren, E., Vial, A., Klein, R., Machine learning and deep learning in medical imaging: Intelligent imaging. *J. Med. Imaging Radiat. Sci.*, 50, 4, 477–487, 2019.

5. Han, T., Nebelung, S., Pedersoli, F., Zimmermann, M., Schulze-Hagen, M., Ho, M., Haarburger, C., Kiessling, F., Kuhl, C., Schulz, V., Truhn, D., Advancing diagnostic performance and clinical usability of neural networks via adversarial training and dual batch normalization. *Nat. Commun.*, 12, 1, 4315, 2021, 14.

6. Parashar, G., Chaudhary, A., Rana, A., Systematic mapping study of AI/machine learning in healthcare and future directions. *SN Comput. Sci.*, 2, 6, 461, 2021.

7. Kyventidis, N. and Angelopoulos, C., Intraoral radiograph anatomical region classification using neural networks. *Int. J. Comput. Assist. Radiol. Surg.*, 16, 3, 447–455, 2021.

8. Yi, P.H., Kim, T.K., Wei, J., Shin, J., Hui, F.K., Sair, H.I., Hager, G.D., Fritz, J., Automated semantic labeling of pediatric musculoskeletal radiographs using deep learning. *Pediatr. Radiol.*, 49, 8, 1066–1070, 2019 Jul.

9. Offiah, A.C., Current and emerging artificial intelligence applications for pediatric musculoskeletal radiology. *Pediatr. Radiol.*, 2021. doi: 10.1007/s00247-021-05130-8. Epub ahead of print. PMID: 34272573.

10. Weisberg, E.M., Chu, L.C., Fishman, E.K., The first use of artificial intelligence (AI) in the ER: Triage not diagnosis. *Emerg. Radiol.*, 27, 4, 361–366, 2020.

11. Jalal, S., Parker, W., Ferguson, D., Nicolaou, S., Exploring the role of artificial intelligence in an emergency and trauma radiology department. *Can. Assoc. Radiol. J.*, 72, 1, 167–174, 2021.

12. Hirschmann, A., Cyriac, J., Stieltjes, B., Kober, T., Richiardi, J., Omoumi, P., Artificial intelligence in musculoskeletal imaging: Review of current literature, challenges, and trends. *Semin. Musculoskelet. Radiol.*, 23, 3, 304–311, 2019 Jun.

13. Chea, P. and Mandell, J.C., Current applications and future directions of deep learning in musculoskeletal radiology. *Skeletal Radiol.*, 49, 2, 183–197, 2020 Feb.

14. Lee, J.H., Kim, D.H., Jeong, S.N., Choi, S.H., Detection and diagnosis of dental caries using a deep learning-based convolutional neural network algorithm. *J. Dent.*, 77, 106–111, 2018 Oct.

15. Hamm, C.A., Wang, C.J., Savic, L.J., Ferrante, M., Schobert, I., Schlachter, T., Lin, M., Duncan, J.S., Weinreb, J.C., Chapiro, J., Letzen, B., Deep learning for liver tumor diagnosis part I: Development of a convolutional neural network classifier for multi-phasic MRI. *Eur. Radiol.*, 29, 7, 3338–3347, 2019 Jul.

16. Lo, E.C., Rucker A, N., Federle, M.P., Hepatocellular Carcinoma and intrahepatic cholangiocarcinoma: Imaging for diagnosis, tumor response to treatment and liver response to radiation. *Semin. Radiat. Oncol.*, 28, 4, 267–276, 2018 Oct.

17. Wo, J.Y., Dawson, L.A., Zhu, A.X., Hong, T.S., An emerging role for radiation therapy in the treatment of hepatocellular carcinoma and intrahepatic cholangiocarcinoma. *Surg. Oncol. Clin. N. Am.*, 23, 2, 353–68, 2014.

18. Stojadinovic, A., Eberhardt, J., Chua, T.C., Pelz, J.O.W., Esquivel, J., Development of a Bayesian belief network model for personalized prognostic risk assessment in colon carcinomatosis. *Am. Surg.*, 77, 221–2, 2011.

19. Gustafson, M.P., Bornschlegl, S., Park, S.S., Gastineau, D.A., Roberts, L.R., Dietz, A.B., Hallemeier, C.L., Comprehensive assessment of circulating immune cell populations in response to stereotactic body radiation therapy in patients with liver cancer. *Adv. Radiat. Oncol.*, 2, 4, 540–547, 2017, 18.

20. Sheng, R.F., Zeng, M.S., Ren, Z.G., Ye, S.L., Zhang, L., Chen, C.Z., Intrahepatic distant recurrence following complete radiofrequency ablation of small hepatocellular carcinoma: Risk factors and early MRI evaluation. *Hepatobiliary Pancreat. Dis. Int.*, 14, 6, 603–12, 2015.

21. Dong, W., Zhang, T., Wang, Z.G., Liu, H., Clinical outcome of small hepatocellular carcinoma after different treatments: A meta-analysis. *World J. Gastroenterol.*, 20, 29, 10174–82, 2014, 7.

22. Dinić, J., Efferth, T., García-Sosa, A.T., Grahovac, J., Padrón, J.M., Pajeva, I., Rizzolio, F., Saponara, S., Spengler, G., Tsakovska, I., Repurposing old drugs to fight multidrug resistant cancers. *Drug Resist. Updat.*, 52, 100713, 2020 Sep.

23. Kuntz, S., Krieghoff-Henning, E., Kather, J.N., Jutzi, T., Höhn, J., Kiehl, L., Hekler, A., Alwers, E., von Kalle, C., Fröhling, S., Utikal, J.S., Brenner, H., Hoffmeister, M., Brinker, T.J., Gastrointestinal cancer classification and prognostication from histology using deep learning: Systematic review. *Eur. J. Cancer*, 155, 200–215, 2021.

24. Zhou, J., Hu, N., Huang, Z.Y., Song, B., Wu, C.C., Zeng, F.X., Wu, M., Application of artificial intelligence in gastrointestinal disease: A narrative review. *Ann. Transl. Med.*, 9, 14, 1188, 2021.

25. Pannala, R., Krishnan, K., Melson, J., Parsi, M.A., Schulman, A.R., Sullivan, S., Trikudanathan, G., Trindade, A.J., Watson, R.R., Maple, J.T., Lichtenstein, D.R., Artificial intelligence in gastrointestinal endoscopy. *VideoGIE*, 5, 12, 598–613, 2020.

26. Parasher, G., Wong, M., Rawat, M., Evolving role of artificial intelligence in gastrointestinal endoscopy. *World J. Gastroenterol.*, 26, 46, 7287–7298, 2020.

27. Iqbal, M.J., Javed, Z., Sadia, H., Qureshi, I.A., Irshad, A., Ahmed, R., Malik, K., Raza, S., Abbas, A., Pezzani, R., Sharifi-Rad, J., Clinical applications of artificial intelligence and machine learning in cancer diagnosis: Looking into the future. *Cancer Cell Int.*, 21, 1, 270, 2021 May 21.

28. Gubatan, J., Levitte, S., Patel, A., Balabanis, T., Wei, M.T., Sinha, S.R., Artificial intelligence applications in inflammatory bowel disease: Emerging technologies and future directions. *World J. Gastroenterol.*, 27, 17, 1920–1935, 2021.

29. Chang, Y., Park, H., Yang, H.J., Lee, S., Lee, K.Y., Kim, T.S., Jung, J., Shin, J.M., Cancer drug response profile scan (CDRscan): A deep learning model that predicts drug effectiveness from cancer genomic signature. *Sci. Rep.*, 8, 1, 8857, 2018 Jun 11.

30. Zhu, W., Xie, L., Han, J., Guo, X., The application of deep learning in cancer prognosis prediction. *Cancers (Basel)*, 12, 3, 603, 2020 Mar 5.

31. Wu, J., Chen, J., Cai, J., Application of artificial intelligence in gastrointestinal endoscopy. *J. Clin. Gastroenterol.*, 55, 2, 110–120, 2021.

32. El Hajjar, A. and Rey, J.F., Artificial intelligence in gastrointestinal endoscopy: General overview. *Chin. Med. J. (Engl)*, 133, 3, 326–334, 2020.

33. Kim, J. and Shin, H., Breast cancer survivability prediction using labeled, unlabeled, and pseudo-labeled patient data. *J. Am. Med. Inform. Assoc.*, 20, 613–618, 2013.

34. Ayer, T., Alagoz, O., Chhatwal, J., Shavlik, J.W., Kahn, C.E., Burnside, E.S., Breast cancer risk estimation with artificial neural networks revisited. *Cancer*, 116, 3310–3321, 2010.

35. Waddell, M., Page, D., Shaughnessy Jr., J., Predicting cancer susceptibility from single-nucleotide polymorphism data: A case study in multiple myeloma. *ACM*, pp. 21–28, 2005.

36. Listgarten, J., Damaraju, S., Poulin, B., Cook, L., Dufour, J., Driga, A. *et al.*, Predictive models for breast cancer susceptibility from multiple single nucleotide polymorphisms. *Clin. Cancer Res.*, 10, 2725–2737, 2004.

37. Chang, S.-W., Abdul-Kareem, S., Merican, A.F., Zain, R.B., Oral cancer prognosis based on clinicopathologic and genomic markers using a hybrid of feature selection and machine learning methods. *BMC Bioinf.*, 14, 170, 2013.

38. Delen, D., Walker, G., Kadam, A., Predicting breast cancer survivability: A comparison of three data mining methods. *Artif. Intell. Med.*, 34, 113–127, 2005.

39. Rosado, P., Lequerica-Fernández, P., Villallaín, L., Peña, I., Sanchez-Lasheras, F., de Vicente, J.C., Survival model in oral squamous cell carcinoma based

on clinicopathological parameters, molecular markers and support vector machines. *Expert Syst. Appl.*, 40, 4770–4776, 2013.

40. Yu, H., Singh, R., Shin, S.H., Ho, K.Y., Artificial intelligence in upper GI endoscopy - current status, challenges and future promise. *J. Gastroenterol. Hepatol.*, 36, 1, 20–24, 2021.

41. Kagiyama, N., Shrestha, S., Farjo, P.D., Sengupta, P.P., Artificial intelligence: Practical primer for clinical research in cardiovascular disease. *J. Am. Heart Assoc.*, 8, 17, e012788, 2019 Sep 3.

42. Young, E., Philpott, H., Singh, R., Endoscopic diagnosis and treatment of gastric dysplasia and early cancer: Current evidence and what the future may hold. *World J. Gastroenterol.*, 27, 31, 5126–5151, 2021.

43. Moon, H.S., Yun, G.Y., Kim, J.S., Eun, H.S., Kang, S.H., Sung, J.K., Jeong, H.Y., Song, K.S., Risk factors for metachronous gastric carcinoma development after endoscopic resection of gastric dysplasia: Retrospective, single-center study. *World J. Gastroenterol.*, 23, 24, 4407–4415, 2017.

44. Jiang, F., Jiang, Y., Zhi, H., Dong, Y., Li, H., Ma, S., Wang, Y., Dong, Q., Shen, H., Wang, Y., Artificial intelligence in healthcare: Past, present and future. *Stroke Vasc. Neurol.*, 2, 4, 230–243, 2017 Jun 21.

45. Kleppe, A., Skrede, O.J., De Raedt, S., Liestøl, K., Kerr, D.J., Danielsen, H.E., Designing deep learning studies in cancer diagnostics. *Nat. Rev. Cancer*, 21, 3, 199–211, 2021.

46. Lee, S., Oh, S.I., Jo, J., Kang, S., Shin, Y., Park, J.W., Deep learning for early dental caries detection in bitewing radiographs. *Sci. Rep.*, 11, 1, 16807, 2021 Aug 19.

47. Kim, S.J., Wang, C., Zhao, B., Im, H., Min, J., Choi, H.J., Tadros, J., Choi, N.R., Castro, C.M., Weissleder, R., Lee, H., Lee, K., Deep transfer learning-based hologram classification for molecular diagnostics. *Sci. Rep.*, 8, 1, 17003, 2018 Nov 19.

48. Huang, S., Yang, J., Fong, S., Zhao, Q., Artificial intelligence in cancer diagnosis and prognosis: Opportunities and challenges. *Cancer Lett.*, 471, 61–71, 2020 Feb 28.

49. He, Y., Zhao, H., Wong, S.T.C., Deep learning powers cancer diagnosis in digital pathology. *Comput. Med. Imaging Graphics*, 88, 101820, 2021 Mar.

50. Arefan, D., Mohamed, A.A., Berg, W.A., Zuley, M.L., Sumkin, J.H., Wu, S., Deep learning modeling using normal mammograms for predicting breast cancer risk. *Med. Phys.*, 47, 1, 110–118, 2020 Jan.

51. Miyagi, Y., Takehara, K., Miyake, T., Application of deep learning to the classification of uterine cervical squamous epithelial lesion from colposcopy images. *Mol. Clin. Oncol.*, 11, 6, 583–589, 2019 Dec.

52. Mohamed, A.A., Berg, W.A., Peng, H., Luo, Y., Jankowitz, R.C., Wu, S., A deep learning method for classifying mammographic breast density categories. *Med. Phys.*, 45, 1, 314–321, 2018 Jan.

53. Mohamed, A.A., Luo, Y., Peng, H., Jankowitz, R.C., Wu, S., Understanding clinical mammographic breast density assessment: A deep learning perspective. *J. Digit. Imaging*, 31, 4, 387–392, 2018 Aug.

54. Munir, K., Elahi, H., Ayub, A., Frezza, F., Rizzi, A., Cancer diagnosis using deep learning: A bibliographic review. *Cancers (Basel)*, 11, 9, 1235, 2019 Aug 23.

55. Lee, J.H., Kim, D.H., Jeong, S.N., Choi, S.H., Diagnosis and prediction of periodontally compromised teeth using a deep learning-based convolutional neural network algorithm. *J. Periodontal. Implant. Sci.*, 48, 2, 114–123, 2018 Apr 30.

56. Lee, Y.H., Efficiency improvement in a busy radiology practice: Determination of musculoskeletal magnetic resonance imaging protocol using deep-learning convolutional neural networks. *J. Digit. Imaging*, 31, 5, 604–610, 2018 Oct.

57. Bai, J., Posner, R., Wang, T., Yang, C., Nabavi, S., Applying deep learning in digital breast tomosynthesis for automatic breast cancer detection: A review. *Med. Image Anal.*, 71, 102049, 2021 Jul.

58. Sutton, R.T., Pincock, D., Baumgart, D.C., Sadowski, D.C., Fedorak, R.N., Kroeker, K.I., An overview of clinical decision support systems: Benefits, risks, and strategies for success. *NPJ Digit. Med.*, 3, 17, 2020 Feb 6.

59. Miyagi, Y., Takehara, K., Nagayasu, Y., Miyake, T., Application of deep learning to the classification of uterine cervical squamous epithelial lesion from colposcopy images combined with HPV types. *Oncol. Lett.*, 19, 2, 1602–1610, 2020 Feb.

60. Pacal, I., Karaboga, D., Basturk, A., Akay, B., Nalbantoglu, U., A comprehensive review of deep learning in colon cancer. *Comput. Biol. Med.*, 126, 104003, 2020 Nov.

61. Liu, L., Wang, Y., Liu, X., Han, S., Jia, L., Meng, L., Yang, Z., Chen, W., Zhang, Y., Qiao, X., Computer-aided diagnostic system based on deep learning for classifying colposcopy images. *Ann. Transl. Med.*, 9, 13, 1045, 2021 Jul.

62. Abdelhafiz, D., Yang, C., Ammar, R., Nabavi, S., Deep convolutional neural networks for mammography: Advances, challenges and applications. *BMC Bioinf.*, 20, Suppl 11, 281, 2019 Jun 6.

63. Min, J.K., Kwak, M.S., Cha, J.M., Overview of deep learning in gastrointestinal endoscopy. *Gut Liver*, 13, 4, 388–393, 2019.

64. Wildeboer, R.R., van Sloun, R.J.G., Wijkstra, H., Mischi, M., Artificial intelligence in multiparametric prostate cancer imaging with focus on deep-learning methods. *Comput. Methods Programs Biomed.*, 189, 105316, 2020 Jun.

65. Chan, H.P., Hadjiiski, L.M., Samala, R.K., Computer-aided diagnosis in the era of deep learning. *Med. Phys.*, 47, 5, e218–e227, 2020 Jun.

9

Applications of Deep Learning in Radiation Therapy

Akanksha Sharma¹*, Ashish Verma², Rishabha Malviya³ and Shalini Yadav⁴

¹Monad College of Pharmacy, Monad University, Delhi Hapur Road, Kastla, Kasmabad, Pilkhuwa, Uttar Pradesh, India
²School of Pharmacy, Monad University, Delhi Hapur Road, Kastla, Kasmabad, Pilkhuwa, Uttar Pradesh, India
³Department of Pharmacy, School of Medical and Allied Sciences, Galgotias University, Greater Noida, Gautam Buddha Nagar, Uttar Pradesh, India
⁴Dr. M. C. Saxena College of Pharmacy, Lucknow, Uttar Pradesh, India

Abstract

Deep learning is a branch of artificial intelligence (AI) that employs neural networks to learn unsupervised from unlabeled or unstructured data. It is an area that is focused on computer algorithms examining and developing on their own. Within healthcare, machine learning approaches to problem solving are quickly expanding, and radiation is no different. Identification and image segmentation, radiomic signature discovery and image phenotyping, image dose quantification, clinical outcome estimation, radiation adaptation, image generation and dose-response modeling are some of the uses of deep learning in radiation therapy. A large number of researches evaluating the success of the deep learning approach in radiation therapy have been published in the last few years.

This chapter describes the significance of radiation therapy with deep learning to treat diseases like cancer. It explains how deep learning–based technologies can support physicians in their everyday practice, whether it is by reducing the time required or by helping in the prediction of treatment effects and toxicities.

*Corresponding author: akankshasona012@gmail.com; 0000-0002-5325-427X
Ashish Verma: ORCID: 0000-0002-8951-4846
Rishabha Malviya: ORCID: 0000-0003-2874-6149

Rishabha Malviya, Gheorghita Ghinea, Rajesh Kumar Dhanaraj, Balamurugan Balusamy
and Sonali Sundram (eds.) Deep Learning for Targeted Treatments: Transformation in Healthcare,
(247–288) © 2022 Scrivener Publishing LLC

Keywords: Deep learning, machine learning, radiation therapy, oncology, disease, healthcare, artificial intelligence

9.1   Introduction

Introduction of Radiation Therapy

The world's greatest cause of death is still cancer. (IARC) The International Agency for Research on Cancer currently anticipated tumor causes 7.6 million deaths worldwide, with new cases reported each year, i.e 12.7 million. Developing countries carry a disproportionate share of the burden; they account for 63% of cancer fatalities. Cancer is a disease that is multicellular and multigenic with a multifactorial etiology that can affect any cell type or organ [1].

Regrettably, at the tissue level, it is a variety of diseases and this variation is a big barrier for its particular diagnosis, followed by therapeutic efficiency. The prostate, bronchus and lung, rectum and colon and urinary bladder all are the organs that have the highest chances to get cancer in men. Breast cancer, lung and bronchus cancer, uterine corpus cancer, thyroid cancer, colon and rectum cancer are the most common cancers in women. This indicates breast and prostate cancer account for a crucial part of carcinoma in men and women, respectively. Blood cancer, as well as malignancies of the brain and lymph nodes, account for the highest percentage of cancer cases in children [2].

The importance of the target's activity in healthy cells poses a challenge to traditional target-directed approaches, which is one of the major concerns in anticancer research. Targeting proteins have important functions that result in chemical entities which have considerable toxicity and limited therapeutic windows. Another problem in cancer cells is epigenetic and unstable genetic status, which is characterized by chromosomal abnormalities, gene copy changes, and numerous mutations, all of these affect anticancer drug effectiveness at various phases of the disease. The specific biomarkers identification, biomarkers validation for the therapeutic targets identification and development of a drug are all necessary steps in the development of individualized and rationalized medicine [3].

Along with chemotherapy and surgery, radiation treatment is one of the modern medicines and is used as the most potent weapon in the fight against cancer. Radiotherapy, commonly called radiation therapy which is referred to as a cancer treatment method that involves the application of radioactive chemicals or high-energy rays to tumor cells to destroy them and stop their growth and proliferation. When considering its usage for both palliative and curative reasons, "Radiotherapy is given to well over 50% of cancer patients at once throughout their treatment." Radiation therapy is administered externally using high-energy X-ray photons and internally, radioactive chemicals are placed in or near a tumor, a technique known as brachytherapy [4, 5].

Due to its large public exposure, systemic therapy may be incorrectly perceived as the cornerstone of curative care. In fact, in high, low and middle income nations, 40 percent of cancer patients who are cured will get radiation therapy during their treatment and roughly 50 percent of patients with cancer will need it during their treatment. External beam therapy (which includes protons, electrons, photons and other particles) and surface or internal medication are types of radiation therapy (radio-pharmaceuticals and brachytherapy) [6, 7].

Megavoltage photon therapy is a type of electromagnetic wave having high energy that is generated with the help of a radiation source, is the most extensively utilized technique. Megavoltage photons may penetrate a wide spectrum of tissue, allowing them to treat deeper inside body structures like pelvic organs and lung tumors. Orthovoltage photons have a shallower penetration in tissue and are utilized in the therapy of skin and soft tissue. Electrons are generally employed to treat superficial and skin tumors since

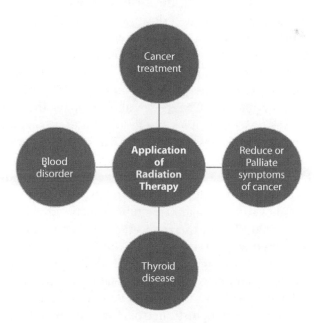

Figure 9.1 Schematic diagram represents the basic use/application of radio therapy for treatment of various diseases.

they have a similarly limited range of tissue penetration as orthovoltage photons but a distinct dosage distribution [7].

Figure 9.1 shows the schematic diagram for the basic use/application of radio therapy for the treatment of various diseases.

9.2   History of Radiotherapy

A growing number of research on the application of X-rays and radium in medicine was published in the first years of the new century. Despite the poor penetration of radiations in the tissue, skin malignancies were the most commonly treated disease by this therapy. Coolidge created a new system in 1910 that could release high energy X-rays for the therapy of deeper malignancies. In actuality, due to less comprehension of the mode of action of RT and properties, the effectiveness, good results in the treatment of tumors were low in contrast to their side effects, forcing physicians to start on new research to better understand the treatments [8, 9].

There have been discoveries of new radioactive isotopes, ray types, and radiation procedures. Scientists started working on comprehending the modes of action, their nature of radiations and the impact of dose and time on the persistence of cells. Until the 1920s doctors does not realise that fractionating the overall radiation dose was better than a single therapy session in terms of cancer control with fewer adverse effects [10].

After radioactive isotopes the ICRP "International Commission on Radiological Protection", is formerly called The International X-Ray and Radium Protection Committee, was inveterate in 1928, which was affiliated with the International Congresses of Radiology. The Commission's primary goal was to set principles and guidelines to protect medical personnel and patients from possible health harm caused by ionizing radiation exposure [11].

From 1930 to 1950, there was a steady stream of scientific advancement in the therapy of patients with profound cancers. This period was marked by the invention of supervoltage X-ray tubes capable of delivering energy between 50 and 200 kV and the application of radium-based interstitial irradiation (brachytherapy) (also called the Orthovoltage era) [12].

Radiotherapy became a recognized medical discipline in the first two decades of the 20th century. New research establishing usefulness of radiotherapy in enhancing patient survival with various kinds of tumors accompanied the introduction of sophisticated devices with computerized controls into medical practice. The fundamental advantage of employing ion beams is that they are more controllable, making them high caliber tools for treating cancer and tough to the treatment of benign illnesses [13].

Considerable advancements in radiation have been made when more improved computers were introduced around the end of the 1990s, the improvement of the 3D conformal radiotherapeutic device which also called stereotactic radiation treatment, capable of treating patients with greater efficacy and safety. Stereotactic radio therapy, which is utilized to treat metastatic cancers, gained popularity in the new millennium, as well as the introduction of (ART) Adaptive radiotherapy, (IGRT) form of image-guided radiation which allows for replanning and occasionally optimization of treatment approach during radiation therapy when clinically suitable [14].

9.3 Principal of Radiotherapy

Radiation therapy is named as radiotherapy, it is a technique of tumor medication which includes the administration of radiation high doses to tumor cells to destroy the cells and shrink the cancer cells. Radiation is utilized in x-rays to look inside the body at low levels like X-rays of fractured bones or teeth. Radiation therapy kills or delays the development of cancer cells by damaging their DNA at high dosages. Cancer cells that have had their DNA damaged beyond repair will either die or proliferation gets ceased.

The body breaks down and removes the damaged cell which died. Radio therapy does not destroy tumor cells immediately. It takes a few days or weeks for treatment before tumor cells DNA is enough destroyed to kill them. After then, cancerous cells endure dying for weeks or months after radio therapy is finished. Although radiation kills both normal and cancer and cells, the radiation treatment has the goal to enhance the radiation dose to aberrant tumor cells while reducing radiation exposure to normal cells closest to cancer cells or in the way of radiation [15].

9.4 Deep Learning

Machine learning (ML) has recently exploded in popularity in research, with different applications ranging from the mining of text to video recommendation, spam detection, multimedia idea retrieval and image categorization. In these applications, deep learning (DL) is among the most extensively utilized machine learning algorithms. Representation learning is another name for DL. The advent of new researches in the distributed and deep learning fields is occurring due to the unpredictability of data availability as well as tremendous advancements in hardware technologies, such as High Performance Computing (HPC). Deep Learning (DL) is based on a standard neural network, however, it performs far better than its predecessors. Furthermore, for purpose of constructing models for multilayer learning, DL uses both transformations and graph technologies at the same time. The most recently developed deep learning approaches have achieved excellent results in a variety of applications, including speech and audio processing, natural language processing (NLP) and visual data processing among others [16].

The input-data representation's integrity depends on the effectiveness of a machine learning algorithm. It is established that a proper representation of data enhances the performance when compared with a poor representation of data. As a result, feature engineering has been a major research topic in machine learning for many years. This method seeks to create characteristics derived from raw data. Furthermore, it's quite field-specific, and it typically necessitates a lot of human effort. In the domain of computer vision, for example, different kinds of characteristics were proposed and compared, like the histogram of directed gradients (HOG), Scale-invariant feature transform (SIFT) and a bag of words (BoW) [16, 17].

The black-box method is a kind of deep learning for inferring robust and scalable insights from complicated and high-dimensional data while reducing the amount of manual labor required. One characteristic that differentiates deep learning as a subset of its superset is the utilization of multilayer models in machine learning that results in a higher level representation of the different databases. Without being expressly instructed, deep learning can extract crucial information, making it more resistant to noisy and unstructured input. Medical imaging, finance, healthcare, geophysical sciences, hydrology and remote sensing are just a few of the fields and businesses where deep learning has been successfully implemented. Due to its high potential and adoption rate to get applied in any sector, open source and for-profit software platforms, control systems, generalized algorithms and educational resources have been given access for usage, bringing up a slew of new avenues for hydrological research [18].

Image detection, image segmentation, radiomic signature finding, image phenotyping, image dose measurement, clinical outcome prediction, radiation adaptation, dose response modeling, and image synthesis are some of the applications/use of deep learning in radio therapy or radiation oncology. Carcinomas of the neck and head are treated by using chemotherapy, pneumonitis in lung cancer, toxicity after prostate cancer, PSA level response and uterus cervical cancer is treated by using radiation exposure and all these techniques have been determined for their activity by using Artificial Neural Networks (ANNs). The models constructed in these experiments functioned well, although the training cohorts were small, and external validation was required.

New methodologies, like (DL) deep learning, are applied to real-world data. All department of radiation oncology uses the record and verify systems so the data quality is good that proactively save every information on the therapy ordered, how it was administered, and any potential deviations. Deep learning could be utilized to build a "learning health system" that may provide a patient's response to the method of treatment or survival while it is continuously upgrading itself with fresh information [19].

Figure 9.2 represents the schematic diagram of different clinical applications of Deep Learning.

Radiation therapy in treatment areas and possible side effects in a cancer patient are shown in Table 9.1.

The advantages and disadvantages of radiation therapy are available in Table 9.2.

Figure 9.2 Schematic representation of clinical application of deep learning.

Table 9.1 Treatment areas and possible side effects of radiation therapy in tumor patients.

S. no.	Parts of the body being treated	Side effects on body parts
1.	Prostate Gland	Fatigue, diarrhea, sleep disruption, urinary problems, skin irritation in the treated area [20].
2.	Brain	Altered function of pituitary, visual disturbance, necrosis of brain and the initiation of new tumors [21].
3.	Cervical	Hematologic toxicities and gastrointestinal toxicity [22].
4.	Breast	Lymphedema, radiation pneumonitis, myocardial infarction, coronary revascularization, ischemic heart disease [23].
5.	Uterine	Loss of appetite, psychological distress (anxiety and depression), pain, nausea/vomiting, diarrhea, insomnia and anorexia syndrome [24].
6.	Eye	Eyelash loss, dry eye, neovascular glaucoma, cataract, optic neuropathy and radiation retinopathy [25].
7.	Rectal	Intestinal obstruction, possibility of venous thromboembolism and femoral neck or pelvic fracture [26].

9.5   Radiation Therapy Techniques

There are various types of radiation methods which are available for the treatment of cancer are explained below.

Figure 9.3 represents the schematic diagram of different types of radiation therapy techniques used for the disease treatment.

Table 9.2 Summary of advantages and disadvantages of different radiation therapy.

Technology	Advantages	Disadvantages
General radiation therapy	No need for routine CT Good rate of cancer treatment Decreased recurrence rate	Risk of second malignancy Most patients get over treated Fertility impairment Cardiotoxicity [27]
Conventional 2-D radiation therapy	Radiotherapy efficacy is demonstrated by reliable clinical data and extensive follow-up	Geometric precision at its most basic level, Do not protect normal tissue [28]
IMRT	Good adjustment of treatment portal to the cancer site	Rigid heat fixation Less patient number with small follow up [28]
Fractionated proton therapy	Optimal coverage of cancer site Maximum sparing of surrounding tissue	Limited access More costly Less patient number [28]
Radiosurgery	For one session only Good coverage of cancer site No dose to non-target or surrounding tissue	The limited set of clinical Less patient number Small time follow up [28]
Cyberknife	Only few session Good coverage of cancer site No dose to non target or surrounding tissue	The role is not clear Few experiences No reliable data related to cancer treatment [28]
Intracavity colloid isotope application	More rate of tumor control	Only cystic tumors are treated Possibility of leakage [28]
Interstitial irradiation	Conformity to dosing Normal tissue is most protected	Less clinical evidence [28]

(Continued)

Table 9.2 Summary of advantages and disadvantages of different radiation therapy. (*Continued*)

Technology	Advantages	Disadvantages
External beam radiation therapy	Inoperable tumors become resectable Small portals of radiation Lows the positive margins intraoperatively During surgery, it reduces tumor seeding Good surgical planning The good wound healing property Surgically easier to remove the tumor	Wound healing gets delayed Complication during surgery Evaluation of margin and histologic diagnosis becomes difficult Possibility to seed other tissue Healing problem delays the external beam radiation [27]
Stereotactic body radiotherapy (SBRT)	Less complication Less toxicity rate Provide local control Used for unresectable tumors Feasible for solitary organ	Pathological evaluation is limited Before SBRT, the lower limit of renal function remains undefined. Requires robust technical and quality assurance [29]

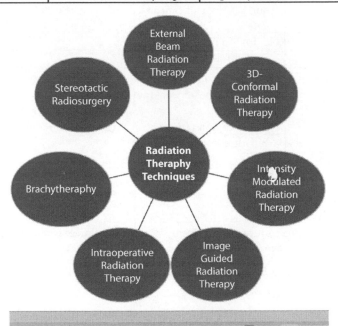

Figure 9.3 Schematic diagram of different types of radiation therapy techniques used for the disease treatment.

9.5.1   External Beam Radiation Therapy

Hepatocellular carcinoma (HCC) is now increasingly commonly treated by the utilization of external beam radiation therapy (EBRT), was formerly uncommon due to liver damage. The supplementation for insufficient transarterial chemoembolization, treatment of portal vein thrombosis and creation of new therapeutic chances employing stereotactic body radiation are all feasible indications for using EBRT. The external beam radiotherapy treatment method differs from conventional medical treatment or surgery in terms of its process, as well as its radiobiological and physical aspects [30].

Through a computerized planning procedure, the EBRT approach employs modulated beams to optimize dose distribution and promote normal tissue sparing for tumors with complex shapes. Its use has risen in tandem with its potency, which has increased the efficacy of treatment while decreasing in side effects. Stereotactic body radiotherapy (SBRT) is a type of EBRT approach utilized to accurately deliver the highest dose of radiation to an extracranial object in one or a few segments. SBRT is becoming more often used as a curable option for tumors that have resisted standard local treatments like as radiofrequency ablation (RFA) or surgery [31].

The distribution of dosage of radiation beams, as well as the numerous dose adaptation and tools for tumor localization, all are important elements in EBRT delivery and planning. At the very same time, the dose recommendation and fractionation strategy should be biologically and medically compatible. It is necessary to increase the expected tumor control rate, the chances of normal tissue problems, and long-term quality of life. The selection process of an EBRT modality, in addition to physical dosage predictions, is projected to improve as a result of treatment planning based on knowledge [32].

Because of the time-consuming preparation and treatment procedure, high facility maintenance costs and reimbursement schedule, single-session or hypofractionation regimens are commonly used in EBRTs like Stereotactic body radiation therapy (SBRT), PBT (Proton Beam Therapy), SRT (Stereotactic Radiotherapy) and CBT (Carbon ion Beam Therapy). Hypofractionation, on the other hand, may not be the top treatment for every malignancy. Hypofractionation, for example, can stop sequential OARs and cause deadly side effects in centralized lung tumors while only causing minor harm in peripheral lung tumors. As a result, in EBRT, it is necessary to have universally acknowledged healthy tissues limits for hypofractionation treatment [33].

Using radiological images, gene expression data, radiomics, genomics and radiogenomics are likely to be effective in patient identification who might benefit through radiation in general, as well as anatomic radioresistant locations identification where an EBRT boost might be advantageous. Imaging of hypoxic may support locating such resistant zones, but more research is needed because the signal to noise ratio of semiconductor positron emission tomography (PET) is yet insufficient for dose escalation investigations [34].

EBRT is a treatment for people who have bone metastases that causes pain in one or a few sites. Although therapy is primarily palliative, it can relieve the pain in 60% to 85% of patients, with 15 to 58% obtaining total pain relief. EBRT may also help to preserve the function of skeletal and their integrity. Disease modification therapy, like EBRT for localized pain and systemic bone pain, is radiopharmaceuticals, should be investigated in addition to analgesic medicines. Cancer pain management is improved when palliative care practitioners or pain medicine physicians are involved. EBRT is convenient for the treatment of localized bone pain initiated by individual metastases. EBRT, on the other hand, is not feasible and would be too toxic for people suffering from diffuse bone pain as a result of broad metastatic disease. Radiopharmaceuticals that serve as calcium mimetics and localize precisely for the bone have been created as a result of this unmet demand [35]. The volume and dose details of external beam radiotherapy are summarized in Table 9.3.

Table 9.3 Volume and dose details of external beam radiotherapy [36, 37].

EBRT technology	Volume	Dose
PTV 1	Whole pelvic	50.40 Gy in 28 fx
SIB 1	Uterus fundus	60.20 Gy in 28 fx
SIB 2	Middle/lower 3rd of vaginal paraurethral area and right inguinal lymph nodes	58.80 Gy in 28 fx

9.5.2   Three-Dimensional Conformal Radiation Therapy (3D-CRT)

Three-dimensional conformal radiation therapy (3D-CRT) became popular in the late 1990s Because it provided improved target covering and greatly diminished bladder radiation exposure, it was chosen as the primary treatment for gynecologic cancers. Though, the quantity of radiation exposure to the rectum and intestine was not significantly reduced using this strategy. Recent advancements in computer technology have resulted in enhancements in the 3D-CRT approach, the most notable advancement is the creation of intensity-modulated radiation therapy (IMRT) [38, 39].

3D-CRT uses radiation beams that are tailored to enter the patient from a variety of angles, as much good tissue as possible to be spared. The term "conformal" refers to the process of shaping the beams to match the structure of the tumor. These treatments are frequently given to patients daily for up to seven weeks. When compared to other types of treatment, 3D CRT has several advantages. It makes use of specialized computers to find the exact area of the tumor. The formation and focusing of radiation beam towards the tumors from a variety of angles, making it less likely that normal tissues will be damaged. Each patient undergoes an initial consultation to see if they are a good candidate for radiation therapy. The next step before therapy is a simulation, which is the process of devising the best cancer treatment strategy. A unique immobilization device may be created to guarantee that the patient remains still during treatment, and a CT scan may be used to aid in the development of the treatment plan [40].

3D-CRT is a frequently accepted method to deliver radiation therapy. The Food and Drug Administration (FDA) has approved various commercial 3D treatment planning systems. 3D-CRT is more than just a supplement to traditional two-dimensional radiation oncology planning methods. In the two-dimensional treatment planning technique, the traditional simulator is utilized to create beam portals utilizing standardized beam arrangements and bone markers are visible on planning radiographs. For characterizing the tumor and organs at risk for specific patients, a visual simulation technique based on volumetric images is emphasized in 3D treatment planning.

The basic premise of 3D-CRT has comprised the dosage to normal and targeted tissue can be pinpointed with greater accuracy may controlled, resulting in better tumor control and lower morbidity. 3D treatment planning systems cost about $250,000 and involve extra resources such as physicians, therapists, physicists, and ancillary services to deliver therapy (radiology department or CT) [41].

9.5.3   Intensity Modulated Radiation Therapy (IMRT)

IMRT is a well-developed and rapidly expanding therapy that is utilized to care a vast variety of cancer around the world, containing deep-seated tumors and complicated anatomical features. Modern imaging procedures like ultrasonography (US), computed tomography (CT), positron emission tomography (PET), magnetic resonance imaging (MRI), as well as advanced delivery strategies, have become a much more effective medication option for patients with cancer. IMRT is popular because of its dose acceleration, increased Organs at Risk (OARs) sparing capabilities and improved exposure of Planning Target Volume (PTV). IMRT is a kind of external beam radiation that modulates the intensity of each beam by dividing it into beamlets. Computerized inverse planning algorithms modify the intensity of each beamlet separately, which is made possible by MLC movements. The varied intensity and changing of the number inside fields of each voxel improve the dose conformation such as concave dosage distribution [42].

IMRT, in contrast to 3D-CRT, utilizes non-uniform beams to give superior intended target volume coverage while reducing unwanted exposure to radiation to healthy organs. As a result, IMRT seems to have become a popular method for whole pelvic radiotherapy (WPRT), with studies showing that it provides more precise distributions of dose and tightened dose patterns to sites, in addition to lowering the probability of toxicity and unwanted complications to the small bowel, rectum, pelvic bones and bladder [38, 43].

Improved target conformity, especially for concave target volumes is one of the benefits of IMRT. It also increases the enables dose escalation, normal tissue sparing, compensates for missing tissue and induces intentional dose inhomogeneity. Disadvantage of IMRT includes that it needs substantial quality assurance program, organ outlining and enhanced medication time for target, enhanced total body irradiation dose and enhanced planning time (initially) with machine treatment time [43].

IMRT has been approved to be a secure and efficient treatment method for malignancies of lung, head, neck, breast, prostate system and central nervous system. While the technique has also been used to treat endometrial and cervical cancers, the results on its safety and efficacy in these patients have been inconsistent. For gynecologic malignancy, the IMRT treatment method was not well-recognized for general prescription, according to the National Comprehensive Cancer Network (NCCN) in late 2000s [44].

In IMRT clinical research, there are two fundamental paradigms have been studied. The first research approach tries to keep current tumor control ratios while reducing risk. For example, in H&N (Head and Neck) cancer research, IMRT aims to keep typical dosage in the malignant tumor and at-risk nodal regions, while reducing the exposure of dose to nearby normal tissue structures like spinal cord and salivary glands. The second technique is used to increase the tumor target dose while keeping toxicity at a manageable level. This strategy has been used in prostate cancer dosage escalation and hypofractionation trials, as well as in lung cancer trials [45].

Because IMRT treatment procedures are provided on daily basis with a linear accelerator, they're very comparable to traditional therapies. However, the patient's treatment may differ in several aspects. Because more individual treatment fields are used so the daily time for the treatment is slightly longer. To deliver the same dose, the higher beam modulation needs longer "beam-on" durations. A conventional neck and head radiation therapy take about 5–10 minutes. On the other hand, an IMRT neck and head treatment can take about 25–30 minutes to complete.

To limit toxicity, IMRT dose assessments usually display strong dose variation between the adjacent normal structures and tumors. As a result, excellent neck and head IMRT patient setup and placement are highly repeatable regularly. In the traditional neck and head radiation, for quality assurance, patients are oriented with basic lasers and mask marks, as well as weekly position check films. With this setup procedure, daily setup adjustments of 3–8 mm are safe.

This daily setup fluctuation is easily accommodated by conventional radiation design with broad lateral fields. More stringent setup verification and immobilization are required for high-quality IMRT. Optical guidance, daily portal filming, and linac/imaging machine hybrids are some of the ways that can be deployed. These procedures may need the use of an extra device, such as a maxillary bite tray which is used in optical guiding or a little extension of treatment time for daily imaging [46].

9.5.4   Image-Guided Radiation Therapy (IGRT)

Method of imaging at the time of administration of highly conformal radiation treatment have the goal to enhance precision and accuracy of target by compensating biological and anatomic aberrations which are called image guided radiation therapy (IGRT). Diminished planning treatment volume (PTV) expansion is possible with IGRT techniques such as volumetric or planar imaging (without or with implanted fiducial marker),

(3D) 3-dimensional surface imaging, electromagnetic and ultrasound transponders, integrated optical imaging by stereoscopic X-ray (ExacTrac). As a result of the reduced setup suspicions, it allows the reliable employment of sharp dose gradients amongst the PTV boundaries and area enclosing vital organs that are at risk. Furthermore, due to the verification process and acquisition of the image, IGRT approaches intensify overall treatment duration and RT team effort which may influence the operating expenses and clinical workflow [47, 48].

The main concept of IGRT is, increase the accuracy and precision of radiation treatment and decrease toxicity. It also allows for escalation of dose which enhances the tumor control. The accuracy of daily therapy distribution becomes even more important as the high-dose envelope conforms to target volumes. Intensity-modulated radiation therapy is linked through a sharp decrease in dosage outside or surrounding the target, necessitating strict management of geometric uncertainties (like organ motion and set-up errors) as well as improved target delineation and target localization before treatment administration. Procedures with more accuracy are generally intolerant during the setup failures and also provide image guidance for precise delivery. As a result, the everyday anatomy and each fraction position of the patient must be as similar as what was planned during therapy. In radiation planning and execution, there are various sources of uncertainty and mistake. Uncertainty in target volume delineation, organ positional change within the patient, unknown degree of microscopic malignancy and set-up errors are just a few examples [49].

The utilization of IGRT techniques in RT has enhanced significantly over last decade, but there has been a lot of heterogeneity in the availability and use of IGRT in medical field around the world. In addition, IGRT techniques are underutilized because of various problems related to gathered imaging exposure and the time utilizing behavior of their implementation [50].

The awareness of individuals for understanding the daily intra and inter fractional setup changes and mobility has been enhanced by the use of the IGRT technique. Intrapatient and interpatient difference in liver and lung tumor motion associated with breathing have been quantified and the complexity of these motions have to get more clearer. Understanding the different IGRT procedures with their relevancy and inadequacies can assist the oncologist related to radiation in making a correct decision on the method which is most suitable for the specific health condition to maximize radiation therapy benefit. IGRT is generally used to benefit medical situations when the tumor is near to healthy and sensitive tissues, when large organ setup and motion errors may result in severe concerns of positional errors or when the doses needed for disease control exceed the levels of tolerance in adjacent normal tissues. With some clinical experience, it is envisaged that upper abdominal and thoracic targets with necessary respiratory motion, obese individuals, neck and head tumors, retroperitoneal and paraspinal sarcomas and prostate cancer will benefit the most. IGRT is predicted to provide the least benefit in medical situations where great local control was achieved by even low dose irradiation, palliative radiation therapy applied in vast fields and in treatment of superficial cancers which are susceptible to direct visual inspection [51].

9.5.5   Intraoperative Radiation Therapy (IORT)

(IORT) Intraoperative radiotherapy is a procedure in which ionizing radiations significant dose is delivered precisely to the cancer cell or during tumor bed surgery. With IORT, this leads to a higher therapeutic ratio. Whereas in it 1960s it was introduced first with the low-kV IORT and self-shielding transportable linear accelerator emergence devices, its comeback was seen as a prominence. These devices have enabled its wider use in the community by removing the logistical issues of transporting patients for radiotherapy during surgery or building a shielded operating room. As part of a multidisciplinary strategy, IORT is frequently utilized in conjunction with different modalities such as external beam radiation (EBRT), maximal surgical resection or chemotherapy. IORT has been determined to be efficacious in a range of cancers, including recurrent and locally progressed rectal cancer, pancreatic cancer, retroperitoneal sarcoma, early breast cancer and several genitourinary and gynecologic malignancies.

IORT has been delivered in a variety of ways. In current clinical practice, X-rays (kV IORT), beams of electrons (electron IORT or IOERT) and (HDR IORT) high-dose-rate brachytherapy are the few examples of IORT techniques that are used regularly [52].

In oncology, with direct visualization inside the operating room, IORT has several advantages. The advantage of IORT is that it can deliver the dose of tumoricidal radiation for a single time with customization of the radiation to the area which has more risk of disease recurrence. This results in a large relative biological efficacy while minimizing dosage to normal tissue through tumor bed devascularization, eradication of interfraction tumor cell repopulation and maybe systemic immunological impact [53].

IOERT (intraoperative electron radiotherapy) is utilized during breast-conserving surgery. It acts as a booster at dose 10-12 Gy for (WBI) whole breast irradiation and dose 20-24 Gy (full dose) for partial breast irradiation (PBI). From all the IORT approaches, IOERT has the most proof in the disease cure. For a long time, follow-up > 5 years, low rate of local recurrence were seen when it is administered as a boost. IOERT has been involved in the long term control of tumors in the local area, mostly in more than 90% of the patient that comes under high risk groups of locally advanced or triple-negative breast cancers. IOERT as PBI with a dose of 21 Gy appears as a promising therapeutic substitute to regular WBI for selected individuals with low risk. IOERT has been recognized as a beneficial method due to several reasons: Due to direct vision of the tumor bed, geographic misses are avoided, allowing a large single dose to be administered with maximum accuracy, entirely restricting the skin and assuring an excellent long time cosmetic result. Likewise, in cell-line experiments, large single doses appear to elicit biological pathways with demonstrable anticancer capacity. Furthermore, in chosen low-risk constellations, IOERT significantly reduces the whole time of treatment when used in conjunction with (generally hypofractionated) PBI or as a WBI [54].

Intraoperative radiation (IORT) was previously only available at centers having shielded operating rooms (ORs) with dedicated linear accelerators, at high expense and in a normal radiotherapy chamber transport from the OR is required. The ability to treat patients by using IORT is no longer limited to the special operating rooms availability, it can also be done in conventional, unshielded ORs employing mobile/portable IORT machines with X-rays of low-kV having steep dosage gradient. Previous IORT systems also include another problem like the anesthetized patient had to be transported from the OR table to the accelerator for treatment [55].

Intraoperative irradiation with high-dose-rate remote-afterloading brachytherapy (HDRIORT) necessitates specialized physical equipment and services, proper software of computer for the planning of treatment and physicians trained in dose delivery, dose planning and quality assurance methods, all of these are act as an important part of the interdisciplinary team. The utilization of HDR-IORT stems benefits in restricting the therapeutic dose towards the highly localized target while protecting normal tissues by shielding them or shifting them away from tumor cells [56].

The Intrabeam® system (Carl Zeiss Meditec, Dublin, CA, USA) utilizes a photon beam mobile X-ray machine of 50 kV which has been in medicinal use since 1999. Tiny accelerator generates low-energy X-rays which act as an isotropic point source by accelerating an electron beam to the drift tube tip. The source is installed permanently in the unit of treatment and is calibrated both externally and internally daily. This system is standardized at a rate of single dosage and output factor and also designed for single fraction IORT. Versatile solid state spherical applicators having a diameter of 1.5–5 cm are used to distribute IORT. Treatment times range from 20 to 45 minutes which depends on the applicator size [57].

Since 2009, the Axxent® System (Xoft Inc., Sunnyvale, CA, USA) has been used as electronic brachytherapy equipment in a medicinal system. An electronic, small, high-dose rate low-energy X-ray tube was built onto the flexible multi lumen catheter which generates X-rays about 40–50 Kv at catheter tip which serves as the radiation source. The system of Axxent was developed by fractionated balloon based partial irradiation of breast with different voltages and currents to accommodate variations in depths or rates of doses, but this is also utilized for single fractions. Disposable balloons with ellipsoidal and spherical shapes are used (5–6 cm elliptical and 3–6 cm spherical) at 10–20 minute intervals during treatment. With simply portable shielding, both systems can be employed in a typical operating room [58].

9.5.6   Brachytherapy

Internal Radiation Therapy, Endocurietherapy, Curietherapy, and Plesiotherapy are all terms used interchangeably to describe brachytherapy. It is defined as the method of delivering radiotherapy by the utilization of sealed sources which are placed close to the treatment location as possible. Brachytherapy comes from the Greek word "Brachys," which denotes

Table 9.4 Some commonly used radioactive sources with their application [59].

Source	Maximum energy	Available in forms	Application
Caesium 137	0.662 MeV	Tubes and Needles	Used as an alternative for Radium in Manual Afterloading
Cobalt 60	1.25 MeV	Needles and Spherical plates	Used as an alternative for Radium Ophthalmic Applicators
Iridium 192	1.5 MeV	Tubes and Flexible Wire	Uterine, Neck and Head, Breast and Cervix Malignancies
Radium 226	2.4 MeV	Tubes and Needles	No longer in use

"short distance." In 1931, Forssell created the term "brachytherapy." Small sources of radioactive substances are inserted within the tumor or close to it during brachytherapy. It can be used to treat tumors by implanting sources using catheters or needles. The most frequent brachytherapy sources release 'photons,' but sources that emit 'beta rays' and 'neutrons' are also utilized [59]. Table 9.4 represents the few examples of radioactive sources with their application.

Brachytherapy is used in cancer treatment with an isotope of different radioactive placed in, on or near the tumors or lesions can be treated across a short distance. Based on dose delivering rates, brachytherapy procedures can be categorized as either low-dose-rate (LDR) or high-dose-rate (HDR). At a distance of 1 cm from the source, HDR systems employed rates of doses up to 12 Gy/h, however, LDR systems use lower values of 0.4-2 Gy/h. Iodine-125 [^{125}I], palladium-103 [^{103}Pd], cobalt-60 [^{60}Co], cesium-137 [^{137}Cs] and iridium-192 [^{192}Ir] are some of the most commonly utilized radioisotopes in brachytherapy. Brachytherapy sources come in a variety of forms (needles, wires, tubes, pellets and seeds), each with distinctive half-life and average photon energy. The dose is administered either for a small time (temporary implants) or a lifetime in brachytherapy system (permanent implants). After the dose has been administered by the temporary implant, the system is removed. Intracavitary brachytherapy is the method in which the systems are implanted inside the body cavities adjacent to interstitial brachytherapy and tumor and in other methods, sources are implanted within the tumor are the two basic forms of brachytherapy implants [60].

Other less common procedures like surface, intraoperative, intraluminal and intravascular implants are also accessible. Prostate, brain, breast and cervical tumors are the most common cancers treated with brachytherapy. However, it can be used to treat a variety of different malignancies. Brachytherapy is a well established prostate cancer treatment method in general. This is a proven method of treatment for both high and low-risk prostate cancer [61].

BT Techniques

Defined by the dosage rate (according to ICRU definitions): They may classify as follows,

1. 0.4-2.0 Gy/h: (LDR) Low-dose-rate
2. 0.5-1.0 Gy/h: (PDR) Pulsed-dose-rate
3. 2-12 Gy/h: (MDR) Medium-dose-rate
4. > 12 Gy/h: (HDR) High-dose-rate [62].

Low-dose-rate (LDR) with Brachytherapy, also named as seed implant or permanent prostate brachytherapy, is a treatment that involves permanently implanting radioactive sources into the prostate. International Commission on Radiologic Units and Measurements defines brachytherapy, as the utilization of a source of radiation with a less than 2 Gy per hour dose rate. With several studies its use and efficacy were proved, brachytherapy increases the LDR administration which become a well established technique of treatment in high-risk prostate cancer [63].

For patients which have a high risk of prostate tumor, researchers performed a randomized controlled trial of LDR brachytherapy by comparing iridium[192] with 35 Gy and 40 Gy in 20 fractions to EBRT. EBRT was administered alone for 66 Gy in 33 fractions. In either arm, no androgen restriction method was provided simultaneously or neoadjuvantly. The clinical or biochemical breakdown was the primary result. The EBRT plus temporary LDR brachytherapy boost arm failed 29 percent of the time which is determined by the median follow-up of 8.2 years as compared to the EBRT single arm which is found to be 61 percent (p = 0.0024; hazard ratio = 0.42). Regardless of this, the dose of EBRT employed in this research was minimal as compared to contemporary standards, it set the framework and verifies the principle that brachytherapy combined with EBRT moderates the doses which result in a higher biochemical control rate rather than the alone EBRT [64].

Pulsed-dose-rate (PDR) utilises a 15-37 GBq (0,5 – 1Ci) single-stepping [192]Iridium source. This results in 3 Gy per hour treatment dose rates, that can be used (pulsed) by each hour for a total of 24 pulses each day. In 2.5 mm long and 1.1 mm wide capsule source is get enclosed. Treatment periods for each place and each pulse may be specified from 0 to 999.9 seconds. A single radioactive stepping system passes via all of the catheters during each pulse. A dedicated computer can accurately configure the single high activity source route via a catheter inserted, which is then carried out by a distant projector source. The isodoses are produced that are improved by varying the stay time of sources as a trajectory function inside the implanted volume. Dose distributions individualization is possible and the medical staff is getting essentially spared from radiation exposure. In HDR source power requirement is less than 10 to 20 times and the shielding requisites are less strict. A regular room of brachytherapy would just need two additional half-valued shielding layers and the use of an accelerator type bunker is not needed [65].

In medium-dose-rate (MDR), the radiation is supplied at 2–12 Gy/h (+/–10 Gy/h) using cesium[137] sources in 1–3 fractions which depends on the dose. Afterloading treatment might be manual or automatic. In comparison to LDR treatments, the total dose must be reduced due to the greater dose rate. During treatment, you will be admitted to the hospital. It is infrequently utilized, and gynecologic malignancies are the most typical application location [66].

Brachytherapy of (HDR) High Dose Rate is a radiation type in which radioactive sources are employed to the nearby proximity of the treatment area. The objective of this technique is to administer high radiation doses to small areas of the body, allowing for better disease management and less treatment toxicity to normal tissues nearby. A small source of iridium linked with the end of a wire may be robotically moved via several channels, halting at specified points (dwell positions) for varying amounts of time, according to HDR brachytherapy a remote afterloading method. HDR brachytherapy utilizes the iridium^{192} isotopes and is supplied at an administration area with > 12 Gy/hour rate. The benefits of HDR brachytherapy include accurate source location, extreme variable dwell positions and lengths that allow dose sculpting, quicker treatment times (minutes versus days) and safety to the medical staff from dangerous radiation [67].

9.5.7   Stereotactic Radiosurgery (SRS)

Radiation therapy is used to remove abnormal tissue, such as tumor cells while causing minimum damage to healthy tissue. In 1951, Lars Leksell created (SRS) stereotactic radiosurgery as a treatment alternative to whole brain irradiation. SRS works by delivering several high-energy convergent beams of gamma rays, protons to discrete or x-rays and radiographically defined treatment volume. Radiation is delivered in a highly conformal manner. The treatment volume receives a high, therapeutic prescription dose from several, intersecting beams of radiation, while normal brain tissue surrounding gets a relatively low dose. This treatment can be precisely customized, following the treatment volume's margins to allow quick energy dissipation beyond the edges while protecting normal tissue. Radiation fall-off into surrounding tissues is steep, which reduces toxicity and adverse effects while maintaining safety. Radiation-induced DNA damage by ions and free radicals is the basis of stereotactic radiosurgery. Endothelial cell death, T-cell response and microvascular dysfunction all contribute to the primary target of the vascular endothelium [68].

The accurate administration of a large radiation dose to a target with a fast drop off of the doses around the normal tissues is a critical SRS component. Cyberknife (Accuray, Sunnyvale, CA, USA), Gamma Knife (Elekta AB, Stockholm, Sweden), gantry–based linear accelerator (LINAC) systems (like BrainLab, Novalis TX) and proton beam based systems are some of the technologies that can be employed [69].

Gamma Knife creates a stereotactic grid "space" for treatment planning by using a fixed immobilization frame and images captured while the frame is in place. For treatment planning, many imaging modalities can be employed, with all scans co-located in the same area. Fine cut post-contrast magnetic resonance imaging is the most common treatment for brain metastases (MRI). When patients have MRI contraindications (like pacemaker or defibrillator), computed tomography (CT) with contrast can be performed instead of MRI. PET (Positron emission tomography) scans are utilized in the planning of therapy to include biologically significant information [69].

Adler *et al.* created Cyberknife (CK) in 1987, a robotic-based SRS device. A linear accelerator with six separate free arm movements in this system can target diverse targets without using stereotactic frames for radiation and can target different lesions in any location. It is utilized after non-radical excision of lesions because of the higher occurrence of hormone-inactive pituitary adenomas. Complications are comparable to those seen with other SRS procedures (most often complication is the development of hypopituitarism) [70].

9.6 Different Role of Deep Learning with Corresponding Role of Medical Physicist

9.6.1 Deep Learning in Patient Assessment

9.6.1.1 Radiotherapy Results Prediction

Currently, treatment of cancer is based on multidisciplinary care, such as chemotherapy, radiation therapy and physical surgery, which have been established. Radiation therapy has been used on approximately 30% of all most cancer patients inside the Republic of Korea and in the United States on 50% of cancer patients. Potential advantages should be examined before the beginning of radio therapy, Tumor Control Probability (TCP) and Normal Tissue Complication Probability (NTCP) were taken into consideration which is involved in the treatment. The aim is to increase the TCP while lowering the NTCP. For instance, if the dose absorption which is delivered to the tumor is very less, the therapeutic response will be reduced, or if an unreasonably large dose to the OARs was administered an immediate or late radiation toxicity (like radiation therapy induced fibrosis or oncogenesis) get developed. As a result, precise assessment and prediction of risk are critical, especially when the alternatives are available like chemotherapy.

The data used to operate radiation outcomes is separated into structured and unstructured categories. While preparing an outcome prediction model only structured data is used, a Deep Learning model based on the Multilayer perceptron (MLP) and (RNN) Recurrent Neural Network family is suggested for this objective. In the event of unstructured data like notes or photos related to medical, a feature extractor is required to obtain useful information as a result for this purpose Convolutional Neural Network (CNN) model is often advised [71].

Although the characteristics of a multivariate model are determined by decisions made during the development process (for instance, the overall prediction accuracy is determined when the features are chosen), the accomplishment of models depends on another factor, like its interactivity and availability, that enhances the acceptability. Models that are based on the vast population of patients have received accurate external validation that can be rejected by medical staff if the interpretation of the result is difficult by the used model, if the medicinal use of the model is not reported or proven and if there is lack of possibility to utilize the model. Though few models like decision trees have an implicitly interpretable visual demonstration which the majority of models do not have. The nomogram is a highly interpretable demonstration of a feature set. In the early 20th century, the nomogram was first utilized to make estimated mathematical problems graphical computations. Nomograms experienced a renewal in medicine which is determined by the growing number of research in this field [72].

In traditional radiomics, quantitative consistency features are extracted from clinical pictures to find correlations between the clinical endpoints. CNNs can improve the traditional radiomics performance by determining picture patterns which are not determined by a typical radiomic framework. This theory was tested by using a CNN to determine the treatment results in the patient having neck and head squamous cell carcinoma, based on their pre-treatment computed tomography imaging. The Cancer Imaging Archive provided the validation sets (106 patients) and training (194 patients) by involving four mutually independent institutions. This technique shows an Area Under Curve (AUC) of 0.88 while used in determining the distant metastasis when compared with a conventional radiomic framework used on the same group of patients. When this model is combined with the prior model, the AUC rises to 0.92 [73].

9.6.1.2 Respiratory Signal Prediction

During radiation therapy, target movements, such as liver and lung cancers, might change dramatically due to changes in respiratory breathing patterns. As a result, to avoid the target area, every treatment area where radiation is applied is often planned to be greater than the targets actual volume, resulting in less radiation exposure to normal tissues. Several motion management techniques are thoroughly examined: The breath-hold approach, in which patients hold their breath for a while during irradiation to reduce respiratory movements. This strategy, although, might not be appropriate for the patients that are unable to hold their breaths for long periods.

Treatments with free breathing are the approach in which the patient is allowed to breathe freely throughout the treatment. During simulation, four-dimensional computed tomography (4D-CT) is utilized to catch the tumors motion range and construct the volume of the internal target. For respiratory motion, the volume of the target is often larger, which may result in a larger dose to the tissues which is present surrounding the target. Respiratory gated treatment is the technology that tracks tumor movements and turns on the beam of radiation when the aimed target of tissue is coming inside the Beam's Eye View (BEV) by using signals of breathing obtained from an external device like Real-time Position Management (RPM). Radiation beams chase the moving target dynamically, ensuring that the target persists within the BEV at all times. The dynamic tracking and respiratory gating are used to decrease the treatment field and reduce harm to the normal tissue caused by radiation. Dynamic tracking provides a greater delivery efficiency than respiratory gating since the radiation is administered constantly while target tracking [74, 75].

Wang *et al.* employed Bi-LSTM (Long Short Term Memory) while testing the precision of respiratory signal and found that its performance is better than the autoregressive integrated moving average (ARIMA), that is often utilized in the analysis of time series and Adaptive Boosting with Multilayer Perceptron (ADMLP). For ADMLP, ARIMA and Bi-LSTM, the normalized root-mean-square error (nRMSE) was 0.228, 0.521 and 0.081, respectively. For respiratory pattern prediction, Bi-LSTM had the best results [76].

9.6.2 Simulation Computed Tomography

In many areas like nursing and Medical Radiation Sciences (MRS), simulation can be employed as an efficacious training method to develop the confidence and skill of students. The utilization of (VR) virtual reality simulation for training of medical staff has been grown as digital technologies and has to gain progress in society. The Virtual Environment Radiotherapy Training (VERT) method has been used to describe and assess the VR usage to help in the learning of radiation therapy (RT) trainees. The utilization of virtual reality simulation helps medical imaging (MI) trainees to improve their general radiography skills [77].

Thoracic surgery with video assistance for the metastatic lung tumors treatment is used currently and segmentectomy and lobectomy have become a conventional surgical method. Several kinds of research have shown that a thoracoscopic technique is as safe and successful as a traditional thoracotomy, with morbidity reduction, better postoperative respiratory function and comparable oncological outcomes. Anatomical variations in pulmonary arteries can result in significant complications, such as sudden bleeding in VATS patients. Preoperative simulations and a detailed understanding of the preoperative surgical anatomy by utilizing image modalities will substantially aid in the safe performance of VATS. Surgeons can create lungs anatomy by using 3-dimensional (3D) images which are captured by the multidetector computed tomography (MDCT). To produce pulmonary arteries 3D images and the tracheobronchial tree for surgical simulations, they utilize 3D lung modeling based on pictures of CT clicked via utilizing the Fujifilm Synapse Vincent system (Fujifilm Corporation, Tokyo, Japan). Several studies have addressed the use of 3D evaluations before or during surgery in the thoracic surgery field [78].

In the literature, 95–98% of Pulmonary artery (PA) branches were identified preoperatively by utilizing 3D-CT angiography in patients undergoing thoracoscopic and open surgery, similar to our findings. Several writers also used 3D reconstruction to study aberrant PA, (Pulmonary Vein) PV, or bronchial abnormalities for surgery. Before performing anatomical segmentectomy of lung cancer, 3D simulation is used in determining the inter-segmental veins as pulmonary segment boundary lines, in determining surgical margins by utilizing the lateral 3D images and identifying the targeted segmental bronchi via vertical 3D images. These studies display that the use of intraoperative visual guidance for the target bronchi and pulmonary vessels as well as their relationship with each other is disclosed by high-quality 3D images. Thoracic surgeons are better prepared for more sophisticated surgeries and can perform safer anatomical resections of the lung [79].

Adaptive radiotherapy (ART) is a treatment that uses one or more plans to repair morphological differences. Imaging is utilized to determine these differences and adjust the treatment approach as needed. Adaptive radiotherapy is described as altering a patient's radiation treatment plan during a period of radiation therapy to determine the temporal alteration alterations in anatomy (like cancer reduction, internal movements and weight loss) as well as changes in tumor function and biology (e.g. hypoxia). Different approaches employed during the treatment course to account for functional and anatomical variables which can affect the dose distribution are referred as adaptive radiotherapy [80].

To offer in-room CT scanners, in-room 3D imaging, gantry-mounted cone beam CT and tomotherapy-based megavoltage CT are accessible now. The choice of an area of interest to identify shifts related to reference simulation images have a specific requirement for verification of 3D position. The algorithms development help in the detection of non-rigid (elastic) deformation which is required for the registration of image. Dose adaptation has been proven in planning experiments to improve the additional dose provided to the irradiated volume, particularly the parotid glands [81].

9.6.3   Targets and Organs-at-Risk Segmentation

Target and OARs segmentation on CT images is the maximum time taking part in planning of radio therapy. To decrease waiting time of patients and enable ART, accurate and quick autosegmentation techniques are required. Recognition and delineation are the two activities that make up segmentation. Features finding (e.g. identification) in the images and assessing the areas based on that features is required for autosegmentation (i.e., delineation). As a result, CNN is extensively utilized and suggested as an automatic feature extractor that could extract images with their optimal features, while MLP is mostly utilized as a predictor to categorize regions based on retrieved features [82].

Prostate cancer treatment planning uses magnetic resonance (MR) which marks a substantial paradigm change from traditional computed tomography (CT)-based planning. The advanced MRI's of soft tissues contrast permits the physicians to describe clinical target volume [CTV] (seminal vesicles and prostate) more precisely and consistently in addition to differentiating organs-at-risk (OARs) which is closer to dangerous regions of the target border (bladder, urethra and rectal wall). This technique is currently carried out manually, which is very time taking for doctors and also susceptible to inter observer variability.

The development of an automated segmentation technique will be useful in streamlining the existing MR-only method and also in the transition for quick online adaptive planning. Aside from time savings, an accurate auto-segmentation technique should allow a single physician's knowledge to be shared as a learning device for those who are new in the treatment modality, improving contour consistency. The result of different studies shows that deep learning based methods for auto-segmentation are considerable in enhancement of traditional atlas-based techniques which can learn complicated feature sets and accurately execute pixel-wise classification of images [83].

Ronneberger *et al.* developed a U-Net network for biomedical images based on Fully Convolutional Network (FCN), which has now become widely utilized in medical image segmentation. U-Net and its derivatives have been widely employed in different sub-fields of computer vision (CV) because of their great performance. This method was first introduced at the MICCAI conference in 2015 and it has since been mentioned over 4000 times. U-Net has a lot of different versions so far. There are numerous new convolutional neural network design approaches. However, many of them still cited the U-Net core idea, incorporating other design elements or adding new modules [84].

Moeskops *et al.* have been evaluated the deep learning method in the brain tissues segmentation and white matter hyperintensities (WMH) via MRI. A T1-weighted image, a T1-weighted inversion recovery (IR) image and a T2-weighted fluid attenuated inversion recovery (FLAIR) image are used as inputs to discover a multi-scale convolutional neural network. White matter (WM), basal ganglia and thalami (BGT), cortical grey matter (cGM), cerebellum (CB), lateral ventricular cerebrospinal fluid (lvCSF), brain stem (BS), white matter hyperintensities (WMH), peripheral cerebrospinal fluid (pCSF) all are automatically segmented by this approach. This study shows that older individuals MR images with varied brain peculiarities degrees and motion artifacts may be get accurately segmented by using a convolutional neural network based segmentation technique [85].

9.6.4 Treatment Planning

9.6.4.1 Beam Angle Optimization

In general, fluence optimization has the main focus on inverse planning of radiation therapy. In intensity modulated radio treatment, beam angle optimization (BAO) contains selecting optimal radiation incidence directions and may affect the IMRT plans property, both to increase tumor coverage and organ sparing. However, in practice, the treatment planner still chooses beam orientations by hand most of the time, without any objective or stringent criterion. Pattern search technique is the derivative-free optimization method that can proceed and converge only a few functions of evaluations and have the potential to prevent local entrapment. Each framework of the pattern search technique includes a poll phase and a search step. The poll step confirms the convergence of a stationary point or local minimizer by doing a local investigation in a mesh neighborhood. Because it supports searches outside of the current iterate's neighborhood it must have the flexibility for search worldwide [86].

Intensity-modulated radiation therapy for tumor cure requires choice of a good set of beam angles, which is a crucial step and yet a difficult task. This problem is called the beam angle optimization (BAO) problem which is handled with a single objective that finding a beam angle configuration (BAC) initiates the optimal distribution of dose. Because there is a trade-off among major objectives of IMRT (to irradiate the tumor according to prescription while avoiding the healthy tissue present around the tumor), solving this difficulty by a multiobjective (MO) perspective makes sense. A deterministic local search algorithm is utilized in the first phase to choose a collection of locally optimal BACs based on a single objective function. Using exact nonlinear programming approach, an optimal dose distribution for every BAC with reference to single goal is determined through this search. During the second phase, for each promising local optimum BAC, a group of nondominated points is constructed and a dominance analysis is performed among them. The approach produces a set of (roughly) efficient BACs with good dosage distributions. The two-phase procedure is used on a prostate case to demonstrate the methods viability [87].

Recent research has been published on beam angle optimization by utilizing a complicated Deep Learning algorithm. Taasti *et al.* brought a Bayesian optimization based beam angle selection technique, in their in-house treatment planning system for pencil beam scanning [88].

Gerlach *et al.* determine the feasibility and analyzes the CNN based candidate for the generation of the beam in robotic radiosurgery. Robotic radiosurgery uses robotic arms flexibility to attain large target conformity and a steep dose gradient. However, because of search space, possible beam directions for dosage distribution are subjectively wide, treatment planning becomes a computationally hard operation. In clinical practice, treatment planning is based on a candidate beams collection created by a randomized heuristic.

To determine interesting candidate beams, a convolutional neural network is utilized. The effect of a candidate beam on the given dosage specifically using radiological aspects of the patient is forecasted and this prediction is used to guide candidate beam selection. During planning, characteristics are characterized as organ systems projections that are relevant.

For the candidate of random and CNN-predicted beams, inverse planning solutions are generated. The researches suggest that deep learning based on radiological capabilities can significantly enhance the quality of treatment plan, decrease treatment time and minimize computation runtime as compared to the heuristic method that is utilized in the hospitals [89].

9.6.4.2   Dose Prediction

The treatment outcomes of cancer patients are gradually increasing as radiation therapy treatment technology advances. In contrast to conventional 3D conformal radio therapy, innovative treatment techniques including intensitmodulation radiation therapy and volumetric arc therapy are recently used to provide larger doses to tumor regions while minimizing efficacious doses to normal organs. Though the capacity of these sophisticated medication approaches is used to create an optimal plan which depends on the planner's experience and a time taking activity must be examined, till treatment objective is realized [90].

Recently, commercial software in shape of RapidPlan is available (version 13.6, Varian Oncology Systems, Palo Alto, CA, USA). A knowledge based planning (KBP) system is constructed by utilizing earlier, medically authorized treatment data based on regression analysis, like dose-volume histogram (DVH) which estimates the algorithm of RapidPlan [91].

For neck and head, prostate, rectal and lung cancer cases, deep learning algorithms based on IMRT plans have been used for the prediction of dose. In addition, VMAT plans have been used to forecast doses for neck and head, prostate and rectal cancers. Other treatment methods like 3D dose prediction for neck and head tumor medication employing helical tomotherapy, have also been developed [92].

Several studies on radiation dosage prediction have been published. Dose prediction studies can be divided into two types. The prediction of dose-volume histograms (DVH) via mathematical frameworks is one example. Without three-dimensional dosage volume information, the research exclusively used DVH indices as model outputs and inputs. They used OARs sparingly to provide probable optimal plan information. The other is neural network-based dose volume prediction based on dosage volumes and images. According to quantitative index comparisons, those investigations revealed very high prediction precision, and the anticipated outcomes, three-dimensional dose volume can offer a probability for all qualitative and quantitative evaluations. The therapeutic effect of prediction models is uncertain because it depends on the action of models which assist in reducing the medicinal practice load [93].

Kandalan *et al.* have been pre-developed a dose prediction model by using deep learning for volumetric modulated arc therapy (VMAT) which is used in the prostate tumors treatment. This model is accepted after utilizing transfer learning with minimum input data such as one external institution planning style and three distinct internal treatment planning styles. The source model properly determines the dose distributions but its performance for the one external and three internal target styles was poor having to mean DSCs of 0.81–0.94 and 0.82–0.91, respectively. The target model predictions enhance mean DSC from 0.88–0.95 to 0.92–0.96 for the internal and exterior styles, by utilizing transfer learning. The source model was effectively adapted into a variety of practice styles. This paves the path for DL-based dose prediction to become more widely used in clinical practice [94].

9.6.5   Other Role of Deep Learning in Corresponds with Medical Physicists

DL is effective for various problems, including diseases diagnosis, where a DL advisor performed better than well-trained clinicians, and data mining in medical informatics, where hidden structures in clinical information were revealed and used to assist the management. Within the medical field of physics, research interests in DL have likewise grown rapidly and steadily in a relatively short time [95].

Medical physicists empowered with these cutting-edge tools should be capable of answering critical difficulties in modern medical oncology in the present big data revolution. A review of the fundamental components of DL model construction for medical physics applications, including model training, data processing and validation is presented and explored here. Deep learning can be classified as unsupervised learning or supervised learning or reinforcement learning, depending on the underlying task; each categories has its own input and output data characteristic and objectives to resolve various types of problems in medical physics which includes process automation to predictive analytics. It's also understood that data capacity prerequisites may vary based on the type of medical physics activity and methods used. Before training a model, it is necessary to do data processing, that is critical for model consistency and precision. Deep learning, a subset of machine learning, can build multilevel representations from raw input data, removing need for hand crafted features in traditional machine learning [96, 97].

It's a multilayer (deep) structure with nonlinear activation functions that's an extension of traditional linear models. The idea of getting "deeper" is linked to learning complicated data patterns and recent advances in parallel computer architectures and the growth of more robust optimization approaches for effective implementation of these algorithms have facilitated its realization. Model validation is a crucial step in the development of DL models. It is impossible to trust the model being constructed to generalize to unknown data without it. When using DL, keep in mind that, according to Amara's rule, people tend to overestimate a technology's abilities in the near term while underestimating its capability in the long run. Models that balance accuracy and interpretability should be created to integrate the DL role into conventional medical practice. Deep-learning algorithms offer the ability to automate routine procedures, improve the safety and efficacy of auto-contouring, medication planning, motion management, quality assurance and result prediction in radiation oncology. Medical physicists have been at the forefront of technological translation into medicine and they should be ready to accept and lead the inevitable role of DL in radiation oncology practice [96, 97].

Deep-learning algorithms have also been utilized in other traditional radiation disciplines, according to recent studies. Processing of simulation and positioning pictures (MRI to pseudo-CT image synthesis, metal artifact correction, image quality enhancement, deformable multimodal imaging registration) are just a few examples. Automatic treatment planning or assurance of quality are two terms that can be used interchangeably. It's worth noting that combining some of these distinct applications could make adaptive radiotherapy easier to implement in clinical practice. Deep learning systems have also been created for managing patient's mobility and anatomy at the time of therapy [98].

In a review of radiation oncology medical physicists, the majority (69 %) said they are utilizing or planning to employ deep learning in the clinic, but they also said they need accessibility to multicenter databases and more training programs. The majority of respondents in a survey of practicing radiation oncology such as physicians, oncologists and radiation therapists found that the possiblity of automation enhanced (including machine learning) in the future, but many of them also concluded that they deficite the training and tools to implement these techniques in the hospitals. Image classification, model quality standards, radiomics, and decision support systems have all been the focus of previous machine learning reviews in radiation oncology. A more general report focuses on the essential considerations for physicians when using deep learning, and just three case studies and algorithms were used to demonstrate the concepts. It offered a summary of machine learning with representations of certain algorithm, as well as single case studies on applications [99].

In chemotherapy, medical physicians have played an important role. Medical physicists have gradually retreated from direct clinical involvement in radiotherapy treatment planning, with medical dosimetrists taking on increased responsibility. Physicists must be involved in medication planning and clinical dosimetry for every patient, at least to some level; otherwise, physicians will no longer be regarded as clinical specialists. This withdrawal may have an adverse effect on the treatment qulaity and patient safety. To be effective partners with radiation oncologists, medical physicians should have a comprehensive understanding of human physiology and anatomy. They must also comprehend the drawbacks of the algorithms employed in radiotherapy and have a solid understanding of the physics of radiation as it interacts with the body's tissues. Medical physicists should also be at forefront of assessing new difficulties in radiation safety and quality. Physicists' input in clinical audits and risk assessments is critical in this regard. The best way forward is to take the required actions ahead of time to ensure that our vital position in clinical medicine is maintained and advanced [100].

Radiation oncologists, especially medical physicists, are at the leading post of developing and implementing novel methods for delivering RT to tumor patient like children. A quality assurance program and safety procedures must be created at each institution to confirm that pediatric patients are cured safely. Medical physicists conduct regular quality assurance tests and measurements on treatment planning systems, RT equipment, imaging equipment for RT simulation and patient placement, verify and record systems for RT delivery and patient-specific dosimetry to ensure consistency and accuracy. Although QA tests for adult and pediatric treatments are similar, there are several differences which medical physicians consider while treating children. Because many child patients are treated in clinical trials, physicists and dosimetrists should be aware of the changes in normal-tissue limits between adults and children. Many exciting technological improvements in RT are being investigated in addition to the activities and advancements outlined above.

The majority are directed by medical physicians and are predicted to have a significant effect on RT efficacy, safety and innovative uses. Automation (organ segmentation, knowledge-based planning, plan QA), machine learning, knowledge-guided prescription, improved biological modeling and optimization, low and fast dose image guidance procedures, dynamic trajectory optimization of beam delivery, online adaptive therapy, ultrahigh dose-rate delivery and big data analytics are all examples of these innovations. Although the impact of these advancements on children is currently minimal, it is likely to grow over the coming years. Future opportunities abound, but to accelerate clinical acceptance and achieve the ultimate objective of treating tumors while limiting damage, physicists must work together with other members of the radiation oncology team [101].

The task of radiotherapy plan validation is a complicated process in which a medical physicist confirms several treatment plan components before delivering radiation. It's a job that frequently necessitates conferring with other practitioners, analyzing data from numerous software systems and QA process outcomes (such as measurements), and relying on the physicist's clinical knowledge and judgment throughout. The primary purpose of these checks is to look for obvious flaws as well as the plan's suitability. As a result, it is a crucial and effective point in radiation oncology safety, as well as an area where ML-based technologies have the potential to have a significant therapeutic impact [102].

9.7   Conclusion

Deep learning is a machine learning subset that utilizes numerous layers to extract higher-level features from raw data. In medical imaging, deep learning is the most extensively used technique, particularly for lesion identification, image classification and segmentation. Deep learning methods are used in radiation oncology that can provide various benefits and significant support to physicians at various stages of treatment, including the ability to improve technical parameters (such as quality of treatment and speed) while also providing medically relevant insights. This book chapter illustrates the role of radiation therapy and deep learning in healthcare. Its focus on the various deep learning programs used in radiation therapy such as IMRT, EBRT, 3D-CRT, IGRT, Intraoperative RT, Brachytherapy, SRS Manuscript also describes the different roles of deep learning with their corresponding role with a medical physicist. Radiologists are unlikely to be replaced by machine learning. Instead, these strategies are expected to assist radiologists, improve radiology efficiency and improve the diagnostic accuracy of radiologists. All therapies have their specific function and help in identification and image segmentation, radiomic signature discovery and image phenotyping, image dose quantification, clinical result estimation, radiation adaptation, image generation and dose-response modeling.

References

1. Baskar, R., Lee, K.A., Yeo, R., Yeoh, K.W., Cancer and radiation therapy: Current advances and future directions. *Int. J. Med. Sci.*, *9*, 3, 193–199, 2012.
2. Hassanpour, S.H. and Dehghani, M., Review of cancer from the perspective of molecular. *J. Cancer Res. Pract.*, *4*, 4, 127–129, 2017.
3. Bansode, S., Cancer biology-causes & biomarkers of cancer. *Curr. Res. Oncol.*, *2019*, 1, 1–9, 2019.
4. Delwiche, F.A., Mapping the literature of radiation therapy. *J. Med. Libr. Assoc.*, *101*, 2, 120–127, 2013.
5. Tward, J.D., Anker, C.J., Gaffney, D.K., Bowen, G.M., Radiation therapy and skin cancer, in: *Modern Practices in Radiation Therapy*, pp. 207–246, 2012.
6. Atun, R., Jaffray, D.A., Barton, M.B., Bray, F., Baumann, M., Vikram, B., Hanna, T.P., Knaul, F.M., Lievens, Y., Lui, T.Y., Milosevic, M., Expanding global access to radiotherapy. *Lancet Oncol.*, *16*, 10, 1153–1186, 2015.
7. Thompson, M.K., Poortmans, P., Chalmers, A.J., Faivre-Finn, C., Hall, E., Huddart, R.A., Lievens, Y., Sebag-Montefiore, D., Coles, C.E., Practice-changing radiation therapy trials for the treatment of cancer: Where are we 150 years after the birth of Marie Curie? *Br. J. Cancer*, *119*, 4, 389–407, 2018.
8. Lederman, M., The early history of radiotherapy: 1895–1939. *Int. J. Radiat. Oncol. Biol. Phys.*, *7*, 5, 639–648, 1981.
9. Gianfaldoni, S., Gianfaldoni, R., Wollina, U., Lotti, J., Tchernev, G., Lotti, T., An overview on radiotherapy: From its history to its current applications in dermatology. *Open Access Maced. J. Med. Sci.*, *5*, 4, 521–525, 2017.
10. Coutard, H., Principles of x ray therapy of malignant diseases. *Lancet*, *224*, 5784, 1–8, 1934.
11. Streffer, C., International commission on radiological protection: Policy and worldwide standards, in: *The politics of scientific advice: Institutional design for quality assurance*, pp. 102–136, 2011.
12. Chao, A. and Chou, W., *Reviews of accelerator science and technology*, vol. 1, pp. 1–5, World Scientific Publishing Company, Singapore, 2008.
13. Price, R.C. and Obe, A.P., The society of radiographers 1920 to 2020. *Radiography (London, England: 1995)*, *26*, 3, 185–188, 2020.
14. Schwartz, D.L., Garden, A.S., Thomas, J., Chen, Y., Zhang, Y., Lewin, J., Chambers, M.S., Dong, L., Adaptive radiotherapy for head-and-neck cancer: Initial clinical outcomes from a prospective trial. *Int. J. Radiat. Oncol. Biol. Phys.*, *83*, 3, 986–993, 2012.
15. https://www.cancer.gov/about-cancer/treatment/types/radiation-therapy
16. Alzubaidi, L., Zhang, J., Humaidi, A.J., Al-Dujaili, A., Duan, Y., Al-Shamma, O., Santamaría, J., Fadhel, M.A., Al-Amidie, M., Farhan, L., Review of deep learning: Concepts, CNN architectures, challenges, applications, future directions. *J. Big Data*, *8*, 1, 1–74, 2021.

17. Dalal, N. and Triggs, B., Histograms of oriented gradients for human detection, in: *2005 IEEE computer society conference on computer vision and pattern recognition (CVPR'05)*, vol. 1, pp. 886–893, 2005.

18. Sit, M., Demiray, B.Z., Xiang, Z., Ewing, G.J., Sermet, Y., Demir, I., A comprehensive review of deep learning applications in hydrology and water resources. *Water Sci. Technol.*, *82*, 12, 2635–2670, 2020.

19. Boldrini, L., Bibault, J.E., Masciocchi, C., Shen, Y., Bittner, M.I., Deep learning: A review for the radiation oncologist. *Front. Oncol.*, *9*, 1–10, 2019.

20. Kim, Y., Roscoe, J.A., Morrow, G.R., The effects of information and negative affect on severity of side effects from radiation therapy for prostate cancer. *Support. Care Cancer*, *10*, 5, 416–421, 2002.

21. Al-Mefty, O., Kersh, J.E., Routh, A., Smith, R.R., The long-term side effects of radiation therapy for benign brain tumors in adults. *J. Neurosurg.*, *73*, 4, 502–512, 1990.

22. Li, X.Y., Liu, L., Xie, X.M., Zhou, C., The role of raltitrexed/cisplatin with concurrent radiation therapy in treating advanced cervical cancer. *Age*, *40*, 57, 3491–3496, 2014.

23. Brown, L.C., Mutter, R.W., Halyard, M.Y., Benefits, risks, and safety of external beam radiation therapy for breast cancer. *Int. J. Womens Health*, *7*, 449–458, 2015.

24. Ahlberg, K., Ekman, T., Gaston-Johansson, F., The experience of fatigue, other symptoms and global quality of life during radiotherapy for uterine cancer. *Int. J. Nurs. Stud.*, *42*, 4, 377–386, 2005.

25. Finger, P.T., Radiation therapy for orbital tumors: Concepts, current use, and ophthalmic radiation side effects. *Surv. Ophthalmol.*, *54*, 5, 545–568, 2009.

26. Birgisson, H., Pahlman, L., Gunnarsson, U., Glimelius, B., Adverse effects of preoperative radiation therapy for rectal cancer: Long-term follow-up of the Swedish Rectal Cancer Trial. *J. Clin. Oncol.*, *23*, 34, 8697–8705, 2005.

27. Boujelbene, N., Cosinschi, A., Boujelbene, N., Khanfir, K., Bhagwati, S., Herrmann, E., Mirimanoff, R.O., Ozsahin, M., Zouhair, A., Pure seminoma: A review and update. *Radiat. Oncol.*, *6*, 1, 1–12, 2011.

28. Rim, C.H. and Yoon, W.S., Leaflet manual of external beam radiation therapy for hepatocellular carcinoma: A review of the indications, evidences, and clinical trials. *OncoTargets Ther.*, *11*, 2865–2874, 2018.

29. https://aboutradiation.blogspot.com/2020/01/vmat-radiation-therapy-ppt.html

30. Sanuki, N., Takeda, A., Kunieda, E., Role of stereotactic body radiation therapy for hepatocellular carcinoma. *World J. Gastroenterol.*, *20*, 12, 3100–3111, 2014.

31. Shirato, H., Le, Q.T., Kobashi, K., Prayongrat, A., Takao, S., Shimizu, S., Giaccia, A., Xing, L., Umegaki, K., Selection of external beam radiotherapy approaches for precise and accurate cancer treatment. *J. Radiat. Res.*, *59*, 1, 2–10, 2018.

32. Timmerman, R., McGarry, R., Yiannoutsos, C., Papiez, L., Tudor, K., DeLuca, J., Ewing, M., Abdulrahman, R., DesRosiers, C., Williams, M., Fletcher, J., Excessive toxicity when treating central tumors in a phase II study of stereotactic body radiation therapy for medically inoperable early-stage lung cancer. *J. Clin. Oncol.*, 24, 30, 4833–4839, 2006.

33. Lambin, P., Van Stiphout, R.G., Starmans, M.H., Rios-Velazquez, E., Nalbantov, G., Aerts, H.J., Roelofs, E., Van Elmpt, W., Boutros, P.C., Granone, P., Valentini, V., Predicting outcomes in radiation oncology—multifactorial decision support systems. *Nat. Rev. Clin. Oncol.*, 10, 1, 27–40, 2013.

34. Pietzak, E. and Mucksavage, P., Bone health in Prostate Cancer, in: *Prostate Cancer*, pp. 491–507, 2016.

35. Yang, B., Zhu, L., Cheng, H., Li, Q., Zhang, Y., Zhao, Y., Dosimetric comparison of intensity modulated radiotherapy and three-dimensional conformal radiotherapy in patients with gynecologic malignancies: a systematic review and meta-analysis. *Radiat. Oncol.*, 7, 1, 1–11, 2012.

36. Giannelli, F., Chiola, I., Belgioia, L., Garelli, S., Pastorino, A., Marcenaro, M., Mammoliti, S., Costantini, S., Bizzarri, N., Vellone, V., Barra, S., Complete response in a patient with gynecological hidradenocarcinoma treated with exclusive external beam radiotherapy and brachytherapy: A case report. *J. Contemp. Brachytherapy*, 9, 6, 572–578, 2017.

37. Bhalavat, R., Chandra, M., Pareek, V., Nellore, L., George, K., Nandakumar, P., Bauskar, P., High-dose-rate interstitial brachytherapy in head and neck cancer: Do we need a look back into a forgotten art–a single institute experience. *J. Contemp. Brachytherapy*, 9, 2, 124–131, 2017.

38. Whitton, A., Warde, P., Sharpe, M., Oliver, T.K., Bak, K., Leszczynski, K., Etheridge, S., Fleming, K., Gutierrez, E., Favell, L., Green, E., Organisational standards for the delivery of intensity-modulated radiation therapy in Ontario. *Clin. Oncol.*, 21, 3, 192–203, 2009.

39. https://www.uabmedicine.org/patient-care/treatments/3d-conformal-radiation-therapy-crt-?medallia=occ-survey

40. Morris, D.E., Emami, B., Mauch, P.M., Konski, A.A., Tao, M.L., Ng, A.K., Klein, E.A., Mohideen, N., Hurwitz, M.D., Fraas, B.A., Roach III, M., Evidence-based review of three-dimensional conformal radiotherapy for localized prostate cancer: An ASTRO outcomes initiative. *Int. J. Radiat. Oncol. Biol. Phys.*, 62, 1, 3–19, 2005.

41. Zahra, J.U., Ahmad, N., Khalid, M., Noor ul Huda Khan Asghar, H.M., Gilani, Z.A., Ullah, I., Nasar, G., Akhtar, M.M., Usmani, M.N., Intensity modulated radiation therapy: A review of current practice and future outlooks. *J. Radiat. Res. Appl. Sci.*, 11, 4, 361–367, 2018.

42. Georg, P., Georg, D., Hillbrand, M., Kirisits, C., Pötter, R., Factors influencing bowel sparing in intensity modulated whole pelvic radiotherapy for gynaecological malignancies. *Radiother. Oncol.*, 80, 1, 19–26, 2006.

43. Taylor, A. and Powell, M.E.B., Intensity-modulated radiotherapy—what is it? *Cancer Imaging*, 4, 2, 68–73, 2004.

44. Iğdem, S., Ercan, T., Alco, G., Zengin, F., Ozgüleş, R., Geceer, G., Okkan, S., Ober, A., Turkan, S., Dosimetric comparison of intensity modulated pelvic radiotherapy with 3D conformal radiotherapy in patients with gynecologic malignancies. *Eur. J. Gynaecol. Oncol.*, *30*, 5, 547–551, 2009.

45. Hong, T.S., Ritter, M.A., Tome, W.A., Harari, P.M., Intensity-modulated radiation therapy: Emerging cancer treatment technology. *Br. J. Cancer*, *92*, 10, 1819–1824, 2005.

46. Hong, T.S., Tomé, W.A., Harari, P.M., Intensity-modulated radiation therapy in the management of head and neck cancer, in: *Squamous Cell Head and Neck Cancer*, pp. 115–124, 2005.

47. Simpson, D.R., Lawson, J.D., Nath, S.K., Rose, B.S., Mundt, A.J., Mell, L.K., A survey of image-guided radiation therapy use in the United States. *Cancer*, *116*, 16, 3953–3960, 2010.

48. Nabavizadeh, N., Elliott, D.A., Chen, Y., Kusano, A.S., Mitin, T., Thomas Jr., C.R., Holland, J.M., Image guided radiation therapy (IGRT) practice patterns and IGRT's impact on workflow and treatment planning: Results from a national survey of American Society for Radiation Oncology members. *Int. J. Radiat. Oncol. Biol. Phys.*, *94*, 4, 850–857, 2016.

49. Gupta, T. and Narayan, C.A., Image-guided radiation therapy: Physician's perspectives. *J. Med. Phys.*, *37*, 4, 174–182, 2012.

50. Kearney, M., Coffey, M., Leong, A., A review of Image Guided Radiation Therapy in head and neck cancer from 2009–2019–best practice recommendations for RTTs in the Clinic. *Tech. Innovations Patient Support Radiat. Oncol.*, *14*, 43–50, 2020.

51. Goyal, S. and Kataria, T., Image guidance in radiation therapy: Techniques and applications. *Radiol. Res. Pract.*, *2014*, 1–10, 2014.

52. Pilar, A., Gupta, M., Laskar, S.G., Laskar, S., Intraoperative radiotherapy: Review of techniques and results. *Ecancermedicalscience*, *11*, 1–33, 2017.

53. Thomas, T.O. and Small Jr., W., Intraoperative Radiotherapy (IORT)—A new frontier for personalized medicine as adjuvant treatment and treatment of locally recurrent advanced malignancy. *Front. Oncol.*, *8*, 1–2, 2018.

54. Kaiser, J., Reitsamer, R., Kopp, P., Gaisberger, C., Kopp, M., Fischer, T., Zehentmayr, F., Sedlmayer, F., Fastner, G., Intraoperative electron radiotherapy (IOERT) in the treatment of primary breast cancer. *Breast Care*, *13*, 3, 162–167, 2018.

55. Kraus-Tiefenbacher, U., Biggs, P., Vaidya, J., Francescatti, D., Electronic brachytherapy/low KV-IORT: Physics and techniques, in: *Intraoperative Irradiation*, pp. 85–98, 2011.

56. Anderson, L.L., Harrington, P.J., Germain, J.S., Physics of intraoperative high-dose-rate brachytherapy, in: *Intraoperative Irradiation*, pp. 87–104, Humana Press, Totowa, NJ, 1999.

57. *INTRABEAM System from ZEISS [Internet]*, Nice accredited, U.K., 2017, Available from: http://www.targit-research.org/clinics/intrabeam/about-intrabeam/.

58. Vaidya, J.S., Tobias, J.S., Baum, M., Keshtgar, M., Joseph, D., Wenz, F., Houghton, J., Saunders, C., Corica, T., D'Souza, D., Sainsbury, R., Intraoperative radiotherapy for breast cancer. *Lancet Oncol.*, 5, 3, 165–173, 2004.

59. Kadam, S., Desai, J., Nimma, V., Ramaswamy, E., Ramchandani, A., Mishra, I., Brachytherapy–principles and practice. *AOHDR*, 2, 2, 21–24, 2018.

60. Podgorsak, E.B., Radiation oncology physics: A handbook for teachers and students, in: *Brachytherapy: Physical and clinical aspects*, N. Suntharalingam, E.B. Podgorsak, H. Tolli (Eds.), pp. 451–484, International Atomic Energy Agency, Vienna, 2005.

61. Dahiya, M., Brachytherapy: A review. *J. Crit. Rev.*, 3, 6–10, 2016.

62. Skowronek, J., Current status of brachytherapy in cancer treatment–short overview. *J. Contemp. Brachytherapy*, 9, 6, 581–589, 2017.

63. Fischer-Valuck, B.W., Gay, H.A., Patel, S., Baumann, B.C., Michalski, J.M., A brief review of low-dose rate (LDR) and high-dose rate (HDR) brachytherapy boost for high-risk prostate. *Front. Oncol.*, 9, 1–7, 2019.

64. Sathya, J.R., Davis, I.R., Julian, J.A., Guo, Q., Daya, D., Dayes, I.S., Lukka, H.R., Levine, M., Randomized trial comparing iridium implant plus external-beam radiation therapy with external-beam radiation therapy alone in node-negative locally advanced cancer of the prostate. *J. Clin. Oncol.*, 23, 1192–1199, 2005.

65. Skowronek, J., Zwierzchowski, G., Piotrowski, T., Pulsed dose rate brachytherapy–description of a method and a review of clinical applications. *Rep. Pract. Oncol. Radiother.*, 6, 4, 197–202, 2001.

66. Yavaş, G., Dose rate definition in brachytherapy. *Turk. J. Oncol.*, 34, 1, 44–55, 2019.

67. Uyeda, M., Friedrich, F., Pellizzon, A.C.A., High dose rate (HDR) brachytherapy in gynecologic cancer regression: A review of the literature. *Appl. Cancer Res.*, 38, 1, 1–5, 2018.

68. Leksell, L., Stereotactic radiosurgery. *J. Neurol. Neurosurg. Psychiatry*, 46, 9, 797–803, 1983.

69. Halasz, L.M. and Rockhill, J.K., Stereotactic radiosurgery and stereotactic radiotherapy for brain metastases. *Surg. Neurol. Int.*, 4, 4, 185–191, 2013.

70. Abdali, A., Astafeva, L., Trunin, Y., Kalinin, P., Golanov, A., Abdali, B., Chmutin, G., Shkarubo, A., Chaurasia, B., Modern methods of stereotactic radiosurgery and radiotherapy for the treatment of Cushing disease. *Neurol. India*, 68, 7, 129–133, 2020.

71. Cheon, W., Kim, H., Kim, J., Deep learning in radiation oncology. *Prog. Med. Phys.*, 31, 3, 111–123, 2020.

72. Lambin, P., Van Stiphout, R.G., Starmans, M.H., Rios-Velazquez, E., Nalbantov, G., Aerts, H.J., Roelofs, E., Van Elmpt, W., Boutros, P.C., Granone, P., Valentini, V., Predicting outcomes in radiation oncology—multifactorial decision support systems. *Nat. Rev. Clin. Oncol.*, 10, 1, 27–40, 2013.

73. Diamant, A., Chatterjee, A., Vallières, M., Shenouda, G., Seuntjens, J., Deep learning in head & neck cancer outcome prediction. *Sci. Rep.*, *9*, 1, 1–10, 2019.

74. Sun, W.Z., Jiang, M.Y., Ren, L., Dang, J., You, T., Yin, F.F., Respiratory signal prediction based on adaptive boosting and multi-layer perceptron neural network. *Phys. Med. Biol.*, *62*, 17, 6822–6835, 2017.

75. Sun, W., Wei, Q., Ren, L., Dang, J., Yin, F.F., Adaptive respiratory signal prediction using dual multi-layer perceptron neural networks. *Phys. Med. Biol.*, *65*, 18, 1–17, 2020.

76. Wang, R., Liang, X., Zhu, X., Xie, Y., A feasibility of respiration prediction based on deep Bi-LSTM for real-time tumor tracking. *IEEE Access*, *6*, 51262–51268, 2018.

77. Gunn, T., Rowntree, P., Starkey, D., Nissen, L., The use of virtual reality computed tomography simulation within a medical imaging and a radiation therapy undergraduate programme. *J. Med. Radiat. Sci.*, *68*, 1, 28–36, 2021.

78. Hagiwara, M., Shimada, Y., Kato, Y., Nawa, K., Makino, Y., Furumoto, H., Akata, S., Kakihana, M., Kajiwara, N., Ohira, T., Saji, H., High-quality 3-dimensional image simulation for pulmonary lobectomy and segmentectomy: Results of preoperative assessment of pulmonary vessels and short-term surgical outcomes in consecutive patients undergoing video-assisted thoracic surgery. *Eur. J. Cardiothorac. Surg.*, *46*, 6, 120–126, 2014.

79. Shimizu, K., Nakano, T., Kamiyoshihara, M., Takeyoshi, I., Segmentectomy guided by three-dimensional computed tomography angiography and bronchography. *Interact. Cardiovasc. Thorac. Surg.*, *15*, 2, 194–196, 2012.

80. Mali, S.B., Adaptive radiotherapy for head neck cancer. *J. Maxillofac. Oral. Surg.*, *15*, 4, 549–554, 2016.

81. Simone II, C.B., Ly, D., Dan, T.D., Ondos, J., Ning, H., Belard, A., O'Connell, J., Miller, R.W., Simone, N.L., Comparison of intensity-modulated radiotherapy, adaptive radiotherapy, proton radiotherapy, and adaptive proton radiotherapy for treatment of locally advanced head and neck cancer. *Radiother. Oncol.*, *101*, 3, 376–382, 2011.

82. Long, J., Shelhamer, E., Darrell, T., Fully convolutional networks for semantic segmentation, in: *Proceedings of the IEEE conference on computer vision and pattern recognition*, pp. 3431–3440, 2015.

83. Elguindi, S., Zelefsky, M.J., Jiang, J., Veeraraghavan, H., Deasy, J.O., Hunt, M.A., Tyagi, N., Deep learning-based auto-segmentation of targets and organs-at-risk for magnetic resonance imaging only planning of prostate radiotherapy. *Phys. Imaging Radiat. Oncol.*, *12*, 80–86, 2019.

84. Liu, X., Song, L., Liu, S., Zhang, Y., A review of deep-learning-based medical image segmentation methods. *Sustainability*, *13*, 3, 1–29, 2021.

85. Moeskops, P., de Bresser, J., Kuijf, H.J., Mendrik, A.M., Biessels, G.J., Pluim, J.P., Išgum, I., Evaluation of a deep learning approach for the segmentation of brain tissues and white matter hyperintensities of presumed vascular origin in MRI. *NeuroImage Clin.*, *17*, 251–262, 2018.

86. Rocha, H., Dias, J.M., Ferreira, B.C., Lopes, M.C., Beam angle optimization for intensity-modulated radiation therapy using a guided pattern search method. *Phys. Med. Biol.*, *58*, 9, 1–18, 2013.

87. Cabrera, G.G., Ehrgott, M., Mason, A.J., Raith, A., A matheuristic approach to solve the multiobjective beam angle optimization problem in intensity-modulated radiation therapy. *Int. Trans. Oper. Res.*, *25*, 1, 243–268, 2018.

88. Taasti, V.T., Hong, L., Shim, J.S.A., Deasy, J.O., Zarepisheh, M., Automating proton treatment planning with beam angle selection using Bayesian optimization. *Med. Phys.*, *47*, 3286–3296, 2020.

89. Gerlach, S., Fürweger, C., Hofmann, T., Schlaefer, A., Feasibility and analysis of CNN-based candidate beam generation for robotic radiosurgery. *Med. Phys.*, *47*, 9, 3806–3815, 2020.

90. Cagni, E., Botti, A., Micera, R., Galeandro, M., Sghedoni, R., Orlandi, M., Iotti, C., Cozzi, L., Iori, M., Knowledge-based treatment planning: An inter-technique and inter-system feasibility study for prostate cancer. *Phys. Med.*, *36*, 38–45, 2017.

91. Fogliata, A., Reggiori, G., Stravato, A., Lobefalo, F., Franzese, C., Franceschini, D., Tomatis, S., Mancosu, P., Scorsetti, M., Cozzi, L., Rapid plan head and neck model: The objectives and possible clinical benefit. *Radiat. Oncol.*, *12*, 1, 1–12, 2017.

92. Ahn, S.H., Kim, E., Kim, C., Cheon, W., Kim, M., Lee, S.B., Lim, Y.K., Kim, H., Shin, D., Kim, D.Y., Jeong, J.H., Deep learning method for prediction of patient-specific dose distribution in breast cancer. *Radiat. Oncol.*, *16*, 1, 1–13, 2021.

93. Song, Y., Hu, J., Liu, Y., Hu, H., Huang, Y., Bai, S., Yi, Z., Dose prediction using a deep neural network for accelerated planning of rectal cancer radiotherapy. *Radiother. Oncol.*, *149*, 111–116, 2020.

94. Kandalan, R.N., Nguyen, D., Rezaeian, N.H., Barragán-Montero, A.M., Breedveld, S., Namuduri, K., Jiang, S., Lin, M.H., Dose prediction with deep learning for prostate cancer radiation therapy: Model adaptation to different treatment planning practices. *Radiother. Oncol.*, *153*, 228–235, 2020.

95. Shen, C., Nguyen, D., Zhou, Z., Jiang, S.B., Dong, B., Jia, X., An introduction to deep learning in medical physics: Advantages, potential, and challenges. *Phys. Med. Biol.*, *65*, 5, 1–46, 2020.

96. Bi, W.L., Hosny, A., Schabath, M.B., Giger, M.L., Birkbak, N.J., Mehrtash, A., Allison, T., Arnaout, O., Abbosh, C., Dunn, I.F., Mak, R.H., Artificial intelligence in cancer imaging: Clinical challenges and applications. *CA Cancer J. Clin.*, *69*, 2, 127–157, 2019.

97. Cui, S., Tseng, H.H., Pakela, J., Ten Haken, R.K., El Naqa, I., Introduction to machine and deep learning for medical physicists. *Med. Phys.*, *47*, 5, 127–147, 2020.

98. Meyer, P., Noblet, V., Lallement, A., Niederst, C., Jarnet, D., Dehaynin, N., Mazzara, C., 41 Deep learning in radiotherapy in 2019: What role for the medical physicist? *Phys. Med.: Eur. J. Med. Phys.*, *68*, 24–25, 2019.

99. Field, M., Hardcastle, N., Jameson, M., Aherne, N., Holloway, L., Machine learning applications in radiation oncology. *Phys. Imaging Radiat. Oncol.*, *19*, 13–24, 2021.

100. Malicki, J., Medical physics in radiotherapy: The importance of preserving clinical responsibilities and expanding the profession's role in research, education, and quality control. *Rep. Pract. Oncol. Radiother.*, *20*, 3, 161–169, 2015.

101. Hua, C.H., Mascia, A.E., Seravalli, E., Lomax, A.J., Seiersen, K., Ulin, K., Advances in radiotherapy technology for pediatric cancer patients and roles of medical physicists: COG and SIOP Europe perspectives. *Pediatr. Blood Cancer*, *68*, 1–9, 2021.

102. Kalet, A.M., Luk, S.M., Phillips, M.H., Radiation therapy quality assurance tasks and tools: The many roles of machine learning. *Med. Phys.*, *47*, 5, 168–177, 2020.

Application of Deep Learning in Radiation Therapy

Shilpa Rawat, Shilpa Singh*, Md. Aftab Alam and Rishabha Malviya

Department of Pharmacy, School of Medical and Allied Sciences,
Galgotias University, Greater Noida, Uttar Pradesh, India

Abstract

It is a computational approach, which uses a deep learning model with an architecture similar to that of biological brain networks, that has been trained using vast amounts of data. Deep reinforcement learning (DRL) is another name for deep learning (DL). By eliminating the need for direct programming in the process, DL functions as a middleman between data collection and meaningful knowledge. It has outperformed the vast majority of classification algorithms and is capable of learning data representations for a broad range of functions by itself. Deep learning applications in cancer include classification, feature extraction, object identification, picture interpretation and translation, sensitively and appropriately, and image annotation and labeling. The goal of this chapter is to gain a better understanding of the possible function of DL and how it may be used more successfully in radiation oncology. With the expansion of DL, a wide range of studies that led to the improvement of radiation oncology were explored more thoroughly than before. This article discussed medical imaging, image segmentation utilizing computers to assist diagnosis, computer-aided detection, treatment planning and delivery, quality assurance, treatment response, and treatment delivery. The studies that utilized DL were classified and organized according to the kind of radiation treatment used. The most current scientific achievements were chosen, and the therapeutic value of their results was assessed. Therapists may profit from employing a deep learning model since it will provide them with more precise and accurate solutions to their problems. A statistical approach to cancer patient safety is obvious, but implementing these concepts would require social adjustments at both the academic and industrial levels, which will take time. The goal of this

**Corresponding author*: shilpasingh43206@gmail.com

Rishabha Malviya, Gheorghita Ghinea, Rajesh Kumar Dhanaraj, Balamurugan Balusamy
and Sonali Sundram (eds.) Deep Learning for Targeted Treatments: Transformation in Healthcare,
(289–332) © 2022 Scrivener Publishing LLC

chapter was to make it as accessible as possible to both radiotherapy and deep learning in order to encourage new collaboration between the two groups in the development of specialized radiation technologies.

Keywords: Deep learning, machine learning, radiation therapy, medical imaging, radiation oncology, artificial intelligence

10.1   Introduction

The widespread use of computers, as well as the increase and rapid development in the amount of data, has benefited artificial intelligence research significantly. In recent decades, artificial intelligence (AI) has become more widely used in healthcare to examine data in oncology, cardiology, pathology, radiology, pharmacology, and genomics to provide accurate data for the prediction of disease, prognosis, diagnosis, treatment, screening, patient care, and also for drug development. Many applied research initiatives presently ongoing could result in more healthcare professionals, particularly radiation oncology doctors, using Artificial Intelligence [1].

For a long time, computer vision (CV) and machine learning (ML) have been used to automate segmentation activities in various phases of medical processes related to cancer. Conventional image segmentation algorithms depend on features, such as texture, shape distributions, and intensity distributions to detect abnormalities [2].

The conclusion is that the emergence of deep learning (DL) algorithms, multimodality medical imaging research has grown, with a concentration on applications that require human interpretation/intervention or manual data processing [3].

Algorithms show significant potential for rapidly learning from data, comprehending it well, and successfully executing specified work following suitable training. Artificial intelligence is gaining attraction in the field of medical science in general due to its ability to handle data overflow, eliminate optimism bias caused by generalization in humans depending upon false personal experiences, manage unusual diseases or incidents that are often neglected, be robust to interpersonal and intrapersonal variabilities, and keep up with minor changes [4].

Computer scientists have focused on discovering better features or feature combinations utilizing anatomy and physiology data to improve these algorithms. Deep learning significantly impacted the game's dynamics. Deep neural networks have only been around since 2010 in terms of real-world implementations and applications. Despite advances in computational and GPU hardware-accelerated, the effectiveness of current deep neural networks is mainly dependent on the supply of large datasets labeled by professionals [5].

As a result of the growing use of DL algorithms, radiation oncology clinicians can now more easily perform tasks such as organ-at-risk (OAR), image fusion, automatic planning (AP), delineation of the clinical target volume (CTV), outcome prediction using convolutional neural networks (CNNs) and dose distribution prediction as well as other DL algorithms [6]. Because of DL, doctors may devote more time to advanced decision making, which not only increases diagnostic accurateness but also objectivity and decreases the work pressure [7].

Deep learning-based systems have made significant contributions to the AI developments outlined above (DL). We increasingly employ DL-based solutions while searching the internet for pictures or communicating with digital assistants on smartphones and home entertainment systems. DL is already years old and is poised to take over medical image analysis, having already had a considerable influence on the field with performance levels attained over a wide variety of tasks and application areas [8].

AI and machine learning (ML)-based technologies are predicted to revolutionize clinical radiation therapy to prepare for future advances [9].

10.2 Radiotherapy

Radiotherapy is a very successful cancer treatments. In 48.3% of all cancers, there is an evidence-based indication [2, 10]. Imaging methods are used extensively in the planning and assessment of treatment results to guarantee that radiation is a realistic choice for a specific patient. Radiotherapy planning is a time-consuming strategy for optimizing radiation beam location to ensure that the tumor receives a suitable dose while sparing healthy tissue in the surrounding area (organs-at-risk) [2, 11]. This technique has been proven to benefit from automated tumor and organ-at-risk volume segmentation [2, 12].

Treatment planning (TP), radiotherapy accessories, radiotherapy verification, simulation, imaging, radiation delivery, and patient monitoring are the seven components of radiotherapy. When a patient is diagnosed with a tumor, the early phase of the imaging procedure is employed to collect vital tumor information for later use. To efficiently give radiation doses, the clinician must have correct information on the tumor amount, shape, location, and any surrounding organs that may be at risk. Thanks to increasingly advanced imaging technologies, therapy can be more focused and effective [13].

Radiation oncologists are concerned about distant metastasis, and if the tumor is not appropriately identified during imaging, it may return and represent an even greater hazard in the future [14, 15]. Today, we have improved imaging modality like computerized tomography, positron emission tomography, and single-photon emission tomography (SPECT) scan that can acquire medical images with incredible precision and with very little radiation exposure [16, 17]. Nonradiative techniques, like magnetic resonance imaging (MRI), as well as ultrasound may produce high-resolution images with amazing precision [13, 18].

During the past years, significant technical developments in radiation treatment have resulted in a rapid shift in clinical practices that have a direct impact on patient outcomes [19].

Using the information acquired during the treatment planning and simulation phases, it is feasible to personalize the therapy to each patient's specific needs. These data comprise tumor mass, height, weight, BMI, previous radiation exposure, and internal medical imaging. The TP process includes risk assessment, failure estimation, and prediction. The treatment planning procedure includes movements of organs, systematic treatment selection, treatment margin, optimization, and beam intensity shaping. Newer approaches, like 3D conformal radiotherapy, which minimizes the dosage to at-risk organs while boosting radiation for volume target, have greatly improved the treatment procedure. Both techniques need a very accurate treatment setup, constant monitoring, and exact target volume placement that accounts for internal organ movements and tumor regression [13, 20]. The TP may be divided into several types, including expert-based, knowledge-based, and artificial intelligence (AI)-based [13, 21]. Following that, treatment planning and dosage calculations will commence. Monte Carlo simulation is commonly acknowledged as per the standard of gold for radiation dosage estimation due to its portrayal of real-world physical processes. PENELOPE, MCNP, and Geant4 are three of the most common MC codes. Completing these simulations necessitates a significant investment of time and computational resources. CloudMC, on the other hand, is a better solution because it is less expensive and less time-consuming in these areas [13, 22]. Radiotherapy equipment is used to immobilize the patient, limiting the patient's mobility and providing an additional precise measurement of the volume target area [13, 23]. Typically, immobilization occurs during the simulation phase. The patient receives a dosage of radiation during radiotherapy. The amount of energy deposited per mass unit is referred to as the dose. The fundamental objective of radiation treatment

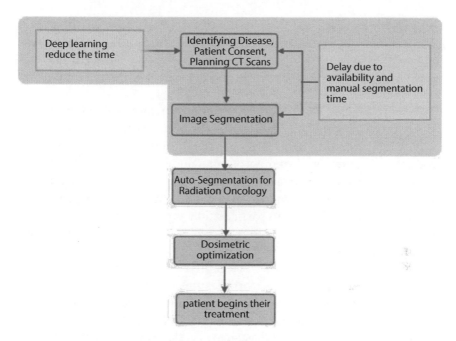

Figure 10.1 Radiotherapy pathway using deep learning.

is to destroy cancer cells while sparing or lowering the amount of energy deposited in healthy cells. Brachytherapy and brachytherapy therapies are available in addition to SBRT, volumetric modulated arc therapy, IMRT, proton therapy, and electron treatment [13, 24]. Following the advances of the treatment plan, a patient specific quality assurance method will use to guarantee that dose-distribution is accurate. A patient is monitored for side effects and result for some time (months to years) after receiving radiation [13, 25]. Deep learning framework can be utilized for radiotherapy management of patients (Figure 10.1).

10.3   Principle of Deep Learning and Machine Learning

"Artificial intelligence" was invented by John McCarthy in the year 1956, a pioneer in the subject [26, 27, 30]. Boden defined AI as a science that tries to produce robots that execute jobs that would otherwise need human intelligence [28, 30]. When it comes to modern AI, various authors have recognized the 1950 paper Computing mechanism and intelligence as one of the foundational works [29, 30]. And then after six-year, Newell and

Simon published the logic theorist algorithm, which is widely regarded as a key achievement in the field of AI [30]. For example, Samuel, introduced the concept of machine learning in 1959 when he created an artificial intelligence (AI) software that could play checkers based on partial settings and experience [31].

The purpose of ML techniques like neural networks will be able to create computer networks that can learn by their mistakes and develop as a result of their own experience, which is stored in the statistical approaches produced from previous instances of input and output data. These systems use statistical patterns revealed by input-output observations to automate the creation of outputs depending on upcoming inputs and design decision rules that need as little human participation as possible [32].

An ideal machine learning system would use computers to predict clinical outcomes, detect disease features, and enhance treatment procedures. This would transform the knowledge gathered into scientific proof [1].

Deep learning algorithms perform feature extraction and classification continuously, removing the need for human participation during training. In a nutshell, end-to-end machine learning. CNNs have regularly outperformed their competitors in ImageNet tasks that employ AI algorithms to correctly categorize animals and objects, explaining their present popularity and the trend away from machine learning in the digital photography industry [33].

CNNs have demonstrated revolutionary in the diagnostic imaging uses like imaging classification (e.g., distinguishing malignant from benign tumors in computer-aided diagnosis in radiology) and image segmentation (e.g., automated delineation of anatomical regions in radiation treatment). Deep learning technologies can progress clinical judgment, treatment planning, operational efficiency, and delivery [34].

10.3.1   Deep Neural Networks (DNN)

The two method based on deep learning such as "deep neural networks" and "convolutional neural networks" were recently developed and employed in radiotherapy for enhanced computing.

Deep neural networks is classified as either supervised or unsupervised, depending on their level of supervision. Reducing input complexity and emphasizing the most important patterns for machine learning algorithms are commonly necessary for this field. In most cases, the success of the AI function is determined by the performance of the learning algorithm [5].

DNNs are self-teaching and need a larger number of them to understand how to represent incoming data in the proper order. This kind of neural network is known as a DNN. DNNs, like ANNs, begin with nodes, then the result of the first layer becomes the intake of the next layer, and so on, with the output of the final layer acting as the derivative output of the system. Because the fundamentals of unsupervised DNN are the same as those of unsupervised learning and ANN, first layer output is used as second layer input and vice versa. Unmonitored DL approaches are preferred over monitored DNN methods because they need less labeled data. It is quite difficult to demonstrate that representation learning is important in an unmonitored DNN [35].

10.3.2   Convolutional Neural Network

Convolutional neural networks (CNN) may be used to handle data collection, such as medical pictures (CNNs). CNN often makes use of convolutional, fully linked layers, and pooling. The convolutional layer's goal is to find feature similarities across preceding layers and to learn feature representations for input. The number of convolution layers used in the creation of convolutional features is proportional to the number of convolution kernels employed. Each neuron in the feature map may be connected to a neuron in the previous layer. The fundamental goal of layer pooling is to lower the quality of a feature space in order to increase the shift variance. The two convolutional layers were often placed between the feature map and the pooling layer in the preceding layers. A wholly linked layer's function is to perform conspicuous thinking by linking all neurons in the previous stage to all neurons in the layer [13].

10.4   Role of AI and Deep Learning in Radiation Therapy

For radiological therapies (RTs), the technology of medical duties is nothing new, since many procedures are obtained very effectively over time, allowing RTs to dedicate more time to patient care and quality assurance (QA). In his study, radiation oncologist Boldrini identifies numerous ways that DL might be utilized to enhance therapeutic practices. RTS has an important role in many aspects of cancer therapy, including those when ML is already acting. Image-guided radiation therapy, treatment planning, and multimodal image fusion are just a few of the numerous applications of this technology that are being researched and developed. Furthermore, it may be possible to offer data on patient survival and toxicity prediction [36].

To plan treatment, modern radiation therapy procedures require good quality of MR and CT images [37, 38].

Mirada Medical in Oxford, UK, has just recently developed DL contouring methods such as "Mirada DLC Expert" [9, 39, 40]. According to a deep CNN-based study, intelligent strategies may surpass atlas-based ones [9, 41]. Zhu *et al.* [9, 42] demonstrate that systems based on CNN with an average Dice similarity coefficient of more than (0.8) can achieve a task in patients with lung cancer compared to atlas-based processes when it comes to automated lungs segmentation, heart as well as in the liver. The spinal cord and esophagus are still able to be shaped even if the Dice similarity coefficients were less exact. CNN is becoming simpler to use in healthcare applications due to automated contouring technology. Varian Ethos, for example, is based on algorithms that segment organ at risk (OAR) structures using kilovoltage (kV) cone-beam CT images and CNN's methods [9, 43]. They have the potential to revolutionize adaptive workflows, especially in neck patients and also in head patients, but radiotherapy in planning treatment positions must be cognizant of the merits as well as demerits of such types of algorithms. Knowledge-based upon planning [9, 44], knowledge-based upon auto contouring [9, 45], and planning automation optimization using multicriteria.

According to the Court *et al.*, the automation advantage in treatment planning is to reduce the time and healthcare operations efficiency [46].

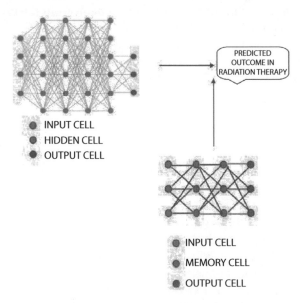

Figure 10.2 AI framework for radiotherapy outcome prediction.

Application of AI framework for radiotherapy outcome prediction can be presented as Figure 10.2.

Zhao *et al.* suggested employing trained DNN layers to assist daily localization in a group of patients of prostate cancer without fiducial markers. The research shows that very exact prostate localization utilising deep learning-based marker less prostate target localization is possible [47].

Radiation therapy planning in current clinical practise is mainly based on CT (computer tomography) pictures, which give electron density data to dose calculation algorithms. As a result, structural contouring on CT scans is now standard practise, using information from additional, extremely delicate imaging modality, either individually or in concert with scheduled computerized tomography (CT) scans [48].

10.5 Platforms for Deep Learning and Tools for Radiotherapy

DL was mainly composed of vast interconnected network systems of Intelligent retrieval that can detect important attributes, which include interpretations of input information (in our particular instance, pictures and videos), for activities like identification and tracking, and provided massive amounts of unmarked or marked statistical data [5, 49].

Deep learning, rather than being a new idea, is mostly an expansion of previously existing types of computational models to incorporate a higher number of hidden nodes and layers inside each layer [50].

Larger data sets grew more prevalent, while commercialized gaming graphics processing units (GPUs) were becoming more commonly available, enabling the quicker examination of higher, denser structural training. GPUs have helped the development of DL by significantly lowering the time for training. When using DL, design decisions must be made regarding the hidden layers, the amount of layers in the network (or the number and quality of kernels in the case of CNNs), the type and level of regularization, the network device setup, whether to contain redistributing layer upon layer and, if that is so, and which category of accumulation, and so on [8, 51].

To predict the huge set of variables in a DL system, a huge number of training data instances are necessary. To teach a huge amount of parameters to hundreds of millions or even billions of parameters, backpropagation across many rounds using the training algorithm technique across micro-batches containing a small amount of data at a time is required. For training, a single and multi-central processor device or a network of multiprocessor modules inside a high-performance computer technology might be utilized, but this would take an unusually sustained duration and would need the deployment of costly equipment.

Furthermore, gaming GPUs have gotten less expensive, more powerful, and simpler to produce during the last decade. As a consequence, the hardware requirements for deep learning execution (as opposed to high-performance computer technology systems) are substantially lower, and training periods are much shorter as compared to a CPU-based technique [52, 53].

The most typical configuration for training DL models is a computer system with one or more fast graphics GPUs that can be quickly installed on a reasonable budget. Users may also train and run their models remotely using cloud-based technologies like Amazon Web Services (AWSs) and NVidia (NVa) GPU cloud. Google has created an application-specific integrated circuit (ASIC) for neural model to enable a broad range of Deep Learning (DL) apps. Tensor processing units (TPUs) that are repeatedly quicker than CPU or GPU solutions are now accessible on Google Cloud.

"Amazon Web Services" is an acronym for "Amazon "NVidia GPU Cloud" is available at https://aws.amazon.com/. Visit https://www.nvidia.com/en-us/gpu-cloud/ for further information. "Google Cloud TPU," as it is known. Visit https://cloud.google.com/tpu/ for further information [8].

Caffe (CE) from Columbia University, Cognitive Toolkit (CNTK) from Microsoft, Tensor Flow (TF) from Google, and Torch (TO), among other deep learning tools, were recently launched to expedite the construction of new deep learning models. CE, CNTK, TF, and TO, among other tools, including Theano (TH), MXNet, and others, are among them. For optimal performance, all of these apps need multicore CPUs and GPUs with a large number of cores. Deep learning's main purpose is to locate a large number of parameters, which may be performed using linear or matrices techniques, respectively. To speed up matrix-related tasks, CE, CNTK, and TO utilize OpenBLAS or cuBLAS, while TensorFlow uses Eigen, an updated matrix processing toolkit [54–62].

End-users may find it challenging to choose the most suitable deep learning tool for their deep learning operations given the wide variety of deep learning software and hardware resources available today. We offer our effort to assess three basic kinds of deep learning models, namely densely integrated feed-forward neural networks (fully convolutional neural networks) and recurrent neural networks, utilizing four cutting-edge GPU-speed-up tools: Caffe (CE), CNTK, Tensor Flow (TF), and Torch (TO) (RNNs). We analyze the performance of two prominent CPUs (PC processor and a grade of service processor) and 3-key NVidia (NVa) GPUs on two distinct systems (Kepler, Maxwell, and Pascal platforms) [63–65].

Table 10.1 An overview of the many deep learning-based applications, sorted by radiation therapy phase.

Phase in radiation treatment	Implementation	Source information	DL approaches	Reference
Images used in radiotherapy treatment planning	Synthesizing of a pseudo-x-ray picture	Magnetic resonance scanning	(UNet) & (ResNet)	[67]
	Synthesis of pseudo magnetic resonance	Computerized tomography	Fully Convolutional Network (Semantic Segmentation)	[68]
Segmentation of image	Tissue from the breasts	Computerized tomography	(UNet)	[69]
	Organs of the Head and Neck	Computerized tomography	2D convolutional kernels	[70]
Computer-aided diagnostic	Pulmonary nodules	Computerized tomography	Deep belief network	[71]
	Breasts cancer	Mammography	Convolutional neural network	[72]
Image identification	Prediction of contraction	Magnetic resonance scanning	Visual geometry group	[73]
	2D/3D X-ray identification	Cone beam computed tomography, 2D X-rays	Fully Convolutional Network (Semantic Segmentation)	[74]
Planning for treatment	Estimate dosage based on organ structure	Radiotherapy structure Dose	(UNet) convolutional kernels	[75]
Data extraction and outcome prediction in therapy	The chances of survival after rectal cancer chemo-radiotherapy are minimal	Positron emission tomography	Convolutional neural network	[76]

Application of deep learning in radiation therapy is shown in Table 10.1.
We chose a small-dimension network and a large-dimension network
for each kind of network to evaluate. The following is a summary of our
primary findings:

❖ The performance of the system does not scale correctly
  when using multi-core CPUs. A little margin separates the
  performance of utilizing 16 CPU cores from that of using 4
  or 8 CPU cores in many situations.
❖ On central processing unit systems, there is no obvious winner. The functioning of any application is entirely dependent on the neural network models utilized, the CPU model
  employed, and the number of processes used. To outperform CE on FCNs, CE outperforms TO on Alex Net (AN),
  Torch outperforms ResNet-50, and CNTK and TF outperform TO on RNNs, for example.
❖ Most devices can achieve significant speedups when using
  advanced graphics processing units (GPUs). When comparing the top GPU and the best CPU performance, we discover
  that the GPU is 10–30% faster than the CPU in most cases.
  CE, CNTK, and TO outperform TO on FCNs and RNNs.
  TO, CNTK, and CE outperform TO on FCNs and RNNs.
❖ In most cases, the GTX1080 outperforms the other two
  GPU platforms because of its highest computational power.
❖ The design of configuration files has an impact on performance. For example, CNTK enables target consumers to
  fine-tune respective systems and pay off GPU storage for
  increased computational performance [66].

10.6   Radiation Therapy Implementation in Deep Learning

Deep learning (DL) algorithms were applied in radiotherapy, which is a
relatively new development. In this section, we will look at recent breakthroughs in machine learning, particularly deep learning, as they relate
to the various stages of radiation therapy treatment planning & treatment
delivery, such as treatment planning optimization, treatment delivery monitoring, outcome prediction, and planning quality assurance. We will high-
light some major studies in each field because it is difficult to summarise

all of the achievements. For those who are interested, more study may be obtained in the literature [77].

10.6.1   Deep Learning and Imaging Techniques

Machine learning (ML) model in medical imaging for a very long time. In the mid-1960s with algorithms to analyze or assist in the interpretation of X-rays. Initially, in the midway 1980s, computer-aided diagnostic algorithms advanced, focusing on cancer diagnosis and detection on mammograms and chest x-ray, then moving to other imaging modalities like ultrasound and CT scans. In the beginning, CAD algorithms, like most DL algorithms today, used a data-driven technique [8].

Modern CT scanners can scan a person in exquisite detail from head to toe. Magnetic Resonance Imaging (MRI) technology is the most often utilized medical image procedure. Although MRI is most suited for acquiring images of soft tissue in joints and ligaments, it may be utilised practically anyplace on the body if the density of the soft tissue differs. Although MRI can provide good imaging than CT scans minus the danger of radioactivity, it can't be utilized if there is any metal present, such as an implant, since the magnetic field of MRI would be changed [78].

There are several limitations to each of these imaging technologies like exposure to radiation, sensitivity to the environment, and expense like algorithms based on AI provide less expensive non-radiative alternatives that have been actively studied in recent decades. Algorithms based upon AI have less risk and raise the probability of systemic mistakes that might have a catastrophic effect [79]. Because of advances in computer science and diagnostic imaging, the precision of radiation dose distribution to the target region has greatly increased, enabling for the use of MRI in conjunction with a LINAC (linear accelerator) to provide real-time (MRI) controlled radiation [80].

10.6.2   Image Segmentation

DL algorithms have broadly been applied in radiology to differentiate imaging collected via various approaches. Segmenting patients' tumors is still substantial time taking and, it will also increase a load of humans in radiotherapy. AI can assist in minimizing interobserver variability and treatment planning time [35].

Image segmentation is a technique used in the early phases of radiation therapy treatment planning to distinguish between images of malignancies and normal tissues. A Dice Similarity Coefficient, abbreviated as a [DSC], is a statistical tool used to compare the similarity of models [81].

Nowadays, conventional clinical practise includes human segmentation of organ at risks (OARs), which is done slice-by-slice by competent physicians for distinct structures. This procedure is time taking (it normally takes hours per patient), costly, and inconclusive because of both intraobserver and interobserver variability [82]. Unquestionably, there is an unfulfilled necessity accurate and automated segmentation technologies. Image segmentation approaches based on deep learning can overcome the constraints of standard atlases and machine learning algorithms, which are not much suitable to generalising for unknown human anatomy. In a medical imaging study, CNNs are commonly utilized, at the same time conventional gradient-based boundary detector has been around for some time, Orasanu *et al.* have come up with an improved model that uses a CNN-based boundary detector [83]. In recent decades, U-Net architectures Ronneberger *et al.* have emerged so as to achieve revolutionary for segmentation of the image [84]. Instances, such as 2-dimensional U-Net is utilized for multiclass image segmentation of Eleven organs of the head, an approach based upon graph is employed to induce connections between adjacent ones [85].

10.6.3   Lesion Segmentation

Lesion segmentation (LS) is comparable to segmentation of organ in some aspects, but it is more complex than segmentation of organ since segmented entity can be taken on a broad range of forms and sizes. Several publications on DL lesion segmentation have been published, encompassing a wide range of lesions. A public data-base containing the training course and test set for use with a brain-tumor segmentation challenge has been a regular activity since the computer-aided diagnostic processing and computer-assisted management workshop, which was held from 2014 to 2016 and will be hosted again in 2017 and 2018. Label map auto-encoders, CNN-based architectures, and HNN were all tested on this set of data [86–90].

10.6.4   Computer-Aided Diagnosis

Several groups have created systems whose results are often contrasted in tasks, like the latest LungX Challenge, to categorize lung nodules on Computed tomography on the report of noncancerous or cancerous type [30].

Hua *et al.* presented the very first study to use deep neural methods to solve issues of spot on the lung identification on (CT) images, demonstrating that a combination of DBN-CNN architecture beat CADx systems using traditional handmade features [91]. Many researchers have now created alternative deep learning algorithms because of this [30]. Ali *et al.* proposed CNN approach is based on reinforcement learning [92]. Kumar *et al.* suggested combining deep learning features collected from an auto-encoder system with such a linear decision graph to build a classification system [93]. Song *et al.* examined the lung cancer classification performance of three deep learning networks, such as CNN, DN, and SAE [94]: CNN came out on top with the best results. Sun *et al.* established and related 3 multi-channel structured deep learning algorithms such as CNN, DBN, and SDAE, as well as a traditional handmade technique [95]. With the CNN, the best results were obtained. Wang *et al.* recently attempted to diagnose pulmonary nodules from positron emission tomography (PET) scans rather than CT images, and contrasted a deep learning algorithm to 4 traditional ML techniques. They have demonstrated that their CNNs result were comparable to that of the good classical approaches, however it could be enhanced by including diagnostic characteristics [96].

Breast cancer is a common malignancy in women all over the world-wide, and radiation therapy is a popular cancer treatment choice. Because of the importance of this endeavour, recent advancements in mammography image interpretation have incorporated the use of CNN approaches.

Aside from MRI, DL-based CADx algorithms have been employed in a variety of studies. Chen and colleagues finished fourth in the ProstateX competition, demonstrating that innovative deep neural networks like as (Visual Geometry Group- 16 could be promptly and properly re-educated with insufficient input (classification of clinically relevant prostate lesions on Magnetic Resonance Imaging) [97].

Banerjee *et al.* employed multiparametric MRI to build a CNNs-based CADx for rhabdomyosarcoma subtype categorization [98].

10.6.5   Computer-Aided Detection

Because of the availability of large-scale data sets, automatic image recognition has advanced significantly in recent years. A better example is the identification of CT lung nodes in CAD. ImageNet has over 1.2 million classified nature pictures divided into over 1,000 classes, which are used to train this complicated CNN. A CAD-based CNN trained with ImageNet shown impressive therapeutic benefits on thoracoabdominal lymph nodes and interstitial lung disease. CAD can also identify polyps and metastases in the colon. Deep learning algorithms have been used in recent developments in colonoscopy computer-aided detection and diagnosis (CADx) research. Polyp detection (CADe) and polyp characterization are two of the AI's key diagnostic tasks (CADx). CADe will lower the number of polyps that are overlooked, allowing for more accurate adenoma diagnosis. The adoption of CADx will considerably increase the accurateness of colonscopy optical diagnosis [76].

Prostatic carcinoma is one of the most common malignancies that kill men over the age of 50 in the Western world. Prostate cancer is currently diagnosed via a transrectal ultrasonography biopsy. Because of its low specificity, MRI becomes very famous in detecting prostate cancer in recent decades. Detecting prostate cancer from an MRI scan requires effort and a team of professionals, but the results are worth it. Computer-aided design can help to solve these issues (CAD). A two-phase CAD system is currently being developed. The primary candidates are identified with the help of multiple-atlas segmentation of prostate, classification, feature extraction and local maxima detection. The prognosis for cancer of every filtered candidate is forecasted by utilizing classification algorithms in the second step. Patients were evaluated, with MR-guided biopsies serving as the gold standard. The outcomes of this study suggested that the gadget may be employed as a 2nd reader and to increase sensitivity of radiologists. However, further study is required before the technology can be efficiently used in first-reader circumstances [99].

Patients with breast cancer who are discovered early enough have a fair prognosis. Every year, around 40 million mammograms are conducted in the United States alone. It is a time-taking and error-cause procedure that needs the assistance of one or more competent readers. Second readers for computer-aided design software (CAD) are a popular way to boost efficiency. The computer is unaffected by your level of focus. It is also feasible that they will be skilled with a massive no. of sample, far more than any radiologist could study in his or her career. Computer-aided design system based on CNNs may be used to recognise patterns and objects with high precision. CNN performs equally well at low and high sensitivity when compared to a manually constructed feature set of 45,000 pictures. On the patch lever, there were no significant variations in outcomes between the CNN network and a qualified screening radiologist [100].

10.6.6 Quality Assurance

DL algorithms was used to make virtual (QA) on planning in order to simplify the quality assurance quality assurance process. Interian *et al.* as well as Tomori *et al.* both utilised CNNs model to forecast a statistic known as the gamma passing rate, which may be used to determine how effectively QA tests are doing. Nyflot *et al.* used a model based on an observation of the beam fluence map to indicate that LINAC's multileaf collimator has flaws. Deep learning methods for quality assurance have also improved proton radiation. A model for predicting the output issues of proton beam therapy treatment fields was created, that may be used to validate output factor data.

10.6.7   Treatment Planning

Throughout the planning phase, each patient's treatment location, strategy, and a variety of tumor and normal anatomic features are taken into account. Individuals' experiences, judgements, and decisions impact plans, which may lead to significant differences between organizations as well as inside them. Treatment planning may suffer from a lack of experience and resources between big academic institutions and smaller community centres among low-volume practitioners. Machine learning-based automated planning strategies may assist standardise and enhance plan quality.

The use of CDS in treatment planning in radiation oncology is rare, as it extends beyond CDS in the exam room. CDS that focuses on treatment planning employs planning automation and knowledge-based planning (KBP) methodologies to save effort, enhance patient outcomes, and integrate data-driven decision making into the planning process (e.g., how much margin to place beyond a target, what lymph node regions to include). Initially, machine learning algorithms were employed to find essential dosage and volume correlations in order to build prediction models [101]. Now, ML algorithms may learn from high-quality past treatment plans in order to predict desirable treatment plan characteristics and assist CDS in treatment planning [102]. Rapid Plan (Varian Medical Systems, Palo Alto, California), a commercial KBP tool, has demonstrated plan optimization success [103, 104]. It is possible to bias forecasts by utilising earlier treatment plans due to changes in medical care or data quality [105].

10.6.8   Treatment Delivery

During therapy, it is vital to guarantee that the patient is situated against the treatment beam according to the stated geometry and that the tumour is correctly targeted with the beam despite practical limits such as tumour movement caused by breathing. This is critical to the treatment's effectiveness. DL modeling are now again being established to address these issues.

In order to determine the right patient posture, patient-specific images must be taken and registered with treatment planning photos. X-ray projections of the patient's anatomy are captured and compared to treatment plans using kV or MV beams. For example, CT volume projections. Zhao *et al.* used a CNN approach to find the prostatic focus on a kV x-ray projected image. Image matching between MV x-ray projections recorded during treatment and kV projections estimated during planning is problematic because various radiation energies yield distinct picture attributes, such as inconsistencies in intensity and contrast [106]. Conditional GAN was created in order to ease the process of matching MV with kV images by converting MV shots into kV images [107]. Patients and tumours must be continuously evaluated throughout therapy to guarantee precision in beam aiming and patient safety. Chen et al employed a CNN to automatically identify the patient surface area visible beneath a surfaces imaging sensor for motion monitoring [108]. Park *et al.* designed an inter and intra fuzzy deep learning algorithm to forecast intra and inter lung tumor migration [109]. The migration of a liver tumor was tracked in real time using a robotic-arm-mounted ultrasound imaging method and an interest CNN with a convolutional LSTM network [110]. Lin *et al.* have created models for real-time prediction of patient respiratory data [111].

10.6.9 Response to Treatment

DL may be utilized to withdrawal of tumour features for detection and prediction, as well as to make therapeutic decisions. Machine learning can combine tumour image-based features into a prediction of response to chemotherapy using a number of classifiers. The use of DL to analyse medical images over time can therefore be utilised to predict response. CNNs were utilized to assess the contribution to neoadjuvant therapy utilizing breast DCE-MRI, with inputs moving throughout several contrast time points and treatment exam durations [112].

Lao *et al.* examined at magnetic resonance imaging radiomic characteristics as well as the DL in glioblastoma multiforme to determine whether they might forecast survivability [112]. Bibault *et al.* employed DL to predict pathological full response following chemotherapy and radiation in the treatment of advanced rectal cancer [113], after liver stereotactic body irradiation. Ibramov *et al.* anticipated hepatobiliary injury. The use of DL as a technique for assessing medication response in non-oncology studies has expanded considerably [114]. Shehata *et al.* used auto encoders to detect and predict acute renal rejection following kidney donation [115]. Nielsen *et al.* assessed recombinant T-PA therapy for ischemic stroke

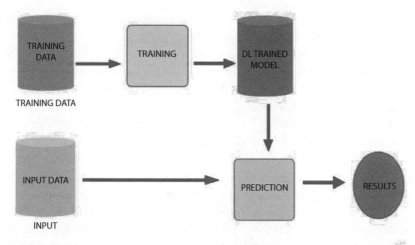

Figure 10.3 Deep learning trained data to predict the outcomes.

patients utilising DL to predict prognosis and quantify treatment success [116]. Role of deep learning data in the prediction of outcomes can be schematically presented as Figure 10.3.

10.7   Prediction of Outcomes

Currently, multidimensional cancer treatment alternatives, such as surgical therapy, chemotherapy therapy, and radiation have been developed and proven effective [117]. The examination of healthcare data has been done using DL approaches (including outcome prediction). DL approaches represents a promising for radiotherapy risk stratification [118, 119]. In prostatic radiation therapy predictive analytics, Coates *et al.* said that DL approaches might be helpful in the context of radioactive material biotic outcomes due to their understanding of the complexities of the biological and chemical systems involved. The delivery of energy to the tumour is accomplished through the use of high-energy radiations in radiation therapy [120].

Extremely high radiation dose are performed in chemotherapy and radiotherapy to help transfer heat to the tumour. To maximise Possibility of tumor control (PTC) while decreasing the risk of probability of a normal tissue damage (PNTD). Potential benefits should be investigated before beginning 0F radiation therapy, taking into account the PTC and PNTD associated with it [121]. PTC should be enhanced, but PNTD should be kept to a minimum. An extremely high dose to the OARs may result in immediate or late radiation damage (e.g., cirrhosis or radiation treatment oncogenesis), whereas a decreased rate of absorption dosage to the tumor may result in a diminished therapeutic response.

As a result, detailed assessments and projections are required, particularly when remedies such as manual surgery or radiation therapy are offered. To anticipate the effects of radiation, two types of data are used: structured data and unstructured data. When dealing with structured data, use a DL model from the MLP (multilayer perceptron) or RNN (recurrent neural network) families (i.e., tabular data) [122].

A high-dimensional retrospective dataset was used to select the most important characteristics for radiotherapy diagnosis and prediction. These characteristics included tumor and lung generalized Equivalent Uniform Dose (gEUDs), one single nucleotide polymorphism (SNP) (cxcr1-Rs2234671), two microRNA (miRNA) (microR-20a-5p and microR-191-5p), one preliminary processing of radio-mic feature metabolic tumour volume (MTV), and three cytokines (IL-15, IL-4, and IL-10) prior to treatment, as shown by The biophysical relationships between the variables examined are represented by the colored edges of the Bayesian network (BN). While BN may be used to examine physiological consequence correlations using archive data, its inference complexity restricts them, and their processing cost rises exponentially as the number of sensor nodes increases [123]. While BN may be used to examine physiological consequence correlations using archive data, its inference complexity restricts them, and their processing cost rises exponentially as the number of sensor nodes increases [124]. Based on radiomic parameters, Jochem *et al.* developed a three layer trained model for lung and H&N cancer death prediction [125]. Furthermore, Li *et al.* used radiological data to determine the survival of rectal cancer patients. According to the researchers, using PET-CT data as a testing phase for a CNN, they were able to reliably estimate tumor recurrence risk more effectively than previous models [126]. Qi *et al.* suggested a DNN model trained on DVH data to predict quality of life (QOL) in the urine and intestinal domains following prostate SBRT [127].

They proved that their system could predict Levels with a 5-point accuracy. Tseng *et al.* proposed combining these three learning components (GAN, DNN, and deep Q network) to create an autonomous health monitoring system for response-based ART. Using their strategy, which took clinical, genetic, and radiomic factors into account, they were able to change patient dosage per fraction in a response-adapted therapy environment [128].

10.7.1   Toxicity

In 2009, Zhang *et al.* published the first deep learning study, establishing a strategy diagnostic and therapeutic issue statistical method in an intensity-modulated platform. A total of 125 methods were produced for a case of brain and neck cancer, while 256 strategies were established for a case of prostate, with saliva rate of flow and G2 rectal bleeding used as prognostic results. When compared to the ground truth produced using the equivalent uniform dose (EUD) exponential model, the mean absolute error for saliva flow rate prediction was 0.42%, while the average forecast accuracy for G2 rectal bleeding was 97.04. As a consequence, given current understanding of computational programming and modeling, direct inference of plan-related challenges mentioned in this paper seems doable and fascinating for future DL applications [129].

The use of DL to predict radiotherapy toxicity is used in a large proportion of DL forecasts of radiation success. Patients undergoing head and neck radiation therapy are more prone to develop xerostomia. Men *et al.* established an approach to anticipate Xerotes after radiation using a 3D residual convolutional neural network (RCNN) on 784 patients with RTOG 0522 neck and head basal cell carcinoma cancer. Sources included CT imaging scans, 3D dosage distribution, and submandibular and sublingual area outlines, with encouraging findings [130]. CNN has been used to predict tumor development and metastasis following stereotactic radiation in patients with non-small-cell lung cancer (NSCLC). This model was created using image data that was examined after treatment. According to a study of 1605 patient characteristics, five individuals predicted local recurrence, three predicted lobar recurrence, and seven predicted overall survival [131]. Liang *et al.* examined a 3D Network model to three multiple logistic regression-based prediction models for predicting radioactive sinusitis after thoracic irradiation. All four prediction models were validated in 70 patients with Non-Small-Cell Lung Cancer who received volume-modulated radiation (VMR). The data demonstrated that CNN outperformed the traditional model, with an Area under the Curve of 0. 842 [132]. Lee *et al.* used machine learning and bioinformatics technologies to predict and understand late genital tract system damage in prostate cancer patients during radiation using genome-wide data. The ability of DL to predict radiation efficacy and unfavorable effects allows doctors to identify possible treatment beneficiaries and prepare for probable negative consequences [133].

Predicting toxic consequences as a valuable decision support system for doctors is one use of DL methods in radiography [134]. A pre-formed CNN, according to Zhen *et al.*, can simulate rectum dose distribution and forecast rectum damage following cervical cancer radiation. They demonstrated that ensemble learning might aid in addressing the difficulty of training a Cnn model, which is difficult owing to the limited sample size [135]. Arefan *et al.* developed a CNN-based 2 different DL model using two approaches to forecast risk of breast cancer [136].

The toxicity prediction accuracy of neural networks and SVM-based methods was equivalent, with an AUC of 0.7. Pella *et al.* collected medical and dosimetric data from 321 individuals with Adenocarcinoma. When it comes to acute gastro-intestinal (AGI) and genitourinary (GU) toxicity, they classified persons as moderate or severe [137]. Adbollahi *et al.* performed a multi-variable simulation study on neural hearing in patients with head and neck patients receiving radiotherapy; the median achieved predictive ability of the examined techniques was greater than 70% in reliability, precision, and AUROC [138].

The CNN outperforms the other algorithms because to the benefits of DL. The DL modeling technique selects the best attributes from the input to satisfy the model's goal. In spite of their difficulty, they allow for excellent performance [117].

10.7.2   Survival and the Ability to Respond

Deep learning algorithms for predicting radiation therapy patient response and survival may enhance decision assistance and provide an accurate evaluation of the relative advantages of different treatment options for patient characteristics [139].

Bryce *et al.* analysis of data from phase 3 clinical research, it was found that 95 patients with advanced or metastatic SCCHN were selected at random to perform in irradiation whether both with and without chemotherapy in phase 3 clinical research. To measure prediction accuracy, round-robin cross-validation (RRCV) and receiver operating characteristic curve (ROCC) assessment were utilized. The best neural model to predict 2-year survival ability has a (ROCC) significance of (0.78) (0.05), suggesting its capacity to uncover & then utilize potential components different from TNM factors, as well as to classify each patient individually [140]. Another study used ANNs to predict recovery in individuals with uterine cervix cancer who had received irradiation. The prediction model only comprised seven criteria: gender, functional condition, haemoglobin, protein content, cancer stage, histology, and the degree of radiation damage as measured by a standard diagnostic test included [141].

In a report by Chen *et al.* six-input aspects were chosen: lung volume receiving > 16 Gy, generalized equivalent uniform dose for the exponent

Table 10.2 Deep learning for toxicity and result prediction in clinical contexts, along with treatment planning.

Result	Organ	Deep learning	Number of subjects	Variable of prediction	Reference
Toxicity	Prostate	(ANN & SVM)	321	Prediction for G2	[137]
Toxicity	Head and neck	(SVM)	256	Rectal haemorrhage in G2	[145]
Toxicity	Cervix	(CNN)	42	Toxicity of G2 in the rectal area	[146]
Response	Prostate	(ANN)	119	2-year survival under biochemical control	[144]
Response	Head and neck	(ANN)	95	Treatment through the internet	[140]
Planning	Lung	(ANN)	5	Online Verification	[147]
Planning	Lung	(IIFDL)	130	Variation within and across functional group	[148]
Planning	Lung	(GAN)	114	Dose adaptation that is automatic	[149]
Planning	Pelvis	(3D FCN)	22	Magnetic resonance Computed tomography image	[150]

a = 1 (mean lung dose), free expiratory volume in 1 s, carbon monoxide diffusion capacity percent, and whether or not the patient had cancer treatment before radiation treatment. Following that, all attributes were removed from the network to determine their relevance [142]. Cha *et al.* examined the prospect of DL using CNNs on pre/post computerized tomography images of prostate carcinoma sufferer to aid in therapy success evaluation. Furthermore, determining a tumor's prognosis aids in treatment selection and survival prediction [143].

Three layers of ANN (Deep Neural) models were used in 119 individuals who had had radical radiation treatment for prostate carcinoma to understand the relationship among the diagnostic dosage, prescription drug, dosing frequency count, and the associated biological impact. When data were dichotomized, an ANN that was more than 55% sensitive and specific could predict physiochemical stability as well as specific urinary tract and cervix abnormalities [144]. Clinical application of deep learning for toxicity and treatment prediction is shown in Table 10.2.

Moreover, survival is not the only essential factor. When planning a cancer patient's journey, it is important to think about the location of tumor recurrence, therapy tolerance, functional abilities, and overall well-being. In addition to death, other outcomes to evaluate include range of metastasis and local recurrence of tissue in cancer. Even though a patient's survival ability may be altered by a number of different factors throughout time, particularly tumors may be judged more crucial to the treatment's success or failure [138].

10.8   Deep Learning in Conjunction With Radiomoic

Radiomic is a game-changing way of identifying therapeutically relevant features in medical image analysis that are hard to observe with the visible to the naked eye. Identification techniques based on machine learning algorithms are being investigated at a fast pace with the objective of improving patient diagnoses, cures, and prognoses. Radiomic is a rapidly evolving clinical image processing subject that has immense potential for aiding in cancer diagnosis and treatment decision making. Given the progress of data sharing and distributed learning technologies to boost data availability across all patient and tumor types, radiomic paired with deep learning has the capability to increase radiomic in the next few years [138]. Radiomic is predicted to play a significant role in precision medicine because of its ability to gather substantial data on tumor features [151]. Because a patient's individual kind of cancer has a significant influence on clinical performance indicators, personalized cancer therapy treatments must be established for each patient. Non-small cell lung cancer possess a low three-year survivability due to the fact that it has a high risk of metastasizing to other regions of the body [152].

Radiomic machine learning methods, particularly deep learning algorithms, may be beneficial to Radiomic. Machine learning algorithms might be used to investigate the co-relationship among images effect by radiomic, clinical results, and radiation dosage data in order to enhance cancer therapy using radiation method. Two major obstacles have surfaced in the use of ML algorithms in diagnostic imaging.

The first is due to a rise in the quantity of available marked radio-imaging information, while the another is owing to computing's massive processing of data capabilities as a result of numerous processors [153]. Lambin *et al.* proposed the terminology "radiomic" to characterize the automated detection of specific prognostic and diagnostic patterns in cancer image sequences.

Radiomics is made up of four primary processes:

- Visualize,
- Categorization
- Extraction of features
- Interpretation [154].

Radiomics are features extracted from clinical images that may subsequently be connected with endpoint data, particularly two-year survivorship, is utilized to improve prediction. The basic purpose of radiomic is to serve as a decision making tool framework that support clinical judgment by giving an exact treatment, allowing for tailored radiation, and therefore improving treatment outcomes [155]. The radiomic techniques used to predict how well a treatment will work and how long it will last are now at a crossroads. Traditional radiomic methods use hand-made features and involve manually segmenting the area of interest on diagnostic imaging as well as retrieving large numbers of hand-crafted numerical characteristics from that area, which are all thought to be characteristics that make up the tumor. These features are thought to be characteristics that make up the tumor. This could make the process less likely to be repeatable because of human bias [138, 156, 157].

Manual tumor segmentation introduces intra- and inter-reader variability, as well as variations in imaging and feature extraction techniques, all of which might have a significant influence on the models developed afterward. Deep learning enables autonomous categorization, withdrawal and learning of critical radiological attributes in the analytic pipeline without the need for human intervention. As a result, DL has the potential to improve repeatability, generalizability, and accuracy while decreasing bias [158].

10.9   Planning for Treatment

The aim of radiation therapy management is to identify the most effective treatment variables (such as the number of emitters and the form of the multi-leaf lens adapter). Despite the fact that this plan was created with the help of a sophisticated software transaction processing system, it is mostly managed by a human operator.

On the other hand, various semi-automated or fully automated design techniques have been established throughout time with the objective of decreasing planning duration while increasing treatment plan accuracy. Some of these technologies have recently been successfully adopted and tested in commercial goods. As a consequence, DL techniques might be employed to address the problem of computerized treatment planning [159–162].

Adaptive radiotherapy is a kind of radiotherapy in which the treatment plan may be altered depending on the outcomes of measurements made during treatment [163], and it is used to treat cancer. The adaptive-radiotherapy technology may be used on a real-time basis while the sufferer is laying on his or her bed within the processing zone [164–166].

In this instance, DL methods for computerized extraction and image restoration, which may be faster than traditional approaches, may be able to reduce patient treatment time in half. The DL accuracy performance may also be advantageous in the ART process in terms of automated segmentation [167]. The process of planning starts with the recognition of both the site and the target audience (OARs).

Following the determination of target quantities and OARs, the planning process includes the following steps:

❖ Dose distribution is planned for both targeted and common tissues.
❖ Considering the best treatment option (for example, 3D, fixed beam intensity-modulated radiotherapy, volumetric modulated arc treatment, or positive charge nucleus).
❖ Modifying the beams/weights/etc. progressively till the designing goals are accomplished.

❖ Remodeling the beams, weights, so up till the designing goals are achieved continuously [168–173].

DL methods are used to optimize radiation arrangements, particularly for cellular breakdown in the lungs. Lin *et al.* developed a Framework for continuous recognition of cellular breakdown in the lungs that focuses on a therapeutic gating window using a set of ten fluoroscopic images of nine patients. Support Vector Machine Algorithms (SVMAs) and Artificial Neural Network Algorithms (ANNAs) were used to examine various fusions of aspect decrease computations with DL-based classifiers (ANNAs Despite using the same person's visual segment for preparation and analysis, ANNAs combined with the primary part of the examination (PPE) approach seemed to be a more effective option for continuous gated radiation than other combinations [174].

The major decision of treatment planning includes this:

❖ Optimization of beam angle
❖ Prediction of Dose

10.9.1   Optimization of Beam Angle

Beam angle (BA) structure is an initial choice affected by the planner's skill or predicted by a pattern. The process may be characterized as creating options for the BA and assessing a fluence pattern for each possibility to establish the best BA while accounting for the dosimetric effect. The difficult properties of the BA optimization problem, on the other hand, make it impossible to construct it concurrently to employ a shuttered equation, which is computationally expensive since it takes a two-step assessment every cycle [175, 176].

Recent research reported on the usage of a sophisticated DL algorithm to enhance BA. Taasti *et al.* used a BN performance tuning BA selection strategy in their internal method proposed for pencil beam monitoring. BN enhancement was used since nonlinear object goal functions may also be improved [177].

10.9.2   Prediction of Dose

In contemporary radiation therapy planning processes, the planning tool specifies the BA configuration, and the dosage supplied to the objective and OAR is efficient given the stated BA parameters. However, this procedure, on the other hand, is time-taking and non-automated. If a radiology section offers a plenty of radiotherapy devices, it must be decided which equipment to employ for the patient's health state (for example, medicinal straight accelerators, the effect of these variables, or radiation treatment. To compare and assess dose distributions, the ideal strategy is to develop competing techniques for all kinds of therapy. Manually developing competing alternatives for each element of treatment systems, on the other hand, is quite tough. If the dose distributions that characterize the features of each radiotherapy equipment could be predicted using a DL system, planning and quality assurance would be improved [117].

Chen *et al.* proposed utilizing a CNN technique to predict permissible input parameters in a pharmaceutical radiation treatment plan document using a CT image and computerized image analysis and communication residual neural network-101. Using input data, they assessed the reliability of (two-dimensional) dose allocation calculations. Images and the radiation treatment structure are mixed in one approach, whereas imaging, the radiotherapy framework, and the beam pattern are combined in the other. As a consequence, when the beam pattern was provided as input, the projected dose-volume histogram was the most similar to the actual dose-volume histogram [178].

10.10   Deep Learning's Challenges and Future Potential

Deep learning is beneficial in both diagnostic radiology and radiation therapy. DL a subset of computer vision, is a rapidly emerging scientific area with significant promise in imaging and medicine. Profound learning has infiltrated and will continue to infiltrate almost every aspect of clinical image management. The purpose of "prevalent" image examination methods was never to expelling oncologists instead of providing a second perspective on images. Similarly, DL-based technology is unlikely to be able to replace human professionals very soon. In non-medical activities like computer gaming, DL has been shown to function, even if it is not as good as in human performance.

As indicated by the various publications cited in this research, DL has also been found to be extremely useful in a range of medical imaging techniques. Despite recent advances, a vast number of medical imaging problems remain unresolved, and the optimum DL technique and structure each and every activity as well as the utility field is still to be found. In academia, the merging of medical image segmentation tools with other patient records such as background, gender, and statistics is still a hot issue. By enhancing data accuracy, this integration has the potential to increase the value of medical judgment systems.

The availability of massive data sets, technological advancements in data mining approaches, and increasing computer power are all contributing reasons to the DL revolution's pace. As previously noted, new research is being conducted to address the problem of limited data sets in diagnostic imaging, and numerous specialized deep learning structures and approaches adapted to diagnostic imaging have been shown to be quite useful.

The majority of DL-related research articles in medical imaging has grown in recent years, with the majority of these studies published in the last decade. This growth is likely to continue. The number of seminars oriented only to deep learning (DL) in medical imaging (MI) has risen (for example, see https://midl.amsterdam/ for the "Medical Imaging (MI) with Deep Learning (DL) Workshop" slated for July 2018). Deep learning's potential in diagnostic imaging has also been acknowledged by the healthcare sector. Huge healthcare image processing suppliers have indeed made major investments, and companies of all sizes are working hard to develop and market breakthrough DL-based solutions. Even if deep learning is here to stay, it seems to have great potential in computed tomography and radiotherapy [179–182].

10.11 Conclusion

Recently, plenty of DL radiation approaches have been revealed. Radiation oncology is still in its infancy, despite the promising findings of these new approaches. The number of programs available and their capabilities are expected to increase over the next decade. In the opinion of many of the researchers surveyed for this study, the greatest obstacle to this breakthrough is the scarcity of data for training purposes. This exciting topic of DL for radiotherapy has a variety of methodologies and applications to choose from.

As far as radiation oncology is concerned, deep learning has the potential to revolutionize the discipline. For this reason, it is more difficult to use than other machine learning (ML) methods like support vector machines algorithms the number of programs available and their capabilities are expected to grow in the next years. (SVMAs), ensemble learning (ANN), and logistic regression since it requires a higher level of technical expertise from researchers and has more hyper-parameters to adjust.

Training neural networks for deep learning is still an art form, although it is becoming more popular in academic circles. Finally, we want to emphasize the need of larger, standardized datasets for future collaborations. As a result, researchers may be able to build more rigorous clinical algorithms, which might lead to better treatment results for cancer patients.

References

1. Huang, D., Bai, H., Wang, L., Hou, Y., Li, L., Xia, Y., Yan, Z., Chen, W., Chang, L., Li, W., The application and development of deep learning in radiotherapy: A systematic review. *Technol. Cancer Res. Treat.*, 20, 15330338211016386, 2021 Jun 17.
2. Samarasinghe, G., Jameson, M., Vinod, S., Field, M., Dowling, J., Sowmya, A., Holloway, L., Deep learning for segmentation in radiation therapy planning: A review. *J. Med. Imaging Radiat. Oncol.*, 65, 5, 578–95, 2021 Aug.
3. Sim, Y., Chung, M.J., Kotter, E., Yune, S., Kim, M., Do, S., Han, K., Kim, H., Yang, S., Lee, D.J., Choi, B.W., Deep convolutional neural network-based software improves radiologist detection of malignant lung nodules on chest radiographs. *Radiology*, 294, 1, 199–209, 2020 Jan.
4. Nensa, F., Demircioglu, A., Rischpler, C., Artificial intelligence in nuclear medicine. *J. Nucl. Med.*, 60, Supplement 2, 29S–37S, 2019 Sep 1.
5. Schmidhuber, J., Deep learning in neural networks: An overview. *Neural Networks*, 61, 85–117, 2015 Jan 1.
6. Francolini, G., Desideri, I., Stocchi, G., Salvestrini, V., Ciccone, L.P., Garlatti, P., Loi, M., Livi, L., Artificial Intelligence in radiotherapy: State of the art and future directions. *Med. Oncol.*, 37, 6, 1–9, 2020 Jun.
7. Mutasa, S., Sun, S., Ha, R., Understanding artificial intelligence-based radiology studies: What is overfitting? *Clin. Imaging*, 65, 96–9, 2020 Sep 1.
8. Sahiner, B., Pezeshk, A., Hadjiiski, L.M., Wang, X., Drukker, K., Cha, K.H., Summers, R.M., Giger, M.L., Deep learning in medical imaging and radiation therapy. *Med. Phys.*, 46, 1, e1–36, 2019 Jan.
9. Chamunyonga, C., Edwards, C., Caldwell, P., Rutledge, P., Burbery, J., The impact of artificial intelligence and machine learning in radiation therapy: Considerations for future curriculum enhancement. *J. Med. Imaging Radiat. Sci.*, 51, 2, 214–20, 2020 Jun 1.
10. Delaney, G.P. and Barton, M.B., Evidence-based estimates of the demand for radiotherapy. *Clin. Oncol.*, 27, 2, 70–6, 2015 Feb 1.
11. Pereira, G.C., Traughber, M., Muzic, R.F., The role of imaging in radiation therapy planning: Past, present, and future. *BioMed. Res. Int.*, 2014, 1–9, 2014 Apr 10.
12. Pham, D.L., Xu, C., Prince, J.L., Current methods in medical image segmentation. *Annu. Rev. Biomed. Eng.*, 2, 1, 315–37, 2000 Aug.

13. Siddique, S. and Chow, J.C., Machine learning in healthcare communication. *Encyclopedia*, 1, 1, 220–39, 2021 Mar.
14. De Felice, F., Piccioli, A., Musio, D., Tombolini, V., The role of radiation therapy in bone metastases management. *Oncotarget.*, 8, 15, 25691, 2017 Apr 11.
15. Deshmukh, P. and Levy, M.S., Effective radiation dose in coronary imaging modalities: Back to Basics. *Catheter. Cardiovasc. Interv.*, 85, 7, 1182–3, 2015 Jun.
16. Weissleder, R. and Nahrendorf, M., Advancing biomedical imaging. *Proc. Natl. Acad. Sci.*, 112, 47, 14424–8, 2015 Nov 24.
17. Hunt, M.A., Pastrana, G., Amols, H.I., Killen, A., Alektiar, K., The impact of new technologies on radiation oncology events and trends in the past decade: An institutional experience. *Int. J. Radiat. Oncol. Biol. Phys.*, 84, 4, 925–31, 2012 Nov 15.
18. van de Bunt, L., Van der Heide, U.A., Ketelaars, M., de Kort, G.A., Jürgenliemk-Schulz, I.M., Conventional, conformal, and intensity-modulated radiation therapy treatment planning of external beam radiotherapy for cervical cancer: The impact of tumor regression. *Int. J. Radiat. Oncol. Biol. Phys.*, 64, 1, 189–96, 2006 Jan 1.
19. Nwankwo, O., Mekdash, H., Sihono, D.S., Wenz, F., Glatting, G., Knowledge-based radiation therapy (KBRT) treatment planning versus planning by experts: Validation of a KBRT algorithm for prostate cancer treatment planning. *Radiat. Oncol.*, 10, 1, 1–5, 2015 Dec.
20. Miras, H., Jiménez, R., Perales, Á., Terrón, J.A., Bertolet, A., Ortiz, A., Macías, J., Monte Carlo verification of radiotherapy treatments with CloudMC. *Radiat. Oncol.*, 13, 1, 1–9, 2018 Dec.
21. Wroe, A.J., Bush, D.A., Schulte, R.W., Slater, J.D., Clinical immobilization techniques for proton therapy. *Technol. Cancer Res. Treat.*, 14, 1, 71–9, 2015 Feb.
22. Shaverdian, N., Verruttipong, D., Wang, P.C., Kishan, A.U., Demanes, D.J., McCloskey, S., Kupelian, P., Steinberg, M.L., King, C.R., Exploring value from the patient's perspective between modern radiation therapy modalities for localized prostate cancer. *Int. J. Radiat. Oncol. Biol. Phys.*, 97, 3, 516–25, 2017 Mar 1.
23. McDonald, D.G., Jacqmin, D.J., Mart, C.J., Koch, N.C., Peng, J.L., Ashenafi, M.S., Fugal, M.A., Vanek, K.N., Validation of a modern second-check dosimetry system using a novel verification phantom. *J. Appl. Clin. Med. Phys.*, 18, 1, 170–7, 2017 Jan.
24. Crevier, D., *AI: The tumultuous history of the search for artificial intelligence*, Basic Books, Inc., New York, 1993 Mar 1.
25. McCarthy, J. and Hayes, P., *Some philosophical problems from the standpoint of artificial intelligence*, vol. 393, pp. 1–51, Read. Plan, California, 1969.
26. Boden, M.A., *Artificial intelligence and natural man*, Basic Books, New York, 1977.

27. Turing, A.M., Computing machinery and intelligence. *Mind*, 59, 433–460, 1950.

28. Newell, A. and Simon, H., The logic theory machine–A complex information processing system. *IRE Trans. Inf. Theory*, 2, 3, 61–79, 1956 Sep.

29. Samuel, A.L., Some studies in machine learning using the game of checkers. *IBM J. Res. Dev.*, 3, 3, 210–29, 1959 Jul.

30. Meyer, P., Noblet, V., Mazzara, C., Lallement, A., Survey on deep learning for radiotherapy. *Comput. Biol. Med.*, 98, 126–46, 2018 Jul 1.

31. Field, M., Hardcastle, N., Jameson, M., Aherne, N., Holloway, L., Machine learning applications in radiation oncology. *Phys. Imaging Radiat. Oncol.*, 19, 13–24, 2021 Jul 1.

32. Zlochower, A., Chow, D.S., Chang, P., Khatri, D., Boockvar, J.A., Filippi, C.G., Deep learning AI applications in the imaging of glioma. *Top. Magn. Reson. Imaging*, 29, 2, 115–00, 2020 Apr 1.

33. Chlap, P., Min, H., Vandenberg, N., Dowling, J., Holloway, L., Haworth, A., A review of medical image data augmentation techniques for deep learning applications. *J. Med. Imaging Radiat. Oncol.*, 65, 5, 543–563, 2021 Jun 19.

34. Sun, Y., Yen, G.G., Yi, Z., Evolving unsupervised deep neural networks for learning meaningful representations. *IEEE Trans. Evol. Comput.*, 23, 1, 89–103, 2019.

35. Boldrini, L., Bibault, J.E., Masciocchi, C., Shen, Y., Bittner, M.I., Deep learning: A review for the radiation oncologist. *Front. Oncol.*, 9, 977, 2019 Oct 1.

36. Wang, T., Manohar, N., Lei, Y., Dhabaan, A., Shu, H.K., Liu, T., Curran, W.J., Yang, X., MRI-based treatment planning for brain stereotactic radiosurgery: Dosimetric validation of a learning-based pseudo-CT generation method. *Med. Dosim.*, 44, 3, 199–204, 2019 Sep 1.

37. Shafai-Erfani, G., Wang, T., Lei, Y., Tian, S., Patel, P., Jani, A.B., Curran, W.J., Liu, T., Yang, X., Dose evaluation of MRI-based synthetic CT generated using a machine learning method for prostate cancer radiotherapy. *Med. Dosim.*, 44, 4, e64–70, 2019 Dec 1.

38. Lustberg, T., van Soest, J., Gooding, M., Peressutti, D., Aljabar, P., van der Stoep, J., van Elmpt, W., Dekker, A., Clinical evaluation of atlas and deep learning based automatic contouring for lung cancer. *Radiother. Oncol.*, 126, 2, 312–7, 2018 Feb 1.

39. Gooding, M.J., Smith, A.J., Tariq, M., Aljabar, P., Peressutti, D., van der Stoep, J., Reymen, B., Emans, D., Hattu, D., van Loon, J., de Rooy, M., Comparative evaluation of autocontouring in clinical practice: A practical method using the Turing test. *Med. Phys.*, 45, 11, 5105–15, 2018 Nov.

40. Zhu, J., Zhang, J., Qiu, B., Liu, Y., Liu, X., Chen, L., Comparison of the automatic segmentation of multiple organs at risk in CT images of lung cancer between deep convolutional neural network-based and atlas-based techniques. *Acta Oncol.*, 58, 2, 257–64, 2019 Feb 1.

41. Varian Medical Systems I. EthosTM therapy AI Technical Brief, 2019, Available at: https://www.varian.com/sites/default/files/resource_attachments/ EthosAITechnicalBrief_RAD10690_Sep19.pdf. Accessed September 30, 2019.

42. Chanyavanich, V., Das, S.K., Lee, W.R., Lo, J.Y., Knowledge-based IMRT treatment planning for prostate cancer. *Med. Phys.*, 38, 5, 2515–22, 2011 May.

43. Chen, H.C., Tan, J., Dolly, S., Kavanaugh, J., Anastasio, M.A., Low, D.A., Harold Li, H., Altman, M., Gay, H., Thorstad, W.L., Mutic, S., Automated contouring error detection based on supervised geometric attribute distribution models for radiation therapy: A general strategy. *Med. Phys.*, 42, 2, 1048–59, 2015 Feb.

44. Kirlik, G., D'Souza, W.D., Zhang, H.H., Fully automated multicriteria optimization (MCO) treatment plan generation for radiation treatment planning. *Int. J. Radiat. Oncol. Biol. Phys.*, 96, 2, S98, 2016 Oct 1.

45. Zhao, W., Han, B., Yang, Y., Buyyounouski, M., Hancock, S.L., Bagshaw, H., Xing, L., Incorporating imaging information from deep neural network layers into image guided radiation therapy (IGRT). *Radiother. Oncol.*, 140, 167–74, 2019 Nov 1.

46. Ruskó, L., Capala, M.E., Czipczer, V., Kolozsvári, B., Deák-Karancsi, B., Czabány, R., Gyalai, B., Tan, T., Végváry, Z., Borzasi, E., Együd, Z., Deep-learning-based segmentation of organs-at-risk in the head for MR-assisted radiation therapy planning, in: *BIOIMAGING*, pp. 31–43, 2021.

47. LeCun, Y., Bengio, Y., Hinton, G., learning D. Deep learning. *Nature*, 521, 436–4, 2015.

48. Caruana, R., Karampatziakis, N., Yessenalina, A., An empirical evaluation of supervised learning in high dimensions, in: *Proceedings of the 25th international conference on Machine learning*, 2008 Jul 5, pp. 96–103.

49. Deng, L., Three classes of deep learning architectures and their applications: A tutorial survey, in: *APSIPA transactions on signal and information processing*, vol. 57, p. 58, 2012.

50. Wan, L., Zeiler, M., Zhang, S., Le Cun, Y., Fergus, R., Regularization of neural networks using drop connect, in: *International conference on machine learning*, 2013 May 26, PMLR, pp. 1058–1066.

51. Coates, A., Huval, B., Wang, T., Wu, D., Catanzaro, B., Andrew, N., Deep learning with COTS HPC systems, in: *International conference on machine learning*, 2013 May 26, PMLR, pp. 1337–1345.

52. Jia, Y., Shelhamer, E., Donahue, J., Karayev, S., Long, J., Girshick, R., Guadarrama, S., Darrell, T., Caffe: Convolutional architecture for fast feature embedding, in: *Proceedings of the 22nd ACM international conference on Multimedia*, 2014 Nov 3, pp. 675–678.

53. D., Eversole, A., Seltzer, M.L., Yao, K., Guenter, B., Kuchaiev, O., Seide, F., Wang, H., Droppo, J., Huang, Z., Zweig, G., An introduction to computational networks and the computational network toolkit (invited talk), in: *Fifteenth Annual Conference of the International Speech Communication Association*, 2014.

54. Abadi, M., Agarwal, A., Barham, P., Brevdo, E., Chen, Z., Citro, C., Corrado, G.S., Davis, A., Dean, J., Devin, M., Ghemawat, S., Tensorflow: Large-scale machine learning on heterogeneous distributed systems. arXiv preprint arXiv:1603.04467, 2016 Mar 14.

55. Collobert, R., Kavukcuoglu, K., Farabet, C., Torch7: A MatLab-like environment for machine learning, in: *BigLearn, NIPS workshop*, 2011, (No. CONF-19237).

56. Team, T.T., Al-Rfou, R., Alain, G., Almahairi, A., Angermueller, C., Bahdanau, D., Ballas, N., Bastien, F., Bayer, J., Belikov, A., Belopolsky, A., Theano: A python framework for fast computation of mathematical expressions. arXiv preprint arXiv:1605.02688, 2016 May 9.

57. Chen, T., Li, M., Li, Y., Lin, M., Wang, N., Wang, M., Xiao, T., Xu, B., Zhang, C., Zhang, Z., Mxnet: A flexible and efficient machine learning library for heterogeneous distributed systems. arXiv preprint arXiv:1512.01274, 2015 Dec 3.

58. *Eigen*, [online] Available: http://eigen.tuxfamily.org/index.php.

59. *Openblas*, [online] Available: http://www.openblas.net/.

60. Toolkit CU, *4.0 cublas library*, vol. 2701, pp. 59–60, Nvidia Corporation, California, 2011.

61. LeCun, Y., Boser, B., Denker, J.S., Henderson, D., Howard, R.E., Hubbard, W., Jackel, L.D., Backpropagation applied to handwritten zip code recognition. *Neural Comput.*, 1, 4, 541–51, 1989 Dec.

62. Krizhevsky, A., Sutskever, I., Hinton, G.E., Imagenet classification with deep convolutional neural networks. *Adv. Neural Inf. Process. Syst.*, 25, 1097–105, 2012.

63. Zaremba, W., Sutskever, I., Vinyals, O., Recurrent neural network regularization. arXiv preprint arXiv:1409.2329, 2014 Sep 8.

64. Shi, S., Wang, Q., Xu, P., Chu, X., Benchmarking state-of-the-art deep learning software tools, in: *2016 7th International Conference on Cloud Computing and Big Data (CCBD)*, 2016 Nov 16, IEEE, pp. 99–104.

65. Stimpel, B., Syben, C., Würfl, T., Mentl, K., Dörfler, A., Maier, A., MR to X-Ray Projection Image Synthesis, ArXiv171007498 Cs, 2017, http://arxiv.org/abs/1710.07498.

66. Zhao, C., Carass, A., Lee, J., He, Y., Prince, J.L., Whole brain segmentation and labeling from CT using synthetic MR images, in: *Mach. Learn. Med. Imaging*, pp. 291–298, Springer, Cham, 2017.

67. Dalmış, M.U., Litjens, G., Holland, K., Setio, A., Mann, R., Karssemeijer, N., Gubern-Mérida, A., Using deep learning to segment breast and fibroglandular tissue in MRI volumes. *Med. Phys.*, 44, 533–546, 2017.

68. Ibragimov, B. and Xing, L., Segmentation of organs-at-risks in head and neck CT images using convolutional neural networks. *Med. Phys.*, 44, 547–557, 2017.

69. Hua, K.-L., Hsu, C.-H., Hidayati, S.C., Cheng, W.-H., Chen, Y.-J., Computer-aided classification of lung nodules on computed tomography images via deep learning technique. *OncoTargets Ther.*, 8, 2015–2022, 2015.

70. Kooi, T., van Ginneken, B., Karssemeijer, N., den Heeten, A., Discriminating solitary cysts from soft tissue lesions in mammography using a pretrained deep convolutional neural network. *Med. Phys.*, 44, 1017–1027, 2017.

71. Yang, X., Kwitt, R., Niethammer, M., Fast predictive image registration, in: *Deep Learn. Data Labeling Med. Appl.*, pp. 48–57, Springer, Cham, 2016.

72. Miao, S., Wang, Z.J., Zheng, Y., Liao, R., Real-time 2D/3D registration via CNN regression, in: *Biomed. Imaging ISBI 2016 IEEE 13th Int. Symp. On*, IEEE, pp. 1430–1434, 2016, http://ieeexplore.ieee.org/abstract/document/7493536/ (accessed February 15, 2017.

73. Nguyen, D., Long, T., Jia, X., Lu, W., Gu, X., Iqbal, Z., Jiang, S., Dose prediction with U-net: A feasibility study for predicting dose distributions from contours using deep learning on prostate IMRT patients, ArXiv Prepr. ArXiv170909233, 2017.

74. Li, H., Zhong, H., Boimel, P.J., Ben-Josef, E., Xiao, Y., Fan, Y., Deep convolutional neural networks for imaging based survival analysis of rectal cancer patients. *Int. J. Radiat. Oncol. Biol.*, 99, S183, 2017.

75. Shan, H., Jia, X., Yan, P., Li, Y., Paganetti, H., Wang, G., Synergizing medical imaging and radiotherapy with deep learning, in: *Machine Learning: Science and Technology*, 1(2), 021001, 2020 Jun 22.

76. Siddique, S. and Chow, J.C., Artificial intelligence in radiotherapy. *Rep. Pract. Oncol. Radiother.*, 25, 4, 656–66, 2020.

77. Geis, J.R., Brady, A.P., Wu, C.C., Spencer, J., Ranschaert, E., Jaremko, J.L., Langer, S.G., Kitts, A.B., Birch, J., Shields, W.F., van den Hoven van Genderen, R., Ethics of artificial intelligence in radiology: Summary of the joint European and North American multisociety statement. *Can. Assoc. Radiol. J.*, 70, 4, 329–34, 2019 Nov.

78. Hall, W.A., Paulson, E.S., van der Heide, U.A., Fuller, C.D., Raaymakers, B.W., Lagendijk, J.J., Li, X.A., Jaffray, D.A., Dawson, L.A., Erickson, B., Verheij, M., The transformation of radiation oncology using real-time magnetic resonance guidance: A review. *Eur. J. Cancer*, 122, 42–52, 2019 Nov 1.

79. Jarrett, D., Stride, E., Vallis, K., Gooding, M.J., Applications and limitations of machine learning in radiation oncology. *Br. J. Radiol.*, 92, 1100, 20190001, 2019 Aug.

80. Chlebus, G., Meine, H., Thoduka, S., Abolmaali, N., Van Ginneken, B., Hahn, H.K., Schenk, A., Reducing inter-observer variability and interaction time of MR liver volumetry by combining automatic CNN-based liver segmentation and manual corrections. *PLoS One*, 14, 5, e0217228, 2019 May 20.

81. Orasanu, E., Brosch, T., Glide-Hurst, C., Renisch, S., Organ-at-risk segmentation in brain MRI using model-based segmentation: Benefits of deep learning-based boundary detectors, in: *International Workshop on Shape in Medical Imaging*, 2018 Sep 20, Springer, Cham, pp. 291–299.

82. Ronneberger, O., Fischer, P., Brox, T., U-net: Convolutional networks for biomedical image segmentation, in: *International Conference on Medical image computing and computer-assisted intervention*, 2015 Oct 5, Springer, Cham, pp. 234–241.

83. Mlynarski, P., Delingette, H., Alghamdi, H., Bondiau, P.Y., Ayache, N., Anatomically consistent segmentation of organs at risk in MRI with convolutional neural networks. arXiv preprint arXiv:1907.02003, 2019 Jul 3.

84. Alex, V., Vaidhya, K., Thirunavukkarasu, S., Kesavadas, C., Krishnamurthi, G., Semisupervised learning using denoising autoencoders for brain lesion detection and segmentation. *J. Med. Imaging*, 4, 4, 041311, 2017 Dec.

85. Korfiatis, P., Kline, T.L., Erickson, B.J., Automated segmentation of hyperintense regions in FLAIR MRI using deep learning. *Tomography*, 2, 4, 334–40, 2016 Dec.

86. Iqbal, S., Ghani, M.U., Saba, T., Rehman, A., Brain tumor segmentation in multi-spectral MRI using convolutional neural networks (CNN). *Microsc. Res. Tech.*, 81, 4, 419–27, 2018 Apr.

87. Zhuge, Y., Krauze, A.V., Ning, H., Cheng, J.Y., Arora, B.C., Camphausen, K., Miller, R.W., Brain tumor segmentation using holistically nested neural networks in MRI images. *Med. Phys.*, 44, 10, 5234–43, 2017 Oct.

88. Hua, K.L., Hsu, C.H., Hidayati, S.C., Cheng, W.H., Chen, Y.J., Computer-aided classification of lung nodules on computed tomography images via deep learning technique. *OncoTargets Ther.*, 8, 2015–2022, 2015.

89. Ali, Hart, G.R., Gunabushanam, G., Liang, Y., Muhammad, W., Nartowt, B., Kane, M., Ma, X., Deng, J., Lung nodule detection via deep reinforcement learning. *Front. Oncol.*, 8, 1–7, 2018. https://doi.org/10.3389/fonc.2018.00108.

90. Kumar, D., Wong, A., Clausi, D.A., Lung nodule classification using deep features in CT images, in: *Comput. Robot Vis. CRV 2015 12th Conf. on*, IEEE, pp. 133–138, 2015, http://ieeexplore.ieee.org/abstract/document/7158331/. (Accessed 6 February 2017).

91. Song, Q., Zhao, L., Luo, X., Dou, X., Using deep learning for classification of lung nodules on computed tomography images. *J. Healthc. Eng.*, 2017, 1–7, 2017, https://doi.org/10.1155/2017/8314740.

92. Sun, W., Zheng, B., Qian, W., Automatic feature learning using multichannel ROI based on deep structured algorithms for computerized lung cancer diagnosis. *Comput. Biol. Med.*, 89, 530–539, 2017, https://doi.org/10.1016/j.compbiomed.2017.04.006.

93. Wang, H., Zhou, Z., Li, Y., Chen, Z., Lu, P., Wang, W., Liu, W., Yu, L., Comparison of machine learning methods for classifying mediastinal lymph node metastasis of non-small cell lung cancer from 18 F-FDG PET/CT images. *EJNMMI Res.*, 7, 11, 2017, https://doi.org/10.1186/s13550-017-0260-9.

94. Meyer, P., Noblet, V., Mazzara, C., Lallement, A., Survey on deep learning for radiotherapy. *Comput. Biol. Med.*, 98, 126–46, 2018 Jul 1.

95. Chen, Q., Xu, X., Hu, S., Li, X., Zou, Q., Li, Y., A transfer learning approach for classification of clinical significant prostate cancers from

MpMRI Scans, Medical Imaging, 10134, 1154–1157, 2017, https://doi. org/10.1117/12.2279021, p. 101344F–101344F–4.

96. Banerjee, A., Crawley, Bhethanabotla, M., Daldrup-Link, H.E., Rubin, D.L., Transfer learning on fused multiparametric MR images for classifying histopathological subtypes of rhabdomyosarcoma. *Comput. Med. Imaging Graph. Off. J. Comput. Med. Imaging Soc.*, 65, 167–175, 2017, https://doi. org/10.1016/j.compmedimag.2017.05.002.

97. Litjens, G., Debats, O., Barentsz, J., Karssemeijer, N., Huisman, H., Computer-aided detection of prostate cancer in MRI. *IEEE Trans. Med. Imaging*, 33, 5, 1083–1092, 2014, http://dx.doi.org/10.1109/TMI.2014. 2303821.

98. Kooi, T., Litjens, G., van Ginneken, B. *et al.*, Large scale deep learning for computer aided detection of mammographic lesions. *Med. Image Anal.*, 35, 303–312, 2017, http://dx.doi.org/10.1016/j.media.2016.07.007.

99. Shan, H., Jia, X., Yan, P., Li, Y., Paganetti, H., Wang, G., Synergizing medical imaging and radiotherapy with deep learning. *Mach. Learn.: Sci. Technol.*, 1, 2, 021001, 2020 Jun 22.

100. Zhang, J., Wu, Q.J., Xie, T., Sheng, Y., Yin, F.-F., Ge, Y., An ensemble approach to knowledge-based intensity-modulated radiation therapy planning. *Front. Oncol.*, 8, 57, 2018.

101. Babier, A., Boutilier, J.J., McNiven, A.L., Chan, T.C.Y., Knowledge-based automated planning for oropharyngeal cancer. *Med. Phys.*, 45, 2875–83, 2018.

102. Tol, J.P., Delaney, A.R., Dahele, M., Slotman, B.J., Verbakel, W.F.A.R., Evaluation of a knowledge-based planning solution for head and neck cancer. *Int. J. Radiat. Oncol. Biol. Phys.*, 91, 612–20, 2015.

103. Fogliata, A., Belosi, F., Clivio, A. *et al.*, On the pre-clinical validation of a commercial model-based optimisation engine: Application to volumetric modulated arc therapy for patients with lung or prostate cancer. *Radiother. Oncol.*, 113, 385–91, 2014.

104. Nguyen, D., Long, T., Jia, X. *et al.*, A feasibility study for predicting optimal radiation therapy dose distributions of prostate cancer patients from patient anatomy using deep learning. arXiv, 9, 1, 1–0. Available at: https://arxiv.org/ abs/1709.09233. Accessed June 17, 2019.

105. Zhao, W., Han, B., Yang, Y., Buyyounouski, M., Hancock, S.L., Bagshaw, H., Xing, L., Incorporating imaging information from deep neural network layers into image guided radiotherapy (IGRT). *Radiother. Oncol.*, 140, 167–74, 2019.

106. Liu, C., Zheming, L., Longhua, M., Wang, L., Jin, X., Wen, S., A modality conversion approach to MV-DRs and KV-DRRs registration using information bottlenecked conditional generative adversarial network. *Med. Phys.*, 46, 4575–87, 2019.

107. Chen, H. *et al.*, Deep-learning based surface region selection for deep inspiration breath hold (DIBH) monitoring in left breast cancer radiotherapy. *Phys. Med. Biol.*, 63, 245013, 2018.

108. Park, S., Lee, S.J., Weiss, E., Motai, Y., Intra-and inter-fractional variation prediction of lung tumors using fuzzy deep learning. *IEEE J. Trans. Eng. Health Med.*, 4, 1–12, 2016.

109. Huang, P., Gang, Y., Hua, L., Liu, D., Xing, L., Yin, Y., Kovalchuk, N., Xing, L., Li, D., Attention-aware fully convolutional neural network with convolutional long short-term memory network for ultrasound-based motion tracking. *Med. Phys.*, 46, 2275–85, 2019.

110. Lin, H., Shi, C., Wang, B., Chan, M.F., Tang, X., Wei, J., Towards real-time respiratory motion prediction based on long short-term memory neural networks. *Phys. Med. Biol.*, 64, 085010, 2019.

111. Cha, K.H., Hadjiiski, L., Chan, H.P., Weizer, A.Z., Alva, A., Cohan, R.H., Caoili, E.M., Paramagul, C., Samala, R.K., Bladder cancer treatment response assessment in CT 2285 using radiomics with deep-learning. *Sci. Rep.*, 7, 1–2, 2017.

112. Lao, J., Chen, Y., Li, Z.C., Li, Q., Zhang, J., Liu, J., Zhai, G., A deep learning-based radiomics model for prediction of survival in glioblastoma multiforme. *Sci. Rep.*, 7, 10353, 2017.

113. Bibault, J.E., Giraud, P., Durdux, C., Taieb, J., Berger, A., Coriat, R., Chaussade, S., Dousset, B., Nordlinger, B., Burgun, A., Deep learning and radiomics predict complete locally advanced rectal cancer, 8, 1, 1–8 response after neoadjuvant chemoradiation for locally advanced rectal cancer. *Sci. Rep.*, 8, 12611, 2018.

114. Ibragimov, B., Toesca, D., Chang, D., Yuan, Y., Koong, A., Xing, L., Development of deep neural network for individualized hepatobiliary toxicity prediction after liver SBRT. *Med. Phys.*, 45, 10, 4763–4774, 2018.

115. Shehata, M., Khalifa, F., Soliman, A., Ghazal, M., Taher, F., Abou El-Ghar, M., Dwyer, A., Gimel'farb, G., Keynton, R., El-Baz, A., Computer-aided diagnostic system for early detection of acute renal transplant rejection using diffusion-weighted MRI. *IEEE Trans. Biomed. Eng.*, 66, 2, 539–552, 2018.

116. Nielsen, M., Hansen, B., Tietze, A., Mouridsen, K., Prediction of tissue outcome and assessment of treatment effect in acute ischemic stroke using deep learning. *Stroke*, 49, 1394–1401, 2018.

117. Cheon, W., Kim, H., Kim, J., Deep learning in radiation oncology. *Prog. Med. Phys.*, 31, 3, 111–23, 2020 Sep 30.

118. Shickel, B., Tighe, P.J., Bihorac, A., Rashidi, P., Deep EHR: A survey of recent advances in deep learning techniques for electronic health record (EHR) analysis. *IEEE J. Biomed. Health Inf.*, 22, 5, 1589–604, 2017 Oct 27.

119. Ravì, D., Wong, C., Deligianni, F., Berthelot, M., Andreu-Perez, J., Lo, B., Yang, G.Z., Deep learning for health informatics. *IEEE J. Biomed. Health Inf.*, 21, 1, 4–21, 2016 Dec 29.

120. Coates, Souhami, L., El Naqa, I., Big data analytics for prostate radiotherapy. *Front. Oncol.*, 6, 1–17, 2016.

121. Chaikh, A., Thariat, J., Thureau, S., Tessonnier, T., Kammerer, E., Fontbonne, C. *et al.*, Construction of radiobiological models as TCP (tumor control probability) and NTCP (normal tissue complication probability): From dose to clinical effects prediction. *Cancer Radiother.*, 24, 247–257, 2020. French.

122. Luo, Y., Chen, S., Valdes, G., Machine learning for radiation outcome modeling and prediction. *Med. Phys.*, 47, e178– e184, 2020.

123. Jochems, A., Deist, T.M., van Soest, J. *et al.*, Distributed learning: Developing a predictive model based on data from multiple hospitals without data leaving the hospital – a real life proof of concept. *Radiother. Oncol.*, 121, 459–467, 2016.

124. Muthalaly, R.S., *Using deep learning to predict the mortality of Leukemia patients*, Queen's University, Kingston, Ont., 2017, http://qspace.library. queensu.ca/handle/1974/15929 (accessed July 12, 2017).

125. Jochems, Deist, T.M., El Naqa, I., Kessler, M., Mayo, C., Reeves, J., Jolly, S., Matuszak, M., Ten Haken, R., van Soest, J., Oberije, C., Faivre-Finn, C., Price, G., de Ruysscher, D., Lambin, P., Dekker, A., Developing and validating a survival prediction model for NSCLC patients through distributed learning across 3 countries. *Int. J. Radiat. Oncol.*, 99, 344–352, 2017.

126. Li, H., Zhong, H., Boimel, P.J., Ben-Josef, E., Xiao, Y., Fan, Y., Deep convolutional neural networks for imaging based survival analysis of rectal cancer patients. *Int. J. Radiat. Oncol. Biol.*, 99, S183, 2017.

127. Qi, X., Neylon, J., Santhanam, A., Dosimetric predictors for quality of life after prostate stereotactic body radiation therapy via deep learning network. *Int. J. Radiat. Oncol. Biol.*, 99, S167, 2017.

128. Tseng, H.-H., Luo, Y., Cui, S., Chien, J.-T., Ten Haken, R.K., Naqa, I.E., Deep reinforcement learning for automated radiation adaptation in lung cancer. *Med. Phys.*, 44, 6690–6705, 2017.

129. Zhang, H.H., D'Souza, W.D., Shi, L., Meyer, R.R., Modeling plan-related clinical complications using machine learning tools in a multiplan IMRT framework. *Int. J. Radiat. Oncol. Biol. Phys.*, 74, 1617–26, 2009.

130. Men, K., Geng, H., Zhong, H., Fan, Y., Lin, A., Xiao, Y., A deep learning model for predicting xerostomia due to radiation therapy for head and neck squamous cell carcinoma in the RTOG 0522 clinical trial. *Int. J. Radiat. Oncol. Biol. Phys.*, 105, 2, 440–447, 2019.

131. Mattonen, S.A., Palma, D.A., Haasbeek, C.J., Senan, S., Ward, A.D., Early prediction of tumor recurrence based on CT texture changes after stereotactic ablative radiotherapy (SABR) for lung cancer. *Med. Phys.*, 41, 3, 033502, 2014.

132. Liang, B., Tian, Y., Chen, X. *et al.*, Prediction of radiation pneumonitis with dose distribution: A convolutional neural network (CNN) based model. *Front. Oncol.*, 9, 1500, 2019.

133. Lee, S., Kerns, S., Ostrer, H., Rosenstein, B., Deasy, J.O., Oh, J.H., Machine learning on a genome-wide association study to predict late genitourinary

toxicity after prostate radiation therapy. *Int. J. Radiat. Oncol. Biol. Phys.*, 101, 1, 128–135, 2018.

134. Kang, J., Schwartz, R., Flickinger, J., Beriwal, S., Machine learning approaches for predicting radiation therapy outcomes: A clinician's perspective. *Int. J. Radiat. Oncol. Biol. Phys.*, 93, 1127–35, 2015.

135. Zhen, X., Chen, J., Zhong, Z., Hrycushko, B.A., Albuquerque, K., Zhou, L., Jiang, S.B., Gu, X., Deep convolutional neural networks with transfer learning for rectum toxicity prediction in combined brachytherapy and external beam radiation therapy for cervical cancer. *Int. J. Radiat. Oncol. Biol.*, 99, S168, 2017.

136. Arefan, D., Mohamed, A.A., Berg, W.A., Zuley, M.L., Sumkin, J.H., Wu, S., Deep learning modeling using normal mammograms for predicting breast cancer risk. *Med. Phys.*, 47, 110–118, 2020.

137. Pella, A., Cambria, R., Riboldi, M., Jereczek-Fossa, B.A., Fodor, C., Zerini, D. *et al.*, Use of machine learning methods for prediction of acute toxicity in organs at risk following prostate radiotherapy. *Med. Phys.*, 38, 2859–67, 2011.

138. Vial, A., Stirling, D., Field, M., Ros, M., Ritz, C., Carolan, M. *et al.*, The role of deep learning and radiomic feature extraction in cancer-specific predictive modelling: A review. *Transl. Cancer Res.*, 7, 803–16, 2018.

139. Boldrini, L., Cusumano, D., Cellini, F., Azario, L., Mattiucci, G.C., Valentini, V., Online adaptive magnetic resonance guided radiotherapy for pancreatic cancer: State of the art, pearls and pitfalls. *Radiat. Oncol.*, 14, 71, 2019.

140. Bryce, T.J., Dewhirst, M.W., Floyd, C.E., Hars, V., Brizel, D.M., Artificial neural network model of survival in patients treated with irradiation with and without concurrent chemotherapy for advanced carcinoma of the head and neck. *Int. J. Radiat. Oncol. Biol. Phys.*, 41, 339–45, 1998.

141. Ochi, T., Murase, K., Fujii, T., Kawamura, M., Ikezoe, J., Survival prediction using artificial neural networks in patients with uterine cervical cancer treated by radiation therapy alone. *Int. J. Clin. Oncol.*, 7, 294–300, 2002.

142. Chen, S., Zhou, S., Zhang, J., Yin, F.-F., Marks, L.B., Das, S.K., A neural network model to predict lung radiation-induced pneumonitis. *Med. Phys.*, 34, 3420–3427, 2007.

143. Cha, K.H., Hadjiiski, L., Chan, H.P., Weizer, A.Z., Alva, A., Cohan, R.H., Caoili, E.M., Paramagul, C., Samala, R.K., Bladder cancer treatment response assessment in CT using radiomics with deep-learning. *Sci. Rep.*, 7, 1–2, 2017.

144. Gulliford, S.L., Webb, S., Rowbottom, C.G., Corne, D.W., Dearnaley, D.P., Use of artificial neural networks to predict biological outcomes for patients receiving radical radiotherapy of the prostate. *Radiother. Oncol.*, 71, 3–12, 2004.

145. Saltz, J., Gupta, R., Hou, L., Kurc, T., Singh, P., Nguyen, V. *et al.*, Spatial organization and molecular correlation of tumor-infiltrating lymphocytes using deep learning on pathology images. *Cell Rep.*, 23, 181–93.e7, 2018.

146. Rios Velazquez, E., Parmar, C., Liu, Y., Coroller, T.P., Cruz, G., Stringfield, O. *et al.*, Somatic mutations drive distinct imaging phenotypes in lung cancer. *Cancer Res.*, 77, 3922–30, 2017.

147. Trebeschi, S., van Griethuysen, J.J.M., Lambregts, D.M.J., Lahaye, M.J., Parmar, C., Bakers, F.C.H. *et al.*, Deep learning for fully-automated localization and segmentation of rectal cancer on multiparametric MR. *Sci. Rep.*, 7, 5301, 2017.

148. Zhen, X., Chen, J., Zhong, Z., Hrycushko, B., Zhou, L., Jiang, S. *et al.*, Deep convolutional neural network with transfer learning for rectum toxicity prediction in cervical cancer radiotherapy: A feasibility study. *Phys. Med. Biol.*, 62, 8246–63, 2017.

149. Gernaat, S.A.M., van Velzen, S.G.M., Koh, V., Emaus, M.J., Išgum, I., Lessmann, N. *et al.*, Automatic quantification of calcifications in the coronary arteries and thoracic aorta on radiotherapy planning CT scans of Western and Asian breast cancer patients. *Radiother. Oncol.*, 127, 487–92, 2018.

150. Boldrini, L., Cusumano, D., Cellini, F., Azario, L., Mattiucci, G.C., Valentini, V., Online adaptive magnetic resonance guided radiotherapy for pancreatic cancer: State of the art, pearls and pitfalls. *Radiat. Oncol.*, 14, 71, 2019, doi: 10.1186/s13014-019-1275-3.

151. Su, M., Miften, M., Whiddon, C., Sun, X., Light, K., Marks, L., An artificial neural network for predicting the incidence of radiation pneumonitis. *Med. Phys.*, 32, 318–325, 2005.

152. Cha, K.H., Hadjiiski, L., Chan, H.P., Weizer, A.Z., Alva, A., Cohan, R.H., Caoili, E.M., Paramagul, C., Samala, R.K., Bladder cancer treatment response assessment in CT using radiomics with deep-learning. *Sci. Rep.*, 7, 1–2, 2017.

153. Chen, B., Zhang, R., Gan, Y. *et al.*, Development and clinical application of radiomics in lung cancer. *Radiat. Oncol.*, 12, 154, 2017.

154. Arrieta, O., Villarreal-Garza, C., Zamora, J. *et al.*, Long-term survival in patients with non-small cell lung cancer and synchronous brain metastasis treated with whole-brain radiotherapy and thoracic chemoradiation. *Radiat. Oncol.*, 6, 166, 2011.

155. Ravi, D., Wong, C., Deligianni, F. *et al.*, Deep learning for health informatics. *IEEE J. Biomed. Health Inform.*, 21, 4–21, 2017.

156. Lambin, P., Rios-Velazquez, E., Leijenaar, R. *et al.*, Radiomics: Extracting more information from medical images using advanced feature analysis. *Eur. J. Cancer*, 48, 441–6, 2012.

157. Dekker, A., Vinod, S., Holloway, L., Oberije, C. *et al.*, Rapid learning in practice: A lung cancer survival decision support system in routine patient care data. *Radiother. Oncol.*, 113, 47–53, 2014.

158. Coy, H., Hsieh, K., Wu, W., Nagarajan, M.B., Young, J.R., Douek, M.L. *et al.*, Deep learning and radiomics: The utility of Google TensorFlowTM Inception in classifying clear cell renal cell carcinoma and oncocytoma on multiphasic CT. *Abdom. Radiol.*, 44, 2009–20, 2019.

159. Parekh, V.S. and Jacobs, M.A., Deep learning and radiomics in precision medicine. *Expert Rev. Precis. Med. Drug Dev.*, 4, 2, 59–72, 2019 Mar 4.

160. Hosny, A., Aerts, H.J., Mak, R.H., Handcrafted versus deep learning radiomics for prediction of cancer therapy response. *Lancet Digit. Health*, 1, 3, e106–7, 2019 Jul 1.

161. Wang, S., Zheng, D., Zhang, C., Ma, R., Bennion, N.R., Lei, Y., Zhu, X., Enke, C.A., Zhou, S., Automatic planning on hippocampal avoidance whole-brain radiotherapy. *Med. Dosim.*, 42, 1, 63–8, 2017 Mar 1.

162. Nawa, K., Haga, A., Nomoto, A., Sarmiento, R.A., Shiraishi, K., Yamashita, H., Nakagawa, K., Evaluation of a commercial automatic treatment planning system for prostate cancers. *Med. Dosim.*, 42, 3, 203–9, 2017 Sep 1.

163. Schubert, C., Waletzko, O., Weiss, C., Voelzke, D., Toperim, S., Roeser, A., Puccini, S., Piroth, M., Mehrens, C., Kueter, J.D., Hierholz, K., Intercenter validation of a knowledge based model for automated planning of volumetric modulated arc therapy for prostate cancer. The experience of the German RapidPlan Consortium. *PLoS One*, 12, 5, e0178034, 2017 May 22.

164. Mitchell, R.A., Wai, P., Colgan, R., Kirby, A.M., Donovan, E.M., Improving the efficiency of breast radiotherapy treatment planning using a semi-automated approach. *J. Appl. Clin. Med. Phys.*, 18, 18–24, 2017.

165. Yan, D., Vicini, F., Wong, J., Martinez, A., Adaptive radiation therapy. *Phys. Med. Biol.*, 42, 123–132, 1997.

166. McPartlin, A.J., Li, X.A., Kershaw, L.E., Heide, U., Kerkmeijer, L., Lawton, C., Mahmood, U., Pos, F., van As, N., van Herk, M., Vesprini, D., van der Voort van Zyp, J., Tree, A., Choudhury, A., MRI guided prostate adaptive radiotherapy – A systematic review. *Radiother. Oncol.*, 119, 371–380, 2016.

167. Colvill, E., Booth, J., Nill, S., Fast, M., Bedford, J., Oelfke, U., Nakamura, M., Poulsen, P., Worm, E., Hansen, R., Ravkilde, T., Rydhög, J.S., Pommer, T., Munck af Rosenschold, P., Lang, S., Guckenberger, M., Groh, C., Herrmann, C., Verellen, D., Poels, K., Wang, L., Hadsell, M., Sothmann, T., Blanck, O., Keall, P., A dosimetric comparison of real-time adaptive and non-adaptive radiotherapy: A multi-institutional study encompassing robotic, gimbaled, multileaf collimator and couch tracking. *Radiother. Oncol.*, 119, 159–165, 2016.

168. Lim-Reinders, S., Keller, B.M., Al-Ward, S., Sahgal, A., Kim, A., Online Adaptive Radiation Therapy. *Int. J. Radiat. Oncol.*, 99, 994–1003, 2017.

169. Meyer, P., Noblet, V., Mazzara, C., Lallement, A., Survey on deep learning for radiotherapy. *Comput. Biol. Med.*, 98, 126–46, 2018 Jul 1.

170. Boutilier, J.J., Craig, T., Sharpe, M.B., Chan, T.C., Sample size requirements for knowledge-based treatment planning. *Med. Phys.*, 43, 1212–21, 2016.

171. Schreibmann, E. and Fox, T., Prior-knowledge treatment planning for volumetric arc therapy using feature-based database mining. *J. Appl. Clin. Med. Phys.*, 15, 4596, 2014. 39. Chanyavanich, V., Das, S.K., Lee, W.R., Lo, J.Y., Knowledge-based IMRT treatment planning for prostate cancer. *Med. Phys.*, 38, 2515–22, 2011.

172. D., Lo, J., Lee, W.R., Wu, Q.J., Yin, F.F., Das, S.K., A knowledge-based approach to improving and homogenizing intensity modulated radiation therapy planning quality among treatment centers: An example application to prostate cancer planning. *Int. J. Radiat. Oncol. Biol. Phys.*, 87, 176–81, 2013.

173. Tol, J.P., Delaney, A.R., Dahele, M., Slotman, B.J., Verbakel, W.F., Evaluation of a knowledge-based planning solution for head and neck cancer. *Int. J. Radiat. Oncol. Biol. Phys.*, 91, 612–20, 2015.

174. Chang, A.T.Y., Hung, A.W.M., Cheung, F.W.K., Lee, M.C.H., Chan, O.S.H., Philips, H. *et al.*, Comparison of planning quality and efficiency between conventional and knowledge-based algorithms in nasopharyngeal cancer patients using intensity modulated radiation therapy. *Int. J. Radiat. Oncol. Biol. Phys.*, 95, 981–90, 2016.

175. Yang, Y. and Xing, L., Clinical knowledge-based inverse treatment planning. *Phys. Med. Biol.*, 49, 5101–17, 2004.

176. Lin, T., Li, R., Tang, X., Dy, J.G., Jiang, S.B., Markerless gating for lung cancer radiotherapy based on machine learning techniques. *Phys. Med. Biol.*, 54, 1555–63, 2009.

177. Cabrera, G.G., Ehrgott, M., Mason, A.J., Raith, A., A matheuristic approach to solve the multiobjective beam angle optimization problem in intensity-modulated radiation therapy. *International transactions in operational research*, 25, 243–268, 2018.

178. Breedveld, S., Storchi, P.R., Voet, P.W., Heijmen, B.J., iCycle: Integrated, multicriterial beam angle, and profile optimization for generation of coplanar and noncoplanar IMRT plans. *Med. Phys.*, 39, 951–963, 2012.

179. Taasti, V.T., Hong, L., Shim, J.S.A., Deasy, J.O., Zarepisheh, M., Automating proton treatment planning with beam angle selection using Bayesian optimization. *Med. Phys.*, 47, 3286–3296, 2020.

180. Chen, X., Men, K., Li, Y., Yi, J., Dai, J., A feasibility study on an automated method to generate patient-specific dose distributions for radiotherapy using deep learning. *Med. Phys.*, 46, 56–64, 2019.

181. Adil, K., Jiang, F., Liu, S.H., Grigorev, A., Gupta, B.B., Rho, S., Training an agent for FPS doom game using visual reinforcement learning and VizDoom. *Int. J. Adv. Comput. Sci. Appl.*, 8, 32–41, 2017.

182. Summers, R.M., Are we at a crossroads or a plateau? Radiomics and machine learning in abdominal oncology imaging. *Abdom. Radiol.*, 44, 6, 1–5, 2018.

11

Deep Learning Framework for Cancer

Pratishtha

School of Pharmacy, Department of Pharmaceutical Sciences, Lingaya's Vidyapeeth, Nachauli, Faridabad, Haryana, India

Abstract

Deep learning is a part of machine-learning. It is based on artificial neural network, in research industry, it provides better treatment results by strategic planning of diagnosis, follow-ups, and treatment module, and now it put down roots in pharmaceutical industries. It helps in diagnosis by digital imaging, drug design, drug response prediction, digital pathology, clinical response prediction, etc. This chapter is aimed to give an insight of deep learning techniques used for cancer detection, diagnosis and treatment. DL data sets collection and literature review were done by authenticated and verified data from different research articles available on trusted websites like Elsevier, PubMed, Springer, Science Direct, Google Scholar, etc. Implementation of deep learning methods in diagnostic, dose predicting and treatment parameters for cancer patients has shown positive and acknowledgeable results. It is economical and less time-consuming process, which enhances the survival chances of cancer patients by better prediction. It also has potential to enhance the diagnostic capability of already existing computer-aided diagnosis system. It is concluded that deep learning methods ensure positive and promising outcomes. Although there are certain factors which limit its implementation in research, advancement in technologies and continuous strive to serve humanity by providing better healthcare services can open the gateways.

Keywords: Deep learning, machine learning, cancer, artificial neural network, convolutional neural network, cancer detection, cancer diagnosis, dose prediction

Email: pratishtha1811@gmail.com

Rishabha Malviya, Gheorghita Ghinea, Rajesh Kumar Dhanaraj, Balamurugan Balusamy
and Sonali Sundram (eds.) Deep Learning for Targeted Treatments: Transformation in Healthcare,
(333–368) © 2022 Scrivener Publishing LLC

11.1   Introduction

Over the past several years, artificial intelligence (AI) had spread in multiple fields along with pharmaceutical industries. Artificial intelligence indulge in accommodating data to serve various purposes, like speech recognition, data interpretation, text recognition, speech to text conversion, image recognition, translating languages, route navigation, personal digital assistant (such as Siri, Google), etc. Advanced computer processing has the ability to solve the non-linear complex problem. From past few years, an approach termed deep learning has gained recognition [1]. Deep learning (DL) is a part of AI. Deep learning has been developed from artificial neural networks (ANN). These standard artificial neural networks involve three layers, which are divided into three separate parts, namely input, hidden, and output layers. All layers possess different functions but are interconnected, and every connection has a weight, whereas they may vary for connecting input to output while training. These layers help in interpreting the data that has been inputted and further conclude the data. It is a widely used method, which suffered from overfitting of data, and with external dataset it has a poor ability to generalize [2], although it is difficult to overtrain the recent versions of artificial neural network, such as Bayesian regularized ANNs. DL or deep neural networks are somewhat similar to the artificial neural networks. DL copies or mimics the brain's action or function. DL also transfers input data to the output layer from input layer to assess as well as to analyze the data, hence, producing the output.

DL represents the forthcoming era of pharmaceutical research that concentrates on extraction of the diverse data that employs sophisticated or modern algorithms like DL for accumulation. Some well-known easily available software like R provides DL tools. Other than that, there are softwares like TensorFlow and Deeplearning4j, whereas, Facebook made their DL software named "Torch," an open source [3, 4] and later Microsoft introduced their DL software CNTK [5].

Cancer is considered the most challenging disease or disorder along with other life-threatening diseases. Major cause of cancer is the rapid increase in cell division, which destroys the normal human cells. This uncontrolled cell division is generally termed as proliferation. These cells form a cluster of multiple cells, which is called as tumor. Cancer can either be malignant also known as invasive or it can be noninvasive. Cancer can be classified depending on the organ where tumor cells originate and grow, for example, pancreatic cancer, breast cancer, lung cancer, blood cancer, etc.

In this chapter, the involvement of DL in different types of cancer will be discussed. We will discuss the advancement of DL in the cancer field, how it can be helpful in treatment, diagnosis and prognosis of cancer. This chapter may also cover the future roles of deep learning in various aspects.

11.2   Brief History of Deep Learning

Deep learning has evolved with time. To acquire the knowledge of earlier stages of artificial intelligence, it is discussed in brief below. See Figure 11.1 for summarized history of deep learning.

> ➢ In 1943, a neural network's first-ever mathematical model was introduced by Walter Pitts and Warren McCulloch. This model was a combination of algorithm and mathematics, which was created to mimic the thought process of humans [6].
> ➢ During the year 1957, a psychologist named Frank Rosenblatt submitted a paper entitled "The Perceptron: A Perceiving and Recognizing Automaton," which was later recognized as Deep Neural Network's foundation.
> ➢ In 1960s, at earlier stage of deep learning, various biological processes of body inspired the ANN. At that time, it was discovered that the different cortex cell can be activated when cats visualized different objects [7].
> ➢ In between 1979 and 1980, artificial neural network (ANN) was able to recognize the visual patterns [8].

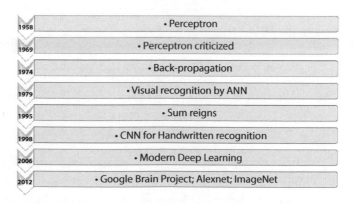

Figure 11.1 Brief history of deep learning.

- ➢ In 1997, Jürgen Schmidhuber and Sepp Hochreiter introduced Long-Short Term Memory (LSTM), a recurrent framework of neural networks.
- ➢ In 1998, Yann LeCun introduced an advanced deep learning approach in his paper titled "Gradient based Learning Applied in Document Recognition".
- ➢ Later from year 2006 onward, new era of advanced or modern deep learning took place which included ImageNet, AlexNet, Face recognition, Google, E-mail, Netflix, etc.

11.3   Types of Deep Learning Methods

Deep learning evolved with time. It was modified as per the requirement to serve different purposes. There are different types of ANNs available that personate or act as the actual neurons and neural networks present in human body. These neural networks were developed to attain qualitative, as well as quantitative data, which may further help in various industries along with the pharmaceutical industry. These neural networks are also termed as deep neural networks (DNNs). Neural networks have three basic layers which are as follows:

1. Input layer
2. Hidden layer or layers
3. Output layer

These layers mimic the function of the interconnected layer(s) of neurons, which illustrate the working of deep learning. Deep learning instructs artificial intelligence to predict the output data with the help of certain input data. The primary layer of the neural network is termed as Input layer in which the data are inserted. Input is further allowed to flow from the input layer to the output layer by passing through the hidden layers. Hidden layers can be numerous. The process in which the flow of input from the input layer to the output layer to form output is known as forward propagation. Whereas the phenomenon of backward propagation is somewhat opposite to the forward propagation, where when output is generated, it is then sent back to the input layer from the output layer passing through the hidden layers. Back propagation takes place only when the generation of output in the output layer differs from the predicted output information. Using this difference loss can be calculated. Thus, the same information is sent to the input layer to adjust the inputs and eventually train the networks.

DNN architectures were divided into different types based on their respective nature or the type of work they perform [9].

These DNN architectures are:

a) Deep autoencoder networks (DAENs)
b) Deep convolutional neural networks (DCNNs)
c) Deep recurrent neural networks (DRNNs)

These networks are further more elaborated and explained in seven models or networks. These models are capable to explain the working of the deep learning in solving the large problems in seconds or minutes.

There are seven different types of deep learning:

i.   Feed-forward neural network
     It is the initial and basic networks among all. Within this neural network, the flow can be controlled from input layer toward the output layer. This may contain probably one layer or only one hidden layer.

ii. Radial basis function neural network
     It includes more than one hidden layer, possibly two hidden layers. In such neural networks, the relative distance is calculated from any point to the center. This is further passed to the next layer. Power restoration systems use these radial basis function neural networks to avoid the blackout. This type of neural network helps in restoration of power in the shortest span of time.

iii. Multilayer Perceptron
     They have more than three layers. Nonlinear data can be classified using these types of neural networks. In this type of neural networks, all the nodes are connected to the network. Such neural networks are widely used for speech recognition. They are also utilized in some of the machine learning technologies.

iv. Convolution Neural Network (CNN)
     They are the advanced version or the variation of the multi-layer perceptron neural network. The presence of more than one convolutional layer can be observed in convolution neural networks (CNN). CNN can be very deep with only fewer parameters due to the presence of

convolutional layers. Image recognition is the spatiality of this type of neural networks, whereas different patterns of images can also be identified with the help of CNN.

v.   Recurrent Neural Network

Recurrent neural networks (RNNs) are those where previously developed output of a particular neuron can be used as an input of the same node. This type of technique helps the neural networks in the prediction of the output(s). Therefore, RNN are capable to maintain small state memory. This type of neural networks can be used to develop the chat-box. RNN may also be used in technologies, which may convert written or typed text into speech.

vi.   Modular Neural Network

Like other neural networks explained above, molecular neural network does not contain any single type of neural network. They are the combination of various smaller neural networks. Plenty neural networks that are termed as subnetworks come together to form a complex or a big neural network. These subnetworks work independently. They achieve a particular or common target by working altogether. Following this kind of technique, these networks may break the larger problems into smaller problems, thus simplifying the problem solving mechanism.

vii.   Sequence to Sequence Model

Sequence to sequence models are usually made up of the combinations of recurrent neural networks (RNN). Such models consist of an encoder. They work on the phenomenon of decoding, as well as on encoding. The encoder present within the neural network may help in encoding the input, whereas the availability of the decoder helps in decoding the output of this neural network. Generally, sequence to sequence neural network models are helpful in processing the text where the length of the output text obtained is observed to be different from the length of the text inputted [10].

Deep Learning Algorithms:

Mathematical representation of deep learning networks is called deep learning algorithm.

a.   Back propagation

    b. Stochastic gradient descent
    c. Learning rate
    d. Batch normalization
    e. Drop out
    f. Bag of words
    g. Long short-term memory

11.4 Applications of Deep Learning

Deep learning works in wide range. In our daily life from asking Google, a question to using social media app, we all are using artificial intelligence.

Deep learning has been applied in bioinformatics. Increased number of publications indicates the requirement and effectiveness of deep learning methods in bioinformatics. Deep learning is being used to simplify various complicated functions. We will discuss about few of the applications of deep learning, see Figure 11.2.

11.4.1 Toxicity Detection for Different Chemical Structures

Among highly reliable applications of deep learning, determination or detection of the toxicity of the naturally available drugs along with the chemically structured drugs were considered most challenging, as well as reliable in research field [11]. The process of drug toxicity detection in time consuming, thus in comparison to the other methods where many scientists took decades for drug toxicity detection, deep learning methods have lessen the time consumption and may determine the specific drug's

Figure 11.2 Applications of deep learning.

toxicity within hour or in days, depending on the intricacy of the molecule [7]. To serve this purpose, DeepTox pipeline was developed with the help of few scientists. Initially, DeepTox helps in normalizing the chemical representation of different compounds. They compute various chemical descriptors, which are useful in machine learning methods as they act as input in such methods. After inputting the data and computation of chemical descriptors, the DeepTox further helps in training the models, their evaluation and then to ensemble they it combines the best among them all. Finally, DeepTox predicts new compound's toxicity [11].

11.4.2   Mitosis Detection

Mitosis is a natural process of cell division where a single divides into two equal and identical daughter cells. These daughter cells carry identical nuclei along with identical genetic information [12]. In the field of research, detection of mitosis is critical has become necessity as it is useful in prognosis or detection of cancer in different phases. Different researchers had invested their time in developing and executing the software in detection of mitosis by making use of deep learning, which also helps in estimating the rate of proliferation. Saha M *et al.* have conducted a research study to suggest a DL model for mitosis signature detection from breast histology WSI image. With the help of deep learning architecture, they designed a DL model with some handcrafted features. The handcrafted features that were used in the study were issued from previous challenges MITOSIS @ ICPR 2012, AMIDA-13 and project (MICO ANR TecSan) expertise.

As explained earlier, these deep learning architectures contains multiple layers. These layers includes, five convolutional layers, four rectified linear units (ReLU), four max-pooling layers and among these layers, whereas two layers are fully connected. Activation function is performed by rectified linear units, therefore, they are present after each convolutional layer and act as an activator. To avoid overfitting, they included the dropout layers after fully connected layers. Handcrafted features of this model mostly consist of intensity, morphological and textural features. They observed an improved precision up to 92%, recall 88% and f-force approximately 90% in the architectural model they proposed.

In breast cancer, the model they proposed provided efficient and effective second opinion to the pathologists in grading of breast cancer. Eventually, the proposed model helped researchers to better understand stages of breast cancer and genesis [13]. In conclusion to the researches, approximately 6000 factors are available in deep learning models which may assist in prediction of chances of patient's survival. As these neural networks effectively contributes in detection, as well as classification of mitosis in patients, thus, proved their efficiency and effectiveness. Also, they participate in investigation of life cycle of cells.

11.4.3   Radiology or Medical Imaging

Radiology is a branch of medicinal science, which utilizes technological imaging for diagnosis and treatment of disease or disorder. The physicians or doctors who have specialization in interpretation of the images for diagnostic purpose are known as diagnostic radiologist.

Hypothetically, radiology is divided into two types, one is diagnostic, whereas other type is interventional radiology. Diagnostic radiology assists professionals, physicians, radiologists, and health providers to look inside the patient's body to identify and diagnose the symptoms of disease. Most commonly used diagnostic radiologies are mammography, positron emission tomography (PET), compute tomography (CT) commonly known as CT scan, PET-CT scan, fluoroscopy, which includes upper gastrointestine and barium enema, Plain or chest x-rays, ultrasound, magnetic resonance angiography (MRA), magnetic resonance imaging (MRI), etc. On the other hand, interventional radiology also involve imaging like CT scan, MRI, fluoroscopy, ultrasound, etc, to assist the radiologists as well as the physicians while operating. It guides them while inserting instruments and tools, such as catheter, camera (also called scope), wires, and other tools for incisions. Some of the interventional radiology are angiography, angioplasty, embolization for bleeding control, chemoembolization, tumor embolization for cancer treatment, etc. [14].

Deep learning in radiology, in breast imaging, cardiothoracic imaging, and other radiological applications of deep learning are expanding with time and demand. Utilization of deep learning ImageNet training data was found to be effective in categorizing chest radiographs, like cardiomegaly, pleural effusion, mediastinal enlargement, etc. [15].

A survey was conducted by Mazurowski et al. on role of DL in radiology focusing on magnetic resonance imaging. The simple and mostly used image segmentation method wax individual voxel classification based on the small patches of images (they include both two dimensional as well as three dimensional image patches) collected from the classified voxel. This method was used in different segmentation issues, such as in the brain tumor segmentation in patients with multiple sclerosis, in segmentation of rectal cancer and in the brain anatomy segmentation [16].

In breast cancer imaging, deep learning was found to be highly accurate diagnostically, it identifies breast cancer with the help of ultrasound, mammograms and MRI. However, with MRI, accuracy was less due to the small datasets and two-dimensional images. However, use of large datasets and multiparametric MRI might increase the diagnostic accuracy [17].

11.4.4   Hallucination

Hallucinations is a symptom of a disease called schizophrenia which is chronic and complex metal health disorder [18]. Schizophrenia is an abnormality in the brain denoted by some behavioral systems for example hallucination, delusions, disturbed perception, and jumbled or disorganized speech [19]. To identify or diagnose brain-related disorders, electroencephalograms (EEG) is used. Shu Lih oh *et al.* conducted a study and collected EEC signals from schizophrenia patients and to analyze the signals they developed an 11-layered convolutional neural network. They opted deep learning algorithm because it is capable to extract the significant features automatically and eventually can classify them. The model they proposed was able to classify accurately non-subject based testing up to 98.07%, whereas it is capable to classify accurately up to 81.26% for subject-based testing [20].

11.4.5   Next-Generation Sequencing (NGS)

Next-generation sequencing (NGS) is a term that represents a DNA sequencing technology. NGS helps scientists in genomic research. With the help of NGS scientists were able to sequence a human genome within a day [21, 22]. Various scientists worked on deep learning model for prediction of NGS. Zhang *et al.* [23] opted the deep learning model, which included bidirectional recurrent neural network, which is capable to take inputs form both DNA nucleotide identities and the probability of unpaired nucleotide. Deep learning models were applied in three different panels of NGS, such as for single nucleotide polymorphism (SNP) of human a 39,144-plex panel, for human long noncoding RNA (lncRNA) a 2000-plex panel, and for storing DNA information a 7373-plex panel targeting non-human sequence. In cross-validation, sequencing depth can be predicted within a factor of 3 with 93% of accuracy for the single nucleotide polymorphism and in nonhuman panel attained accuracy of 99%. When trained on the SNP panel the deep learning model predicted the lncRNA panel with approximately 89% accuracy and also predicted the measured single-plex kinetic rate constants of strand displacement, as well as of DNA hybridization [24].

Initially and successfully applied convolutional neural models were DeepBind [25] and DeepSEA [26] for modeling the specific binding of protein sequence from large-scale chromatin-profile data. With the help of this given technique, it can automatically learn informative sequence features and may achieve superior performance to conventional methods. Also, DanQ [27], a hybrid model, was designed for the task that combines a CNN with long short-term memory (LTSM). Recently, somewhat similar to DeepCpG approach, a joint neural network module named DeepHistone [28] was proposed.

11.4.6 Drug Discovery

Discovering a new drug or new pharmacological effect of preexisting drug is long process and deep learning methods are useful for it. Different deep learning architectures, such as deep autoencoder network, deep feed-forward network, deep restricted Boltzmann machine, recursive neural network, deep convolutional network, deep cascaded network, etc. were used for virtual screening of drug, protein structure and functions, monitoring absorption, distribution, metabolism, and excretion (ADME) properties of drug, proteome mining, qualitative structure activity relationship (QSAR), and other applications for drug discovery [29].

11.4.7 Sequence or Video Generation

Creation of new video after observing various video games, learning their mechanism, etc. Deep learning plays an important role in preparation of video generation.

11.4.8 Other Applications

There are plenty other DL applications like recognition of speech, text recognition, text extraction, earthquake prediction, prediction of frauds or threats, market prediction, digital advertising, email, etc. [30, 31].

11.5 Cancer

Cancer is considered most challenging disease or disorder along with other life-threatening diseases. Major cause of cancer is the rapid increase in cell division, which destroys the normal human cells. This uncontrolled cell division is generally termed as proliferation. These cells form a cluster of multiple cells, which is called as tumor. Cancer can either be malignant also known as invasive or it can be noninvasive. Cancer can be classified depending on the organ where tumor cells originate and grow for example pancreatic, breast, lung, blood cancers, etc.

11.5.1   Factors

Cancer can be caused due to various factors, which are responsible for proliferation or migration of cancer causing cells. People these days are leading stressful lifestyles, which promotes cancer. Cancer can be hereditary or may transfer genetically from parents to child. Apart from that some chemical substances, imbalanced dietary habits may also cause cancer. There are few other factor discussed briefly below. See Table 11.1.

Table 11.1 Cancer-causing factors.

S. no.	Cancer-causing factors	Reason
1.	Age	Age above 65 is more susceptible to cancer than 45 and above.
2.	Virus	They promote the malignancy of carcinogenic cells and increase the chances of malignant cancer.
3.	Chemical substances	Chemical substances, such as tobacco, benzene, nickel, etc. are carcinogenic.
4.	Estrogen	May cause breast cancer.
5.	Heredity	Family history of cancer.
6.	Stress	Stress affects immune systems, thymus gland, and hormones and eventually causes cancer.
7.	Ionizing radiation	Radiations, such as x-rays, UV-rays, etc. damages cells, ruptures DNA and may cause cancer.
8.	Diet	Alcohol, meat, fat, nitrates, energy balance, protein, etc.

11.5.1.1   Heredity

When children inherit any disease or disorder from their parents then that said disease is termed as hereditary. Family history of a particular disease is also considered because there are chances for children to have a disease or disorder form their grand or grand grandparents. When diseased or carcinogenic genes undergoes mutations and passes to the children while in mother's womb, then it increases the risk for children to have cancer. Also, it is dangerous to treat cancer at that early stage and young age.

11.5.1.2   Ionizing Radiation

Ionizing radiations are harmful and as per the studies, these radiations are responsible to cause cancer. These radiations can be ultraviolet rays, uranium, X-rays, etc. Exposure to such radiations may lead to different type of cancer for example, in Japan, the few of the bomb survivors in Hiroshima and Nagasaki were diagnosed with leukemia, underground miners were susceptible to lung cancer, skin cancer can be caused due to exposure of radiations like radiologists and luminous dial painters are usually exposed to radium, which may cause bone cancer.

11.5.1.3   Chemical Substances

Chemical substances can be carcinogenic, which means they may cause cancer and may promote proliferation of carcinogenic or cancer causing cells. These carcinogens can be tobacco (generally found in cigarette), nickel, benzene, benzidine, asbestos, cadmium, ethyl acrylate, ethylene oxide, acrylonitrile, vinyl chloride, mustard gas, N-nitrosamines, lead and lead containing compounds, etc.

11.5.1.4   Dietary Factors

Dietary habits have a major effect on healthy lifestyle of a person. Some of these dietary habits may cause cancer.

- **Meat:** Generally, meat intake or raw (or partially cooked) meat intake can cause cancer. Digestive tract cancer can be associated with meat intake. Colon cancer can be caused due to red and white meat intake, whereas fish sauce consumption in excessive amount may cause gastric cancer.

- **Energy balance:** Energy balance is a relationship maintained between body mass index (BMI), body weight and relative body weight. It has been observed that some specific cancers are associated with it and few organs for example gall bladder cancer, breast cancer, endometrium, kidney etc. High intake of energy with no physical activity and large body mass may cause colon cancer.
- **Fat:** Saturated fats are generally considered unhealthy. Therefore, it may cause prostate cancer if a person consumes high amount of saturated fat.
- **Protein:** As discussed earlier, meat intake can be cancerous and excessive meat consumption may cause colon and advanced stage of prostate cancers.
- **Alcohol:** As we all know excessive consumption of alcohol mostly affects the liver but it may be carcinogenic for the mouth, as well as for pharynx. The tissues that get directly exposed to the alcohol during consumption acts synergistically in the presence of tobacco. The risk of colorectal cancer increases with beer consumption.
- **Nitrates:** Nitrates can be carcinogenic. They are usually present in daily diet, such as inn drinking water, various food items and other dietary sources like vegetables. Processing of salt involves sodium nitrate and potassium nitrate. Pickle processing and food curing also includes sodium and potassium nitrates. Tobacco contains nitrosamines, which may get converted into nitrates and may leads to cancer.

11.5.1.5   Estrogen

Estrogens are given to prevent osteoporosis and for the relief of postmenopausal symptoms. Estrogens may produce breast cancer and endometrial cancer.

11.5.1.6   Viruses

Viruses affects the immune systems of the human and in some cases may act as cofactors, which promotes some of the malignant diseases, including cancer. Hepatitis B virus acts as a co-factor in primary liver cancer.

11.5.1.7   Stress

Stress is the major cause of plenty health issues. It damages the cells and eventually may damage thymus gland. Stress is responsible for imbalanced hormonal behavior. This promotes malignancy and promote malignant cancer.

11.5.1.8   Age

People above 65 years are more susceptible to develop cancer in comparison to others. Likelihood of colorectal cancer development increases in older age and it is higher in people of 65 years and older if compared with the people of age between 40 and 64 years.

11.5.2   Signs and Symptoms of Cancer

Every disease or disorder is diagnosed based on some signs, also known as symptoms of that specific disease and these symptoms signify the presence of that disease. In case of cancer, it is devious to predict their symptoms. Its symptoms depend on the cancer type, its location, and the nature of the carcinogenic cells, if they are migrant or not. For example, a lump could be found in the breast in case of breast cancer, whereas, discharge from nipple may be observed in metastatic breast cancer. In some cases, patients claims to have pain in bones, fatigue (associated with lungs), episodes of seizures, etc. There is a possibility for few patients to not to express any kind of signs or symptoms before it reaches the advanced stage of cancer.

Seven signs or symptoms that indicate the presence of cancer and which suggest to seek medical attention.

- Bowel changes or abnormal habits of bladder,
- Soreness of throat that may not heal,
- Unexpected and unwanted discharge or bleeding,
- Mass development in breast, testicles, or elsewhere which may thickens and forms cluster of cells,
- Problem in engulfing,
- Sometimes visible shape or size change and color change of mole is observed,
- Hoarseness of throat and cough are also considered as the symptoms of cancer.

Other signs or symptoms:

- Unexpected and sudden loss of weight with loss of appetite
- Body ache
- Persistent fatigue, nausea, and vomiting
- Persistent fever or frequent change in body temperature
- Delay recovery of infection or recurring infections which does not get treated with routine treatment.

11.5.3   Types of Cancer Treatment Available

There are several types of cancer treatments but the types of treatment given to the patient depends on the severity of the cancer. The location or the site of cancer also plays a major role in treatment selection. Sometimes only one treatment is given to some patients with initial stage of cancer. But mostly combination of treatments are provided to cancer patients that may include surgery along with radiation therapy and chemotherapy.

11.5.3.1   Surgery

Surgery is a type of cancer treatment where the surgeon removes the cancerous cells from the part of the body.

11.5.3.2   Radiation Therapy

Radiations are given to cancer patients to destroy carcinogenic cells or to diminish tumors.

11.5.3.3   Chemotherapy

Chemotherapy is a type of cancer treatment that uses drugs or pharmacologically active agents to kill cancer cells.

11.5.3.4   Immunotherapy

This therapy boost the immune system of human so the patient's immune system become strong enough to overcome the cancer cells and cause apoptosis of cancer cells.

11.5.3.5   Targeted Therapy

They use targeted drug delivery via parenteral routes at the site of action or cancer. It targets the cancer causing cells, reduces the size of tumor or cancerous cells, and stops them from growing and spreading or migrating into nearest organs and blood.

11.5.3.6   Hormone Therapy

Hormone therapy slows down the growing or proliferating breast and prostate cancers and for this purpose it utilizes hormones.

11.5.3.7   Stem Cell Transplant

There are chances for cancer patients to damage their blood forming cells due to high dose of chemotherapy or radiation therapy. Transplanting stem cell is an advanced technique that helps in restoring blood-forming stem cell in such patients.

11.5.3.8   Precision Medicine

Based on genetic understanding of cancer patient selection of treatment becomes easier for physicians using Precision medicine.

11.5.4   Types of Cancer

11.5.4.1   Carcinoma

Cancer cell when begins to proliferate around internal organs like ovary, skin and lungs causing ovarian cancer, skin cancer and lung cancer respectively. Whereas other type of carcinomas are Papillomas, Melanomas, Adenomas, squamous carcinomas, epithelial carcinomas and basal cell carcinomas.

11.5.4.2   Sarcoma

Sarcomas originate in connective tissues, bone, fat, muscles, cartilages, blood vessels and therefore, causes soft tissue cancer, osteosarcoma, bone cancer, rhabdosarcoma, synovial sarcoma, fibrosarcoma, liposarcoma and angiosarcoma.

11.5.4.3   Leukemia

When blood-forming tissues like bone marrow get affected by carcinogenic agents, they enhances the proliferation of these abnormal blood cells which enters the blood stream and this is termed as "leukemia."

11.5.4.4   Lymphoma and Myeloma

Lymphoma or T-cell lymphomas take place when abnormal cell proliferation takes place in the immune system.

11.5.4.5   Central Nervous System (CNS) Cancers

Brain and spinal cord tumors" Cancer cells when proliferate in the brain tissues and in spinal cord are called CNS cancers.

11.5.5   The Development of Cancer (Pathogenesis) Cancer

The carcinogenic agent does not immediately produce tumor, they have other applications too. Carcinogens are potent to make changes after the initiation step gets induced. Some carcinogenic agents or substances promote the activity of tumor. 'Initiation' means starting of something', as the term indicates, initiation is the first or primary step of cancer development and it is rapid. Al though there are other possibilities but generally, the initiation or the primary step takes place in the genetic material (like DNA). It is expected that carcinogens destroy the stem cell population of specific genes that are said to interact with DNA and probably lead to mutagen, which is also known as genetic makeup of the cell. A complete carcinogen is the one that acts as both promoter and initiator of cancer cell.

11.6   Role of Deep Learning in Various Types of Cancer

Deep learning has shown tremendous and promising effects in the field of cancer. In this era of advanced technology, deep learning plays a vital role in cancer prediction, monitoring, and even in cancer treatment. In this chapter, we will discuss a few of the various cancers and the role of deep learning in them.

11.6.1   Skin Cancer

The skin is outermost surface of human body that acts as a barrier against external environment. The exterior skin layer is called epidermis which consists of different types of cells namely keratinocytes, merkel, melanocytes, etc. whereas, connective tissues are present in dermis where it contains some memory cells and some mast cells. Skin also contains some nerves, sweat glands, pigment layer, sebaceous gland, etc. to serve necessary functions.

Skin cancer is a dangerous and widespread disease. The skin cancer cases are escalating in people these days. Mostly, UV exposure is the topmost reason for skin cancer. These radiations affect skin cells and cause them to proliferate in abnormal way. Skin cancer is divided into these two basic types.

a. Malignant melanoma (MM)
b. Non malignant melanoma

Skin cancer can further be divided into "basal cell carcinoma" (BCC) and "squamous cell carcinoma" (SCC). SCC and BCC generally, takes place due to direct exposure to sunlight having UV radiations. Intense or excessive exposure to sun exposes the skin to the UV radiations that comes from the sun, which leads to malignant melanoma. Among all the nonmelanoma skin cancer, approximately 80% to 85% are found to be SCC and BCC. SCC is more dangerous in comparison and is more likely to cause death. Early stage detection is necessary in skin cancer as it can be treated easily using simple method along with medications in its early stage than in advanced stage. Hypothetically, 80% of skin cancers are BCC, whereas 16% and 4% of skin cancer are SCC and melanoma, respectively.

11.6.1.1   Common Symptoms of Melanoma

Generally, people with pigmented hair other than black, light color eyes are more are at risk of skin cancer. However, generally, there are few symptoms that may be observed in patients suffering from melanoma that are enlisted below:

- Varying size of mole, change in its shape and color.
- Bleeding mole.
- Hard, swollen and itchy mole.

11.6.1.2 Types of Skin Cancer

Skin cancer can be classified into different types based on their nature.

11.6.1.2.1 Basal Cell Carcinoma

Basal cell carcinoma (BCC) are commonly occurring skin cancer that usually starts spreading from head or from neck region to trunk. BCC initiates from basal part of epidermis layer. BCC is divided into 3 basic types; nodular, superficial and morpheaform. Superficial BCC is generally observed in trunk and later as an erythematous plague. Nodular type are usually observed on head, neck and looks like pearly vessels or overlying ulcer [33].

11.6.1.2.2 Squamous Cell Carcinoma

In the US, squamous cell carcinoma (SCC) is diagnosed in approximately 250,000 patients annually and that is why it is said to be common kind of cancer after BCC. It is generally observed in people with more melanin count like in dark skin colored people and also in Asian Indians showing approximately 30% to 65% of skin cancers in both type of races mentioned earlier. It develops on the parts of head and neck that are usually exposed to the sun directly. In general, long-term results are favorable with only 4% or less SCC cases leading to metastasis or even death [33].

11.6.1.2.3 Kaposi Sarcoma

Mostly, old age people are affected by this type of cancer. A virus named KS is the cause of Kaposi sarcoma (KS). KS is associated with human herpes virus (KSHV). This type of cancer mainly affects regions around lower limbs, trunk, and upper limbs. It may also occur in oral mucosa, lymph nodes, stomach, and duodenum [34].

11.6.1.2.4 Mutations of p53 Gene in Skin Cancer

P53 maintains the integrity of genomes by obstructing DNA replication as a reaction to damage of DNA due to exposure to carcinogenic agents like UV-radiation. Exposure to UV radiation increases the level of p53 protein and eventually, affect the cell cycle by restricting the G1 phase. Therefore, UV- induced carcinogenesis may show mutations of p53. SCC development is associated with P53 gene which plays a predominant role in that [35].

11.6.1.3   Prevention

The necessity to educate the people to promote the awareness about the causes of skin cancer that can be avoided to prevent skin cancer is required. These measures help in prevention to some extents. The precautions to be taken for skin cancer prevention includes avoiding direct exposure to sun or UV radiations coming from sun by application of sunscreen lotion if skin is exposed to sunlight, avoiding exposure to sunlamps radiating UV just like in UV-chamber used for sterilization purpose. Using sun bed should be avoided. Wearing protective clothes to avoid sun exposure is an effective method for prevention of skin cancer. Sun screen lotions are found effective in preventing direct sun exposure as well as UV light. Sunscreen lotions have capable to block the formation either SCC or BCC. Primarily sunscreen needs to be applied regularly with other protective aspects suggested by the World Health Organization (WHO), the International Commission on Non-Ionizing Radiation Protection (ICNIRP) and the European Society of Skin Cancer Prevention (EUROSKIN). Secondly, other preventive measures includes malignancy detection in early phase so that the required treatment could help cure it in its early stages when development has initiated, because complete cure of skin cancer isn't available thus, treating it in later stage might complicate the situation.

11.6.1.4   Treatment

Patient's history is the initial step taken in the treatment of skin cancer as it is inclusive of previous drug history, treatment history, family medical history, skin cancer history of skin cancer, sun exposure, etc. determination of size, shape and type of lesion is second measure considered in skin cancer treatment because treatment type vary with the different type of lesions as the main aim of treatment is tumor removal, function prevention, and a good cosmetic outcome.

Treatments or therapies available for skin cancer are as follow: radiotherapy, Mohs micrographic surgery, cryosurgery, conventional surgical excision, topical chemotherapy, electro desiccation, laser surgery, immunotherapy, and other treatments or therapies are available for BCC. Initiation of Skin cancer treatment should be done soon after diagnosis at its early stage for better treatment effects. Radiotherapy is considered effective in early stage treatment of skin cancer lesions. Skin cancer treatments also include some advanced molecular therapeutic approaches, which involve several medications such as immunomodulation with 5-flourouracil, radiation therapy, imiquimod and photodynamic therapy. It had been recognized that small molecule regulators have numerous pathways that results in causing skin cancer. Main focus in research are pathways and skin cancer treatment that can be elevated by smallest adjustment in pathways.

11.6.2   Deep Learning in Skin Cancer

DL algorithm was used in the identification or diagnosis of skin cancer at different sensitivities. It has been observed that skin cancer diagnosing using dermoscopy can be enhanced by the implementation of sonification layer on DL algorithm. Processing of dermoscopy images that were obtained from skin magnifier with polarized light (SMP) was done with the help of primary DL algorithm and was later sonified. Secondary deep learning that was different from first deep learning algorithm helped in further analyzing the audio output. The SMP metrics results includes the receiver operative area under the curve of 0.814, 91.7% sensitivity, 41.8% specificity and 57.3% positive predictive value. Whereas, the diagnostic results by advanced dermoscopy of same set of patients includes 89.5% sensitivity, 57.8% specificity, and 59.9% positive predictive value. Processing of dermoscopic images by deep learning method is followed by sonification method. These results prove the improved diagnostic ability of skin cancer by deep learning after implying the sonification methods [36].

In another study, skin lesion images were used to detect skin cancer and to serve this purpose, a pre-trained deep learning convolutional neural network with AlexNet was used. This model was developed malignant classes and to classify the images. The images or databases includes images of both melanoma and nonmelanoma and were collected from dermoscopy image HAM10000. The raw images were used as input in the said proposed deep learning model which further automatically classify these images and learn useful features from those images. Therefore, this technique helps in avoiding the complex method of extraction of lesions and segmentation of lesions. It resulted in receiver operating characteristic curve (ROC) of 0.91, 84% accuracy, 81% sensitivity, and 88% specificity. The results show the high potential of the employed deep learning model in detection of both melanoma and nonmelanoma skin cancer [37].

11.6.3   Pancreatic Cancer

As the name signifies pancreatic cancer takes place in pancreas. Pancreas is an accessary digestive gland, which is responsible to secrete pancreatic juice

[38, 39]. Along with the pancreatic juice, pancreas secrete digestive juice, enzymes (for example, trypsinogen, amylase, pancreatic lipase, nuclease, etc.) and hormones (for example, insulin from beta cells, glucagon from alpha cells and some of amylin and gastrin) [40].

11.6.3.1 Symptoms of Pancreatic Cancer

Although, the symptoms of pancreatic cancer are not predictable but in a few cases patients might suffer from some uncomfortable situations that can be considered as symptoms. Among those symptoms, most prominent ones are as follow:

- Abdominal pain
- Vomiting and nausea
- Jaundice
- Weight loss
- Change in bowel
- Indigestion

11.6.3.2 Causes or Risk Factors of Pancreatic Cancer:

- Smoking
- Age
- Family history of cancer or genetic factor
- Alcohol consumption
- Diabetes
- Obesity
- Chronic pancreatitis

11.6.3.3 Treatments of Pancreatic Cancer

- Surgery
- Endoscopic treatment
- Chemotherapy or radiation therapy
- Combination treatment (includes two or more of the treatments available for cancer)

11.6.4 Deep Learning in Pancreatic Cancer

Liu *et al.* worked on pancreatic cancer and they incorporated deep learning methodology to differentiate healthy or non-cancerous pancreatic tissues from pancreatic cancer tissues. For this diagnostic study, they collected contrast enhanced computed tomography images of 370 patients suffering from pancreatic cancer. From Taiwanese center, they collected 320 controls, labelled them manually and divided for validation, testing and training. Images were pre-processed into patches and then then convolutional neural network was trained to differentiate these patches as cancerous and noncancerous. These convolutional neural networks (CNN) then tested for other local test set including US datasets. For the comparison between cancerous and noncancerous, the pancreatic cancer image radiologist reports were retrieved, whereas for the diagnosis of pancreatic cystic neoplasm, segmentations of pancreas and neuroendocrine tumors, deep learning has been studied thoroughly. Initially, the CNN were trained after excluding the unwanted or neighboring structures and organs to yield better results. The analysis based on CNN yielded approximately 99% accurate results of multiple local test sets. CNN is capable to capture pancreatic cancer's complex images and process them. It was then observed concluded, that analysis based on CNN can identify the actual site of the tumor even in the presence of dilated pancreatic ducts or presence of other tumor resembling findings [41].

Other than that, for the diagnosis of pancreatic cancer, DL model or architecture such as EfficientNet B1 [42] which is the smaller and advanced version of EfficientNet architecture that has achieved good compromise in performance and the size of model. This model was trained with the help of fully supervised learning along with transfer learning. This deep learning model was trained for evaluation of pancreatic ductal adenocarcinoma (PDAC) in endoscopic ultrasonography-guided fine-needle aspiration cytology (EUS-FNA) whole slide images (WSIs). This study was conducted by Naito et al., in this study, they collected the data sets from Kurume University. The model was evaluated on the test sets, and a metric combination was computed. The receiver operator curve (ROC) was high in models, the area under the curve (AUC) (0.9836; CI, 0.9603–0.9977), specificity (0.9706; CI, 0.9091–1), accuracy (0.9417; CI, 0.8917–0.9750), sensitivity (0.9302; CI, 0.8602–0.9753), and f1-score (0.9581; CI, 0.915–0.9827). In true positives, cancer cells were detected with accuracy without detecting any background blood calls or contaminations. Interestingly, even after the Invasive ductal carcinoma component (IDC) inclusion, there were some nests left in the true positives that were not recognized. Moreover, small cancer nests of isolated carcinoma component (ICC) in false negatives were not detected. However, accuracy in invasive cancer cell detection was not achieved. It was difficult to detect the small cluster area of cancer cells. The cancer cell foci area was larger in true positive than in the false negative. No significant difference was found in the number of cancer call foci between the false-negative and true-positive [43].

11.6.5   Tobacco-Driven Lung Cancer

Lung cancer takes place in lungs. Lungs are responsible for gaseous exchange. They are responsible to supply oxygen to the blood. Lungs are the part of the respiratory system, which is divided into two parts, i.e., airways and lung parenchyma. The airways include bronchus, which bifurcates trachea and further divides it into bronchioles and alveoli. The gaseous exchange takes place with the help of parenchyma, which involves bronchioles, alveoli along with alveolar. Lungs have a spongy texture and pinkish grey hue [44–46]. Lung cancer is usually found to be driven by tobacco. People with smoking habits are most likely to get affected by lung cancer. Generally, it is classified into small cell lung cancer (SCLC) and nonsmall cell lung cancer (NSCLC) [47]. Although the combined therapies of chemotherapy along with radiation therapy has shown improved treatment results, but proper cure is yet to be determine. Thus, new improved techniques for diagnostic and treatment purposes are being introduced in medicinal world [48].

11.6.5.1   Symptoms of Lung Cancer

Lung cancer is one of the major cause of death in humans. Therefore, it is necessary to predict it in its early stage so as to avoid severe consequences otherwise it might lead to death. There are certain symptoms observed in patients with lung cancer which may help the physicians in diagnosis [47, 49]. Few of these symptoms or signs are listed below:

- Abnormal breathing pattern
- Cough
- Chest pain
- Dyspnea
- Hoarseness
- Hemoptysis
- Malaise
- Weight loss
- Loss of appetite
- Fatigue

11.6.5.2   Causes or Risk Factors of Lung Cancer

Lung cancer is mostly caused due to excessive cigarette (tobacco) smoking or polluted environment. But there are other carcinogenic risk factors present that may cause lung cancer [49, 50]. Those factors can be:

- Smoking
- Pollution
- Family history of cancer or genetic factor
- Age
- Pre-existing lung disease or disorder
- Radiation exposure
- Occupational exposure to toxic gases
- Poor diet

11.6.5.3   Treatments Available for Lung Cancer

There are numerous treatment options available for lung cancer which may help in either restricting the proliferation of carcinogenic cells or it may cause apoptosis of those carcinogenic cells [51]. Some of the treatment options can be as follow:

- Surgery
- Radiation therapy
- Chemotherapy
- Targeted treatment
- Combination treatment (includes two or more of the treatments available for cancer)

11.6.5.4   Deep Learning in Lung Cancer

According to various studies conducted worldwide by researchers, tobacco was found responsible for the Lung cancer development. Every year, several cases of patients are being reported to be diagnosed of lung cancer. it is a commonly occurring cancer. Around year 2008, approximately 1.61 million lung cancer cases were reported, which represented 12.7% new cases that year. Death rate is also high in lung cancer. The developing countries are majorly affected by lung cancer, which can either be due to excessive tobacco smoking habit or due to increase in air pollution. Generally, the rate of men being diagnosed with lung cancer is higher in comparison with the rate of women with lung cancer. Lung cancer is usually highly reported in Eastern Asia, Europe (included Central, Southern and Eastern Europe) and America. North America is observed to be highly affected by lung cancer whereas the lowest rate is observed in Central Africa [52].

Medical images were being used to monitor the changes in lesions throughout the treatment. But, it is challenging to evaluate those imaging data. Thus, DL networks for prediction of clinical results were evaluated by analyzing CT images of patients diagnosed with non-small cell lung cancer (NSCLC). With the help of time series scans, deep learning models were able to predict durability and cancer specific results, such as distant metastases, progression, and local-regional recurrence. Along with every additional follow-up scan in the convolutional neural networks model, enhanced model performance was observed. These models grouped or differentiated low mortality risk patients from patients with high mortality risk. Therefore, it was concluded that the deep models can combine imaging scans at different and numerous time-points to attain better results of clinical prediction. Hence, artificial intelligence-based noninvasive radiomics biomarkers can have a notable impression in the clinic given their low-cost and minimal requirements for human input [53].

11.6.6 Breast Cancer

As the name signifies, breast cancer (BC) takes place in the breast or mammary gland itself. There is a possibility for breast cancer cells to invade into other tissues or in other words, breast cancer may be malignant and may reoccur. It is possible for tumor cells to develop in different organ other than breast and then spread in breast, this type of invasion can be termed as malignant breast cancer. Breast cancer can be treated but there are chances of reoccurrence. Based on studies, it was observed that tumor cells present in breast have the tendency to spread in different parts of body, specifically those part which resides near breast, for example: it can spread in neck by invading tissues and also, cancer cells can enter blood stream through veins or arteries, which further can be responsible for blood cancer and may lead to death. Mostly, women (mostly aged 45 years or above) are susceptible to breast cancer and is a major cause of death among women as on date there is no permanent or proper cure for cancer. In year 2008, approximately 1.38 million cases were reported of nonmetastatic breast cancer whereas the reports of metastatic breast cancer were lesser in number. The patients with metastatic breast cancer have privilege because there are chances of survival with the disease for many years. Since 1990, annually approximately 1.5% of incidence rate is increasing. It do not have reliable cure. Survival chances are approx. 12 months for women with metastatic disease without any treatment [54].

11.6.6.1 Symptoms of Breast Cancer

In females, Breast cancer is most common. But, the symptoms of breast cancer are not that prominent whereas, it is important to identify any sign that indicates the presence carcinogenic cells. It may help physicians in diagnosis of breast cancer at its early stage. Few symptoms were observed by physicians, which they found common in different patients suffering from breast cancer. These symptoms are enlisted below [55]:

- Enlargement of mammary gland
- Inversion of nipple
- Lump in breast or mammary gland
- Skin reddening or rash around nipples
- Irritation on skin around breast
- Dimpling of breast skin
- Thickening or swelling of breast
- Pain in mammary gland
- Breathlessness
- Fatigue
- Neck lump
- Chest pain

11.6.6.2 Causes or Risk Factors of Breast Cancer

Breast cancer can be caused due to various reasons that may be the family history or previous breast related disease or disorders. There are other factors too which may help diagnosing the breast cancer, such as:

- Family history of cancer or genetic factor
- Age
- Pre-existing breast disease or disorder
- Radiation exposure
- Malignancy of carcinogenic cells
- Occupational exposure to toxic gases
- Poor diet

11.6.6.3   Treatments Available for Breast Cancer

There are different treatments for breast cancer, which may help in patients. Some of the treatment options can be as follow:

- Surgery
- Radiation therapy
- Chemotherapy
- Targeted treatment
- Combination treatment (includes two or more of the treatments available for cancer)

11.6.7   Deep Learning in Breast Cancer

The accuracy of breast cancer risk models can be improved via mammographic density. Use of density of breast is restricted by variation across radiologists, subjective assessments and constricted data. Thus, DL models based on mammograms may predict the risk more accurately. Patient's questionnaires were used to obtain risk factor information, which along with electronic medical records review were utilized to develop three deep learning models. These models are able to assess breast cancer risk within 5 years.

a. A risk factor based logistic regression model (RF-LR) which utilized traditional risk factor.
b. A deep learning model (includes images only deep learning) which utilizes only mammograms.
c. A hybrid deep learning model, which utilizes both mammograms as well as traditional risk factors.

These models, mentioned above were differentiated. This comparison was done on the risk model of breast cancer which includes density of the breast (Tyrer-Cuzick model, version 8 [TC]). The models were compared on the basis of their performance. The DL models that used full field mammograms attained comparatively better risk discrimination than with the Tyrer-Cuzick (version 8) model [56].

11.6.8   Prostate Cancer

Prostate cancer is another type of cancer. It is most common in men of all ages. It is second most frequently diagnosed cancer among men. Prostate cancer takes place in the prostate gland which is a small walnut shaped gland present in males. Prostate gland is responsible to produce the seminal fluid which nourishes sperms and transport them. Increase in use of Computer Aided Diagnosis (CAD). Prostate cancer is considered fourth leading cause of death among men or males. Prostate cancer is highly reported in New Zealand, Australia, Western America, and Europe (includes both northern and western Europe) because in those regions subsequent biopsy and prostate specific antigen testing has become widespread. Amid all the men that are diagnosed with any type of cancer approximately 16% of them are diagnosed with prostate cancer. Where in America, around 2.2 million men are suffering from prostate cancer. South central Asia was estimated to have lowest age incident rate. Although, rate of these incidence is higher in the developing countries like South America, Caribbean and sub-Saharan Africa. As for other type of cancers, the risk of prostate cancer also increases with age more like in men above 45 years of age. Some of the autopsy reports suggests that approximately 75% of men who died at age of 85 years or above were suffering from prostate cancer at the time of their death. In countries like Sub-Saharan Africa and Caribbean, mortality rates were predominantly high. Whereas, in Europe and Asia, the mortality rates were wound to be intermediate or low.

11.6.9   Deep Learning in Prostate Cancer

Promising results were obtained by automated deep learning systems that were collected from histological images for accurate grading of prostate cancer. For detection of prostate cancer, ConvNets, a convolutional neural network was used which also a feed forward network. The images become smaller when networks go deeper and deeper. There are different convolutional network architectures which can be used for detection or diagnosis of prostate cancer such as AlexNet, LeNet, VGG-16, GoogleNet, Inception-v3, ResNet, UNet, MobileNet, etc. [57].

Different methods were used to compare different methodology for prostate cancer detection in MRI images, which were examined with the help of enhanced convolutional neural network like FocalNet [58].

11.7   Future Aspects of Deep Learning in Cancer

As we have already seen how deep learning has managed to establish its place in the field of cancer. It has been proven that deep learning can achieve heights in case of cancer prediction.

Deep learning helps in early diagnosis of cancer, which in the future will serve as a life-saving technology. Also, deep learning provides insight of ongoing treatment of cancer [59]. Deep learning has enabled the extraction of previously hidden information directly from routine histologic cancer images, which provides potentially clinically useful images. The analysis of image task consists of grading, detection, and subtyping of tumor tissues in histology image. This affects the process of clinical decision making. All these advanced approaches involve molecular feature interference, survival prediction, and therapy prediction [60].

11.8   Conclusion

In this chapter, we discussed about how DL methods plays a vital role in cancer. We discussed about different neural networks available fin deep learning, which help in diagnostic parameters, monitoring ongoing cancer treatment, and helps in predicting better treatment for cancer patients. In the near future, evolving deep learning methods may further enhance the medical science for the betterment of healthcare systems.

References

1. Ekins, S., The next era: Deep learning in pharmaceutical research. *Pharm. Res.*, 33, 11, 2594–603, 2016 Nov.
2. Mitchell, J.B.O., Machine learning methods in chemoinformatics. *Wiley Interdiscip. Rev. Comput. Mol. Sci.*, 4, 5, 468–81, 2014 Sep.
3. Alves, V.M., Braga, R.C., Andrade, C.H., Computational approaches for predicting hERG Activity, in: *Computational toxicology [internet]*, vol. [cited 2021 Oct 3], pp. 69–91, John Wiley & Sons, Ltd, Hoboken, New Jersey, United States, 2018, Available from: https://onlinelibrary.wiley.com/doi/abs/10.1002/9781119282594.ch3.
4. Benfenati, E., Lombardo, A., Roncaglioni, A., Computational toxicology and reach, in: *Computational toxicology [internet]*, vol. 2018 [cited 2021 Oct 3],

pp. 245–68, John Wiley & Sons, Ltd, Hoboken, New Jersey, United States. Available from: https://onlinelibrary.wiley.com/doi/abs/10.1002/9781119282594.ch9.

5. Microsoft releases CNTK, its open source deep learning toolkit, on GitHub [Internet], in: *The AI Blog*, vol. [cited 2021 Oct 3], 2016, Available from: https://blogs.microsoft.com/ai/microsoft-releases-cntk-its-open-source-deep-learning-toolkit-on-github/.

6. *Deep learning: History and state-of-the-Arts. In: The development of deep learning technologies: Research on the development of electronic information engineering technology in china [internet]*, vol. [cited 2021 Dec 4, pp. 1–11. Springer, Singapore, 2020, https://doi.org/10.1007/978-981-15-4584-9_1.

7. Cao, C., Liu, F., Tan, H., Song, D., Shu, W., Li, W. *et al.*, Deep learning and its applications in biomedicine. *GPB*, 16, 1, 17–32, 2018 Feb.

8. Foote, K.D., A brief history of deep learning [internet]. *Dataversity*, [cited 2021 Dec 4], 2017. Available from: https://www.dataversity.net/brief-history-deep-learning/.

9. Pastur-Romay, L.A., Cedrón, F., Pazos, A., Porto-Pazos, A.B., Deep artificial neural networks and neuromorphic chips for big data Analysis: Pharmaceutical and bioinformatics applications. *Int. J. Mol. Sci.*, 17, 8, 1313, 2016 Aug 11.

10. Emmert-Streib, F., Yang, Z., Feng, H., Tripathi, S., Dehmer, M., An Introductory review of deep learning for prediction models With big data. *Front. Artif. Intell.*, 3, 4, 2020.

11. Mayr, A., Klambauer, G., Unterthiner, T., Hochreiter, S., DeepTox: Toxicity prediction using deep learning. *Front. Environ. Sci.*, 3, 80, 2016.

12. McIntosh, J.R., Mitosis. *Cold Spring Harb. Perspect. Biol.*, 8, 9, a023218, 2016 Sep.

13. Saha, M., Chakraborty, C., Racoceanu, D., Efficient deep learning model for mitosis detection using breast histopathology images. *Comput. Med. Imaging Graph.*, 64, 29–40, 2018 Mar.

14. Imaging and radiology: MedlinePlus medical encyclopedia [Internet]. [cited 2021 Oct 15]. Available from: https://medlineplus.gov/ency/article/007451.htm.

15. McBee, M.P., Awan, O.A., Colucci, A.T., Ghobadi, C.W., Kadom, N., Kansagra, A.P. *et al.*, Deep learning in radiology. *Acad. Radiol.*, 25, 11, 1472–80, 2018 Nov 1.

16. Mazurowski, M.A., Buda, M., Saha, A., Bashir, M.R., Deep learning in radiology: An overview of the concepts and a survey of the state of the art with focus on MRI. *J. Magn. Reson Imaging.*, 49, 4, 939–54, 2019 Apr.

17. Aggarwal, R., Sounderajah, V., Martin, G., Ting, D.S.W., Karthikesalingam, A., King, D. *et al.*, Diagnostic accuracy of deep learning in medical imaging: A systematic review and meta-analysis. *NPJ Digit Med.*, 4, 1, 1–23, 2021 Apr 7.

18. Patel, K.R., Cherian, J., Gohil, K., Atkinson, D., Schizophrenia: Overview and treatment options. *P T*, 39, 9, 638–45, 2014 Sep.

19. Hany, M., Rehman, B., Azhar, Y., Chapman, J., Schizophrenia, in: *StatPearls [Internet]*, vol. [cited 2021 Oct 18], StatPearls Publishing, Treasure Island (FL), 2021, Available from: http://www.ncbi.nlm.nih.gov/books/NBK539864/.

20. Oh, S.L., Vicnesh, J., Ciaccio, E.J., Yuvaraj, R., Acharya, U.R., Deep convolutional neural network model for automated diagnosis of schizophrenia using EEG signals. *Appl. Sc.*, 9, 14, 2870, 2019 Jan.

21. Behjati, S. and Tarpey, P.S., What is next generation sequencing? *Arch. Dis. Child Educ. Pract. Ed.*, 98, 6, 236–8, 2013 Dec.

22. Slatko, B.E., Gardner, A.F., Ausubel, F.M., Overview of next-generation sequencing technologies. *Curr. Protoc. Mol. Biol.*, 122, 1, e59, 2018 Apr.

23. Zhang, J.X., Yordanov, B., Gaunt, A., Wang, M.X., Dai, P., Chen, Y.-J. *et al.*, A deep learning model for predicting next-generation sequencing depth from DNA sequence. *Nat. Commun.*, 12, 1, 4387, 2021 Jul 19.

24. Schmidt, B. and Hildebrandt, A., Deep learning in next-generation sequencing. *Drug Discovery Today*, 26, 1, 173–80, 2021 Jan.

25. Alipanahi, B., Delong, A., Weirauch, M.T., Frey, B.J., Predicting the sequence specificities of DNA- and RNA-binding proteins by deep learning. *Nat. Biotechnol.*, 33, 8, 831–8, 2015 Aug.

26. Zhou, J. and Troyanskaya, O.G., Predicting effects of noncoding variants with deep learning–based sequence model. *Nat. Methods*, 12, 10, 931–4, 2015 Oct.

27. Quang, D. and Xie, X., DanQ: A hybrid convolutional and recurrent deep neural network for quantifying the function of DNA sequences. *Nucleic Acids Res.*, 44, 11, e107, 2016 Jun 20.

28. Yin, Q., Wu, M., Liu, Q., Lv, H., Jiang, R., DeepHistone: A deep learning approach to predicting histone modifications. *BMC Genomics*, 20, Suppl 2, 193, 2019 Apr 4.

29. Deep Learning in Drug Discovery - Gawehn, in: *Molecular Informatics*, vol. [cited 2021 Dec 4], Wiley Online Library [Internet], Hoboken, New Jersey, United States, 2016, Available from: https://onlinelibrary.wiley.com/doi/abs/10.1002/minf.201501008.

30. Arabi, H. and Zaidi, H., Applications of artificial intelligence and deep learning in molecular imaging and radiotherapy. *Eur. J. Hybrid Imaging.*, 4, 1, 17, 2020 Sep 23.

31. Chen, D., Liu, S., Kingsbury, P., Sohn, S., Storlie, C.B., Habermann, E.B. *et al.*, Deep learning and alternative learning strategies for retrospective real-world clinical data. *NPJ Digit Med.*, 2, 1, 1–5, 2019 May 30.

32. McDaniel, B., Badri, T., Steele, R.B., Basal cell carcinoma, in: *StatPearls [Internet]*, vol. [cited 2021 Nov 7], StatPearls Publishing, Treasure Island (FL), 2021, Available from: http://www.ncbi.nlm.nih.gov/books/NBK482439/.

33. Howell, J.Y. and Ramsey, M.L., Squamous cell skin cancer, in: *StatPearls [Internet]*, vol. [cited 2021 Nov 7], StatPearls Publishing, Treasure Island (FL), 2021, Available from: http://www.ncbi.nlm.nih.gov/books/NBK441939/.

34. Bishop, B.N. and Lynch, D.T., Kaposi Sarcoma, in: *StatPearls [Internet]*, vol. [cited 2021 Nov 7], StatPearls Publishing, Treasure Island (FL), 2021, Available from: http://www.ncbi.nlm.nih.gov/books/NBK534839/.

35. Rivlin, N., Brosh, R., Oren, M., Rotter, V., Mutations in the p53 Tumor Suppressor gene: Important milestones at the various steps of tumorigenesis. *Genes Cancer.*, 2, 4, 466–74, 2011 Apr.

36. Dascalu, A. and David, E.O., Skin cancer detection by deep learning and sound analysis algorithms: A prospective clinical study of an elementary dermoscope. *EBioMedicine.*, 43, 107–13, 2019 May 1.

37. A. A. A Deep learning approach to skin cancer detection in dermoscopy images. *J. Biomed. Phys. Eng.*, 10, 6, 801–6, 2020 Dec 1.

38. Talathi, S.S., Zimmerman, R., Young, M., Anatomy, Abdomen and Pelvis, Pancreas, in: *StatPearls [Internet]*, vol. [cited 2021 Oct 21], StatPearls Publishing, Treasure Island (FL), 2021, Available from: http://www.ncbi.nlm. nih.gov/books/NBK532912/.

39. Chandra, R. and Liddle, R.A., Recent advances in the regulation of pancreatic secretion. *Curr. Opin. Gastroenterol.*, 30, 5, 490–4, 2014 Sep.

40. Paniccia, A. and Schulick, R.D., Chapter 4 - Pancreatic physiology and functional assessment, in: *Blumgart's surgery of the liver, biliary tract and pancreas, 2-volume set (Sixth Edition) [Internet]*, vol. [cited 2021 Oct 22], W.R. Jarnagin (Ed.), pp. 66–76.e3, Elsevier, Philadelphia, 2017, Available from: https://www.sciencedirect.com/science/article/pii/B9780323340625000042.

41. Liu, K.-L., Wu, T., Chen, P.-T., Tsai, Y.M., Roth, H., Wu, M.-S. *et al.*, Deep learning to distinguish pancreatic cancer tissue from non-cancerous pancreatic tissue: A retrospective study with cross-racial external validation. *Lancet Digit. Health*, 2, 6, e303–13, 2020 Jun.

42. Tan, M. and Le, Q., EfficientNet: Rethinking model scaling for convolutional neural networks, in: *Proceedings of the 36th International Conference on Machine Learning [Internet]*. PMLR, vol. [cited 2021 Nov 9], pp. 6105–14, 2019, Available from: https://proceedings.mlr.press/v97/tan19a.html.

43. Naito, Y., Tsuneki, M., Fukushima, N., Koga, Y., Higashi, M., Notohara, K. *et al.*, A deep learning model to detect pancreatic ductal adenocarcinoma on endoscopic ultrasound-guided fine-needle biopsy. *Sci. Rep.*, 11, 1, 8454, 2021 Apr 19.

44. Donley, E.R., Holme, M.R., Loyd, J.W., Anatomy, Thorax, Wall Movements, in: *StatPearls [Internet]*, vol. [cited 2021 Nov 25], StatPearls Publishing, Treasure Island (FL), 2021, Available from: http://www.ncbi.nlm.nih.gov/ books/NBK526023/.

45. Tucker, W.D., Weber, C., Burns, B., Anatomy, Thorax, Heart Pulmonary Arteries, in: *StatPearls [Internet]*, vol. [cited 2021 Nov 25], StatPearls Publishing, Treasure Island (FL), 2021, Available from: http://www.ncbi.nlm. nih.gov/books/NBK534812/.

46. Chaudhry, R. and Bordoni, B., Anatomy, Thorax, Lungs, in: *StatPearls [Internet]*, vol. [cited 2021 Nov 25], Treasure Island (FL): StatPearls Publishing, 2021, Available from: http://www.ncbi.nlm.nih.gov/books/NBK470197/.

47. Bradley, S.H., Kennedy, M.P.T., Neal, R.D., Recognising lung cancer in primary care. *Adv. Ther.*, 36, 1, 19–30, 2019.

48. Hoffman, P.C., Mauer, A.M., Vokes, E.E., Lung cancer. *Lancet.*, 355, 9202, 479–85, 2000 Feb 5.

49. de Groot, P. and Munden, R.F., Lung cancer epidemiology, risk factors, and prevention. *Radiol. Clin. North Am.*, 50, 5, 863–76, 2012 Sep.

50. Malhotra, J., Malvezzi, M., Negri, E., La Vecchia, C., Boffetta, P., Risk factors for lung cancer worldwide. *Eur. Respir. J.*, 48, 3, 889–902, 2016 Sep.

51. Lemjabbar-Alaoui, H., Hassan, O., Yang, Y.-W., Buchanan, P., Lung cancer: Biology and treatment options. *Biochim. Biophys. Acta*, 1856, 2, 189–210, 2015 Dec.

52. Siddiqui, F. and Siddiqui, A.H., Lung Cancer, in: *StatPearls*, StatPearls Publishing, Treasure Island (FL), 2021, [cited 2021 Nov 26]. Available from: http://www.ncbi.nlm.nih.gov/books/NBK482357/.

53. Xu, Y., Hosny, A., Zeleznik, R., Parmar, C., Coroller, T., Franco, I. *et al.*, Deep learning predicts lung cancer treatment response from serial medical imaging. *Clin. Cancer Res.*, 25, 11, 3266–75, 2019 Jun 1.

54. Alkabban, F.M. and Ferguson, T., Breast Cancer, in: *StatPearls*, StatPearls Publishing, Treasure Island (FL), 2021, [cited 2021 Nov 26]. Available from: http://www.ncbi.nlm.nih.gov/books/NBK482286/.

55. Koo, M.M., von Wagner, C., Abel, G.A., McPhail, S., Rubin, G.P., Lyratzopoulos, G., Typical and atypical presenting symptoms of breast cancer and their associations with diagnostic intervals: Evidence from a national audit of cancer diagnosis. *Cancer Epidemiol.*, 48, 140–6, 2017 Jun.

56. Yala, A., Lehman, C., Schuster, T., Portnoi, T., Barzilay, R., A deep learning mammography-based model for improved breast cancer risk prediction. *Radiology*, 292, 1, 60–6, 2019 Jul 1.

57. Linkon, A.H.M., Labib, M.M., Hasan, T., Hossain, M., Jannat, M.-E.-., Deep learning in prostate cancer diagnosis and Gleason grading in histopathology images: An extensive study. *Inform. Med. Unlocked.*, 24, 100582, 2021 Jan 1.

58. Patel, A., Singh, S.K., Khamparia, A., Detection of prostate cancer using deep learning framework. *IOP Conf Ser: Mater Sci. Eng.*, 1022, 012073, 2021 Jan.

59. Koc, P., Yalcin, C., Kose, U., Alzubi, J., Future of deep learning for cancer diagnosis, in: *Deep learning for cancer diagnosis [Internet] (Studies in Computational Intelligence)*, vol. [cited 2021 Dec 2], pp. 227–38, Springer, Singapore, 2021, Available from: https://doi.org/10.1007/978-981-15-6321-8_13.

60. Echle, A., Rindtorff, N.T., Brinker, T.J., Luedde, T., Pearson, A.T., Kather, J.N., Deep learning in cancer pathology: A new generation of clinical biomarkers. *Br. J. Cancer.*, 124, 4, 686–96, 2021 Feb.

12

Cardiovascular Disease Prediction Using Deep Neural Network for Older People

Nagarjuna Telagam*, B.Venkata Kranti and Nikhil Chandra Devarasetti

Dept of Electrical Electronics and Communication Engineering, GITAM University, Bengaluru, Karnataka, India

Abstract

Cardiovascular disease is the primary reason for people's demise rate, and the rate is increasing globally every year, especially in older adults. Nearly 20 million people are dying with heart-related problems every year across the globe. It was estimated that the numbers would increase by 75 million by the end of 2040. The doctors or medical professionals in the medical field can only predict the disease with an accuracy of 67%. Doctors' unrealistic current situation needs a supporting machine learning model for accurate results. This book chapter presents the study of machine learning and deep learning algorithms with detailed and analytical comparisons, which may help new and inexperienced medical professionals or researchers in the medical field. Extracting medical data is becoming more and more necessary for predicting and treating high death rates due to heart attacks. Every day, the hospitals produce tons of terabytes of data, and the hospitals will use clinical tests for decision-making about heart data. The decision tree algorithm predicts heart disease with 86.72% and 75.40% accuracy on the train and test sets, respectively. We saw the difference between training and testing accuracy, which makes decision tree models less reliable. Hence, the Random Forest algorithm with the best hyperparameters is chosen to obtain 90.16% and 87.6% accuracy for the testing and training data set. The training is done using a four-fold cross-validation scheme, ensuring our test set accuracy is better than training set accuracy. The proposed machine learning model has an accurate algorithm that

Corresponding author: nagarjuna473@gmail.com
Nagarjuna Telagam: ORCID: 0000-0002-6184-6283
B.Venkata Kranti: ORCID: 0000-0003-3177-6250
Nikhil Chandra devarasetti: ORCID: 0000-0001-7770-5306

Rishabha Malviya, Gheorghita Ghinea, Rajesh Kumar Dhanaraj, Balamurugan Balusamy and Sonali Sundram (eds.) Deep Learning for Targeted Treatments: Transformation in Healthcare, (369–406) © 2022 Scrivener Publishing LLC

works with rich healthcare data, a high-dimensional data handling system, and an intelligent framework that uses different data sources to predict heart disease. This book chapter used an ensemble-based deep learning model with optimal feature selection to improve accuracy. The sigmoid function is used for true class or false class identification, and it is also used to calculate the loss or error in the last year in the neural network. The Adam optimizer is used to adjust the three-layer neural network architecture weights. The proposed model shows an accuracy of 97% higher than conventional methods.

Keywords: Decision tree, random forest, confusion matrix, machine learning. artificial intelligence, neural networks, electrocardiogram

12.1 Introduction

The complex problem researchers face in any field is to predict the outcome with some certainty. It is essential to predict any disease and prevent it from affecting people in the medical area. Many high revenue-generating countries Worldwide have been spending billions of dollars on heart disease treatment per day. Therefore, a system is needed to detect cardiovascular disease early for the treatment of patients effectively, preventing a possible heart stroke. Heart diseases can be identified by wearing sensors throughout the human body and extracting the data by conducting medical tests. The physicians or doctors will examine the data generated by the sensors and diagnose the patients accurately. The main problem in wearable sensors is that signal artefacts may corrupt the data, i.e., data has more missing values, and more noise is present in the sensor device. These two problems impact the system degradation performance, and these sensor devices will generate inaccurate results. Electronic Medical Records (EMR) and sensor data analysis are challenging tasks for monitoring cardiac patients. The extraction of features from the data set is vital in predicting disease. Intelligent systems to predict heart disease automatically fuse the information from sensors and EMR.

The hybrid model is the combination of two models. The first model is the feature selection weighting approach to recognize the exact feature weight. The second model utilizes weights as input for machine learning method classifiers to predict disease exactly. Most heart data have invalid, repeated, or missing data, which means redundant and irrelevant features. This kind of data will create confusion among the doctors to define the target class. The time-consuming process is very high in handling this kind of data. The existing methods have heart disease diagnosis depending on the weighting of features methods. Due to the weight allocation, the uncertain combination of operations may increase mean square error values and decrease the effectiveness of the predictive model. The theoretical support will not be present if the mean square error values are present. The specific weight needs to be applied to the features concerning classification models to avoid such situations. The latest technologies in computer science have brought many opportunities for medical researchers, and computer science is used as an instrument for medical professionals to predict diseases. Medical science with artificial intelligence has gained tremendous momentum since the last decade. Machine learning is such a tool used in different domains, and it works on datasets. The best part of machine learning modelling is that reprogramming is possible at any time if the results are not effective. It has much strength and has enormous opportunities for medical professionals. Heart disease prediction has significant challenges because of different parameters utilized for target values. The numerous data types for various conditions to predict heart disease have many approaches, such as Naïve Bayes, K-means nearest neighboring (KNN), Decision tree, Random Forest, and Neural networks, to indicate any disease with high accuracy. Each algorithm has its speciality for feature classification or accuracy. The neural network models have great potential to reduce the error in heart disease prediction.

The UCI dataset [1] is most predominantly used to evaluate heart attack, and it includes the data of 303 people. It has two classes: one class is for people with No Heart Disease, and the other is for heart disease. The authors use the binary cuckoo optimization algorithm to construct the feature selection and support vector machine. The accuracy achieved is 84.44%, sensitivity 86.49%, and specificity 81.49%. The following article [2] is a cascade correlation neural network [CNN] used to predict the disease. This work accuracy depends on 270 data samples, in which 150 samples are taken for training, and the rest are used to stimulate network architecture. CNN architecture depends on 13 input neurons and one output neuron, and obtained accuracy is 78% for training and 85% for testing with less time complexity. The deep belief network [3] for heart disease prediction for likelihood percentage is designed in MATLAB software, and the CNN method provides an accuracy of 82%.

The dataset's illustration for heart disease is usually raw and inconsistent. The pre-processing of the high-dimensional dataset is compulsory for any researcher to reduce it to a common dataset. The extraction of variables from the available dataset is needed to train the algorithm with less time complexity. Many research articles used time as a parameter and compared other parameters such as accuracy and efficiency. The performance of Sequential Minimal Optimization (SMO) classifiers has more efficiency than Multilayer Perceptron (MLP) classifiers [4]. The machine learning methods have advantages and disadvantages, and feature optimization provides high Classification in decision tree efficiency [5]. Early detection of heart disease has feature utilization and includes research for medical professionals to perfect heart disease. This article [6] has collected raw data from electrocardiogram devices and used the dataset for training purposes in a neural network model to classify the patterns in the dataset. This article also shows that 95% is achieved with the support vector machine method and neural network for training data classification. It is also used to achieve better results. If the data are multidimensional and nonlinear, this neural network method provides high efficiency relative to other methods. The robust algorithm-based machine learning helps reduce unwanted noise in any dataset, and the redundant data can be eliminated. The deep learning algorithm has a high chance of increasing efficiency and has high accuracy for heart disease detection. The multilayer perceptron [8] with a backprop-agation algorithm predicts cardiovascular disease accurately. The authors used artificial neural networks and obtained 88.46% and 80.17% for train-ing and validation sets. Overall, the accuracy is increased by 1.1% for the training set and 0.82% for the validation dataset. The weighted associative classifier (WAC) [9] predicts heart disease with a Guided user interface (GUI) interface connected to the patient records. More than 13 attributes and 303 features are used for testing and training.

The target values are chosen in binary format if it is 1, the patient has heart disease. Similarly, if it is 0, the patient does not have heart disease. The classifier used here is Classification based on multiple association rules (CMAR), Classification based on Associations (CBA), and Classification based on predictive association rules (CPAR), and the authors obtained an accuracy of 81.51%. The article [10] supports the innovative decision system for heart disease prediction. Mitral stenosis and ventricular septal defects are three heart diseases predicted using an artificial neural network decision system. The sound of the heart is gathered for devices such as a stethoscope and microphone. The microphone device is placed between the stethoscope and PCI card to strengthen the sound signals. This ANN-based system identifies the three types of heart disease accurately. The principal component analysis (PCA) [5] and regression technique are mainly used for feature selection, and the prediction accuracy is around 92% is achieved for the heart disease dataset. The feed-forward neural net-work achieves 95% efficiency. The feed-forward back propagation neural network is used to predict the disease, and it consists of 13 input layers, 20 hidden layers, and one output layer. This network achieves 88% accu-racy with 20% of the testing dataset, 20% of the validation dataset, and 60% for training purposes. The robust algorithm-based machine learning helps reduce unwanted noise in any dataset, and the redundant data can be eliminated [7]. The microphone device is placed between the stethoscope and PCI card to strengthen the sound signals [11].

The article uses feed-forward multilayer perceptron [12] and supports vector machines to obtain 85% and 87.5% accuracy, out of which 270 samples are used. The division ratio used here is 60 to 40. Samples used for training is 162 and for testing is 108. Target values are usually the same (0,1). In [13], the authors used an entropy ensemble of neural networks with recursive feature elimination [EENNRFE] algorithm for feature extraction. The data set used by the authors is Cleveland from the UCI database. The correlation coefficient is found among the feature classification and, with the help of artificial neural networks, will measure the mean of an ensemble in neural networks. The accuracy of 85.66% is obtained for training data.

Deep learning is used to design a prediction model in medical science. It becomes challenging to achieve higher precision due to the unavailability of values in specific data set fields. The missing values are identified using a systematic methodology. The Cleveland dataset for heart disease is used to test the different models in this book chapter. The authors used the imputation methods for classifying the dataset and identified the MICE imputation method for missing value distribution [27]. Researchers worldwide were working on machine learning algorithms to reduce the death rate. The researchers or doctors entirely depend on the accuracy. The authors used hybrid methods, i.e., combining more than two methods to detect disease with increased accuracy with the importance of feature selection. The two methods are radial basis function and genetic algorithm, and the accuracy increased to 94.2% with nine different characteristics for attribute reduction [28]. The dataset contains some irrelevant features, and the authors used the isolation forest method for improved results. The confusion matrix is used to analyze 14 main attributes in the UCI dataset. The authors achieved 94.2% accuracy using the deep learning approach [29]. Nearly 18 million people are affected by heart disease every year, and overall, 32% of the population suffers from death worldwide. So to identify the disease at an early stage is mandatory for doctors. The authors used the UCI heart disease dataset to determine kernel values. The kernel has a low correlation coefficient and a less mean absolute error, concluding that the proposed model is comparatively good [30]. The authors designed a healthcare application system that depends on an optimal artificial neural network to diagnose heart disease. The proposed method uses two types of processes, i.e. the first process is distance-based misclassified instance removal, and the next one is learning-based optimization. They designed using the Apache spark method for training and testing data [31]. The dataset has many clinical parameters and has proposed a hybrid decision system. With the help of Python language, the hybrid decision system was successfully implemented in the simulation environment, and an accuracy of 87% was achieved by the authors [32]. The authors used the hybrid method, a combination of random forest and decision tree, and achieved an accuracy of 89% [33]. The artificial intelligence methods are high-speed growing techniques for predicting heart disease. Data mining techniques efficiently provide disease identification based on patient data such as age, chest pain, and blood pressure [34]. Heart diseases can be reduced by early diagnosis methods with the help of using machine learning models. The authors used the Cleveland dataset to pre-process data and new hybrid classifiers for the training process. The sensitivity and precision FI score is calculated along with pessimistic prediction and false rate. The authors achieved high accuracy of around 99.05% using RFBM and relief feature selection methods [35]. Type 2 diabetes in older adults will likely result in heart diseases. The authors proposed a risk prediction model which uses a machine-learning algorithm to identify heart disease in type 2 diabetes patients. The classifiers' accuracy is in the range of 79% to 88% [36]. The four different types of machine learning models are compared with accuracy and macro-FI as performance metrics. The dataset was collected from 17661 patients. The authors concluded that features such as age and oxygen saturation play a significant role in heart disease prediction [37]. The machine learning models detect the receiver operator curve based on cardiovascular disease. The detected CVD less various levels of intervals for different machine learning algorithms [38]. The authors used ten-fold cross-validation for twenty-four variables based model developing in the training set [39]. The deep neural network is used for the risk prediction model with 834 patients with type two diabetes conditions [40]. This proposed research utilizes 14 features for predicting heart disease with various comparative analyses of machine learning algorithms [41]. The patient has 15 years of suffering from heart disease, and his mortality risk is identified using four machine learning models developed and compared to conventional methods. The accuracy is increased to 5.2% with Australian cohorts [42]. The classifiers are based on many machine learning models from the fifth Korea National health survey dataset. The authors developed models based on age groups for giving the dose of influenza [43]. The proposed model effectively detects the abnormal left ventricular geometry at the early stages based on different features such as age, body mass index and hypertension [44]. The authors conducted the study based on Qatar Biobank's most extensive collection of biomedical measurements and various factors of heart disease patients. The association of the proposed risk factors and comorbidities must be investigated in clinical setup better to understand their role in CVD [45]. This Review explains the clinical prediction models are analyzed to develop the machine learning counterparts [46]. The best average prediction accuracy is used as the performance metric for various machine learning algorithms for various studies. This proposed research work also validates the area under the receiver operating characteristic curve [47]. The research develops a heart disease prediction based on the ensemble method of multilayer dynamic systems in every layer [48]. The review article has designed a system to integrate the data from omics data to approach the full potential [49]. The artificial intelligence-based heart disease method is developed using a support vector machine with kernel techniques [50]. The cardiovascular disease prediction has made researchers contribute work on many machine learning algorithms. In the medical field, machine learning produces valuable patterns and provide huge helpful information for the researchers, and this study analyzes the documents to provide the disease dataset [51–56].

12.2 Proposed System Model

12.2.1 Decision Tree Algorithm

This algorithm will predict the output based on a tree-type structure. Each branch/set is further divided into subsets to reach the decision finally. It works on nested structures, i.e., each node divides the data into either left or right direction. We imported the required libraries to analyze data, to build the predictive model using different techniques like linear regression, logistic regression, etc. Some of the python libraries used are NumPy, pandas, matplotlib, and seaborn are used for Exploratory Data Analytics [EDA] and Data visualization.

For pre-processing the data, the model building we used is SCIKIT-learn which has StandardScalar, MinMaxScalar, and Robust scalar to rescale the numerical values. MinMaxScalar is used to rescale the values between 0 and 1. StandardScalar is used to bring the data points so that the whole data is around mean 0.

With the help of the panda's library, the excel sheet data are imported into python and stored in a data frame called "df" and checks whether there are any duplicates in the data set and removes drop_duplicates syntax considering all the features into account. Typically, any dataset needs to be split into training and testing sets before modeling. In this proposed model, a four-fold cross-validation scheme is used to divide the training set into four folds and use three folds to train and one fold to validate. 80%

of the data set is used for training, and the remaining 20% is used for testing. Training also involves a validation set.

Basically, in the UCI repository, the data set has 1024×14 rows and columns, i.e., 1024 patients with 14 features are considered in our proposed system, with duplicates. Later the data is cleaned, i.e., we have removed the duplicates, the matrix size is converted to 302×14. Initially, the data is divided into two data frames so that one data frame should have all the variables except the target variable. The other should have only the target variable, i.e., the target variable is popped out and assigned to a data frame Y with all the existing rows of the original data frame and has a matrix size of 302×1 (302 patients with one target value). Table 12.1 shows the data variables, and their values are represented in df format.

Similarly, the remaining variables are assigned to data frame X with all the existing rows with a matrix size of 302×13, i.e., 302 patients with 13 features except the target variable. Table 12.1 shows the features imported in df format. Now it is time to split the data into training and testing sets. Imported train_test_split from sklearn.model_selection library helps split X and Y data frames into train and test sets. As mentioned earlier, the data was split in the 80:20 ratio, i.e., train_size=80% of rows (20% given to validation) and test_size is 20% of rows. After splitting the data, X_train and X_test sizes are (241x13) and (61x13), respectively.

After setting up the data frames, instantiate DecisionTreeClassifier as df format by importing it from sklearn.tree library and fit the data. We instantiated the decision tree classifier with only one hyperparameter, the max_depth = 3, and kept all the other parameters as default. Graphviz software and imported pydotplus library to visualize the tree graph libraries and packages have been imported installed to observe a decision tree graph. We were using export_graphviz, which is imported from sklearn.tree library. We defined the class_names as No Disease and Disease. So, with the help of pydotplus and Graphviz libraries, We obtained a Decision tree graph by considering only max_depth(3) as a predefined parameter, as shown in Figure 12.1.

From sklearn. The metrics import confusion matrix gives the information about the correctly predicted and wrongly predicted values compared to the actual values.

12.2.1.1   Confusion Matrix

This Confusion matrix technique will summarize the performance of any machine learning algorithm. Therefore, other parameters like sensitivity, specificity, precision, recall also play an essential role in understanding the effectiveness of an algorithm. Confusion matrix is a performance measurement

Table 12.1 Features imported into "df" data form.

	Age	Sex	cp	trestbps	Chol	Fbs	Restecg	Thalch	Exang	Oldpeak	Slope	Ca	thal	Target
0	52	1	0	125	212	0	1	168	0	1.0	2	2	3	0
1	53	1	0	140	203	1	0	155	1	3.1	0	0	3	0
2	70	1	0	145	174	0	1	125	1	2.6	0	0	3	0
3	61	1	0	148	203	0	1	161	0	0.0	2	1	3	0
4	62	0	0	138	294	1	1	106	0	1.9	1	3	2	0

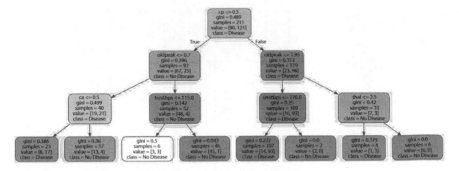

Figure 12.1 Decision tree graph for maximum depth of 3.

for machine learning classification as shown in Figure 12.2. Hyperparameter tuning is searching the hyperparameter space for a set of values that will optimize the machine learning model as shown in Figure 12.3.

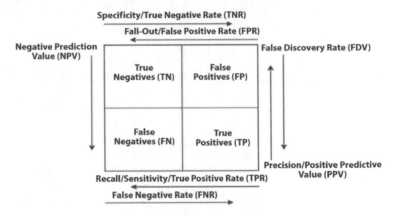

Figure 12.2 Confusion matrix.

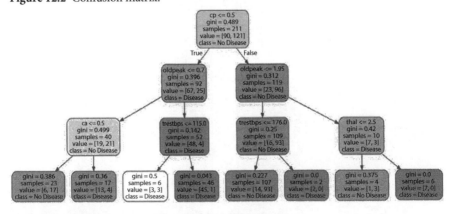

Figure 12.3 Decision tree with best hyperparameters.

Table 12.2 UCI dataset for predicting heart disease.

Data type	Variable name	Input attributes	Specification/range	Predictable attribute
Numerical	AGE	Age	Above 50 [50-79]	Target Values Value 1=< 50% [No heart disease] Value 0 => 50% [patient suffering from heart disease]
Nominal	SEX	Sex	1- Male 2- Female	
Nominal	CP	Chest pain	1. Angina 2. typical type angina 3. non-angina pain 4. asymptomatic	
Numeric	TRESTBPS	Resting blood pressure	(mm Hg)	
Numeric	CHOL	Serum cholesterol	(mg/dl)	
Numeric	FBS	Fasting blood sugar	>120 mg/dl 1. >120 mg/dl	

(Continued)

Table 12.2 UCI Dataset for predicting heart disease. (*Continued*)

Data type	Variable name	Input attributes	Specification/Range	Predictable attribute
Nominal	RESTECG	Resting electrocardiographic results	0. Normal 1. Suffering from ST-TWave abnormality 2. Definite leftventricular hypertrophy	Target Values Value 1=< 50% [No heart disease] Value 0 => 50% [patient suffering from heart disease]
Nominal	THALCH	Heart rate maximum	Beats Per Second	
Nominal	EXANG	Exercise-induced angina	1.Yes 0. No	
Numeric	OLDPEAK	Old peak	ST depression induced by exercise relative to rest	
Nominal	SLOPE	The slope of thepeak exercise ST segment	1. Unsloping 2. Flat 3. Down sloping	
Numeric	CA	No of major vesselscolored by fluoroscopy	Values rangingfrom 0-3	
Nominal	THAL	Thal	3. Normal, 6. Fixed defect, 7. Reversible defect	

Table 12.2 shows the UCI dataset parameters for deep learning model. The confusion matrix output for a sample decision tree is shown below

$$\text{Training set Confusion Matrix} = \begin{bmatrix} 79 & 27 \\ 10 & 125 \end{bmatrix} \qquad (12.1)$$

$$\text{Testing set Confusion Matrix} = \begin{bmatrix} 24 & 8 \\ 5 & 24 \end{bmatrix} \qquad (12.2)$$

Accuracy can be calculated as the ratio of correctly predicted labels to the total number of labels, the training accuracy is 84.64%, and the testing accuracy is 78.68% which is less efficient. So, to improve the algorithm's effectiveness, hyperparameter tuning is done and with GridSearchCV, imported from sklearn.model_selection, best hyperparameters were obtained. The entropy criterion is better than the Gini index, maximum depth of tree to be five and the minimum sample per leaf to be 10. Then instantiated the decision tree on best hyperparameters and fit the training and test sets model. The confusion matrix is being obtained after fitting the model. The confusion matrix calculation as shown in and calculated values for training and testing are shown in equations (12.1), (12.2), (12.3) and (12.4).

$$\text{Training set Confusion Matrix} = \begin{bmatrix} 90 & 16 \\ 16 & 119 \end{bmatrix} \qquad (12.3)$$

$$\text{Testing set Confusion Matrix} = \begin{bmatrix} 24 & 8 \\ 7 & 2 \end{bmatrix} \qquad (12.4)$$

The training and testing accuracy obtained is 86.72% and 75.40%, respectively, which is again a poor test accuracy and ineffective in predicting heart disease correctly. So, the random forests technique could be a better alternative to the decision tree, an ensemble of decision trees or an ensemble of different predictive algorithms.

12.3   Random Forest Algorithm

The Random Forest Classifier is being imported from sklearn.ensemble. Using GridSearchCV, imported from sklearn.model_selection, best hyperparameters were obtained. The best hyperparameters obtained are maximum depth = 10, maximum features =4, min_sample_leaf = 5, number of estimators=10. Later, Instantiated grid_search and fit the model considering the best hyperparameters. We obtained a confusion matrix for the random forest model.

The confusion matrix values for training and testing are shown in equations [12.5] and [12.6].

$$Training\ set\ Confusion\ Matrix = \begin{bmatrix} 93 & 13 \\ 17 & 118 \end{bmatrix} \qquad (12.5)$$

$$Testing\ set\ Confusion\ Matrix = \begin{bmatrix} 27 & 5 \\ 1 & 28 \end{bmatrix} \qquad (12.6)$$

From that, the training accuracy comes out to be 87.67%, and the test set accuracy is about 90.16%, the best accuracy any machine learning model can get.

Here, False Negatives are more dangerous than False Positives. Since we know, the model predicting not having a disease when people have the disease is much more complicated than the opposite case. Therefore, the recall percentage must be as close to 100% as possible. In this case, recall is around 96.55%, which is an encouraging factor. So, we say our model predicts that having heart disease with a 96.6% certainty helps them prevent death. The Random Forest algorithm, as shown in Figure 12.4 hence proved extremely reliable to predict heart disease before the attack. Furthermore, this helps people to take necessary actions to prevent fatal heart stroke.

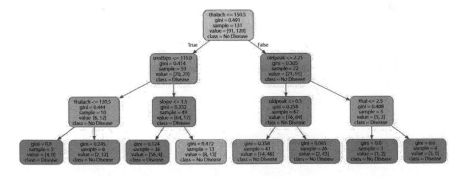

Figure 12.4 Random forest with best hyperparameters.

12.4   Variable Importance for Random Forests

From the tree diagram for random forests, it is seen on the top that cp(chest pain) is the most important feature of all, followed by thalach, ca, thal (thalassemia), exang, sex and so on. Table 12.2 shows the list of variables in the dataset. Chest pain (Cp) has four different values representing 0, 1, 2, 3, and a specific meaning. From the random forests tree diagram, it is clear that if the value is 0, most people will not have heart disease. If cp <= 0.5 is true, the value is 0. Else the condition is false, and then the value can be either 1 or 2 or 3. Let us consider whether the condition is false, as most people have heart disease when the condition is false. Now if cp <= 0.5 is false, we reach one more condition, thal <= 2.5, that means thalassemia. Thal feature too has four different values (0, 1, 2, 3). From the random forests, we can say that if the people with a thal value greater than 2.5 and cp>= 0.5, it can be confirmed that they have heart disease. Now, if thal <= 2.5, there might be no heart disease. After that, we reach a condition, thalach <= 118.5, which means the maximum heart rate achieved in beats per minute(bpm). If that condition is true, then it can be concluded that

Table 12.3 Variable representing feature importance.

Variable number	Variable name	Importance
2	CP	0.238423
7	THALCH	0.137478
11	CA	0.135503
12	THAL	0.120802
8	EXANG	0.092325
1	SEX	0.060381
9	OLDPEAK	0.049703
3	TRESTBPS	0.046792
0	AGE	0.042766
10	SLOPE	0.031194
4	CHOL	0.029229
6	RESTECG	0.015404
5	FBS	0.00000

the person has heart disease, and if not, the probability of a person having heart disease is very less. This way, we understand the random forest ensemble simply by looking at the graph. Table 12.3 shows the variable importance for the random forest algorithm.

12.5   The Proposed Method Using a Deep Learning Model

Since our model will work only for older people, we converted the data with more senior people by sorting the age above 50. We have seen 230 patients from the UCI repository. After Ensembling, the training data is 80%, and data are 20% for testing. The duplicates are removed. The total data from the UCI repository has 1025 entries or patients. We have sorted the patient's age above 50. We got 732 entries. Even after removing the duplicates, 216 entries are used. The number of features we have used to predict heart disease is 13. From there, we generated 60 features, i.e., by combining the elements by multiplication or division or adding, 60 features are used to predict heart disease with 216 entries. Using machine learning techniques like Pearson correlation, linear support vector classifier (SVC), Lasso, select K best with chi-z, random forest method, and variance threshold algorithms. From the 60 features, only 26 are selected as final features. So, therefore, the matrix size is converted to 216 × 26, i.e., 216 patients and 26 features.

In this proposed model, 4096 neurons are used in the first layer, and each neuron has a certain number of inputs with a bias value. Each signal is multiplied by a weighted value. Here 4096 neurons are used, so it has

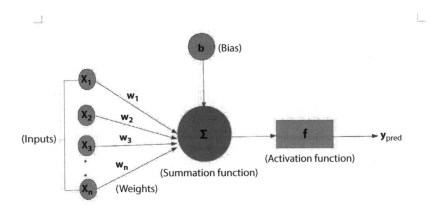

Figure 12.5 Deep learning model.

4096 neurons, and values are adjusted during training time. An activation function as shown in Figure 12.5 decides whether a neuron should be activated or not. This means that it will decide whether the neuron's input to the network is important or not in the process of prediction using simpler mathematical operations. As shown in Figure 12.6, the hidden layers connect one neuron in the input layer to another neuron in the second layer. Each connection always has weight values. The training algorithm updates the weight value to reduce the errors. The activation used in Figure 12.5 has nonlinearity to neural networks. This activation function always squashes the values in a smaller range with a sigmoid function and has values between 0 and 1, as shown in Figure 12.7.

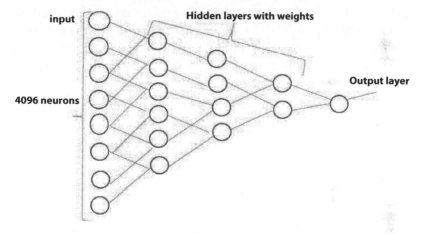

Figure 12.6 Applied deep neural network model with 4096 neurons on the first layer.

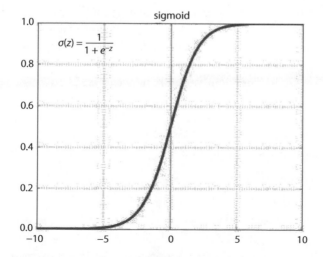

Figure 12.7 Sigmoid activation function range between 0 and 1.

12.5.1   Prevention of Overfitting

We have two methods to prevent the overfitting problem in deep learning.

12.5.2   Batch Normalization

Batch normalization is a technique for training very deep neural networks that standardizes the inputs to a layer for each mini-batch.

12.5.3   Dropout Technique

Here the number of classes is only two, i.e., the target values are 0 or 1. To calculate the losses in the last layer, we have used the sigmoid function.

Since the binary cross-entropy and backpropagation method is used to adjust the weights, the data's training is 94%. Using the confusion matrix, all ML models are used to compare the accuracy, nearly 20 models are tested, and accuracy is obtained by 94%.

12.6   Results and Discussions

Table 12.4 shows that the top 20 models for heart disease prediction are compared.

Each method has its unique feature.

12.6.1   Linear Regression

Linear regression performs supervised learning for the given data. It is based on a statistical method primarily used for predictive analysis. This algorithm makes continuous predictions and has a decent relationship between dependent variables or independent variables. The dependent variable is kept on changing for the independent variable; hence, it is called linear regression. Generally, the plot between the independent and dependent variables is a sloped straight line, which shows that the direct relationship between the variables is linear. The linear relationship can be positive or negative. The mathematical equation for the linear regression is shown in below equation

$$Y = a + bX1 + cX2 + dX3 \ldots + \varepsilon \qquad (12.4)$$

X1, X2, X3 are explanatory variables, Y is the dependent variable, and ε is the random error. If the data is wrongly categorized, errors will occur in the algorithm's accuracy. A linear regression algorithm can easily categorize

Table 12.4 20 models comparison for accuracy training and testing.

Model	Acc_train	Acc_test	Acc_diff
Deep Neural Network model	**97**	**94**	**3**
XGB Classifier	98.84	86.05	12.79
Ridge CV	83.72	86.05	-2.33
Random Forest Classifier	83.14	86.05	-2.91
Gaussian Process Classification	99.42	83.72	15.7
Support Vector Machines	89.53	83.72	5.81
Linear SVC	84.88	83.72	1.16
Stochastic Gradient Decent	84.3	83.72	0.58
Gradient Boosting Classifier	100	81.4	18.6
LGBM Classifier	96.51	81.4	15.11
AdaBoost Classifier	87.79	81.4	6.39
KNN	87.79	81.4	6.39
Extra Trees Classifier	84.3	81.4	2.9
Logistic Regression	82.56	81.4	1.16
Naive Bayes	79.65	81.4	-1.75
Bagging Classifier	97.67	79.07	18.6
Voting Classifier	84.3	79.07	5.23
Decision Tree Classifier	88.95	74.42	14.53
Linear Regression	59.3	48.84	10.46

all the linearly separable datasets. The linear regression is again classified into two types, i.e., multiple and straightforward linear regression. A single independent variable is used to predict the single dependent variable, which comes under simple linear regression.

Similarly, more than one independent variable predicts the single dependent variable's value, which comes under multiple linear regression. Here the linear regression method indicates heart disease, an accuracy of 59.3% for training data, 48.84% for testing data. The difference between the accuracy is very high, and it is not suitable for predicting heart data. Hence, the decision tree classifier improves accuracy, which is the better linear regression version.

12.6.2   Decision Tree Classifier

The decision tree algorithm has the human thinking ability to decide easily, and the essential logic behind this decision depends on the tree-like structure. The algorithm of the decision tree classifier has five steps, and, for the prediction of the class of a given dataset, the algorithm starts from the root node of any tree. This method compares the different values of root features or attributes with the exact dataset, comparing the branches and jumps to the next node. The first step is to begin the tree with the root node, which contains the dataset completely. The second step depends on attribute selection measures for finding the best attribute in the dataset. The third step is to divide the complete dataset into subsets with the best attributes. The fourth step is to generate the decision tree nodes. The final step is to generate different decision trees with subsets formed in the third step and continue this process until the classification of the nodes cannot be done, i.e., the leaf node is generated. Here, the decision tree classifier method predicts heart disease, 88.95% for training data and 74.42% for testing data. The difference between the accuracy is very high, and it is not suitable for predicting heart data. Hence, the voting classifier improves accuracy, which is a better version of the decision tree classifier.

The decision tree algorithm has the human thinking ability to decide easily, and the essential logic behind this decision depends on the tree-like structure. The algorithm of the decision tree classifier has five steps, and, for the prediction of the class of a given dataset, the algorithm starts from the root node of any tree. This method compares the different values of root features or attributes with the exact dataset, comparing the branches and jumps to the next node. The first step is to begin the tree with the root node, which contains the dataset completely. The second step depends on attribute selection measures for finding the best attribute in the dataset. The third step is to divide the complete dataset into subsets with the best attributes. The fourth step is to generate the decision tree nodes. The final step is to generate different decision trees with subsets formed in the third step and continue this process until the classification of the nodes cannot be done, i.e., the leaf node is generated. Here, the decision tree classifier method predicts heart disease, 88.95% for training data and 74.42% for testing data. The difference between the accuracy is very high, and it is not suitable for predicting heart data. Hence, the voting classifier improves accuracy, which is a better version of the decision tree classifier.

12.6.3   Voting Classifier

The output of this model will be predicted based on the highest chance of the chosen class appearing at the output. This technique predicts the output class with the largest majority voting by merging many different elements of each classifier supplied into the voting classifier. The fundamental idea behind this model is to develop a single model that trains all of the individual dedicated models to find accuracy and forecast output based on the majority of votes for each output class. This model has two types of voting, the first one is hard voting, and the second one is soft voting. The prediction depends on the highest probability of the class, with the majority of votes coming under the hard voting category. In soft voting, the prognosis of the output depends on the average probability of the given class. In this book chapter, the majority voting technique based ensemble approach is used, which combines different types of multiple classifiers to increase the accuracy. Primarily based on the UCI dataset, the Cleveland coronary heart dataset includes 14 attributes, out of which 8 are specific attributes, and six are numerical attributes, and 303 patient statistics are discovered. Based on the voting classifier output prediction, an ensemble of vulnerable classifiers with sturdy classifiers using the most people voting technique improved the accuracy of vulnerable classifiers to a positive extent. The bagging classifier is chosen to improve accuracy—an accuracy of 84.30% for training data and 79.42% for testing data. The difference between the accuracy is minimal, and it is not suitable for the best prediction of heart data. Hence, the bagging classifier improves accuracy, which is the better version of the voting classifier.

12.6.4   Bagging Classifier

This model is an ensemble-based meta estimator that fits base classifiers on the original subset's random subsets and then aggregates their predictions to form a final prediction. This meta estimator reduces the variance of the decision tree with randomization. This classifier eases the variance by voting, and the drawback is that it increases bias, which reduces variance. It combines the predictions from many decision trees. Another name for the bagging ensemble algorithm is bootstrap aggregation. It works on the bootstrap sample, a dataset sample with replacement, i.e., the sample taken from the dataset is replaced, which allows the sample to be selected again and even multiple times in the new sample. It provides an objective approach to estimating the statistical quantities in the dataset and creating an ensemble-based decision tree model. The bagging algorithm is used to identify the warning signs of heart disease in patients. This method generates multiple versions of any predictor by making bootstrap replicates of learning sets and using these as new learning sets. This book chapter conducted tests on actual and simulated datasets available in the machine learning repository. It used different classification and regression trees with specific subsets of data. The bagging classifier has shown substantial accuracy gains, 97.07% accuracy for training data, and 79.07% accuracy for testing data. The difference between this accuracy is very high; hence, it is not suitable for best heart disease prediction, so we have used the Naïve Bayes method to improve accuracy, which is a better version than the bagging classifier.

12.6.5   Naïve Bayes

One of the supervised learning algorithms depends on the Bayes theorem for solving classification problems for any dataset. Many researchers use this model for text classification, which includes high dimensional training dataset. This model can make quick predictions. This algorithm is comprised of two words, i.e. Naïve and Bayes. Naïve comes because of the assumption that the occurrence of a particular feature is independent of other features. Bayes comes because this model depends on the principles of the Bayes theorem. The main advantages of this model are that it performs well in multiclass predictions. The main disadvantage is that it assumes all features are independent or unrelated to each other so that it cannot learn the relationship between characteristics. In this book chapter, the Naïve Bayes classifiers predict heart disease with the fastest probabilistic classifier, especially for the training phase. The feature selection is a process of removing the irrelevant features from the dataset. This process involves three classes, i.e. filter, wrapper and embedded method. Here the medical dataset is based on types present or absent. This model could classify 79.65% of input instances correctly, and the remaining are incorrect instances. Based on the Naïve Bayes algorithm, diabetic patients with high cholesterol values are in the age group of 45-55, the bodyweight of humans is 60-71, and blood pressure value is 148-230. Furthermore, 79.65% of the accuracy for training data and 81.4% of the testing data are obtained. This accuracy is negligible; hence, it is not suitable for best heart disease prediction, so we have used the logistic regression method to improve accuracy, a better version than the Naïve Bayes classifier.

12.6.6   Logistic Regression

It is also a supervised learning algorithm; it also uses the probability of the target variable to predict the outcome. The dependent variable is always binary. i.e., either 1 or 0. Logistic regression has binary target variables. It can be divided into several categories: binomial, multinomial, ordinal, etc. the logistic regression method can apply to both datasets, i.e., continuous and discrete datasets. It will classify the observations using different data types to find efficient variables. In this book chapter, the logistic regression model is applied to predict heart disease, based on the logistic results if the probability is greater than 0.05, which shows a less statistically significant relationship with the outcome of the dataset. The logistic regression method predicts heart disease, 82.46% for training data, 81.2% for testing data. The difference between the accuracy is shallow, and it is not suitable for predicting heart data. Hence, the extra trees classifier is used to improve accuracy.

12.6.7   Extra Trees Classifier

This method is also an ensemble technique formed by combining multiple decor-related decision trees in the forest to output its classification result. The only difference between random forest and this extra tree classifier is that each decision tree in the different trees' forest is built from the original training sample. Another name of this algorithm is highly randomized trees. It is mainly related to the decision trees such as bootstrap and decision tree algorithms. Here the extra tree classifier method predicts heart disease, 84.3% for training data, 81.2% for testing data. The difference between the accuracy is significantly less, and it is not suitable for predicting heart data. Hence, the KNN improves accuracy, which is the better version of the extra tree classifier.

12.6.8   K-Nearest Neighbor [KNN] Algorithm

The improvement in artificial intelligence or deep learning methods plays a significant role in identifying how people getting heart disease in the earliest stages is possible with the possible da aset. Here, the KNN algorithm is a supervised learning method and initially assumes the similarity between the new data and already available data and puts the new data into the most similar category to the general data categories. It is also called the non-parametric algorithm, i.e. this algorithm does not consider any assumption data. Sometimes it is also called a lazy learner algorithm, i.e., it will not learn from the training dataset immediately; instead, it acts only on the dataset at the time of Classification. The KNN algorithm mainly helps the identification of a category or any class of a particular dataset. It will work by selecting number K of the neighbors and Euclidean distance of number K. Then, take the K nearest neighbors per the already calculated Euclidean distance. This algorithm is preferred only if all the features are continuous. It is also chosen based on its high speed of convergence.

The dataset contains a huge number of features that can be used to predict cardiac disease. The majority of the dataset has noisy characteristics. Any classifier's performance will be lowered when the dataset contains more and more noisy features. In this book chapter, the irrelevant dataset is being removed by cleansing. The features, such as weight, height, and ap_lo, are removed in this scenario the KNN provides the accuracy of 61%. This algorithm provides higher accuracy for higher values of K, the improvement in accuracy was observed from 61% to 65% for values of K from 1 to 5. Apart from the value of K, some other features also play a significant role in the excellent accuracy. The main drawback of the KNN algorithm is with large datasets and more considerable dimensional data. The distance calculation between each data point is complicated for large datasets. The KNN machine learning method predicts heart disease, 87.31% for training data, 81.2% for testing data. The difference between the accuracy is significantly less, and it is not suitable for predicting heart data. Hence, the Adaboost classifier improves accuracy, which is the better version of the extra tree classifier.

12.6.9   Adaboost Classifier

It is also known as an adaptive boosting technique. It is mainly used as an ensemble method in machine learning. The weights of the branches are assigned to every instance. It is also used to reduce the bias and variance in supervised learning. Initially, the number of decision trees is made in the mandatory training period of data boosting. So it was developed for binary Classification and can be used to increase performance. The weak models are added one by one, with the weighted training data used to train them. The process of adding soft models continues until the training dataset can no longer be improved. The weak classifiers' prediction or detection of heart disease is made possible via a weighted average. Boosting is an ensemble language for building a reliable classifier. It creates a model using training data and then creates a second model to rectify the first model's inaccuracy. The AdaBoost classifier is a very short decision tree that uses only a single split, i.e. decision stump. Here the Adaboost classifier method predicts heart disease, 87.31% for training data, 81.2% for testing data. The difference between the accuracy is significantly less, and it is not suitable for predicting heart data. Hence, the LGBM classifier improves accuracy, which is the better version of the Adaboost classifier.

12.6.10   Light Gradient Boost Classifier

This algorithm depends on a decision tree algorithm and can predict the accuracy of heart disease with high accuracy. It is also an open-source library, and it extends the boosting gradient algorithm and provides high, more significant gradients. It can give a high predictive performance for complex data. The ensembles are created using decision tree models, and these trees are added one by one and fit the corrected prediction errors. The gradient boosting method speeds up learning and reduces computational complexity. The LGBM classifier method predicts heart disease, 96.31% for training data, 81.2% for testing data. The difference between the accuracy is very high, and it is not suitable for predicting heart data. Hence, the Gradient Boosting classifier improves accuracy, which is the better version of the Light Gradient Boost classifier.

12.6.11   Gradient Boosting Classifier

This classifier depends on three elements, i.e. loss function, weak learner and additive model. The loss function solves different problems, and the issues may be differentiable or squared errors. The process determines the differentiable loss for the framework. The weak learner is decision trees, and the regression trees are built greedily, with split points depending on purity scores such as Gini. The Additive model is the final component, in which all trees are added one at a time, with no changes to previous trees. It is used to reduce the loss after the trees have been added. The parameters are also minimized, such as coefficients in weights or regression equations in neural networks. The weights are updated automatically to reduce the error. The parameters of the tree depend on functional gradient descent. This classifier depends on four enhancements: tree constraints, random sampling, shrinkage, and penalized learning. The LGBM classifier method predicts heart disease, 100 % for training data, 81.2% for testing data. The difference between the accuracy is very high, and it is not suitable for predicting heart data. Hence, the Stochastic Gradient Descent Algorithm improves accuracy, the better version of the Gradient Boost classifier.

12.6.12   Stochastic Gradient Descent Algorithm

This algorithm is mainly used to find the values of coefficients of a function which reduce the cost function. It is primarily used to search for an optimization algorithm. It is also a supervised learning-based machine learning algorithm and the best way to find the target function which maps input data and output variables. Many algorithms have many representations with different coefficients, and the optimization process is entirely different for machine learning algorithms. The cost function plays a significant role in evaluating the coefficients in any model by prediction calculation and training dataset. It even compares the actual output values predictions and calculates average error. The cost is calculated for each coefficient and can be updated for every dataset with each iteration in the gradient descent algorithm. Each iteration is called a batch, so the other name is called batch gradient descent. The Stochastic Gradient Descent algorithm predicts heart disease, 84.31% for training data and 83.2% for testing data. The difference between the accuracy is significantly less, and it is not suitable for predicting heart data. Hence, the linear support vector classifier improves accuracy, the better version of the stochastic gradient descent algorithm.

12.6.13   Linear Support Vector Classifier

This classifier is like SVC, but the parameter kernel is linear. Sometimes the kernel can be non-linear also. The linear SVC uses one vs the rest classifier wrapper. It performs Classification, and it performs well with a large number of samples. It uses penalty normalization and loss function apart from the support vector classifier algorithm. The Linear support vector classifier method predicts heart disease, 84.31% for training data, 83.2% for testing data. The difference between the accuracy is negligible, and it is not suitable for predicting heart data. Hence, the support vector machine improves accuracy, which is the better version of the linear support vector classifier.

12.6.14   Support Vector Machines

The backing vector machine is a managed learning framework utilized for arrangement and relapse issues. Numerous individuals incredibly prefer backing vector machines as it produces eminent rightness with less calculation power. It is generally used in order issues. We have three sorts of learning: directed, unaided and support learning. A help vector machine is a specific classifier officially characterized by separating the hyperplane. This is the most popular supervised learning algorithm used for regression problems. The main aim is to create the decision boundary of n-dimensional space into new classes. Usually, the decision boundary is called a hyperplane. The support vector machine mainly helps in choosing the vectors to create the hyperplane. The data points that are always close to the hyperplane and affect the hyperplane's position are termed a support vector. These hyperplanes are decision boundaries and can be helped in the Classification of data points. The support vector machine is classified into two types, i.e., linear and non-linear. The linear support vector machine mainly separates the data into linear wise, called a linear SVM classifier.

Similarly, the nonlinear SVM is primarily used for nonlinearly separated data. The Support vector machine predicts heart disease, 89.31% for training data and 83.2% for testing data. The difference between the accuracy is significantly less, and it is not suitable for predicting heart data. Hence, the Gaussian process classification algorithm improves accuracy, which is the better version of the support vector machine.

12.6.15   Gaussian Process Classification

Gaussian processes are mostly generalized to the probability distribution. It is used for complicated non-parametric machine learning algorithms. This Classification is the type of kernel model and can predict the probabilities of the class. The Gaussian process classifier method predicts heart disease, 99.31% for training data, 83.2% for testing data. The difference between the accuracy is very high, and it is not suitable for predicting heart data. Hence, the random forest classifier improves accuracy, the better version of the Gaussian process classification.

12.6.16   Random Forest Classifier

Random Forest is a well-known artificial intelligence calculation that is used in the implemented learning approach. In machine learning, it is commonly used for both classification and regression problems. It is based on the concept of gathering realization, which is a cycle of combining multiple classifiers to deal with an unforeseen situation and work on the model's exhibition. Random Forest is a classifier that uses the normal to operate on the prescient precision and contains numerous choice trees on different subsets of that dataset, as the name suggests. Instead of depending on one choice tree, the arbitrary backwoods take the expectation from each tree and because of the more significant part votes of forecasts, it predicts the final output. The more prominent number of trees in the timberland prompts higher exactness and forestalls the issue of overfitting. Since the random forest consolidates numerous trees to foresee the class of the dataset, it is conceivable that some decision trees may anticipate the correct output while others may not. In any case, together, every one of the trees foresees a suitable yield. In this manner, beneath are two suspicions for a superior Random Forest classifier. The Random Forest classifier method predicts heart disease, 83.31% for training data, 86.2% for testing data. The difference between the accuracy is significantly less, and it is not suitable for predicting heart data.

12.7   Evaluation Metrics

Different performance metrics were utilized to determine the Machine Learning model's efficiency, shown in Table 12.5. Table 12.5 shows three parameters and their formulas accuracy, recall. and RMSE. Figure 12.8 shows the comparison of 20 different machine learning models.

Feature importance is a technique that refers the score to certain input features and tells the user about predicting a target variable. Depending on the algorithm, many types of features are essential concerning variable parameters such as correlation scores, decision trees, and essential scores, which helps in improving the efficiency of the heart disease model. The feature importance score will provide high insight into the heart dataset and the most relevant feature to the target. The feature importance also helps predict the specific model and improves the model's accuracy. Figure 12.9 shows the feature importance of the variables used to predict heart disease.

Figure 12.10 shows the recall criteria for twenty machine learning algorithms, plotted for training and testing data. It is also called sensitivity. This performance parameter measured the patients with cardiovascular disease and diagnosed the deep learning model as having heart stroke. The patients with true positives and false negatives are actual positives, considering cardiovascular disease is true positives. The proposed deep neural network method and linear regression model have high recall value regarding other algorithms. The Gaussian process classification, gradient

Table 12.5 Performance metrics used for efficiency calculation in machine learning models.

Name	Description
Accuracy	$(TP + TN)/$ $(TP + TN) + (FP + FN)$
Recall (re)	$(TP)/(TP + FN)$
RMSE	$\Sigma. \left\lvert (xi - xi^\wedge)^2 \right\rvert$

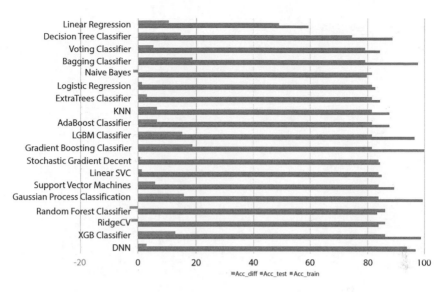

Figure 12.8 Comparison of 20 different models for accuracy of testing, training data.

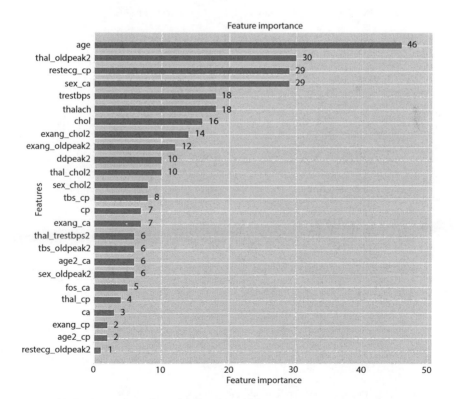

Figure 12.9 Feature importance of different variables.

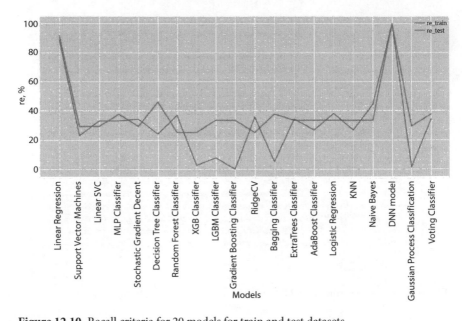

Figure 12.10 Recall criteria for 20 models for train and test datasets.

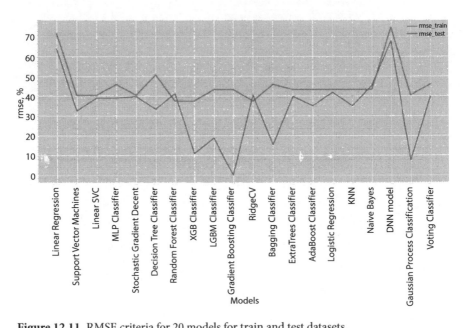

Figure 12.11 RMSE criteria for 20 models for train and test datasets.

Table 12.6 Detailed comparison of existing methods using heart disease dataset.

References	Year	Classification used	Evaluation metrics
Khemphila et al. [14]	2011	Multilayer perceptron with backpropagation machine learning	Accuracy: Training: 89.56%, Testing: 80.99%
Soni et al. [15]	2011	Weighted associative classifier	Accuracy: 81%
Ghwanmeh et al. [16]	2013	Artificial neural network	Accuracy: 92%
Santhanam et al. [17]	2013	Feed forward neural network	Accuracy: 95.2%
Ajam et al. [18]	2015	Feed forward back propagation neural network	Accuracy: 88%
Olaniyi et al. [19]	2015	Feed forward multilayer perceptron	Accuracy: Training: 85%, Testing: 87%
Roostaee et al. [20]	2016	Support vector machine	Accuracy: 84.4%
Karthikeyan et al. [21]	2017	Deep belief network	Accuracy: 90%
Silvia priscila et al. [22]	2017	Support vector machine with recursive feature elimination	Accuracy: 85.6%

(Continued)

Table 12.6 Detailed comparison of existing methods using heart disease dataset. (*Continued*)

References	Year	Classification used	Evaluation metrics
Kishore *et al.* [23]	2018	Adaptive neuro-fuzzy	Accuracy: 94.1%
Latha *et al.* [24]	2019	Ensemble classifiers	Accuracy: 85.4%
Ahmed *et al.* [25]	2019	Decision tree	Accuracy:92.8%
Tuli *et al.* [26]	2019	Deep learning	Accuracy: 89%
Proposed method	**2021**	**Deep Neural network architecture**	**Accuracy:** Training: **97%**, Testing: **94%**

boosting classifier and bagging classifier has significantly less recall value for the training dataset.

Similarly, the deep learning neural network model has a very high recall value for testing datasets concerning other algorithms. The recall value is almost flat for 17 models, and it does not impact performance because the data is not predicted accurately by 17 models. The most negligible value is noticed in the decision tree classifier machine learning model.

Figure 12.11 shows the RMSE criteria for 20 machine learning algorithms, plotted for training and testing data. The thumb rule represents it. The RMSE normal range is around 0.2 and 0.5, i.e., if the model produces a value between 0.2 and 0.5, that model will predict the data accurately. The proposed deep neural network method and linear regression model have high RMSE values with other algorithms. The Gaussian process classification, gradient boosting classifier and bagging classifier has significantly less RMSE value for the training dataset. Similarly, the deep learning neural network model has a very high recall value for testing datasets concerning other algorithms. The RMSE value is almost 0.4 for the other 15 models, which means data are not predicted accurately. The Ridge CV classifier machine learning model notices the most negligible value. Table 12.6 shows that the comparison of conventional machine learning methods accuracy to the proposed system.

Figure 12.9 shows the feature importance of variables used for heart disease prediction. Figure 12.10 shows the plot of recall for 20 different models for train and test datasets. Deep learning neural network shows the highest re value with maximum accuracy. Similarly, Figure 12.11 shows the plot of RMSE values for different machine learning methods and deep learning neural networks. Our paper investigates the various works on machine learning and deep learning techniques to predict the different types of cardiovascular diseases. The feature selection can improve the accuracy, and vital tasks, i.e., the relevant and irrelevant, can be identified for the proposed system. The neural network is a training method and can predict the relationship between input and output values. It used the backpropagation algorithm as support to predict the disease accurately.

12.8   Conclusion

According to the World Health Organization, nearly 32% of global deaths are heart disease. The crucial health problem in society is a heart attack, and this article has used machine learning methods and deep learning. This deep learning method predicts heart disease prediction and compares it with other strategies for different datasets. An efficient and accurate forecast of heart disease is needed. Various ML methods and neural network-based architecture help find the feature selection and precise prediction. This book chapter uses the ensemble-based framework deep learning model and feature selection to improve accuracy. We have obtained an accuracy of 94% by using three layers of neural networks. This book chapter explains the different machine learning models and deep learning neural network models to predict heart disease with the UCI Cleveland dataset. Each machine learning model is explained briefly, and its outcome is compared with other models. We have obtained high accuracy of about 97% by using the deep learning neural network model, the performance parameters used. In this simulation environment are recall, RMSE, and confusion matrix to obtain the accuracy calculation.

References

1. Carroll, W. and Miller, G. E. Heart Disease among Elderly Americans: Estimates for the U.S. Civilian Noninstitutionalized Population, 2010. Statistical Brief #409. Agency for Healthcare Research and Quality, Rockville, MD, June 2013. http://www.meps.ahrq.gov/mepsweb/data_files/publications/st409/stat409.shtml

2. Kirubha, V. and Priya, S.M., Survey on data mining algorithms in disease prediction. *Int. J. Comput. Trend. Technol.*, 38, 3, 124–128, 2016.

3. Chandra, P. and Deekshatulu, B.L., Prediction of risk score for heart disease using associative Classification and hybrid feature subset selection, in: *2012 12th International Conference on Intelligent Systems Design and Applications (ISDA)*, IEEE, pp. 628–634, 2012, November.

4. Sultana, M., Haider, A., Uddin, M.S., Analysis of data mining techniques for heart disease prediction, in: *2016 3rd international conference on electrical engineering and information communication technology (ICEEICT)*, IEEE, pp. 1– 5, 2016, September.

5. Deekshatulu, B.L. and Chandra, P., Classification of heart disease using k-nearest neighbor and genetic algorithm. *Proc. Technol.*, 10, 2013, 85–94, 2013.

6. Yogeswaran, M. and Ponnambalam, S.G., An extensive review of research in swarm robotics. In V. Pai, C. Rajendran, & A. Carvalho (Eds.), *Proceedings of the 2009 World Congress on Nature & Biologically Inspired Computing* (Vol. 1, pp. 140–145), Institute of Electrical and Electronics Engineers (IEEE), 2009.

7. Lakshmi, T.M., Martin, A., Begum, R.M., Venkatesan, V.P., An analysis on performance of decision tree algorithms using student's qualitative data. *Int. J. Mod. Educ. Comput. Sci.*, 5, 5, 18–27, 2013.

8. Sharma, P. and Bhartiya, A.P.R., Implementation of decision tree algorithm to analysis the performance. *Int. J. Adv. Res. Comput. Commun. Eng.*, 1, 10, 861–864, 2012.

9. Srivastava, D.K. and Bhambhu, L., Data classification using support vector machine. *J. Theor. Appl. Inf. Technol.*, 12, 1, 1–7, 2009.

10. Bhatia, N. and Author, C., Survey of nearest neighbor techniques. *Int. J. Comput. Sci. Inf. Secur., (IJCSIS)*, 8, 2, 302–305, 2010.

11. Schmidhuber, J., Deep learning in neural networks: An overview. *Neural Netw.*, 61, 85–117, 2015.

12. Hochreiter, S. and Urgen Schmidhuber, J., Long short-term memory. *Neural Comput.*, 9, 8, 1735–1780, 1997.

13. Palaniappan, S. and Awang, R., Intelligent heart disease prediction system using data mining techniques. *2008 IEEE/ACS International Conference on Computer Systems and Applications*, pp. 108–115, 2008.

14. Khemphila, A. and Boonjing, V., Heart disease classification using neural network and feature selection, in: *2011 21st International Conference on Systems Engineering*, IEEE, pp. 406–409, 2011, August.

15. Soni, J., Ansari, U., Sharma, D., Soni, S., Predictive data mining for medical diagnosis: An overview of heart disease prediction. *Int. J. Comput. Appl.*, 17, 8, 43–48, 2011.

16. Ghwanmeh, S., Mohammad, A., Al-Ibrahim, A., Innovative artificial neural networks-based decision support system for heart diseases diagnosis. JILSA, 5, 3, Article ID:35396,1–8, 2013.

17. Santhanam, T. and Ephzibah, E.P., Heart disease classification using PCA and feed forward neural networks, in: *Mining Intelligence and Knowledge Exploration*, pp. 90–99, Springer, Cham, 2013.

18. Ajam, N., Heart diseases diagnoses using artificial neural network. *Int. J. Complex Syst.*, 5, 4, 7–10, 2015.

19. Olaniyi, E.O., Oyedotun, O.K., Adnan, K., Heart diseases diagnosis using neural networks arbitration. *Int. J. Intell. Syst. Appl.*, 7, 12, 72, 2015.

20. Roostaee, S. and Ghaffary, H.R., Diagnosis of heart disease based on meta heuristic algorithms and clustering methods. *J. Electr. Comput. Eng. Innov. (JECEI)*, 4, 2, 105–110, 2016.

21. Karthikeyan, . and Kanimozhi, V., Deep learning approach for prediction of heart disease using data mining classification algorithm deep belief approach. *Int. J. Adv. Res. Sci., Eng. Technol.*, 4, 3194–3201, 2017.

22. Priscila, S.S. and Hemalatha, M., Improving the performance of entropy ensembles of neural networks (EENNS) on Classification of heart disease prediction. *Int. J. Pure Appl. Math.*, 117, 7, 371–386, 2017.

23. Nandhu Kishore, A.H. and Jayanthi, V.E., Neuro-fuzzy based medical decision support system for coronary artery disease diagnosis and risk level prediction. *J. Comput. Theor. Nanosci.*, 15, 1027–1037, 2018.

24. Latha, C.B.C. and Jeeva, S.C., Improving the accuracy of prediction of heart disease risk based on ensemble classification techniques. *Inform. Med. Unlocked*, 16, 100203, 2019.

25. Ahmed, H., Younis, E.M.G., Hendawi, A., Ali, A.A., Heart disease identification from patients' social posts, machine learning solution on Spark. *Futur. Gener. Comput. Syst.*, 111, 714–722, 2020.

26. Tuli, S., Basumatary, N., Gill, S.S., Kahani, M., Arya, R.C., Wander, G.S., Buyya, R., HealthFog: An ensemble deep learning based smart healthcare system for automatic diagnosis of heart diseases in integrated IoT and fog computing environments. *Futur. Generation Comput. Syst.*, 104, 187–200, 2020.

27. Rani, P., Kumar, R., Jain, A., Multistage model for accurate prediction of missing values using imputation methods in heart disease dataset, in: *Innovative Data Communication Technologies and Application*, pp. 637–653, Springer, Singapore, 2021.

28. Doppala, B.P., Bhattacharyya, D., Chakkravarthy, M., Kim, T.-H., A hybrid machine learning approach to identify coronary diseases using feature selection mechanism on heart disease dataset. *Distrib. Parallel Database*, 2021. https://doi.org/10.1007/s10619-021-07329-

29. Bharti, R., Khamparia, A., Shabaz, M., Dhiman, G., Pande, S., Singh, P., Prediction of heart disease using a combination of machine learning and deep learning. *Comput. Intell. Neurosci.*, 2021, 8387680, 11, 2021.

30. Jebakumar, A.Z. and Ravanan, R., A novel machine learning approaches for heart disease dataset. *Elementary Educ. Online*, 20, 5, 7391–7400, 2021.

31. Selvi, R. and Muthulakshmi, I., An optimal artificial neural network based big data application for heart disease diagnosis and classification model. *J. Ambient Intell. Humaniz. Comput.*, 12, 6, 6129–6139, 2021.

32. Rani, P., Kumar, R., Ahmed, N.M., Jain, A., A decision support system for heart disease prediction based upon machine learning. *J. Reliab. Intell. Environ.*, 7, 3, 263–275, 2021.

33. Kavitha, M., Gnaneswar, G., Dinesh, R., Rohith Sai, Y., Sai Suraj, R., Heart disease prediction using hybrid machine learning model, in: *2021 6th International Conference on Inventive Computation Technologies (ICICT)*, IEEE, pp. 1329–1333, 2021.

34. Pavithra, M., Sindhana, A.M., Subajanaki, T., Mahalakshmi, S., Effective heart disease prediction systems using data mining techniques. *Ann. Romanian Soc. Cell Biol.*, 25, 3, 6566–6571, 2021.

35. Ghosh, P., Azam, S., Jonkman, M., Karim, A., Javed Mehedi Shamrat, F.M., Ignatious, E., Shultana, S., Beeravolu, A.R., De Boer, F., Efficient prediction of cardiovascular disease using machine learning algorithms with relief and LASSO feature selection techniques. *IEEE Access*, 9, 19304–19326, 2021.

36. Hossain, M.E., Uddin, S., Khan, A., Network analytics and machine learning for predictive risk modelling of cardiovascular disease in patients with type 2 diabetes. *Expert Syst. Appl.*, 164, 113918, 2021.

37. Jiang, H., Mao, H., Lu, H., Lin, P., Garry, W., Lu, H., Yang, G., Chen, X., Machine learning-based models to support decision-making in emergency department triage for patients with suspected cardiovascular disease. *Int. J. Med. Inform.*, 145, 104326, 2021.

38. Pollard, J.D., Haq, K.T., Lutz, K.J., Rogovoy, N.M., Paternostro, K.A., Soliman, E.Z., Maher, J., Lima, J.A.C., Musani, S.K., Tereshchenko, L.G., Electrocardiogram machine learning for detection of cardiovascular disease in African Americans: the Jackson Heart Study. *Eur. Heart J. Digit. Health*, 2, 1, 137–151, 2021.

39. Jiang, Y., Zhang, X., Ma, R., Wang, X., Liu, J., Keerman, M., Yan, Y. *et al.*, Cardiovascular disease prediction by machine learning algorithms based on cytokines in Kazakhs of China. *Clin. Epidemiol.*, 13, 417, 2021.

40. Chu, H., Chen, L., Yang, X., Qiu, X., Qiao, Z., Song, X., Zhao, E., Zhou, J., Zhang, W., Mehmood, A., Pan, H., Yang, Y., Roles of anxiety and depression in predicting cardiovascular disease among patients with type 2 diabetes mellitus: A machine learning approach. *Front. Psychol.*, 12, 645418, 2021. https://doi.org/10.3389/fpsyg.2021.645418

41. Rubini, P.E., Subasini, C.A., Vanitha Katharine, A., Kumaresan, V., Kumar, S.G., Nithya, T.M., A cardiovascular disease prediction using machine learning algorithms. *Ann. Romanian Soc. Cell Biol.*, 25, 2, 904–912, 2021.

42. Sajeev, S., Champion, S., Beleigoli, A., Chew, D., Reed, R.L., Magliano, D.J., Shaw, J.E. *et al.*, Predicting Australian adults at high risk of cardiovascular disease mortality using standard risk factors and machine learning. *Int. J. Environ. Res. Public Health*, 18, 6, 3187, 2021.

43. Kim, M., Kim, Y.J., Park, S.J., Kim, K.G., Oh, P.C., Kim, Y.S., Kim, E.Y., Machine learning models to identify low adherence to influenza vaccination among Korean adults with cardiovascular disease. *BMC Cardiovasc. Disord.*, 21, 1, 1–8, 2021.

44. Angelaki, E., Maria, E., Marketou, G.D., Barmparis, A.P., Vardas, P.E., Parthenakis, F., Tsironis, G.P., Detection of abnormal left ventricular geometry in patients without cardiovascular disease through machine learning: An ECG-based approach. *J. Clin. Hypertens.*, 235, 935–945, 2021.

45. Al-Absi, H.R.H., Refaee, M.A., Rehman, A.U., Islam, M.T., Belhaouari, S.B., Alam, T., Risk factors and comorbidities associated to cardiovascular disease in Qatar: A machine learning based case-control study. *IEEE Access*, 9, 29929–29941, 2021.

46. Allan, S., Olaiya, R., Burhan, R., Reviewing the use and quality of machine learning in developing clinical prediction models for cardiovascular disease. *Postgrad. Med. J.*, 2021.

47. Kim, J.O.R., Jeong, Y.-S., Kim, J.H., Lee, J.-W., Kim, H.-S., Machine learning-based cardiovascular disease prediction model: A cohort study on the Korean national health insurance service health screening database. *Diagnostics*, 11, 6, 943, 2021.

48. Uddin, M.N. and Halder, R.K., An ensemble method based multilayer dynamic system to predict cardiovascular disease using machine learning approach. *Inform. Med. Unlocked*, 24, 100584, 2021.

49. Joshi, A., Rienks, M., Theofilatos, K., Mayr, M., Systems biology in cardiovascular disease: A multiomics approach. *Nat. Rev. Cardiol.*, 18, 5, 313–330, 2021.

50. Sun, W., Zhang, P., Wang, Z., Li, D., Prediction of cardiovascular diseases based on machine learning. *ASP Trans. Internet Things*, 1, 1, 30–35, 2021.

51. Garg, H., Machine Learning techniques for cardiovascular disease, in: *IOP Conference Series: Materials Science and Engineering*, vol. 1116, IOP Publishing, p. 012140, 2021.

52. Telagam, N. and Kandasamy, N., Review of the medical Internet of Things-based RFID security protocols, in: *Nanoelectronic Devices for Hardware and Software Security*, pp. 163–178, CRC Press, 2021. https://doi.org/10.1201/9781003126645

53. Nagarjuna, T., Overview of THz applications, in: *Advanced Indium Arsenide-Based HEMT Architectures for Terahertz Applications*, vol. 45, 2021.

54. Telagam, N., Ajitha, D., Kandasamy, N., Review on hardware attacks and security challenges in IoT edge nodes, in: *Security of Internet of Things Nodes: Challenges, Attacks, and Countermeasures*, p. 211, 2021.

55. Dioline, S., Arunkumar, M., Dinesh, V., Nagarjuna, T., Karuppanan, S., Radiology: Clinical trials implemented by composite test-beds via MVDR beamformer system. *Materials Today: Proceedings*, 2021.

56. Gantala, A., Telagam, N., Kumar, G.V., Anjaneyulu, P., Prasad, R.M., Content-based image retrieval using genetic algorithm retrieval effectiveness in terms of precision and recall. *J. Adv. Res. Dyn. Control Syst.*, 9, 18, 2020–2028, 2017.

13

Machine Learning: The Capabilities and Efficiency of Computers in Life Sciences

Shalini Yadav[1], Saurav Yadav[1], Shobhit Prakash Srivastava[1], Saurabh Kumar Gupta[2] and Sudhanshu Mishra[3]*

[1]Dr. M.C. Saxena College of Pharmacy, Lucknow, Uttar Pradesh, India
[2]Rameshwaram Institute of Technology and Management, Lucknow, Uttar Pradesh, India
[3]Department of Pharmaceutical Science & Technology, Madan Mohan Malaviya University of Technology, Gorakhpur, Uttar Pradesh, India

Abstract

Machine learning is an artificial intelligence branch that includes computers to learn progressively from examples, data, and experience. It is a technique for teaching computers how to manage data more effectively. Machine learning's key aim is to teach machines how to solve problems using data or background knowledge. It is becoming more common as outcome of the abundance of datasets available. Artificial intelligence is a field of research that aspires to give machines the capability to learn and acquire to certain behaviors in the same way that humans do. Neo-cognition, an Artificial Neuron Network (ANN), is the source of deep learning. An artificial neural network (ANN) is a linked network of processing units that mimics the brain's network of neurons. Deep learning is a concept for training multilayer ANNs with minimal data. To compare machine learning and deep learning, consider this: a machine learning algorithm will learn parts of the face, such as the eyes and nose for a face recognition task, while a deep learning algorithm will learn extra features, such as the distance between the eyes and the

**Corresponding author*: msudhanshu22@gmail.com
Shalini Yadav: ORCID: 0000-0001-6667-3935
Saurav Yadav: ORCID: 0000-0002-0521-1339
Shobhit Prakash Srivastava: ORCID: 0000-0002-9744-0875
Saurabh Kumar Gupta: ORCID: 0000-0003-0431-4106
Sudhanshu Mishra: ORCID: 0000-0001-5009-4736

Rishabha Malviya, Gheorghita Ghinea, Rajesh Kumar Dhanaraj, Balamurugan Balusamy and Sonali Sundram (eds.) Deep Learning for Targeted Treatments: Transformation in Healthcare, (407–430) © 2022 Scrivener Publishing LLC

length of the nose. Machine learning is used in a variety of fields, from medicine to the military, to extract relevant data. Machine learning has the potential to support potentially revolutionary developments in a variety of fields as the field grows, with important social and economic implications. Machine learning is being used in healthcare to develop applications the ability to learn and adapt to physicians in providing more reliable or efficient diagnoses for specific elements through advanced research that improves decision-making.

Keywords: Machine learning, artificial intelligence, deep learning, artificial neuron network (ANN)

13.1   Introduction

Machine Learning as a Scientific Discipline

For the past decade, statistical estimate models' dismal performance outcomes have swamped the estimating field [1]. Due to their failure to manage categorical data, deal with missing data points, spread of data points, and, most crucially, lack of reasoning abilities, the number of researches utilizing non-traditional methodologies such as machine learning is assisting much in this regard [2]. It's a sub-discipline of artificial intelligence that allows machines that can learn from their mistakes and examples in the same way that people do, and to discover fascinating patterns without having to be programmed. The algorithm is fed data, which is then used to create a model. It can forecast new values using this model. It assists us in locating something unfamiliar to us, which may lead to the discovery of many new things [3].

By definition, machine learning is considered to be the subset of computer science that arose from artificial intelligence research into pattern recognition and computational learning theory. Machine learning systems may undertake difficult tasks instead of just pre-programming by learning from data by enabling computers to accomplish certain jobs intelligently [4].

Machine learning has made significant advancements in the last few years, expanding its capabilities across a wide range of applications. Machine learning algorithms can now be trained on a vast pool of instances thanks to increased data availability, and their analytical skills have been bolstered by increased computer processing power. There have been statistical advancements within the sector, giving machine learning more strength. As a result of these advancements, computers that performed considerably below human levels only a few years ago can now surpass humans at some tasks [5].

Many individuals today engage with machine learning-based systems on a periodic basis, such as social network photo identification schemes, speech processing platforms used by virtual agents, and online store systems for advocacy. Machine learning has the ability to assist potentially transformational advancements as the discipline evolves, with substantial social and economic Implications. Machine learning is currently in use in healthcare to develop algorithms that can assist clinicians in making more accurate or effective diagnosis for specific ailments.

Three abilities are required when machine learning systems grow increasingly prevalent or important in specific sectors. To begin with, as most people's daily encounters with machine information become the paradigm, a fundamental grasp of how data and these systems are used will become a crucial skill for individuals of all ages and backgrounds. This may be ensured by introducing essential ideas in machine learning at a young age. Second, new methods to build a pool of knowledgeable users or practitioners are required to guarantee that a variety of industries and professions have the tendency to accumulate machine learning and implement in its activities that will enhance them. Third, more assistance is required to develop sophisticated machine learning capabilities [6]. Machine learning algorithms are capable of excelling at specialized tasks. It may be utilized to supplement human duties in various circumstances. Even though it is evident that advances in machine learning will have an impact on workplace, forecasting how it might eventuate seems challenging, and projections from prior studies vary widely. Figure 13.1 shows the comparison between traditional programming and machine learning.

Machine learning is required in the following scenarios:

- Human expertise isn't available.
- Humans are unable to articulate their knowledge.
- The solution must be customized to the circumstances.
- The severity of the problem is too large for our limited reasoning powers.

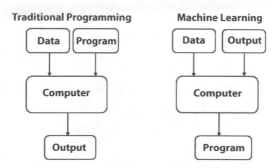

Figure 13.1 Comparison between traditional and machine learning [7].

13.2   Supervised Learning

The machine learning classified in various types (shown in Figure 13.2) like supervised learning. Algorithms that require external aid are known as supervised machine learning algorithms. The resources for training and testing are separated from the input dataset. From input to output, an algorithm can generate a function. If we have results data, we need to predict, we use it. Data is divided into two categories: training data and test data. It examines the training data and generates an inferred function that may be used to map test data for classification or prediction [10].

13.2.1   Workflow of Supervised Learning

Summarized below in Figure 13.3.
   Here are three most frequently used approaches for supervised learning.

13.2.2   Decision Tree

Decision Tree Induction is among the predominant supervised learning tools and methodologies of machine learning. In several domains, such as identification with character, geospatial, drug delivery, knowledge-based systems and information retrieval. Decision Tree classification systems can be effective, to mention only a couple. It employs the method of division and conquest. The structure is of a tree kind with an internal node, branches and leaf nodes (Figure 13.4). The root node signifies the largest information attribute. Branches indicate the outcome of the internal node test and the class label indicates the leaf node. The tree where the class label accepts actual values is referred to as a regression tree and the class label is

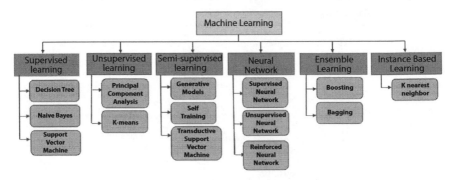

Figure 13.2 Machine learning and their types [8, 9].

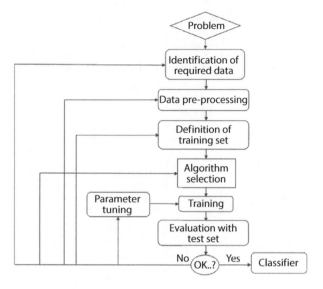

Figure 13.3 Supervised learning workflow [10].

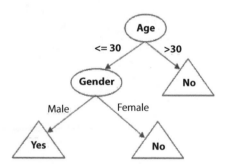

Figure 13.4 Decision tree.

referred to as a classification tree. Benefits and downsides of decision tree is summarized below in Table 13.1 [11].

13.2.3   Support Vector Machine (SVM)

Support vector machine is another of the approach extensively utilized advanced machine learning methods. It is used mostly to classify. In the margin calculation principle, SVM operates. It draws margins among the classes, essentially. Input variables are taken into consideration and a hyperplane is given as an output to categorizes fresh cases. We must divide

Table 13.1 Decision tree benefits and downsides are.

Benefits	Downsides
i. You can grasp this very easily.	i. Complexity: The large tree can get complex with plenty of data.
ii. Handles categorical as well as numerical data.	ii. Cost: Increasing complexity might result in higher costs.
iii. Data preparation is not necessary.	iii. Instability: Modifying data or variables might cause the entire tree to beredrawn.

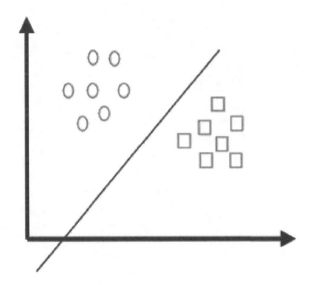

Figure 13.5 Hyperplane to separate circle and square.

Table 13.2 SVM's benefits and drawbacks are.

Benefits	Drawback
i. It works well even if there are very huge numbers of characteristics. It scales to high dimensional data reasonably well.	i. It's not a simple process to choose asuitable kernel function.
ii. Since SVM is built on the kernel it canmodel complicated situations in the actual world.	ii. If the dataset is huge, a long trainingperiod is necessary.

circles and squares, for example as indicated in Figure 13.5 below. SVM draws just one line between these two [12]. SVMs benefits and drawbacks are summarized below in Table 13.2.

13.2.4   Naive Bayes

The texting business is Naive Bayes' principal purpose. It is used mostly for Clumping and categorization purposes. It's grounded on the Bayes

Table 13.3 Various other machine learning method with their features, advantages and their disadvantages [14–16].

Methods	Elucidation	Advantages	Disadvantages
Regularization	Penalize calculators with more variables, particularly linked variables, for reducing overfitting (multicollinearity).	• Yields more (simple) parsimonious estimators. • Enhances generalization. • Contributes tosteady resultssmaller modifications of estimator choices less sensitive.	• Can choose the "worst" predictor if numerous strongly linked predictors are available. • Increases computer complexity.
Deep learning: neural networks	A set of data transformations thatinfluence the inputs to the nextseries of transformations through several layersof transformations and which finallyproduce abstraction/ generalization from the data.	• Can assist to forecast results with extremely complicated nonlinear linkages and interactions. • The danger ofresult from excessively huge and noisy and nontabular	• High computer power required.

probability hypothesis. The idea works that all characteristics are mutually independent. We can categorize the fresh samples based on training data and training data attributes [13]. For instance, if we wish to identify men and women on the basis of the colors of the hair, the height, the eye color, etc. Various other categories along with their description, advantages and disadvantages are described below there in Table 13.3.

13.3   Deep Learning: A New Era of Machine Learning

The foundations of deep learning are Neocognitron; Kunihiko's Fukushima presented the Artificial Neuron Network (ANN) in 1980 [17]. You ought to understand how a neuron operates to comprehend the neural network. A neuron contains four primary components: dendrites, nuclides, cytoplasm, and axonal. Electrical impulses are sent to the dendrites. Soma processes the electrical signal. The process output is transported by the axon to the dendrite terminals, where the output is delivered to the following neuron. The core of the neuron is the nucleus (Portrait below in Figure 13.6).

Deep neural networks (DNNs) are a collection of techniques used to develop sophisticated learning systems; they are also called Artificial Neural Network (ANN) [18]. It (ANN) works in three different tiers. Enter the input layer (much like dendrites). The covered layer processes the entry (like soma and axon). Finally, the output layer transmits the output computed (like dendrite terminals) (shown below in Figure 13.7).

Deep learning is a way to use little data for training multi- (this is why the phrase "deep") ANN. That's why ANN has returned to the game. For example, a profound learning algorithm might learn additional functions, such as proximity of nose and eyes, if a hidden layer learns facial features, eyes and nose for facial identification. By using the example, we compare machine learning to deep learning. Therefore, the deep step from Shallow Learning Algorithms is important [19].

DNNs encompass a wide variety of neural architectures, the most famous being [20]:

- Neural Networks Recurring (NNR)—a network of neurons sending each other feedback signals.
- Convolutional Neural Networks (CNN)—a feed forward ANN generally for visual and image recognition coevolutionary neural networks.

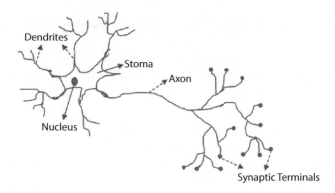

Figure 13.6 A neuron.

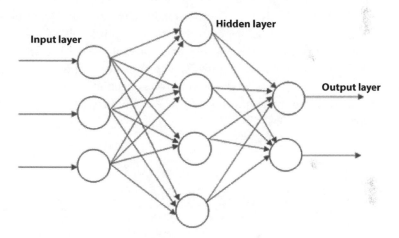

Figure 13.7 Structure of an artificial neural networks (ANNs).

The following are the application of profound learning [21].

- Recognition of optical character for example, to scan a picture and extract text from it.
- Acknowledgement of speech, e.g., generate voice text from the sound clip textual representation.
- Artificial intelligence, e.g., robotic surgery
- Automotive technologies, e.g., self-driving cars
- Governance and security apparatus, e.g., drones

13.4   Deep Learning in Artificial Intelligence (AI)

A new machine study topic, designed to bring machine study reasonably close to a basic objective: artificial intelligence. Profound erudition is the basic degree of efforts to accomplish this aim. It's used in visual acuity, linguistic acknowledgement, entertainment, organizations, selections, healthcare facilities, aviation and language understanding [22].

The word AI has a variety of connotations, from particular kinds of AI, such machine learning, to the hypothetical AI which fits awareness and sensitivity criteria [23]. The Oxford English Dictionary begins with a formal definition of AI: "The ability of computers or other devices to display or mimic intelligent behavior; this is the topic of research [24]. " The emerging field of science and technology is the Artificial Intelligence (AI) (Figure 13.8). It already includes numerous human activities, from people to social organizations, businesses and nations, at all levels of society. In practically every industrial, economic and societal area, AI is spreading fast from IT to trade, manufacturing to space, remote sensing, security and military services, to transport and cars and has been effective at medicine and healthcare since the beginning of the 21st century [25, 26] (summarized below in Table 13.4).

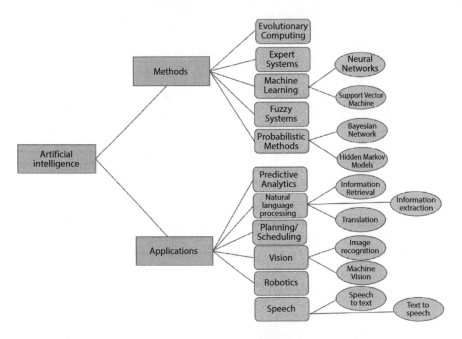

Figure 13.8 A outline of the areas of artificial intelligence.

Table 13.4 Benchmarks examples of AI applications for various groups [29–32].

User groups	Class	Examples of applications	Technology
Patients and Families	Aid of health control/risk assessment.	• Tablet applications, smartphones and webpages. • Devices and wearables.	Machine learning, natural language processing (NLP), Acceptance of speech, chatbots.
	Preventing and managing diseases.	• Preventing and managingdiabetes. • Support formental andemotional health. • Reduction of obesity.	Conversational AI, NLP, Acceptance ofspeech, chatbots.
	Management of drugs	• Adherence to medicines.	Robotic home telehealth.
Teams of clinicians	Tools for early detection, diagnostics and prediction.	• Cardiac arrhythmia, retinopathy imaging. • Screening of early cancer (e.g., melanoma)	Machine Learning

Generally, AI systems range from those which attempts to precisely model human reasoning to resolve a problem, to those which ignore human reasoning and use large amounts of data to generate a framework for responding to interest questions, to those which try to include aspects of human intelligence without exact modelling of the human process [27, 28].

13.5 Using ML to Enhance Preventive and Treatment Insights

ML, given the vast volumes of data coming from multiple sources (e.g., research and research, development, physicians and clinics, non-physician medical staff, wearables, patients, etc.), In the world of healthcare, it has become a rapidly expanding trend business. ML can assist develop ways to collect and analyze this data more successfully in order to prevent disease more efficiently and improve treatment of people and communities [33].

In healthcare, machine learning may contribute with enhanced analytics, which improve decision making to give more accurate diagnostics and more efficient healthcare services [34].

This role can be shown by a breast cancer diagnosis. Breast cancer diagnoses often entail a tissue sample examination by pathologists, in which physicians seek for particular characteristics which signal disease presence or extent. By detecting and utilizing elements of an image that were likely to be associated, but had not previously been employed in pathological evaluations, a machine learning scheme trained on tissue imagery has achieved more precision than pathologists. This helped doctors to estimate a patient's prognosis more precisely. There are many additional approaches of machine learning that can benefit doctors in making decisions. One is the processing of natural languages machine learning that enables computers to access documented or vocal content [35, 36].

Forwards, the potential to support physicians using machine learning algorithms is considerable. Tasks like the extraction of functions from complex information sets such as image data, ECGs and other surveillance devices, or the exploration of configurations for wellness or ailments among medical history individuals, portable sensors, or the combination of relevant information to reach diagnosis and hospitalization options are all suitable to mechanical approaches for learning [37–40].

13.6   Different Additional Emergent Machine Learning Uses

13.6.1   Education

In education machine learning may assist teaching people construct personalized learning plans for individual students and do certain regular task modes of delivery of educational materials, especially in the online context [41]. An application that uses machine education to assist teachers study students' papers effectively is being developed, for instance. A grade scope examines the replies of pupils to questions and group them according to the answers they provide. Then the instructor may examine these groups, verify that the system has appropriately assigned pupils to teams or individually change who is assigned to which category. After the teacher admits, marks may be awarded appropriately [42, 43]. The system improves its future performance by offering this input. In massive Open Online Courses (MOOCs, for example), student inputs, graduation examinations or other computer-based tasks, as well as some computer-vision functions are analyzed. This allows organizers to support huge numbers of students by using machine learning [44].

13.6.2   Pharmaceuticals

The drug sector relies on data from clinical research, drugs' effectiveness studies and genetic investigations and generates a high volume of data. These enormous datasets require analytical approaches to provide significant information which can enhance processes of research and development and to produce diagnostic tools for patients who benefit greatest from medicinal products [45]. Machine learning might improve the drug discovery process to boost efficiency. In the case of machine learning, for example, chemical structures of potentially active drugs compounds may be analyzed and predicted. Such analyses may assist to boost the scoreboard hit rate and so detect more successful medication candidates faster. [46].

13.6.3   Manufacturing

Machine learning in manufacturing has the potential to automate or improve processes, creating individual goods, or allowing predictive maintenance. Aside from automating production processes, the way manufacturing equipment or manufactured items may for instance be serviced and maintained may be altered. Learning programs can construct predictive maintenance systems by gathering data on how equipment operates and whether equipment is not operational. These systems would predict that the assets would fail and direct maintenance operations would thus save expensive repairs for the equipment that was in failure at a later date or longer downtime times [47].

13.7   Machine Learning

Machine learning might be a crucial facilitator for a number of experimental domains, extending the limits of knowledge, by analyzing the massive amounts of data already being created in subjects like biological sciences, particle physics, astronomy, the social sciences, and more. Researchers may use machine learning to analyze these big datasets, identifying previously unknown patterns or extracting surprising insights [48]. Below are some early instances of its use in scientific investigations; its prospective uses in scientific research span a wide range of disciplines and will encompass a variety of topics not covered in depth here.

13.7.1   Neuroscience Research Advancements

Machine learning has had and continues to have a significant impact on modern neuroscience in a variety of ways, most prominently through research methodology and statistical modeling approaches [49, 50]. Because neuroscience has a lot of data processing and stats challenges, supervised, semi-supervised, and unsupervised learning approaches are indeed useful for data analysis in a variety of investigations [51]. Machine learning can help map how the brain accomplishes its functions by detecting patterns of movement in massive datasets acquired through investigations of electrical stimulation. Machine learning can associate regions of activity with specific activities, such as detecting graphic symbols, by analyzing brain data, including those obtained by operational MRI scans [52, 53]. The intricacies in these photographs are frequently too tiny for human analysts to perceive, but machine learning algorithms can find patterns in them. Machine learning might help diagnose or cure disease in the future by offering a richer knowledge of the brain in this way. Neuroscience has also influenced machine learning advances, such as work in convolutional networks, computer vision, and episodic memory, to name a few examples [54].

13.7.2   Finding Patterns in Astronomical Data

Astronomical research creates a lot of data. The Large Synoptic Survey Telescope (LSST), for example, is predicted to generate over 15 terabytes of astronomical data per night once it is up and running [55]. A fundamental difficulty for astronomy in analyzing these data is to separate important characteristics or sensory information's from the chaos and assigning them to the appropriate class or phenomena. The Kepler mission, for example, is looking for Earth-sized celestial bodies circling other stars by gathering information from surveys of the Orion Spur and beyond that might confirms the existence of galaxies or planets. However, not all of this information is meaningful; it might be skewed by on-board thruster action, changes in stellar activity, or other systemic tendencies. These "instrumental artefacts" must be eliminated from the system before the data can be analyzed. Researchers have developed a machine learning technique that can identify and eliminate these imperfections from the network, allowing it to be cleaned for further examination [56]. Machine learning is already being used by the Dark Energy Survey to determine photometric redshifts [57].

13.8   Ethical and Social Issues Raised.... ! ! !

A lot of ethical and societal challenges highlighted by machine learning overlap with those posed by data use, automation, technology dependency more generally, and problems arising with the use of assistive and "tele-health" technologies [58]. Many machines learning approaches that have contributed to AI's present success are based on neural artificial networks. Ethics are caused by opacity, unpredictability and the necessity for enormous datasets to develop technology. The characteristics of such techniques normally neither the developer nor the user(s) (see box) know how the system reacts with a certain set of inputs in advance [59].

13.8.1   Reliability and Safety

Trustworthiness and security are major challenges in which AI is employed in monitoring equipment, providing therapy, or taking healthcare choices. AI may make mistakes, which can have serious repercussions if the error is difficult to detect or has a cascading impact [60].

13.8.2   Transparency and Accountability

The underlying logic of AI outputs can be difficult or impossible to identify. Some AIs are private and confidential, but certain are just too complicated to be understood by a human. Machine learning technology may be especially opaque by constantly changing its individual settings and rules as it learns. This leads to validated AI system outputs and to inaccuracies or mistakes in the data being identified [61, 62].

13.8.3   Data Privacy and Security

AI healthcare apps employ data that would be confidential and private to many. This is open to legal scrutiny [63]. However, other forms of data, such as social media activity and internet search history, that are clearly not about health state, might be applied to disclose health status information about the user and people around him [64].

13.8.4　Malicious Use of AI

While AI may be utilized for beneficial reasons, it may also be employed for malevolent reasons. There are suspicions, for example, that AI may be used for hidden monitoring or screening. Analyzing motor behavior, AI technologies (e.g., how somebody types on a keyboard) and the mobility patterns found by tracking cellphones, could disclose health information without knowing [65]. AI may be utilized to perform cyberattacks at cheaper cost and to a larger extent. This has pushed policymakers, researchers and engineers to think about the dual-use characteristics of AI, as well as how to anticipate for possible undesirable applications of AI technology [66].

13.8.5　Effects on Healthcare Professionals

If AI questions healthcare practitioners' expertise, they might perceive as if their independence and authority are being challenged. The advent of AI, like many new technologies, is expected to impact the abilities and knowledge of healthcare practitioners. In some fields, AI may allow jobs formerly performed by humans to be automated. This might allow health providers to dedicate more time to contacting patients directly. However, there are worries to justify employing a less trained workforce by introducing AI systems [67]. This might be troublesome if the technology fails, and the workers cannot detect faults without computer direction or carry out the essential activities [68].

13.9　Future of Machine Learning in Healthcare

In the future, AI systems such as machine learning are anticipated to be further developed and be able to do a broad range of positions without the control or input of people. While we cannot fully forecast the future, the future situations that are likely to occur can be considered [69].

13.9.1　A Better Patient Journey

While every existing technology used to leverage NLP and ML has its own distinct value, the main advantage of healthcare in the future will probably be the synergies generated by integrating the powers of AI-related technology throughout the patient's journey. Take, for example, an upcoming scenario in which an overweight man is an ex-diabetes smoker with auric fibrillation. The wearable gadgets are anticipated to be used to monitor hyperglycemia, cardiac rates and rhythms as well as the amounts of activity over time in future. These can be synchronized to a central surveillance system that utilizes ML to identify unusual and unwanted changes in patterns (Figure 13.9). The surveillance system can automatically contact the provider and instruct the patient to arrange for appointments when an aberrant pattern change is observed. The provider may study the relevant data supplied by wearable devices of the patient prior to visiting the patient, together with the reasons why the alert is created and a list of potentials of diagnosis provided by the AI capabilities of the wearable monitoring system. The provider will then issue a visit notice once the patient has been seen and examined [70]. The oncologist may examine the patient's medical electronic record and imagery results before he meets the patient, then use NLP and ML to examine evidence-based medical literature on viable therapeutic alternatives or clinical trial applicable directly to the patient. Once a therapeutic solution is decided, ML will adapt the therapeutic plan to the individual clinical situation of the patient. The wearable gadgets will monitor the patient and alert both the patient and its provider if an AI-enabled monitoring system conclude that intervention is necessary, both while the patient is getting therapy and after treatment [71].

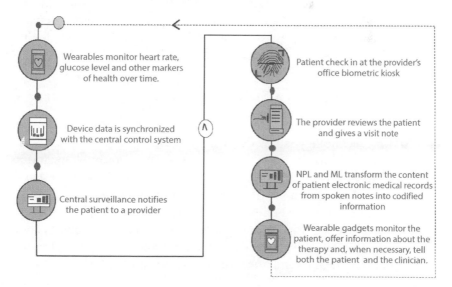

Figure 13.9 Schematic representation of patient journey.

13.9.2   New Ways to Deliver Care

The wider use of machine learning in healthcare will also affect the sorts of new people in the healthcare sector and the future working of providers, clinicians and other employees. The use of technologies such as NLP and ML in their day-to-day operations is likely to be considered a need in order to produce the competitive benefits of new healthcare market participants (whether payers, providers, pharmaceutical firms, technology or other healthcare enterprises). As such, a bigger percentage of operations associated with healthcare will be automated, enabling providers, clinicians and employees to focus on skills setting and high-level license operations that produce more added value. The usage of NLP and ML may also influence the models of the health talent itself, since they influence how and where the job is being done. The AI provider, physician and staff will concentrate on more top-of-the-line activities and skill sets [72]. In conjunction with NLP and ML (as well as physician supervision), more dependency on the doctor extender is likely to be made to decrease costs and leverage the doctor's time. There are also going to be developments in new forms of talent model.

13.10   Challenges and Hesitations [73–75]

Although machine learning has demonstrated to have a dramatic influence on many industries, uncertainties and technological obstacles remain. Some of the potential threats associated with the usage of technologies like NLP and ML must also be understood.

13.10.1   Not Overlord Assistant Intelligent

The dread of technology overcoming people is first and foremost. As we have shown, technology is not flawless and frequently needs the help of people to maintain precision. However, the power of technology and its propensity to be wiser than we are still have great dread and uncertainty [73]. At its heart, AI is a set of algorithms and mathematical equations which require training for humans. That implies AI and machine learning are just as intelligent as we educate them. AI is ideal helping people become more productive when deployed correctly. Technology is not here to overwhelm us, but to help us and improve our quality of life [74].

13.10.2   Issues with Unlabeled Data

The ability of technology to effectively manage unlabeled data seems to be a more sophisticated issue that affects both machine and intelligent systems. As machine learning is rely on data information, a huge number of labeled information are naturally needed to function the most efficiently. There are, however, numerous circumstances when data are not publicly available or unlabeled. This makes it more difficult to create algorithms [75]. We are teaching these algorithms to be cleverer and to achieve human precision with continuous study and new improvements, which means that unmarked data are as adequate as labeled data 1 day.

13.11   Concluding Thoughts

The positions of this technology are endless in the future. Progress in some fields of study on machine learning will affect the societal acceptability of applied machine learning and thus public trust. ML along with AL and NLP is used at several levels in the healthcare setting and its usage in healthcare is becoming increasingly essential as a technique to:

- Improving the productivity and quality of treatment of providers and clinicians.
- Improve patient involvement and improve access to treatment.
- Speed up the development of novel pharmaceutical therapies while cutting costs.

Although each such technology has its own worth, its ultimate worth comes in the synergies achieved by its application. Furthermore, greater usage of NLP and ML also means that organizational rules and procedures (and possibly legislation and laws) need to be developed to regulate their application. More crucially, NLP and ML should be regarded instruments to encourage providers and clinicians to perform medicine, but should not rely on them to the degree that they have lost the art of medicine itself.

Acknowledgments

I'd like to express my gratitude to my co-authors for their contributions of expertise and effort, as well as their participation in compiling the work.

References

1. McCrea, N., An Introduction to Machine Learning Theory and Its Applications: A Visual Tutorial with Examples, Toptal, United States, 2016.
2. Vasilev, I., *A deep learning tutorial: From perceptrons to deep networks*, Toptal, United States, 2017.
3. Kumar, R., Machine learning: Concept, deep learning and application. *Wirel. Commun. Math.*, 49, 2019.
4. Deng, L. and Hinton, G., Brian Kingsbury Microsoft Research, in: New types of deep learning for speech recognition and related applications: An overview. *IEEE International Conference on Acoustics, Speech, and Signal Processing (ICASSP)*, Redmond, WA, USA, May 2013.
5. Sharma, B., An explanation of machine learning. *IJCSMC*, 8, 4, 78–82, 2019.
6. Simon, A., Deo, M.S., Venkatesan, S., Babu, D.R., An overview of machine learning and its applications. *Int. J. Electr. Sci. Eng.*, 1, 1, 22–24, 2016.
7. Dietterich, T.G., Machine-learning research. *AI magazine*, 18, 4, 97–97, 1997.
8. Aniesch, C., Zschech, P., Heinrich, K., Machine learning and deep learning. *Electron Markets,* 31, 685–695, 2021..
9. Bowles, M., *Machine learning in Python: Essential techniques for predictive analysis.* John Wiley & Sons, 2015.
10. Kotsiantis, S.B., Zaharakis, I., Pintelas, P., Supervised machine learning: A review of classification techniques. *J. Informatica Emerging Artif. Intell. Appl. Comput. Eng.,* 1, 3–24, 160, 2007.
11. Alsabti, K., Ranka, S., Singh, V., An efficient k-means clustering algorithm. *Electr. Eng. Comput. Sci.,* paper 43, 1997.
12. Zhu, X. and Goldberg, A.B., Introduction to semi-supervised learning. *Synthesis Lectures on Artificial Intelligence and Machine Learning,* Vol. 3, pp. 1–130, Morgan and Claypool Publishers, 2009.
13. Caruana, R., Multitask learning. *Mach. Learn.*, 28, 1, 41–75, 1997.
14. Lowd, D. and Domingos, P., Naive Bayes models for probability estimation, in: *Proceedings of the 22nd international conference on Machine learning*, pp. 529–536, 2005.
15. Sharma, V., Rai, S., Dev, A., A comprehensive study of artificial neural networks. *Int. J. Adv. Res. Comput. Sci. Eng. Inf. Technol.*, 2, 10, 2012.
16. Hiregoudar, S.B., Manjunath, K., Patil, K.S., A survey: Research summary on neural networks. *Int. J. Res. Eng.*, 3, 3, 385–389, 2014.

17. Dey, A., Machine learning algorithms: A review. *Int. J. Comput. Sci. Inf. Technol. Res.*, 7, 3, 1174–1179, 2016.
18. Bengio, S., Deng, L., Larochelle, H., Lee, H., Salakhutdinov, R., Guest editors' introduction: Special section on learning deep architectures. *IEEE Trans. Pattern Anal. Mach. Intell.*, 35, 8, 1795–1797, 2013.
19. Zheng, Q., Wu, Z., Cheng, X., Jiang, L., Liu, J., Learning to crawl deep web. *Inf. Syste. J.*, 38, 6, 801–819, 2013.
20. Krizhevsky, A., Sutskever, I., Hinton, G.E., Imagenet classification with deep convolutional neural networks. *Adv. Neural Inf. Process. Sys.*, 25, 1097–1105, 2012.
21. Arel, I., Rose, D.C., Karnowski, T.P., Deep machine learning-a new frontier in artificial intelligence research [research frontier]. *IEEE Comput. Intell.*, 5, 4, 13–18, 2010.
22. Parvin, H., Alizadeh, H., Minati, B., A modification on k-nearest neighbor classifier. *J. Comput. Sci. Technol.*, 10, 14, 38–40, 2010.
23. Manning, C. and Schutze, H., Foundation of statistical natural learning processing. *Journal of Information Security*, Vol. 8, MIT Press, Cambridge, 1999.
24. Long, E., Lin, H., Liu, Z., Wu, X., Wang, L., Jiang, J., Liu, Y., An artificial intelligence platform for the multihospital collaborative management of congenital cataracts. *Nat. Biomed. Eng.*, 1, 2, 1–8, 2017.
25. Bengio, S., Deng, L., Larochelle, H., Lee, H., Salakhutdinov, R., Guest editors' introduction: Special section on learning deep architectures. *IEEE Trans. Patt. Anal. Mach. Intell.*, 35, 8, 1795–1797, 2013.
26. Zheng, Q., Wu, Z., Cheng, X., Jiang, L., Liu, J., Learning to crawl deep web. *Inf. Syst.*, 38, 6, 801–819, 2013.
27. Muhammad, I. and Yan, Z., Supervised machine learning approaches: A survey. *ICTACT J. Soft Comput.*, 5, 3, 2015.
28. Gulshan, V., Peng, L., Coram, M., Stumpe, M.C., Wu, D., Narayanaswamy, A., Webster, D.R., Development and validation of a deep learning algorithm for detection of diabetic retinopathy in retinal fundus photographs. *Jama*, 316, 22, 2402–2410, 2016.
29. Esteva, A., Dermatologist-level classification of skin cancer with deep neural networks. *Nat.*, 542, 115118, 2017.
30. Varnek, A. and Baskin, I., Machine learning methods for property prediction in chemoinformatics: quo vadis. *J. Chem. Inf. Model.*, 52, 6, 1413–1437, 2012.
31. Caruana, R., Lou, Y., Gehrke, J., Koch, P., Sturm, M., Elhadad, N., Intelligible models for healthcare: Predicting pneumonia risk and hospital 30-day readmission, in: *Proceedings of the 21th ACM SIGKDD international conference on knowledge discovery and data mining*, pp. 1721–1730, 2015.
32. Singh, Y., Bhatia, P.K., Sangwan, O., A review of studies on machine learning techniques. *Int. J. Comput. Sci. Secur.*, 1, 1, 70–84, 2007.
33. Wang, H., Ma, C., Zhou, L., (2009, December). A brief review of machine learning and its application, in: *2009 international conference on information engineering and computer science*, IEEE, pp. 1–4, 2009.

34. Dilsizian, S.E. and Siegel, E.L., Artificial intelligence in medicine and cardiac imaging: Harnessing big data and advanced computing to provide personalized medical diagnosis and treatment. *Curr. Cardio. Rep.*, 16, 1, 441, 2014.

35. Jiang, F., Jiang, Y., Zhi, H., Dong, Y., Li, H., Ma, S., Wang, Y., Artificial intelligence in healthcare: Past, present and futur. *Stroke Vas. Neuro.*, 2, 4, 2017.

36. Buruk, B., Ekmekci, P.E., Arda, B., A critical perspective on guidelines for responsible and trustworthy artificial intelligence. *Med. Healthcare Phil.*, 23, 3, 387–399, 2020.

37. Cockburn, I.M., Henderson, R., Stern, S., The impact of artificial intelligence on innovation. *NBER*, 5, 17, 23–30, 2018.

38. Shalev-Shwartz, S. and Ben-David, S., *Understanding machine learning: From theory to algorithms.* Cambridge University Press, 2014.

39. Angra, S. and Ahuja, S., Machine learning and its applications: A review, in: *2017 International Conference on Big Data Analytics and Computational Intelligence (ICBDAC)*, IEEE, pp. 57–60, 2017.

40. Doupe, P., Faghmous, J., Basu, S., Machine learning for health services researchers. *Value Health*, 22, 7, 808–815, 2019.

41. Jabbar, M.A., Samreen, S., Aluvalu, R., The future of healthcare: Machine learning. *Int. J. Eng. Technol.*, 7, 4, 23–5, 2018.

42. Gupta, P., Machine learning: The future of healthcare. *Harvard Sci. Rev.*, (May 16), 2017.

43. Varnek, A. and Baskin, I., Machine learning methods for property prediction in chemoinformatics: Quo vadis. *J. Chem. Inf. Model.*, 52, 6, 1413–1437, 2012.

44. Beck, A.H., Sangoi, A.R., Leung, S., Marinelli, R.J., Nielsen, T.O., van de Vijver, M.J., Koller, D., Systematic analysis of breast cancer morphology uncovers stromal features associated with survival. *Sci. Transl. Med.*, 3, 108ra113, 2011.

45. Gulshan, V., Peng, L., Coram, M., Stumpe, M.C., Wu, D., Narayanaswamy, A., Webster, D.R., Development and validation of a deep learning algorithm for detection of diabetic retinopathy in retinal fundus photographs. *Jama*, 316, 22, 2402–2410, 2016.

46. Khare, A., Jeon, M., Sethi, I.K., Xu, B., Machine learning theory and applications for healthcare. *J. Healthc. Eng.*, 2017, 1–2, 2017.

47. LeCun, Y., Bengio, Y., Hinton, G., Deep learning. *Nature*, 521, 7553, 436–444, 2015.

48. Hollands, F.M. and Tirthali, D., MOOCs: Expectations and reality, in: *Center for Benefit-Cost Studies of Education*, vol. 138, Teachers College, Columbia University, 2014.

49. Kass, R., Eden, U., Brown, E., *Analysis of neural data*, Springer Verlag, Berlin, Germany, 2014.

50. Yamins, D.L. and DiCarlo, J.J., Using goal-driven deep learning models to understand sensory cortex. *Nat. Neurosci.*, 19, 3, 356–365, 2016.

51. Grabska-Barwinska, A., Barthelme, S., Beck, J., Mainen, Z.F., Pouget, A., Latham, P.E., A probabilistic approach to demixing odors. *Nat. Neurosci.*, 20, 1, 98–106, 2017.

52. Jas, M., Engemann, D.A., Bekhti, Y., Raimondo, F., Gramfort, A., Autoreject: Automated artifact rejection for MEG and EEG data. *Neuro. Image*, 159, 417–429, 2017.

53. Naselaris, T., Olman, C.A., Stansbury, D.E., Ugurbil, K., Gallant, J.L., A voxel-wise encoding model for early visual areas decodes mental images of remembered scenes. *Neuroimage*, 105, 215–228, 2015.

54. Liu, F. and Perez, J., Gated end-to-end memory networks, in: *Proceedings of the 15th Conference of the European Chapter of the Association for Computational Linguistics*, vol. 1, Long Papers, pp. 1–10, 2017.

55. Borgman, C.L., The lives and after lives of data. *Harvard Data Sci. Rev.*, 1, 2019. https://doi.org/10.1162/99608f92.9a36bdb6

56. Roberts, S., McQuillan, A., Reece, S., Aigrain, S., Astrophysically robust systematics removal using variational inference: application to the first month of Kepler data. *Mon. Notices R. Astron. Soc*, 435, 4, 3639–3653, 2013.

57. Sadeh, I., Abdalla, F.B., Lahav, O., ANNz2: Photometric redshift and probability distribution function estimation using machine learning. *Publ. Astron. Soc Pac.*, 128, 968, 104502, 2016.

58. The Collection, Linking and Use of Data in Biomedical Research and Health Care: Ethical Issues: A Guide to the Report, Nuffield Council on Bioethics, 2015.

59. Caruana, R., Lou, Y., Gehrke, J., Koch, P., Sturm, M., Elhadad, N., Intelligible models for healthcare: Predicting pneumonia risk and hospital 30-day readmission, in: *Proceedings of the 21th ACM SIGKDD international conference on knowledge discovery and data mining*, pp. 1721–1730, 2015.

60. Knight, W., The dark secret at the heart of AI. *MIT Technol. Rev.*, 120, 54–61, 2017.

61. Burrell, J., How the machine thinks: Understanding opacity in machine learning algorithms. *BIG Data Soc.*, 1–3, 2016.

62. Stahl, B.C., Ethical issues of AI. *Artificial Intelligence for a Better Future: An Ecosystem Perspective on the Ethics of AI and Emerging Digital Technologies*, pp. 35–53, 2021.

63. Bird, S., Barocas, S., Crawford, K., Diaz, F., Wallach, H., Exploring or exploiting? Social and ethical implications of autonomous experimentation in AI, in: *Workshop on Fairness, Accountability, and Transparency in Machine Learning*, 2016.

64. Crawford, K., Artificial intelligences white guy problem. *Computer Science - The New York Times*, 25, 2016.

65. Polonski, V., People Dont Trust AIHeres How We Can Change That, in: *The Conversation*, vol. 9, 35–53, 2018.

66. Yuste, R., Goering, S., Bi, G., Carmena, J.M., Carter, A., Fins, J.J., Wolpaw, J., Four ethical priorities for neurotechnologies and AI. *Nat. News*, 551, 7679, 159, 2017.

67. Brundage, M., Avin, S., Clark, J., Toner, H., Eckersley, P., Garfinkel, B., Amodei, D., The malicious use of artificial intelligence: Forecasting, prevention, and mitigation. *Cornell University – Comput. Sci. Artif. Intell.*, 2018.

68. Bostrom, N. and Yudkowsky, E., The ethics of artificial intelligence, in: *The Cambridge handbook of artificial intelligence*, vol. 1, pp. 316–334, 2014.

69. Safdar, N.M., Banja, J.D., Meltzer, C.C., Ethical considerations in artificial intelligence. *Eur. J. Radiol.*, 122, 2020.

70. Frankish, K. and Ramsey, W.M., *The Cambridge handbook of artificial intelligence*, Cambridge University Press, 2014.

71. Hamid, S., The opportunities and risks of artificial intelligence in medicine and healthcare. CUSPE Communications, pp. 1–4, 2016.

72. Charniak, E., *Introduction to artificial intelligence*, Addison Wesley Publishing Company, Pearson Education India, 1985.

73. Bundy, A., Preparing for the future of artificial intelligence. *AI Soc.*, 32, 2, 285–287, 2017.

74. Lords, H.O., AI in the UK: Ready, willing and able, Parliament Business, p. 100, 2018.

75. Brooks, R.A., Intelligence without representation. *Artif. Intell.*, 47, 1–3, 139–159, 1991.

Index

Printed and bound by CPI Group (UK) Ltd, Croydon, CR0 4YY
11/10/2022
03153969-0001